Early Intervention

Early Intervention

Implementing Child and Family Services for Infants and Toddlers Who Are At Risk or Disabled

Second Edition

Marci J. Hanson
Eleanor W. Lynch

pro·ed

8700 Shoal Creek Boulevard
Austin, Texas 78757

pro·ed

© 1995, 1989 by PRO-ED, Inc.
8700 Shoal Creek Boulevard
Austin, Texas 78757-6897

All rights reserved. No part of the material protected by this copyright notice may be reproduced or utilized in any form or by any means, electronic or mechanical, including photocopying, recording, or by any information storage and retrieval system, without the prior written permission of the copyright owner.

Library of Congress Cataloging-in-Publication Data

Hanson, Marci J.
    Early intervention : implementing child and family services for infants and toddlers who are at-risk and disabled / Marci J. Hanson, Eleanor W. Lynch.
        p.   cm.
    Includes bibliographical references (p.   ) and index.
    ISBN 0-89079-621-1
       1. Handicapped children—Education (Preschool)—United States.
    2. Socially handicapped children—Education (Preschool)—United States.   3. Special education—United States.   I. Lynch, Eleanor W.
II. Title
LC4019.2.H37   1995   94-41958
371.9—dc20   CIP

This book is designed in Caslon

Production Manager: Alan Grimes
Production Coordinator: Karen Swain
Art Director: Lori Kopp
Reprints Buyer: Alicia Woods
Editor: Debra Berman
Editorial Assistant: Claudette Landry

Printed in the United States of America

1 2 3 4 5 6 7 8 9 10   99 98 97 96 95

To our families:

Laura and Jillian Campbell
Max and Maxine Hanson
Patrick Harrison
Leo and Virginia Whiteside

Contents

PREFACE • *xi*

ACKNOWLEDGMENTS • *xiv*

SECTION I BACKGROUND AND INTRODUCTION • *1*

CHAPTER 1 Historical Perspectives and Current Practices • *2*
The Importance of Early Intervention • *3*
Effectiveness of Early Intervention • *10*
Preferred Practices • *14*
Summary • *15*
References • *16*

CHAPTER 2 Children and Families in Early Intervention: Defining Disabilities and Risk Conditions • *20*
Infants and Toddlers with Established Risk Conditions • *21*
Infants and Toddlers At Biological Risk • *32*
Infants Born At Environmental Risk • *38*
Summary • *39*
References • *39*
Selected Readings • *42*

CHAPTER 3 Serving Diverse Populations • *44*
Changing Demographics • *44*
The Importance of Cultural Competence and Respecting Diversity • *46*
Applying Principles of Cross-Cultural Competence in Early Intervention • *52*
Other Dimensions of Diversity • *60*
Summary • *64*
Preferred Practices • *65*
References • *65*
Selected Readings • *67*

SECTION II MODEL COMPONENTS • *69*

CHAPTER 4 Developing a Model • *70*
Components of an Optimal Model • *70*
Service Delivery Systems • *82*
A Synthesized, Dynamic Approach • *84*
Summary • *84*
Preferred Practices • *86*
References • *86*

CHAPTER 5 Working in Partnership with Families • *90*
Family Interactions and Adjustments • *90*
The Family as a System • *96*
Rationale for Family-Centered Models • *99*
Types of Family Services • *100*
Strategies for Working with Families • *106*

A Family-Centered Approach to Early Intervention • *110*
Summary • *111*
Preferred Practices • *111*
References • *112*
Selected Readings • *114*

CHAPTER 6 **Staffing and Staff Development • *118***
Team Membership • *118*
Staff Competencies • *123*
Staff Development • *125*
Personnel Issues • *129*
Summary • *132*
Preferred Practices • *132*
References • *133*
Selected Readings • *135*

CHAPTER 7 **Coordinating Screening and Identification Efforts • *136***
Screening • *137*
Identification and Referral for Further Assessment and Diagnosis • *141*
Interface Between the Referral Source and the Early Intervention Program • *142*
Summary • *143*
Preferred Practices • *144*
References • *145*
Selected Readings • *145*

CHAPTER 8 **Assessing Children and Identifying Family Concerns, Priorities, and Resources • *146***
Child Assessment • *147*
Identifying Family Concerns, Priorities, and Resources • *168*
Summary • *178*
Preferred Practices • *179*
References • *180*
Selected Readings • *183*

CHAPTER 9 **Designing the Curriculum • *184***
Definition of Curriculum • *185*
Theoretical Approaches • *185*
Developmentally Appropriate Practice • *187*
Curricular Content • *188*
Method • *190*
Activity-Based Intervention • *198*
Putting It All Together • *198*
Summary • *198*
Preferred Practices • *199*
References • *200*
Selected Readings • *201*
Curriculum, Equipment, and Supply Resources • *202*
Selected Early Intervention Curricula • *202*

CHAPTER 10   Creating Learning Environments • *206*
  Learning Through Social Interactions and Play • *206*
  Characteristics of Quality Learning Environments • *208*
  Home Environments • *217*
  Center Environments • *223*
  Working in Inclusive Settings • *227*
  Summary • *230*
  Preferred Practices • *230*
  References • *231*
  Selected Readings • *233*
  Recommended Equipment and Materials • *234*
  Resources for Adaptive Equipment • *235*

SECTION III   ADMINISTRATIVE ISSUES • *237*

CHAPTER 11   Managing Program Components • *238*
  Strategic Planning • *240*
  Operational Planning • *240*
  Organizing • *243*
  Directing • *265*
  Controlling • *272*
  Summary • *272*
  Preferred Practices • *272*
  References • *273*
  Selected Readings • *273*

CHAPTER 12   Developing Community Collaboration • *274*
  Why Collaborate? • *275*
  How to Develop Community Collaboration • *278*
  The Collaboration Cascade • *281*
  Barriers and Facilitating Factors in Interagency Collaboration • *284*
  Summary • *285*
  Preferred Practices • *285*
  References • *286*
  Selected Readings • *287*

CHAPTER 13   Evaluating Programs *(Contributed by Patrick J. Harrison, San Diego State University)* • *288*
  Determining the Kinds of Questions To Be Answered • *290*
  Approaches to Evaluation • *294*
  Evaluation Models • *295*
  Planning and Conducting an Evaluation • *296*
  Summary • *320*
  Preferred Practices • *320*
  References • *321*
  Selected Readings • *322*

EPILOGUE • *323*		
APPENDIX A	Public Law 99-457 (Title 1, Part H) • *327*	
APPENDIX B	Professional and Parent Organizations and Information Resources • *341*	
APPENDIX C	Council for Exceptional Children (CEC) Code of Ethics and Standards for Educators • *345*	
APPENDIX D	Early Childhood Special Education Journals • *349*	
APPENDIX E	Individualized Family Service Plan • *351*	
APPENDIX F	Typical Developmental Milestones • *363*	
APPENDIX G	Resources for Equipment and Education Materials • *369*	
AUTHOR INDEX • *373*		
SUBJECT INDEX • *383*		

Preface

Attention to the needs of infants who are disabled or at risk for developing disabilities has increased rapidly. Early intervention services are now found throughout the United States, and the numbers and types of such services are expanding. This increase in early intervention services has risen from the defined needs of children and families, the identification of children at risk for early assistance, and federal legislation. Although services are being developed at a growing rate, relatively few resources are available for assisting in this process. Thus, our purpose in this book is to provide a practical, comprehensive guide to planning and implementing early intervention services.

The term *early intervention* carries many meanings. For the purposes of this book, the term will be used in reference to a comprehensive cluster of services that incorporate goals in education, health care, and social service for young children who are disabled or at risk for developing disabilities and their families. Such services appropriate for children ranging in age from birth to 3 years are discussed.

In defining children for whom early intervention may be warranted, three types of risk conditions typically are considered: established risk, biological risk, and environmental risk (Tjossem, 1976). Briefly, children who are at established risk are those who have developmental disabilities associated with defined medical disorders (e.g., Down syndrome). Biological risk conditions, on the other hand, refer to prenatal, perinatal, postnatal, and early developmental events resulting in biological damage that may increase the likelihood of developmental delays or differences. Children born at extreme prematurity or with low birth weight and/or complex birth complications may fall into this category. Finally, environmental risks are those life experiences (e.g., poor health, lack of social and/or learning opportunities) that, without intervention, may result in developmental delays.

Early intervention programs around the country may include children from all three risk categories, or they may focus on a particular group of children. However, by and large, most states and localities have focused early intervention efforts on children at established risk, with a growing number including children who experience delays due to biological risk. Most topics covered in this book are appropriate to programs serving a range of children. However, the various risk conditions do necessitate different approaches and different emphases in terms of services delivered. Our purpose is to present a full range and comprehensive continuum of services for discussion, recognizing that all services will not be provided by all programs. Further, the emphasis is placed on the group of children needing the widest range and most intensive services—children who are at established risk.

We do not attempt to present all types of service approaches that may be implemented as early intervention services. Rather, several major principles or biases reflect the approach advocated in this book: (a) a transactional model of child development; (b) a family-centered model; (c) a collaborative, community-based, interdisciplinary approach; (d) a comprehensive continuum of services; and (e) an approach that is systematically planned and structured around the achievement of specific goals and desired outcomes. Each of these principles is briefly examined.

First, most scientists and practitioners accept that a child's development is a product of both the child's inherited or constitutional characteristics and the child's interaction with the environment—a position that has been termed an interactional model of child development. Today, this model is carried even further and discussed in terms of the child's "transactions" with the environment. The transactional model, as articulated by Sameroff and Chandler (1975), emphasizes the importance of the "continual and progressive" interactions between the child and the environment. Thus, a child's status at any one point is shaped by the previous history of environmental interaction, such that development represents a constantly evolving interplay between the active influence of child characteristics and environmental response to them. Sameroff and Chandler discussed two types of risk—reproductive risk and caretaking risk. Reproductive risk refers to biological (e.g., prematurity, birth complications) and genetic constitutional factors affecting the child, whereas caretaking risk applies to the social and physical environment of the child (e.g., child-rearing practices, socioeconomic factors). These risks are examined as varying along a continuum, and the interactional effects of both are considered. For example, a child born with significant biological insults but reared in a supportive environment is expected to develop more optimally than the child with biological insults that are compounded by rearing in a poor caregiving environment. Given the powerful effects of these early interactions, early intervention efforts are marshaled around creating nurturing, supportive environments for infants to facilitate optimal development and prevent secondary difficulties. Thus, a transactional approach to viewing developmental changes is essential to the concept of early intervention.

A second essential element is the view of early intervention as a family-centered network of services. From an educational standpoint it is impossible to view the needs and goals for the child apart from those of the family. The infant's time and primary learning opportunities are spent in the context of the family, and it is the early relationships the baby develops with the significant adult caregivers that underpin social-emotional development and communication. Given the transactional model just discussed, it is logical that emphasis in early intervention will be placed on enhancing nurturing home and family environments, supporting family–professional partnerships, and respecting family diversity, to assure the best outcomes for children regardless of disability or risk.

A third element of early intervention is an emphasis on a coordinated, community-based, interdisciplinary service approach. The needs of the young child who is disabled or at risk and the needs of the family are diverse and span across professional disciplines. Typically, parents must seek out medical and other health care services, educational services, and social services. It is essential that these service providers have training in child development, a knowledge of various disabilities and risk factors, and the ability to work with families. Further, parents should be entitled to select from a range of service options in their community to meet their specific needs. Perhaps at no other time in the life cycle is the need for service delivery from a multitude of professionals so great. The needs of the baby almost always involve health care, social services, and developmental and educational consultation and services. Thus, the more professionals work in concerted efforts with one another to provide coordinated, interdisciplinary services, the better families and children will be served.

Fourth, a menu of services in the community should be available to families. These services should range from early screening and periodic follow-up of children considered at risk, to a comprehensive early intervention "package" tailored for those children considered at established risk or in need of intensive services and their families. This range of services should be activated at the point at which concern first is expressed, and parents should be provided clear, accurate information to enable them to make fully informed decisions regarding service needs.

Finally, the approach advocated in this book emphasizes carefully planned and structured interventions that are designed around clearly specified intervention goals and outcomes. That is not to say that the instructional setting must always be structured, but rather that intervention efforts must be planned and carefully articulated. Such efforts should be systematically examined and evaluated so that the most effective models can be identified and used. A program without an underlying structure is like a boat without a rudder. Especially because early intervention services represent a considerable economic as well as social outlay, services should be well designed, data based, and thoroughly evaluated.

Our society has made a commitment to supporting the lives of young children who are born at considerable risk or placed at risk by subsequent developmental events. Emerging information suggests that children for whom such early support is provided go on to lead lives characterized by higher quality and the need for less intensive and less expensive services.

Quality early intervention services are aimed at facilitating or enhancing the development of infants and toddlers, preventing additional or secondary developmental effects, and supporting families in caring for children who are disabled or at risk. It is our hope that this book contributes practical guidance and information to allow parents and professionals to advocate for early services and to design and implement appropriate services for infants and toddlers and their families.

The second edition of this book has been changed to reflect the growing knowledge in the field of early intervention, the full implementation of federal and state legislation related to infants and toddlers with disabilities and their families, and the changing demographics of the United States. In addition to major revisions in each of the chapters and the appendices, two additional chapters have been added. Chapter 2, Children and Families in Early Intervention: Defining Disabilities and Risk Conditions, discusses the range of disabilities and risk conditions that children referred to early intervention programs might have. The chapter presents information about diagnostic categories, health and medical issues, and risk factors in relation to developmental needs and implications for support and intervention. It also discusses larger societal issues, such as prenatal drug exposure, poverty, and violence, that negatively affect infant and family outcomes. Chapter 3, Serving Diverse Populations, focuses on family diversity in relation to the changing demographics of the United States and discusses the importance of cross-cultural competence when serving families from diverse ethnic, cultural, and language groups. It also provides suggestions for serving families who differ from providers in other dimensions, with special attention given to serving families when the parents have mental retardation, are teens, or face multiple risks. These changes reflect new knowledge, new concerns, and emerging practices in the field of early intervention. It is hoped that they will encourage families and professionals to consider new challenges and develop improved practices.

References

Sameroff, A. J., & Chandler, M. J. (1975). Reproductive risk and the continuum of caretaking causality. In F. D. Horowitz (Ed.), *Review of child development research* (Vol. 4, pp. 187–244). Chicago: University of Chicago Press.

Tjossem, T. D. (Ed.). (1976). *Intervention strategies for high-risk infants and young children*. Baltimore: University Park Press.

Acknowledgments

The authors gratefully acknowledge the staff members, parents, and children of the San Francisco Special Infant Services program of San Francisco State University, Department of Special Education, for allowing us to photograph and use project forms. The services provided there have been a major source of inspiration for this book.

We would also like to thank the administrator and the parents and children at the San Diego State University Child Study Center for their willingness to allow us to photograph an exemplary program.

Finally, we sincerely appreciate Dr. Patrick Harrison for his continuing contributions to this edition of the book and to the authors' understanding of and approach to evaluation and management.

SECTION I

Background and Introduction

Historical Perspectives and Current Practices

CHAPTER 1

Miles has come a long way since those early days when we peered into his incubator and wondered what the future would hold for him. Now we have seen what a positive difference early intervention can make.

(Kathy Reed, parent, in Hanson & Harris, 1986, p. 6)

Once we were over the week of tears and shock, Kathleen became our sweetheart.... She continues to be a challenge and a source of great joy....

We do not know what is down the road, so we take one step at a time. I could stew and fret continually, but then I would not have enough energy to do what needs to be done....

No one knows the child as well as the parents, and they must stand up for the child, because no one else is going to. They must get involved and make changes and make it better for their child. We have truly learned the meaning of "Life (happiness) is a journey, not a destination."

(NayDean Daily, parent, in Hanson, 1987, pp. 1–2)

For most parents the birth of a baby is a joyous event—the culmination of months of planning and expectations. But for some parents, hopes and plans are shattered by the birth of a child with developmental problems. These parents are thrust into a whole new world of responsibilities above and beyond caregiving and loving. For them this world is filled with a myriad of professionals and new and complicated questions about their child's growth and development. For some parents the early difficulties faced by their babies will be transient; for others the problems will necessitate lifelong adjustments. It is the early support and assistance that caring friends, relatives, and professionals provide that can influence the family's ability to cope with the issues posed by a child who is born disabled or at risk for developing disabilities.

The early service delivery needs of these babies vary greatly. For many the needs are primarily medical, involving health care and life support, as well as the family's understanding and adjustment to these interventions. For others a comprehensive service delivery model of health care and educational and social services is warranted. The provision of these early, comprehensive services is typically referred to as early intervention. Our purpose in this book is to outline and discuss the development and implementation of early intervention services. These procedures are designed to assist the reader to establish community-based services for infants from birth to 3 years utilizing a family-oriented program perspective.

The Importance of Early Intervention

This section covers the importance of early intervention, both currently and over the years, and presents extensive rationale for these programs.

Current Perspectives

The importance of early intervention has been underscored by a major policy commitment in the United States—the passage of Public Law (P.L.) 99-457, the Education of the Handicapped Act (EHA) Amendments, in 1986 (see Appendix A). This law is now retitled the Individuals with Disabilities Education Act (IDEA), P.L. 102-119 of 1991. The early education of infants and toddlers with disabilities is addressed specifically in Title I of this landmark piece of legislation. It states that the early intervention program for infants and toddlers with disabilities is intended to:

(a) Develop and implement a statewide, comprehensive, coordinated, multidisciplinary, interagency program of early intervention services for infants and toddlers with disabilities and their families;

(b) Facilitate the coordination of payment for early intervention services from Federal, State, local, and private sources (including public and private insurance coverage);

(c) Enhance the States' capacity to provide quality early intervention services and expand and improve existing early intervention services being provided to infants and toddlers with disabilities and their families; and

(d) Enhance the capacity of State and local agencies and service providers to identify, evaluate, and meet the needs of historically underrepresented populations, particularly minority, low-income, inner-city, and rural populations. (34 C.F.R., Part 303, Early Intervention Programs for Infants and Toddlers with Disabilities)

The law further specified that children are to receive comprehensive, multidisciplinary evaluations and that an Individualized Family Service Plan (IFSP) is to be developed for each eligible child and family. The passage of this law was based on findings that make it clear that early services to young children with disabilities enhance their abilities to develop to their maximum potential, minimize later educational costs to society, and reduce the likelihood of institutionalization for children with handicaps.

Historical Roots

Early intervention services have increased steadily in the last two decades. Attention to this field has resulted from trends and legislation in three related fields: early childhood education, compensatory education for the disadvantaged, and special education. Each area is briefly reviewed below. More detailed reviews are found in Peters, Neisworth, and Yawkey (1985) and Peterson (1987).

Early childhood educational programs were first established in the United States in the late 1800s. In many ways these early programs for nondisabled children paved the way for programs that would later be offered for children at risk through both environmental and biologically based factors. These early programs were kindergarten programs grounded primarily in the philosophies of Europeans such as Froebel, who emphasized the importance of child-centered learning and children's play. Subsequent innovations came from the work of educators such as John Dewey who championed the importance of active learning through social and child-initiated interactions. A second major influence on the developing U.S. programs was the nursery school movement in both England and Italy. In the early 1900s the MacMillan sisters began the first nursery schools in England whose purpose was to provide for the emotional and physical well-being of "slum" children. At around the same time, Maria Montessori began her nursery schools in Rome. Montessori's work has particular significance for the influence it later exercised over the development of educational programs for children with disabilities. Montessori's philosophy emphasized learning in graded sequences, self-paced and self-correcting instructional materials, and learning through the sensory modalities through active involvement with the environment.

The nursery school movement, transported to the United States along with other social and economic forces, resulted in an increase in early childhood education and child care programs. These other forces included the Depression, during which a great many nursery school jobs were created for unemployed teachers, and World War II, which necessitated the entrance of many women into the labor force. The need for child care for working mothers has continued to grow as more and more women have entered and remained in the workforce. Thus, the child care movement too has influenced the proliferation of early childhood education programs. Today, these programs are characterized by a diversity of models and philosophies.

Another educational movement that has exercised tremendous influence on the development of early intervention services is the compensatory education movement. Head Start was begun in the mid-1960s in an effort to help young disadvantaged children to enter and cope with regular school programs. The child's early environment and early learning were recognized as factors crucial to the child's later success in school. Given that many children were growing up in suboptimal conditions, early childhood educational programs designed to "compensate" for these conditions were developed. Head Start efforts were unique in that they were community based, stressed parent involvement, and required a comprehensive approach with the participation of different types of professionals. Although the effects of these compensatory programs, specifically Head Start and its offspring Follow-Through, have been hotly debated and analyzed over the years, society has made a commitment to the continuation of these early educational intervention services. Other more family-oriented approaches to service delivery also grew out of these efforts. This produced a broad range of program models that included home visitors, early childhood centers, and combinations of home- and center-based programs. The development of these programs has resulted in a focus downward in terms of the ages of children served. Although the original Head Start programs concentrated on preschool-age children, subsequent efforts attended to the needs of the young child under age 3 as well.

The early intervention movement of today also has been shaped to a large degree by the overall special education movement in the United States. The earliest services in this country for individuals with disabilities consisted primarily of residential facilities for groups with specific disabilities (e.g., deafness, blindness). Although programs for children with disabilities continued to grow over the years, most were segregated and many children were denied equal access to a public education. Parent groups began to organize and demand appropriate educational services for their children. Several landmark legal cases, such as *Pennsylvania Association for Retarded Children (PARC) v. Commonwealth of Pennsylvania* (1971), brought attention to the educational rights of children with disabilities and their need for equal protection and due process procedures under the law. These legal and social forces resulted in the passage in 1975 of a significant piece of legislation, the Education for All Handicapped Children Act, P.L. 94-142. This law defines six major principles: a zero reject model entitling children to a free, appropriate education; nondiscriminatory testing, classification, and placement; an appropriate and individualized education; education in the least restrictive appropriate placement; procedural due process; and parent participation and shared decision making. Although this law did not apply to the very young child under age 3 except in states where services to this age group were mandated, the principles it defined played an important role in the development of early intervention services.

Several other laws of importance to children with disabilities deserve mention. These include the Handicapped Children's Early Education Assistance Act (HCEEAA) (P.L. 90-538) and the 1972 Economic Opportunity Amendments (P.L. 92-424). The former established funds to encourage and improve programs for young children with disabilities. From it the Handicapped Children's Early Education Program (HCEEP) Model Demonstration Programs, also known as First Chance Programs, were developed. These demonstration programs are funded through 3-year grants awarded to projects throughout the country to establish exemplary models. The models and products developed by these programs have had a tremendous influence on the quality of early intervention services today. Finally, the Economic Opportunity Amendments mandated that Head Start services be offered to children with disabilities from low income families. Thus, this requirement provided further incentives for expanding services to the young child with disabilities.

This brief review of the historical factors that influenced the development and increase of early intervention programs in this country underscores the multifaceted nature of early intervention. Such services are born from traditions steeped in community-based services, active parent involvement, active child-centered learning, and services designed to enhance learning and developmental potential for children at special risk or need.

Developmental Principles

The developmental theoretical and empirical literature points to several underlying tenets for understanding early development. Lewis (1984) described five principles that he called "important guideposts" for designing assessment and education/intervention programs for the very young child who is disabled or at risk for disability. These five principles, discussed briefly in the following paragraphs, are:

1. The infant as a competent organism
2. The infant as a social organism
3. The infant as an active organism
4. The infant's development as proceeding from undifferentiated to differentiated abilities
5. The infant's development as an interactive process between the infant's status at any point in time and the environment in which the infant is immersed. (Lewis, 1984, p. 3)

Research from the mid-1950s to 1970s documented the perceptual and sensory capabilities of the young infant from birth. These findings led to the view of infants as competent and capable. Findings showed that babies shortly after birth are able to process information and develop complex skills. At the same time, a great deal of research was conducted on the earliest relationships that infants have with their caregivers and on early infant social development. The link between social and cognitive development was further substantiated. Studies examining how infants interact with their environment, both with social and nonsocial elements, further established that infants are active learners. These tenets underscore the importance of supporting infants' development early in their lives and of designing interventions that are interactive in nature and that recognize the contributions the infant makes to the interaction process.

The fourth principle discussed by Lewis (1984) is the notion that development proceeds from undifferentiated to increasingly differentiated skills. The infant's competencies thus are viewed as interrelated and interdependent. Lewis likened the child's development to that of a tree with core areas of development integrated at the core or trunk and skills that, like the branches, are more differentiated. The implications for assessment and intervention are great given this concept. Independent areas and skills cannot be examined separately or in isolation; rather the whole of the child's development and the interrelatedness of developmental areas must be considered. Early intervention as such holds promise for reducing the likelihood of further impairment or secondary impairments in related areas.

Finally, Lewis (1984) described an interactive model of development. This model also has been labeled a transactional model by Sameroff and Chandler (1975). According to this model, a child's developmental outcome is a product of the child's constitutional status and environment, and the interactions or transactions between these variables. Thus, to support or enhance a child's development through early intervention, the child must be supported to develop more fully and competently and the child's environment must provide supportive relationships. This notion argues for intervention at the earliest point and for interventions that support all aspects of the infant's development within the context of the family.

Rationale for Early Intervention

Theoretical arguments, empirical evidence, and societal needs have formed the strong rationale for intervening early in the lives of children born at risk or disabled. Four bases for this rationale are considered:

1. The importance of early environmental interactions
2. The prevention of secondary disabilities/effects
3. The needs of families of children who are disabled or at risk
4. Benefits of early intervention to society

Importance of the early years to later development

Research investigations in the 1950s and 1960s ascertained the incredible capabilities of the human infant (Stone, Smith, & Murphy, 1973). This body of evidence helped to shift the beliefs of many professionals away from an outdated perspective that infants had relatively unorganized and limited sensate capabilities to a more accurate view of the infant's abilities to process and organize sensory information. Related studies on infant learning documented the ability of the infant to learn from birth.

The effects of the infant's environment on learning and subsequent development became an area of great interest. Hunt's (1961) important book *Intelligence and Experience* called particular attention in professional circles to the significance of early environmental influences on later development. Hunt recommended the provision of optimal environments for young children to increase their intellectual growth. Furthermore, landmark investigations, such as that of Skeels and Dye (1939) and Skeels's (1966) follow-up, underscored the importance of the child's early environment. Skeels and Dye studied a group of children who had been raised in an orphanage, then transferred to a ward where they were cared for in part by women with mental retardation who gave them a great deal of attention and care. These children showed a dramatic IQ gain when compared with children who had not been transferred. Clearly, the new environment provided more stimulation and learning experiences for the children. In the follow-up of these children some 25 years later, Skeels noted that differences remained between the experimental group (children who had been transferred) and the control group (children who had remained in the orphanage conditions). The experimental group, as adults, showed higher academic education levels and more advanced levels of occupational achievement. Finally, other research, primarily animal studies, appeared to lend support to the importance of the early years to subsequent development by the identification of critical periods of development (periods during which certain stimuli are necessary for a given aspect of development to occur) (e.g., Lorenz, 1937).

Later work has questioned the notion of critical periods of human development. Furthermore, it has been argued that the early years are not the only crucial period of development and that development in fact continues throughout the life span (Clarke & Clarke, 1976). However, regardless of the controversy surrounding the critical nature of the very early years, few professionals would debate the importance of the early years to subsequent development. The foundations for many behavior patterns are set in these early years, and subsequent developmental growth is based on these foundations.

The *transactional model of development* further highlights the importance of the early years as a period worthy of attention for the prevention or amelioration of developmental difficulties. This model posits that development occurs through a "continual and progressive interplay between the organism and its environment" (Sameroff & Chandler, 1975, p. 234). This model highlights the importance of interactions or transactions as determinants of subsequent developmental outcomes. For example, an infant born at significant health risk and raised in an optimal supportive environment would be expected to fare much better than an infant raised in a less sustaining environment. In fact, the baby with the most significant health risk may actually develop more favorably than a baby born at less risk but raised in a suboptimal environment. Thus, the interactions between the baby's constitutional makeup and environmental factors are paramount to deciding the infant's subsequent developmental status.

Finally, most theories of child development recognize the tremendous growth that occurs during early childhood and emphasize the relationships between early growth and development and later development. Piaget's theory of cognitive development (Phillips, 1975; Piaget, 1952) has exerted perhaps the greatest influence on notions of children's intellectual growth and development. Central to Piaget's theory is the idea that the intellectual developmental process results from adaptations the individual makes in interactions with the environment. Further, he postulated that cognitive development occurs in stages or set sequences and that subsequent stages are built upon preceding intellectual developments.

These theoretical underpinnings and research studies establish the early years as important to the child's later development. Although the earliest years are not the only crucial period of development, clearly an attempt at enhancing development must begin during this significant time. Failure to address the earliest interactions of the child with the environment may result in wasted time or developmental lags for the child who is born at risk or disabled.

Prevention of secondary disabilities or effects

The specific conditions that create at-risk developmental circumstances for the child represent only part of the picture. As can be seen from the transactional model of development, the response of the environment to these conditions may greatly influence the child's subsequent growth and development. For example, the baby born with hearing and visual impairments who is unable to make eye contact with the parents and "signal" the parents in the way that babies typically do may be "at risk" in the interactions he or she has with the parents, as well as in the manner that the disabling visual and hearing conditions influence the child's development. Thus, the attitudes and behaviors that others exhibit toward the child with a disability may result in other disabilities, such as behavioral difficulties. Further, the disabling condition itself, if left untreated, may result in additional effects. Take for example the case of children with severe physical impairments that limit their movements. Over time these movement difficulties may result in more physical impairments such as the development of contractures (the permanent shortening of muscles or tendons). Likewise, a child who is born congenitally blind will be unable to glean certain types of information from the environment that are provided through the visual modality. This lack of information hinders the child's ability to move about the environment, inhibits reaching and walking, and even delays the child's development of language, because the child's world is limited initially to the here and now and to the self. Early interventions can be employed to adapt the child's environment—both the social (e.g., families) and the nonsocial (e.g., toys, equipment, and materials)—to prevent the occurrence of secondary disabilities or effects that result from the interaction between the child's disabling condition and environmental factors.

Family concerns and priorities

The birth of a child with disabilities or one who is at risk for developing difficulties presents many new challenges to family members and caregivers. Most families must work with a variety of professionals in the health care, education, and social service professions in order to meet the baby's special needs. These extra responsibilities are thrust upon the family at a vulnerable time when the family is adjusting to the addition of a new member and the changes that event brings even under the best of circumstances.

Families often express needs for support and information. Many families desire basic information and support in dealing with the myriad of professional services and agencies they must encounter. For some, different periods of adjustment will be particularly trying or stressful and may necessitate counseling or emotional support. For others, accurate, factual information surrounding the disability or risk condition may be needed to assist in decision making regarding appropriate actions or treatments for that child and family. Some family members will need very specific information and training in particular aspects of child care and education, for example, positioning and handling. Finally, given the atypical behavior patterns that babies may exhibit due to the disability or risk conditions, parents may need assistance in understanding their child's unique behavior and cues. Such assistance can be provided early in the developing parent–child relationship so that healthy and mutually satisfying interactions between parents and their children result.

Benefits to society

Early intervention services also have been developed and expanded predicated on the notion that such services are cost-effective. Such arguments are based primarily on data indicating savings in educational costs in the elementary years. Findings showed that children receiving early intervention are more likely to go on to regular education services or less intensive and restrictive (and thus less expensive) special education. Several studies are relevant to the discussion. First, the long-term follow-up of the Ypsilanti Perry Preschool Project (Berrueta-Clement, Schweinhart, Barnett, Epstein, & Weikart, 1984; Schweinhart, Barnes, & Weikart, 1993; Schweinhart, Berrueta-Clement, Barnett, Epstein, & Weikart, 1985; Weber, Foster, & Weikart, 1978) found that preschool graduates were less likely to require more costly and intensive special education programs in later years and that the projected lifetime earnings for program participants were greater than those for control group children. Projected benefits were estimated at over $14,000 per child. Furthermore, a long-term follow-up of the graduates showed that the program group (as contrasted with the control group) had completed higher levels of schooling and had significantly higher earnings and percentages of home ownership. Also, lower percentages of the program group received social services or had been arrested (Schweinhart, Barnes, & Weikart, 1993).

Garland, Stone, Swanson, and Woodruff (1981) also reported a study on the economic analysis of the effects of early intervention services. The results of this study showed projected educational costs at $37,273 for children whose intervention began at birth, $37,600 for those beginning at age 2, $46,816 for those beginning at age 6 with attrition and entrance to regular education, and $53,340 for those beginning at age 6 and remaining in special educational services. Bricker (1989) reviewed other studies of the economic benefits of early intervention services.

Effectiveness of Early Intervention

The question of early intervention efficacy has received a great deal of attention in recent years. Although the final "verdict" most likely awaits the long-term analysis of the developmental growth of children who participated in quality, well-defined early intervention services, the wealth of information in this area does suggest positive intervention effects. Specifically, these effects are examined in terms of benefits to children and benefits to families.

Many attempts to study the effects of specific early intervention programs have been made in the last several decades. Most represent short-term studies conducted with limited resources by the specific intervention program. As a result many of the investigations are seriously flawed methodologically, particularly those studies that have focused on early intervention for children at established risk for disability. Some of these methodological difficulties include the following: (a) failure to include a control group because of difficulties in matching children and/or ethical issues related to depriving certain children of services; (b) limited documentation of the type or degree of "treatment"; (c) failure to document or control for effects of related services (e.g., parent instruction and participation); (d) heterogeneity of the population; (e) small sample sizes due to the population; (f) lack of direct correspondence between the dependent variables or outcomes analyzed and the program's objectives and components; and (g) lack of or inappropriateness of measurement instruments to the populations examined (e.g., standardized IQ tests designed for use with normally developing children). Furthermore, given that most studies have been conducted with limited project resources and without the benefit of large-scale collaborative efforts, many different program models, outcomes, and instruments have been used, making cross-study comparisons difficult. These frustrations are inherent in research efforts in the area of early intervention. However, despite these tremendous limitations, some conclusions can be drawn with regard to early intervention effectiveness. These conclusions are summarized below.

Benefits to Children

Benefits to children are described in terms of the general target group of children served in an effort to sort out program outcomes in a meaningful fashion. Children are grouped by type of risk (using risk factors as categorized by Tjossem, 1976) and include those at environmental risk (e.g., disadvantaged children), those at established risk (e.g., children with specific disabilities, such as Down syndrome, cerebral palsy, spina bifida), and those at biological risk (e.g., children who are medically fragile due to birth complications and/or extreme prematurity or low birth weight).

Children at environmental risk

The most substantial body of early intervention efficacy literature is for children at environmental risk. Several major reviews concluded that early intervention is effective for this group of children (Beller, 1979; Bronfenbrenner, 1975; Casto & White, 1984; Lazar & Darlington, 1982). Many of the studies that examined this group of children were able to use experimental control group designs and otherwise satisfy the requirements for a sound evaluation research design. In a comprehensive review, Lazar and Darlington (1982) reported that experimental group children (those who received early intervention), when examined in follow-up studies, were more likely to meet their school's requirements, outperformed control group children on intelligence test measures, and were more likely to provide achievement-related reasons for being proud of themselves. Effects for families were noted as well and are reviewed in a later section.

A recent monograph, *At Risk Does Not Mean Doomed* (Ramey & Ramey, 1992), further underscores the importance and effectiveness of intervention in the early years for children at risk. Three early educational intervention programs aimed at preventing mental retardation and improving school readiness were examined. Two of the programs focused on children primarily at environmental risk. One program, the Abecedarian Project, provided high-quality programs for children shortly after birth and continuing through kindergarten. This well-designed longitudinal research project has provided extensive documentation of the benefit to children in terms of intellectual and academic performance (Martin, Ramey, & Ramey, 1990; Ramey & Campbell, 1987). The second program, Project CARE, was a successor to the Abecedarian Project and examined the effects of home-based early intervention. Results presented in this monograph suggested that children of mothers with low IQs benefited from early intervention, as demonstrated by a dramatic improvement in their intellectual performance. Further, early center-based programs supplemented by home-based visits were more effective than either home- or center-based programs. Also, the more intensively a family participated the greater the developmental benefits for children (Ramey & Ramey, 1992).

Finally, as previously reviewed, the longitudinal study of children enrolled in the preschool years in the High/Scope Perry Preschool Project strongly supports the efficacy of early intervention for children at environmental risk. Children who participated in the original project have been followed for nearly three decades. Findings contrasting the experimental group of children who received the preschool intervention with a control group of children who did not, indicated that, at age 27, the experimental group participants had higher earnings; higher levels of schooling achieved; and higher intellectual performance, general literacy, and school achievement (Schweinhart, Barnes, & Weikart, 1993). In summary, substantial evidence exists to support the effects of early intervention in improving the lives of children at environmental risk.

Children at established risk

Although the effects of early intervention are less well documented and substantiated for children with known or established risks, the data suggest that early intervention is effective (Bailey & Bricker, 1984; Casto & White,

1984; Dunst & Rheingrover, 1981; Simeonsson, Cooper, & Scheiner, 1982; Strain, 1984). A number of studies have been conducted on specific groups of children with disabilities. One of the most extensively examined groups is children with Down syndrome. Most investigations with this group reported substantial gains for children receiving early intervention, and many supported the use of structured models with active parental involvement (Aronson & Fallstrom, 1977; Bidder, Bryant, & Gray, 1975; Clunies-Ross, 1978; Connolly & Russell, 1976; Hanson, 1981; Hanson & Schwarz, 1979; Hayden & Dmitriev, 1975; Ludlow & Allen, 1979; Rynders & Horrobin, 1980). Similar findings have been noted for children with visual impairments (Adelson & Fraiberg, 1974) and hearing impairments (Horton, 1976). Finally, several investigations have focused on children with multiple and/or severe disabilities (Bricker & Dow, 1980; Fredericks, Baldwin, Moore, Templeman, & Anderson, 1980; Hanson, 1985). These studies also showed gains for children involved in early intervention regimens.

The Early Intervention Research Institute at Utah State University conducted a meta-analysis of over 70 early intervention studies for children with disabilities. Findings from this research concluded that early intervention does result in sizable and positive program effects and that the more intensive (involving more instructional time) and structured programs offer greater effects (Casto & Mastropieri, 1985, 1986; White & Casto, 1985; White, Mastropieri, & Casto, 1984). The findings were less optimistic with regard to parent involvement and age of onset of intervention. The methodology and conclusions from this research have been questioned by other researchers (Dunst & Snyder, 1986; Strain & Smith, 1986).

Another large study of children from multi-intervention sites was conducted by Shonkoff and colleagues (Shonkoff & Hauser-Cram, 1987; Shonkoff, Hauser-Cram, Krauss, & Upshur, 1988). Their results supported the provision of early intervention services on improving child outcomes and found that greater parent participation was associated with more child progress.

Despite the research difficulties and pitfalls in examining the effectiveness of early intervention with children at established risk as a group, substantial evidence exists to support the provision of early services. Early intervention has been shown to improve a variety of developmental outcomes for these children.

Children at biological risk

The final group of children to be considered includes those children born at biological risk. Like the children with disabilities, this group represents a particularly heterogeneous group, making controlled research efforts difficult to achieve. Gorski (1984) reviewed a number of investigations performed with these children in intensive care nurseries. Typically, interventions focused on stimulating children through a regimen of touching, holding, rocking, and/or sensory stimulation. Most studies reported favorable results of early stimulation. However, most were short term in nature and did not involve long-term follow-up of children's developmental status.

One intensive project was conducted with children born prematurely at 37 weeks gestational age and at low birth weight (2,500 grams, about 5.5 pounds). This large study, the Infant Health and Development Program, was conducted at eight sites throughout the United States and involved nearly 1,000 children and families (The Infant Health and Development Program, 1990; Ramey et al., 1992). Findings indicated that children who participated in the intervention program (center- and home-based programs modeled on the Abecedarian Project) benefited from the intervention. Children in the experimental group outperformed control group children on intellectual performance measures, and babies who were the heavier of the low birth weight babies benefited more than the smaller babies (Ramey & Ramey, 1992).

It also should be noted that most investigations (see review in Gorski, 1984) involved premature and/or low birth weight children who were at the least high risk by today's standards. Today, extreme prematurity is typically considered 25 to 26 weeks gestational age, and very low birth weight is defined as 1,500 grams or lower. Gorski (1984) cautioned that stimulation efforts in the neonatal intensive care unit must be carefully examined and monitored for use as intervention strategies given the baby's fragile physiological status.

Biologically at-risk children represent major challenges, and insufficient evidence exists to generalize about overall educational and developmental intervention protocols, especially for the children at greatest risk. As with other children with developmental difficulties, interventions must be carefully tailored to each child's individual needs. The issue is complicated further by the fact that many children born at biological or medical risk recover without formal interventions. Scott and Masi (1979) reported that approximately 30% of infants discharged from neonatal intensive care units will require some form of intervention by age 6, whereas 70% will "recover." To date, no reliable set of predictors has been found to identify absolutely those at-risk children at greatest need for intervention.

Summary

Many questions are left unanswered in the movement to document the effects of early intervention for children at risk. Although more research is needed for all types of risk conditions, reviews of the relevant literature generally conclude that intensive, high-quality intervention efforts are effective. The evidence appears strong enough to warrant the continuation and expansion of such services.

Benefits to Families

Although fewer investigations have attempted to document the effects of early intervention efforts on families than on the children, these data do suggest positive outcomes. Lazar and Darlington (1982), for example, reported that mothers of experimental group children were more positive regarding school and vocational issues related to the children. The Carolina Abecedarian Project, an early intervention program for children from impoverished conditions (environmental risk), reported improved mother–infant interactions (Ramey, MacPhee, & Yeates, 1983) and greater dyadic involvement (i.e., mother and infant playing together) (Ramey, Sparling, & Wasik, 1981). Studies done with mothers of children with cerebral palsy also reported more positive interactional styles for mothers who had undergone training with respect to behavioral and interactional strategies (Gordon & Kogan, 1975; Tyler & Kogan, 1977). Finally, the work of Field and colleagues with teenage mothers indicated that mothers who received training showed a higher rate of return to work and/or school and lower repeat pregnancy rates (Field, Widmayer, Greenberg, & Stoller, 1982).

Parents have also been found to be effective teachers or change agents for their children. Many of the studies previously reviewed have emphasized facilitating children's behavior through a parent-implemented training model (e.g., Bidder, Bryant, & Gray, 1975; Hanson & Schwarz, 1978). Baker and colleagues (Baker & Heifetz, 1976; Baker, Heifetz, & Murphy, 1980) also documented the positive effects of parent training. Mothers who received special training via manuals, phone calls, and group training on specific behavioral vignettes, improved their skills when compared with parents who did not receive the training. Furthermore, their children acquired skills in target areas at more advanced levels than did the control group children.

With respect to social support and stress, Shonkoff and Hauser-Cram (1987) reported that families that were provided opportunities to interact with other families showed greater changes in the intervention period in terms of maternal support. However, services delivered by a single provider and in an individualized manner were associated with greater child gains and decreased maternal stress. Services delivered through a transdisciplinary model also were associated with greater decreases in maternal parenting stress.

The effects of early intervention on family members are not well documented empirically. Given the complexity in studying family variables and the influence of other factors, such as socioeconomic status, on one's well-being, the issue of efficacy of early intervention as an entity is difficult to determine. However, the existing body of evidence does suggest that family members are affected by early intervention and that the effects appear to be positive attitudinal and behavioral changes and greater support networks.

Our society has made a commitment to the provision of early intervention services, particularly for children born with established risks. In general, early intervention as a concept appears sound and beneficial to the lives of children and their families. However, further research is needed to determine the types of intervention that are best suited for given children and their families, the length and intensity of the interventions, and the age of onset for intervention that is most beneficial.

Denhoff (1981) summarized some of the issues faced in evaluating the effects of early intervention:

> (1) They provide the infant and his/her parents with opportunities for both to develop to full potential. (2) Strengthening of the natural interactions between infant and parents that these programs provide is fundamental to good family development. (3) Various and numerous problems that produce parent guilt, anger, and frustration are lessened in a supportive milieu. (4) Constant reinforcement between infant and parents during the almost 3-year program may lay the groundwork for the eventual emergence of positive developmental patterns. (p. 35)

Preferred Practices

Although early intervention as a concept appears to be valid, not all programs are equally effective or appropriate. The following discussion highlights those variables that have been identified through clinical practice as indicative of the highest quality service delivery to infants and their families. These indicators of best practices include individualized programs for children and families, a family-oriented approach, a curricular model that emphasizes both a developmental and a functional approach to child education, a transdisciplinary model approach to service delivery, and interagency coordination and collaboration.

Individualized Programs

Given the heterogeneity of the population of children served in early intervention programs, no one set of curricular objectives is appropriate for all children. Rather, the needs of children and their families must be individually assessed, and from that assessment a plan specifically tailored to the child and family must be developed. Family participation in a manner that is consistent with the family's beliefs and values is essential. With the variety of needs peculiar to this age group (medical, educational, social, basic caregiving), an individualized approach is particularly necessary to ensure a comprehensive and appropriate program.

Family-Oriented Approach

The needs and life of the very young child are integrally intertwined with the family. Rather than "serving" the young child as an entity, the service delivery system must see the child and family as a unit or a system. Any intervention attempt with an infant would be limited indeed were it to focus solely on the child. Furthermore, attempts to "teach" or provide therapy to a child exclusive of the parent's wants and involvement may actually be deleterious to the evolving parent–child relationship. The early years are an important time for the formation of this relationship, and families are best served by professionals who support parents in their roles, rather than by professionals who try to assume these roles.

Developmental and Functional Curricular Approach

Infancy is a period of rapid growth and development, and many developmental changes are predicated on the achievement of earlier ones. Therefore, a developmental approach is warranted for use with very young children and infants. However, not all children, such as those with multiple and/or severe handicaps, will develop quickly or according to the normal developmental sequence. Therefore, it is necessary also to teach those skills or promote those actions that are functional for the child or family. To be included in the "curriculum" of a program, any goal should be (a) developmentally appropriate and (b) functional for the child and desired by the family. For example, working on assisting a child to reach may be seen as developmentally appropriate for an infant and also functional in that the child can use this behavior to engage the environment.

Transdisciplinary Staffing Model

The need for professionals from a variety of disciplines is particularly acute in infancy. Many children have medical and educational needs, and many families desire social service network supports. Moreover, families must often initiate contact with a variety of professionals in their quest to work out the best set of services for their children. The approach that offers the highest degree of coordinated services and involvement of parents is the transdisciplinary approach. In this approach professionals from a variety of disciplines form a team and, together with the family members, evaluate, plan, and implement child and family programs. A major emphasis is placed on ongoing staff development, role sharing, and collaboration. Such a model appears to offer both professional development opportunities for staff members and a truly coordinated system of service delivery for families.

Interagency Collaboration

Given the diversity of child and family needs, families are likely to interact with a variety of agencies to procure services for their children. This situation often results in multiple assessments, many appointments, and confusion for families. A coordinated system of defined interagency collaborative arrangements in a community can save duplication of efforts across agencies and afford families a more manageable system with which to work. At a time when the stresses of child care may be major, such collaborative efforts can be particularly needed and welcomed by families. The potential cost-effectiveness of such efforts provides a benefit to society as well.

Summary

Early intervention for infants born at risk or disabled requires a comprehensive, planned system of service delivery. The provision of such services in the United States is grounded in a long and rich history of services to young children and children with special needs and their families. Despite this history, many questions remain as to the best means and best types of early intervention services. However baffling some of these questions remain, there is a significant amount of experience in this country in early intervention and a defined commitment to providing services to young children and their families in need. The purpose of this text is to define current "preferred practices" in early intervention and outline strategies that can be used for implementing these practices.

References

Adelson, E., & Fraiberg, S. (1974). Gross motor development in infants blind from birth. *Child Development, 45,* 114–126.

Aronson, M., & Fallstrom, K. (1977). Immediate and long-term effects of developmental training in children with Down's syndrome. *Developmental Medicine and Child Neurology, 19,* 489–494.

Bailey, E. J., & Bricker, D. D. (1984). The efficacy of early intervention for severely handicapped infants and young children. *Topics in Early Childhood Special Education, 4*(3), 30–51.

Baker, B., & Heifetz, L. (1976). The Read Project: Teaching manuals for parents of retarded children. In T. Tjossem (Ed), *Intervention strategies for high-risk infants and young children* (pp. 351–369). Baltimore: University Park Press.

Baker, B., Heifetz, L., & Murphy, D. (1980). Behavioral training for parents of mentally retarded children: One year follow-up. *American Journal of Mental Deficiency, 85,* 31–38.

Beller, E. K. (1979). Early intervention programs. In J. D. Osofsky (Ed.), *Handbook of infant development* (pp. 852–894). New York: Wiley.

Berrueta-Clement, J. R., Schweinhart, L. J., Barnett, W. S., Epstein, A. S., & Weikart, D. P. (1984). *Changed lives: The effects of the Perry Preschool Program on youths through age 19.* Ypsilanti, MI: High/Scope Press.

Bidder, R. T., Bryant, G., & Gray, O. P. (1975). Benefits to Down's syndrome children through training their mothers. *Archives of Disease in Childhood, 50,* 383–386.

Bricker, D. D. (1989). *Early intervention for at-risk and handicapped infants, toddlers, and preschool children* (2nd ed.). Palo Alto, CA: VORT.

Bricker, D. D., & Dow, M. G. (1980). Early intervention with the young severely handicapped child. *Journal of the Association for the Severely Handicapped, 5*(2), 130–142.

Bronfenbrenner, U. (1975). Is early intervention effective? In B. Z. Friedlander, G. M. Sterritt, & G. E. Kirk (Eds.), *Exceptional infant: Assessment and intervention* (Vol. 3, pp. 449–475). New York: Brunner/Mazel.

Casto, G., & Mastropieri, M. A. (1985). *The efficacy of early intervention programs for handicapped children: A meta-analysis.* Unpublished manuscript, Early Intervention Research Institute, Utah State University, Logan.

Casto, G., & Mastropieri, M. (1986). The efficacy of early intervention programs. A meta-analysis. *Exceptional Children, 52*(5), 417–424.

Casto, G., & White, K. (1984). The efficacy of early intervention programs with environmentally at-risk infants. *Journal of Children in Contemporary Society, 17,* 37–48.

Clarke, A. D. B., & Clarke, A. M. (1976). *Early experience: Myth and evidence.* New York: Free Press.

Clunies-Ross, G. G. (1979). Accelerating the development of Down's syndrome infants and young children. *The Journal of Special Education, 13*(2), 169–177.

Connolly, B., & Russell, F. (1976). Interdisciplinary early intervention program. *Physical Therapy, 56*(2), 155–158.

Denhoff, E. (1981). Current status of infant stimulation or enrichment programs for children with developmental disabilities. *Pediatrics, 67*(1), 32–46.

Dunst, C. J., & Rheingrover, R. M. (1981). Analysis of the efficacy of infant intervention programs for handicapped children. *Evaluation and Program Planning, 4,* 287–323.

Dunst, C. J., & Snyder, S. W. (1986). A critique of the Utah State University early intervention meta-analysis research. *Exceptional Children, 53*(3), 269–279.

Field, T., Widmayer, S., Greenberg, R., & Stoller, S. (1982). Effects of parent training on teenager mothers and their infants. *Pediatrics, 69*(6), 703–707.

Fredericks, B., Baldwin, V., Moore, W., Templeman, T., & Anderson, R. (1980). The Teaching

Research data-based classroom model. *Journal of the Association for the Severely Handicapped, 5*(3), 211–223.

Garland, C., Stone, N. W., Swanson, J., & Woodruff, G. (Eds.). (1981). *Early intervention for children with special needs and their families.* Monmouth, OR: Western States Technical Assistance Resource (WESTAR).

Gordon, N., & Kogan, K. (1975). A mother instruction program: Behavior changes with and without therapeutic intervention. *Child Psychiatry and Human Development, 6,* 89–105.

Gorski, P. A. (1984). Infants at risk. In M. J. Hanson (Ed.), *Atypical infant development* (pp. 57–80). Austin, TX: PRO-ED.

Hanson, M. J. (1981). Down's syndrome children: Characteristics and intervention research. In M. Lewis & L. Rosenblum (Eds.), *The uncommon child* (pp. 83–114). New York: Plenum.

Hanson, M. J. (1985). An analysis of the effects of early intervention services for infants and toddlers with moderate and severe handicaps. *Topics in Early Childhood Special Education, 5*(2), 36–51.

Hanson, M. J. (1987). *Teaching the infant with Down syndrome: A guide for parents and professionals* (2nd ed.). Austin, TX: PRO-ED.

Hanson, M. J., & Harris, S. R. (1986). *Teaching the young child with motor delays.* Austin, TX: PRO-ED.

Hanson, M. J., & Schwarz, R. H. (1978). Results of a longitudinal intervention program for Down's syndrome infants and their families. *Education and Training of the Mentally Retarded, 13*(4), 403–407.

Hayden, A. H., & Dmitriev, V. (1975). The multidisciplinary preschool program for Down's syndrome children at the University of Washington Model Preschool Center. In B. Z. Friedlander, B. M. Sterritt, & G. E. Kirk (Eds.), *Exceptional infant: Assessment and intervention* (Vol. 3, pp. 193–221). New York: Brunner/Mazel.

Horton, K. (1976). Early intervention of hearing-impaired infants and young children. In T. Tjossem (Ed.), *Intervention strategies for high-risk infants and young children* (pp. 371–380). Baltimore: University Park Press.

Hunt, J. M. (1961). *Intelligence and experience.* New York: Ronald Press.

Infant Health and Development Program. (1990). Enhancing the outcomes of low-birth-weight, premature infants. *Journal of the American Medical Association, 263*(22), 3035–3042.

Lazar, I., & Darlington, R. (1982). Lasting effects of early intervention: A report from the Consortium for Longitudinal Studies. *Monographs of the Society for Research in Child Development, 47*(Serial No. 195).

Lewis, M. (1984). Developmental principles and their implications for at-risk and handicapped infants. In M. J. Hanson (Ed.), *Atypical infant development* (pp. 3–24). Austin, TX: PRO-ED.

Lorenz, K. Z. (1937). The companion in the bird's world. *Auk, 54,* 245–273.

Ludlow, J. R., & Allen, L. M. (1979). The effect of early intervention and preschool stimulus on the development of the Down's syndrome child. *Journal of Mental Deficiency Research, 23,* 29–44.

Martin, S. L., Ramey, C. T., & Ramey, S. L. (1990). The prevention of intellectual impairment in children of impoverished families: Findings of a randomized trial of educational daycare. *American Journal of Public Health, 80,* 844–847.

Pennsylvania Association for Retarded Children (PARC) v. Commonwealth of Pennsylvania, 334 F. Supp. 1257, 343 F. Supp. 279 (E.D. Pa. 1971, 1972).

Peters, D. L., Neisworth, J. T., & Yawkey, T. D. (1985). *Early childhood education: From theory to practice.* Monterey, CA: Brooks/Cole.

Peterson, N. L. (1987). *Early intervention for handicapped and at-risk children.* Denver: Love.

Phillips, J. L. (1975). *The origins of intellect: Piaget's theory* (2nd ed.). San Francisco: W. H. Freeman.

Piaget, J. (1952). *The origins of intelligence in children* (M. Cook, Trans.). New York: International Universities Press. (Original French edition, 1936)

Ramey, C. T., Bryant, D. M., Wasik, B. H., Sparling, J. J., Fendt, D. H., & Lavange, L. M. (1992). The Infant Health and Development Program for low birthweight, premature infants: Program elements, family participation, and child intelligence. *Pediatrics, 89,* 454–465.

Ramey, C. T., & Campbell, F. A. (1987). The Carolina Abecedarian Project: An educational experiment concerning human malleability. In J. J. Gallagher & C. T. Ramey (Eds.), *The malleability of children* (pp. 127–139). Baltimore: Brookes.

Ramey, C., MacPhee, D., & Yeates, K. (1983). Preventing developmental retardation: A general systems model. In L. Bond & J. Joffe (Eds.), *Facilitating infant and early childhood development* (pp. 343–401). Hanover, NH: University Press of New England.

Ramey, C. T., & Ramey, S. L. (1992). *At risk does not mean doomed: National Health/Education Consortium Occasional Paper #4*. Birmingham: Civitan International Research Center, University of Alabama at Birmingham.

Ramey, C. T., Sparling, J. J., & Wasik, B. (1981). Creating social environments to facilitate language development. In R. Schiefelbusch & D. Bricker (Eds.), *Early language: Acquisition and intervention* (pp. 447–476). Austin, TX: PRO-Ed.

Rynders, J. E., & Horrobin, J. M. (1980). Educational provisions for young children with Down's syndrome. In J. Gottlieb (Ed.), *Educating mentally retarded persons in the mainstream* (pp. 173–191). Baltimore: University Park Press.

Sameroff, A. J., & Chandler, M. J. (1975). Reproductive risk and the continuum of caretaking causality. In F. D. Horowitz (Ed.), *Review of child development research* (Vol. 4, pp. 187–244). Chicago: University of Chicago Press.

Schweinhart, L. J., Barnes, H. V., & Weikart, D. P. (1993). *Significant benefits: The High/Scope Perry Preschool Study Through Age 27. Monographs of the High/Scope Educational Research Foundation Number Ten*. Ypsilanti, MI: High/Scope Educational Research Foundation.

Schweinhart, L. J., Berrueta-Clement, J. R., Barnett, W. S., Epstein, A. S., & Weikart, D. P. (1985). Effects of the Perry Preschool Program on youths through age 19: A summary. *Topics in Early Childhood Special Education, 5*(2), 26–35.

Scott, K., & Masi, W. (1979). The outcome from the utility of registers of risk. In T. Field, A. Sostek, S. Godberg, & H. Shuman (Eds.), *Infants born at risk* (pp. 485–496). Jamaica, NY: Spectrum.

Shonkoff, J., & Hauser-Cram, P. (1987). Early intervention for disabled infants and their families: A quantitative analysis. *Pediatrics, 80*(5), 650–658.

Shonkoff, J., Hauser-Cram, P., Krauss, M., & Upshur, C. (1988). Early intervention efficacy research: What have we learned and where do we go from here? *Topics in Early Childhood Special Education, 8*(1), 81–93.

Simeonsson, R. J., Cooper, D. H., & Scheiner, A. P. (1982). A review and analysis of the effectiveness of early intervention programs. *Pediatrics, 69*(5), 635–641.

Skeels, H. M. (1966). Adult status of children with contrasting early life experiences. *Monographs of the Society for Research in Child Development, 31*(3, Serial No. 105).

Skeels, H. M., & Dye, H. B. (1939). A study of the effects of differential stimulation on mentally retarded children. *Proceedings and Addresses of the American Association on Mental Deficiency, 44*, 114–136.

Stone, J. L., Smith, H. T., & Murphy, L. B. (Eds.). (1973). *The competent infant*. New York: Basic Books.

Strain, P. (1984). Efficacy research with young handicapped children: A critique of the status quo. *Journal of the Division for Early Childhood, 9*, 4–10.

Strain, P., & Smith, B. (1986). A counter-interpretation of early intervention effects: A response to Casto and Mastropieri. *Exceptional Children, 53*(3), 260–265.

Tjossem, T. D. (Ed.). (1976) *Intervention strategies for high-risk infants and young children*. Baltimore: University Park Press.

Tyler, N., & Kogan, K. (1977). Reduction of stress between mothers and their handicapped children. *The American Journal of Occupational Therapy, 31*, 151–155.

Weber, C. U., Foster, P. W., & Weikart, D. P. (1978). *An economic analysis of the Ypsilanti Perry Preschool Project* (Monograph No. 5). Ypsilanti, MI: High/Scope Foundation Press.

White, K., & Casto, G. (1985). An integrative review of early intervention efficacy studies with at-risk children: Implications for the handicapped. *Analysis and Intervention in Developmental Disabilities, 5*, 7–31.

White, K. R., Mastropieri, M., & Casto, G. (1984). An analysis of special education early childhood projects approved by the Joint Dissemination Review Panel. *Journal of the Division of Early Childhood, 9*, 11–26.

Notes

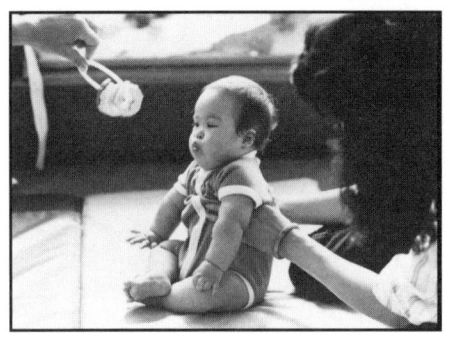

Children and Families in Early Intervention: Defining Disabilities and Risk Conditions

CHAPTER 2

All infants and toddlers who receive early intervention services have one thing in common: Because of a known disability or set of risk factors, they and their families have been identified as being eligible for services. The criteria for eligibility vary from state to state, but children with identified disabilities or risk conditions known to cause developmental delays are typically included in early intervention programs and services (Harbin, Gallagher, & Terry, 1991).

A wide range of biomedical conditions and risks can interfere with development. To assist in understanding these multiple factors, Tjossem (1976) developed a framework for defining risk factors that lead to developmental delay and disability. He proposed three categories of risk that often overlap: established, biological, and environmental. *Established risk* refers to medical disorders such as Down syndrome or Fragile X syndrome that have a known etiology and relatively predictable pattern of development that is associated with some level of developmental delay. *Biological risk* includes those conditions in which there is a history of complications in prenatal, perinatal, neonatal, or early development that suggests that there was an insult to the central nervous system.

Infants who are born prematurely, who are small for gestational age, or who are prenatally substance exposed are at biological risk. *Environmental risk* refers to situations and conditions in the child's life that interfere with development such as poor nutrition, or physical or psychological abuse. The possibility of overlap in these definitions is evident. For example, a premature infant who is difficult to feed and calm may be more likely to elicit abusive behavior in a situation in which parents are already stressed and having difficulty coping with life circumstances. Thus, environmental risk may be added to the existing biological risk. These definitions have gained wide acceptance across many professional disciplines and service delivery systems and can be used to consider the range of developmental issues that may make a child eligible for early intervention programs and services.

Although a child's medical diagnosis and its characteristics do not lead directly to a plan of developmental or educational intervention, they provide important information. Knowing a diagnosis can help the interventionist ask the right questions and be more effective in monitoring the child's progress. For example, knowing that young children with Down syndrome often have other medical and health-related problems allows the interventionist to be alert to these conditions and their impact on development. Because of the higher incidence of congenital heart disease, lowered resistance to infection, and a higher than average incidence of vision problems and hearing loss among infants and toddlers with Down syndrome (Blackman, 1990a), an interventionist needs to be alert to fatigue or restrictions in activity imposed by the heart condition, fluctuating hearing that may result from frequent ear infections, and developmental delays that may be the result of a vision problem rather than cognitive delay.

This chapter provides an overview of some of the major categories of established, biological, and environmental risks that are frequently encountered in early intervention settings. Because the categories often overlap, a condition discussed in one category might also be appropriate for inclusion in another. Several of the most common conditions are highlighted in each of the three risk areas, but the conditions presented and their discussion are not exhaustive. For more comprehensive information, a list of suggested readings is included at the end of the chapter.

Infants and Toddlers with Established Risk Conditions

Established risk conditions include genetic and biomedical causes of developmental delay and disability, such as chromosomal disorders, inborn errors of metabolism, congenital

malformations, neural tube defects, congenital infections, sensory loss, and injuries that result in disability and/or developmental delay. Although each child's developmental rate is unique, a direct link exists between the risk condition and the disability. Children may be minimally or significantly affected, but in nearly all instances an established risk results in developmental differences.

Chromosomal Disorders

Many children in early intervention programs have chromosomal disorders. Some of these disorders may be inherited and their occurrence in the family statistically predictable; others are the result of randomly occurring alterations in the genetic material during early cell division. To be inherited, one or both of the biological parents must have the gene. Although the pattern of transmission varies, achondroplasia (a type of dwarfism), cystic fibrosis, phenylketonuria (PKU), Tay-Sachs disease, Fragile X syndrome, Duchenne and Becker types of muscular dystrophy, and hemophilia are all examples of inherited chromosomal disorders. Down syndrome (in the majority of cases), Turner syndrome, and Cri-du-chat ("cat cry") syndrome are examples of disorders caused by noninherited chromosomal abnormalities.

Down syndrome

Perhaps the most recognizable and commonly known chromosomal disorder is Down syndrome (Crain, 1984). Although several genetic patterns or karotypes result in Down syndrome, 95% of those with Down syndrome have Trisomy 21, so named because of the extra chromosome attached to the 21st chromosome pair. Although developmental and educational outcomes vary widely, individuals with Down syndrome are often recognized by their physical features. Common features evident in infants include decreased muscle tone (hypotonia), small heads with a flattened back, upward slanting eyes with epicanthal folds at the inner corners, a single crease across the palm and soles of the feet, and short, wide hands with an inward curve of the little finger (Batshaw & Perret, 1992).

In absolute numbers the majority of children with Down syndrome are born to mothers under the age of 30, but the risk of having a child with Down syndrome increases significantly with parental age. Women between 35 and 39 are 6.5 times more likely and women between 40 and 44 are 20.5 times more likely to have a child with Down syndrome than those 20 to 24 years old (Batshaw & Perret, 1992). Although the numbers presented are based on maternal age, recent studies suggest that the father's aging is also a contributing factor (Batshaw & Perret, 1992).

Developmental Issues. During the early weeks and months of life, the greatest concerns for children with Down syndrome and their families is ensuring their survival and growth. Medical management of congenital heart or gastrointestinal problems takes priority in infants with these complications. Although development is delayed, many children with Down syndrome are closest to their age-mates during infancy and toddlerhood, with greater discrepancies emerging when faced with the demands of language and higher order cognitive tasks (Batshaw & Perret, 1992).

Implications for Support and Intervention. As children become medically stable, other developmental issues can be addressed. Emphasis on developing motor, communication, and cognitive skills is typical in early intervention programs. Playing and learning alongside typically developing peers often provides the motivation that children with Down syndrome need to increase motor and communication skills, as well as opportunities to practice social interactions that form the foundation for later relationships. Monitoring the child's vision and hearing is also important during early intervention. Seventy percent of those with Down syndrome have refractive errors that require glasses, and 60% to 80% have a hearing loss. To prevent additional disabilities, the early interventionist needs to work with the child's family to ensure that the child is carefully monitored and routinely assessed for vision and hearing problems.

Of equal importance is the provision of information and support for families based upon their requests. Several organizations have long been active in providing parent-to-parent and professional support to parents who have a child with Down syndrome. Through their publications, annual conferences, and local chapter meetings, a wealth of information is available. (A list of organizations and information resources is provided in Appendix B.)

Fragile X syndrome

As the second leading genetic cause of mental retardation (Down syndrome is first) and the most common inherited cause, Fragile X syndrome has been identified only recently (Lubs, 1969; Mazzocco & O'Connor, 1993; Verkerk et al., 1991). In males, Fragile X syndrome is associated with mental retardation that tends to become more significant during childhood, delayed communication skills, and behavioral difficulties similar to autism (Batshaw & Perret, 1992). In females, cognitive skills are less affected, but learning disabilities and mild mental retardation are common. Communication patterns differ and are characterized by cluttered speech and a high-pitched tone of voice (Batshaw & Perret, 1992). Girls with Fragile X often are described as being shy and withdrawn, and approximately 20% reportedly have psychiatric disorders (Reiss & Freund, 1990).

As with most syndromes, certain physical features are common. In Fragile X these include long, narrow faces; prominent ears and jaw; and large testicles in postpubescent males (Batshaw & Perret, 1992). Among infants and toddlers, the physical characteristics may not be pronounced, but delays in communication, cognitive skill development, and motor behavior become evident.

Developmental Issues. Because of the impact of the syndrome on the acquisition of cognitive, communicative, motor skills, and adaptive behavior, all of these areas are appropriate targets for intervention. Although each child's program is individually tailored to meet his or her own needs as well as those of the family, general strategies that are effective in all early intervention are appropriate for children with Fragile X syndrome.

Implications for Support and Intervention. For young children who manifest the delays associated with Fragile X syndrome, a transdisciplinary approach to early intervention is recommended. Because of the language, cognitive, and behavioral difficulties that often emerge as children grow and develop, a team of professionals working together can provide the most appropriate interventions.

As with all areas of early intervention, support and information for families is also an important function of the early intervention team. Because Fragile X is an inherited disability, knowledge about and access to genetic counseling is critical. One or more members of the early intervention team should be aware of resources for genetic counseling in the community or region and be able to talk with families about the process.

Phenylketonuria

Phenylketonuria (PKU) is a metabolic disease caused by an inherited chromosomal disorder. Chromosomal disorders that result in metabolic diseases are often referred to as inborn errors of metabolism. PKU is a model for examining these diseases because of the success that has been achieved in its diagnosis and treatment. Undetected or untreated PKU results in severe mental retardation, seizures, and behavior disorders; however, with detection and treatment, individuals with PKU function normally (Blackman, 1990a).

Individuals with untreated PKU are unable to convert phenylalanine to tyrosine; phenylalanine is an essential amino acid that is found in high protein foods. Although infants may appear normal at birth, the accumulation of unconverted phenylalanine in the blood and brain becomes toxic and causes mental retardation (Batshaw & Perret, 1992; Blackman, 1990a). The breakthrough in treating PKU came with the development of the first newborn screening test by Robert Guthrie in 1959 (Guthrie & Susi, 1963). By analyzing a few drops of blood from a heel stick, a diagnosis of PKU can be made before an infant is 2 weeks old, and a diet in which phenylalanine is restricted can be initiated to prevent mental retardation and accompanying disabilities (Batshaw & Perret, 1992).

The number of inborn errors of metabolism that can be detected shortly after birth has increased, and states typically mandate such testing before a newborn is released from a hospital. One of the goals of *Healthy People 2000: National Health Promotion and Disease Prevention Objectives,* developed under the auspices of the U.S. Department of Health and Human Services Public Health Service (1990), is to "increase to at least 95 percent the proportion of newborns that are screened by State-sponsored programs for genetic disorders and other disabling conditions and to 90 percent the proportion of newborns testing positive for disease who receive appropriate treatment" (p. 111).

Developmental Issues. When PKU is diagnosed and treated, developmental issues are the same as those for all young children. However, it is critical that the phenylalanine-restricted diet be observed through the early years of life and that the child's growth, development, and metabolic status be routinely monitored.

Implications for Support and Intervention. Developmental and educational support and intervention typically are not required for a young child with PKU whose condition is being treated. However, families may want information about the disease, its heritability, and strategies that other families have used to maintain the restrictions of their child's diet. Women who have been treated for PKU also need to visit genetics specialists when they are planning to become pregnant. Recent findings suggest that they must resume phenylalanine-restricted diets during pregnancy to prevent retardation caused by the higher levels of phenylalanine being transferred to the developing fetus (Hanley, Clarke, & Schoonheyt, 1987; Krywawych, Haseler, & Brenton, 1991).

Congenital Malformations

Malformations that occur during fetal development can be caused by a variety of agents. Although some are due to chromosomal disorders, the largest percentage (65%) are due to currently unknown causes (Beckman & Brent, 1986). Although many individuals have slight physical differences that have been present since birth, such as a birthmark, a crooked toe or finger, or pinched cartilage in the ear, congenital malformations are physical differences originating in the prenatal period that are significant enough to interfere with typical development (Buyse, 1990).

Agents that cause abnormalities in a developing fetus are called teratogens. Public health agencies in many large communities maintain a teratogen registry, which pregnant women can consult when they have been exposed to a chemical, substance, or other agent that they are afraid might affect their developing fetus. The extent of damage that a teratogen can cause depends on the timing and degree of the exposure (Batshaw & Perret, 1992). Two of the most commonly known teratogens are radiation and thalidomide. According to Batshaw and Perret (1992), "radiation was the first agent shown to cause birth defects, initially in animals and later in survivors of Hiroshima and Nagasaki" (p. 41). Thalidomide, the medication used to control nausea in pregnancy, was used extensively in Europe in the 1950s. Shortly thereafter a previously rare condition known as phocomelia began to appear. Individuals with phocomelia have short or missing limbs. Epidemiological studies determined that the increased incidence of phocomelia was a result of taking thalidomide during the first trimester of pregnancy (Batshaw & Perret, 1992).

Technologies such as ultrasonography often allow for prenatal detection of congenital malformations; however, when teratogens are known and avoided, their effects on the developing fetus can be prevented. To achieve the goal of primary prevention, more needs to be known about which agents interfere with normal fetal development, and efforts to inform the public about the risks of these agents must continue so that women planning pregnancies can avoid potentially harmful substances. For example, a medication used to treat severe acne (isotretinoin, or Accutane) is known to cause malformations of the face and head (Rosa, 1983). Tetracycline, also used to treat acne and a variety of infections, causes staining of the teeth. Although permanent teeth are not visible for many years after birth, the damage done during their formation in utero is evident when they do emerge (Batshaw & Perret, 1992). Current research suggests that 10% to 20% of infants born to mothers taking anticonvulsant medications have congenital malformations (Batshaw & Perret, 1992). Although anticonvulsant medications may be needed for the mother's safety, information about the risks and a carefully monitored pregnancy may help to reduce the chance that the baby will be affected.

Developmental issues

No single developmental issue pervades the wide range of congenital malformations that exist. In some instances, the severity of the malformation makes the infant's survival the primary concern. For example, infants born with exposed organs require immediate and intensive medical and surgical treatment to sustain life. Malformations that are not life-threatening may still require multiple surgeries over a long period of time. For example, children with craniofacial anomalies may require periodic surgery throughout their entire growth period. Other malformations, such as phocomelia, may not be surgically correctable but require a series of educational and therapeutic interventions that enable children to compensate for their physical differences.

Implications for support and intervention

Just as no two children are alike, no two children with malformations require exactly the same interventions. Each child's needs and each family's concerns and priorities will determine the range of early intervention programs and services to be provided. A child with cleft lip and palate, for instance, may be involved in a long course of surgeries, intensive assistance with communication, support from an occupational therapist or nurse around feeding issues, and inclusion in a toddler program that provides opportunities for interactions with nondisabled peers. The child's family may choose to become involved with a support group for families of children with cleft lip and palate, may request help in finding babysitting services to care for their other children during their child's surgeries, and may want to talk with a professional about the impact of frequent hospitalizations on developmental milestones and behavior. Regardless of the condition, a transdisciplinary approach that considers the whole child in the context of the family is an essential aspect of early intervention for children with congenital malformations.

Neural Tube Defects

The neural tube includes the vertebrae and the spinal cord, and neural tube defects encompass a number of congenital anomalies and malformations that affect this area. Although neural tube defects include malformations, they are discussed separately because of their unique nature and their prevalence among children in early intervention programs. Neural tube defects can be detected prenatally through ultrasonography, by measuring maternal blood serum alpha-fetoprotein (AFP) levels during the 12th to 14th weeks of pregnancy, or through amniocentesis (Blackman, 1990a; Committee on Genetics, 1991). An increasing amount is being learned about neural tube defects, and recent studies suggest that folate supplementation for the mother during the periconceptual period can significantly reduce the occurrence of neural tube defects (Blackman, personal communication; Czeizel & Dudas, 1992).

Spina bifida with myelomeningocele is the most common neural tube defect (Charney, 1992). Infants born with this condition have an opening in the back that allows a fluid-filled sac containing portions of malformed vertebrae as well as surrounding membranes to protrude out of an opening in the back. Nerves below the opening are affected with resulting paralysis, lack of sensation, and compromised bowel and bladder control (Charney, 1992). Hydrocephaly, an increased head size due to the body's inability to reabsorb cerebral spinal fluid, is present in 80% of children with myelomeningocele (Chauvel, 1991). Within the first few days of life, the opening in the back is surgically closed and often a ventriculoperitoneal shunt is implanted. The shunt, or tube, allows the cerebrospinal fluid to drain from the ventricles down to the abdominal cavity, where it is reabsorbed by blood vessels in membranes that surround the internal organs (Blackman, 1990a). Because shunts are mechanical, they can malfunction, so parents and interventionists must be alert to sudden illnesses, fevers, and vomiting that are signs of malfunctions or infections. As children grow shunts can be replaced, and some children outgrow the need for the shunt (Blackman, 1990a).

The prognosis for infants with myelomeningocele is variable, but many children who receive appropriate medical, developmental, and educational interventions have positive outcomes. Like children with Down syndrome who were once institutionalized at birth, children with myelomeningocele were assumed to have little hope for a future that included education, friendship, and successful careers. This is no longer true.

Developmental issues

Depending on the location of the opening in the back, various functions will be affected. The higher the lesion, the more systems are affected and the poorer the prognosis for walking and for bowel and bladder control (Chauvel, 1991). Due to the different possibilities, a variety of developmental issues must be addressed by the transdisciplinary team. Because even in the least affected child locomotor activity will be delayed because of surgeries and hospitalizations, physical therapists, medical professionals, and orthotists will be called on to work with the family on ambulation. For some children bracing is used to allow them to walk independently; others will learn to travel in a wheelchair. Early stages of independence that come with the ability to crawl and walk may not occur for toddlers with myelomeningocele; therefore, other opportunities for them to assert themselves become especially important. Decreased bowel and bladder control also interfere with individuation and autonomy, so strategies for maximizing independence in this area often occupy considerable time for families and interventionists well past the child's third birthday. Because of the higher incidence of learning disabilities among children with myelomeningocele, emphasis on maximizing chronologically age-appropriate exploration, problem-solving, and language skills is also important in early intervention programs.

Implications for support and intervention

All of the developmental issues mentioned in the previous section are used as a framework for providing support and intervention. Depending on each child's individual pattern of development, medical needs, and health status and the family's concerns and priorities, the Individualized Family Service Plan (IFSP) is developed and implemented. Like most toddlers and preschoolers, those with neural tube defects need to be with same-age peers without disabilities as an important part of learning and social development.

Families with children with myelomeningocele often interact with many medical and allied health professionals. Working to ensure coordination within and across systems, providing information and support as requested, and providing flexibility in the programs and services available can increase the likelihood of successful outcomes for children with myelomeningocele and their families.

Congenital Infections

Infections contracted after birth, such as encephalitis and meningitis, can result in severe disability including mental retardation, but this section addresses only those acquired before or during birth. These infections can be caused by bacteria, viruses, or protozoan organisms and can result in a wide range of outcomes from minimal effect on the developing organism to significant, lifelong disabilities. As Blackman (1990a) stated, the most is known about six infections often referred to as the TORCH-S or STORCH infections. The acronym stands for: *t*oxoplasmosis, *o*ther infections, *r*ubella, *c*ytomegalic inclusion disease, *h*erpes, and *s*yphilis. Several of these infections are discussed in the following paragraphs; for more complete information, see the suggested readings at the end of the chapter.

Toxoplasmosis

A protozoan organism carried by many animals is responsible for toxoplasmosis; however, its transmission is most commonly associated with cats. The tiny organisms exist in cysts that are eliminated with cats' feces into the soil or litter box cats use, creating an opportunity for infection (Blackman, 1990a). Raw meat and eggs from infected animals can also contain the protozoa, so uncooked meat and fish, as well as cookie dough and salad dressings made with uncooked eggs, should be avoided. Williamson and Demmler (1992) suggested that eating unwashed fruits and vegetables or inhaling materials from soil or litter boxes that contain cat feces should also be avoided. Healthy women who are infected with toxoplasmosis usually have no symptoms, but during an active infection, the organism can pass through the placenta to the developing fetus (Blackman, 1990a; Williamson & Demmler, 1992).

The results of prenatal infection vary. Spontaneous abortion may occur, or in a few cases the fetus may be born preterm with a series of health problems and mental retardation. In the largest percentage of infants born with toxoplasmosis who show no or minimal signs at birth, eye problems may occur later in development, and approximately 20% of those with no clinical symptoms show later neurodevelopmental difficulties (Wilson et al., as cited in Williamson & Demmler, 1992). Because transmission of toxoplasmosis does not occur from person to person, working with children who are born with the infection does not put the interventionist at risk (Blackman, 1990).

Human immunodeficiency virus/acquired immune deficiency syndrome

Although there has been debate in recent literature related to acquired immune deficiency syndrome (AIDS) and its cause (Duesberg, undated), this section relies on the dominant paradigm—that AIDS is a primarily sexually transmitted disease caused by the human immunodeficiency virus (HIV). AIDS has been added under the category of "other" to the list of congenital infections that can seriously compromise fetal and early childhood development. An individual who tests positive for HIV is said to be HIV positive; the diagnosis of AIDS is not made until the individual displays symptoms of the disease. According to Conlon (1992), 80% of the children who are HIV positive or have AIDS have contracted it from their mother. Three routes of transmission from mother to child have been identified: passage of the virus through the placental barrier; infant exposure to blood and vaginal secretions at birth; and infant exposure through breast milk (Batshaw & Perret, 1992; Caldwell & Rogers, 1991). According to Chu et al. (cited in Batshaw & Perret, 1992), AIDS "has become a disease of the inner city poor, with African Americans representing 58% of the children with the virus and Latinos another 26%. It is one of the top two causes of death in children age 1–4 years in these groups" (p. 122). However, anyone engaging in high-risk sexual behavior or intravenous drug use is a candidate for AIDS.

The course of AIDS in young children differs from that in adult AIDS. Among children, the incubation period is shorter, and the associated, opportunistic infections differ (Caldwell & Rogers, 1991; Calvelli & Rubenstein, 1990). Infants born to mothers who are HIV infected or who have AIDS usually fall into one of three categories: those under 15 months of age whose status cannot be determined until they lose their mother's antibodies; infants and young children who are proven to be infected but show no symptoms; and those who are infected and symptomatic (Johnson, 1993). AIDS-related cancers often seen in adults are rare in children, but bacterial infections, lung diseases, and failure to thrive are common (Johnson, 1993). Among children who are symptomatic, 78% to 93% have neurological problems (Calvelli & Rubenstein, 1990; Johnson, 1993). In addition to the problems of coping with a chronic disease, a high likelihood of parental loss, and out-of-home placement, children with HIV or AIDS face an additional threat: Lack of accurate information, fear, and prejudice in the general public lead to stigmatization.

Developmental Issues. In children who are HIV infected or have AIDS, nearly every issue of development is made more complex. For those who are infected and symptomatic, all areas of development are compromised by the disease. In addition to medical management issues, attachment is another major issue. Because of the frequent loss of the mother through death or debilitating illness and changes in primary caregivers because of hospitalizations or changing foster placements, children who are symptomatic or asymptomatic are at risk for attachment disorders.

Implications for Support and Intervention. Because of the complexity of issues involved in HIV infection, coordinated, comprehensive early intervention services are required. Although children with AIDS benefit from typical early childhood programs with special supports when they are healthy, where and how services are delivered depends upon the child's health and vulnerability to other infections. The only reason not to integrate a child with HIV infection is to protect the child, not for the safety of others in his or her environment (Batshaw & Perret, 1992).

Because AIDS is becoming a family disease (Krener & Miller, 1989), family support is a critical component of early intervention. Assisting families or primary caregivers to find a wide range of services, from respite care to financial support, from nutritional counseling to housekeeping and laundry services, may be part of the early interventionist's role. Providing or finding support for family members facing their own death as well as experiencing the loss of loved ones, is one of the most difficult roles that early interventionists may encounter as they work with children and families with AIDS (Lesar & Maldonado, 1994).

Rubella

Maternal rubella, or German measles, has long been known to affect the developing fetus. An epidemic in the United States in the mid-1960s resulted in more than 20,000 infants born with congenital rubella syndrome, a complex of problems most often associated with vision and hearing impairments that require early intervention (Williamson & Demmler, 1992). Although the number of children in the United States being born with congenital rubella syndrome has significantly decreased since the 1960s, in recent years there has been a steady rise in the number of cases reported to the Centers for Disease Control (Williamson & Demmler, 1992). Because infants born with congenital rubella syndrome continue to excrete infectious concentrations of the virus through saliva, nasal mucus, and urine for 3 to 6 months after birth, women who are pregnant or planning to become pregnant need to be aware of the possibility of contagion.

Developmental Issues. Depending on the type and extent of disability caused by prenatal rubella infection, developmental issues differ. However, the most common concerns relate to the child's vision, hearing, and rate of cognitive development. Significant vision or hearing loss affects all other developmental areas. Loss of vision not only delays mobility but also has an impact on the rate of language acquisition and social interaction. Hearing losses also delay language acquisition and social interaction. For a child with congenital rubella syndrome, like all young children with special needs, an IFSP is needed that addresses their particular needs as well as those of the family.

Implications for Support and Intervention. Early attention to hearing and vision loss or impairment is one of the primary goals of early intervention. Because both disabilities significantly impact communication, assisting the child and his or her family to find ways of communicating is a priority. Cognitive and motor delays should also be assessed and addressed by service providers. Although addressing sensory losses is critical, it is important to remember that all children need opportunities for social interactions and opportunities to practice emerging skills in natural environments. This suggests that, regardless of the intensity of intervention related to vision and hearing, young children need not be separated from their peers for all of their learning.

Cytomegalovirus infection

Cytomegalovirus (CMV) is a commonly occurring virus among children and adults, and it is estimated that one third to one half of the women in the United States have had a CMV infection at some time in their lives (Stagno et al., as cited by Williamson & Demmler, 1992). Approximately 40% of pregnant women who have a primary CMV infection during pregnancy transmit the virus to the fetus (Stagno et al. as cited by Williamson & Demmler, 1992). Although the infection may go unnoticed in an otherwise healthy adult or cause mild, flu-like symptoms, the consequences for the developing fetus are much greater. Of the 10% who are identified at birth, almost all have developmental hearing or neurological problems (Pass, Stagno, Myers, & Alford, 1980). Cerebral palsy and vision problems have also been found in those children who show symptoms at birth. According to Williamson and Demmler (1992), the outcomes for children who are asymptomatic at birth are less clear. Although sensory loss has been observed, data in existing studies conflict.

Infants and young children infected with CMV, whether symptomatic or asymptomatic, shed the virus, as do children and adults with postnatal CMV. Therefore, pregnant women should follow universal health precautions in all situations in which CMV might be present, including typical day care settings (Williamson & Demmler, 1992).

Developmental Issues. The developmental issues associated with congenital CMV vary depending on the extent and type of disability. For children with significant delays, all areas of development are affected. For those with delays or disabilities in specific areas, development within these areas becomes the focus of early intervention.

Implications for Support and Intervention. A comprehensive early intervention program tailored to the child's needs and the family's concerns and priorities is most often suggested for children known to have congenital CMV with symptoms that suggest developmental delays and differences. For those children with specific sensory, motor, or language disabilities, emphasis may be placed upon development or compensatory skills in these areas.

Cerebral palsy and other established risks

In addition to the conditions discussed in the previous paragraphs, many others frequently lead to disabilities or delays. Cerebral palsy, childhood accidents, injuries from abuse, deafness, blindness, organic or nonorganic failure to thrive, chronic diseases such as cystic fibrosis or muscular dystrophy, regulatory or behavioral difficulties, as well as delays of unknown etiology are common diagnoses in early intervention programs. Because many children who receive early intervention services have cerebral palsy, it is highlighted in this section.

Cerebral palsy (CP) is a medical diagnosis that refers to any disorder of movement or posture that occurs as a result of damage to the immature brain (Batshaw, Perret, & Kurtz, 1992). Cerebral palsy can be caused by multiple factors and can occur prenatally, perinatally, or postnatally. The way in which cerebral palsy is classified also varies. One classification system uses a three-group model that refers to the site of the damage. In this system, pyramidal CP indicates that the motor cortex or pyramidal tract have been damaged, causing spastic movements. Extrapyramidal CP refers to damage that is outside the pyramidal tract. The insult or injury may be to a tract that passes through the basal ganglia or comes from the cerebellum. This type of cerebral palsy typically results in fluctuating muscle tone and abrupt, uncontrollable movement. When both pyramidal and extrapyramidal types of CP occur together, the type of cerebral palsy is described as mixed (Batshaw et al., 1992). Another system classifies CP by the part of the body that is affected. In that system, hemiplegia refers to involvement of the arm and leg on one side of the body, quadriplegia involves all four limbs, and paraplegia involves the legs only (Fraser & Hensinger, 1983). Interventionists may see medical records in which both classification systems are used to describe a child's motor disability, so the diagnosis could be written as spastic hemiplegia.

The diagnosis of cerebral palsy is usually made late in the child's first year or during the second year of life, because the signs and symptoms are variable and some cannot be detected until certain milestones are reached. However, children who are born prematurely, those who weigh less than 1,500 grams at birth, and twins are at greater risk for cerebral palsy (Batshaw et al., 1992). Once the diagnosis is made, the most important issue is treatment. Treatment includes strategies that prevent additional disability, as well as adaptations that allow the child to function as comfortably and normally as possible. Although CP is not degenerative, its consequences on movement and posture can cause additional disabilities if left untreated.

Developmental Issues. Because cerebral palsy is a motor disability, many systems and areas of development can be affected. For some children, sitting, standing, walking, and running may be significantly delayed or require special assistance because of abnormal muscle tone or movement patterns. For children whose mouth and tongue movements are involved, both feeding and speech production may be limited. Even vision may be affected because of muscle tone abnormalities that make it difficult or impossible for the child to track objects visually. In addition to motor problems, many children with cerebral palsy also have mental retardation. Although the incidence of mental retardation varies with the type of cerebral palsy, approximately 66% of those with CP also have cognitive limitations (Batshaw et al., 1992). Whenever delays and disabilities affect physical development, it is likely that social and emotional development will also be affected. Inability to achieve independence at the expected ages, continued dependency on others to have one's basic needs met, and difficulty with communication put additional stress on the young child struggling for autonomy.

Implications for Support and Intervention. Perhaps the single most critical factor in creating effective early intervention programs for children with cerebral palsy is the emphasis on adaptation (M. D. Klein, personal communication, August 15, 1994). Positioning the child to interact with the world and handling the child in ways that do not increase irritability or create discomfort are prerequisites to any other intervention. With the support and instruction of physical and occupational therapists, families and service providers can learn appropriate positioning and handling techniques. Interventionists can also learn ways to help children strengthen their muscles and bones to prevent contractures and improve overall motor skills (Batshaw et al., 1992). Speech–language therapists and audiologists are important members of the early intervention team to support the child's communication. For some children, speech therapy may be sufficient; for others, adaptive or augmentative communication devices may be required to enable them to communicate. Careful, ongoing assessments of cognitive skills through observation and report are equally critical to intervention. Because motor behavior is so highly related to the expression of cognitive ability in young children, children with cerebral palsy sometimes are assumed to be far more intellectually limited than they actually are. Therefore, it becomes especially important for the early intervention team to guard against underestimating the child's capabilities.

Because adaptations may need to be made in many environments, working closely with family members is especially important. Feeding, dressing, bathing, developing communication strategies, and other issues are critical for families and often require that specialists spend time in the home adapting equipment to the setting, the space available, and the family's lifestyle.

Each child, each family, and each situation differ, but in every instance, children are referred for early intervention programs and services to optimize physical, developmental, and social outcomes. Regardless of the risk condition(s), it is the responsibility of the early intervention team to work with the family to support the child's development in the context of the family.

Infants and Toddlers At Biological Risk

An increasing proportion of infants born in the United States are born at biological risk. In some instances high-risk behaviors of parents have put the infants at risk for a variety of conditions associated with poor developmental outcomes. In other instances the scientific and technological advances that have enabled them to be born impose risks. Regardless of the cause, all of these infants have been exposed to some condition or situation that increases the likelihood that they and their families will need early intervention programs or services. This section of the chapter discusses several of the conditions known to put children at biological risk. As stated early in the chapter, risk conditions are often overlapping and many could be included under established, biological, or environmental risks; therefore, the decision to place the conditions discussed in this section under biological risk could be debated.

Prematurity, Illness, and/or Low Birth Weight

Medical and technological advances in the last several decades have had tremendous implications for infants born at risk due to prematurity, illness, and/or low birth weight. Today, the lives of many babies are being saved, even those born so small that they can fit into the palm of an adult hand. Although responsible for saving lives, these advances also have introduced new challenges for care providers in the health professions and early intervention. Not only does the condition itself (e.g., preterm birth or illness) create risk, but this early treatment may introduce new risks. For example, in the hospital intensive care nursery, the excessive stimulation from handling in routine care and from noise created by the equipment may negatively affect the baby born preterm (Slavik, Holloway, & Milburn, 1989). Many of these infants will overcome the trauma of their earliest experiences; others will demonstrate developmental delays or difficulties.

Infants born prematurely

Preterm birth is typically defined as birth before the 37th week of pregnancy (full-term gestation is 40 weeks). Healthy premature infants (usually born between 32 and 36 weeks gestational age) may show initial variations in development from the healthy full-term baby. Typically, these babies are hospitalized for a relatively short time while their development is monitored, their growth is completed, and they learn to feed adequately without complications before they are released home. They may demonstrate differences in motor development, such as less flexion, especially when placed on their back, and increased extension in their arms and legs with jerky movements. Some motor behaviors such as mild asymmetry, low muscle tone, or extensor tone and arching may persist into the second year (Dubowitz, 1988; Thom, 1988). When examining the development of these babies, one must adjust the infant's developmental age to account for the degree of prematurity so that development is viewed with more realistic expectations.

Some babies born prematurely, especially those born at extreme prematurity, may face complications and illness. These complications or conditions in the postnatal period are respiratory distress syndrome (also called hyaline membrane disease), infection, intracranial hemorrhage, malnutrition created by feeding difficulties, jaundice, apnea (pause in respiration), necrotizing enterocolitis (inflammation of the intestinal wall tissue), and patent ductus arteriosus (failure of a small blood vessel in the heart, the ductus arteriosus, to close) (Blackman, 1990b). The nature and degree of these complications will affect the baby's development.

Infants born with significant illnesses

Full-term infants who are hospitalized at or shortly after birth due to severe illness may demonstrate particular developmental needs. Following surgery or illness, they may need recovery time to heal and grow. Most will need sensitive care in early handling to establish feeding and sleeping routines, to help them sustain attention, and to conserve their energy for growth.

For infants who are chronically ill, such as babies with bronchopulmonary dysplasia, a chronic lung disease usually produced by prolonged mechanical ventilation, the increased risk of repeated rehospitalizations may negatively affect their developmental progress. These babies often demonstrate low thresholds for stimulation and will need modulated and careful caregiving and developmental support.

Infants born at low birth weight

Infants born at low birth weight may be born prematurely or at full term. Low birth weight is defined as below 2,500 grams (approximately 5.5 pounds). Population statistics reveal that approximately 7% of babies born in the United States weigh below 2,500 grams (United States Department of Health and Human Services, National Center for Health Statistics, 1991). Furthermore, as noted by the Children's Defense Fund (1994), African American infants are twice as likely to be born at low birth weight (13.6%) as White infants (5.8%).

Very low birth weight (associated with even greater risk) is typically considered to be below 1,500 grams. The developmental outcome for these babies in terms of degree of risk is greatly affected by the baby's environment. Factors such as socioeconomic status and maternal education are powerful predictors of outcome for these infants (Heyne, 1989).

Low birth weight may be due to premature birth, intrauterine growth retardation, or both (Blackman, 1990b). Genetic or inherited factors may produce intrauterine growth retardation, or it may be caused by infection (e.g., cytomegalovirus or rubella), environmental stress in the uterus, or placental insufficiency. "Intrauterine growth retardation is also associated with multiple births, cigarette smoking, high altitudes, drug addiction, alcohol abuse, toxemia, and hypertension" (Blackman 1990b, p. 184). When the stress occurs early in the pregnancy or is chronic, brain growth may be affected, leading to greater developmental risk than if the stress occurs later in the pregnancy. Whereas healthy preterm babies will likely catch up in growth during the second year of life, some babies born at low birth weight (also called small for gestational age) tend to remain smaller than average (Blackman, 1990b).

Development issues

Infants born at biological risk begin their lives in *neonatal intensive care units* (NICUs), also referred to as neonatal intensive care nurseries (NICNs). These units provide the highly specialized care needed by these babies who often experience prolonged and repeated hospitalizations. Researchers have begun to focus on the effects of the treatment itself on the fragile newborn's development. In the 1970s these units were believed to provide sensory deprivation, and regimens designed to stimulate infants were advocated. As smaller and sicker babies have been saved, this notion has been replaced. Studies have more closely examined the effects of stimulation, such as excessive auditory input from nursery equipment and excessive stimulation from handling to perform medical treatments, on the development of the fragile newborn whose immature physiological system may be unable to cope (Gorski, Hole, & Leonard, 1983; Long, Lucey, & Philip, 1980; Long, Philip, & Lucey, 1980). This body of research has led to greater attention to the effects of handling, the type of handling, and the overall impact of the NICU on the infant's development (Als, 1982, 1986). More information on the development of babies born at risk can be found in the resources listed at the end of this chapter.

Implications for support and intervention

Infants born at risk often need carefully tailored and modulated interventions, particularly during their early months. These babies tend to benefit from less stimulation and carefully modulated input because they often have very low thresholds to stimuli. Again, the references listed at the end of this chapter provide more in-depth information regarding the special intervention needs of these infants; several are of particular value to early interventionists who will work with families in the babies' early years (Hanson & VandenBerg, 1993; Hussey, 1988; Semmler & Butcher, 1990; VandenBerg & Hanson, 1993). Major areas of concern in tailoring these interventions are discussed briefly below.

Behavioral organization is one of the primary frameworks used to access and provide intervention for infants who are preterm, sick, or low birth weight. Babies born early will show signs of physiological stress due to their immaturity. Als (1982) described a model for understanding the behavior of the recovering neonate who is born at risk. She described infant behavior in five areas or subsystems: physiological, motor, state, attention, and self-regulatory. Each is discussed as it relates to intervention issues.

When recovering infants are discharged from NICUs, they are still in the process of recovery. Most of their means of communication early on will be expressed by *physiological* signs. Some of these signs include changes in respiration and heart rate (e.g., a pause in breathing due to intense stimuli such as noise, and a drop in heart rate) and changes in skin color (e.g., becoming less pink and more pale). These babies may also show startles or tremors from time to time and changes in muscle tone, gaze aversion, hiccoughing, spitting up, gagging, or bowel movements in response to increased activity (Als, 1982).

With respect to the *motor system*, these infants may demonstrate flailing or arching when held or repositioned and their muscle tone may fluctuate. Thom (1988) described sensorimotor patterns that are typical of infants born preterm. Some of these patterns include the tendency toward extensor tone, arching of the neck and upper trunk, less flexor tone, "jittery" appearing movements, decreased midline movements, greater likelihood of supported standing in tiptoe stance, and the tendency to retain primitive reflexes beyond the ages expected.

The infant's *state* early on is often difficult to differentiate, and the recovering premature infant is in the process of moving to a wider range of available states including the alert state. States progress from poorly differentiated to increasingly clearer and defined states, with smoother transitions between states.

The infant's *attention system* also may show differences from the full-term infant. In the early months these babies still do not have all their functions under control and they may show intense reactions or no responses at all to stimuli such as their parents' voices and faces. As they are able to maintain an alert state for longer periods of time, they become better able to attend to both visual and auditory stimuli separately and then at the same time.

Finally, the *self-regulatory system* is of special importance for caregivers. These recovering babies will typically differ from healthy full-term babies with regard to their abilities to maintain or control their states (e.g., sleep, alertness) and move from state to state. For example, they may be less able to soothe themselves by bringing their hand to mouth due to their history of positioning in the hospital and differences in their motor control. They may not be able to make smooth transitions from one state to another such as from alert to sleeping. Many of these infants are characterized as "fussy" and some cry uncontrollably for periods of time, whereas others sleep for seemingly endless periods. The inabilities of these infants to self-regulate effectively leave them at the mercy of their caregivers.

What can caregivers and interventionists do to more effectively support these infants? Suggestions include reading infants' cues and adjusting the environment. *Reading the infants' cues* requires careful observation. These babies give cues that indicate they are stressed and need a break, as well as cues that they are stable and ready for interaction (Hanson & VandenBerg, 1993; Hussey, 1988; Semmler & Butcher, 1990; VandenBerg & Hanson, 1993). Some of the *cues for stress or fatigue* include changes in breathing to faster breathing or pausing or gasping for breath; becoming pale or blue; showing gastrointestinal upset such as spitting up, gagging, hiccoughing, or bowel straining; startling or tremoring; coughing and sighing; becoming limp or stiff; arching; expressions characterized by a hyperalert or panicked look; dull expressions; and frantic or disorganized activity. *Cues indicating stability and readiness* include regular breathing; stable pink color; absence of coughing, gagging, and so forth; smooth limb movements; bringing hands to mouth and/or sucking on fingers or fist; ability to calm self by bracing foot against something like a bed; and maintaining a calm posture. These cues are the means by which the young baby can communicate. Caregivers can observe the infant's behavior carefully to know when to talk to the baby, handle the baby, or introduce something visually to the baby. When the baby shows signs of stress, the caregiver can understand that it is time to stop the stimulation and give the baby a chance to regroup and recover before providing more input.

Caregivers and interventionists can do a number of things to *adjust the environment to support the infant's early development.* These infants often need to be protected from overstimulation. Some suggestions for the early weeks and months include reducing light and noise until the infant indicates that he or she can cope with the more active world. Some infants can cope with only one activity at a time, such as dressing or being held or being talked to by the caregiver. Particularly during feeding, they need to conserve their energy to concentrate on one activity. Certain positions may be useful. These infants may benefit from being swaddled or wrapped or being placed in a kind of "nest" with blanket rolls tucked at their sides and feet. When up and awake, they may tire quickly. They may be able to tolerate baby seats or being held for only short periods of time initially. Toys including sounds and sights should be introduced one at a time and for short periods until the child indicates that these stimuli can be tolerated. As these infants grow and recover, they can tolerate increasing amounts of stimulation. However, caregivers and interventionists are cautioned to carefully watch the infant's cues and modulate the stimuli accordingly.

Infants Born At Risk Due to Prenatal Drug Exposure

One major risk factor is drug use by women of childbearing age. One national epidemiological report estimated that in 1990 in a given month, 4.8 million women of childbearing age used an illicit drug, 30.5 million used alcohol, and 17.4 million used nicotine (Khalsa & Gfroerer, 1991). Although an alarm has been sounded in the public media and professional literature, a great deal of research is needed in certain areas before long-term implications can be determined about drug effects for children exposed prenatally. It is important to keep in mind that a range of effects has been associated with drug exposure and that children who fall into this category do not represent a homogeneous group. Furthermore, given methodological and research difficulties in conducting research on drug use, many questions remain, particularly with regard to long-term outcomes. Research in this area is further complicated by difficulty in determining the contributions or effects of adverse living environments on the development of these children.

A recent literature review by Shriver and Piersel (1994) provides an excellent summary of the long-term physiological effects of intrauterine drug exposure on child development. Their findings are briefly reviewed in the following discussion in relation to existing knowledge about commonly used drugs.

Alcohol

The effect of prenatal alcohol exposure has received a great deal of research attention. Fetal alcohol syndrome (FAS) has been identified in children whose development is most adversely affected. FAS is associated with certain characteristics, including pre- and postnatal growth deficiency, facial malformations, and some central nervous system effects that may result in mental retardation, hyperactivity, or motor problems (Clarren, 1981; Streissguth, 1986). Children who demonstrate some, but not all of these characteristics, may be identified as having fetal alcohol effects (FAE). As indicated by Shriver and Piersel (1994), children who are diagnosed with FAS or FAE typically perform more poorly on measures of intelligence and achievement, exhibit difficulties in motor coordination, demonstrate behavioral difficulties such as poor attention, and show some physical difficulties and growth retardation. However, a continuum of effects were noted for those children who do not receive this diagnosis but who are believed to have been exposed prenatally to alcohol.

Cocaine

As Shriver and Piersel (1994) indicated, few studies have examined the long-term effects of intrauterine cocaine exposure. Most studies have documented effects in the first year of life. Effects have included decreased head circumference, increased prematurity and low birth weight, intrauterine growth retardation, congenital malformations of the genitourinary tract, and behavioral difficulties such as hyperexcitability and poor ability to self-regulate.

Heroin

Again, Shriver and Piersel (1994) pointed out the paucity of research on the effects of heroin use. Effects are not clear in that outcomes appear significantly related to the quality of the child's home environment.

Marijuana

The studies cited in Shriver and Piersel's (1994) review reported few differences in the development of children exposed prenatally to marijuana. Several studies indicated poorer performance on memory tasks in the preschool years, but the effects of environment were not controlled.

Multiple and polydrug use

The use of multiple drugs deserves special mention because it is believed that individuals who use drugs generally use more than one (Day & Richardson, 1991). Again, studies of long-term outcome are few. Research in this area is particularly difficult, given the interaction of drugs. Studies, however, have suggested behavioral differences in the children who were drug exposed with regard to state control, greater lability, and poorer consolability (Chasnoff, Burns, Burns, & Schnoll, 1986).

The area of prenatal substance exposure is of intense interest to professionals and the public alike, and information is being published at a rapid rate. *Topics in Early Childhood Special Education* (Hanson, 1994) devoted an entire issue to the topic of developmental effects of prenatal substance exposure, and the reader is directed to this volume for more specific information. The Early Childhood Research Institute of Substance Abuse, which is a consortium of researchers from the University of Kansas, the University of Minnesota, and the University of South Dakota, is an excellent source of information. Researchers from this institute, Carta et al. (1994), presented a comprehensive review and analysis of the experimental literature on behavioral outcomes of children prenatally exposed to illicit drugs.

Implications for support and intervention

Given the dearth of information regarding the long-term development outcomes for children exposed to drugs prenatally, it is difficult to plan interventions specifically related to this group. Furthermore, even if studies were conclusive as to developmental effects, the often overriding effect of the child's home environment must not be underestimated. Finally, as previously stated, this group of children does not represent a homogeneous group.

These issues point to several intervention concerns. Interventions aimed at supporting the development of children prenatally exposed to drugs must take a comprehensive, family-focused, systems-level approach. The child cannot be examined separately from the family, and the needs of the families who may be living in an at-risk environment must be considered. Poulsen (1994) outlined such a comprehensive stance in a review of the policy recommendations made by a California task force. Among the recommendations are the avoidance of a "label" for this group of children; the provision of comprehensive and family-centered services for infants, their mothers, and other family members; treatments that address drug recovery; appropriate assessment and identification; coordination of management and follow-up; attention to out-of-home placement issues, such as recruitment of and training for foster families; the need for appropriately trained personnel in the child care, health, and education fields; and interagency collaboration.

The early interventionist is cautioned to avoid labeling or overgeneralizing about this group of children. The same preferred practices that are identified in this volume are advocated for children who are at risk due to prenatal drug exposure. In addition, the reader is directed to the discussion of support and interventions for children born at risk due to prematurity, low birth weight, and illness, because many of the children who have been prenatally drug exposed also fall into this risk category. Further, the strategies for reading infants' cues and adapting the environment are appropriate considerations for this group of children as well, given the difficulties often reported with behavioral regulation.

As with all risk conditions, the needs of each child and family should be individually determined through a joint partnership between family members and professionals. Because many children who have been exposed to drugs prenatally may be living in an out-of-home placement, working with foster families and nonbiological parents, instead of or in addition to biological parents, may present additional challenges for the early interventionist. Hanson, Poulsen, and McKinney (1995) more fully describe issues associated with family foster care. Although the number of contacts and the complications in the child's life may increase the work load and challenge for the service providers, coordinated service delivery with all the agencies and caregivers concerned with the child is essential to effective interventions that are child and family focused.

Infants Born At Environmental Risk

Environmental risks include life circumstances and situations that interfere with healthy development. These risks are often cumulative and lead to a variety of developmental and behavioral difficulties that intensify as children grow older. For example, lack of adequate nutrition, housing, and a basic sense of safety and well-being in early life may lead to poor attachment, attention, and school failure in childhood. In adolescence, these may lead to alienation, identification with gangs to gain personal and social validation, and early school leaving, which result in poorly educated, poorly socialized, and ineffective adults. Although many children who are exposed to environmental risks find personal support through caring family members, teachers, or other significant adults in their lives, many do not. Perhaps the greatest tragedy is that many of the environmental risks to which infants and young children are exposed are preventable. This section discusses one of the major environmental risks in the United States today—poverty.

The effects of poverty can be pervasive and overriding in a child's life. The transactional model presented by Sameroff and Chandler (1975) underscores the overarching influence of the caregiving environment. In reviewing longitudinal studies of developmental outcomes for children, these researchers point to the powerful effects of the environment in compensating for or negatively interacting with other risks, such as biological risk conditions, in producing child outcomes. These studies suggested that children born at greater biological risk but raised in nurturing environments often fared better than those born at lesser biological risk but reared in a non-nurturing milieu.

The issue of children growing up in poverty is of tremendous concern in this society. A recent publication from the Children's Defense Fund (1994) reported an increase in the number of children living in poverty from 14.3 million in 1991 to 14.6 million in 1992 based upon census data. This report further stated that "One in every four children younger than six was poor, as were 27 percent of all children younger than three" (p. 2). The 1993 poverty line (defined by the U.S. Department of Health and Human Services guidelines) was an income below $11,890 for a three-person family. Based on the data reviewed by the Children's Defense Fund (1994), the child poverty rate in 1992 was 21.9%. These data also indicated that, in female-headed households where no other adults were present, 54% of the 14.8 million children in these households were poor.

Children living in poverty may be deeply and negatively affected. Poverty is associated with many other risk conditions, including greater risk of infectious and parasitic disease, accidents, poor health and nutrition, health and learning problems, and exposure to toxic environments (Children's Defense Fund, 1994). The effects of one of these risks, inadequate nutrition, are documented in the National Center for Children in Poverty (Klerman & Parker, 1990) report, indicating that impoverished children under age 6 are more likely than their peers to present signs of malnutrition, which include growth retardation, iron deficiency, and anemia.

Other risks associated with living in poverty are homelessness and exposure to violent situations. The Children's Defense Fund (1994) estimated that 100,000 children are homeless each night in this country and that the proportion of the homeless who are families with children is 36%. The Children's Defense Fund (1994) report also sounded the alarm on the number of violent incidents in the lives of the nation's children.

The Child Welfare League of America (Merkel-Holguin & Sobel, 1993) stated that "Young children are more likely to be poor than any other age group in the United States" (p. 153). The implications of living in poverty are overwhelming for many children. Early interventionists are cautioned to recognize the *potential* effects of poverty, while taking care not to assume that all individuals living in poverty will have children who are deleteriously affected. Again, a family-centered, coordinated approach to early intervention will assist the interventionist in supporting family strengths while providing families the resources that they identify and request.

Summary

Infants and toddlers may be referred to early intervention programs and services for a variety of reasons. Some have identified disabilities or conditions that are recognizable at birth and are highly correlated with developmental delay or other special needs. For these children, developmental and educational early intervention may ameliorate the delay and prevent additional disabilities from occurring. Other children may experience an event in utero, at birth, or shortly thereafter that may or may not lead to developmental problems. Infants born prematurely, those prenatally drug exposed, and those who are seriously ill may need the extra support that early intervention provides but soon move past the need for specialized services; others in this group will need ongoing services. Another group of infants and toddlers will enter the world intact but encounter environmental conditions that interfere with healthy development. For these children, individual as well as systemwide intervention can make a positive difference in their outcomes.

Although each child's needs and each family's concerns, priorities, and resources differ, some generalizations can be made about serving children and families in early intervention programs:

- Although a young child's special need may appear to be limited to one area of development, it is important to consider the whole child and implement strategies that fit with family preferences and total development.
- All infants and toddlers are more like their peers than they are different. Regardless of their medical condition, disability, or developmental difference, they are children who deserve opportunities to be a part of everyday life with their families and peers.
- Infants have their own cues that enable parents, interventionists, and caregivers to understand their needs. An important part of early intervention is learning to read the babies' cues and teaching those around them to read and respond appropriately.
- Comprehensive, coordinated, family-centered, interagency services improve outcomes for families, children, and the service systems involved. There is too much to do for one family or professional to do it alone.

References

Als, H. (1982). Towards a research instrument for the assessment of preterm infants' behavior and manual for the Assessment of Preterm Infants' Behavior (APIB). In H. D. Fitzgerald, B. M. Lester, & M. W. Yogman (Eds.), *Theory and research in behavioral pediatrics* (pp. 35–132). New York: Plenum Press.

Als, H. (1986). A synactive model of neonatal behavioral organization: Framework for assessment and support of the neurobehavioral development of the premature infant and his parents in the environment of the neonatal intensive care unit. In J. K. Sweeney (Ed.), *The high risk neonate: Developmental therapy perspectives* (pp. 3–55). New York: Haworth Press.

Batshaw, M. L., & Perret, Y. M. (1992). *Children with disabilities: A medical primer* (3rd ed.). Baltimore: Brookes.

Batshaw, M. L., Perret, Y. M., & Kurtz, L. A. (1992). Cerebral palsy. In M. L. Batshaw & Y. M. Perret, *Children with disabilities: A medical primer* (3rd ed., pp. 441–469). Baltimore: Brookes.

Beckman, A. A., & Brent, R. L. (1986). Mechanism of known environmental teratogens: Drugs and chemicals. *Clinics in Perinatology, 13,* 649–687.

Blackman, J. A. (1990a). Down syndrome. In J. A. Blackman (Ed.), *Medical aspects of developmental disabilities in children birth to three* (2nd ed., pp. 107–111). Rockville, MD: Aspen.

Blackman, J. A. (1990b). Low birth weight. In J. A. Blackman (Ed.), *Medical aspects of developmental disabilities in children birth to three* (2nd ed., pp. 181–184). Rockville, MD: Aspen.

Buyse, M. L. (1990). *Birth defects encyclopedia.* Dover, MA: Center for Birth Defects Information Services.

Caldwell, M. B., & Rogers, M. F. (1991). Epidemiology of pediatric HIV infection. *Pediatric Clinics of North America, 38,* 45–67.

Calvelli, T. A., & Rubenstein, A. (1990). Pediatric HIV infection: A review. *Immunodeficiency Review, 2,* 83–127.

Carta, J. J., Sideridis, G., Rinkel, P., Guimaraes, S., Greenwood, C., Baggett, K., Peterson, P., & Atwater, J. (1994). Behavioral outcomes of infants and young children prenatally exposed to illicit drugs: A review of analysis of the experimental literature. *Topics in Early Childhood Special Education, 14,* 184–216.

Charney, E. B. (1992). Neural tube defects: Spina bifida and myelomeningocele. In M. L. Batshaw & Y. M. Perret, *Children with disabilities: A medical primer* (pp. 471–488). Baltimore: Brookes.

Chasnoff, I. J., Burns, K. A., Burns, W. J., & Schnoll, S. H. (1986). Prenatal drug exposure: Effects on neonatal and infant growth and development. *Neurobehavioral Toxicology and Teratology, 8,* 357–362.

Chauvel, P. (1991). Spina bifida and hydrocephalus. In A. J. Capute & P. J. Accardo (Eds.), *Developmental disabilities in infancy and early childhood* (pp. 383–393). Baltimore: Brookes.

Children's Defense Fund. (1994). *The state of America's children: Yearbook 1994.* Washington, DC: Author.

Clarren, S. K. (1981). Recognition of fetal alcohol syndrome. *The Journal of the American Medical Association, 245,* 2436–2439.

Committee on Genetics. (1991). Maternal serum alpha-fetoprotein screening. *Pediatrics, 75,* 58–64.

Conlon, C. J. (1992). New threats to development. In M. L. Batshaw & Y. M. Perret, *Children with disabilities: A medical primer* (pp. 111–136). Baltimore: Brookes.

Crain, L. S. (1984). Prenatal causes of atypical development. In M. J. Hanson (Ed.), *Atypical infant development* (pp. 27–55). Austin, TX: PRO-ED.

Czeizel, A. E., & Dudas, I. (1992). Prevention of the first occurrence of neural-tube defects by periconceptional vitamin supplementation. *New England Journal of Medicine, 327,* 1832–1835.

Day, N. L., & Richardson, G. A. (1991). Prenatal alcohol exposure: A continuum of effects. *Seminars in Perinatology, 15,* 271–279.

Dubowitz, L. M. S. (1988). Neurologic assessment. In R. Ballard (Ed.), *Pediatric care of the ICN graduate* (pp. 59–85). Philadelphia: Saunders.

Duesberg, P. (undated). HIV is not the cause of AIDS—Rethinking AIDS. (Available from Group for the Scientific Reappraisal of the HIV/AIDS Hypothesis, 2040 Polk Street, Suite 321, San Francisco, CA 94109)

Fraser, B. A., & Hensinger, R. N. (1983). *Managing physical handicaps: A practical guide for parents, care providers, and educators.* Baltimore: Brookes.

Gorski, P. A., Hole, W. T., & Leonard, C. H. (1983). Direct computer recording of premature infants and nursery care: Distress following two interventions. *Pediatrics, 72*(2), 198–202.

Guthrie, R., & Susi, A. (1963). A simple method for detecting phenylketonuria in large populations of newborn infants. *Pediatrics, 32,* 338–343.

Hanley, W. B., Clarke, J. T., & Schoonheyt, W. (1987). Maternal phenylketonuria (PKU)—A review. *Clinical Biochemistry, 20,* 149–156.

Hanson, M. J. (Ed.). (1994). Substance abuse and early intervention [Special issue]. *Topics in Early Childhood Special Education, 14*(2).

Hanson, M. J., Poulsen, M. K., & McKinney, L. E. (1995). The impact of family diversity on addiction, treatment, and recovery. In K. D. Lewis (Ed.), *Maternal drug use: Effect on the infant and the young child.* North Branch, MN: Sunrise River Press.

Hanson, M. J., & VandenBerg, K. A. (1993). *Homecoming for babies after the intensive care nursery: A guide for parents in supporting their baby's early development.* Austin, TX: PRO-ED.

Harbin, G. L., Gallagher, J. J., & Terry, D. V. (1991). Defining the eligible population: Policy issues and challenges. *Journal of Early Intervention, 15,* 13–20.

Heyne, E. (1989). Low birth weight infant follow-up at Children's Medical Center, Dallas. In C. J. Semmler (Ed.), *A guide to care and management of very low birth weight infants: A team approach* (pp. 124–135). Tucson, AZ: Therapy Skill Builders.

Hussey, B. (1988). *Understanding my signals: Help for parents of premature infants*. Palo Alto, CA: VORT.

Johnson, C. B. (1993). Developmental issues: Children infected with the human immunodeficiency virus. *Infants and Young Children, 6*(1), 1–10.

Khalsa, J. H., & Gfroerer, J. (1991). Epidemiology and health consequences of drug abuse among pregnant women. *Seminars in Perinatology, 15,* 265–270.

Klerman, L. V., & Parker, M. (1990). *Alive and well? A review of health policies and programs for young children*. New York: National Center for Children in Poverty.

Krener, P., & Miller, F. B. (1989). Psychiatric response to HIV spectrum of disease in children and adolescents. *Journal of the American Academy of Child and Adolescent Psychiatry, 28,* 596–605.

Krywawych, S., Haseler, M., & Brenton, D. P. (1991). Theoretical and practical aspects of preventing fetal damage in women with phenylketonuria. In J. Schaub, F. Van Hoof, & H. L. Vis (Eds.), *Inborn errors of metabolism* (pp. 125–135). New York: Raven Press.

Lesar, S., & Maldonado, Y. A. (1994). Infants and young children with HIV infection: Service delivery considerations for family support. *Infants and Young Children, 6*(4), 70–81.

Long, J. G., Lucey, J. F., & Philip, A. G. (1980). Noise and hypoxemia in the intensive care nursery. *Pediatrics, 65,* 143–145.

Long, J. G., Philip, A. G., & Lucey, J. F. (1980). Excessive handling as a cause of hypoxemia. *Pediatrics, 65,* 203–207.

Lubs, H. A. (1969). A marker X chromosome. *American Journal of Human Genetics, 21,* 231–244.

Mazzocco, M. M., & O'Connor, R. (1993). Fragile X syndrome: A guide for teachers of young children. *Young Children, 49*(1), 73–77.

Merkel-Holguin, L. A., & Sobel, A. J. (1993). *The child welfare stat book 1993*. Washington, DC: Child Welfare League of America.

Pass, R. F., Stagno, A., Myers, J. J., & Alford, C. A. (1980). Outcome of symptomatic congenital cytomegalovirus infection: Results of long-term longitudinal follow up. *Pediatrics, 66,* 758–762.

Poulsen, M. K. (1994). The development of policy recommendations to address the individual and family needs of infants and young children affected by perinatal substance use. *Topics in Early Childhood Special Education, 14,* 275–291.

Reiss, A. L., & Freund, L. (1990). Fragile-X syndrome. *Biological Psychiatry, 27,* 223–240.

Rosa, F. W. (1983). Teratogenicity of isotretinoin. *Lancet, 2,* 513.

Sameroff, A. J., & Chandler, M. J. (1975). Reproductive risk and the continuum of caretaking casualty. In F. D. Horowitz (Ed.), *Review of child development research* (Vol. 4, pp. 187–244). Chicago: University of Chicago Press.

Semmler, C. J., & Butcher, S. D. (1990). *Handle with care: Articles about the at-risk neonate*. Tucson, AZ: Therapy Skill Builders.

Shriver, M. D., & Piersel, W. (1994). The long term effects of intrauterine drug exposure: A review of recent research and implications for early childhood special education. *Topics in Early Childhood Special Education, 14,* 161–183.

Slavik, B., Holloway, E., & Milburn, D. (1989). A changing perspective: Early intervention. In C. J. Semmler (Ed.), *A guide to care and management of very low birth weight infants: A team approach* (pp. 53–76). Tucson, AZ: Therapy Skill Builders.

Streissguth, A. P. (1986). The behavioral teratology of alcohol: Performance, behavioral, and intellectual deficits in prenatally exposed children. In J. West (Ed.), *Alcohol and brain development* (pp. 3–44). New York: Oxford University Press.

Thom, V. A. (1988). Physical therapy: Follow-up of the special-care infant. In R. Ballard (Ed.), *Pediatric care of the ICN graduate* (pp. 86–93). Philadelphia: Saunders.

Tjossem, T. (1976). Early intervention: Issues and approaches. In T. Tjossem (Ed.), *Intervention strategies for high-risk and handicapped children* (pp. 3–33). Baltimore: University Park Press.

United States Department of Health and Human Services, National Center for Health Statistics. (1991). *Vital statistics of the United States: 1991. Volume 1—Natality*. Washington, DC: Author.

United States Department of Health and Human Services Public Health Service. (1990). *Healthy people 2000: National health promotion and disease prevention objectives.* Washington, DC: U.S. Government Printing Office.

VandenBerg, K. A., & Hanson, M. J. (1993). *Homecoming for babies after the neonatal intensive care nursery: A guide for professionals in supporting their baby's early development.* Austin, TX: PRO-ED.

Verkerk, A. J. M. H., Plerettl, M., Sutcliffe, J. S., Fu, Y.-H., Kuhl, D. P. A., Pizzuti, A., Reinder, O., Richards, S., Victoria, M. F., Zhang, F., Eussen, B. E., van Ommen, G.-J. B., Blonden, L. A. J., Riggins, G. J., Chastain, J. L., Kunst, C. B., Galjaard, H., Caskey, C. T., Nelson, D. L., Oostra, B. A., & Warren, S. T. (1991). Identification of a gene (FMR-1) containing a CGG repeat coincipent with a breakpoint cluster regions exhibiting length variation in Fragile X syndrome. *Cell, 65,* 905–914.

Williamson, W. D., & Demmler, G. J. (1992). Congenital infections: Clinical outcome and educational implications. *Infants and Young Children, 4*(4), 1–10.

Selected Readings

Readings on Specific Disabilities and Risk Conditions

Batshaw, M. L., & Perret, Y. M. (1992). *Children with disabilities: A medical primer* (3rd ed.). Baltimore: Brookes.

This extremely readable book is frequently revised and updated for accuracy. It includes chapters on specific disabilities, conditions, and risk factors as well as an overview of genetics and discussions of specific interventions. Although it addresses many medical and health-related issues in technical terms, it is very useful to readers outside the health professions.

Blackman, J. A. (1990). *Medical aspects of developmental disabilities in children birth to three* (2nd ed.). Rockville, MD: Aspen.

Organized in alphabetical order, this reference for non-medical and health-related professionals and parents is extremely useful. It provides basic information in extremely readable, non-technical language that makes even the most complicated medical concerns clear. The book also contains many illustrations of equipment, orthotic, and prosthetic devices that provide the reader with an excellent overview.

Capute, A. J., & Accardo, P. J. (Eds.). (1991). *Developmental disabilities in infancy and childhood.* Baltimore: Brookes.

In spite of the technical nature of this textbook on disabilities in young children, the authors have made it understandable to readers outside of the medical and health professions who have been exposed to medical terms and descriptions. All 32 chapters are written by physicians, and each chapter focuses on a specific condition or one of the basics of developmental pediatrics. This is an excellent, advanced resource.

Readings on Prematurity, Low Birth Weight, and Early Illness

Hanson, M. J., & VandenBerg, K. A. (1993). *Homecoming for babies after the intensive care nursery: A guide for parents in supporting their baby's early development.* Austin, TX: PRO-ED.

VandenBerg, K. A., & Hanson, M. J. (1983). *Homecoming for babies after the neonatal intensive care nursery: A guide for professionals in supporting their baby's early development.* Austin, TX: PRO-ED.

The following list of readings was compiled in the two references listed above and is reprinted by permission.

Flushman, B., Gale, G., Lackey, S., Sweet, N., & VandenBerg, K. (1991). *My special start: A guide for parents in the neonatal intensive care unit.* Palo Alto, CA: VORT Corporation.

This small, readable manual is written for parents of premature infants who are hospitalized in the neonatal intensive care unit (NICU). It describes the ways in which parents can support their baby's development in the early days and weeks of the child's life in the NICU. Many photographs are provided to illustrate techniques.

Flushman, B. L., & VandenBerg, K. A. (1986). *Developmental steps: A guide for parents to infant development in the intensive care nursery.* Oakland,

CA: Children's Hospital Medical Center. (Distributed by Education Programs Associates, Inc., 1 W. Campbell Avenue, Building C, Campbell, CA 95008)

This easy-to-read guide provides helpful information to parents while their babies are in intensive care nurseries. Directions and illustrations related to handling and care of at-risk babies in the nurseries are described for all phases of infant recovery.

Goldberg, S., & Divitto, B. A. (1983). *Born too soon: Preterm birth and early development.* San Francisco: W. H. Freeman.

Topics related to all aspects of treatment and care of infants born prematurely are discussed in this paperback book. These topics include intensive care; mental, motor, sensory, and social development; parenting issues; and interventions.

Harrison, H. (1983). *The premature baby book: A parents' guide to coping and caring in the first years.* New York: St. Martin's Press.

This comprehensive guide for parents presents basic medical information about prematurity, the treatments used, and associated conditions. It also provides information for parents while babies are in intensive care nurseries and as they bring their babies home and care for them. Families' feelings and experiences are presented throughout.

Hussey, B. (1988). *Understanding my signals: Help for parents of premature infants.* Palo Alto, CA: VORT.

This small booklet presents photographs of babies' cues and signals and helpful tips for parents on interpreting these behaviors.

Semmler, C. (Ed.). (1989). *A guide to care and management of very low birth weight infants: A team approach.* Tucson, AZ: Therapy Skill Builders.

This book provides comprehensive information for professionals on all aspects of high-risk infant care. Contributors to the volume come from a range of professional disciplines, including nursing, nutrition–dietetics, occupational therapy, physical therapy, psychology, special education, and communication disorders. A team approach to treatment and care is emphasized.

Semmler, C. J., & Butcher, S. D. (1990). *Handle with care: Articles about the at-risk neonate.* Tucson, AZ: Therapy Skill Builders.

This easy-to-read paperback provides information to parents and professionals on interventions in the intensive care nursery, developmental issues and interventions for babies born at risk, and characteristics of infants born at risk. Useful glossaries and tables are provided including practical information on topics such as car seat selection.

Serving Diverse Populations

CHAPTER 3

Families vary from one another along a number of dimensions. They come in all sizes and configurations. Some families are large and others small. Some include members who are young children, whereas others do not. Caregivers may be single parents, two parents, extended family members, friends, or neighbors. In addition, families come from a wide range of cultural and linguistic backgrounds. Thus, the early interventionist is challenged to provide support and services to a wide range of individuals and families, many of whom differ markedly from one another and from the early interventionist in terms of beliefs, values, lifestyles, and even languages spoken. The purpose of this chapter is to examine the changing demographics in the United States and explore methods that early interventionists can use to become more culturally competent, sensitive, and responsive to families from diverse backgrounds.

Changing Demographics

The majority of families in the United States today differ from the "typical" family of 20 to 30 years ago in a number of respects (Hanson & Lynch, 1992). The population has become increasingly diverse in terms of cultural orientation, ethnicity, and languages spoken. Other family characteristics also have changed. The average size of the family, age of childbearing, and family composition are a few of the variables in which changes have been noted.

Culture, Ethnicity, and Language

The cultural, linguistic, and ethnic makeup of the United States has changed dramatically over the last decade and is expected to continue changing. These changes are reflected in the fact that, in some parts of the country, groups that were formerly referred to as minorities make up more than 50% of the population; in some areas, in fact, no "majority" group (over 50% of the population) exists. Immigration and differential birthrates across cultural and ethnic groups are contributing to the increasing diversification of the nation's population.

The most recent census data of 1990 revealed that, of a total population in the United States of 248,709,873 persons, 60,581,577 persons were Hispanic or non-White (U.S. Department of Commerce, 1992). In 1984, 36% of the infants born in this country were from ethnolinguistically diverse families, and it was estimated that by the year 2000, 38% of the children under 18 will be from non-White, non-Anglo groups (Research and Policy Committee of the Committee for Economic Development, 1987). The Children's Defense Fund (1989) estimated that, in comparison to the year 1985, by the year 2000 there will be "2.4 million more Hispanic children; 1.7 million more African-American children; 483,000 more children of other races; and 66,000 more white, non-Hispanic children" (p. 116). Furthermore, projections for the year 2030 indicate that there will be "5.5 million more Hispanic children; 2.6 million more African-American children; 1.5 million more children of other races; and 6.2 million fewer white, non-Hispanic children" (Children's Defense Fund, 1989, p. 166). Using these estimated figures, approximately 41% of the children in this country will be Latino or children of color by the year 2030 (Hanson, Lynch, & Wayman, 1990).

Although the children receiving early intervention services are likely to be increasingly diverse culturally, linguistically, and ethnically, this degree of diversity is not reflected in the backgrounds of service providers at the current time (Lynch & Hanson, 1993). As Lynch and Hanson (1993) suggested, this issue must be addressed at several levels. First, personnel preparation programs across early intervention disciplines must encourage and support diversity in recruitment and retention. Additionally, curricula in these programs must include skill building in cultural competence. Particularly with the trend and advocacy for providing services through a family-centered approach, sensitivity and respect for differences among families must be a primary component in this training.

Family Characteristics

One cannot make generalizations about families because of the great variability in family characteristics. One factor that has affected family demographics is the *age of childbearing*.

Current trends reveal increases at both ends of the childbearing age spectrum (Levitan, Belous, & Gallo, 1988; Rosenbaum, Layton, & Liu, 1991). Of concern are increases in the number of children born to teenage mothers. Rosenbaum et al. (1991), for instance, reported that 12.5% of births in the United States in 1988 were to women under age 20 and that the number of births to teens (ages 15–19) increased between 1987 and 1988, with birthrates of 43.7 per 1,000 for white women and 105.9 per 1,000 for African American women. These researchers also noted the strong association between teenage parenting and long-term poverty. Teenage parents also are more likely to be single parents. As indicated by the Children's Defense Fund (1991), "Every 31 seconds an infant is born to an unmarried mother. Every 64 seconds an infant is born to a teenager mother" (p. 5).

Family size too has changed over the years; families today are generally smaller. However, as previously noted, fertility rates differ across ethnic and cultural groups, with some groups showing increased rates of childbirth.

Changes in *family structure* also have occurred. Families of today include those with two parents, single parents, teen parents, couples without children, and gay or lesbian parents, as well as divorced, blended, extended, adoptive, and foster families. Terms such as "traditional" and "nuclear" are no longer meaningful for describing families.

Changes in family composition and structure are reflected in shifts in the numbers of children living with their biological parents. One study, the National Health Interview Survey, indicated that in 1960 almost 75% of children in the United States lived with both biological parents, each of whom had been married only once (Dawson, 1991). Later studies performed by the Joint Center for Urban Studies revealed that by 1975 the proportion fell to slightly over 65%, and by 1990 the proportion was projected to fall to 28% (Masnick & Bane, 1980).

Summary

Because the population of the United States is becoming increasingly diverse and the composition and characteristics of families are changing, early interventionists are challenged to be knowledgeable and respectful of a wide range of family options and to individualize approaches to meet the needs and concerns of individual families and their children.

The Importance of Cultural Competence and Respecting Diversity

Although the United States has never had a culturally homogeneous population, for many years it was characterized as a "melting pot" society. From this perspective, it was assumed that citizens and immigrants to the country would merge and forge together a new society. This view of a melting pot acculturation has been replaced today by a recognition of the pluralistic nature of U.S. society. In another publication (Lynch & Hanson, 1992a), we likened today's society to a garden filled with varied plants. While these plants share many things, such as the need for sun, soil, and water, they differ radically in the amount and type of these essential supports needed to sustain their growth and allow them to reach their potential. Likewise, the members of the U.S. population share many common needs, yet individuals differ markedly in the types of support and the manner in which supports are delivered to foster their growth and fulfill their needs.

The tremendous individual differences in families' needs present an opportunity for service providers to gain knowledge of and familiarity with a variety of lifestyles and perspectives. These variations also present a challenge to those who provide services. The service challenge is heightened by the fact that the nature of early intervention places the service provider in contact with a family at a sensitive time—shortly after the birth or addition of a new child to the family. This contact with the family is often very close in that early interventionists often work in the child's home and work closely with all members of the family.

Given the wide range of families receiving early intervention services, the lifestyle and background of the early interventionist are likely to differ from those of the family. Without a knowledge of and respect for the language, lifestyle, beliefs, and values of family members, early interventionists run the risk of being offensive or ineffective when working with families.

Even in a group of individuals from the same neighborhood, office, or school, tremendous differences may be apparent in how individuals view such complex issues as child rearing and disability. As early interventionists traverse their communities working with families from diverse perspectives, they too will encounter a wide range of beliefs and values. Hanson et al. (1990) discussed several central variables upon which families may differ with respect to their values and beliefs. These include views on children and child rearing, disability and causation, change and intervention, medicine and healing, the family and family roles, and language and communication styles.

Children and Child Rearing

Societal mores play a tremendous role in determining current child rearing practices. For instance, at different times in U.S. society, two diametrically opposed philosophies on feeding babies have been advocated. One view supported the belief that infants should be fed on demand or whenever the baby indicated a desire to eat. The opposite view was that babies should be fed on a fixed, caregiver-determined schedule. In addition to the current trends and fads in society, one's cultural orientation affects families' values. For some families highly compliant and obedient children are valued, whereas for others children who "test" and explore are the norm. Likewise, the type and degree of physical contact, the ages at which developmental milestones such as toilet training are expected, the amount and type of parent–child communication, and routines for daily living such as eating, sleeping, and bathing, are all dictated in part by one's cultural framework. Thus, the interventionist must use caution not to impose her or his own style and values for caring for children upon a parent or caregiver whose values may differ.

Disability and Causation

The meaning of a disability or risk condition may take on very different patterns across families. For some the disability and the explanation for its causation may be viewed as something to be accepted and tolerated; for others it may bring shame; and yet for others it may be viewed as a challenge that must be faced and overcome. Each of these perspectives will likely result in differences in terms of the willingness of families to be involved in intervention and, if involved, different goals surrounding the intervention itself.

Change and Intervention

Related to the issue of causation is the view of change and intervention. Families may look to different sources for support and to different methods for achieving their goals. Some families may seek spiritual assistance; others may seek help from healers whom they believe have special powers; and still others may look to traditional or nontraditional medical interventions. Some families may highly regard and adopt the conventional services that are available through agencies in their communities, whereas others may choose more personal supports and/or less conventional ones.

Medicine and Healing

Tremendous differences can be noted across cultural groups with respect to the person who is considered a medical provider or healer, the view of the link between mind and body, and specific healing strategies or practices. What one group may hold fervently as a healing truth, another group may view as bizarre. The early interventionist may often be confronted with practices that are unfamiliar, and she or he may need to seek additional information while showing respect for the family's practices.

Definition of Family and Family Roles

The values and beliefs of the cultural community with which the family identifies heavily influence the family's ideas about the child's place within the family, the definition of caregiver, the practice of caregiving, and the roles played by family members. Making predetermined assumptions about who should or should not do caregiving and how it should be done, can be unwise for the early interventionist concerned with delivering services that are sensitive to family choices and needs.

Language and Communication Styles

Anyone who has traveled outside of her or his own community has encountered difficulties at some time or another with understanding, navigating, or getting information from persons in the unfamiliar environs. Particularly for families who have recently emigrated to the United States, this discomfort with communication may be felt every day. Cultural mores dictate how persons are greeted, who speaks to whom, whether eye contact is made, whether physical contact is made and how it is made, what gestures and verbal statements are appropriate, and even what position one uses to sit or stand. Thus, issues of language and communication style may play a crucial role in the abilities of family members and early interventionists to establish rapport and exchange information.

Summary

The dimensions discussed in the previous sections represent only a few of the variables upon which family values and beliefs may differ. For the early interventionist, such variations underscore the importance of individualizing services and attaining cross-cultural competence.

The Meaning and Influence of Culture

Culture can be viewed as a framework that "guides and bounds life practices" (Hanson, 1992, p. 3). This framework is not rigid or prescriptive but rather, as Anderson and Fenichel (1989) suggested, "must be viewed as a set of tendencies or possibilities from which to choose" (p. 8). As previously noted, cultural influences may play a key role as service providers work with families to define and meet families' concerns and priorities.

As one examines the issue of cultural orientation, it is important to keep in mind that the members of any cultural group, or even the members of a given family, may differ in terms of their degree of identification with the cultural group and that group's cultural beliefs and practices. Some individuals hold a primary identification with one particular group. Other individuals can be viewed as "bicultural" and move across several groups easily. Some individuals may choose to identify primarily with one cultural orientation at work and demonstrate another orientation in the home. Furthermore, some people identify strongly with their primary culture for some life practices (e.g., social relationships, dating, family roles) but select or identify with other cultural groups for other practices (e.g., health care, recreational activities).

Although cultural identity is an important contributor to one's life practices, it is not the only factor in determining behavioral practices and beliefs. Other factors that influence the individual's goals, concerns, and beliefs may include socioeconomic status, age, gender, educational level, length of residence in the United States, family supports, language spoken and degree of fluency, and, for immigrants, the time and reason for immigration. These factors can play an even more crucial role in determining a person's behavior than does the person's primary cultural affiliation.

Developing Cross-Cultural Competence

It is evident from the previous discussion that early interventionists work with a wide range of families and will often confront beliefs and practices that may differ from those they personally hold dear. How then can the early interventionist acquire the knowledge and skills to work effectively with a diverse population?

Governments, business, and industry have been concerned with the development of cross-cultural competence for many years. Thus, the rationale for such competence and the issues surrounding training in this area are not new. To be effective working across different countries and cultures, governmental and business enterprises have devoted much attention to this issue. The literature from this experience was considered by Lynch and Hanson (1993), who recommended several necessary components for interventionists learning to be cross-culturally competent. These components are (a) clarifying one's own cultural heritage, values, beliefs, and behaviors; (b) obtaining culture-specific information about the cultures with whom one will be working; and (c) applying that knowledge in practice or real situations. Each of these components is examined briefly in the following sections with respect to training in the field of early intervention.

Values clarification

One's cultural orientation is often so subtle and so taken for granted that an individual may be unaware of its influence. Thus, a necessary first step is for the individual to become aware of and clear about her or his values, beliefs, and behaviors with regard to many facets of daily life. For example, how a person eats, sleeps, works, recreates, and with whom the person interacts in all these activities are largely influenced by cultural heritage and the degree to which the individual chooses to identify with a given cultural perspective. Becoming aware of one's own orientation allows the individual to appreciate the influence of culture on the behavior of the individuals with whom one works. For instance, an early interventionist may become troubled because a baby sleeps in the same bed as the parents, or because parents introduce a new food to the baby, or because the parents seem unconcerned that the child is not yet toilet trained. On all these behaviors, a wide range of cultural perspectives may be seen. Opportunities for "cultural clashes" exist unless early interventionists become aware of their own biases and those of the families and appreciate the wide range of styles and perspectives in "normal" development and family functioning.

Individuals can learn more about and clarify their own culturally determined values in a number of ways. Valuable exercises for examining one's own beliefs, behaviors, and biases include formal training sessions and workshops; reading autobiography, fiction, poetry, and plays by writers from different cultural groups; participating in community events and activities outside one's own cultural, religious, or ethnic group; and finding cultural guides or mediators who can share and discuss alternative perspectives. One exercise that has been particularly effective in training sessions we have conducted is the use of the "Cultural Journey," shown in Table 3.1. Responding to the questions posed in the Cultural Journey and sharing one's responses in small groups with diverse membership can help each individual recognize the ways in which culture, ethnicity, religion, and life experience influence activities, actions, and expectations.

Obtaining information about specific cultures

The goal for early interventionists is not to become experts on cultures that differ from their own or to adopt the culture of the families with whom they work. Rather, the goal is for early interventionists to achieve some basic understanding of cultural practices and a facility for interacting with individuals who may believe and behave differently from the service provider. Obtaining information on cultural preferences, customs, and courtesies, as well as the cultural group's general orientation to issues such as disability, intervention, child rearing, and health care, can be extremely useful in developing rapport with family members and working together as partners in the intervention process. This type of information can be obtained from many different sources. One major source is individuals who can function as "cultural guides" in that they may be able to move in and out of several cultural groups because of their own ethnic or linguistic background, and thus impart information to individuals who may be unfamiliar with a given orientation. Other sources are reading and literature, the arts (e.g., movies and films), exploring areas of a city or town where a particular cultural group may be represented in eating establishments and business, traveling, and attending events of cultural interest such as holiday festivals.

Application of new cultural knowledge

Once the interventionist has obtained information about various cultures, she or he needs to apply the knowledge. "As with any practice component, coaching, feedback, and support for approximations from cultural mediators or guides are important to gaining mastery over newly learned behaviors" (Lynch & Hanson, 1993, p. 54). Once again, consulting with individuals who are knowledgeable about or members of the culture one wishes to learn about is extremely useful. Likewise, developing effective working relationships with translators is also necessary (the use of translators is discussed later in this chapter). In addition, as in so many other areas of early intervention, the provision of staff development activities, feedback, and team support is crucial to the success and retention of individuals working in this field.

Summary

The early interventionist's task is not an easy one. It is difficult to work with families whose perspective may differ or even be at odds with one's own. It is also difficult to work with a wide range of families that may differ widely from one another. However, as Lynch (1992) related, communication between individuals is undoubtedly strengthened when the early interventionist demonstrates the following behaviors:

- Respects individuals from other cultures
- Makes continued and sincere attempts to understand the world from others' points of view
- Is open to new learning
- Is flexible

Table 3.1. A Cultural Journey

Culture isn't just something that someone else has. Everyone has a cultural, ethnic, and linguistic heritage that influences their current beliefs, values, and behaviors. To learn a little more about your own, take this simple cultural journey.

ORIGINS

1. When you think about your roots, what country(ies) other than the United States do you identify as a place of origin for you or your family?
2. Have you ever heard any stories about how your family or your ancestors came to the United States? Briefly, what was the story?
3. Are there any foods that you or someone else prepares that are traditional for your country(ies) of origin? What are they?
4. Are there any celebrations, ceremonies, rituals, holidays that your family continues to celebrate that reflect your country(ies) of origin? What are they? How are they celebrated?
5. Do you or anyone in your family speak a language other than English because of your original origins? If so, what language?
6. Can you think of one piece of advice that has been handed down through your family that reflects the values held by your ancestors in the country(ies) of origin? What is it?

BELIEFS, BIASES, AND BEHAVIORS

7. Have you ever heard anyone make a negative comment about people from your country(ies) of origin? If so, what was it?
8. As you were growing up, do you remember discovering that your family did anything differently from other families that you were exposed to because of your culture, religion, or ethnicity? Name something that you remember that was different.
9. Have you ever been with someone in a work situation that did something because of their culture, religion, or ethnicity that seemed unusual to you? What was it?
   Why did it seem unusual?
10. Have you ever felt shocked, upset, or appalled by something that you saw when you were traveling in another part of the world? If so, what was it?
    How did it make you feel? Pick some descriptive words to explain your feelings.
    How did you react?
    In retrospect, how do you wish you would have reacted?
11. Have you ever done anything that you think was culturally inappropriate when you have been in another country or with someone from a different culture? In other words, have you ever done something that you think might have been upsetting or embarrassing to them? What was it?
    What did you do to try to improve the situation?

IMAGINE

12. If you could be from another culture or ethnic group, what culture would it be?
    Why?
13. What is one value from that culture or ethnic group that attracts you to it?
14. Is there anything about that culture or ethnic group that concerns or frightens you? What is it?
15. Name one concrete way in which you think your life would be different if you were from that culture or ethnic group?

From "Developing Cross-Cultural Competence" by E. W. Lynch, 1992, in E. W. Lynch and M. J. Hanson (Eds.), *Developing Cross-Cultural Competence: A Guide for Working with Young Children and Their Families* (pp. 60–62). Baltimore: Paul H. Brookes. Copyright 1992 by Paul H. Brookes Publishing Co. Reprinted by permission.

- Has a sense of humor
- Tolerates ambiguity well
- Approaches others with a desire to learn. (pp. 51–52)

These perspectives are shared by Green (1982), who described the attributes of individual service providers and the needed organizational supports for facilitating "ethnic competence." These include (a) the awareness of one's own cultural limitations; (b) an openness to cultural differences; (c) the adoption of a learning style that is client oriented, interactive, and flexible; (d) the ability to help someone recognize and use resources; and (e) a recognition of the integrity of all cultures (Green, 1982, pp. 54–58). These characteristics form a foundation for the development of cross-cultural competence.

Applying Principles of Cross-Cultural Competence in Early Intervention

Cross-cultural competence is essential to effective, family-focused early intervention at three levels: personal, programmatic, and policy. The chapter thus far has focused primarily on personal competence—the ability of individuals on the early intervention team to work effectively with families who differ from themselves. The following sections of the chapter highlight the need for cross-cultural competence at the programmatic and policy levels. The ways in which services are delivered and the policies that govern their delivery warrant examination.

The central feature of early intervention is the Individualized Family Service Plan (IFSP). The IFSP process can be viewed as having multiple steps (e.g., Lynch, Jackson, Mendoza, & English, 1991; McGonigel, Kaufmann, & Hurth, 1991), each of which has implications for establishing cross-culturally competent practices. In the model presented by Lynch et al. (1991), the process is described as a five-step sequence including (a) first contacts; (b) child assessment and determination of the family's concerns, priorities, and resources; (c) program planning and IFSP development; (d) implementation and monitoring; and (e) IFSP review, evaluation, and transition. Underlying each of these steps is the personal competence in cross-cultural transactions that each interventionist brings to the process; however, each step in the sequence has implications for cross-cultural competence at the programmatic level. These steps and their implications are discussed in the sections that follow.

First Contacts

Many children in early intervention programs are not identified at birth. The largest percentage have disabilities or delays that are apparent only when they lag behind other children in the accomplishment of major milestones such as sitting, standing, walking, babbling, saying their first words, or initiating social contact. As a result, most families must learn about early intervention after they have left the hospital or birthing center where their child was delivered. Traditional forms of outreach have included informing primary care physicians, disseminating print material through existing agencies that serve children with disabilities, making presentations at local meetings or service clubs, or providing toll-free phone numbers that families or other concerned people can call for information. Although these methods may ultimately reach the majority of middle class, Anglo-European American families, other strategies may be more effective in reaching families from diverse ethnic, cultural, and language groups (Anderson & Fenichel, 1989; Sontag & Schacht, 1994).

To reach families, it is important that information be available in the language that they speak; from respected people within their own cultural, religious, or ethnic community; and in places where they go. Because religious leaders are an important source of information for some families, it is important that priests, monks, or other clergy understand the purposes and benefits of early intervention and the organization of services in their community. Respected political or community leaders at the neighborhood level can also be important conduits of information for families. These avenues of outreach provide families the link to services through a trusted relationship, as well as enable families who may not be literate to obtain verbal information (Anderson & Fenichel, 1989).

Material printed in the language of the family and made easily accessible is another form of outreach. One large grocery chain agreed to print on grocery bags basic information about child development along with a number that families could call if they had concerns about their child. Other communities distribute fliers or brochures at church or temple services; in neighborhood stores, parks, and gas stations; and in area health clinics, refugee centers, and employment and social services offices. In the community in which one of us works, information about an early intervention project was advertised on the billboards inside public buses. Public service announcements on local television and radio stations, with particular attention to non-English stations, are another way to reach families who do not have a primary care physician, speak a language other than English, or are wary of formal programs and agencies because of their lack of experience, negative past experiences, or overall confusion about the many systems they encounter. Yonemitsu and Cleveland (1992), in their training manual on culturally competent service delivery for Southeast Asian refugee families, stated that even bilingual–bicultural interventionists must do some " 'detective work' . . . to locate [families] through neighborhood grapevines and extended family ties

. . . [because] families would, in a sense, 'go underground' in response to the fear they felt when teams of the health care personnel such as nurses, respiratory technicians, social workers, etc. descended on them soon after their baby was discharged from the hospital" (pp. 12–13).

When outreach efforts are successful and families reach an early intervention program, their initial contacts with interventionists are critical in determining whether the family decides to participate. According to an old adage, "you never get a second chance to make a first impression." If initial contacts are respectful, the family's concerns and priorities are listened to, and the interventionist is knowledgeable without being intimidating, families are more likely to maintain contact. If these things do not occur, families may elect not to participate.

Respect, valuing family input, and knowledge are expected of all professionals in their interactions with families, but the ways in which one shows respect, listens to families' concerns, and shares knowledge vary across cultural groups (Lynch & Hanson, 1992a). Therefore, what the interventionist perceives as respect and collaboration may be different from what the family from a different ethnic or cultural group perceives. Programs that are more effective in transcultural interactions invest time in helping staff members learn culture-specific information about preferred ways of communicating and sharing information; views of disability, health, and healing; and family structure. For example, the wordy explanations and desire to avoid silence that are characteristic of low-context cultures, such as that of Anglo-Europeans, may create discomfort in members of high-context cultures, such as traditional Asian or American Indian families (Lynch, 1992). Likewise, the informality of addressing family members by their first names before a relationship has been formed or permission given may be viewed as disrespectful by African American families (Willis, 1992).

The kinds of information that interventionists might want to know are included in Table 3.2, Guidelines for the Home Visitor. The questions presented in these guidelines can be answered broadly about various cultural, ethnic, and religious groups, then used to examine each family's preferences. These guidelines are not meant to be used as an interview but as a framework for gathering information that interventionists can use to tailor the interventions to the individual child and family. Although the interventionist needs to recognize that *as many differences exist within groups as across groups* and that culture-specific information can be no more than a guideline for initial interactions, learning about general cultural preferences can help programs be more responsive to families from diverse cultures. (For additional information, see Lynch and Hanson, 1992a.)

Assessment

Assessment of infants and toddlers for early intervention programs has two overlapping but distinct components: the assessment of the child's strengths and needs and, with the family's concurrence, a determination of the family's concerns, priorities, and resources. These two components require multiple approaches and data points for all children and families, and each component has implications for culturally competent service delivery.

Assessing the child's strengths and needs

The appropriate assessment of young children has been a topic of debate for many years (e.g., Escalona, 1950; Hobbs, 1975; Mercer, Algozzine, & Trifiletti, 1979), as has the appropriateness of existing assessment procedures for children from non–English-speaking, culturally diverse families (e.g., Cummins, 1986; Figueroa, 1989; Hilliard, 1984; Jones, 1988; Lidz, 1987). When the two issues—assessment of young children and assessment of non–English-speaking children or those from diverse cultural backgrounds—are combined, the complexity is magnified (Barrera, 1994). However, as Barrera (1994) pointed out, "diversity between an assessor and a child cannot be judged solely by the child's apparent group membership. Rather, diversity must be judged reciprocally and relationally" (p. 10). She further stated that diversity can be assumed to be present "whenever there is the probability that, in interaction with a particular child or family, the assessor might attribute different meanings or values to behaviors or events than would the family or someone from the family's environment" (p. 10). This much broader definition of diversity could include differences in socioeconomic status, educational level, and experience, as well as differences within and between cultures. Although the broader definition of diversity must be considered, the discussion that follows focuses on issues that may arise when ethnic, cultural, and linguistic differences exist between the assessor and the child and family.

After the areas of child assessment have been planned with the family, members of the assessment team must select strategies that will be most effective in gathering the information needed. Although the appropriateness of using standardized instruments can be questioned for any young child, the use of these tests is inappropriate when the instrument is not in the child's primary language; developmental expectations differ in the child's culture; and significant differences in child-rearing practices are present. Alternative approaches such as observation and interviewing should be used (Lynch & Hanson, in press).

During the assessment cultural taboos may arise. Using objects found in the home as part of the assessment can result in cultural misunderstandings. For example, checking a child's hearing with a rattle found in an American Indian home or asking a child to point to the

Table 3.2. Guidelines for the Home Visitor

PART I—FAMILY STRUCTURE AND CHILDREARING PRACTICES

- **Family Structure**

  - *Family Composition*
    - Who are the members of the family system?
    - Who are the key decision makers?
    - Is decision making related to specific situations?
    - Is decision making individual or group oriented?
    - Do family members all live in the same household?
    - What is the relationship of friends to the family system?
    - What is the hierarchy within the family? Is status related to gender or age?

  - *Primary Caregiver(s)*
    - Who is the primary caregiver?
    - Who else participates in the caregiving?
    - What is the amount of care given by mother vs. others?
    - How much time does the infant spend away from the primary caregiver?
    - Is there conflict between (among) caregivers regarding appropriate practices?
    - What ecological/environmental issues impinge upon general caregiving (i.e., housing, jobs, etc.)?

- **Childrearing Practices**

  - *Family Feeding Practices*
    - What are the family feeding practices?
    - What are the beliefs regarding breastfeeding and weaning?
    - What are the beliefs regarding bottle feeding?
    - What are the family practices when transitioning to solid food?
    - Which family member(s) prepare food?
    - Is food purchased or homemade?
    - Which family member(s) feed the child?
    - What is the configuration of the family mealtime?
    - What are the family's views on independent feeding?
    - Is there a discrepancy among family members regarding the beliefs and practices related to feeding an infant/toddler?

  - *Family Sleeping Patterns*
    - Does the infant sleep in the same room/bed as the parents?
    - At what age is the infant moved away from close proximity to the mother?
    - Is there an established bedtime?
    - What is the family response to an infant when he/she awakes at night?
    - What practices surround daytime napping?

  - *Family's Response to Disobedience and Aggression*
    - What are the parameters of acceptable child behavior?
    - What form does the discipline take?
    - Who metes out the disciplinary action?

  - *Family's Response to a Crying Infant*
    - Temporal qualities—How long before the caregiver picks up a crying infant?
    - How does the caregiver calm an upset infant?

(continues)

Table 3.2. *Continued*

PART II—FAMILY PERCEPTIONS AND ATTITUDES

- **Family Perception of Child's Disability**
  - Are there cultural or religious factors that would shape family perceptions?
  - To what/where/whom does the family assign responsibility for their child's disability?
  - How does the family view the role of fate in their lives?
  - How does the family view their role in intervening with their child? Do they feel they can make a difference or do they consider it hopeless?

- **Family's Perception of Health and Healing**
  - What is the family's approach to medical needs?
  - Do they rely solely on Western medical services?
  - Do they rely solely on holistic approaches?
  - Do they utilize a combination of these approaches?
  - Who is the primary medical provider or conveyer of medical information? Family members? Elders? Friends? Folk healers? Family doctor? Medical specialists?
  - Do all members of the family agree on approaches to medical needs?

- **Family's Perception of Help-Seeking and Intervention**
  - Who does the family seek help from—family members or outside agencies/individuals?
  - Does the family seek help directly or indirectly?
  - What are the general feelings of family when seeking assistance—ashamed, angry, demand as a right, view as unnecessary?
  - With which community systems does the family interact (educational/medical/social)?
  - How are these interactions completed (face-to-face, telephone, letter)?
  - Which family member interacts with other systems?
  - Does that family member feel comfortable when interacting with other systems?

PART III: LANGUAGE AND COMMUNICATION STYLES

- **Language**
  - *To what degree:*
    - Is the home visitor proficient in the family's native language?
    - Is the family proficient in English?

  - *If an interpreter is used:*
    - With which culture is the interpreter primarily affiliated?
    - Is the interpreter familiar with the colloquialisms of the family members' country/region of origin?
    - Is the family member comfortable with the interpreter? (Would the family member feel more comfortable with an interpreter of the same sex?)
    - If written materials are used, are they in the family's native language?

- **Interaction Styles**
  - Does the family communicate with each other in a direct or indirect style?
  - Do family members share feelings when discussing emotional issues?
  - Does the family ask you direct questions?
  - Does the family value a lengthy social time at each home visit unrelated to the early childhood services program goals?
  - Is it important for the family to know about the home visitor's extended family? Is the home visitor comfortable sharing that information?

From "Home-Based Early Childhood Services: Cultural Sensitivity in a Family Systems Approach" by K. I. Wayman, E. W. Lynch, and M. J. Hanson, 1990, *Topics in Early Childhood Special Education, 10,* pp. 65–66. Copyright 1990 by PRO-ED, Inc. Reprinted by permission.

orange taken from the altar of a Buddhist or Hindu shrine in the home is a desecration of the sacred. Likewise, patting a Muslim child on the head or commenting effusively over a Latino or East Indian child's beauty may cause consternation in traditional families. The head should not be touched because it is the seat of the soul, and comments about children's attractiveness may call undue attention to them, putting them in danger (Lynch, 1992; Lynch & Hanson, in press). Learning more about general cultural or religious mores before meeting the family can help interventionists avoid embarrassing mistakes.

A bilingual–bicultural mediator should be present throughout the child's assessment to translate what is occurring and how families are responding. What the interventionist is learning from observation of routine activities or play is not intuitively obvious, so the mediator helps family members understand the purpose and the findings of the observation (Lynch & Hanson, in press). The use of interpreters or translators, however, raises additional concerns that must be addressed at the programmatic level. These concerns are discussed in the paragraphs that follow.

Determining family concerns, priorities, and resources

Strategies for determining the family's concerns, priorities, and resources are still being refined and are new to many early interventionists. Cultural and language differences are particularly salient in this area of assessment. For example, to learn what families want for their child, the interventionist and the family members have to be able to talk together. When they do not share the same language, a translator or interpreter is needed; however, the introduction of a third party into such an emotionally loaded situation adds an additional element of stress and discomfort. Many translators are not professionally trained in translation; even though they may be familiar with early intervention and fluent in both languages being used, the conventions of translation are not observed. Sometimes a family member, often an adolescent who has learned English, is forced into the role of translator; however, putting a younger family member into this position results in role reversals, resentment, and interference with family dynamics (Chan, as cited in Lynch, 1992). Likewise, using a relative, neighbor, or friend as the translator may compromise the family's right to and desire for privacy. Finally, because of the shortage of well-trained, bilingual–bicultural personnel, many programs rely on a single individual to translate for families of a particular language group. This responsibility often creates hardships for the translator and the families that they serve. The translator may become overburdened by the number of requests and the desire to ensure that families have access to everything that they need (Chan as cited in Lynch, 1992). Of equal danger is that families have access through only one individual who controls communication. As a result, families may be reluctant to voice any concerns about the translator's competence (Harrison & Lynch, 1994).

Chan (as cited in Lynch, 1992) provided a number of suggestions for working more effectively with interpreters and translators. Those suggestions are summarized in Table 3.3.

Other issues that emerge when gathering information about families' concerns, priorities, and resources need attention at the programmatic level. For families that have recently arrived in the United States, nearly everything is new. Their concept of disability may be different (Harry, 1992), the fact that early intervention programs exist may be new to them, and the emphasis on family–professional collaboration may be unknown (Lynch & Hanson, 1992a). Therefore, programs and their staff need to develop ways to explain their services clearly and work with families over time to build partnerships that are comfortable for families. To help families who are unfamiliar with the system inform themselves when they are ready, program

Table 3.3. Guidelines for Working with Interpreters

- Learn proper protocols and forms of address (including a few greetings and social phrases) in the family's primary language, the name they wish to be called, and the correct pronunciation.
- Introduce yourself and the interpreter, describe your respective roles, and clarify mutual expectations and the purpose of the encounter.
- Learn basic words and sentences in the family's language and become familiar with special terminology they may use so you can selectively attend to them during interpreter–family exchanges.
- During the interaction, address your remarks and questions directly to the family (not the interpreter); look at and listen to family members as they speak and observe their nonverbal communication.
- Avoid body language or gestures that may be offensive or misunderstood.
- Use a positive tone of voice and facial expressions that sincerely convey respect and your interest in the family; and address them in a calm, unhurried manner.
- Speak clearly and somewhat more slowly, but *not* more loudly.
- Limit your remarks and questions to a few sentences between translations and avoid giving too much information or long, complex discussions of several topics in a single session.
- Avoid technical jargon, colloquialisms, idioms, slang, and abstractions.
- Give instructions in a clear, logical sequence; emphasize key words or points; and offer reasons for specific recommendations.
- Periodically check on the family's understanding and the accuracy of the translation by asking the family to repeat instructions or whatever has been communicated in their own words, with the interpreter facilitating; but avoid literally asking, "Do you understand?"
- When possible, reinforce verbal information with materials written in the family's language and visual aids or behavioral modeling if appropriate. Before introducing written materials, tactfully determine the client's literacy level through the interpreter.
- Be patient and prepared for the additional time that will inevitably be required for careful interpretation.

From "Developing Cross-Cultural Competence" by E. W. Lynch, 1992, in E. W. Lynch and M. J. Hanson (Eds.), *Developing Cross-Cultural Competence: A Guide for Working with Young Children and Their Families* (pp. 55–56). Baltimore: Paul H. Brookes. Copyright 1992 by Paul H. Brookes Publishing Co. Reprinted by permission.

---

staff can provide menus of services; videotapes that give short, clear explanations; and booklets in the family's language.

A final important issue relates to the level of disclosure with which families are comfortable. For some families, regardless of culture, ethnicity, or language, sharing information with professional strangers is uncomfortable. They may feel that it is a matter for the family, not something in which outsiders should become involved. Others may want to share but feel that they should not because they have been brought up to believe that having a child with a disability means that they have done something wrong or that they are bad people (Yonemitsu & Cleveland, 1992). To reach these families yet honor their concerns, programs must develop policies and procedures that allow for the family's reticence and do not intrude upon the family's preferences. Cultural guides or mediators from the community are often most helpful as program staff develop a range of approaches to meet each family's needs.

Program Planning

The IFSP is developed following assessment. Like all other aspects of early intervention, the development of this document is meant to be interactive and to rely on the partnership between families and the professionals involved. As mentioned in the previous paragraph, it is difficult for parents to be active partners when information is being translated, when the system is unfamiliar, and when there may be an underlying belief that professionals know best. For these reasons, professionals may find that they are taking more of a lead than their interpretation of family–professional collaboration allows. However, it is important to remember that everybody—including interventionists—consults professionals for their special expertise at various times, and often the language, processes, and procedures that they use are unfamiliar. Typically, professionals' expertise is used to increase understanding in hopes that their assistance and instruction will enable the consultee to take over management of the issue or to resolve a similar issue with less help in the future. This analogy can be used as a framework for working with families. The goal is to provide the level of support they request and the information that enables them to assume greater responsibility in the future.

The outcomes that are developed for the child and recorded on the IFSP should reflect not only the child's needs but also the family's priorities and goals. As an example, eating with a spoon is a common priority in many families, but forks are never used in a number of cultures. Thus, the outcome should match the family's way of eating. Also, for any child and family, the strategies that are employed to achieve these outcomes should be easily incorporated into the child's and family's life.

As program staff members encounter cultural, ethnic, and religious differences, they may need to remind themselves that developmental milestones are not immutable. How they are expressed may vary considerably from group to group and family to family, and the emphasis on milestones that is common in the Anglo-European tradition may not be as rigidly observed among other groups. Although it is important to share information with families from diverse cultures about the milestones and behaviors that are emphasized in the systems that they and their child will encounter, it is rarely the interventionist's role to convince families to abandon traditional practices. Such advice would be given only in those situations in which the child was being harmed or the practice would lead to legal action in the United States.

Implementation and Monitoring

After the plan has been developed, it is implemented and monitored. When the outcomes included in the IFSP match the family's concerns and priorities, they are more likely to be achieved (Lynch & Hanson, 1992b). Careful attention to these family issues when the IFSP is developed shows when it is being monitored. Perhaps of greatest importance during the monitoring phase is the development of processes and procedures that do not make family members feel as if they are being evaluated.

IFSP Review, Evaluation, and Transition

Of the elements of the IFSP process, the one that we have not yet addressed is transition. By law, transition planning is mandated prior to the child's third birthday. In reality, however, many transitions may occur prior to that time that need careful planning, coordination, and follow through. When a child leaves the hospital after an extended stay, when a child begins attending programs outside the home, or when a new interventionist becomes involved with the family, the transition should be addressed. Wolery (1989), in a comprehensive discussion of transition issues, emphasized the importance of designing processes and procedures that minimize disruptions for the child and family. This is especially important for families from diverse cultures and language groups. Procedures that programs have developed can be affirmed or improved by family input and by suggestions from cultural guides or mediators. Procedures that families view as supportive have the greatest chance for success.

Summary

In addition to ensuring that individual staff members are culturally competent, the policies and practices of the program must also be considered. The goal is to make early intervention programs and services accessible to and comfortable for families with widely varying backgrounds, languages, worldviews, and lifestyles. Thus, a program's policies and procedures may need to be reviewed, reconsidered, and revised to meet the needs of the communities being served.

Other Dimensions of Diversity

Cultural, ethnic, and language differences are not the only dimensions of diversity among families in early intervention. Families with infants and toddlers with or at risk for disabilities come from all walks of life and all segments of the community. In addition to those families from different language and ethnic backgrounds, three additional family populations with their own special needs are increasingly represented in early intervention programs. They include families in which one or more of the parents is mentally retarded, teen parents, and families who face multiple risks. Although families cannot be stereotyped, each of these three groups may require a different approach. In the sections that follow, each group is briefly discussed with suggestions for incorporating them into early intervention programs.

Parents with Mental Retardation

Community-based services and the inclusion of individuals with cognitive limitations into the mainstream of education, society, and the work world have dramatically increased the opportunities available to these individuals. Throughout the country, an increasing number of adults with mental retardation are becoming parents, and early interventionists often work with these families and their children. Child rearing is complex, and because of the limitations that mental retardation imposes on generalization, attention, memory, judgment, and adaptive behavior, child rearing presents major challenges for individuals with cognitive limitations. Research with this population is limited, and the reports from special projects designed to work with parents with mental retardation present differing perspectives and evaluations of their success (e.g., Espe-Sherwindt, 1991; Espe-Sherwindt & Kerlin, 1990; Lynch & Bakley, 1989). Although the data base is limited, more and more programs are finding a need to develop effective strategies to incorporate these families into early intervention programs.

Children of parents with mental retardation are often in early intervention programs because they are at risk, not because they have a diagnosed disability. The primary goals are typically twofold: The first is to help the family parent effectively, and the second is to monitor the child's progress to prevent environmentally caused delays. Bakley (1986) identified 22 problems interventionists confront when working with parents with mental retardation. Several of these problems are highlighted in the following paragraphs, with suggested solutions.

Parents may have difficulty following through with activities that have been suggested or in doing routine activities with their infant or toddler, such as bathing, feeding, and diaper changing. Explaining the activity simply, demonstrating it, watching the parent as she or he does the activity with the child, reviewing the steps, reinforcing the parent, and reviewing at the next visit are steps that have been used to help parents learn the activity, realize their own ability to perform it, and recognize its importance. Bakley (1986) also suggested using an instant camera to photograph each step of the activity and leaving the pictures to help the parent remember the steps.

Parent–child interaction may be limited or inappropriate, and the interventionist may need to model ways to play with the baby, point out the child's cues, and interpret the child's responses. Many parents with retardation seem not to be attuned to their child or the environment. Teaching games such as peek-a-boo or simple nursery rhymes can help the parent get involved with the child. Modeling these games during home visits and complimenting the parents when they interact positively with the child can improve parent–child interaction and increase the parents' own self-esteem. This is particularly important because of the loss of self-esteem that many of these parents have experienced (Espe-Sherwindt, 1991). Parents with retardation may misinterpret cries and vocalizations, and then inappropriately punish the child for "bad behavior." The early interventionist can help the parent interpret the different cries, explaining that they are the only way the baby knows how to "talk to you."

Using good judgment in selecting toys, preparing food, and creating a safe environment for a small child is often difficult for parents with mental retardation. Like all parents, parents with retardation may select toys that appeal to them rather than toys that are developmentally appropriate. This becomes a concern when the toy may be dangerous for a young child. The interventionist may want to go on a shopping trip with the parents, bring safe toys into the home, or provide some guidelines about toy selection.

Parents may have limited food preparation skills and little information about nutrition, especially for a young child. Simple cookbooks designed for people with limited reading skills, pictures of the various food groups, and cooking lessons provided by the interventionist can help assure that all family members receive a more balanced diet.

Recognizing safety hazards within the home may also be a problem. The early interventionist may want to conduct a "safety check" with the parents to see that cleaning fluids, medicines, and other harmful or dangerous materials are out of reach.

Finally, *problems in daily living*, such as instability, isolation, and difficulty with home and money management, often present challenges to both the family and the interventionist. Because most parents with mental retardation are in the lowest socioeconomic bracket, money for housing, food, transportation, and basic needs is usually limited. Coupled with parents' limited skill in budgeting, families are often in economic crises. Helping parents plan budgets and follow them often becomes one of the early interventionist's tasks. Managing the home is also an area in which parents with mental retardation need support. Keeping things clean, understanding that certain foods must be refrigerated, and developing routines for the child are all issues that the interventionist may need to address with the family.

Because of the range of needs, multiple agencies are typically involved to assist parents with mental retardation with housing, employment, child care, and health issues. However, these parents are usually not prepared to deal with multiple people. For these families in particular, it is critical to have a coordinated intervention plan with frequent communication among all of those involved.

Espe-Sherwindt (1991) described the use of the IFSP as a vehicle for empowerment with parents with mental retardation and as a way to promote problem-solving skills. This approach and the family focus of P.L. 99-457 and its amendments may increase positive outcomes for parents with mental retardation and their children. There may still be times, however, when family support is not enough to assure that the child can grow and develop adequately in the home. In these instances the early interventionist must advocate exclusively for the child and work with other agencies to seek a placement outside the home. Although this is not the primary goal of early intervention with these families, it may become a necessity. When this occurs it is extremely hard on everyone involved, and program administrators need to be sensitive to the additional support that staff members and families may need during this process.

Parents with mental retardation are some of the most challenging families represented in early intervention programs. The early intervention team typically plays a key role in providing and/or coordinating a multifaceted intervention plan. With the current emphasis on family-focused intervention, both children and families can be served optimally.

Teen Parents

Teen parents are also appearing in increasing numbers in early intervention programs. According to a report of the Children's Defense Fund (1994), data released in mid-1993 show that the number of births to teen parents rose for the fifth year in a row in 1991. In 1991 an estimated 1.1 million teenage girls became pregnant, and 519,577 babies were born to girls between 15 and 19 years of age (Children's Defense Fund, 1994). Two thirds (68.9%) of these births were to unmarried girls (Children's Defense Fund, 1994).

It is well documented that teen mothers, when compared with their older counterparts, may be less effective in their ability to interact with their infants, have less knowledge of child development, and are more likely to be abusive (Anastasiow, 1982; Thurman & Gonsalves, 1993). It is also clear that adolescent mothers and their children have short- and long-term problems in the psychological, vocational, and social spheres of their lives (Brooks-Gunn & Furstenberg, 1986). As would be expected from their age of childbearing, the environmental factors that lead to early pregnancy in the United States, and the life circumstances of teen parents, they are at increased risk for having an infant born prematurely or a child with disabilities or delays (Osofsky, Hann, & Peebles, 1993).

Although a great deal has been written about teen pregnancy, relatively little has focused on the needs of young teens who have a child with a disability. Findings of studies focused on mother–infant interaction among adolescent mothers are increasingly consistent in their findings that these interactions are not optimal (Osofsky et al., 1993). Thus, the case for early intervention may be made for many babies of teen parents, but it is especially compelling for those infants or young children with diagnosed disabilities. Teen parents typically need emotional support, instruction in child care and child rearing, and assistance that will help them develop and meet some of their own goals. The suggestions that follow have been used to support teen parents and their infants.

Building the teen parent's self-esteem can have positive consequences for both the parent and the infant. Acknowledging all of the things that the parent is doing right and providing emotional support for the parent's own needs can help build the bridge to more positive outcomes. This is not an easy task because self-esteem is peer-based in adolescence and early interventionists are more often more representative of authority figures. However, communicating, caring, supporting, and having high expectations for the parents can help develop self-esteem.

Providing information about child development, child care, and the disability is essential in the intervention process. An interventionist can help young parents become more competent by showing them how to take care of the child, modeling how to interact positively, and modeling acceptance and enjoyment of the child.

Helping teen parents establish and meet their own goals can have positive outcomes for the child as well. Linking parents to education, respite care, social groups, and agencies that provide a wide range of support can provide them with the skills they need to create a more positive and stable environment for themselves and their child. Teen parents present a unique set of concerns, risks, and challenges and can often benefit from strategies used with other families who face multiple risks.

Families Who Face Multiple Risks

An increasing number of infants and toddlers from families who face multiple risks are entering early intervention programs. These families, as defined by Greenspan (1982), have a broad range of economic, social, medical, mental health, and emotional problems that make effective parenting difficult for them. Poverty, limited education, poor nutrition, and homelessness present almost insurmountable obstacles to child rearing, bringing into early intervention programs an increasing number of families that have no material resources. Unlike the well-educated, middle income families served by many infant programs of the 1970s and 1980s, these families need help meeting the basic needs for food and shelter before they can focus any energy on the needs of their child who is high risk or has a disability.

In addition, a rise in substance abuse has created a new population of infants who have been prenatally drug exposed to cocaine, alcohol, heroin, methamphetamines, or other damaging substances (Zuckerman & Brown, 1993). According to figures released to Congress in 1990 by the U.S. General Accounting Office, between 100,000 and 375,000 women each year give birth to infants exposed to illegal drugs. The numbers who give birth to infants exposed to alcohol and tobacco, whose negative consequences are much easier to predict, are far higher (Bloch, 1992; Olson, Burgess, & Streissguth, 1992). In addition to the developmental difficulties created by maternal substance abuse, home environments in which drugs are being used and sold are poorly suited for fostering healthy growth and development of young children.

The increasing use of intravenous drugs in the U.S. population and early pregnancy among teens who engage in high-risk sexual behavior have resulted in a new population of terminally ill infants with AIDS and their families who need intervention services. As reported by Johnson (1993), between 12% and 35% of infants born to HIV-infected mothers are infected themselves. In 1992, there were twice as many infected infants as in 1991 (Lesar & Maldonado, 1994). These children and their families typically need a wide range of medical, social, educational, and personal support services in addition to early intervention.

The final group of children and families that face multiple risks are those that live in violent environments. In the United States physical abuse is the leading cause of death among children under a year of age (Osofsky, 1993–1994), and a far greater number of young children are disabled by abuse. However, child abuse is only part of the picture of violence in the United States. According to a poll conducted by the Children's Defense Fund and *Newsweek* magazine, 75% of the parents surveyed and more than 50% of the children described their greatest worry as fear that someone they love would become a victim of a violent crime (Children's Defense Fund, 1994). Gun violence is the most pervasive. The Children's Defense Fund (1994) reported compelling figures: "An American child dies of a gunshot wound every two hours, and every two days 25 children—the equivalent of a classroomful—lose their lives to guns.... For every child killed by a gun, several are injured, with estimates ranging between 30 and 67 each day" (pp. 63, 64). Community violence seriously threatens many young children and their families in the United States.

Many of the risks described above are intertwined. In communities where there is high drug use, infants and their parents often face, in addition, poverty, greater violence, and poorer health. Families who face these multiple risks present a range of needs that are new to many early intervention programs. To meet these needs, broad-based changes in social and political systems are needed; however, until changes occur, early interventionists must find ways to help families and children who need help now. The suggestions that follow are a sampling of strategies presented by Carson (1986).

Communicate respect and genuineness to families regardless of their circumstances. The inability to provide for one's children often lowers parents' self-esteem, making it more difficult to make constructive changes. The genuineness of the early interventionist, respect for the family's concerns, and belief that the family can make changes are important to improving the family's ability to cope.

Provide clear information as needed and requested by families. Many families who face multiple risks have serious gaps in their knowledge of health, child rearing, growth, and development. They are also unaware of or unable to utilize community resources. By providing education and information as it is needed and can be applied, the early interventionist can help families gain skills and self-respect. Assisting families to set small goals and helping them meet those goals is one strategy for helping families regain control of their lives.

Isolation from the mainstream of life is a frequent problem encountered by families in multiple-risk situations. Single mothers living in poverty often have little contact with the world outside the home. The *support and companionship of the home visitor can be a first step in helping families reduce isolation*. Having someone who cares, is dependable, and is rooting for their success can help families become more involved in the community. Helping families identify ways to increase control over their own lives and developing strategies for making that possible are steps to help reduce isolation.

Helping families become motivated is one of the most difficult challenges for the early interventionist. After years of poverty, addiction, low self-esteem, and incompetence, it is often difficult for families to feel that there is a way out. Many may have never been exposed to another way of life and have no confidence in themselves or in the system. Although motivation comes from within, the early interventionist can help families identify small attainable changes that they would like to make. Success with these small changes can provide the encouragement to seek greater changes in their lives.

There are no magic answers for working successfully with families who face multiple risks, but belief that change is possible is a first step. As early interventionists work more closely with all of the families that they serve, it may become easier to find ways to work in partnership with those families that have the greatest needs.

Summary

Early intervention programs are serving a more diverse group of children and families than ever before. Whether differences are due to culture, ethnicity, language, or other variables, staff members and the programs in which they work are challenged to find new approaches to service delivery. For some of the groups, approaches have been developed and strategies are suggested in the literature that can be applied and adapted to a particular community or program. For other groups, such as parents with mental retardation, families in violent environments, and families with individuals with AIDS, the strategies are still evolving. Regardless of the availability of research, several things are clear. Programs with visionary administrators, knowledgeable and respectful staff, and flexible models of service delivery that focus on children and their families are most likely to be successful.

Preferred Practices

The following questions can be used to review and evaluate early intervention programs in relation to what are currently known to be preferred practices.

1. Does the program have staff members who represent the ethnic,cultural, and language diversity of the children and families being served?

2. Have staff members been trained in and do they apply culturally competent strategies in their interactions with one another and the families they serve?

3. Are trained interpreters and translators available, and have staff members been trained to work with them effectively?

4. Have the program's policies and procedures been reviewed by families, staff, and cultural guides or mediators for their sensitivity to family diversity?

5. Can staff members accurately describe the demographics of the population that they serve, and do they have information about the communities in which the families live?

6. In what ways has the program been changed in the past 5 years to become more family focused and meet the changing needs of families served?

7. Are family members representing diverse groups involved in program review and policy development?

8. Does the program work with cultural advocacy groups and leaders in the families' communities to help improve services to diverse families?

9. Have staff members received training about the various risks that many families currently encounter, such as violence, teen parents, and AIDS?

10. Does the program administrator or other staff members work with the larger community to help improve the social system that puts families at multiple risk?

References

Anastasiow, N. J. (Ed.). (1982). *The adolescent parent*. Baltimore: Brookes.

Anderson, P. P., & Fenichel, E. S. (1989). *Serving culturally diverse families of infants and toddlers with disabilities*. Washington, DC: National Center for Clinical Infant Programs.

Bakley, S. (1986). *But I wasn't trained for this: A manual for working with mothers who are retarded*. San Diego: Department of Special Education, San Diego State University.

Barrera, I. (1994). Thoughts on the assessment of young children whose sociocultural background is unfamiliar to the assessor. *Zero to Three, 14*(6), 9–13.

Bloch, M. (1992). Tobacco control advocacy: Winning the war on tobacco. *Zero to Three, 13*(1), 29–34.

Brooks-Gunn, J., & Furstenberg, F. F. (1986). The children of adolescent mothers: Physical, academic, and psychological outcomes. *Developmental Review, 6*, 224–251.

Carson, A. T. (1986). *A professional challenge: Working with multi-problem families*. San Diego: Department of Special Education, San Diego State University.

Children's Defense Fund. (1989). *A vision for America's future*. Washington, DC: Author.

Children's Defense Fund. (1991). *The state of America's children 1991.* Washington, DC: Author.

Children's Defense Fund. (1994). *The state of America's children: Yearbook 1994.* Washington, DC: Author.

Cummins, J. (1986). Empowering minority students: A framework for intervention. *Harvard Educational Review, 56,* 16–36.

Dawson, D. A. (1991). Family structure and children's health and well-being: Data from the 1988 national health interview survey on child health. *Journal of Marriage and the Family, 53,* 573–584.

Escalona, S. K. (1950). The use of infant tests for predictive purposes. *Bulletin of the Meninger Clinic, 14,* 117–128.

Espe-Sherwindt, M. (1991). The IFSP and parents with special needs/mental retardation. *Topics in Early Childhood Special Education, 11,* 107–120.

Espe-Sherwindt, M., & Kerlin, S. L. (1990). Early intervention with parents with mental retardation: Do we empower or impair? *Infants and Young Children, 2*(4), 21–28.

Figueroa, R. A. (1989). Psychological testing of linguistic-minority students: Knowledge gaps and regulations. *Exceptional Children, 56,* 145–152.

Green, J. W. (1982). *Cultural awareness in the human services.* Englewood Cliffs, NJ: Prentice-Hall.

Greenspan, S. I. (1982). Developmental morbidity in infants in multi–risk-factor families: Clinical perspectives. *Public Health Reports, 97*(1), 16–23.

Hanson, M. J. (1992). Ethnic, cultural, and language diversity in intervention settings. In E. W. Lynch & M. J. Hanson (Eds.), *Developing cross-cultural competence: A guide for working with young children and their families* (pp. 3–18). Baltimore: Brookes.

Hanson, M. J., & Lynch, E. W. (1992). Family diversity: Implications for policy and practice. *Topics in Early Childhood Special Education, 12*(3), 283–306.

Hanson, M. J., Lynch, E. W., & Wayman, K. I. (1990). Honoring the cultural diversity of families when gathering data. *Topics in Early Childhood Special Education, 10*(1), 112–131.

Harrison, P. J., & Lynch, E. W. (1994). *Sacramento County Office of Education Infant Development Program: Families' evaluation of services.* Unpublished evaluation study.

Harry, B. (1992). *Cultural diversity, families, and the special education system: Communication and empowerment.* New York: Teachers College Press.

Hilliard, A. G., III. (1984). I.Q. testing as the emperor's new clothes: A critique of bias in mental testing. In C. Reynolds & R. E. Brown (Eds.), *Perspectives on bias in mental testing* (pp. 139–169). New York: Plenum Press.

Hobbs, N. (1975). *The futures of children.* San Francisco: Jossey-Bass.

Johnson, C. B. (1993). Developmental issues: Children infected with the human immunodeficiency virus. *Infants and Young Children, 6*(1), 1–10.

Jones, R. L. (Ed.). (1988). *Psychoeducational assessment of minority group children: A casebook.* Berkeley, CA: Cobb & Henry.

Lesar, S., & Maldonado, Y. A. (1994). Infants and young children with HIV infection: Service delivery considerations for family support. *Infants and Young Children, 6*(4), 70–81.

Levitan, S. A., Belous, R. S., & Gallo, F. (1988). *What's happening to the American family? Tensions, hopes, and realities* (rev. ed.). Baltimore: Johns Hopkins University Press.

Lidz, C. S. (Ed.). (1987). *Dynamic assessment: An interactional approach to evaluating learning potential.* New York: Guilford Press.

Lynch, E. W. (1992). Developing cross-cultural competence. In E. W. Lynch & M. J. Hanson (Eds.), *Developing cross-cultural competence: A guide for working with young children and their families* (pp. 35–62). Baltimore: Brookes.

Lynch, E. W., & Bakley, S. (1989). Serving young children whose parents are mentally retarded. *Infants and Young Children, 1*(3), 26–38.

Lynch, E. W., & Hanson, M. J. (Eds.). (1992a). *Developing cross-cultural competence: A guide for working with young children and their families.* Baltimore: Brookes.

Lynch, E. W., & Hanson, M. J. (1992b). Steps in the right direction. In E. W. Lynch & M. J. Hanson (Eds.), *Developing cross-cultural competence: A guide for working with young children and their families* (pp. 355–370). Baltimore: Brookes.

Lynch, E. W., & Hanson, M. J. (1993). Changing demographics: Implications for training in early intervention. *Infants and Young Children, 6*(1), 50–55.

Lynch, E. W., & Hanson, M. J. (in press). Ensuring cultural competence in assessment. In

M. McLean, D. Bailey, & M. Wolery (Eds.), *Assessing infants and toddlers with special needs.* Columbus, OH: Merrill.

Lynch, E. W., Jackson, J. A., Mendoza, J., & English, K. (1991). The merging of best practices and state policy in the IFSP process in California. *Topics in Early Childhood Special Education, 11,* 32–53.

Masnick, G., & Bane, M. J. (1980). *The nation's families: 1960–1990.* Boston: Auburn House.

McGonigel, M. J., Kaufmann, R. K., & Hurth, J. L. (1991). The IFSP sequence. In M. J. McGonigel, R. K. Kaufmann, & J. L. Hurth (Eds.), *Guidelines and recommended practices for the Individualized Family Service Plan* (2nd ed.). Washington, DC: Association for the Care of Children's Health.

Mercer, C. D., Algozzine, B., & Trifiletti, J. J. (1979). Early identification issues and considerations. *Exceptional Children, 46,* 52–54.

Olson, H. C., Burgess, D. M., & Streissguth, A. P. (1992). Fetal alcohol syndrome (FAS) and fetal alcohol effects (FAE): A lifespan view, with implications for early intervention. *Zero to Three, 13*(1), 24–29.

Osofsky, J. D. (1993–1994). Introduction: Hurt, healing hope—Caring for infants and toddlers in violent environments. *Zero to Three, 14*(3), 3–6.

Osofsky, J. D., Hann, D. M., & Peebles, C. (1993). Adolescent parenthood: Risks and opportunities for mothers and infants. In C. H. Zeanah, Jr. (Ed.), *Handbook of infant mental health* (pp. 106–119). New York: Guilford Press.

Research and Policy Committee of the Committee for Economic Development. (1987). *Children in need—Investment strategies for the educationally disadvantaged.* New York: Author.

Rosenbaum, S., Layton, C., & Liu, J. (1991). *The health of America's children.* Washington, DC: Children's Defense Fund.

Sontag, J. C., & Schacht, R. (1994). An ethnic comparison of parent participation and information needs in early intervention. *Exceptional Children, 60,* 422–433.

Thurman, S. K., & Gonsalves, S. V. (1993). Adolescent mothers and their premature infants: Responding to double risk. *Infants and Young Children, 5*(4), 44–51.

U.S. Department of Commerce. (1992). *1990 Census of population and housing: Summary population and housing characteristic United States.* Washington, DC: Author.

U.S. General Accounting Office. (1990, June 28). *Drug-exposed infants: A generation at risk* (Report to the Chairman, Committee on Finance, U.S. Senate). Washington, DC: U.S. Government Printing Office.

Wayman, K. I., Lynch, E. W., & Hanson, M. J. (1990). Home-based early childhood services: Cultural sensitivity in a family systems approach. *Topics in Early Childhood Special Education, 10*(4), 56–75.

Willis, W. (1992). Families with African American roots. In E. W. Lynch & M. J. Hanson (Eds.), *Developing cross-cultural competence: A guide for working with young children and their families* (pp. 121–150). Baltimore: Brookes.

Wolery, M. (1989). Transitions in early childhood special education: Issues and procedures. *Focus on Exceptional Children, 22*(2), 1–16.

Yonemitsu, D. M., & Cleveland, J. O. (1992). *Culturally competent service delivery: A training manual for bilingual/bicultural casemanagers.* (Available from SEADD Project, c/o San Diego Imperial Counties Developmental Services, Inc., 4355 Ruffin Road, San Diego, CA 92123)

Zuckerman, B., & Brown, E. R. (1993). Maternal substance abuse and infant development. In C. H. Zeanah, Jr. (Ed.), *Handbook of infant mental health* (pp. 143–158). New York: Guilford Press.

Selected Readings

Chan, S. (1990). Early intervention with culturally diverse families of infants and toddlers with disabilities. *Infants and Young Children, 3*(2), 78–87.

This article describes the Multicultural Trainer of Trainers (MTOT) Program designed by and for Asian American and Latin American parents of young children with disabilities. The article describes the process that was used to develop the model, the model itself, and the program outcomes. The information provided is especially useful to those working to develop parent training and support programs in multicultural communities.

Harry, B. (1992). *Cultural diversity, families, and the special education system: Communication and empowerment.* New York: Teachers College Press.

This resource is a qualitative study of 12 Puerto Rican families and their encounters with the special education system. The book is a powerful commentary on the disadvantages and difficulties faced by poor parents from underrepresented groups when they attempt to interact with the school system. Although the book focuses on the special education system, almost any other system could be substituted. With its many rich quotes from the extensive interviews, the book is truly a window into how families feel and how systems fail families.

Lynch, E. W., & Hanson, M. J. (1992). *Developing cross-cultural competence: A guide for working with young children and their families*. Baltimore: Brookes.

This extremely readable and informative book provides information about working cross-culturally, culture-specific information about many ethnic groups in the United States, and suggestions for applying the information in any setting that serves young children. The information provided is useful, interesting, and respectfully presented. For those seeking to improve their own cross-cultural competence or trying to ensure that programs and policies support diversity, this book is an invaluable resource.

SECTION II

Model Components

CHAPTER 4

Developing a Model

Designing an early intervention program is similar to building a house. The architects must have a vision in mind, an idea of what is needed and what they want to create. In addition to the dream, the architects must keep in mind who will live in the house and what features are most important to them. They must also have knowledge about the rules and regulations for building in the state, neighborhood, or community; knowledge about best practices in construction; and an openness to changes in plans, modifications in the design, and information about new and more effective methods of building. There are many parallels in developing an effective early intervention program. Just as the architects begin with a set of plans, the early interventionist begins with a program model—an integrated, comprehensive approach to providing services to infants and toddlers who are at risk or disabled and their families.

Components of an Optimal Model

Exemplary program models consist of multiple components. The components that must be a part of any comprehensive early intervention program include program philosophy, staffing, identification procedures, assessment procedures for children and their families, curriculum, family–professional collaboration, opportunities for integration and inclusion, transition services, systems for assuring health and safety of children and staff, administration and management, and evaluation. Each of the components requires knowledge about preferred practices in the fields of child development and early intervention, consideration of needs that are specific to the particular families and communities in the service area, awareness of available resources, and commitment to a transdisciplinary and interagency approach. This chapter provides an overview of each of the components of an optimal model. Section II of this book, Model Components, addresses these areas in depth.

Program Philosophy

The philosophy provides the foundation of the program, and all of the components are shaped by it. The program philosophy embodies the theoretical biases of the program developers and serves as a framework for all other aspects of service delivery. A philosophy used in medically based interventions and at least six different educational models based on different philosophies, theories, and beliefs about development and intervention have emerged (Linder, 1983). Each model represents a slightly different view of how children learn and develop and how they should be treated or taught. Both the medical model and the six educational models presented in this chapter are comprehensive models of service that include program content and goals, staffing patterns, degree of structure, and other aspects of how programs are organized and delivered. In current practice, models are often blended to maximize the strengths of several different approaches.

Medical Model

For many infants who are at risk or have disabilities, the first interventions are medical; they may occur in utero, in the delivery room, or shortly after birth in a neonatal intensive care unit (Klaus & Fanaroff, 1979). The Medical Model is characterized by the participation of teams of physicians and allied health professionals such as nurses, occupational and physical therapists, and a host of technicians. Social workers are also included as members of most medical teams dealing with newborns who are high risk, disabled, or critically ill. The Medical Model has its roots in medical research and is characterized by hierarchical decision making (by the physician in charge), quick action, high technology, technical language, and continuous monitoring and data gathering on the infant's state and progress. Environments in which medical interventions take place rely heavily on prevention of additional health problems, protection from anything that could

slow improvement, and attempts to "cure" the patient. Roles are clearly defined with most decisions reserved for physicians and implementation of those decisions delegated to nurses and other health professionals or paraprofessionals.

Medical models are highly suited to medical facilities and life or death situations. In those settings and at those times, it is critically important for the person with the most knowledge to take charge and act quickly without a long team process. However, a purely medical model is less well suited to educationally oriented early intervention programs. Hierarchical decision making and the lack of team process and consultation can result in intervention plans that are not comprehensive, do not reflect family priorities, and an overemphasis on cure that can result in disillusionment and burnout when the child remains disabled. However, working together, medical and educational teams can forge an alliance that supports both the child's and the family's needs.

Child Development Model

The Child Development Model (Ackerman & Moore, 1976) or Normal Developmental Model (Anastasiow, 1978) is based on the belief that children unfold and will learn when they are developmentally ready to learn. In this approach the interventionist's role is relatively passive. His or her role is to make developmentally appropriate materials available but not to be intrusive. The environment is usually characterized by activity areas such as the "housekeeping corner," "book nook," and painting area filled with attractive, child-size materials, and children choose the area in which they want to spend time.

For many years this model was considered to be inappropriate for children with more severe and pervasive disabilities (e.g., Alberto, Briggs, & Goldstein, 1983; Cicchetti & Sroufe, 1976; Warren & Rogers-Warren, 1982). However, the recent emphasis on the inclusion of children with disabilities in settings with other children of the same age, such as play groups, family day care, and preschools, has resulted in a reconsideration of the Child Development Model. Documents on the importance of developmentally appropriate practice published by the National Association for the Education of Young Children (NAEYC) (Bredekamp, 1987) have suggested that some practices are appropriate for all children, regardless of their disability. Although there is little about developmentally appropriate practice that is inappropriate for children with disabilities, many would argue that developmentally appropriate practice as outlined by NAEYC does not go far enough in outlining the range of programs and strategies that are necessary to serve children who are at risk or who have disabilities (e.g., Carta, Atwater, Schwartz, & McConnell, 1993; Carta, Schwartz, Atwater, & McConnell, 1991; McLean & Odom, 1993; Wolery, Strain, & Bailey, 1992). As early intervention programs and services are offered more frequently in typical community settings, it is important that developmentally appropriate practice be combined with the approaches and strategies that have been demonstrated to be effective with children with disabilities. Strategies such as those proposed by Cavallaro, Haney, and Cabello (1993) that focus on attention and responsiveness to children, environmental structuring, adult mediation, and peer mediation combine developmentally appropriate practice with tested approaches from early childhood special education.

Montessori Model

The model developed by Maria Montessori (1964), sometimes referred to as the Sensory Cognitive Model, is based on a belief that children will learn spontaneously in a well-organized environment. In this model the teacher plays the role of facilitator and carefully observes children to determine their readiness for tasks of greater difficulty. In this model the classroom is structured through a variety of materials of increasing complexity, and children learn at their own pace as they interact with the materials. The Montessori Model has been shown to have positive effects in a number of areas such as general verbal intelligence and perceptual and motor performance as well as on concentration and attention to task (Chatlin-McNichols, 1981); however, little recent research has been conducted on its effectiveness with young children with disabilities.

Cognitive Model

The Cognitive Interactional or Cognitive Developmental Model is a fusion of the ideas of many of the best known educators and psychologists, including John Dewey, Susan Isaacs, Erik Erikson, Anna Freud, Jean Piaget, and others (Linder, 1983). The model focuses on the interaction between the child and the environment, as well as on the child's genetic makeup and maturation. The environment is typically organized into activity or learning centers where a wide range of play and learning opportunities is available. Children's maturation is facilitated through manipulative activities and continuous verbal interactions; the emphasis is on learning to think and to solve problems (Lerner, Mardell-Czudnowski, & Goldenberg, 1987). Teachers take an active role in encouraging children to attempt new things and in questioning children about their experiences, but they do not intervene to prevent failure. Failure is viewed as an important aspect of learning and as a motivator for learning. This model is often used in preschool programs that integrate children with disabilities because of its dual emphases on cognitive and language development and its ability to incorporate children at differing performance levels (Bricker & Bricker, 1976; Hohman, Banet, & Weikart, 1979).

Applied Behavioral Analysis Model

In the development of educational programs for children with disabilities, one of the most frequently used models of intervention has been the Applied Behavioral Analysis Model, or its corollary the Precision Teaching Model (Bailey & Wolery, 1984; Snell & Zirpoli, 1987). Based on the principles of behavioral psychology, this model is highly structured and organized with an emphasis on behavioral specificity and data collection. In a behavioral model, specific behaviors are targeted for change and taught using modeling, prompting, fading, chaining, shaping, and reinforcement of successive approximations. The criteria for successful performance are set, and data collection is a routine part of monitoring the child's progress. When the child has mastered the behavior, continued opportunities to practice are provided on a maintenance schedule to ensure that the behavior is not forgotten. This model of intervention resulted in an important milestone in the education of individuals with severe disabilities for it clearly demonstrated that all children can learn, regardless of the extent of their disability. Because of its success, it was widely used as the primary mode of intervention in many early intervention and early childhood special education programs in the 1970s and 1980s.

Although the Applied Behavioral Analysis Model continues to provide effective strategies that early interventionists may use to teach certain skills or behaviors, it is no longer the primary mode of intervention. A more transactional model that requires that the child act, rather than be acted upon, and a more constructivist philosophy have replaced a strictly behavioral approach in most early intervention programs in the 1990s.

Activity-Based Model

The model of early intervention and early childhood special education that is currently receiving the most attention is the Activity-Based Model. Although it has roots in the developmental learning model (Klein & Campbell, 1991) and some of its elements have been used in high-quality programs for many years, Bricker (1989) and Bricker and Cripe (1992) have elaborated and extended the approach into a comprehensive model. Drawn from the theories of Piaget, Dewey, and Vygotsky, the Activity-Based Model is based on three themes: "(a) the influence and interaction of both the immediate and larger social-cultural environment, (b) the need for active involvement by the learner, (c) the enhancement of learning by engaging children in functional and meaningful activities" (Bricker & Cripe, 1992, p. 16). In this model of intervention, the child's individual objectives and outcomes are addressed in activities that occur naturally, that the child initiates, or that the interventionist plans. Naturally occurring events are used as antecedents or consequences to help the child develop functional and higher order cognitive skills. To ensure that the child is progressing, curriculum-based assessment is linked with intervention, and a series of activity opportunities are provided to allow children to practice what they are learning. This approach results in a highly transactional model that occurs in the context of the child's experience and borrows from behavioral principles.

Ecological Model

Within the past decade the Ecological or Functional Model has been used in many programs for students with moderate, severe, and profound disabilities. Although it emerged from work with older students, it may in part be applied to younger children with developmental disabilities. This model is based on several premises regarding individuals with severe handicaps: (a) They have an extremely limited ability to generalize and use old learnings to solve new problems; (b) they learn at a much slower rate than their nondisabled peers; and (c) education should focus on those skills that they will need to function most effectively currently and in the future. Thus, the curriculum is based on skills that will increase students' self-sufficiency, independence, and general quality of life such as daily living or domestic skills, vocational skills, recreation and leisure skills, communication skills, and interactions with nonhandicapped peers (Brown, Evans, Weed, & Owen, 1987; Brown, Branston, et al., 1979; Brown, Branston-McLean, et al., 1979). Instruction takes place in the settings where the skills will be needed. For example, toothbrushing would be taught at the sink in the bathroom and making a sandwich in the kitchen. For older students, the majority of the instruction takes place in the community. Instructors in this model use a variety of direct instructional techniques as well as modeling to teach the necessary skills. Although this model has revolutionized instruction for many students with severe disabilities from the elementary grades through young adulthood, its effects on infants, preschoolers, and toddlers have been less dramatic. The lessened impact of the model on this age group is not difficult to understand, because many of the basic developmental milestones on which the typical infant and toddler curriculum focuses are functional skills. However, as programs for infants and toddlers who are disabled or at risk for disabilities become more refined, functionality is becoming a more important criterion.

Summary

It is evident from the diversity of the models described in the preceding paragraphs that one's philosophy of child development, understanding of disabilities and risk conditions, knowledge of child and family needs, and individual skills, values, and biases will affect the program philosophy. Regardless of those factors, however, every early intervention program needs to have a stated philosophy—one that is explicit and shared with all staff members and families—for it is the philosophy that drives all other aspects of the program. Few programs today subscribe exclusively to one model. Instead most combine elements to meet the increasingly diverse needs of the children and families that they serve.

Many programs that are just beginning find it helpful to develop their philosophy as a group and to use the process as a vehicle for building the early intervention team. Teams of early intervention programs that have been in operation for a period of years often review their philosophy to assure that their practice is still a reflection of their basic beliefs about optimal service delivery. They may also develop interview questions for prospective employees based on their philosophy to assure that any new team member will be compatible with the philosophy and goals of the program.

Staffing and Staff Development

A well-trained, knowledgeable, sensitive staff is the most critical component of any program. Because of the complexity of the needs of infants and toddlers with disabilities, no single professional discipline is capable of providing all of the services; therefore, staff members are organized into teams. Although early childhood special educators may predominate in educationally based early intervention programs, teams may be organized in a variety of ways. Most frequently, teams are described as multidisciplinary, interdisciplinary, or transdisciplinary. In *multidisciplinary* teams, staff members representing different disciplines, such as education, physical therapy, psychology, and social work, assess the child and provide programs in isolation from one another. In *interdisciplinary* models, team members assess individually or with some collaboration and share information with one another so that program goals can be facilitated by all team members as they work with the child and family. In *transdisciplinary* models, the roles of the team members blend. Each team member shares skills with others so that each person's role is less differentiated. They may do joint assessments, and one or two people may be designated to be the primary interveners. In this model, family members are considered to be team members, and the primary intervener works with the mother, father, or other primary caregiver to see that services are delivered. Other team members provide consultation to the family and the primary intervener as needed (Raver, 1991). This transdisciplinary programming model is the goal of most early intervention programs, although in many programs throughout the country it is not yet a reality.

Determining who should be on the team depends upon the general needs of children and families that the program serves, resources within the community, and the program philosophy. Although it is often easiest to think about staff members in terms of their professional training, that is not always the most functional way to determine what staff members are needed. At a minimum, early intervention teams need staff members with expertise in the following areas: typical and atypical child development; assessment and intervention strategies in language–communication, social, motor, and cognitive skills; and working with families with diverse backgrounds and preferences. Because training in these skills is part of many professional preparation programs, the program administrator can select individuals with the greatest overall strength. For example, some professionals from special education, psychology, social work, and nursing have specialized in working with families of children with exceptionalities; thus, the individual hired to assure service in that area of the program might come from a wide range of disciplines. Likewise, individuals from nursing, occupational therapy, and physical therapy can bring expertise in motor assessment and intervention to the team. Because the various skills and knowledge needed can come from a variety of training backgrounds, the opportunities for hiring a team that combines the necessary expertise are more likely. The bottom line in staff recruitment and hiring is the need for training and experience in working with infants, toddlers, and their families and working effectively with team members from other professional disciplines and agencies. The needs and demands of infants and toddlers who are at risk or disabled and their families are different from those of older children and their families, and those differences must be accounted for in every interaction. Thus, regardless of the staff member's professional discipline, the focus of the training, or later experience, all team members should have been trained to work with very young children and their families.

A final note about staffing relates to the use of paraprofessionals. Many excellent programs throughout the country have used paraprofessionals very successfully in circumscribed ways. Working under the supervision of professionals, paraprofessionals have been hired to carry out or work with families to implement programs. For example, the language specialist may have designed a communication program for the child that involves talking to the child, imitating the sounds the child makes, and trying to get the child to imitate certain sounds like "ma ma ma" or "ba ba ba." A paraprofessional may help the family integrate those activities into the daily routine of feeding, changing, and playing with the baby. In some programs paraprofessionals who are also parents of children with disabilities work with families to provide support and assistance in working with a variety of community agencies. Paraprofessionals such as occupational or physical therapy aides may be used to implement and monitor motor or therapy programs. Using paraprofessionals can also help programs respond to the cultural and language diversity of the families that they serve. However, ongoing training and supervision of paraprofessionals cannot be overemphasized. With the focus on family-centered services, delivery models that rely on serving families in their homes, and the growing number of technical and process skills that are needed to be an effective early interventionist, supervision is a critical factor for all staff members; it is especially important for monitoring the effectiveness of paraprofessionals.

Incorporating paraprofessionals into early intervention programs has allowed some programs to extend services within their budget. However, for every paraprofessional team member, time for training and supervision must be figured into the responsibilities of the administrative and professional staff.

Like any other field, early intervention is not static. Changes in knowledge about disabilities, new technologies, and new or altered legislation bring about changes that must be incorporated into ongoing programs. Staff development is the vehicle that is used to keep staff members abreast of new developments. It may also be used to work on team building and sharing of knowledge, because people not trained in inter- or transdisciplinary programs may have to add knowledge and process skills to their repertoire.

Staff development should be an integral part of any early intervention program. It should be based on a comprehensive needs assessment of staff members, and a number of options for training should be available. In communities where there are university programs and comprehensive community resources, staff members often have more opportunities than time to keep up in the field. In areas that are more isolated, alternate staff development models must be created. In remote areas, consultants who provide training and follow-up technical assistance may be a wise investment. Videotapes or interactive video training packages can be rented, or staff members may form journal groups who read the most recent journal articles and meet as a group to discuss those readings. As the technologies available increase, distance learning may provide increasingly effective ways to conduct staff development activities. Interactive teleconferences that link participants via integrated voice, video, and data can reduce costs without losing the sense of connectedness that is often desired. Electronic mail services that allow interventionists to communicate throughout their agency, community, state, and the world can also be used to gather information and maintain support networks.

Recognition that individuals new to any job require support has led to the development of induction year and mentoring programs. Hanson (1990) described such an approach that supports the idea of using experienced early interventionists to mentor new colleagues. Although staff development activities are typically limited by economic factors, the range of cost-effective, meaningful strategies is increasing.

Identification

Part H of P.L. 99-457, the Education of the Handicapped Act, and its subsequent amendments [see Appendix A (P.L. 99-457)] require that each state participating in the legislation have a comprehensive child-find system to identify children eligible for early intervention programs and services. The legislation also requires states to have a public awareness program that focuses on early intervention, referral sources, and informational materials for parents. In addition, it is the responsibility of each state to establish and maintain a central directory that includes information about early intervention services, the resources available in the state, the experts in early intervention, and special projects within the state involved in early intervention research or demonstration. As a result of these requirements, states, and the communities within them, have developed ways to identify infants and toddlers who may be eligible for services. Screening and referral processes that identify eligible children and help families locate services require cooperation among public and private health care providers, and education, social service, and other agencies that have contact with young children and their families. Because of the time lines involved in the referral process, assessment, and development of the IFSP, carefully coordinated, interagency approaches to identification have become especially important.

In some communities early intervention programs have developed strong relationships with physicians, nurses, social workers, and discharge planners in hospital neonatal intensive care units. Whenever a child is born with a disability, the hospital personnel know whom to call and how to make a referral. Pediatricians, primary care physicians, and nurse practitioners are also informed in many communities about available early intervention programs. In those areas where the medical and educational communities have not yet developed a system of collaboration, the social service system or parent organizations link families to services.

To be effective, practices used to identify infants and toddlers who are at risk or disabled must be based on criteria that can be operationalized and procedures that are systematic. Programs must meet professional guidelines for appropriateness and be humane in their treatment of families who are being confronted by many professionals at a time of extreme stress.

Child Assessment and Determination of Family Concerns, Priorities, and Resources

Assessment is the most common strategy for determining eligibility for services, strengths, and needs of the child, and the concerns, priorities, and resources of the families being served. Educationally focused early intervention programs must include assessments that address each of these concerns.

Initial assessments are typically done by intervention team members to determine whether the child is eligible to receive services. Usually this inter- or transdisciplinary assessment examines those areas in which families have expressed concern; the child's cognitive abilities; and the child's gross and fine motor, communication, self-help, and social and emotional skills. Measures of physical and health status are also included in the eligibility "workup." All assessments must be conducted with parents' permissions and input by trained professionals using instruments and procedures designed for the purpose for which they are being used. Assessments must also be conducted in the child's and family's primary language (i.e., the language used in the home). Information about the child gathered in this assessment is compared with the criteria for program entrance (eligibility criteria), and the team decides whether the child meets those criteria.

As approaches to child assessment have evolved, so have the assessment strategies. In many states and communities the eligibility assessment described in the previous paragraph may take other forms. For example, gathering information through a review of records of previous assessments might be adequate to qualify a child for services, or an assessment that relied on a combination of observation, parent report, and clinical judgment might substitute for the administration of standardized instruments. Regardless of the strategies used, assessments can be conducted only after obtaining parental permission and must be conducted in the language appropriate to the child and family unless it is clearly not feasible to do so.

The curriculum of any program provides the scope and sequence of skills to be learned, but the specific objectives selected for each child are based on a careful assessment of the child's individual strengths and needs and the family's priorities. This curriculum-based assessment is conducted after the child enters the program. Although information from the eligibility assessment may be used to help develop the IFSP, additional criterion-referenced measures and information gathered from families are usually used to plan a comprehensive intervention (Neisworth & Bagnato, 1988). This assessment is an ongoing process that enables interventionists and families to measure the child's skill attainment and monitor the success of the interventions.

With the implementation of P.L. 99-457 and its subsequent amendments, the identification of family concerns, priorities, and resources has become an important part of the assessment process. With the family's concurrence, interventionists can gather information about family issues, concerns, priorities, goals, and resources related to facilitating their child's development. With family permission, this information can be incorporated into the IFSP and the family may choose to develop outcomes for themselves that are separate from individual child outcomes. In other words, the family may want to include an outcome on the IFSP that focuses on spending more time with other children in the family, helping the grandparents understand their child's disability, or learning sign language so that they can support their child's communication more effectively.

The idea of determining family concerns, priorities, and resources and incorporating them into an intervention plan is new to most early interventionists. Although a great deal has been written about the process and procedures since P.L. 99-457 was enacted, this area continues to be poorly defined (e.g., Bailey, Winton, Rouse, & Turnbull, 1990; Beckman & Bristol, 1991; Bennett, Lingerfelt, & Nelson, 1990; Dunst, Trivette, & Deal, 1988; McGonigel, Kaufmann, & Johnson, 1991).

Curriculum

The curriculum is the anchor for any early intervention program. It, in combination with family priorities, defines the overall goals and objectives as well as the skills that children are taught. It is a planned sequence of learning activities. An increasing number of commercially available curriculum packages for infants and toddlers who are at risk or disabled are now available. The majority of these are based on developmental tasks in cognitive, receptive and expressive language, gross and fine motor, social, emotional, and self-care skills, and are structured with the belief that these infants and toddlers follow the same developmental sequences as normally developing children. Although this assumption is currently being questioned, far fewer curricula have been designed for children with specific developmental needs, such as those by Hanson and Harris (1986) for children with motor delays, Hanson (1987) for infants with Down syndrome, and Fewell and Sandall (1983) for infants with sensory or physical impairments.

The comprehensiveness of curricular packages varies, but many include strategies and procedures for teaching and maintaining skills. One of the current emphases in curriculum development is functionality, the importance of the skill in current and future environments. Although it has been assumed that all developmental skills are functional, this needs further examination. Future curricula may be based less on traditional milestones than are the curricula of the present. They may also be designed to account for quantitative and qualitative differences in children who have disabilities and those who are at risk.

Family–Professional Collaboration

Infants and toddlers can be viewed only in the context of the family. In recent years, the critical importance of the family to all aspects of intervention has been recognized and supported through legislation and changes in the ways in which programs and services are delivered. As a part of these changes, the relationship between families and professionals has also changed. Instead of emphasizing family involvement in early intervention, the emphasis is on family–professional partnerships and collaboration (Lynch, Jackson, Mendoza, & English, 1991). These collaborative partnerships are designed to help interventionists more effectively meet the needs of the child and his or her family and to help families acquire the skills, knowledge, and confidence that they need to become equal partners in decision making for their child (Healy, Keesee, & Smith, 1985; Singer & Powers, 1993; Turnbull et al., 1993).

The changing demographics of families in recent years have increased the complexity of early intervention. Many families are headed by single mothers with limited resources; others are headed by grandmothers. An increasing number of families are non–English speaking; and a growing number have multiple problems that limit their ability to cope effectively with the added responsibility of an infant or toddler who is at risk or disabled (Greenspan, 1982). Empowering families who face multiple risks poses new challenges for early intervention teams and demands the expertise of someone with special training in working with families (Cicchetti & Toth, 1987; Harris, 1993; Myers, Olson, & Kaltenbach, 1992; Osofsky & Fenichel, 1994).

Opportunities for Inclusion with Nondisabled Peers

The concept of inclusion with nondisabled peers has been described in a variety of ways. Public Law 94-142 used the term *least restrictive environment* (LRE) to describe settings for children with disabilities that are as close to those of their nondisabled peers as possible. For example, most nondisabled preschoolers live at home and spend some time in a child care or preschool program in their community. A similar arrangement would be the least restrictive and the most appropriate environment for the majority of preschoolers with disabilities. On the other hand, placing preschoolers with disabilities in a large, residential institution far from their families would be a very restrictive environment, one that is very different from the lives of their nonhandicapped peers.

In addition to LRE, opportunities to spend time with nondisabled peers are sometimes referred to as *integration* or *mainstreaming*. Another term that has been used to describe a merging of programs for children with and without disabilities is *inclusion*. In inclusive environments, children with disabilities are included in the same settings as their nondisabled peers, and supports are provided as needed. For example, instead of placing Tyrone in a toddler program for children with disabilities and then scheduling time for him to participate in a regular child care setting in his neighborhood, the opposite would be done. The neighborhood child care setting would be Tyrone's primary placement, and support services would be provided there along with training for the child care providers. In some instances, specialized services might be provided in another setting, but the emphasis is on ensuring that the child and the family are included in programs and services for children who are developing normally.

Issues related to inclusion, integration, mainstreaming, and LRE are somewhat different for infants and toddlers than for older children. The least restrictive environment for most infants and toddlers is in their own home or in a homelike child care setting. As advocacy for inclusion of older students gains strength, it is critical for early interventionists and families to define inclusion for young children. What is appropriate for older students with disabilities does not constitute the least restrictive placement for a baby.

Two final issues regarding opportunities for very young children who are at risk and disabled to interact with nondisabled peers must be considered. The first relates to the importance of opportunities for families of young children with disabilities to participate in the same educational, recreational, and social support programs in which families of nondisabled infants and toddlers participate. Being a part of the community, recognizing that babies are babies regardless of their special needs, and receiving understanding and support from other new parents has not always been available to families with a child with disabilities. Therefore, one of the goals of inclusion efforts is to ensure that families, as well as young children with disabilities, are an integral part of the larger community. The second issue relates to the family's preferences regarding inclusion opportunities. Some families may want to begin receiving services for their child in fully included settings. Others, for their own reasons, may prefer to wait several months or more before becoming involved in settings that include nondisabled children and their families. Although the ultimate goal is inclusion and full participation, it is important to respect family wishes and let them set the pace on inclusion.

Transition Services

One of the primary purposes for early intervention programs is to give young children who are at risk and disabled the head start that they need to increase competence and function more effectively and independently in the future. For many young children who are at risk or disabled, the first transition is from the hospital to the home—from medical support to more educationally oriented intervention. Early interventionists can ease this transition for both the child and the family by working closely with the medical system.

Infants and toddlers who have been identified for services usually leave the early intervention program at age 3 and enter a preschool program. One of the primary jobs of early interventionists is to ease that transition for the child and the family. Part H of P.L. 99-457 is clear about procedures for transition. Each IFSP, as appropriate, must address the steps that will be taken to support the child's transition to the next environment, and interventionists are charged with working with families to develop the steps that will be undertaken in making the transition. Knowing community resources, initiating planning well before the change is to take place, providing support to the family, and being available to follow up on the child's new placement are all aspects of successful transitions (Neisworth & Fewell, 1990). Moving from the nurturing environment of most infant and toddler programs to the hurly-burly of preschool causes stress for both parent and child, but that stress can be channeled into eagerness and enthusiasm if the early intervention team, family, and preschool team work together on the transition.

Health and Safety

Assuring the health and safety of young children is important in any environment, but it may be even more so in early intervention programs. Children at risk for disabilities or those who have disabilities that are identified in infancy may be more vulnerable to a variety of health problems, and many of the children have chronic illnesses. In addition to knowing how to respond to general medical emergencies, early interventionists need to be knowledgeable about individual children's health problems and needs (Walker, 1986). Procedures for administering medication, catheterization, or making behavioral observations when a child's medication is being altered by the physician may be the responsibility of an early intervention team member.

Health issues relate to the early intervention team members as well as to the children. Infections such as rubella and cytomegalovirus (CMV), which often cause disabilities when acquired in utero, may be active for several years after birth (Batshaw & Perret, 1992). Thus, early interventionists in close contact with the child (e.g., those who change diapers) may be exposed to the infection. For most generally healthy adults such exposure is little more than an inconvenient irritant if they become ill, but women who are pregnant at the time they are infected run the risk of infecting the fetus they carry. Because of the incidence of infectious disease among young children, it becomes even more important for early interventionists to use universal health precautions to prevent the spread of infection to children in the program and themselves.

Safety for children and staff members alike is an ongoing part of any program. Being alert to hazards, following all fire and safety codes with diligence, and conducting routine inspections with the help of community experts can help to prevent accidents. Because of the immobility of very young children, plans for evacuating the building in case of fire or explosion need to be carefully developed and frequent drills need to be conducted.

Program Administration and Management

In every type of program or service, leadership and effective management improve the quality of services (Lay-Dopyera & Dopyera, 1985). In early intervention programs administrators are responsible for hiring of personnel, managing day-to-day operations, keeping records, interfacing with district or agency management as well as their own staff members, developing collaborative interagency efforts, designing staff development programs, managing the budget, evaluating program effectiveness, engaging in future planning, and mediating disputes. They may also find themselves lobbying for their program's needs in a larger system where there is competition for resources or selling their program when they are not part of a larger organization. Yet, with all of these tasks, administrators are, most importantly, the programmatic leaders of early intervention programs.

Administrators of early intervention programs often have developed their skills from on-the-job training, because administering these programs has not yet evolved into a specialty area. Although models of early childhood special education administrator preparation have been proposed (Wimpelberg, Abroms, & Catardi, 1985), few people have had the benefit of systematic training. The importance of a strong administrator who understands the unique needs of infants, toddlers, and their families cannot be overestimated in the development of an optimal model.

Program Evaluation

Because of the relative newness of early intervention programs, the diversity of children and families served, the wide range of models that have been employed, and the overall commitment to high-quality programs and services, optimal programs include routine, periodic evaluations of their effectiveness. In recent years considerable attention has been given to the overall efficacy and cost-effectiveness of early intervention programs (e.g., Garwood, Neisworth, Mori, & Fewell, 1985; Lazar & Darlington, 1982; Weikart, 1980), bringing program evaluation to public attention. Although most early intervention programs do not have the resources to conduct comprehensive evaluations of all aspects of their programs, including cost-effectiveness, some basic evaluation of services and child and family outcomes is a necessity. These routine evaluations provide formative evaluation data that enable programs to change to better meet the needs of the children and families they serve.

Summary

Optimal early intervention programs are made up of separate but interrelated components, which include philosophy and theory as well as the day-to-day, operational aspects of the program. Early intervention programs are built on a philosophy that states the program's beliefs about children and families. The program philosophy serves as a framework for selecting staff members; assessing children; determining family concerns, priorities, and resources; and selecting and implementing the curriculum. High-quality early intervention programs also have well-developed procedures for identifying children in need of service and for collaborating with families through support and instruction. Although the types of opportunities for children and families to interact with nondisabled peers may vary, inclusion is a component of any optimal program, as is a carefully designed transition plan for moving from hospital to early intervention settings and from early intervention programs into preschool. Early intervention team members and the program administrator may come from a variety of disciplines, but they should have knowledge about typical and atypical development and skill in assessing, designing, and implementing programs for atypical infants and toddlers across all areas of development. Additionally, they should be skilled in working with diverse families and able to share their own expertise with parents and colleagues to improve services to the child. Finally, the effectiveness of early intervention programs is measured by carefully designed, routine program evaluation, and data gathered in these evaluations are used to improve existing services.

Service Delivery Systems

After the components of the model have been determined and developed, the issue of location of services remains. Services are usually described as home based, center based, or combination home and center based (Lewis & Lynch, 1988). As the names suggest, home-based services are delivered in the child's own home or the home of his or her primary caregiver. The early interventionist usually makes weekly home visits to work with the child and family. Kelly (1980) suggested that providing services in the home has multiple advantages, including greater comfort for the child and family, causing them to be more natural in their interactions; protection of the child's health; less disruption in the child's and family's routines; greater regularity in sessions; greater likelihood of full family involvement in the interventions; and opportunities for the interventionist to help modify the child's environment in ways that promote development.

Center-based models are generally group oriented. The infant or toddler who is at risk or disabled is brought to the center for early intervention services. In many programs a parent or primary caregiver accompanies the child. Parents or caregivers may spend part of the session working with the child with the assistance of the early intervention team and part of the session observing or meeting together in a parent group. Sometimes, parents are encouraged to leave the child and take a break from caregiving. Kelly (1980) listed the following advantages of center-based programs: greater access to the full early intervention team, opportunities for parents to spend time with other parents, opportunities for both children and families to model from others, reduced costs, and opportunities to create a much more specialized learning environment for the child.

In reality, many programs use both the home- and center-based models in combination. Some programs serve infants at home until they are at least 18 months old, at which time they may go to a center for a few hours once or twice a week, increasing their time at the center as they get older. Other programs combine home visits with center-based programs for all children. At this time there is no clear research evidence on the superiority of any of the models (Filler, 1983); however, the philosophies of individualization for child and family and least restrictive environment suggest that a range of options, including home, center, and combination programs, is probably best.

In addition to the location of the service, the agency or agencies responsible for providing early intervention services must also be determined. Public Law 99-457 and its subsequent amendments require that services for children who are at risk and disabled from birth to 3 years demonstrate interagency planning and coordination. In recent years, considerable attention has been given to developing collaborative models of service delivery that involve health, education, social, and developmental service agencies (e.g., Elder & Magrab, 1980; Lynch & Harrison, 1986; Rossi, Gilmartin, & Dayton, 1982). Collaborative planning and programming should result in a greater range of options, reduced duplication of service, assurance that gaps in the service delivery system are filled, and elimination of fragmentation, thus improving services to children and families (Lynch & Harrison, 1986).

Service delivery systems can be conceptualized in relation to the location of services and the agency or agencies providing the service. Home-based, center-based, and combination models are the descriptors used most often to identify the location of early intervention services. The location of services depends on the age of the child, the outcomes desired for the child by the family, and the resources available. Because research does not suggest that one model is superior to another, best practice suggests that the full range of models be available to increase the availability of services for families. A current trend in service delivery supported by the Individuals with Disabilities Education Act (IDEA) is the collaboration among agencies to provide the multiple services needed by infants and toddlers who are at risk or disabled and their families. Interagency collaboration increases the likelihood that the full range of necessary services will be available, reduces costs by eliminating duplication, and improves the quality of services by eliminating fragmentation.

A Synthesized, Dynamic Approach

Services for infants and toddlers who are at risk and disabled and their families differ quantitatively and qualitatively from services for older children with disabilities. A wide range of services may be needed as families discover that their child is disabled or at risk for disability. Coupled with the changes that all families face whenever there is a new member, the advent of an infant or toddler who is at risk or disabled may cause stress, which further taxes the family's ability to cope (Beckman, Pokorni, Maza, & Balzer-Martin, 1986; Beckman-Bell, 1981; Kornblatt & Heinrich, 1985; Salisbury, 1987). The infant may need intensive medical treatment and constant monitoring, followed by therapy and educational intervention. The parents may need moral support, financial assistance, counseling, and respite from the demands of caring for the child (Blacher, 1984). Other siblings may need information about what is happening and what to expect, assurance that they are not responsible for the child's problems, and attention from parents to let them know that they are still loved and valued family members (Meyer, Vadasy, & Fewell, 1985). Grandparents may need information about the child's condition and emotional support as they grieve for themselves and their own children. No single discipline or agency can meet all of these needs, but models that include transdisciplinary teams and collaboration among agencies and that are committed to continuous reevaluation and needed change can be responsive. To meet the ever-changing needs of children and families, the service system must be dynamic (Yando & Zigler, 1984).

The needs of infants and toddlers themselves are also different from those of older children. Interventions must be tailored to their temperament, rhythm, patterns of sleep and wakefulness, and their total dependence on caregivers. Infants cannot be viewed separately from the family unit. The transactional nature of the infant–caregiver dyad necessitates intervention strategies that may be quite different from those that would be recommended for an older child (e.g., Bromwich, 1981; Hanson, 1982; Healy et al., 1985; Klaus & Kennell, 1982).

Finally, early intervention services must be based on an assessment of community needs. The size, location, number of individuals of childbearing age, economic stability, diversity of cultures and languages represented, incidence of disabilities in the community, and the generic and specialized services already available will influence the number and type of services that are developed. The needs for early intervention services in retirement communities in the nation's sunbelts, for example, are far different from those in major cities. Early intervention programs in communities with large numbers of teenage parents may differ from those in affluent areas where the average age at the birth of the first child is 33. Also, like all other aspects of early intervention, programs in all of these areas will need to grow and change in relation to the changing needs of the community.

Thus, a model that is synthesized, yet dynamic and responsive to change, is the ideal. When programs cease to be responsive to child, family, and community needs, they become obsolete.

Summary

Program models in early intervention have multiple components that must be developed for new programs and reviewed periodically in established programs. Optimal programs are based on a philosophy that incorporates research, theory, and experiential wisdom about best practices for very young children and families. Various models have emerged in educationally based early intervention programs, but each can be traced to theoretical underpinnings in developmental psychology and behavioral psychology.

Staffing patterns for early intervention programs are generally inter- or transdisciplinary, with a variety of professionals working together on teams. Because of the nature of child and family needs, individuals with expertise in typical and atypical development, working with families, assessment and intervention, and medical and health issues are essential to optimal programming. The field of early intervention is growing and changing rapidly, and best practice 5 years ago may no longer represent the optimum. Thus, staff development must become an integral part of any program.

Programs also need procedures for identifying children who are appropriate for services and for conducting comprehensive evaluations to determine the nature of the intervention. In some communities hospitals screen, identify, and refer those infants and toddlers who are at risk or disabled; in other communities other agencies fulfill that function. Once the child's eligibility for service has been determined, the early intervention team conducts curriculum-based assessments to determine the child's strengths and needs. Family concerns, priorities, and resources may also be assessed in early intervention programs.

The overall curriculum for an early intervention program includes the scope and sequence of skills that are taught. In most programs for very young children, the curriculum incorporates the early developmental milestones related to communication, mobility, self-care, and cognitive, gross and fine motor, and personal–social development, as well as those skills or behaviors that are priorities for the family. One of the current themes in early intervention is the functionality of the curriculum—the need to teach those skills that will increase the child's later independence and be useful in the future.

Infants and toddlers cannot be considered separate from their families, so the child and family become the unit for intervention. Because parents or primary caregivers are the most important individuals in an infant's or toddler's life, family–professional collaboration is stressed. Family members are encouraged to determine the ways in which they want to be involved in the child's program and helped to find ways to participate that are appropriate to their culture, personal preferences, and wishes.

Based on parental wishes, programs are encouraged to develop inclusion opportunities for infants and toddlers who are at risk or disabled and their families. The extent and type of inclusion will vary with the child's age and the family's preferences, but as infants grow into toddlers, nondisabled peers can provide excellent models, and families can benefit from participation in the broader community.

Early intervention programs tend to be unique in their creation of a supportive and nurturant environment for children and families, yet this environment may also impede the child's and family's comfort with subsequent programs. Consequently, early intervention programs must look to the future and develop strategies that help the child and the family make the transition to preschool programs.

The health and safety of infants and young children is always an issue, but it takes on added importance in settings in which the children are more vulnerable to disease or accidents. In addition to developing procedures that promote the health and safety of the children, early intervention programs must also consider the health of staff members. Some children receiving services in infancy carry infectious diseases that could be hazardous to pregnant staff members. Personal hygiene with an emphasis on universal health precautions as well as procedures for handling diapers and feeding children must be developed, and staff members must receive training in their implementation.

Optimal models have strong administrators who combine skill in both leadership and management. Early intervention administrators need to understand the unique features of programs for very young children and their families, provide programmatic leadership, work with their supervisors in the organization, and interact with colleagues in other programs and agencies.

A final, essential component of an optimal early intervention program is evaluation. In order to continue to improve services, routine periodic evaluations should be conducted on all aspects of the program.

As early intervention programs have developed, several locations have been used for delivering services. Home-based, center-based, and combination home- and center-based programs are used throughout the nation. Programs that combine all three models are preferred, because it enables the program to be more responsive to family needs and acknowledges the range of inclusive environments that can be appropriate for infants and toddlers who are at risk or disabled.

Services to infants and toddlers who are at risk or disabled and their families are not merely downward extensions of special education services to older students. They are different in kind and in degree and require skills, knowledge, and understanding of these differences. Optimal programs for the youngest children with special needs are, themselves, very special.

Preferred Practices

The following questions can be used to review an early intervention program in relation to preferred practices.

1. Does the program have a written program philosophy?
2. Can all staff members describe the model that provides the foundation for the program's operation?
3. Are staff members well trained and from a variety of professional disciplines?
4. Do staff members function as a transdisciplinary team that includes families?
5. Are opportunities for staff development made available to all staff members?
6. Is there a systematic set of procedures for identifying children who may be eligible for the program?
7. Does the child's assessment lead to programming?
8. Are families' concerns, priorities, and resources determined and used in the development of the IFSP?
9. Is there an agreed-upon curriculum that is appropriate for the children and families served and consistent with the program philosophy?
10. Are families encouraged to take responsibility and control, and are they treated as equal team members?
11. Are there opportunities for interactions with nondisabled peers?
12. Are there systematic procedures to ease transitions from one environment to the next?
13. Are health and safety procedures that protect children, family, and staff members in place?
14. Is the management system consistent with program needs?
15. Is there an ongoing evaluation process?

References

Ackerman, P. R., Jr., & Moore, M. G. (1976). Delivery of educational services to preschool handicapped children. In T. Tjossem (Ed.), *Intervention strategies for high-risk infants and young children* (pp. 669–688). Baltimore: University Park Press.

Alberto, P. A., Briggs, T., & Goldstein, D. (1983). Managing learning in handicapped infants. In S. G. Garwood & R. R. Fewell (Eds.), *Educating handicapped infants* (pp. 417–454). Rockville, MD: Aspen.

Anastasiow, N. J. (1978). Strategies and models for early childhood intervention programs in integrated settings. In M. Guralnick (Ed.), *Early intervention and the integration of handicapped and non-handicapped children* (pp. 85–111). Baltimore: University Park Press.

Bailey, D. B., Winton, P. J., Rouse, L., & Turnbull, A. P. (1990). Family goals in infant intervention: Analysis and issues. *Journal of Early Intervention, 14,* 15–26.

Bailey, D. B., & Wolery, M. (1984). *Teaching infants and preschoolers with handicaps.* Columbus, OH: Merrill.

Batshaw, M. L., & Perret, Y. M. (1992). *Children with disabilities: A medical primer.* Baltimore: Brookes.

Beckman, P. J., & Bristol, M. M. (1991). Issues in developing the IFSP: A framework for establishing family outcomes. *Topics in Early Childhood Special Education, 11,* 19–31.

Beckman, P., Pokorni, J., Maza, R., & Balzer-Martin, L. (1986). A longitudinal study of stress and support in families of preterm and full-term infants. *Journal of the Division of Early Childhood, 11*(1), 2–9

Beckman-Bell, P. J. (1981). Child related stress in families of handicapped children. *Topics in Early Childhood Special Education, 1*(3), 45–53.

Bennett, T., Lingerfelt, B. V., & Nelson, D. E. (1990). *Developing individualized family support plans: A training manual.* Cambridge, MA: Brookline Books.

Blacher, J. (1984). A dynamic perspective on the impact of a severely handicapped child on the family. In J. Blacher (Ed.), *Severely handicapped young children and their families* (pp. 3–50). Orlando, FL: Academic Press.

Bredekamp, S. (Ed.). (1987). *Developmentally appropriate practice in early childhood programs serving children birth through age 8.* Washington, DC: National Association for the Education of Young Children.

Bricker, D. D. (1989). *Early intervention for at-risk and handicapped infants, toddlers, and preschool children.* Palo Alto, CA: VORT.

Bricker, D. D., & Cripe, J. (1992). *An activity-based approach to early intervention.* Baltimore: Brookes.

Bricker, W. A., & Bricker, D. D. (1976). The infant, toddler, and preschool research and intervention project. In T. D. Tjossem (Ed.), *Intervention strategies for high-risk infants and young children* (pp. 545–572). Baltimore: University Park Press.

Bromwich, R. (1981). *Working with parents and infants.* Austin, TX: PRO-ED.

Brown, F., Evans, I. M., Weed, K. A., & Owen, V. (1987). Delineating functional competencies: A component model. *The Journal of the Association for Persons with Severe Handicaps, 12,* 117–124.

Brown, L., Branston, M. B., Hamre-Nietupski, S., Pumpian, I., Certo, N., & Gruenwald, L. (1979). A strategy for developing chronological age-appropriate and functional curricular content for severely handicapped adolescents and young adults. *The Journal of Special Education, 13,* 81–90.

Brown, L., Branston-McLean, M., Baumgart, D., Vincent, L., Falvey, M., & Schroeder, J. (1979). Using the characteristics of current and subsequent least restrictive environments in the development of curricular content for severely handicapped students. *AAESPH Review, 4,* 407–424.

Carta, J. J., Atwater, J. B., Schwartz, I. S., & McConnell, S. R. (1993). Developmentally appropriate practices and early childhood special education: A reaction to Johnson and McChesney Johnson, *Topics in Early Childhood Special Education, 13,* 243–254.

Carta, J. J., Schwartz, I. S., Atwater, J. B., & McConnell, S. R. (1991). Developmentally appropriate practice: Appraising its usefulness for young children with disabilities. *Topics in Early Childhood Special Education, 11,* 1–20.

Cavallaro, C. C., Haney, M., & Cabello, B. (1993). Developmentally appropriate strategies for promoting full participation in early childhood settings. *Topics in Early Childhood Special Education, 13,* 293–307.

Chatlin-McNichols, J. P. (1981). The effects of Montessori school experience. *Young Children, 36*(5), 49–66.

Cicchetti, D., & Sroufe, A. (1976). The relationship between affective and cognitive development in Down's syndrome infants. *Child Development, 46,* 920–929.

Cicchetti, D., & Toth, S. L. (1987). The application of a transactional risk model to intervention with multi-risk maltreating families. *Zero to Three, 7*(5), 1–8.

Dunst, C. J., Trivette, C. M., & Deal, A. G. (1988). *Enabling and empowering families: Principles and guidelines for practice.* Cambridge, MA: Brookline.

Elder, J. O., & Magrab, P. R. (1980). *Coordinating services to handicapped children—A handbook for interagency collaboration.* Baltimore: Brookes.

Fewell, R. R., & Sandall, S. R. (1983). Curricula adaptations for young children: Visually impaired, hearing impaired, and physically impaired. *Topics in Early Childhood Special Education, 2*(4), 51–66.

Filler, J. W. (1983). Service models for handicapped infants. In S. G. Garwood & R. R. Fewell (Eds.), *Educating handicapped infants* (pp. 369–386). Rockville, MD: Aspen.

Garwood, S. G., Neisworth, J. T., Mori, A. A., & Fewell, R. R. (Eds.). (1985). Efficacy studies: Programs for young handicapped children [Special issue]. *Topics in Early Childhood Special Education, 5*(2).

Greenspan, S. I. (1982). Developmental morbidity in infants in multi-risk-factor families: Clinical perspectives. *Public Health Reports, 97*(1), 16–23.

Hanson, M. J. (1982). Issues in designing intervention approaches from developmental theory and research. In D. D. Bricker (Ed.), *Intervention with at-risk and handicapped infants* (pp. 249–267). Austin, TX: PRO-ED.

Hanson, M. J. (1987). *Teaching the infant with Down syndrome: A guide for parents and professionals* (2nd ed.). Austin, TX: PRO-ED.

Hanson, M. J. (1990). *Final report: California early intervention personnel model, personnel standards, and personnel preparation plan.* San Francisco: Department of Special Education, San Francisco State University. (Available from Ben Traverso, Department of Developmental Services, P. O. Box 944202, Sacramento, CA 94244-2020)

Hanson, M. J., & Harris, S. R. (1986). *Teaching the young child with motor delays.* Austin, TX: PRO-ED.

Harris, J. (1993). Babies in prison. *Zero to Three, 13*(3), 17–21.

Healy, A., Keesee, P. D., & Smith, B. S. (1985). *Early services for children with special needs: Transactions for family support.* Iowa City: Division of Developmental Disabilities, University Hospital School, University of Iowa.

Hohman, M., Banet, B., & Weikart, D. P. (1979). *Young children in action.* Ypsilanti, MI: High/Scope Educational Research Foundation.

Kelly, J. F. (1980). *Analysis of service delivery to children birth to three years, and their families.* Monmouth, OR: WESTAR.

Klaus, M. H., & Fanaroff, A. A. (1979). *Care of the high-risk neonate* (2nd ed.). Philadelphia: W. B. Saunders.

Klaus, M. H., & Kennell, J. H. (1982). *Parent–infant bonding* (2nd ed.). St. Louis: Mosby.

Klein, N., & Campbell, P. (1991). Preparing personnel to serve at-risk and disabled infants, toddlers, and preschoolers. In S. Meisels & J. Shonkoff (Eds.), *Handbook of early intervention* (pp. 671–699). New York: Cambridge University Press.

Kornblatt, E. S., & Heinrich, J. (1985). Needs and coping abilities in families of children with developmental disabilities. *Mental Retardation, 23,* 13–19.

Lay-Dopyera, M., & Dopyera, J. E. (1985). Administrative leadership: Styles, competencies, repertoire. *Topics in Early Childhood Special Education, 5*(1), 15–23.

Lazar, I., & Darlington, R. (1982). Lasting effects of early education: A report from the consortium for longitudinal studies. *Monographs of the Society for Research in Child Development, 47*(2–3, Serial No. 195).

Lerner, J., Mardell-Czudnowski, C., & Goldenberg, D. (1987). *Special education for the early childhood years* (2nd ed.). Englewood Cliffs, NJ: Prentice-Hall.

Lewis, R. B., & Lynch, E. W. (1988). Services for exceptional people. In E. W. Lynch & R. B. Lewis (Eds.), *Exceptional children and adults: An introduction to special education* (pp. 46–93). Glenview, IL: Scott, Foresman.

Linder, T. (1983). *Early childhood special education.* Baltimore: Brookes.

Lynch, E. W., & Harrison, P. J. (1986). *Interagency collaboration: Making magic happen.* San Diego:

Department of Special Education, San Diego State University.

Lynch, E. W., Jackson, J. A., Mendoza, J. M., & English, K. (1991). The merging of best practices and state policy in the IFSP process in California. *Topics in Early Childhood Special Education, 11,* 32–53.

McGonigel, M. J., Kaufmann, R. K., & Johnson, B. J. (1991). *Guidelines and recommended practices for the Individualized Family Service Plan* (2nd ed.). Bethesda, MD: Association for the Care of Children's Health.

McLean, M. E., & Odom, S. L. (1993). Practices for young children with and without disabilities: A comparison of DEC and NAEYC identified practices. *Topics in Early Childhood Special Education, 13,* 274–292.

Meyer, D. J., Vadasy, P. F., & Fewell, R. R. (1985). *Living with a brother or sister with special needs—A book for sibs.* Seattle: University of Washington Press.

Montessori, M. (1964). *The Montessori method.* New York: Schocken.

Myers, B. J., Olson, H. C., & Kaltenbach, K. (1992). Cocaine-exposed infants: Myths and misunderstandings. *Zero to Three, 13*(1), 1–5.

Neisworth, J. T., & Bagnato, S. J. (1988). Assessment in early childhood special education. In S. L. Odom & M. B. Karnes (Eds.), *Early intervention for infants and children with handicaps: An empirical base* (pp. 23–49). Baltimore: Brookes.

Neisworth, J. T., & Fewell, R. R. (1990). Transition [Special issue]. *Topics in Early Childhood Special Education, 9*(4).

Osofsky, J. D., & Fenichel, E. (Eds.). (1994). Caring for infants and toddlers in violent environments: Hurt, healing, and hope [Special issue]. *Zero to Three, 14*(3).

Raver, S. A. (1991). *Strategies for teaching at-risk and handicapped infants and toddlers: A transdisciplinary approach.* Columbus, OH: Merrill.

Rossi, R. J., Gilmartin, K. J., & Dayton, C. W. (1982). *Agencies working together—A guide to coordination and planning.* Beverly Hills, CA: Sage.

Salisbury, C. (1987). Stressors of parents with young handicapped and nonhandicapped children. *Journal of the Division of Early Childhood, 11*(2), 154–160.

Singer, G. H. S., & Powers, L. E. (1993). *Families, disability, and empowerment: Active coping skills and strategies for family interventions.* Baltimore: Brookes.

Snell, M. E., & Zirpoli, T. J. (1987). Intervention strategies. In M. E. Snell (Ed.), *Systematic instruction of persons with severe handicaps* (3rd ed., pp. 110–149). Columbus, OH: Merrill.

Turnbull, A. P., Patterson, J. M., Behr, S. K., Murphy, D. L., Marquis, J. G., & Blue-Banning, M. J. (1993). *Cognitive coping, families, and disability.* Baltimore: Brookes.

Walker, D. K. (1986). Chronically ill children in early childhood education programs. *Topics in Early Childhood Special Education, 5*(4), 12–22.

Warren, S. F., & Rogers-Warren, A. (1982). Language acquisition patterns in normal and handicapped children. *Topics in Early Childhood Special Education, 2*(2), 70–79.

Weikart, D. P. (1980, December). *Effects of the Perry Preschool Program on youths through age 15.* Paper presented at the meeting of the Handicapped Children's Early Education Program, Washington, DC.

Wimpelberg, R. K., Abroms, K. I., & Catardi, C. L. (1985). Multiple models for administrator preparation in early childhood special education. *Topics in Early Childhood Special Education, 5*(1), 1–14.

Wolery, M., Strain, P. S., & Bailey, D. B. (1992). Reaching potentials of children with special needs. In S. Bredekamp & T. Rosegrant (Eds.), *Reaching potentials: Appropriate curriculum and assessment for young children* (pp. 92–111). Washington, DC: National Association for the Education of Young Children.

Yando, R., & Zigler, E. (1984). Severely handicapped children and their families: A synthesis. In J. Blacher (Ed.), *Severely handicapped young children and their families* (pp. 401–416). Orlando, FL: Academic Press.

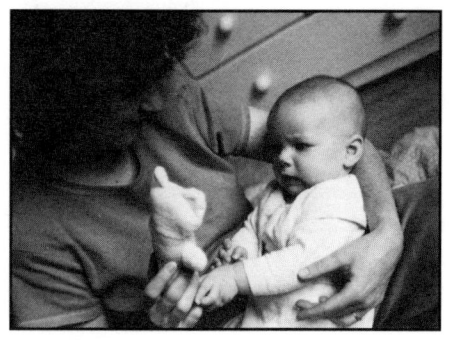

Working in Partnership with Families

CHAPTER 5

Once we got over the dismay and shock at the hospital, and picked up our shattered dreams and hopes, we began the slow process of reorienting and reorganizing those dreams and hopes into a different set of rules, a different lifestyle. No, maybe our little Down syndrome boy wouldn't be able to realize some of those high dreams we had composed before his birth, but with a little reshuffling (and a lot of hard work) he will be able to realize other dreams that we are composing day by day. So the song will have different words and a different melody, but will still be a masterpiece.

(Timothy and Marilyn Sullivan, parents, in Hanson & Harris, 1986, p. 8)

Family Interactions and Adjustments

The birth of a child brings a multitude of changes and challenges to a family. Prior to the birth all family members have expectations, anxieties, and excitement over the impending event. With the arrival of the new baby, many emotional, behavioral, and lifestyle changes occur. Parents often experience the whole gamut of emotions—joy, frustration, fear, relief, excitement, exhaustion, and uncertainty. As stated in the following quote, perhaps no responsibility or challenge is greater than that of rearing a child: "Motherhood brings as much joy as ever, but it still brings boredom, exhaustion, and sorrow too. Nothing else ever will make you as happy or as sad, as proud or as tired, for nothing is quite as hard as helping a person develop his own individuality, especially while you struggle to keep your own" (Marguerite Kelly & Elia Parsons). The depth of emotional response and role changes for family members is unparalleled. One mother described the first 2 years of raising her typically developing son: "It's the highest highs and the lowest lows I've ever experienced."

Given adequate resources and support, most families manage these initial adaptations brought by the addition of a new family member within the early months and years. Family roles and responsibilities become established, and the newest member of the family becomes incorporated into the family whole. However, when a child is born with a disability or at significant risk for developmental difficulties, the adjustments may be more pronounced and prolonged—perhaps for years. The family also may encounter additional challenges and stresses. Consider the following statements by parents:

> I felt that my ego had been wiped out. My superego with all its guilts had become the most prominent part of my personality, and I had completely lost my self-esteem. Any credits of self-worth that I could give myself from any of my personal endeavors meant nothing. Graduating from college and a first-rate medical school, surviving an internship, practicing medicine, and having two beautiful sons and a good marriage counted for nil. All I knew at this point was that I was the mother of an abnormal and most likely retarded child.
>
> It took about a year until I came home from working in a clinic and said to my husband, "Today I had a problem that was greater than Jennie." My very wise husband said, "That must mean you're getting better." It did mean that I was getting better, but it took a few more very painful months, and easily another 2 years, until I believed again that I was more than the mother of a retarded child. I decided that I did not want the major distinction of my life to be the fact that I was the mother of a retarded child. I finally was able to pick up the pieces of my life and proceed. (Ziskin, 1985, pp. 68–69)

Disabled children use up enormous amounts of their parents' physical and psychic energy. These children require more of everything, and those who take parenting seriously give it to them. Yet all the rest of life goes on and also demands its due from us. And the collective demands must be met within the same 24-hour day allotted to everyone.

But there is more to it than just that. There is an expectation by others that we should live normally, as if, in fact, there

were nothing abnormal about our lives. Who—besides another parent of a handicapped child—understands the extraordinary effort it takes to hang onto friends, respond to family, attend back-to-school nights, take children to dentists, entertain for husbands, shop for groceries, do the housework, take the car to be fixed, drop one child off to play with a friend, pick up another after a piano lesson, or, heaven forbid, hold down a job while attending to the needs of a child who is disabled and needs extraordinary care?

It is not a one-time demand. (Morton, 1985, p. 143)

These quotations underscore the enormous changes and challenges that individuals may face when they become parents of a child with special needs. Early intervention services must be planned to take into account the demands facing families and the individual needs of families. Such services can play an important role in providing support to families as they begin their journeys with their new family members and adjust to the new challenges and responsibilities. The provision of an array of appropriate support systems and services can help ease families through the early adaptations and enhance positive family relationships early on, and thus prevent or lessen some of the potential difficulties.

The purpose of this chapter is twofold: (a) to advocate a family-centered approach to early intervention that emphasizes working not only with the child but with the child and family as a system and (b) to describe exemplary family service practices in early intervention settings. The nature and development of early parent–child relationships are reviewed, and stresses and challenges that parents of children who are at risk or disabled may face are described. Furthermore, the rationale for family involvement in early intervention is outlined, and types of services common to intervention programs are discussed. Finally, recommended guidelines or principles for working with families are provided, and specific strategies that can be used for communicating with families and establishing parent–professional partnerships are presented.

More than ample justification for working closely and in partnership with families come from research, theory, and clinical findings and practice. As is so clearly pointed out by a transactional model of child development, the child's environment is crucial to determining the child's ultimate developmental outcome. For the very young child, the parents are the key people in that environment. Many research investigations have substantiated the influence that parental behavior has on child development. For example, maternal responsiveness and stimulation have been linked to infant cognitive, language, and affective development (Bell & Ainsworth, 1972; Clarke-Stewart, 1973; Tulkin & Covitz, 1975; Yarrow, Rubenstein, Pedersen, & Jankowski, 1972). For babies born at risk or with disabilities, a nurturing environment is particularly important so that these children are not at double risk from both physical and social environmental factors. Early services can support parents to form satisfying and nurturing relationships with their infants and also learn ways to enhance and support their babies' development.

Early Attachment

The earliest attachments or bonds that babies form with significant adult caregivers (typically the child's parents) are viewed as crucial to the child's social-emotional development and the ability to form subsequent relationships (Ainsworth, 1973; Bowlby, 1969). Attachment is seen as a process characterized by several developmental phases. Bowlby (1969) described four major developmental phases: (a) a phase of social responsiveness that is relatively nondiscriminating when the baby orients to people but does so unselectively; (b) a phase of discriminating social responsiveness where the baby recognizes familiar, primary caregivers and shows a preference for them; (c) a phase characterized by active proximity-seeking, contact-seeking, and contact-maintaining behavior as the baby chooses to be near the parent; and (d) a phase identified as a "goal-corrected partnership" in which the baby attempts to alter the parent's behavior to bring the parent into proximity and interaction. These phases in the development of attachment are closely linked to the attainment of cognitive milestones (Ainsworth, 1973). Examples include the ability to differentiate among people in order to discriminate caregivers from others and the attainment of object/person permanence so that the child can appreciate that the parent is there even if not in sight for the moment.

Both partners—the parent and the child—play an active role in this attachment process (Bell, 1968). Developmental theorists have stressed the influence that each partner has on the other and have outlined developmental adaptations or issues faced by the pair in the early years. One such theoretical perspective is that outlined by Sander (1969), who identified five developmental issues or adaptations in the parent–infant relationship in the first years:

1. *Initial regulation* (1–3 months). The caregiver and infant are concerned with regulation of biological functions such as feeding, sleeping, and states of arousal.
2. *Reciprocal exchange* (4–6 months). Reciprocal coordination of caregiving activities and social play is demonstrated. Back and forth exchanges occur between the caregiver and the infant, and the infant is able to smile and become involved in the interaction using vocal and motor behavior.
3. *Initiative* (7–9 months). Infants become more active in initiating and getting a social exchange with the parent. They develop an understanding of means–ends relationships.
4. *Focalization* (10–13 months). Infants can establish proximity to their caregivers using locomotion and begin to determine the caregiver's availability through their own initiatives. The demands are typically focalized on the mother.
5. *Self-assertion* (14–20 months). Infants determine their own activities and widen the range of activities. They may do so in the face of parental opposition.

These issues or adaptations are derived from the study of typically developing children. For caregiver–infant pairs in which the infant is behaviorally at risk or disabled, the issues or adaptations may be somewhat different or additional issues may be posed. The developmental differences or delays that arise from the infant's risk condition or disability may have an impact on the caregiver–infant relationship and interactions.

Interactional Issues

Given the tremendous influence that parents have on babies and babies have on their parents, one can see how the presence of a disability or risk condition that creates developmental and behavioral differences in the infant can influence the interactions between parent and child. For example, the baby who

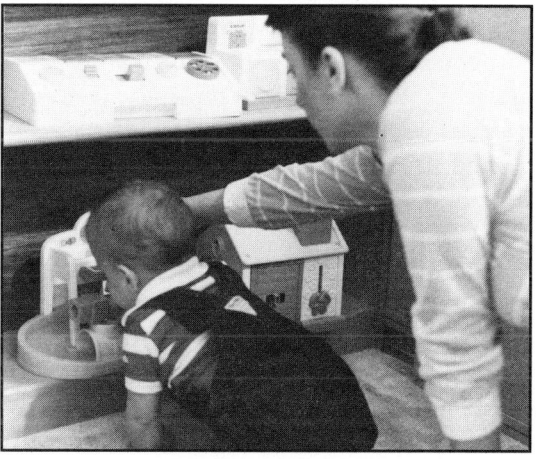

does not clearly communicate differentiation among caregivers may fail to elicit the feelings of being "special" from the parent, or the baby whose states are highly volatile may make even initial regulation of caregiving and interactional activities difficult for the caregiver.

Several investigations have documented the potential differences or disruptions in the interactional process. One of the clearest examples comes from Fraiberg's (1975) classic work with infants with visual impairments. She observed that parents of these children were unable to rely upon the visual cues (e.g., reciprocal smiling, gaze) of the typical infant–parent pair. Rather, parents learned to "read" their babies' hand signals and behavioral changes as signals of interactional initiations. Research on children with cognitive delays, such as Down syndrome, also has shown some potential differences. Emde, Katz, and Thorpe (1978) observed qualitative differences in the affective behavior (e.g., smiling, eye contact) of children with Down syndrome and indicated that these babies presented somewhat "dampened" affect. Delays in affective behavior (e.g., smiling and laughter) and temperamental differences (e.g., approach to novel stimuli, persistence, and threshold of stimulation) when infants with Down syndrome were compared with typically developing infants have been noted as well (Bridges & Cicchetti, 1982; Cicchetti & Sroufe, 1976; Rothbart & Hanson, 1983).

Differences in interactional and communication styles between parents of children with cognitive delays and their young children when compared with typically developing child–mother pairs have also been documented (Buium, Rynders, & Turnure, 1974; Crawley & Spiker, 1983; Garrard, 1989; Gutmann & Rondal, 1979; Jones, 1977, 1980; Mahoney, Finger, & Powell, 1985; Marshall, Hegrenes, & Goldstein, 1973; Maurer & Sherrod, 1987; McCollum, 1987). Additionally, communication differences, such as fewer social initiations and differences in response to communicative attempts, were observed in young children with hearing impairments (Greenberg & Marvin, 1979; Schlesinger & Meadow, 1972).

Finally, the preterm baby also presents behavioral differences from the full-term baby that appear to affect interactional patterns with caregivers. These babies appear to require more stimulation to become attentive and responsive, but when stimulated have a lower threshold for stimulation than do babies born at term (Field, 1977a, 1979). Mothers were observed to provide more intensive stimulation during interactions, such as feeding, in order to interact with their babies (Brown & Bakeman, 1979; DiVitto & Goldberg, 1979; Field, 1977b). It is likely that the developmental and behavioral differences noted in these babies born at risk or disabled trigger differences in interactional patterns. That is not to say that these differences are maladaptive. Rather, many adjustments made by caregivers, such as talking in more simple sentences or providing higher levels of stimulation to arouse the infant, may be highly adaptive in particular interactional situations. Although these developmental and behavioral differences appear to affect parent–infant interactions, it is also noteworthy that relatively few differences have been shown when dyads in which the baby is disabled or at risk are compared with dyads in which the baby is developing typically.

A comprehensive review of the literature on parent–child (with a disability) interactions is found in Rosenberg and Robinson (1988). The relationship between interactional variables and child development is examined and assessment and intervention strategies are reviewed.

Documentation of these potential differences and disruptions is useful from an intervention standpoint. In remediating interactional difficulties, given the developmental dependence and needs of the baby, the burden falls primarily to the parent or the caregiver to modify the interactions. As these factors are observed and documented, parents and other primary caregivers can be helped to understand the behavior of their infants and learn to read the children's unique cues. Thus, a primary goal of early intervention must be to support these early interactions and assist parents and infants to engage in mutually satisfying interactions and relationships. Such support helps parents to include the new baby in the family structure, provide the baby with more normative experiences, and feel competent and positive as parents of this new child.

Sources of Stress for Families

The birth of a child brings adjustments for any family. Certain types of adjustments can cause significant stress. Typically, family interaction patterns and roles change (e.g., the mother becomes increasingly involved with feeding and care of the new baby). Other stressful events may include financial burdens and increased expenses, changes in work patterns particularly for mothers, child care needs, lack of sleep, less time for friendships and leisure activities, and increased responsibilities during the care of the baby.

Certainly, these same potentially stressful events may be associated with the birth of a child who is at risk or disabled. In fact, the child born with developmental difficulties may necessitate even more adjustments in each of these areas or may heighten family concerns. For example, the hospitalization period may be long and the expenses staggering. Studies have shown that financial costs associated with neonatal care are among the highest hospital costs (Schroeder, Showstack, & Roberts, 1979). Furthermore, the demands associated with child care routines, such as feeding, dressing, bathing, may be much more difficult or problematic. Essentially, parents of children born at risk or disabled face the same demands as do other parents, but these demands may be heightened and prolonged over typical demands, and additional adjustments and burdens may be placed in their path.

A number of studies have identified these additional factors. For instance, investigations have focused on the relationship of particular child characteristics to parental (maternal) stress. Child responsiveness, temperament, repetitive behavior patterns, and the presence of unusual or additional caregiving demands were all found to be significantly related to maternal stress (Beckman, 1983). Rate of child progress was not significantly related. Other factors identified in the clinical research as related to parental stress included fears and problems of attachment, child behaviors such as lack of responsiveness, prolonged separation due to extended hospitalization, fears about parental competence particularly when faced with the need to rely on sophisticated technology and highly skilled professionals for the baby's survival, and the failure to produce the hoped for and expected baby (Taylor & Hall, 1979).

Recent research studies have also examined the relationships between parent stress and parent resources and support (Beckman, 1991; Hanson & Hanline, 1990; Sexton, Burrell, Thompson, & Sharpton, 1992). These studies confirm a link between child characteristics and parental stress. They also found a negative relationship between stress and support, in that those families with less support scored higher on measures of stress.

A great deal of clinical attention has been given to parental reaction to the birth of a child with a disability. Solnit and Stark (1961) have likened these reactions to a mourning process in that the parents mourn the loss of the expected child. Several hypothetical models have presented a series of stages through which parents may pass in the adjustment process. One such model is that identified by Drotar, Baskiewicz, Irvin, Kennell, and Klaus (1975). The model outlines five stages: shock, denial or disbelief, sadness and anger, adaptation, and reorganization. It is possible that parents do pass through stages and highly likely that parents may experience a range of emotions such as shock, anger, envy, denial, guilt, depression, and adjustment or acceptance. However, just as no two individuals are alike, no two persons' responses to any stressful event are the same.

These clinical models and studies are important for identifying possible parental and familial reactions to the stressful event of the birth of a child with developmental difficulties. However, early interventionists must appreciate the wide range of individual responses and also the variability of time that it takes to pass through stages and emotions. Some people pass through stages of emotions very quickly, whereas others may spend a lifetime in the resolution of a particular issue. Furthermore, individual needs and responses are not fixed but may vary markedly over time—even day to day. Intervention models that emphasize individual differences and individualized, flexible service options will best suit the needs of families who experience the birth of a child who is at risk or disabled.

The Family as a System

For many years the focus in early intervention was almost exclusively on the child. Most medical and educational efforts were aimed at assisting the child to develop more normally. The role of parents in early intervention programs was typically that of teachers of their children. Furthermore, parental involvement in early intervention was generally synonymous with maternal involvement.

Although mothers are more often the parents actively involved in programs for their children because of the age of the children and traditional parental roles, the contemporary view of parental involvement focuses not only on the child, or the mother and child, but on the entire family. The family is seen as a system with interacting subsystems. This view of the family as a system acknowledges that no family member functions in isolation from other family members. Thus, an event or intervention with one family member is likely to have an impact on other members and interactions in the family. This family systems perspective has led early interventionists to define intervention efforts much more broadly. The needs of the child with an exceptionality are examined within the context of the family, and assessments and program plans reflect an appreciation of family dynamics and interactions, as well as individual child needs. This perspective is reinforced in the Individuals with Disabilities Education Act, which requires that Individualized Family Service Plans (IFSPs) that focus on the child and family replace the traditional Individualized Education Program (IEP) for children from birth to age 3.

Bronfenbrenner's (1979) "ecology of human development" model expands the concept of family systems theory and describes the individual or child and family as nested within several systems. The systems in this social ecology model include (a) the *microsystem*—the relations and roles within the family; (b) the *mesosystem*—the settings and persons with whom the family interacts, such as other extended family members, neighbors, education and health workers, and work and school associates; (c) the *exosystem*—settings that influence the family and individual but with which the family does not directly interact, such as the social welfare, health care, and education systems; and (d) the *macrosystem*—the belief systems and elements in societal systems (e.g., economic, cultural, socioeconomic, political). This model provides a means for examining the many influences on the family. As can be seen, while each family member brings individual needs, expectations, and abilities to the family interaction and roles within the family, each is closely interlocked with the other family members and influenced by outside elements (Figure 5.1). The notion of the family as a system is derived from these interrelationships.

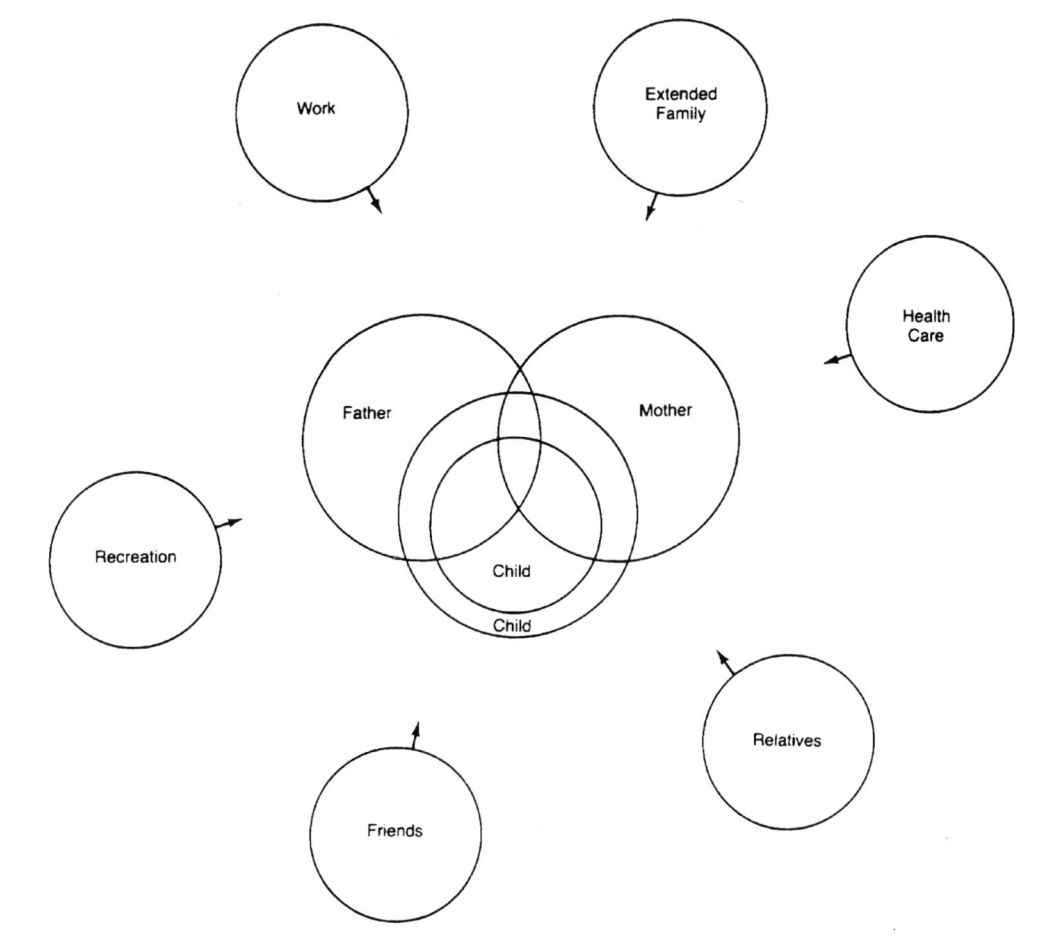

Figure 5.1. Influences on the family system.

The family is also composed of subsystems. Minuchin (1974) and Turnbull, Summers, and Brotherson (1984) described four such subsystems: parent–parent (marital subsystem), parent–child (parental subsystem), child–child (sibling subsystem), and family–extrafamily (extrafamilial subsystem). Subsystems, of course, vary across families. For example, the single-parent family will have no marital subsystem; the family with extended family members may have a parental subsystem that involves more than one or two parents; and the family with one child will have no sibling subsystem.

The ability of a family member to function in one role in a subsystem may not be predictive or reflective of his or her behavior in other subsystems. A man or woman may behave very differently when functioning as mother or father than as husband or wife or as neighbor or colleague. The birth of a child may influence a family member's behavior and roles within one subsystem but not within others. Several typical examples include the negative or jealous responses that young siblings may make toward a new baby or the difficulties experienced between spouses when the new baby demands so much time and energy that the partners have little time to themselves or with each other. It is not the role of early interventionists to intervene in these areas, but they can better appreciate family interactions with an awareness of the entire family system and the various subsystems within families.

Although early intervention programs are not typically developed or equipped to provide services to the entire family, a knowledge and appreciation of the family is crucial to the planning and implementation of intervention strategies. Turnbull et al. (1984) proposed that the family systems approach has the following implications for the design of intervention efforts. First, each family is unique and has different characteristics and styles. Thus, interventionists must be aware that family characteristics, such as cultural background, religious beliefs, and socioeconomic status, will have a tremendous influence on the family's response to a child with a disability or at-risk condition. For example, the beliefs concerning the importance of academic achievement or the notions of disability causation will influence the family's reaction to the child with developmental difficulties. Second, each family system has boundaries that are constantly changing. Brothers and sisters may become more or less involved in care for the child over time, for instance, or outside supports such as relatives and neighbors may change. Third, different functions for individual members are filled by the family. The family functions to meet the needs of an individual member in a number of areas such as economic, social, recreational, and domestic care. Intervention efforts should support, not jeopardize, needed family functions, and the early interventionist must be aware that the family serves many functions beyond those of direct concern in early intervention (e.g., educational). Finally, interventionists should acknowledge that families undergo changes, and these changes affect all family members.

Interventions planned from the perspective of the family as a system can be designed to better promote the needs and priorities of all family members, rather than solely the needs of the member with the disability. Turnbull and Turnbull (1990) described a family systems framework for understanding and working with families. They outlined four major components that should be considered in establishing parent–professional partnerships. These include family resources, family interactions, family functions, and the family's life cycle. Family resources represent the *inputs* into family interactions and include characteristics of the exceptionality (e.g., type and severity), family characteristics (e.g., size, socioeconomic status, geographical location, cultural background), and personal family member characteristics (e.g., health and coping styles). Family interaction focuses on the *processes* of interaction and how family member relationships meet individual and family needs. Family functions represent the *outputs* of family interactions and refer to the different needs families address (e.g., economic, domestic and health care, recreational, social, self-identity, affection, educational and vocational). Finally, the family life cycle defines the developmental and nondevelopmental changes that affect families (e.g., issues associated with birth and diagnosis, finding services, transitions to school, sibling rivalry). This framework can be used to identify family variables that must be considered as IFSPs are developed and early intervention strategies are designed.

Any interaction an early interventionist has with a child or the child's family member can be construed as an intervention. Any intervention, likewise, may produce a "ripple in the pond," as it affects not only the individual but also other family members within the system. Thus, early interventionists must be vigilant and thoughtful in the design and implementation of services. Every effort must be made to ensure that, insofar as possible, the needs of the entire family are regarded. Consider, for example, the following scenario.

Richard and Kathryn are the parents of Alexander, who was born prematurely at 26 weeks gestational age. When Alexander is 8 months old, Kathryn elects to enroll Alexander in an early intervention program because she believes his muscles are "too stiff." Alexander is accepted into the program, and he and Kathryn begin to attend on a regular basis. Kathryn reports that she feels support from the early intervention staff members and from the other parents and that the activities seem to be helping Alexander. Richard, her husband, on the other hand, feels that Kathryn should be following the doctor's orders which were to wait and see for a while. He is not adamantly opposed to their participation in the program, but resents the amount of time Kathryn is now spending on special exercises and activities for Alexander. He complains that they have no time together, that Kathryn's whole life is becoming Alexander and "going to school," and that none of this is needed anyway because "nothing is wrong with his son." Clearly, participation in an early intervention program is having an effect on this family, and the activities could provide both positive (for the child) and negative (spousal) outcomes. Once again, an intervention affects not only the target individual but the entire family. Early interventionists can best serve families by remembering that the family is an interacting system and that the needs of all family members must be considered as intervention strategies are designed and implemented. Furthermore, just as special education has so appropriately underscored the need for individualizing programs for children, so too must the individualized needs of the family be acknowledged.

Rationale for Family-Centered Models

The family systems perspective provides ample rationale for the inclusion of family members in early intervention services. However, a number of other factors also underscore the importance of this involvement. These factors include the following:

1. *Parents and significant caregivers are the most important people in the child's life.* Child development theory and research establish that social-emotional development and one's feelings of self-worth are predicated upon early attachments and relationships. Further, learning, particularly during the early years, is largely social in nature. Babies are attuned to social stimuli such as parents' faces and voices from birth, and most early learning occurs through social interactions. Early intervention services should support these important relationships and capitalize on early social interactions as learning opportunities.

2. *It is the parents' right to make decisions regarding their child.* Parents hold the rights and responsibilities for making decisions regarding all aspects of the child's life. Thus, initial and continuous parental input and decision making regarding educational strategies are paramount.

3. *Parents have legal rights for input and decision making in the educational process.* P.L. 94-142, the Education for All Handicapped Children Act of 1975, established the right of parents of school-aged children to be involved in the assessment and educational planning of programs for their children. P.L. 99-457 extended these rights to parents of young children from birth. The regulations under these laws outline the mechanisms for parent involvement in the assessment process and in the development of IFSPs and IEPs and specify due process procedures for parents under the law.

4. *Parental input and carryover in the home are essential for optimal effects of early intervention efforts.* It is not only the law but also common sense that the parents of young children should be actively involved in their children's educational programs. Children spend the majority of their time in their homes with their parents or caregivers. Intervention efforts

implemented by professionals for a few minutes or hours each week have little benefit if carryover into the home situation is not considered or if the goals of the professional are at odds with those of the parents. Furthermore, once children make gains in a particular area, experiences in the home are crucial for the generalization and maintenance of those gains.

5. *Early intervention can assist parents to experience positive relationships with their children and support parents to keep their children in their homes.* For years many parents were counseled to institutionalize children with significant impairments, and little community support existed for the families who chose to rear their children in their homes. Early services and interventions today are more supportive and available to parents so that institutionalization can be avoided. Moreover, early services, such as counseling, respite, and interactional support, can assist parents in their parenting roles and improve family interactions and satisfaction.

6. *Early services can provide information and support to parents to more effectively use community resources.* Although a full complement of social, medical, and educational resources is not available in every community, each state does have agencies charged with the responsibility for providing or locating services for families that include individuals with disabilities. Early interventionists can best serve families by providing them with information regarding the range and location of available resources, showing them how to use these resources, and supporting them to use the services as needed on their own.

7. *Active parental involvement and input can ensure more fully coordinated services.* Families of children with disabilities often work with a variety of service providers from different agencies and professions. Coordination among services may or may not occur optimally in all communities. The active and informed parent is more likely to advocate for needed services for the child and ensure that services are consistent or complementary to one another rather than duplicative or contradictory.

8. *Parental involvement in programs may be more economical.* Few early intervention services are adequately funded to provide the breadth of services desired. The inclusion of parents as teaching assistants or paraprofessionals in programs and the ability of parents to implement teaching programs at home ensure that children receive more instruction without the cost of additional professional personnel. Parents who elect to be involved in teaching roles bring motivation and understanding to the role because of their personal commitment and experience.

In summary, a number of factors, ranging from legal to economical to theoretical, argue for the involvement of families in early intervention programs. Given the age and developmental needs of the young child, early intervention regimens must be committed to family involvement. Programs that limit the focus solely to the child not only fail to utilize the most important learning opportunities in the child's life, but also run the risk of actually disrupting family interactions by inattention to family needs and concerns and by failure to support and nurture the parent–child interactions and relationships. Family involvement is the *sine qua non* of early intervention.

Types of Family Services

To meet the varied needs of families, a "menu" of services must be available. A range of services will ensure that intervention programs are able to tailor services to the individualized concerns of families. Family needs vary from family to family, and the needs of any given family are likely to change over time. For example, most families initially request information and support surrounding the diagnosis of the child. As the child grows and develops, families may request assistance in reading the child's cues and in networking with other families.

Family services can be provided through a number of options, such as parent meetings with staff members in the home or center, parent support groups, parent-to-parent networks, and parent training sessions that may include presentations, demonstrations, and/or role playing. Many families use several different service delivery options to obtain the type of services they need.

Programs also must develop a mechanism for matching appropriate services to individual families. Many programs achieve this matching through a needs assessment conducted with the family. Family needs can be determined through an extensive interview and discussion with the family and/or through a questionnaire. This process is described more fully in Chapter 8.

The needs assessment can occur in conjunction with the development of the IFSP. Once family needs are identified, the early intervention program staff members and families arrive at consensus as to which services are needed and which services can be provided by the program. Families are referred to other outside services when their needs go beyond those offered in the early intervention program. Program staff members are responsible for being knowledgeable about community resources so that they can make appropriate referrals to other services as needed.

Hanson (1984) described four major areas of family service needs that are commonly addressed in early intervention programs. These include the need for (a) general information, (b) support, (c) education and training, and (d) assistance and support in parent–child interactions. A fifth area is that of effectively using community resources (Linder, 1983). Each is discussed in the following sections.

General Information

The earliest contact in the service delivery system occurs around the time of the child's birth and/or diagnosis. From the moment of diagnosis or determination of developmental difficulties, most families seek out information concerning the child's condition. Research suggests that parents need to be informed of the diagnosis as early as possible and that they need to be given specific and accurate information (Cunningham & Sloper, 1977; Lipton & Svarstad, 1977). It is likely that this information needs to be repeated and presented at different times and in various ways for many families.

The need for information does not end at the point of diagnosis. Rather, as the child grows and develops, so do the questions. Most parents have concerns related to children's feeding, sleeping, elimination, and crying and communication patterns. For parents of children who are disabled or at risk, additional questions represent concerns with prognosis, general developmental patterns and difficulties, and strategies or treatment for remediation of the difficulties. Early intervention programs can be a major source of information in all these areas and also can provide appropriate referrals to other sources of information as needed.

Information can be provided through a variety of avenues. One source is written materials. Many programs provide a lending library for parents and annotated bibliographies in specific areas. Interviews and conferences with staff professionals either on a one-to-one or small group basis also provide a major vehicle for the exchange of information. Parent groups also serve this purpose and have the added advantage of giving parents the opportunity to exchange helpful tips with one another. Group sessions may be used to transmit information in a variety of ways, such as presentation, films and slides, and demonstration. Most parents appreciate having several optional methods through which to obtain specific information so that they can select the optimal method for their family. Different options are valuable too in that the wide range of languages spoken and literacy levels can be taken into account so that family members are provided resources that are most appropriate to their styles and preferences.

Early intervention programs also should actively coordinate with other agencies and service providers in order to provide information for families. For example, in helping families to make the transition from the hospital to an early intervention program, hospital and early intervention personnel may work together to provide information and instruction in areas such as tube feeding; positioning and handling for holding, feeding, bathing, and dressing; infant state regulation; and regulation of stimulation to the baby. Likewise, when the child makes the transition from the early intervention program to a preschool program, intervention staff members and preschool teachers may work together in describing the preschool demands and objectives to parents.

Another source of information for families is established, formal parent-to-parent networks. Through these networks families are linked to parents of children with the same or similar conditions. Typically, families are "hooked up" to these services shortly after the child's birth or through contacts in early intervention programs. Effective parent-to-parent networks are organized and managed by parents who are trained in the subject matter and skilled in working with families. Although no empirical documentation is available for determining the crucial characteristics of these networks, clinical experience suggests that the following components are important: (a) The network is established and maintained by parents with professional consultation as needed; (b) "visitor" or "contact" parents must be carefully screened to ensure that those selected are emotionally stable and available at a variety of times; (c) "contact" parents must undergo extensive training on methods of assisting families; and (d) networks that receive outside funding to pay key staff members and manage resources are more likely to survive and grow than those managed solely on a volunteer basis. Informal parent-to-parent networks around the country are becoming increasingly formalized and provide an important service that can supplement early intervention services.

In summary, the provision of information to families is a major role of early intervention services. Information needs begin at the time of diagnosis or identification of developmental difficulties and continue as the needs of the families and children change. This vital need for information can be met through a variety of methods including written materials and individual and group meetings in the family's primary language or language of choice. Various options are desirable so that the needs of individual families can be addressed.

Support

Just as all families need basic factual information upon the birth of a child, so too do all families need support. Some communities meet this need by providing trained personnel, typically nurses, as home visitors to all families of newborns. This professional gives families basic information on caregiving and areas of concern and provides a tremendous support to new parents.

The support needs of families of children born with disabilities or conditions that place them at risk developmentally are likely to be even more profound. The time and financial demands of the child alone may reduce the degree to which these families can tap traditional sources of support, such as visits with relatives and friends. Also, the needs of these families for both formal and informal support systems are likely to be even greater than for the family of a typically developing child because of the questions and stresses posed by the child's condition.

The importance of support networks to child and family functioning has been documented. Dunst (1985), for instance, found that most measures of social support in their study were significantly correlated to parent and family dependent measures. Increased provision of support was related to decreased emotional and physical problems and time demands for parents. Based on this research, Dunst, Trivette, and Deal (1988) developed an assessment and intervention model for supporting families.

Early intervention personnel are well advised to identify the sources of social support for families so that intervention routines can be integrated into those family practices that enhance family functioning and well-being. Cultural values will play a strong part in determining these sources of support. Supports for some families will come primarily from family and neighbors and for others from religious or spiritual sources.

Some families will need sources of formal support as well. These may include agencies that provide or finance services such as respite care and counseling. The early intervention program can be an important source of information and referral to these other community agencies.

The staff members of the intervention program also can serve as a tremendous source of direct support for families. For some families the intervention program is the first and only contact outside of the home. If the program provides flexible services in the family's native language by culturally sensitive and informed staff members, the individual needs of various families can be met. One caveat is in order, however: Early interventionists should be vigilant that their support is not fostering overdependence on the program or that their intimacy with the family is not overstepping the professional bounds of the intervention program. Periodic staff discussions and conferences regarding the needs of specific families can ensure that appropriate bounds are being observed and that families are referred to other services as warranted.

Early intervention programs can provide family support services through a variety of avenues. Individual discussions between families and staff members and parent support groups are primary methods. Many programs find it useful to assign a particular staff member as the family liaison or family services coordinator for a specific family. Although the family may be involved with other staff members while receiving services, this provides the family with a primary contact person who is thoroughly versed in the family's concerns and intervention plans. The family services coordinator can monitor the family's service plan and ensure that all needs are being met. The coordinator also can serve as the family's liaison with other staff members (e.g., taking charge of "staffings" for a particular family) and with other community service providers when necessary to guarantee consistent and thorough services for a family.

Services that encourage families to include the child who is at risk or disabled in the family fold and assist families in negotiating the developmental changes and stresses that will be encountered over time can help optimize family functioning. The early intervention program can be an important source of this support. The program can facilitate and complement existing formal and informal sources of support.

Education and Training

Traditionally, the focus of early intervention programs was almost exclusively on training parents to teach their children in various areas. Although the breadth of services has changed over the years and program personnel have become increasingly sensitive to the range of service needs for families, the need for education and training remains a primary service of early intervention programs.

The need for training is not limited to parents of children who are at risk or disabled. The new parent of a typically developing

child often goes to a grandmother or neighbor for tips on how to bathe, feed, diaper, and otherwise care for a new baby. This means of information exchange and training has been invaluable throughout the years. As families in the United States have become more mobile, these sources of support and training have become less available.

Families of babies who are at risk or disabled may need this education and training even more. The demands of their daily tasks often necessitate extraordinary technical know-how, such as tube feeding, equipment monitoring, proper positioning and handling, and state regulation. Furthermore, their children may require special techniques in order to feed, play with toys and other objects, or even communicate effectively with others. These are skills that must be learned. The early intervention program is typically *the* major source of these educational training opportunities.

Staff members representing various disciplines, such as early childhood special education, occupational and physical therapy, speech–language therapy, and nursing, can provide this specialized information and training to family members to assist them in working with the children. Family members can benefit from training through a variety of methods, such as demonstration, role playing, oral presentations, and written instructional materials.

Early intervention programs generally provide the major source of educational and training activities for families of children who are disabled or at risk for developing disabilities. These activities should be implemented in such a fashion that they facilitate, rather than interfere with, family routines. In addition, staff members should be careful to plan activities that do not necessitate unrealistic time or personnel demands for families. Family needs are best served when programs furnish a variety of training options and families are free to choose when, what, and how they would like to participate in educational training activities.

Parent–Child Interaction

All parents encounter difficulties from time to time in understanding their baby's cues and in developing strategies for changing the child's behavior. For example, it is probably fair to assume that all parents have experienced frustration at one time or another with a crying baby—frustration in identifying why the child was crying and frustration in identifying a strategy for quieting the child. Typically, under these circumstances parents reach into their bag of tricks—all the advice they have received from other parents, relatives, and professionals such as pediatricians—and proceed to try out different possibilities. When a successful strategy is identified, parents are relieved and encouraged, and their sense of competency as parents in this situation is increased. For parents with children who show unusual behavioral patterns or who exhibit a preponderance of negative responses such as crying, whining, and turning away, their feelings of competency may be compromised.

Goldberg (1977) observed that most parents monitor their infant's behavior and that their feelings of competency are undoubtedly linked to their infant's responsiveness to their attempts to intervene. She noted that individual differences across infants can be considered in three different dimensions: (a) *readability*, "the extent to which an infant's behaviors are clearly defined and provide distinctive signals and cues for adults"; (b) *predictability*, "the extent to which an adult can reliably anticipate behavior from contextual events and/or immediately preceding behaviors"; and (c) *responsiveness*, "the quality and extent of infant reactions to stimulation" (pp. 171–172).

Early interventionists can be instrumental in assisting parents to read their infant's cues and in developing techniques for responding to those cues and initiating to the baby. The goal in supporting parents to interact with their babies is a more enjoyable and mutually satisfying interaction for both parents and babies. Such assistance is aimed at supporting early attachment relationships between parents and infants.

Using Community Resources

Services for families are not necessarily under the domain of one agency, but rather represent a continuum of community service options. This first point of service contact typically comes with care in the hospital. This is followed by transitions to the home and to early intervention programs when warranted.

Early intervention staff members can be most effective if they are a part of the service delivery network from the outset of involvement with a family. This can best be accomplished through an overlap strategy in which a

staff member from the early intervention program coordinates with the appropriate hospital contact person(s) or agency in charge of diagnosis and referral. In this fashion families "hook up" with the early intervention service while they are still receiving beginning services so that they may make a comfortable transition to the next level of services.

Families may benefit from a wide variety of community services. The role of the early interventionist is to furnish families with information on the services available and assistance in learning how to use these services. This information can be provided in early intervention programs through individual discussions, group meetings, and written materials. Early interventionists, however, should be cautioned against trying to be all things to families and in so doing take over parental responsibilities. Families need information on how to negotiate the service delivery system and procure the services they desire; they are not best served by well-meaning staff members who take over this role. Families will be involved with community services for a long time—for many, throughout the child's life. The better able they are to use services independently and productively and to become their child's case manager, the more effective they can be as advocates for their children in the community.

Summary

Early intervention programs provide a range of services for families. Common areas of service needs include (a) procuring general information, (b) receiving support, (c) obtaining education and training, (d) receiving support in parent–child interactions, and (e) learning to use community resources. These services can be implemented through a variety of forums such as individual discussions between parent and staff members, group meetings, and written materials. Parents are best served when they are given a range of services from which they can select and when services are adapted to the families' languages, styles, and values.

Strategies for Working with Families

One of the primary competencies of the early interventionist is the ability to communicate with and respect families. Fruitful parent–professional partnerships can be fostered by staff members who are able to effectively coordinate with family members in intervention planning and implementation. General principles to be considered in working with families are outlined in this section. Further, specific intervention strategies for communicating and coordinating with parents are presented.

General Principles

Early interventionists must have technical skills in their areas of expertise. However, their effectiveness in applying these skills is strongly influenced by their ability to communicate with families. The following considerations provide basic guidelines for working with families in early intervention programs.

1. *View parents as parents, not only as parents of a child who is disabled.* Although children who are at risk or disabled may pose special challenges for parents, their parents also have the same concerns and needs that all parents do. Like all parents, those participating in early intervention programs have concerns about their children's health, growth, and development, and they share the same difficulties that all families experience, such as juggling schedules, financial concerns, and meeting the needs of all family members.

2. *Be sensitive to and respectful of the different styles, cultural backgrounds, needs, and concerns posed by families.* Observe and listen to what the

family members have to say. All staff members should respect the family's values and attitudes and their goals and strategies for intervention. Cultural beliefs and practices must be attended to and tolerated, not labeled (e.g., overprotective, rejecting) according to preconceived notions by staff members who may differ in beliefs. Furthermore, it is parents and other closely involved family members who know their children best, and their observations, opinions, and concerns must be honored. Finally, during discussions "jargonese" is best avoided so that parents are actively included and not isolated from the conversation.

3. *Provide families the opportunities to become involved in all aspects of the intervention program.* Family members should be a part of the process of goal setting, as well as program planning, implementation, and evaluation. It is the parents' right and sound educational practice. Although family members may alter their level of involvement based on life circumstances, encouragement and opportunities for participation must be maintained.

4. *Keep in mind that the family is an interacting system.* Early intervention programs best address the needs of the child when the child's family is included in all planning and program implementation. All interventions have a ripple effect so that influencing one family member will have carryover of some kind to other members. At times what is best for the child with developmental difficulties is not best for the family. Early interventionists must accept the validity of family choices that sometimes place the good of the family as a whole above the good of an individual family member.

5. *Be flexible to accommodate the diverse and changing needs of families.* As the transactional model makes so apparent, the transactions among family members and between family members and others produce a constantly changing situation. Therefore, the concerns and needs at any given time are likely to be different than at other times. Service plans should be individualized for families just as they are for children to include diverse methods and strategies that are continuously updated as needed.

6. *Be aware and respectful of parent needs when setting program expectations.* The type and degree of family participation may shift over time just as the family's needs and goals shift. Some families may choose not to participate, and others may participate actively through a variety of roles. Winton and Turnbull (1981) noted "the very legitimate need that some parents have to not be formally involved at times" (p. 18). Some documentation also shows that intensive early intervention regimens and requirements can increase parent burnout (Bristol & Schopler, 1983).

7. *Help parents to feel competent in their parenting role.* Discuss the things parents are doing right, not merely potential areas of need. Encourage positive parent–child interactions; ensure that parents experience their children's successes and smiles rather than early interventionists taking the spotlight. Assist parents to become involved in the IFSP process. Parents may feel they are being examined or critiqued in their parenting skills by virtue of their participation in the program. All parents have good days and bad days, and staff members can assist parents to feel comfortable and competent as they perform their daily routines and responsibilities.

8. *Provide an open forum for communication.* Parents need to have opportunities for informal as well as formal discussions with staff members. Communication is enhanced if parents are made to feel that staff members are available to them and interested in them. Professionals can engage in warm and friendly relationships without overstepping professional bounds. Open and effective communication can occur only if family members are able to communicate in their language of choice, and if differences in opinions, concerns, beliefs, and values are respected.

In summary, true parent–professional partnerships grow from mutual understanding and respect. The early interventionist can facilitate these interactions by genuinely seeking and acknowledging parental input and by establishing open and clear lines of communication. Such communication will lead to more individualized, flexible, and appropriate services for families.

Communicating with Family Members and Building Partnerships

Specific techniques for communicating with family members and building effective family–professional partnerships are discussed in this section. Several early intervention projects have outlined such intervention strategies for working with families (Bromwich, 1981; Hanson & Krentz, 1986). Although a primary aim of these intervention programs was to facilitate parent–child interaction, the strategies outlined can be used in communicating and coordinating with parents around a wide variety of intervention goals and issues.

Bromwich (1981) and colleagues at the Intervention Program of the University of California, Los Angeles (UCLA), Infant Studies Project outlined eight steps or strategies that were implemented in their parent–infant interaction intervention program for mothers and high-risk babies from birth to 3 years. The eight modes of intervention for early interventionists included (a) listening empathically, (b) observing, (c) commenting positively, (d) discussing, (e) asking, (f) modeling, (g) experimenting, and (h) encouraging. The beginning approach to a new issue involved listening to the parents carefully and acknowledging their feelings. Staff members communicated empathically with parents while being careful not to push the parents to discuss issues that they did not wish to discuss or to become involved in personal matters unrelated to the issue at hand. This approach was followed by helping the parents to become astute observers of the child. Staff members shared their observations with the parents and also tried to understand the parents' perceptions of the child's behavior. The third strategy involved helping parents to gain self-confidence by commenting on the interactions where parents and infants were in sync or in tune with one another. Staff members also commented positively on the child's behavior so that parents were able to identify areas of progress. The fourth strategy, discussion, was most used. Discussions occurred through informal conversations between parents and staff members and served to gain information, suggest alternatives, answer parent questions, and/or introduce new areas of interest to the parents. The fifth strategy, asking, was used to elicit from parents their concerns and observations about the child. Modeling was implemented to demonstrate a particular behavior or way of interacting with the child in the hope that the parents would imitate the behavior. The seventh strategy, experimenting, involved working with the child to try out different methods by getting the child to respond or interact. Finally, the staff members used encouragement to help parents to respond in a particular fashion to the child's behavior, to take initiative, and to take care of their own needs in cases of overinvolvement with the babies.

Hanson and Krentz (1986) outlined an intervention process or loop that consisted of

four steps: alerting, guiding, practicing, and assessing. Briefly, either the parent or the professional brings to the attention of the other an area of need (alerting). This is followed by the planning of strategies for meeting the need (guiding). Subsequently, the parent tries out the strategies in his or her interactions with the child (practicing), and then the effectiveness of the techniques is analyzed by parents and staff members (assessing). These four steps were used to establish common grounds and goals for parent–professional communication.

Intervention is viewed as a process of change using this system, where each interaction or communication has an effect on subsequent interactions. Further, either partner—the parent or the early interventionist—can initiate an activity or particular step at any time. The process may proceed at different rates at different times and sometimes may move slowly in a certain phase (e.g., guiding).

The first steps outlined in this intervention process can be broken into several specific techniques. *Alerting* provides a common focus for the parent and early interventionist. Alerting may be accomplished through several avenues. One option is *commenting or sharing observations*. Either the parent or the professional may point out an area of need (e.g., "Marisela always arches when I pick her up"). Another optional method of alerting is to speak for the baby or *serve as the infant's interpreter*. An example is: "Oh, Justin, is that too much noise and excitement? You're just shutting down from too much stimulation." The alerting process provides the other member of the partnership—the parent or the professional—with information on the other's observations and perceptions.

Guiding involves specific techniques for changing a behavior that has been identified through the alerting process as an area of need. Again, several optional avenues for guiding are discussed. One strategy involves *informing*. Parents often request specific information on a disability or method of treatment (e.g., the cognitive development and the educational possibilities for young children with Down syndrome). Likewise, the parent may inform the staff member about some aspect of the child's behavior (e.g., "Molly prefers bright and shiny objects such as pinwheels. I think she can detect some light and movement"). Another strategy is that of *reframing a behavior* (either the child's or the parent's) in a more positive manner. An example is, in response to the baby's restlessness: "Jamal really knows his mother. He starts to move when you come near. I don't think he's trying to kick you. I think he's just excited that you're holding him." Another example is: "Laura certainly does like to resist you when you help her with the spoon. I think she's trying to tell us she's becoming more grown-up and independent!" A third strategy is *commenting* on the unique qualities of the parent or child (e.g., "Kaitlin uses her hands and fingers to communicate with you since she can't see you," or "Anthony always uses that sound when he's hungry"). A fourth strategy described is that of *modeling*. When modeling, either the parent or the professional demonstrates a particular method for working with the child. For example, the physical therapist may show a parent how to pick up a child with spasticity so that more normalized muscle tone can be achieved and maintained. Or the special educator may demonstrate waiting for the child to make a sound before giving the child a food or a favorite toy. The parent may show staff members how to hold the child or calm the child most effectively. A fifth strategy is *experimenting*. This strategy involves the parent and early interventionist working together to try out different techniques. Each can contribute suggestions and observations. The sixth strategy discussed is that of *highlighting*. Through this process either the parent or the professional can positively comment on some aspect of the child's or other's behavior. For instance, "Dean, what a great idea that you put her in the baby seat while you're eating dinner. That way she can see what is going on and you can be there to calm her when she needs you." These strategies can all be used in establishing new behaviors or reinforcing changes that are being made. Again, their use assumes that a common focus or ground has been reached between the parent and the professional regarding goals.

The third and fourth steps of this intervention approach are *practicing* and *assessing*. As in any intervention, a plan must be tried and evaluated. For intervention plans developed for babies, this usually means having parents practice activities in their daily routines. One measure of the worth of the intervention plan is how willing and able the parent is to integrate the activity into the family's lifestyle. Those procedures that can be readily incorporated into existing routines are more likely to be feasible and helpful. The assessment step allows adjustments to be made and the effects or repercussions of the interventions to be discussed. Both positive and negative effects can be noted and changes made as needed.

In summary, these two intervention models suggest techniques for communicating with families and ways in which to view the working parent–professional partnership. Communication is a two-way process. Professionals must be sensitive to listening first to parents' needs and concerns, and then join with the parent to form a plan for meeting those needs.

A Family-Centered Approach to Early Intervention

All aspects of early intervention reviewed thus far point in one direction—the need for models of service that are *family centered*. The fields of early education and early intervention have a long and proud history of family involvement; however, recently the types and levels of involvement have undergone further scrutiny, and a more clear definition of the relationship between family members and professionals in early intervention is emerging. This focus has been termed family centered, family guided, and family focused to name several predominant terms. In this volume, we do not attempt to separate or differentiate among these terms.

A subtle but profound distinction emerges when early intervention is viewed as family centered. Family members are placed in the "driver's seat" in that they are the beginning and the end points for determining and implementing intervention goals for that child and family. The shift is away from the professional as the all-knowing guide for families to the professional as a consultant and support for families as they use their own strengths and resources. Dunst et al. (1988) discussed this philosophy as *enabling* in that it functions for "creating opportunities for competence to be displayed" (p. 4). They further described the process as facilitating *empowerment* as "the person who is the help seeker, learner, or client must attribute behavior change to his or her own actions if one is to acquire a sense of control necessary to manage family affairs" (Dunst et al., 1988, p. 4).

The philosophical shift to a family-centered perspective influences all aspects of early intervention services and cannot be entered into without a thoughtful analysis of the relationship between families and the early intervention program (Bailey et al., 1986; Brinker, 1992; Kaiser & Hemmeter, 1989; McBride, Brotherson, Joanning, Whiddon, & Demmitt, 1993). Families cannot be viewed as "cases" to be managed with problems to be solved. Rather, families are allowed to express their concerns and priorities in a manner that is culturally and personally appropriate and desired. Their strengths and resources for meeting the needs that arise as their concerns and priorities are articulated are then identified and applied in a manner that is appropriate to the family's lifeways. Professionals may participate in this process in many different ways. The partnerships formed with families will vary depending on the family's individual needs and the resources of the program and staff members. Just as no two individuals look or act the same or have exactly the same needs, no two families have precisely the same concerns, priorities, and resources. Once staff members take the leap of faith and openly and actively listen to and respect the family's perspective, the opportunity for an open and honest exchange of ideas and a fruitful working partnership will be provided for planning and implementing early intervention services.

Summary

Early intervention services must focus not only on the child, but on the child within the context of the family. The most important environment for the young child is the family. It is with the child's parents that early attachments and relationships are formed that lay the basis for subsequent development.

Families are best served in family-centered early intervention programs when they are provided with a range and continuum of service options. Such a flexible model allows for each family to receive individualized services based on their identified concerns and priorities. By supporting families to fulfill their functions, the early intervention program can help to facilitate the growth and development of young children who are at risk or disabled.

Preferred Practices

The following questions provide a guide for practitioners in evaluating the services provided to families in the early intervention program. Given the importance of this area to the development and implementation of the program, each of the following issues should be addressed.

1. Do *all* early intervention staff members have commitment to and skill in communicating with families with diverse backgrounds and lifeways and have a knowledge of family systems, needs, and services?

2. Are family members encouraged to become involved in all aspects of the program and decision making—goal setting, implementation, and evaluation?

3. Does the program provide a wide range of opportunities for families to become involved in culturally appropriate ways (e.g., observation, participation in program planning, implementation of strategies, assessment of the program)?

4. Are services for families individualized so that the specific needs and concerns, priorities, and resources of each family are addressed and the family characteristics (e.g., cultural background, language spoken, socioeconomic level, values, and priorities) are considered and respected?

5. Do staff members focus on children's and families' strengths, priorities, and resources, rather than view them from a deficit model?

6. Does the program have a well-defined procedure for identifying family needs and establishing a working partnership with parents?

7. Do staff members view the family as a system so that intervention program strategies take into consideration the dynamics of the entire family, not merely the child or the child and one parent?

8. Are parents supported to experience positive relationships with their children and competency in their parenting roles?

9. Does the early intervention program enable and support parents to assume the various roles that they are required to play?

10. Are various types of services provided by the early intervention program—general information, support, education and training, support in parent–child interactions, and help in using community resources?

11. Does the program actively coordinate with other community agencies that provide services to families so that families are able to procure the range of services they may need (e.g., respite, financial, and health insurance)?

References

Ainsworth, M. D. S. (1973). The development of infant–mother attachment. In B. M. Caldwell & H. Ricciutti (Eds.), *Review of child development research* (pp. 1–94). Chicago: University of Chicago Press.

Bailey, D. B., Simeonsson, R. J., Winton, P. J., Huntington, G. S., Comfort, M., Isbell, P., O'Donnell, K. J., & Helm, J. M. (1986). Family-focused intervention: A functional model for planning, implementing, and evaluating individualized family services in early intervention. *Journal of the Division for Early Childhood, 10*(2), 156–171.

Beckman, P. J. (1983). Influence of selected child characteristics on stress in families of handicapped infants. *American Journal of Mental Deficiency, 88*(2), 150–156.

Beckman, P. J. (1991). Comparison of mothers' and fathers' perceptions of the effect of young children with and without disabilities. *American Journal of Mental Retardation, 95*(5), 585–595.

Bell, R. Q. (1968). A reinterpretation of the direct effects of studies of socialization. *Psychological Review, 75*, 81–95.

Bell, R. Q., & Ainsworth, M. D. S. (1972). Infant crying and maternal responsiveness. *Child Development, 43*, 1171–1190.

Bowlby, F. (1969). *Attachment*. New York: Basic Books.

Bridges, F. A., & Cicchetti, E. (1982). Mothers' ratings of the temperament characteristics of Down syndrome infants. *Developmental Psychology, 18*(2), 238–244.

Brinker, R. P. (1992). Family involvement in early intervention: Accepting the unchangeable, changing the changeable, and knowing the difference. *Topics in Early Childhood Special Education, 12*(3), 307–332.

Bristol, M. M., & Schopler, E. (1983). Stress and coping in families of autistic adolescents. In E. Schopler & G. B. Mesibov (Eds.), *Autism in adolescents and adults* (pp. 251–258). New York: Plenum.

Bromwich, R. M. (1981). *Working with parents and infants*. Austin, TX: PRO-ED.

Bronfenbrenner, U. (1979). *The ecology of human development*. Cambridge, MA: Harvard University Press.

Brown, J. V., & Bakeman, R. (1979). Relationship of human mothers with their infants during the first year of life. In R. W. Bell & W. P. Smotherman (Eds.), *Maternal influences and early behavior* (pp. 353–373). New York: Spectrum.

Buium, N., Rynders, J., & Turnure, J. (1974). Early maternal linguistic environments of normal and Down's syndrome language-learning children. *American Journal of Mental Deficiency, 79*, 52–58.

Cicchetti, D., & Sroufe, L. A. (1976). The relationship between affective and cognitive development in Down's syndrome infants. *Child Development, 47*, 920–929.

Clarke-Stewart, K. A. (1973). Interactions between mothers and their young children: Characteristics and consequences. *Monographs of the Society for Research in Child Development, 38*(6–7, Serial No. 153), 1–109.

Crawley, S. G., & Spiker, D. (1983). Mother–child interactions involving two-year-olds with Down syndrome: A look at individual differences. *Child Development, 54*, 1312–1323.

Cunningham, C. C., & Sloper, T. (1977). Parents of Down's syndrome babies: Their early needs. *Child: Care, Health, and Development, 3*, 325–347.

DiVitto, B., & Goldberg, S. (1979). The effects of newborn medical status on early parent–infant interaction. In T. M. Field, A. M. Sostek, S. Goldberg, & H. H. Shuman (Eds.), *Infants born at risk: Behavior and development* (pp. 311–332). New York: Spectrum.

Drotar, D., Baskiewicz, A., Irvin, N., Kennell, J. H., & Klaus, M. H. (1975). The adaptation of parents to the birth of an infant with a congenital malformation: A hypothetical model. *Pediatrics, 56*, 710–717.

Dunst, C. J. (1985). Rethinking early intervention. *Analysis and Intervention in Developmental Disabilities, 5*, 165–201.

Dunst, C., Trivette, C., & Deal, A. (1988). *Enabling and empowering families: Principles and guidelines for practice.* Cambridge, MA: Brookline Books.

Emde, R. N., Katz, E. L., & Thorpe, J. K. (1978). Emotional expression in infancy: II. Early deviations in Down's syndrome. In M. Lewis & L. Rosenblum (Eds.), *The development of affect: Genesis of behavior* (Vol. 1, pp. 125–148). New York: Plenum.

Field, T. M. (1977a). Effects of early separation, interactive deficits, and experimental manipulations on infant–mother face-to-face interaction. *Child Development, 48*, 763–771.

Field, T. M. (1977b). Maternal stimulation during infant feeding. *Developmental Psychology, 13*, 539–540.

Field, T. M. (1979). Interaction patterns of preterm and term infants. In T. M. Field, A. M. Sostek, S. Goldberg, & H. H. Shuman (Eds.), *Infants born at risk: Behavior and development* (pp. 333–356). New York: Spectrum.

Fraiberg, S. (1975). Intervention in infancy: A program for blind infants. In B. Z. Friedlander, G. M. Sterritt, & G. E. Kirk (Eds.), *Exceptional infant: Assessment and intervention* (pp. 40–62). New York: Brunner/Mazel.

Garrard, K. R. (1989). Mothers' verbal directives to delayed and nondelayed children. *Mental Retardation, 27*(1), 11–18.

Goldberg, S. (1977). Social competence in infancy: A model of parent–infant interaction. *Merrill-Palmer Quarterly, 23*, 163–177.

Greenberg, M. T., & Marvin, R. S. (1979). Attachment patterns of profoundly deaf preschool children. *Merrill-Palmer Quarterly, 25*(4), 265–279.

Gutman, A. J., & Rondal, J. A. (1979). Verbal operants in mothers' speech to nonretarded and Down's syndrome children matched for linguistic level. *American Journal of Mental Deficiency, 83*, 446–452.

Hanson, M. J. (1984). Early intervention: Models and practices. In M. J. Hanson (Ed.), *Atypical infant development* (pp. 361–384). Austin, TX: PRO-ED.

Hanson, M. J., & Hanline, M. F. (1990). Parenting a child with a disability: A longitudinal study of parental stress and adaptation. *Journal of Early Intervention, 14*(3), 234–248.

Hanson, M. J., & Harris, S. R. (1986). *Teaching the young child with motor delays.* Austin, TX: PRO-ED.

Hanson, M. J., & Krentz, M. S. (1986). *Supporting parent–child interactions: A guide for early intervention program personnel.* San Francisco: San Francisco State University, Department of Special Education.

Jones, O. H. M. (1977). Mother–child communication with prelinguistic Down's syndrome and normal infants. In H. R. Schaffer (Ed.), *Studies in mother–infant interaction* (pp. 379–401). New York: Academic Press.

Jones, O. H. M. (1980). Prelinguistic communication skills in Down's syndrome and normal infants. In T. M. Field, S. Goldberg, D. Stern, & A. M. Sostek (Eds.), *High-risk infants and children: Adult and peer interactions* (pp. 205–225). New York: Academic Press.

Kaiser, A. P., & Hemmeter, M. L. (1989). Value-based approaches to family intervention. *Topics in Early Childhood Special Education, 8*(4), 72–86.

Linder, T. W. (1983). *Early childhood special education: Program development and administration.* Baltimore: Brookes.

Lipton, H. L., & Svarstad, B. (1977). Sources of variation in clinician's communication to parents about mental retardation. *American Journal of Mental Deficiency, 82*, 155–161.

Mahoney, G., Finger, I., & Powell, A. (1985). Relationship of material behavioral style to the development of organically impaired mentally retarded infants. *American Journal of Mental Deficiency, 90*(3), 296–302.

Marshall, N. R., Hegrenes, J. R., & Goldstein, S. (1973). Verbal interactions: Mothers and their retarded children vs. mothers and their nonretarded children. *American Journal of Mental Deficiency, 77*, 415–419.

Maurer, H., & Sherrod, K. B. (1987). Context of directives given to young children with Down syndrome and nonretarded children: Development over two years. *American Journal of Mental Deficiency, 91*(6), 579–590.

McBride, S. L., Brotherson, M. J., Joanning, H., Whiddon, D., & Demmitt, A. (1993). Implementation of family-centered services: Perceptions of families and professionals. *Journal of Early Intervention, 17*(4), 414–430.

McCollum, J. A. (1987). Looking patterns of mentally retarded and nonretarded infants in play and instructional interactions. *American Journal of Mental Deficiency, 91*(5), 516–523.

Minuchin, S. (1974). *Families and family therapy.* Cambridge, MA: Harvard University Press.

Morton, K. (1985). Identifying the enemy—A parent's complaint. In H. R. Turnbull & A. P. Turnbull (Eds.), *Parents speak out—Then and now* (pp. 143–147). Columbus, OH: Merrill.

Rosenberg, S. A., & Robinson, C. C. (1988). Interactions of parents with their young handicapped children. In S. L. Odom & M. B. Karnes (Eds.), *Early intervention for infants and children with handicaps* (pp. 159–177). Baltimore: Brookes.

Rothbart, M. K., & Hanson, M. J. (1983). A caregiver report comparison of temperamental characteristics of Down syndrome and normal infants. *Developmental Psychology, 19,* 766–769.

Sander, L. W. (1969). The longitudinal course of early mother–child interaction: Cross case comparison in a sample of mother–child pairs. In B. M. Foss (Ed.), *Determinants of infant behavior* (Vol. 4, pp. 189–228). London: Methuen.

Schlesinger, H. S., & Meadow, K. P. (1972). *Sound and sign: Childhood deafness and mental health.* Berkeley: University of California Press.

Schroeder, S., Showstack, J., & Roberts, H. (1979). Frequency and clinical description of high cost patients in 17 acute care hospitals. *New England Journal of Medicine, 300,* 1706–1709.

Sexton, D., Burrell, B., Thompson, B., & Sharpton, W. R. (1992). Measuring stress in families of children with disabilities. *Early Education and Development, 3*(1), 60–66.

Solnit, A., & Stark, M. (1961). Mourning the birth of a defective child. *The Psychoanalytic Study of the Child, 16,* 523–527.

Taylor, P., & Hall, B. (1979). Parent–infant bonding and opportunities in perinatal center. *Seminars in Perinatology, 3,* 73–79.

Tulkin, S. R., & Covitz, F. E. (1975, April). *Mother–infant interaction and intellectual functioning at age six.* Paper presented at the biennial meeting of The Society for Research in Child Development, Denver.

Turnbull, A. P., Summers, J. A., & Brotherson, M. J. (1984). *Working with families with disabled members: A family systems approach.* Lawrence: University of Kansas, Kansas University Affiliated Facility.

Turnbull, A. P., & Turnbull, H. R. (1990). *Families, professionals, and exceptionality: A special partnership* (2nd ed.). Columbus, OH: Merrill.

Winton, P., & Turnbull, A. P. (1981). Parent involvement as viewed by parents of preschool handicapped children. *Topics in Early Childhood Special Education, 1*(3), 11–19.

Yarrow, L. J., Rubenstein, J. L., Pedersen, F. A., & Jankowski, J. J. (1972). Dimensions of early stimulation and their different effect on infant development. *Merrill-Palmer Quarterly, 18,* 205–218.

Ziskin, L. (1985). The story of Jennie. In H. R. Turnbull & A. P. Turnbull (Eds.), *Parents speak out—Then and now* (pp. 65–73). Columbus, OH: Merrill.

Selected Readings

About Families

The following texts provide valuable theoretical and clinical information to professionals regarding research with families of children with special needs.

Fewell, R. R., & Vadasy, P. F. (Eds.). (1986). *Families of handicapped children.* Austin, TX: PRO-ED.

Gallagher, J. J., & Vietze, P. M. (Eds.). (1986). *Families of handicapped persons.* Baltimore: Brookes.

Harry, B. (1992). *Cultural diversity, families, and the special education system: Communication and empowerment.* New York: Teachers College Press.

Lynch, E. W., & Hanson, M. J. (1992). *Developing cross-cultural competence: A guide for working with young children and their families.* Baltimore: Brookes.

McWilliam, P. J., & Bailey, D. B. (Eds.). (1993). *Working together with children and families: Case studies of early intervention.* Baltimore: Brookes.

Mori, A. A. (1983). *Families of children with special needs.* Austin, TX: PRO-ED.

Mullick, J. A., & Pueschel, S. M. (Eds.). (1983). *Parent–professional partnerships in developmental disability services.* Cambridge, MA: Ware Press.

Paul, J. L. (Ed.). (1981). *Understanding and working with parents of children with special needs.* New York: Holt, Rinehart & Winston.

Powell, T. H., & Ogle, P. A. (1985). *Brothers and sisters—A special part of exceptional families.* Baltimore: Brookes.

Schulz, J. B. (1987). *Parents and professionals in special education.* Boston: Allyn & Bacon.

Seligman, M. (Ed.). (1983). *The family with a handicapped child: Understanding and treatment.* New York: Grune & Stratton.

Seligman, M., & Darling, R. B. (1989). *Ordinary families, special children.* New York: Guilford Press.

Singer, G. H. S., & Irvin, L. K. (1989). *Support for caregiving families: Enabling positive adaptation to disability.* Baltimore: Brookes.

Singer, G. H. S., & Powers, L. E. (1993). *Families, disability, and empowerment: Active coping skills and strategies for family interventions.* Baltimore: Brookes.

Turnbull, A. P., Patterson, J. M., Behr, S. K., Murphy, D. L., Marquis, J. G., & Blue-Banning, M. J. (Eds.). (1993). *Cognitive coping, families and disability.* Baltimore: Brookes.

Turnbull, A. P., & Turnbull, H. R. (1990). *Families, professionals, and exceptionality: A special partnership* (2nd ed.). Columbus, OH: Merrill.

By Families/About Families

These books were written by parents of children with disabilities. They provide excellent resources to professionals and parents about parental perceptions, experiences, and adjustments.

Featherstone, H. (1981). *A difference in the family: Living with a disabled child.* New York: Penguin.

Simons, R. (1987). *After the tears: Parents talk about raising a child with a disability.* San Diego: Harcourt Brace Jovanovich.

Turnbull, H. R., & Turnbull, A. P. (1985). *Parents speak out—Then and now.* Columbus, OH: Merrill.

Communicating and Working with Families

One of the most important tasks of the early interventionist is the ability to communicate with and work with families in a partnership. These resources provide important clinical strategies for this work.

Gargiulo, R. M. (1985). *Working with parents of exceptional children: A guide for professionals.* Boston: Houghton Mifflin.

Kroth, R. L. (1985). *Communicating with parents of exceptional children* (2nd ed.). Denver: Love.

McConkey, R. (1985). *Working with parents: A practical guide for teachers and therapists.* Cambridge, MA: Brookline.

Simpson, R. L. (1982). *Conferencing parents of exceptional children.* Austin, TX: PRO-ED.

Stewart, J. C. (1986). *Counseling parents of exceptional children* (2nd ed.). Columbus, OH: Merrill.

Resources for Parents About Specific Disabilities/Risks

The following texts are written for parents and professionals to guide them in working with and raising a child who is at risk or disabled.

Cunningham, C. (1987). *Down's syndrome: An introduction for parents.* Cambridge, MA: Brookline.

Finnie, N. H. (1975). *Handling the young cerebral palsied child at home.* New York: Dutton.

Fraser, B. S., & Hensinger, R. N. (1983). *Managing physical handicaps: A practical guide for parents, care providers, and educators.* Baltimore: Brookes.

Freeman, R. D., Carbin, C. F., & Boese, R. J. (1981). *Can't your child hear?* Austin, TX: PRO-ED.

Golbin, A. (Ed.). (1977). *Cerebral palsy and communication: What parents can do.* Washington, DC: Job Development Laboratory, Division of Rehabilitation Medicine, George Washington University. (Available from 2300 I Street N.W., Room 420, Washington, DC 20037)

Hanson, M. J. (1987). *Teaching the infant with Down syndrome: A guide for parents and professionals* (2nd ed.). Austin, TX: PRO-ED.

Hanson, M. J., & Harris, S. R. (1986). *Teaching the young child with motor delays.* Austin, TX: PRO-ED.

Harrison, H. (1983). *The premature baby book.* New York: St. Martin's Press.

Jan, J. E., Ziegler, R. G., & Erba, G. (1983). *Does your child have epilepsy?* Austin, TX: PRO-ED.

Pueschel, S. M. (1990). *A parent's guide to Down syndrome.* Baltimore: Brookes.

Pueschel, S. M., Bernier, J. C., & Weidenman, L. E. (1988). *The special child: A source book for parents of children with developmental disabilities.* Baltimore: Brookes.

Scott, E. P., Jan, J. E., & Freeman, R. D. (1985). *Can't your child see?* (2nd ed.). Austin, TX: PRO-ED.

Schleichkorn, J. (1983). *Coping with cerebral palsy.* Austin, TX: PRO-ED.

Stray-Gundersen, K. (Ed.). (1986). *Babies with Down syndrome: A new parents' guide.* Kinsington, MD: Woodbine House.

Publications for Parents

The Exceptional Parent. Psy-Ed Corporation, 605 Commonwealth Ave., Boston, MA 02115, (617) 482-0480. This magazine provides articles on topics of interest to parents of children with disabilities. It presents information on new developments in products and services, programs designed to help children with disabilities, and articles written by and about parents of children with disabilities. Many parents appreciate the wide range of advertisers in this magazine and the resource information on a variety of topics. This publication is a "must" for any parent resource library.

The Growing Child and *The Growing Parent.* Dunn & Hargitt, Inc., 22 North Second St., Lafayette, IN 47902, (317) 423-2626. These monthly newsletters present development information and recommend appropriate playthings for the typically developing child each month. *The Growing Parent* discusses issues designed to assist parents in coping with parenthood.

Notes

CHAPTER 6

Staffing and Staff Development

The most important ingredient in any educationally oriented, early intervention program is a skilled, knowledgeable, and sensitive team of staff members representing a variety of disciplines. Early intervention is a people-oriented profession; as such, it demands people who are technical experts in their own disciplines as well as in interpersonal interactions. Being knowledgeable and skillful in using one's professional skills as an early childhood special educator, family counselor, pediatric nurse practitioner, or pediatric occupational or physical therapist is essential, but it is not enough. In addition to those skills, the early intervention professional must be able to work equally effectively with very young children, their families, and colleagues with different training, priorities, experiences, and perspectives. Team members must be able and willing to learn and use skills that were not part of their basic disciplinary training, and develop skills in teamwork, compromise, and shared responsibility. Working in an early intervention program is not merely taking care of babies; it requires a highly demanding set of professional and interpersonal skills. This chapter is organized around five major areas: team membership, staff competencies, staff development, personnel issues of special significance in early intervention, and preferred practices in staffing and staff development.

Team Membership

Optimal early intervention programs are staffed by professionals from a wide range of disciplines; trained paraprofessionals who function under professional supervision are also included in many early intervention programs throughout the country. Staff members are typically organized into teams with varying structures.

Multidisciplinary, Interdisciplinary, and Transdisciplinary Teams

Three types of team structures have been used in early intervention programs and described in the literature: multidisciplinary, interdisciplinary, and transdisciplinary (Allen, Holm, & Schiefelbusch, 1978; Campbell, 1987; Lyon & Lyon, 1980; McCormick & Goldman, 1979). As described by Lynch and Lewis (1988), *multidisciplinary* usually means that professionals representing several different disciplines work on different aspects of the same case. For example, the speech–language therapist would assess and intervene only in the area of speech or language, with little input or information from individuals from other disciplines who are also working with the child and family.

Members of *interdisciplinary* teams may conduct separate assessments or collaborate to some extent in the assessment phase. Following assessment they meet to share results and develop a treatment plan that includes recommendations for all areas of need. In this model team members continue to communicate about the case through team meetings, allowing each team member to facilitate all of the educational and treatment goals, but the direct services are often provided in isolation. Thus, the speech–language therapist might collect a language sample while observing the early childhood special education assessment, making it unnecessary to work directly with the child; the speech–language therapist, physical therapist, and early childhood special educator would share their findings in the interdisciplinary team meetings. However, direct speech–language, physical therapy, and early childhood special education services would typically be offered separately from one another.

The hallmark of the *transdisciplinary* model is the extent of collaboration, communication, and shared responsibility among team members. Each team member teaches many of his or her disciplinary skills to the other team members, resulting in some blended roles that make each discipline less distinct. As a result, one team member can act as the primary interventionist with assistance and consultation from the others. This model does not rule out

individual therapies, but they typically are used far less frequently in an attempt to integrate all services into the daily life and program of the child and family. To illustrate, the early childhood special educator might conduct the developmental assessment following discussion and input from other team members. If the child's movement patterns were extremely atypical and beyond the early childhood special educator's training and experience, the special educator would call upon the physical therapist for assistance. If the team determined that the child's primary needs were related to these atypical movement patterns, the physical therapist might be assigned as the primary interventionist. As such, this team member would incorporate the speech–language and educational goals into the therapy program with consultation from the early childhood special educator and speech–language therapist. As the child's needs changed or whenever the physical therapist or parent felt a need for more expertise in speech–language or special education programming, the early childhood special educator or speech–language therapist could be called in as a resource person.

Transdisciplinary as the Optimal Model

Legislation, training programs, and model early intervention programs began by focusing on developing interdisciplinary teams to work with young children with disabilities and their families (Linder, 1983; Trohanis, Cox, & Meyer, 1982). However, transdisciplinary programming has evolved as the optimal model in early intervention. It allows one team member to be the primary liaison with families, reducing the number of professionals in the home and the number of people with whom parents have to relate. It increases the competence of all team members and enables them to be more effective with a wider range of children and families, and it increases professionals' opportunities to grow and learn. Furthermore, a research study on early intervention efficacy by Shonkoff and Hauser-Cram (1987) identified the transdisciplinary model as most effective in decreasing maternal parenting stress.

However, nothing is without its costs. To develop effective transdisciplinary teams, certain conditions must be met. There must be time for team members to train one another and time for specific members or the whole team to discuss and consult around cases. Team members need to be well trained and secure in their own disciplinary expertise and willing to share what they know with others. Also, team members must respect, value, and trust one another and the skills that each person brings to the team (Linder, 1983; Lynch & Lewis, 1988). Furthermore, although teams represent an optimal model, for some families and circumstances a team model is neither necessary nor desired. As with other facets of early intervention, an individualized approach to family and community needs is warranted.

In summary, several models have been used to provide educational intervention to infants who are at risk or disabled and their families. Initially, models were multidisciplinary in nature, with team members from various disciplines functioning autonomously. Interdisciplinary models followed, which included more collaboration among disciplines in both the assessment and delivery phases. More recently, transdisciplinary models have evolved. Although this model does not rule out individual therapies, it does emphasize shared professional skills and the blending of disciplinary roles.

Professional Skills and Disciplines

Integrated early intervention programs that are educationally oriented and family focused require a wide range of expertise among staff members (Hanson, Hanline, & Petersen, 1987). Early interventionists must have skills that include typical and atypical child development, family support and involvement, program planning and implementation, child and family assessment, program evaluation, and professional conduct (Hanson, 1990; Hanson & Brekken, 1991; Hanson et al., 1987; Zeitlin, du Verglas, & Windhover, 1982). Fewell (1983) and Linder (1983) suggested that Bricker's (1976) view of the special educator as "synthesizer" or "generative teacher" is an appropriate way to describe the early intervention professional, and Bailey, Farel, O'Donnell, Simeonsson, and Miller (1987) emphasized the importance of knowledge about biomedical risk factors and disabilities as well as the ability to work with medical and allied health professionals. Moreover, the current family-centered approach to early intervention stresses the importance of establishing partnerships with families and focusing on child and family strengths rather than deficits. Because no single professional discipline includes training in all of these competencies, programs need to hire individuals from a variety of disciplinary backgrounds and expand training curricula in all professional disciplines (Hanson & Lovett, 1992).

Determining who should be on the team depends on the general needs of the infants, toddlers, and families that the program serves; the resources within the community; and the program philosophy. Although team composition is typically viewed in terms of specific professions or disciplines, that is not always the most functional way to determine what staff members will be needed. Outlining the specific knowledge and skills that are needed, then looking for individuals from a variety of disciplines who may meet these criteria, is usually a more expeditious way of selecting staff. For example, programs need individuals who are knowledgeable about typical and atypical infant development; who can assess and program in all of the developmental areas with particular emphasis on motor, language, and cognitive skills; and who can work effectively with families. Instead of deciding that the program must hire a physical therapist to get the necessary level of expertise in motor development, assessment, and programming, the administrator may seek someone with those skills from a wide range of disciplines, including physical therapy, occupational therapy, nursing, or perhaps even adaptive physical education. By broadening the range of acceptable disciplines, the administrator has more flexibility in finding someone with the greatest overall strength for the program. The same is true in other areas as well. Although psychology and social work are traditionally considered to be disciplines that work with families, some early childhood special educators, child development specialists, nurses, and counselors may have focused on this area in their training and have the skills the program needs.

Three things are more important than the specific course of study that a potential staff member has completed: (a) the extent of training and experience related to infants, toddlers, and their families; (b) professional licensure or certification in the discipline; and (c) the individual's ability to work as a team member and with families. Even the most highly skilled professionals may have been trained to work with older children, adolescents, or young adults but have no training or experience related to children from birth to 3 years. Providing educational services to a 2-year-old with severe motor delays is considerably different from providing spelling instruction to adolescents with learning disabilities, just as pediatric nursing is different from nursing in a cardiology intensive care unit. Thus, early intervention teams need a mix of individuals with special disciplinary training and expertise as well as training and experience related to infants and toddlers.

Team members should also be certified, licensed, or registered (depending upon the profession and state requirements) in their own professional disciplines. Although such an endorsement from the state or profession does not guarantee professional expertise, it does assure basic levels of training, practicum experience, and knowledge of the professional code of conduct. Appendix C provides an example of a code of ethics for educators of persons with disabilities.

Finally, staff members selected need to be good team members and team players. Providing optimal early intervention services is not an individual or professional popularity contest; it is a carefully orchestrated team effort that requires commitment, respect, and compromise.

Given the caveats above, there are team configurations that are fairly typical in model early intervention programs. Many educationally oriented, family-focused early intervention programs include early childhood special educators and at least one speech–language therapist, occupational or physical therapist, nurse, psychologist, or social worker. In small programs or those in areas lacking professional resources, team composition may consist of three core disciplines or staff members with others involved on a consulting basis. For example, an early childhood special educator, physical or occupational therapist, and speech–language therapist may be hired as the early intervention team, with health care and psychological and/or social services provided either directly or in consultation by staff from other community agencies. In larger metropolitan areas, or in those areas of the United States where professional services are more available, early intervention programs may be staffed by a full complement of professionals with additional consultations provided by nutritionists, pediatricians, and other specialists.

Paraprofessional Team Members

Paraprofessionals have recently been added to many early intervention teams. Decisions to include paraprofessionals have been influenced by two major factors—responsiveness to family needs and cost. Many programs hire parents of children who are disabled, since families of children who are at risk or who have diagnosed disabilities report that during the initial crisis they most want to talk with other parents of children who are at risk or developmentally disabled (Harrison & Kositsky, 1983; Lynch, 1981; Simons, 1987; Simpson, 1987; Stoneman, 1985). Talking to someone who "has been through it" is comforting, for there is a special bond among people who have shared similar experiences. Because they have experienced some of the same feelings firsthand and have had to face similar challenges, they can be asked the "unaskable questions"—those questions that lurk near the surface but are too embarrassing, too personal, or too emotional to ask those who have not shared the experience. Parents of children who are at risk or disabled have gained considerable experience and can also provide practical, down-to-earth advice about everything from breast-feeding, to car seats, to finding and using community services. Consequently, many early intervention programs have hired and trained parents of children who are at risk or disabled to work in early intervention programs. These staff members are sometimes called parent liaisons, parent–community workers, or parent facilitators. They function as team members and work under the supervision of professional staff members with circumscribed responsibilities.

Key to the success of such programs is the initial and ongoing training and supervision of the parent paraprofessionals. Although being the parent of (or having served in a parenting role for) a child who is at risk or who has a disability is a necessary criterion, it is not the sole criterion. The role is to support other parents, not simply to have a forum to repeat one's own story. Thus, parents selected for such roles need to have progressed beyond an exclusively "I-centered" view of disability and its impact on families to a more global perspective.

Sometimes paraprofessionals are recruited and hired from the linguistic and cultural community of the families served in the program. These staff members can be invaluable in establishing rapport and effective communication with families and in ensuring that services are culturally appropriate for the families served in the community.

In sum, paraprofessionals who are parents of children who are at risk or who have disabilities can be an extremely valuable resource to programs, and paraprofessionals (whether parents or not) provide additional resources at lower costs. However, critical to determining the feasibility of including paraprofessionals is the program's ability (time, resources, and expertise) to provide the ongoing training and supervision required. If the program can obtain or provide the training, paraprofessionals may be an excellent way to improve and extend services.

Parents and Families as Team Members

Parents and other family members have been recognized for a long time as important members of the early intervention team (e.g., Jones, 1977; Lynch, 1978; Moersch, 1978). By law and by philosophy, they continue to be central figures in the assessment and programming that is designed for their child. Because Chapter 5 deals extensively with families, they are not discussed in this chapter.

Staff Competencies

Working with infants and toddlers with special needs and their families requires special skills. Training programs in many disciplines are expanding their personnel preparation efforts to reflect the uniqueness of this early developmental period, the differences in intervention and assessment efforts for infants and toddlers, the importance of working with a diverse population of families as well as children, the need for interdisciplinary practices and team coordination efforts, and the importance of the practical and interpersonal skills of the personnel providing early intervention services.

A number of professionals have described the competencies and characteristics of training that are needed for this age group (Bailey et al., 1987; Bailey, Palsha, & Huntington, 1990; Bricker & Slentz, 1987; Bruder & McLean, 1988; Fenichel & Eggbeer, 1989; Hanson et al., 1987; Linder, 1982; McCollum & Thorp, 1988; Thorp & McCollum, 1988). Fenichel and Eggbeer (1989) also outlined the seven knowledge areas that they felt were essential for working with infants and toddlers and their families: "1) endowment, maturation and individual differences in the first three years of life; 2) the power of human relationships; 3) transactions between the child and environment; 4) parenthood as a developmental process; 5) developmental processes and their interrelationship; 6) risk, coping, adaptation and mastery; and 7) the helping relationship" (p. 5).

Professionals from specific disciplines are beginning to map out specialization in early intervention within their disciplines and also articulate training needs and strategies. A number of articles address these issues in the following disciplines: special education (McCollum, McLean, McCartan, & Kaiser, 1989; Thorp & McCollum, 1988); nursing and public health (Brandt & Magyary, 1989; Farel, 1988); nutrition and dietetics (Hine, Cloud, Carithers, Hickey, & Hinton, 1989; Kaufman, 1989; Lucas, 1989); occupational therapy (Dunn et al., 1989; Hanft & Humphry, 1989); physical therapy (Scull & Deitz, 1989); psychology (Drotar & Sturm, 1989); social work (Nover & Timberlake, 1989); and speech pathology (Crais & Leonard, 1988).

The development of *personnel standards* for early interventionists is essential to defining exemplary practice. A number of groups have undertaken this effort. The original comprehensive examination and definition of standards was conducted by INTER-ACT, the National Committee for Services to Very Young Children with Special Needs and Their Families, and resulted in the publication of *Basic Competencies for Personnel in Early Intervention*

Programs (Zeitlin et al., 1982). This study was extended in California by the California Early Intervention Personnel Study Project (Hanson, 1990). This project defined a personnel model for early interventionists and developed a recommended set of competencies (Hanson, 1990; Hanson & Brekken, 1991). The philosophy upon which these standards was based is presented in Table 6.1, and the major competency areas are presented in Table 6.2 (Hanson, 1990; Hanson & Brekken, 1991). These standards are constantly undergoing scrutiny and updating; in recent months, standards related to working with families from diverse

Table 6.1. Philosophical Tenets Underlying Personnel Standards

- The period of development from birth to 3 years is a dynamic period. This dynamic nature renders it both full of potential for positive, long-lasting influence upon children and families and extremely vulnerable to negative forces and events. For this reason, the personnel working in this area must be extremely well qualified in order to capitalize on the potential for positive change, as well as to prevent harm.
- Infants and toddlers are unique because of their dependence on their families. This dependence necessitates a family-focused approach to early intervention.
- Responsibility for a child's development rests with the family. Programs must support, not supplant, the family's role.
- No one agency or discipline can meet the diverse and complex needs of very young children with special needs and their families. A coordinated interagency and interdisciplinary approach to planning and delivery of services is necessary.
- Very young children and their families have a wide variety of needs and resources. Therefore, early intervention services need to be individualized and flexible to accommodate to changing needs of families and children. Some infants considered at high risk may need only periodic assessment and follow-up, while other infants and families may need intensive intervention and support.
- Individualized early intervention services can reduce significantly the potential impact of many handicapping and at-risk conditions and positively influence later development.
- Early intervention systems must include the continuum of services necessary to address the varied needs of infants and families. Systems must assure accessibility, availability, and accountability for individual families.
- Center-based and group services should maximize opportunities for integration with nondisabled infants and children. All services must be provided in a setting and context that recognizes cultural and linguistic diversity and acknowledges the value of each individual served.
- Due to the size and diversity of many states, the needs and resources vary significantly on a geographic basis. Any system must acknowledge and accommodate these differences to be effective.
- A statewide early intervention system must allow and encourage local decision making.
- The quality and effectiveness of services depends on well-trained early intervention personnel. A team of professionals who are knowledgeable in child development, atypical development, and family systems, as well as the specific requirements of their unique disciplines, is critical.
- As the state of the art in early intervention changes, these guidelines will also change. Periodic review of the proposed standards by a qualified statewide, interdisciplinary body concerned with early intervention services will assure that the standards remain appropriate.

From *Final Report: California Early Intervention Personnel Model, Personnel Standards, and Personnel Preparation Plan* by M. J. Hanson, 1990, San Francisco: Department of Special Education, San Francisco State University. From "Early Intervention Personnel Model and Standards: An Interdisciplinary Field-Developed Approach" by M. J. Hanson and L. Brekken, 1991, *Infants and Young Children*, 4(1), p. 58. Copyright 1991 by Aspen Publishers, Inc. Reprinted with permission.

backgrounds, service coordination, and working in a range of community environments have been added.

Regardless of the discipline, key concepts such as those outlined above are considered to be both crucial to training in early intervention and also universal across these disciplines or professions. Most experts agree that a unique body of knowledge is needed for working with infants and toddlers and their families.

Staff Development

The previous sections of this chapter have dealt with team membership and staff competencies, with the underlying assumption that staff members will be selected for their professional training as well as their training and experience with young children. However, early intervention is a rapidly changing field, and even the best qualified staff members need opportunities to expand their skills. Consequently, staff development (inservice training) is an important component of early intervention programs. Appendixes B and D, respectively, provide lists of professional and parent organizations and journals that may be used for staff development.

Assessing Needs

A first step in staff development is assessing staff needs. Many programs find that an annual needs assessment is an effective way to

---

Table 6.2. Basic Competency Areas for Early Intervention Personnel

---

I. **Child development**

   A. *Typical child development*

     Demonstrates knowledge of:

     1. Prenatal and perinatal development.
     2. Development in the early years.
     3. Interaction between the environment and the developing child.
     4. Interaction among familial, cultural, social, and physical environments which enhance an infant and young child's development.
     5. Theory and research in typical infant and child development.

   B. *Atypical child development*

     Demonstrates knowledge of:

     1. Prenatal and perinatal developmental risk factors.
     2. Handicapping and at-risk conditions (e.g., prematurity, perinatal substance exposure, abuse and neglect, chronic illness) and their effects on early development.
     3. Interactions among the familial, cultural, social, and physical environments that may influence the infant and young child in achieving maximum growth and development.
     4. Theory and research in atypical child development.

II. **Family involvement**

   A. *Demonstrates the ability to:*

     1. Recognize and strengthen family capabilities.
     2. Establish and maintain a relationship with the family.

(continues)

Table 6.2. *Continued*

    3. Assess issues within the family.
    4. Meet family needs.
    5. Encourage the infant's and young child's development by increasing the family's knowledge and involvement.
    6. Help families use support systems.

  B. *Demonstrates knowledge:*
    Of theory and research related to family development and functioning, and family systems.

III. Assessment

Demonstrates the ability to:
1. Use assessment practices appropriate to the infant and toddler with special developmental needs.
2. Select and utilize assessment strategies and tools appropriately.
3. Accurately and appropriately interpret and report assessment results.

IV. Development and implementation of individualized intervention program plans

  A. *Demonstrates knowledge:*
    Of current trends and practices.

  B. *Demonstrates the ability to:*
    1. Plan intervention programs.
    2. Implement intervention programs for infants, toddlers, and families.
    3. Evaluate intervention programs for infants, toddlers, and their families.

V. Professional interaction skills

Demonstrates the ability to:
1. Work collaboratively with families.
2. Work collaboratively with team members.

VI. Personal interaction skills

In addition to the knowledge and skills described in the previous sections, all early intervention staff members should have personal characteristics which enable them to function successfully with infants or toddlers and their families and other team members.

Personal characteristics of *all* early intervention personnel:
- Enjoy and appreciate infants and toddlers.
- Exhibit gentle, nurturing, accepting style.
- Maintain collaborative attitude.
- Maintain optimistic, yet realistic attitude and expectations for families, colleagues, and oneself.
- Exhibit flexibility and sensitivity to changing conditions.
- Exhibit openness to diversity in lifestyles, culture, religious beliefs, and language.
- Exhibit self-awareness related to personal mental health, issues of codependence, and personal strengths and weaknesses.
- Maintain a positive attitude and belief in families' abilities to identify and meet their own and their infant's or toddler's needs with support.
- Exhibit self-control and handle stressful situations calmly.
- Maintain a sense of humor.

From "Early Intervention Personnel Model and Standards: An Interdisciplinary Field-Developed Approach" by M. J. Hanson and L. Brekken, 1991, *Infants and Young Children*, 4(1), pp. 59–60. Copyright 1991 by Aspen Publishers, Inc. Reprinted with permission.

plan training opportunities for the year. A needs assessment developed by the program administrator or a staff subcommittee can be distributed to team members, allowing each person to indicate the areas in which she or he would like to receive training. A sample needs assessment is presented in Figure 6.1. In this example staff members are asked to rate their interest in each of the topics listed, add topics not listed, suggest people who might provide the training, and list any areas in which they would like to provide training.

Needs assessments often culminate in individualized staff development plans that enable staff members to learn those things they perceive as most important. Plans are usually negotiated with the program administrator or staff member responsible for inservice training, and they are formalized in writing with specified time lines and activities. For example, a new staff member who has never worked with premature infants may want to be paired with an experienced team member as part of her or his staff development plan. She or he may also spend several days observing in a neonatal intensive care unit, attend a local nursing conference that has multiple sessions on premature infants, and read three books related to early intervention with premature infants as part of the plan. Such individualization is consistent with the principles of adult learning, because it allows for diversity in content needs and learning preferences.

Required Staff Development Activities

In addition to staff members' perceived needs, there may also be topics on which everyone needs additional training. As legal mandates and the clients being served change and as new practices become validated, all staff members will need additional training. For example, as smaller and smaller infants survive and enter programs, staff members may need more information about the children's condition, restrictions, and needs. As the demographics of a community change, resulting in more children entering the program from non–English speaking homes and diverse cultures, staff members may need to learn more about the impact of culture on child-rearing practices, health care, and acceptance of intervention. Thus, the annual inservice calendar will need to leave some openings for changing needs.

Staff Development as a Team-Building Activity

Some programs use one or two staff development sessions each year for team-building activities. These sessions may be facilitated by a consultant on group dynamics, human resource development, or team building with group exercises that lead to improved team functioning, or they may be loosely structured group activities such as lunches, picnics, or retreats that allow team members to be together without the pressure of client demands. Activities that focus on team cohesion contribute to more efficient and effective functioning on the job (Rogers, Lewis, & Reis, 1987).

Collaborative Staff Development and Training Options

To minimize the costs of staff development activities and broaden the range of opportunities, programs may collaborate on training activities. An early intervention program administered by a school district may want to arrange some of its training activities in conjunction with the local hospital, the health department, or the department of social services. If multiple agencies work together, the cost to any single agency is significantly reduced. Coordinating training efforts is also a vehicle for community collaboration discussed in Chapter 12. Shared training experiences can

Staff Needs Assessment

The Staff Development Task Force has started to plan this year's staff development activities and would appreciate your input. Please take a few minutes to review the following list of proposed activities, and circle your level of interest in each. If you have other topics you would like to have addressed, please list them in the blank spaces.

		Interest Level	
Topic	Low	Medium	High
1. Making battery-operated toys accessible by constructing adaptive switches	1	2	3
2. Cultural customs, values, health care, and child-rearing practices of the Hmong people of Southeast Asia	1	2	3
3. Procedures for clean, intermittent catheterization	1	2	3
4. Services provided by Home Intervention, Incorporated	1	2	3
5. National trends in services for high-risk infants and their families	1	2	3
6. Procedures to prevent the spread of infectious disease	1	2	3
7. Preparing children and families for the transition from early intervention to preschool programs	1	2	3
8. New techniques for feeding children with severe oral/motor involvement	1	2	3
9. Parent/professional partnerships: development and maintenance	1	2	3
10.	1	2	3
11.	1	2	3
12.	1	2	3

Please think about some of the best staff development or conference sessions you have attended, and list those speakers that you think would be especially good at addressing any of the topics mentioned above.

Name	Topic	Address/Phone/Organization

Please list any areas of expertise in which you would be willing to provide training to our staff.

_____
_____
_____
_____
_____

Thank you for your suggestions. Our Task Force will be reporting the results of this needs assessment at the next scheduled staff meeting. In the meantime, if there is anything that you would like to add, please let Connie or Jeff know.

Figure 6.1. Sample staff needs assessment form.

enhance the relationships among programs and providers in the community (Lynch & Harrison, 1986).

The range of training options is broad; staff development does not need to be a 2-hour lecture. Instead, staff development can include coaching and mentoring by experienced staff members; advanced university course work; attendance at local, state, and national conferences; ongoing consultation from experts; visitations to exemplary programs; journal groups with discussions based on the professional literature; or development and implementation of new procedures or practices within one's own program. Imagination is the only limit to the variety of ways that staff development activities can be delivered.

Even in remote areas where universities, professionals, and colleagues with similar jobs do not exist, "distance education" is an option. An increasing number of colleges and universities are transmitting course work via satellite to remote rural areas as well as to specific locations within metropolitan areas. A number of high-quality videotapes and films related to early intervention practice as well as to medical and ethical issues have also been developed for training. These are available for rent or purchase for use in programs throughout the nation.

In summary, staff development is an integral part of all model early intervention programs. An annual staff needs assessment allows program administrators to plan training activities that will be the most meaningful and motivating to staff members, and an annual calendar of training events enables staff members to get the most out of each activity. Sharing staff development resources with other community agencies is one way to extend the amount and extent of training and to increase collaboration among community providers. Many activities, from reading and discussing articles in the latest professional journals, to visiting other programs, to watching videotapes of infant assessment, to being observed and coached by peers, are appropriate staff development activities. Staff development does not occur on one or two occasions. It is a continuous process. A range of training options must be made available to staff members throughout their professional lives.

Personnel Issues

Many personnel issues are generic. Managers in businesses, agencies, and organizations grapple with similar issues such as rates of pay, benefits, and performance evaluation. These are also issues in early intervention programs; however, several additional concerns are likely to emerge in these programs. These issues are not necessarily documented in the literature, nor are they areas of extensive research, but they have been noted consistently in our experience as staff members, managers, and university trainers. The issues are described in the following sections.

Credentialing and Licensure

Administering organizations for early intervention programs are not always designed to recruit, hire, and promote individuals from a variety of disciplines. As mentioned earlier in the chapter, some school districts require that anyone hired as a certified employee must have a teaching credential. As a result, physical and occupational therapists, child development specialists, social workers, and some psychologists may not be employable on a professional salary schedule or, in some instances, may not be employable by the district at all. Similarly, medically based facilities may not have the flexibility to hire staff members who are not physicians or allied health professionals. Until this issue is resolved throughout the nation, it will continue to have a negative impact on early intervention programs. Although there may not always be a resolution, it behooves program administrators to voice their concerns, demonstrate the need for professional diversity, and fight for administrative policies that serve their programs.

Burnout

Although sometimes an overused word, staff burnout is not unheard of in early intervention programs. Staff members work closely with families in crisis and with children who have serious, often life-threatening problems. Regardless of the individual's skills and inner strengths, the stress of other people's pain takes its toll. When a definite diagnosis is made, a family splits up, child abuse is suspected, or an infant dies, staff members share in the pain. As a result staff members may show signs of burnout. They may seem to care less; may become irritable or depressed; or may appear to be in a rut. They may lose their enthusiasm, inventiveness, and sense of worth. Regardless of how they express their symptoms, they need opportunities to regain their equilibrium. For some it may be a vacation, for others a complete change of clients or assignment. A few may ultimately decide on a career change. Regardless of the outcome, staff members who are showing signs of burnout need help.

Although it is not always possible to prevent staff burnout, some strategies can be used to decrease its frequency. Selectivity in hiring is the first line of defense. All helping professions attract some people who simply want to make everything right. Although this is a worthy goal, it is not the primary goal of early intervention.

A second strategy is to develop programmatic policies that establish realistic limits on staff members' accessibility. For example, it is unrealistic for team members to be on call at all times. Although staff members may choose to give families their home phone numbers, the program may decide that numbers should be given only in limited circumstances. Staff members need respite, and being available 24 hours a day, 7 days a week is not reasonable.

Finally, developing a system that rotates family client responsibilities on an annual basis can help to alleviate enmeshed relationships between families and staff members. Changing primary interventionists also brings a fresh perspective to the program implementation.

Mentoring and Support

Being an early interventionist can be extremely rewarding, but it is not an easy job. Early interventionists typically work closely with families and often work with them in their homes and neighborhoods. Staff members may experience a variety of stresses associated with the illness or death of a child, family disruptions, cultural clashes, and an overload of families assigned to their service, to name a few. Furthermore, the early interventionist may have entered the field with minimal background or experience working with very young children and their families due to the newness of the field and the lack of training opportunities in many areas. One strategy that can help retain staff members is the provision of support and training through a mentorship arrangement (Fenichel, 1991). The type and duration of the arrangement will vary according to the resources and needs of agencies and individuals. However, the underlying idea is that staff members are paired or matched with others who have more experience or training in an area of need. The mentor staff person is available to provide guidance, information, or even a friendly ear as the interventionist conducts her or his duties. The importance of mentorship arrangements are being increasingly recognized as crucial to staff support and retention, particularly in today's busy world with a vast range of early intervention challenges.

Turnover and Continuity

As in any new and growing field, many early interventionists are young and in the early stages of their own lives and careers. This demographic reality contributes to staff turnover as team members elect to move to other areas of the country, begin their own families, and/or return to school for advanced degrees. Although turnover is often positive, continuity of services is particularly important in early intervention programs. Services are often provided year-round with little time for extended training of new staff members. Thus, the program administrator must develop strategies to bring people on board quickly and efficiently. Maintaining a file of applicants, pairing old and new staff members for the first months of service delivery, hiring one "floating" staff member who can fill in when there are extended absences or resignations, providing written handbooks and policy manuals for all staff members, and videotaping training sessions for use with new employees can help to reduce problems created by turnover.

Health and Safety Precautions

Many diseases and bacterial and viral agents are present in centers where young children and families are served. Diseases such as hepatitis and tuberculosis are on the increase in many areas. Early intervention personnel are cautioned to use universal health care precautions, including frequent and thorough hand washing and cleansing of diapering and food preparation surfaces.

Infants who are at risk or have disabilities because of infections contracted in utero, such as rubella, cytomegalic inclusion disease (cytomegalovirus or CMV), or herpes, often continue to shed the virus as infants and toddlers. Viruses may be present in secretions such as saliva or urine or found in active herpes lesions. As staff members feed, diaper, and handle the infants, they are at risk for contracting the infection. Although these viruses usually have little impact on healthy adults, they can have devastating effects on the fetus; thus, staff members who are pregnant or considering becoming pregnant need to be informed about safe handling techniques.

The number of newborns infected with the HIV or AIDS virus is on the increase. As these infants enter early intervention programs, procedures that protect the infants from infection in the environment and assure the safety of others must be implemented. These policies require consultation from physicians and/or other allied health personnel, and involve simple procedures that are standard in hospitals and clinics but less familiar in educational settings. Staff and parent understanding of the procedures and their implementation help to create a safe environment for everyone.

Early interventionists also may be required to work in neighborhoods or communities characterized by violence. Caution is warranted. Programs are advised to consult with local safety officers and develop protocols for home visits and travel.

Personal Needs

A primary goal of all early intervention programs is to assist parents to locate and use resources, develop systems of support, and become advocates for their own child. Doing this takes time and practice, but the skills can be used for a lifetime. Early interventionists are available to help, to coach, and to provide support as parents learn, but early interventionists are *not* to usurp the parents' responsibility. Early interventionists who "take over" parental roles and responsibilities deprive parents of opportunities to grow and develop and contribute to family dependence rather than independence. When a staff member accompanies a family on every visit to the pediatrician, drives them around to look for a different apartment, and spends part of every weekend talking to parents on the phone, there is a good chance that the interventionist's need to be needed has replaced the family's needs as the top priority. This situation calls for a discussion within the team and often for a change in the staff member's assignment.

Similarly, interventionists may sometimes venture beyond their areas of expertise in an attempt to help family members. The bond between a home visitor and the family (particularly the mother, since she is usually the most involved with the infant and the program) is often strong and intimate. As a result a family member may share information with interventionists that is quite private or may seek advice about matters that are beyond the interventionist's ability to handle. Although the request to give advice is impossible for many to refuse, giving the advice is seldom a wise decision. For example, few educational interventionists have also been trained to handle drug and alcohol problems, to provide marriage counseling, or to help control spousal abuse; however, many are flattered to be asked for help. An educational interventionist is available to provide support and appropriate referrals, not family therapy. It is the interventionist's professional responsibility to acknowledge his or her limitations and help the mother or other family member find other resources.

All people in the helping professions become overprotective at times, unconsciously put their needs or the agency's needs above those of the client, or take on responsibility that is not theirs. This section has not been aimed at those occasional occurrences. Instead, it is intended to describe consistent patterns of behavior that suggest a staff member is not working toward program goals. Such behavior patterns are incompatible with effective functioning in an early intervention program.

Summary

The needs of infants who are at risk or disabled and their families are diverse, and no single discipline trains professionals who are able to meet all of the needs. As a result, inter- or transdisciplinary teams have evolved to provide early intervention services. In educationally oriented, family-centered early intervention programs, staff members must have skills in typical and atypical child development, family support and involvement, program planning and implementation, child and family assessment, program evaluation, and professional conduct. In addition, they must be able to work effectively with families from diverse backgrounds with lifeways that may differ from their own and with a range of other professionals. In the development of an early intervention team, the professional competencies of team members are as important as their professional disciplines. Trained paraprofessionals have become extremely important to many teams because of the understanding and practicality they bring from their own experiences. Although selecting staff members with excellent professional training and experience with young children is essential, staff development is an important component of early intervention programs. Although many of the personnel issues within early intervention programs are generic, several require special consideration. Issues of credentialing and licensure, burnout, mentoring and support, turnover and continuity, health precautions, and personal needs are all of special significance in early intervention.

Preferred Practices

The following list of questions can be used to guide the reader in developing an intervention team, organizing staff development activities, and supporting staff members on the job.

1. What are the primary needs of the infants, toddlers, and their families served in the program, and are the areas of expertise needed to meet those needs represented on the team?

2. Are parents of the children being served by the program participating as equal team members?

3. Are staff members sensitive to, respectful of, and knowledgeable about the wide range of families served by the program (as they differ in terms of language, culture, ethnicity, religion, lifestyle, and socioeconomic status)?

4. Is adequate time being allocated for communication among team members?

5. Is adequate time being allocated for team members to share skills?

6. Are all staff members credentialed, registered, or licensed in their own professional disciplines?

7. Have all team members had experience with young children and families?

8. Is there a plan for conducting staff development activities?

9. Is a staff needs assessment conducted at least annually and used to plan staff development activities?

10. Is a range of staff development activities available to team members?

11. Do programs and agencies within the community collaborate in staff development activities?

12. Are staff members encouraged to increase their skills and knowledge and incorporate newly validated practices into the program?

13. Do opportunities exist for staff members to get together on an informal basis to develop team cohesion?

14. Are staff members supervised, supported, and assisted in their roles by the administration?

15. Are rules of professional conduct discussed, and are appropriate policies in place?

References

Allen, K. E., Holm, V. A., & Schiefelbusch, R. L. (Eds.). (1978). *Early intervention—A team approach.* Austin, TX: PRO-ED.

Bailey, D., Farel, A., O'Donnell, K., Simeonsson, R., & Miller, C. (1987). Preparing infant interventionists: Interdepartmental training in special education and maternal and child health. *The Journal of the Division for Early Childhood, 11*(1), 67–77.

Bailey, D., Palsha, S. A., & Huntington, G. S. (1990). Preservice preparation of special educators to serve infants with handicaps and their families: Current status and training needs. *Journal of Early Intervention, 14*(2), 43–54.

Brandt, P. A., & Magyary, D. L. (1989). Preparation of clinical nurse specialists for family-centered early intervention. *Infants and Young Children, 1*(3), 51–62.

Bricker, D. (1976). Educational synthesizer. In A. Thomas (Ed.), *Hey, don't forget about me!* (pp. 84–97). Reston, VA: Council for Exceptional Children.

Bricker, D., & Slentz, K. (1987). Personnel preparation: Handicapped infants. In M. C. Wang, M. C. Reynolds, & H. J. Walberg (Eds.), *Handbook of special education: Research and practice* (Vol. 3, pp. 319–345). Elmsford, NY: Pergamon Books.

Bruder, M., & McLean, M. (1988). Personnel preparation for infant interventionists: A review of federally funded projects. *The Journal of the Division for Early Childhood, 12*(4), 299–305.

Campbell, P. H. (1987). The integrated programming team: An approach for coordinating professionals of various disciplines in programs for students with severe handicaps. *Journal of the Association for Persons with Severe Handicaps, 12,* 107–116.

Crais, E. R., & Leonard, C. R. (1988). *P.L. 99-457: Are speech/language pathologists trained and ready?* Unpublished manuscript, University of North Carolina, Chapel Hill.

Drotar, D., & Sturm, L. (1989). Training psychologists as infant specialists. *Infants and Young Children, 2*(2), 58–66.

Dunn, W., Campbell, P. H., Oetter, P. L., Hall, S., Berger, E., & Strickland, L. R. (1989). *Guidelines for occupational therapy services in early intervention and preschool services.* Rockville, MD: American Occupational Therapy Association.

Farel, A. M. (1988). Public health in early intervention: Historic foundations for contemporary training. *Infants and Young Children, 1*(1), 63–70.

Fenichel, E. (1991). Learning through supervision and mentorship to support the development of infants, toddlers and their families. *Zero to Three, 12*(2), 1–6.

Fenichel, E. S., & Eggbeer, L. (1989). Educating allies: Issues and recommendations in the training of practitioners to work with infants, toddlers, and their families. *Zero to Three, 10*(1), 1–7.

Fewell, R. R. (1983). The team approach to infant education. In S. G. Garwood & R. R. Fewell (Eds.), *Educating handicapped infants* (pp. 299–322). Rockville, MD: Aspen.

Hanft, B. E., & Humphry, R. (1989). Training occupational therapists in early intervention. *Infants and Young Children, 1*(4), 54–65.

Hanson, M. J. (1990). *Final report: California early intervention personnel model, personnel standards, and personnel preparation plan*. San Francisco: San Francisco State University, Department of Special Education.

Hanson, M. J., & Brekken, L. (1991). Early intervention personnel model and standards: An interdisciplinary field-developed approach. *Infants and Young Children, 4*(1), 54–61.

Hanson, M. J., Hanline, M. F., & Petersen, S. (1987). Addressing state and local needs: A model for interdisciplinary preservice training in early childhood special education. *Topics in Early Childhood Special Education, 7*(3), 36–47.

Hanson, M. J., & Lovett, D. (1992). Personnel preparation for early interventionists: A cross-disciplinary survey. *Journal of Early Intervention, 16*(2), 123–135.

Harrison, H., & Kositsky, A. (1983). *The premature baby book*. New York: St. Martin's Press.

Hine, R. J., Cloud, H. H., Carithers, T., Hickey, C., & Hinton, A. W. (1989). Early nutrition intervention services for children with special health care needs. *Journal of the American Dietetic Association, 89*(11), 1636–1639.

Jones, M. H. (1977). Intervention programs for children under three years. In B. M. Caldwell & D. J. Stedman (Eds.), *Infant education: A guide for helping handicapped children in the first three years* (pp. 123–145). New York: Walker.

Kaufman, M. (1989). Are dietitians prepared to work with handicapped infants? P.L. 99-457 offers new opportunities. *Journal of the American Dietetic Association, 89*(11), 1602–1605.

Linder, T. (1982). A national study of competencies for early childhood special education. *Educational and Psychological Research, 2*, 31–42.

Linder, T. W. (1983). *Early childhood special education*. Baltimore: Brookes.

Lucas, B. L. (1989). Serving infants and children with special health care needs in the 1990s—Are we ready? *Journal of the American Dietetic Association, 89*(11), 1599–1601.

Lynch, E. W. (1978). The home–school partnership. In S. L. Brown & M. S. Moersch (Eds.), *Parents on the team* (pp. 21–24). Ann Arbor: University of Michigan Press.

Lynch, E. W. (1981). *But I've tried everything! A special educator's guide to working with parents*. San Diego: San Diego State University.

Lynch, E. W., & Harrison, P. J. (1986). *Interagency collaboration: Making magic happen*. San Diego: San Diego State University.

Lynch, E. W., & Lewis, R. B. (1988). The nature and needs of exceptional people. In E. W. Lynch & R. B. Lewis (Eds.), *Exceptional children and adults* (pp. 4–45). Glenview, IL: Scott, Foresman.

Lyon, S., & Lyon, G. (1980). Team functioning and staff development: A role release approach to providing integrated educational services for severely handicapped students. *Journal of the Association for the Severely Handicapped, 5*(3), 250–263.

McCollum, J., McLean, M., McCartan, K., & Kaiser, C. (1989). Recommendations for certification in early childhood special education. *Journal of Early Intervention, 13*(3), 195–211.

McCollum, J., & Thorp, E. K. (1988). Training of infant specialists: A look to the future. *Infants and Young Children, 1*(2), 55–65.

McCormick, L., & Goldman, R. (1979). The transdisciplinary model: Implications for service delivery and personnel preparation for the severely and profoundly handicapped. *AAESPH Review, 4*, 152–161.

Moersch, M. S. (1978). History and rationale for parent involvement. In S. L. Brown & M. S. Moersch (Eds.), *Parents on the team* (pp. 1–10). Ann Arbor: University of Michigan Press.

Nover, A. R., & Timberlake, E. M. (1989). Meeting the challenge: The educational preparation of social workers for practice with at-risk children (0–3) and their families. *Infants and Young Children, 2*(1), 59–65.

Rogers, S. J., Lewis, H. C., & Reis, K. (1987). An effective procedure for training early special education teams to implement a model program. *Journal of the Division of Early Childhood, 11,* 180–188.

Scull, S., & Deitz, J. (1989). Competencies for the physical therapist in the neonatal intensive care unit (NICU). *Pediatric Physical Therapy, 1*(1), 11–14.

Shonkoff, J., & Hauser-Cram, P. (1987). Early intervention for disabled infants and their families—A quantitative analysis. *Pediatrics, 80,* 650–658.

Simons, R. (1987). *After the tears—Parents talk about raising a child with a disability.* San Diego: Harcourt Brace Jovanovich.

Simpson, C. (1987). Parents need parents. *Special Care, 2*(2), 14–15.

Stoneman, Z. (1985). Family involvement in early childhood special education programs. In N. H. Fallen & W. Umansky (Eds.), *Young children with special needs* (pp. 442–469). Columbus, OH: Merrill.

Thorp, E. V., & McCollum, J. A. (1988). Defining the infancy specialization in early childhood special education. In J. B. Jordan, J. J. Gallagher, P. L. Hutinger, & M. B. Karnes (Eds.), *Early childhood special education: Birth to three* (pp. 147–161). Reston, VA: Council for Exceptional Children.

Trohanis, P. L., Cox, J. O., & Meyer, R. A. (1982). A report on selected demonstration programs for infant intervention. In C. T. Ramey & P. L. Trohanis (Eds.), *Finding and educating high-risk and handicapped infants* (pp. 163–191). Austin, TX: PRO-ED.

Zeitlin, S., du Verglas, G., & Windhover, R. (Eds.). (1982). *Basic competencies for personnel in early intervention programs.* Monmouth, OR: Western Technical Assistance Resources (WESTAR).

Selected Readings

In addition to the references cited in the chapter, the following selected readings may be of interest.

Bailey, D. B. (1989). Issues and directions in preparing professionals to work with young handicapped children and their families. In J. J. Gallagher, P. L. Trohanis, & R. M. Clifford (Eds.), *Policy implementation and PL 99-457: Planning for young children with special needs* (pp. 97–132). Baltimore: Brookes.

Crais, E. R. (1991). *A practical guide to embedding family-centered content into existing speech–language pathology coursework.* Chapel Hill: University of North Carolina at Chapel Hill, Frank Porter Graham Child Development Center.

Donahue-Kilburg, G. (1992). *Family-centered early intervention for communication disorders.* Gaithersburg, MD: Aspen.

Edelman, L. (1991). *Getting on board: Training activities to promote the practice of family-centered care.* Bethesda, MD: Association for the Care of Children's Health.

Edelman, L. (1992). *Project Copernicus train—The trainer series in family-centered service delivery.* St. Paul, MN: Pathfinder Resources.

This training package includes the following manuals:

Edelman, L., Elsayed, S. S., & McGonigel, M. (1992). *Overview of family-centered service coordination. Facilitors' guide.*

Edelman, L., Greenland, B., & Mills, B. L. (1992). *Family-centered communication skills: Facilitors' guide.*

Edelman, L., Greenland, B., & Mills, B. L. (1992). *Building parent/professional collaboration: Facilitors' guide.*

Fenichel, E. S., & Eggbeer, L. (1990). *Preparing practitioners to work with infants, toddlers, and their families.* Washington, DC: National Center for Clinical Infant Programs.

There are four documents in this series:
(1) *Issues and recommendations for the professions.*
(2) *Issues and recommendations for policymakers.*
(3) *Issues and recommendations for educators and trainers.*
(4) *Issues and recommendations for parents.*

Hanft, B., Burke, J., Cahill, M., Swenson-Miller, K., & Humphry, R. (1992). *Working with families: A curriculum guide for pediatric occupational therapists.* Chapel Hill: University of North Carolina at Chapel Hill, Frank Porter Graham Child Development Center.

Phi Delta Kappa, Center on Evaluation, Development, Research. (1989). *Teacher peer coaching.* Bloomington, IN: Author.

Spencer, P. E., & Coye, R. W. (1988). Project BRIDGE: A team approach to decision-making for early services. *Infants and Young Children, 1*(1), 82–92.

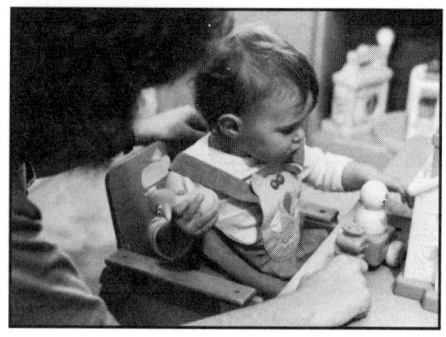

Coordinating Screening and Identification Efforts

CHAPTER 7

Identifying infants and toddlers who are at risk for disability or those who have a diagnosed disability is one of the functions of screening programs. This process can be thought of as a funnel-like system that starts with broad screening measures for all children and gradually narrows to provide more comprehensive and specific assessments of fewer and fewer children. Although identification of eligible infants and toddlers is a requirement of the Individuals with Disabilities Education Act (IDEA), screening and identification programs are a wider community responsibility. Many people and agencies, including primary care physicians, public health nurses, school districts, and health agencies, typically identify and refer children in need of services to early intervention programs. The way in which referrals are made through IDEA varies by state and community.

The following is a typical example of the way the identification process works. Mrs. Ruiz has noticed that her 12-month-old son, Alfonso, makes very few sounds compared with the number of vocalizations her other children made at the same age. One day at a nearby shopping center, she notices a large van from the community hospital with a banner inviting parents to bring their children in for free hearing, vision, and movement screenings. Although Mrs. Ruiz did not think much could be learned about a 12-month-old, she decided to go in and ask. The nurse and volunteers in the van talked with Mrs. Ruiz and spent some time playing with Alfonso. They also shook rattles, tapped a drum, and rang a bell near his ears but out of his sight to see whether he noticed the sounds. After they had played with him for a while, the nurse told Mrs. Ruiz that she shared her concern. She explained that Alfonso did not seem to be responding to sounds, which could explain why he was not vocalizing. The nurse explained that the next step was to have a more formal hearing test done by the audiologists at the health service the Ruiz family belonged to. Mrs. Ruiz made the appointment and took Alfonso for the test. On the day of the test he was fussy, and it was very difficult for the audiologist to get a clear picture of how well he could hear. The audiologist suggested that Mrs. Ruiz make an appointment at the community hospital to do a more specialized hearing test designed for very young children. The audiologist explained that the test was much more sophisticated and would be done while Alfonso was sleeping. The test in the hospital showed that Alfonso had a moderate hearing loss in both ears. At that point the audiologist suggested that Alfonso be referred to the local early intervention program so that he could be taught language and his family could learn how to work with him.

In this example a parent's concern caused her to seek assistance. The general screening suggested that the child might have problems, and a referral for a more refined assessment was made. Following that assessment another referral was made for a more sophisticated assessment. When the results of that assessment confirmed that Alfonso had a hearing loss, the Ruiz family was referred to an early intervention program for services.

The way in which risk is defined, the comprehensiveness of the screening process used to find children and families who are eligible for services, and the extent of community collaboration all influence the numbers of children that will be identified. This chapter focuses on screening, identification and referral, and the interface between referral sources and the early intervention program.

Screening

One of the clearest definitions of screening is that of Dumars, Duran-Flores, Foster, and Stills (1987): "Screening is the application of a simple accurate method for determining which children in the population are likely to be in need of special services in order to develop optimally" (p. 111). Effective screening procedures have a single purpose, to divide

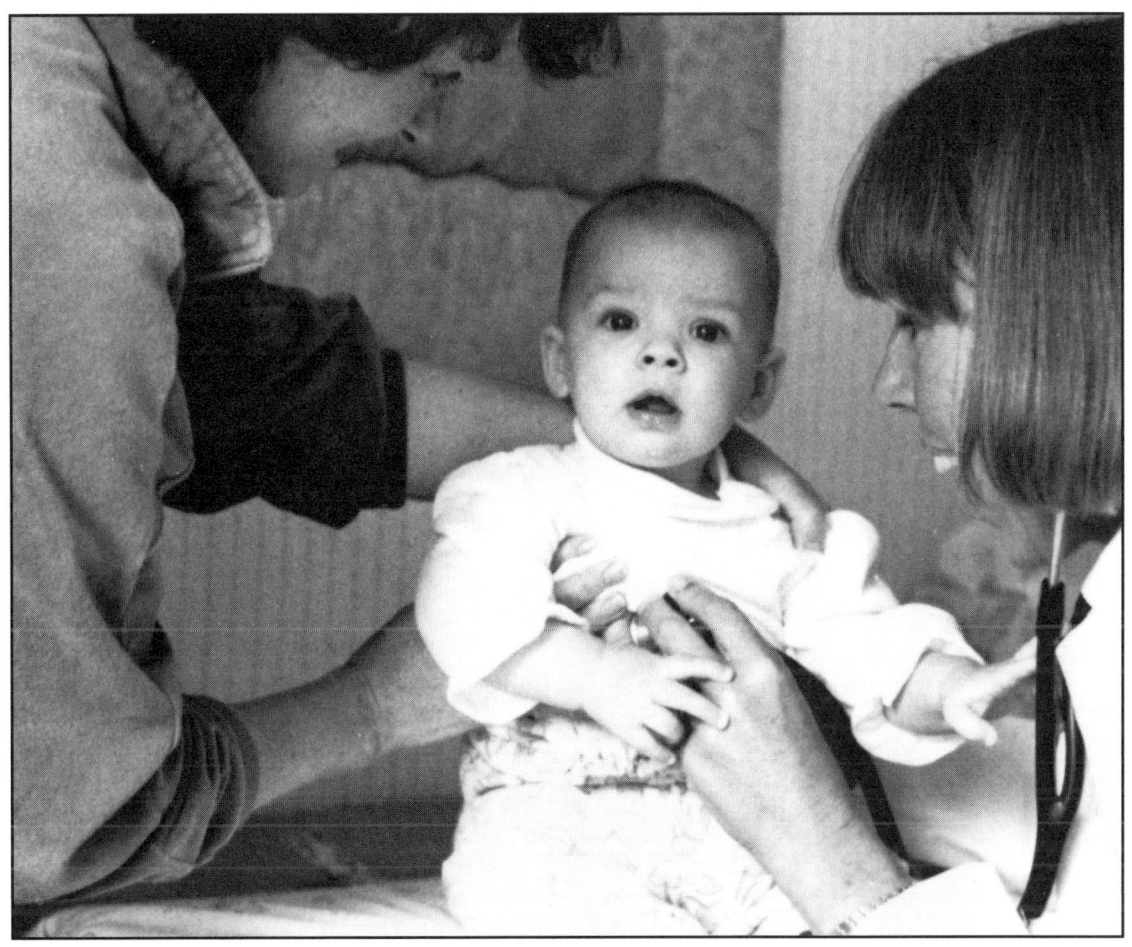

children into two groups: those who are at risk and those who are not (Brooks-Gunn & Lewis, 1983; Dumars et al., 1987; Thurman & Widerstrom, 1990). Because screening is the first step in determining eligibility for services, exemplary screening programs are designed to include all infants and toddlers in the community.

Until the implementation of P.L. 99-457 and its subsequent amendments (IDEA), no federally sponsored screening program was available for all infants and toddlers suspected of delay or developmental disabilities. Although large-scale programs did exist for those children eligible for Medicaid, they reached only a small fraction of the nation's population. Under the mandates of P.L. 94-142, the Education of the Handicapped Act of 1975, school districts were tasked with identifying all children and youth with disabilities from birth through age 21. However, as the number of school-aged children requiring special services increased and resources remained static, child-find efforts were given a lower priority in many states and districts.

Comprehensive child-find systems are now a requirement throughout the United States. Subchapter VIII of IDEA requires that states develop a system that incorporates primary referral sources and includes time lines for referrals. Because professionals in private medical offices, health maintenance organizations, and clinics often have the greatest opportunity to notice atypical development, their inclusion in the legislation as primary referral sources was an important step in ensuring information and access to early intervention programs and services for families.

Optimal screening models rely on interagency efforts that provide periodic checks of children who appear to be developing normally and continuous surveillance of at-risk infants through the first 3 years of life. A combination of screening settings, such as hospital health fairs, neighborhood health clinics, and mobile screening units that can be taken to grocery stores, community recreation centers, churches, and other places where people gather, can be used to reach segments of the population that do not seek routine care from physicians. With agreements among groups and agencies providing screening and signed parent permission forms, information gathered in the screening can be shared with agencies providing programs, allowing them to follow up on infants and toddlers who need further evaluation. The regulations that specify the way Part H of IDEA is to be implemented include time lines for referral for those children who appear to be disabled or delayed.

Criteria for Exemplary Screening Programs

Such large-scale efforts require that screening programs meet a number of specific criteria. These criteria have been frequently described in the literature (e.g., Anastasiow, Frankenburg, & Fandal, 1982; Brooks-Gunn & Lewis, 1983; Dumars et al., 1987; Lillie, 1977). In general, effective screening programs are simple, accurate, comprehensive, cost-effective, and involve parents. These characteristics and their implications for practice are detailed in Table 7.1.

Definitions of Risk

The definition used to determine which infants and toddlers are eligible for services and which are not is a critical factor in screening programs. It is necessary to know whom one is searching for before one begins to look. Both risk and disability must be defined before screening can begin.

The concept of risk is extremely broad. Some individuals would include all children from low income families in a high-risk group; others use more stringent definitions in which a specific medical condition is the determiner of risk. To reduce confusion Tjossem (1976) proposed definitions and de-

Table 7.1. Criteria for Exemplary Screening Programs

Criterion	Implementation Implications
Simple	Instruments or strategies should be short, easy to administer or implement, and usable by professionals from a variety of disciplines as well as paraprofessionals.
	Scoring should be quick and easy to do.
	The program should be systematized for easy implementation and replication at different locations over time.
Accurate	Instruments should be valid and reliable for the purpose for which they are being used.
	Instruments should not generate an excess of false positives (children without problems identified as having a problem) or false negatives (children with problems who are not identified).
	Instruments should be appropriate for the ethnic and language groups with whom they are used.
Comprehensive	The program should be multidimensional and include screening for educational, health, behavioral, and environmental problems.
	The program should be available to and designed to reach the entire community.
Cost-effective	Programs should lead to appropriate and timely interventions.
	Inappropriate referrals should be minimized.
	Instruments and strategies should be inexpensive.
	Personnel costs should be reduced through the use of trained paraprofessionals.
Partnership with Parents	Programs should include family input and contribute to family–professional collaboration.
	Referrals should be thoroughly and sensitively explained to families, and they should be part of the referral process.
	Programs should provide information for families as requested (e.g., developmental milestones, child management, nutrition, community resources).

scriptions of three major types of risk: established risk, environmental risk, and biological risk. Since their introduction they have become the standard definitions across many professional disciplines. The three are not mutually exclusive and, in fact, often overlap; however, they do provide a helpful schema for determining which infants and young children are at risk.

Established risk describes those children who have a definite medical disorder of known etiology and a relatively predictable developmental prognosis that includes developmental delay. Infants with Down syndrome are one example of those with established risk. Infants and young children who are biologically healthy but whose life experiences or living conditions are limited to the extent that without intervention the children are likely to experience developmental delay are considered to be at *environmental risk*. Lack of care from and interaction with the mother or family, limited opportunities for expression, lack of health care, neglect, and abuse are examples of environmental risk factors. Infants at *biological risk* have a history of prenatal, perinatal, neonatal, and early developmental complications, which suggests that there has been some insult to their central nervous system. Although the etiology is unknown and the specific insult undocumented, there is a greater than normal likelihood that these children will develop atypically. Infants who are born prematurely or who are small for gestational age fall into this risk group.

These definitions can be used to develop more specific criteria for determining which children are eligible for early intervention.

Table 7.2 lists some of the more specific risk factors that are used in some states to identify infants at risk for developmental problems.

The overlap among the categories of risk described in the previous paragraphs and clinical practice with young children and their families have given rise to another perspective on the impact of risk factors on children's development. Some children experience multiple or cumulative risks that combine to interfere with healthy development and optimal outcomes (e.g., Gabarino, 1990; Greenspan, 1990; Sameroff, Seifer, Barocas, Zax, & Greenspan, 1987; Werner, 1990). Infants who

Table 7.2. Risk Factors in Newborns

Factors Pertaining to the Infant
    Admitted to neonatal intensive care unit following birth
        Required 1-to-1 or 1-to-2 nurse-to-patient ratio for longer than 24 hours
        Under 32 weeks gestation
        Under 1,500 grams
        Small for gestational age
        Severe respiratory distress requiring assisted ventilation for over 48 hours during the first 4 weeks of life
        Asphyxia with a 5-minute apgar of 5 or less
        Sustained hypoxemia, acidemia, hypoglycemia, or frequent apnea
        Hyperbilirubinemia requiring an exchange transfusion
        Severe, persistent metabolic abnormality
        Neonatal seizures or nonfebrile seizures during the first 3 years of life
        Seizure activity during the first week of life
        Evidence of intracranial hemorrhage
        Central nervous system lesion or abnormality
        Central nervous system infection
        Congenital anomalies that may affect developmental outcome
        Serious biomedical insult that may affect developmental outcome
        Positive neonatal toxicology screen, symptomatic neonatal drug withdrawal, or known prenatal drug exposure
        Prenatal exposure to known teratogens
        Persistent muscle tone abnormality
        Failure to thrive

Factors Pertaining to the Family
    Infant born with evidence of prenatal substance exposure
    Infant born to a parent with developmental disabilities
    Infant born HIV positive
    Infant born to a mother under the age of 18 or over 35 years of age
    Infant born to a mother with an educational level of less than 10th grade
    Poor maternal attachment
    Home environment lacks stimulation
    Developmental delay as a consequence of biomedical and/or environmental factors

are born prematurely to single, teenage mothers who use drugs, have limited financial resources, and live in violent neighborhoods are being exposed to a multitude of risks. Likewise, infants born to families who are socially isolated, non-nurturing, and psychologically unavailable to their children are exposed to multiple risk factors. Early research focused on single risk factors and the negative outcomes associated with biological and environmental vulnerability. More recent research has examined resilience and protective factors in children's lives (Poulsen, 1993; Werner, 1990). Although still in its infancy, this research is beginning to set directions for early intervention programs that serve children and families who experience multiple risks. The importance of assessing and building upon the protective factors in the child's and family's life, provision of consistent nurturance, predictable environments, and opportunities for mastery and competence are key elements in increasing resilience and reducing the impact of risk.

Definitions of Disability

Defining disability is less ambiguous than defining risk, but it is not always clear-cut. The primary difficulty in defining disability is related to the differences in terminology used by the various service delivery systems. Medical settings use medical diagnoses, such as cerebral palsy, meningocele, and respiratory distress syndrome, to describe patients' needs. Educational systems use levels of disability, such as mild to severe, or categorical areas, such as learning disability, mental retardation, physical disability, or chronic illness, to define service needs. Other agencies may use descriptors such as developmentally disabled, which includes only some of the categories recognized in education. Consequently, an infant or toddler with cerebral palsy might qualify as having a mild or severe disability, depending on the extent of motor involvement, or as having a physical disability. Later, during the school years, this child might not need any further special education services, or the child might qualify because of a learning disability, mental retardation, or physical disability, depending on the extent of motor and cognitive involvement.

To reduce these definitional problems and the potential stigma in labeling, federal law allows early intervention programs to provide services without assigning a disability or severity label to children. Establishing that the child is at risk or is developmentally delayed by state eligibility criteria is sufficient cause to provide services. Thus, programs use state legislation and regulations to determine whom they may serve. Because serving infants and toddlers who are at risk or have disabilities is an interagency task with each state having a lead agency, the responsible state agency varies. Departments of public health, departments of education, departments of social service, and many others may serve as the lead agency in a state; therefore, early interventionists need to know state regulations and guidelines as well as the requirements of the local district or agency.

Screening is the first step in determining which infants and toddlers may need early intervention services. Exemplary screening programs are simple, accurate, comprehensive, and cost-effective, and they demonstrate their commitment to a partnership with families. They represent an interagency approach and reach out to all segments of the community. As communities develop their screening programs, those involved must grapple with the definitions of risk and disability that are used in the state.

Identification and Referral for Further Assessment and Diagnosis

Screening programs are designed to locate those infants and toddlers who need further assessment. The suspected problems could be related to development, health, or environmental issues (Barnard & Magyary, 1987). If a child is identified by the screening program as needing a more in-depth assessment or evaluation, the screening program typically provides referrals for that assessment.

Referrals may be provided in several ways. At a minimum, families may be told what the concern is and referred, with their permission, to their family physician, local health clinic, school district, or other agency designated by state guidelines for the implementation of Part H of IDEA.

Effective screening programs have a high rate of follow-through. Identifying children with potential problems is only the first step; encouraging families to seek further assessment for their child is the next. The partnership between parents and screeners is important to the follow-through effort. Asking family members to share information about their child as a valued part of the screening program and giving information about the findings of the screening in a clear yet supportive manner increase the chances that parents or caregivers will feel concerned and confident enough to obtain a more in-depth evaluation. Providing screening that is culturally competent—that is, done in a manner that is consistent with family beliefs, values, and language preferences; conducted in settings that families frequent and in which they are comfortable; and performed by people that families trust—also increases the chances that families will pursue more in-depth assessment.

Assessments to make a diagnosis or to determine eligibility for early intervention programs and services may be done by a variety of agencies, depending on state law and regulations, and they should focus not only on the results of screening tests but on the family's concerns. Diagnostic assessments for medical and health-related problems are conducted by physicians and allied health personnel. Assessments to determine the child's mental health are often conducted by clinical psychologists, social workers, counselors, or psychiatrists; and assessments to determine the child's cognitive and developmental status are typically conducted by early childhood special educators and school psychologists. As stressed throughout this book, assessments involve a team of professionals in collaboration with the family and follow state-determined guidelines for the implementation of Part H of IDEA.

Eligibility assessments are to be family centered and usually rely on observations, interviews with parents or caregivers, and standardized instruments that compare the child's health, development, and/or behavior with that of a normative group. However, standardized measures are now used less frequently than in the past. If the child's performance differs significantly, as determined by state regulation, from what one would expect of other children of the same chronological age, culture, and language background, the child is eligible for services. Once eligibility has been determined and the Individualized Family Service Plan (IFSP) written, curriculum-based assessment becomes an ongoing part of the intervention. Chapter 8 elaborates on all aspects of the assessment process.

Interface Between the Referral Source and the Early Intervention Program

Depending on state law and regulations, in some communities the early intervention program may receive a referral directly from the screening program, and the early intervention team may do the eligibility assessment. In other communities the early intervention program receives the referral after the child has already been assessed and found eligible for its services. However, the order in which this happens is far less important than the process that is used to cause it to happen. At every step children and their families are involved, because every interaction and piece of information that is shared has an impact on the family system. Many of these first contacts with professionals set the tone for parents' future perspectives on programs and services (McGonigel, Kaufmann, & Johnson, 1991). Professionals who respect and seek family input, speak honestly yet compassionately with family members, and use up-to-date, validated practices can assist in developing partnerships with families that foster positive outcomes for all involved.

One strategy for linking referrals to services is a collaborative community team composed of representatives from each of the agencies that provide services to infants and toddlers who are at risk or disabled and their families (Commission for Cooperative Services for Young Handicapped Children and Their Families, 1988; Lynch, Jackson, Mendoza, & English, 1991). Children who are suspected of being disabled or at risk are referred, with parental permission, to the team to determine their eligibility for services. Using a single intake form that all agencies within the community have agreed to accept, all of the information is collected about the child and family, and direct referrals to services are then made. In this model families are asked to provide basic information only one time, and representatives from all of the community's services are present to provide information, guidance, and support. Such a model, which utilizes a single point of contact for families, reduces duplication, assures that the family is made aware of all services, and increases the likelihood that services will be coordinated. If the number of team members involved is large, smaller subgroups of the team can meet with families in a more comfortable environment.

As this model evolves, it is likely that the initial service coordinator will be appointed from the group and will support the child and family through the assessment process. Technology may also influence the development of this model. It is now possible to have all of the necessary information about a particular child and family on a microchip stored on something no larger than a plastic credit card. In the not-so-distant future, programs may be able to read a family's card into the agency computer for immediate access to all or part of the child's and family's file. Because families would keep the card and provide the access codes to agencies, they would have complete control over what information was shared and with whom it was shared.

Even without such advanced technology, strategies can be used to assure a positive and productive relationship between referral sources and programs. These include (a) time for updating staff members from each program about the services provided; (b) quick and efficient responding to referrals within mandated time lines; and (c) follow-up with the referring agency or individual regarding the assessments that have been done, the services that have been provided, and the current status of the child and family.

Summary

Comprehensive child-find programs to identify those infants and toddlers who are at risk or disabled are mandated by Part H of the Individuals with Disabilities Education Act. States must develop strategies and procedures that make these services accessible to families and result in a timely referral process for additional assessment if developmental difficulties are suspected or determined. The ways in which these screening programs are conducted vary from state to state and community to community, but all should share a common set of characteristics. All screening programs should be simple to implement, accurate, comprehensive, cost-effective, and conducted in partnership with family members or caregivers who know the most about the child's development.

Because of the time lines included in the regulations for Part H of IDEA, any professional who suspects that a child needs further assessment should be acquainted with referral processes, reporting procedures, and assessment resources within the community. They should also be trained in communicating with parents and family members about their concerns, the referral process, and the implications that their concerns may have for the child and family. Being able to explain clearly the next steps in assessment, the agencies or systems that will be involved, and how these resources are coordinated in the community will help to ensure that families feel comfortable giving their permission for the referral.

Once family permission is given and the referral made for eligibility assessment, those legally responsible through the state's regulations for implementing Part H of IDEA have a limited time period in which to conduct the assessment and determine whether the child is eligible for services. When conducting an eligibility assessment, professionals are faced with an inherent conflict in the letter and the spirit of Part H. The letter of the law involves specific time lines and assessment across developmental areas by a multidisciplinary team, whereas the spirit of the law focuses on family partnerships and emphasizes the importance of conducting assessments that specifically address family concerns with as little intrusion as possible. As a result, legal requirements may interfere with a totally family-focused process. However, agencies responsible for implementation, service providers, and family members are working together throughout the United States to find ways of meeting legal requirements while honoring families' preferences.

As implementation of Part H continues, understanding each agency's definition of risk and disability, being aware of services available, maintaining contact with agencies, sharing information, and involving families in policy and practice decision making will lead to positive and productive relationships and more effective screening and identification.

Preferred Practices

The following questions can be used to review and evaluate screening and identification procedures that are being used to refer children and families for more comprehensive assessments.

1. Does the community have a comprehensive screening and identification program?
2. Does screening lead to more extensive diagnostic assessment and intervention services when appropriate?
3. Are the existing screening and identification programs reaching all members of the community, particularly low socioeconomic status families, teen parents, families who are non–English speaking, and those from diverse cultural backgrounds?
4. Are screening and identification efforts well publicized, nonthreatening, and positive in their approach?
5. Does the screening program follow through with agencies and families to determine the outcome of referrals?
6. Is time allocated for those involved in screening and identification to meet with those offering assessment and intervention services?
7. Are referrals for further assessment or for services usually accurate? In other words, are there very few false positives or false negatives?
8. Do various agencies within the community share the same definitions of risk and disability? If not, is each aware of the others' definitions?
9. Does a child receive one comprehensive, coordinated assessment rather than multiple, duplicate assessments by each agency?
10. Do referral and assessment processes and procedures honor family preferences as well as comply with state regulations?

11. Do procedures exist for including families in all parts of the screening and identification process, and do professionals value and utilize their input?

References

Anastasiow, N. J., Frankenburg, W. K., & Fandal, A. W. (Eds.). (1982). *Identifying the developmentally delayed child*. Baltimore: University Park Press.

Barnard, K. E., & Magyary, D. L. (1987). Early identification. In H. M. Wallace, R. F. Biehl, L. Taft, & A. C. Oglesby (Eds.), *Handicapped children and youth* (pp. 99–110). New York: Human Sciences Press.

Brooks-Gunn, J., & Lewis, M. (1983). Screening and diagnosing handicapped infants. *Topics in Early Childhood Special Education, 3*(1), 14–28.

Commission for Cooperative Services for Young Handicapped Children and Their Families. (1988). *Getting started: A guidebook for interagency collaboration*. (Available from Infant/Toddler Interagency Collaboration Project, 9245 Sky Park Court, Suite 130, San Diego, CA 92123)

Dumars, K. W., Duran-Flores, D., Foster, C., & Stills, S. (1987). Screening for developmental disabilities. H. M. Wallace, R. F. Biehl, L. Taft, & A. C. Oglesby (Eds.), *Handicapped children and youth* (pp. 111–125). New York: Human Sciences Press.

Gabarino, J. (1990). The human ecology of early risk. In S. J. Meisels & J. P. Shonkoff (Eds.), *Handbook of early childhood intervention* (pp. 78–96). New York: Cambridge University Press.

Greenspan, S. I. (1990). Comprehensive clinical approaches to infants and their families: Psychodynamic and developmental perspectives. In S. J. Meisels & J. P. Shonkoff (Eds.), *Handbook of early childhood intervention* (pp. 150–172). New York: Cambridge University Press.

Lillie, D. L. (1977). Screening. In L. Cross & K. W. Goin (Eds.), *Identifying handicapped children: A guide to casefinding, screening, diagnosis, assessment and evaluation* (pp. 17–24). New York: Walker.

Lynch, E. W., Jackson, J. A., Mendoza, J. M., & English, K. (1991). The merging of best practices and state policy in the IFSP process in California. *Topics in Early Childhood Special Education, 11*, 32–53.

McGonigel, M. J., Kaufmann, R. K., & Johnson, B. H. (1991). *Guidelines and recommended practices for the Individualized Family Service Plan* (2nd ed.). Bethesda, MD: Association for the Care of Children's Health.

Poulsen, M. K. (1993). Strategies for building resilience in infants and young children at risk. *Infants and Young Children, 6*(2), 29–40.

Sameroff, A., Seifer, R., Barocas, R., Zax, M., & Greenspan, S. (1987). Intelligence quotient scores of 4-year-old children: Social environmental risk factors. *Pediatrics, 79*, 343–350.

Thurman, S. K., & Widerstrom, A. H. (1990). *Infants and young children with special needs* (2nd ed.). Baltimore: Brookes.

Tjossem, T. (1976). Early intervention: Issues and approaches. In T. Tjossem (Ed.), *Intervention strategies for high-risk and handicapped children* (pp. 3–33). Baltimore: University Park Press.

Werner, E. E. (1990). Protective factors and individual resilience. In S. J. Meisels & J. P. Shonkoff (Eds.), *Handbook of early childhood intervention* (pp. 97–116). New York: Cambridge University Press.

Selected Readings

The following references provide general information about screening and identification as well as discussions of policy issues.

Harbin, G. L., Gallagher, J. J., & Terry, D. V. (1991). Defining the eligible populations: Policy issues and challenges. *Journal of Early Intervention, 15*, 13–20.

Meisels, S. J., & Wasik, B. A. (1990). Who should be served? Identifying children in need of early intervention. In S. J. Meisels & J. P. Shonkoff (Eds.), *Handbook of early childhood intervention* (pp. 605–632). New York: Cambridge University Press.

Peterson, N. L. (1991). Interagency collaboration under Part H: The key to comprehensive, multidisciplinary, coordinated infant/toddler intervention services. *Journal of Early Intervention, 15*, 89–105.

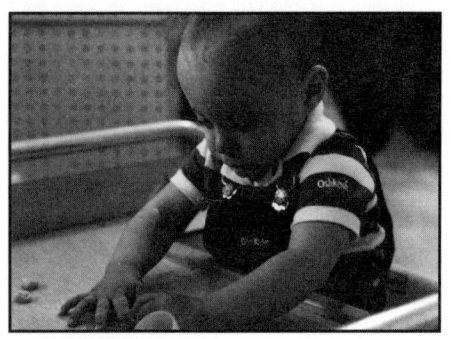

Assessing Children and Identifying Family Concerns, Priorities, and Resources

CHAPTER 8

Assessment is a complex yet exciting process. It demands extensive planning, flexibility, considerable knowledge about development and human behavior, skill in working collaboratively with families, and a systematic approach. Yet, with all the rigor that is required, each assessment is a little like being the detective in a well-written mystery. The job is absorbing and dependent to a large extent on one's skills in listening and observation. When all of the clues lead to an appropriate solution, it provides an exhilarating sense of accomplishment. Learning more about how an infant or toddler who is at risk or disabled thinks, learns, moves, communicates, and experiences the world takes the team one step closer to developing a program that will help that child continue to grow and develop. Learning what is important to the family is the next step. Assessment provides the map that guides program development and evaluates program effectiveness. It is an ongoing process that enables early interventionists and family members to work together to determine the child's strengths and needs and the outcomes that the family wants to achieve.

Assessment over time also provides a yardstick for measuring one aspect of program success. When children are growing, learning, and accomplishing objectives, their program plan is effective; however, when repeated assessments demonstrate that no growth is being made, the objectives and the intervention strategies need to be reviewed and revised. The same is true for families. If they are accomplishing the outcomes that they included for themselves in the Individualized Family Service Plan (IFSP), both early interventionists and family members can be pleased. However, if families are not accomplishing their goals, the IFSP may need to be reexamined and modified.

Until the passage of P.L. 99-457, now retitled the Individuals with Disabilities Education Act (IDEA), many early intervention programs focused almost exclusively on child assessment. Although early interventionists often worked closely with families and learned about their special circumstances, priorities, and needs, formally identifying family concerns, priorities, and resources and building those into the services being delivered were not viewed as part of the early intervention program's responsibility. With the implementation of P.L. 99-457, assessing family concerns, priorities, and resources and helping families achieve desired outcomes have become a part of all early intervention programs. This chapter focuses on the assessment of the child and the determination of family concerns, priorities, and resources in ways that are culturally competent and collaborative.

Child Assessment

The first sections of this chapter focus on general information about assessment and specific considerations and issues related to assessing infants and toddlers. Later sections highlight assessment strategies, techniques, and instruments that are appropriate for these young children.

Purposes of Assessment

Assessments vary in their purpose, scope, and content. In general, assessments are conducted for one of four purposes: detection, diagnosis, planning, and program monitoring (McLoughlin & Lewis, 1994). Detection, or screening, described in the previous chapter, is the first level of fact finding. Screening programs identify those children who are suspected of being at risk or of having a disability.

Those children identified through the screening process are referred to the second level of assessment—diagnosis or determination of eligibility for services. Diagnostic assessments are designed to provide an in-depth study of the child, to answer the questions

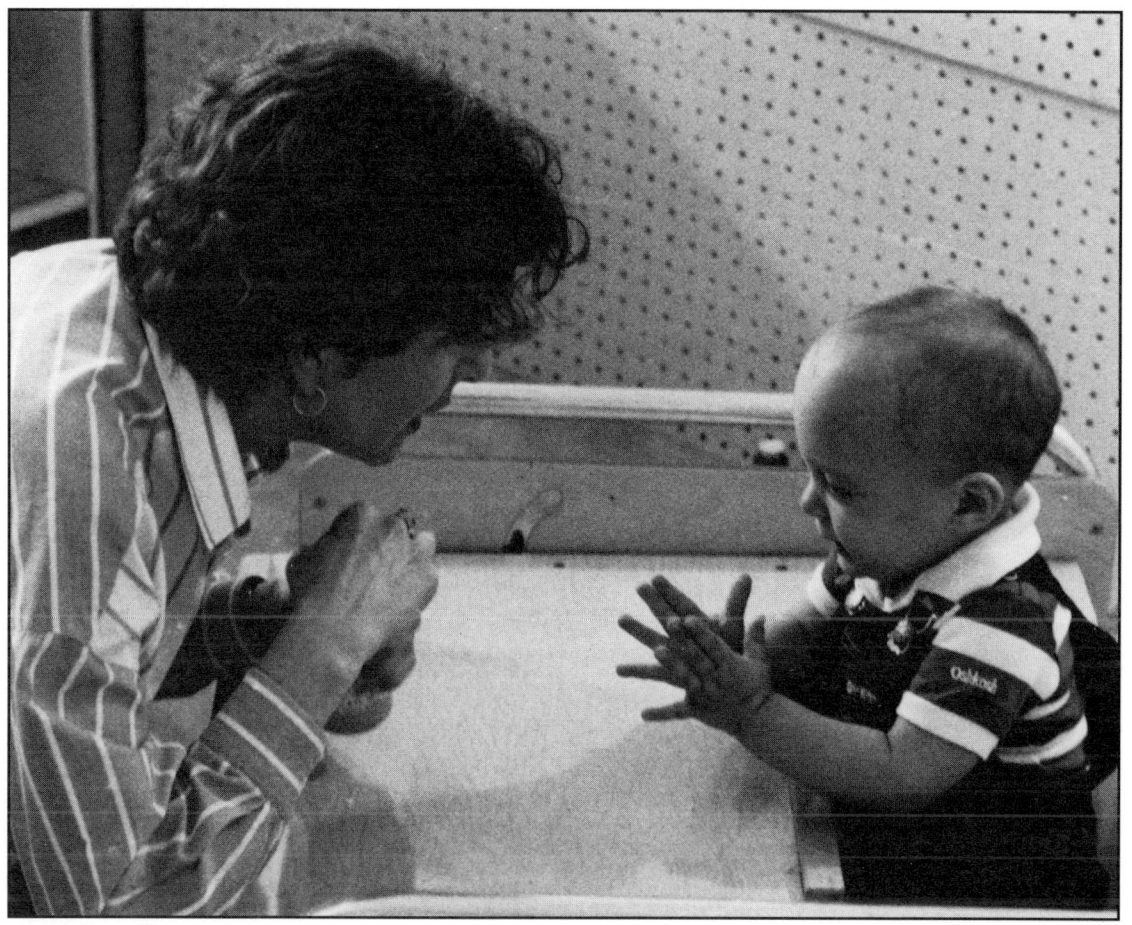

raised by the screening, and to address the family's concerns. The word *diagnosis* is most often used by health professionals to describe a medical condition. For example, the child's medical diagnosis may be that she or he has Down syndrome, cerebral palsy, respiratory distress syndrome, a seizure disorder, or apnea. Educational diagnoses are more often stated as levels of performance or intensity of need. For example, the child may be described as developmentally delayed or as having a mild, moderate, or severe disability. Although early interventionists use categories of disability such as visual impairment, hearing impairment, or physical disability to describe those disorders, many prefer not to describe children as mentally retarded at such an early age. This reluctance is based on the limited range of repertoires for assessment in very young infants (Teti & Gibbs, 1990), limited predictability of later performance of at-risk or mildly delayed children based on early assessment (Dunst & Rheingrover, 1981), and concern that negative labels may become self-fulfilling prophecies (Hunt, 1976; Zelazo, 1979). The diagnostic assessment also determines a child's eligibility for early intervention programs and services. Part H of IDEA requires that eligibility assessments be conducted by a multidisciplinary team; however, preferred practice suggests that inter- or transdisciplinary teams, described in Chapters 4 and 6 of this book, are more appropriate for assessing young children.

After the child's eligibility for services has been determined, the third type of assessment begins. Descriptive, or curriculum-based, assessment is ongoing. Although it uses and builds upon information gathered in the diagnostic assessment, its purpose is to provide a more detailed description of the child's strengths and needs for day-to-day programming (Bagnato, Neisworth, & Munson, 1993). Staff and family members who work with the child on a daily basis collect the information and use it to refine instructional targets and strategies and improve the service delivery.

The fourth type of assessment is also mandated by Part H of IDEA. The IFSP must be reviewed at 6-month intervals and evaluated annually. These checkpoints provide opportunities for interventionists and staff members to assess the child's progress, review family outcomes, and examine the effectiveness of the strategies and approaches that are being used. This monitoring provides an opportunity to evaluate individual programs as well as gather information on the overall effects of the program on child and family outcomes.

Interactive, Family-Focused Approaches to Assessment

Historically, three approaches have been used to assess infants and young children. All of the approaches were based on models for older children and adults. Simeonsson (1986) described these approaches to assessment as psychometric, behavioral, and qualitative-developmental. The purpose of the psychometric approach is to compare the child to normal standards of development, intelligence, or achievement, and determine performance discrepancies. Comparisons are usually made in relation to chronological or mental age. Diagnostic decisions in which IQ is one of the determiners of eligibility for services typically rely on a psychometric approach.

The behavioral approach to assessment relies on examining those variables that govern behavior in various situations. This approach describes behaviors; documents their antecedents, consequences, and the context in which they occur; and suggests strategies for manipulating or changing variables to change responses. Negative behaviors such as hitting, kicking, and biting are often studied using this approach, but the approach need not be limited to the assessment of maladaptive behavior. Skills such as eating, smiling, grasping, and using language can all be assessed using a behavioral approach.

The third approach Simeonsson (1986) described is the qualitative-developmental approach. This approach attempts to determine the child's stage of functioning independent of age. Based on Piaget's theory of development and the changes in the quality of a child's interactions over time, this approach is often used in assessing young children. The qualitative-developmental approach enables the early interventionist to examine the child's skills as well as the child's approach to people and tasks, providing rich information for program development.

As theory, research, and practice with infants and young children have expanded in recent years and the emphasis in early intervention has shifted from the child to the child within the context of the family, so have the approaches to assessment. It has become increasingly clear that the models described in the previous paragraphs were far too narrow and limiting and that they often perpetuated the deficit model in viewing children and their families (Meisels & Provence, 1989). Likewise, these approaches were not consistent with the belief that a primary goal of assessment is to address the concerns of the family. As a result, a paradigm shift is occurring in the area of assessment of infants and young children. This shift is based on a commitment to family-focused assessment and intervention (Dunst, Trivette, & Deal, 1988; McGonigel, Kaufmann, & Johnson, 1991; StevensDominguez, Beam, & Thomas, 1989) and the belief that "The cornerstone of assessment should be the observation of the child in interaction with trusted caregivers and appreciation of the child's core functional capacities. Assessment involves multiple sources of information, organized and integrated in a landmark-based model of development" (Greenspan & Meisels, 1994, p. 8).

The reorientation toward assessment that focuses on multiple variables and the interplay of child, family, and environmental characteristics has been aided by another perspective sometimes referred to as judgment-based assessment (Neisworth & Bagnato, 1988). Judgment-based assessment attempts to capture, organize, and quantify the impressions of professionals and caregivers about the child and the environmental characteristics (Neisworth & Bagnato, 1988). Judgment-based assessment is an attempt to legitimize and use the rich body of knowledge that families and caregivers have about their own children or those for whom they are the primary adult. It also acknowledges the extensive body of knowledge that professionals have gained from their training and clinical practice. Rather than assuming that statistical validity and reliability are the only measures by which the value of information can be judged, judgment-based assessment assumes that observation, reports from a single individual, and perceptions contribute insight about a child and her or his interactions with the environment (Hayes, 1990).

This major change in the way that the assessment of young children is conceptualized and conducted has resulted in the widespread use of ecological approaches and play-based approaches to information gathering. Neisworth and Bagnato (1988) defined ecological assessment as "the examination and recording of the physical, social, and psychological features of a child's developmental context" (p. 39). This approach to assessment focuses on multiple aspects of the child as well as the interplay of child characteristics, caregiver characteristics, and the environment. Examining the multiple variables that influence growth and development gives interventionists and families alike a more comprehensive picture of children's strengths and needs in the context of their family. Such an approach assumes that interventions can be made in multiple aspects of the child, family, and environmental systems and does not assume that only child characteristics determine intervention strategies. Ecological assessments are conducted in children's natural environments—the settings where children spend their time, such as in their home, at a toddler center, in a hospital, or at a grandparent's house (Thurman & Widerstrom, 1990). In addition to assessing the child, the environments and interactions within them are also part of the assessment process, helping to ensure that sociocultural and language variables are considered in both the assessment and the recommendations for intervention.

Another approach to assessment that has gained widespread attention and use is play-based assessment. Although it has been an informal part of some assessors' repertoires for many years (e.g., Cohen & Spenciner, 1994; DuBose, 1981; Garwood, 1982), Linder's (1990) work has brought play-based assessment into the forefront of assessment strategies. Transdisciplinary play-based assessment is an interactive, flexible method of data gathering that relies on child, team, and family involvement in a play session designed to provide information about the child's patterns of interaction, developmental levels, and preferred ways of learning. Behaviors to observe in each area of development are carefully described and sequenced to provide a framework for observation during the play session and a structure for organizing the observations. The functional, interactive nature of play-based assessment is consistent with the paradigm shift in assessment.

The Assessment Team

Part H of IDEA mandates that a multidisciplinary team be involved in the child's assessment; however, inter- or transdisciplinary teams are preferred in early intervention and early childhood programs. The team is composed of the parents or other appropriate family members, caregivers, and professionals from a variety of disciplines. The team determines what is to be assessed and how the information will be gathered.

The families' and professionals' concerns about the child will determine the assessment questions, and many times the concerns and questions will be broad ranging. Because of this, professionals with expertise in a variety of areas may be needed to address the assessment questions. However, a primary consideration is to ensure that the child and family are not overwhelmed by a multitude of assessors. Transdisciplinary teams make this easier because one person can often gather information for another. Usually, two to three people should be adequate for gathering information. For example, a speech–language pathologist may not conduct an initial, "hands-on" assessment of the child, but may ask that the special educator audiotape or keep a log of all of the child's vocalizations while conducting a play-based assessment. If the child's needs are primarily related to motor development, a physical or occupational therapist and someone with knowledge about working with families may be the only ones involved in the assessment; or if an infant has just been released from a neonatal intensive care unit, a nurse and another staff member with expertise in working with families may review the hospital records and use them as the assessment for the IFSP.

Law and preferred practice dictate that assessments should be conducted by a team that includes the parents and professionals from a variety of disciplines; however, sensitivity to family desires and needs suggests that a parade of professionals may not be in the child's or family's best interests. Like all other decisions that must be made by early intervention professionals and families, the decision about who should conduct the assessment is one that must be individualized for each child and family.

A Family-Focused, Child Assessment Process

For an individual assessor or for a member of an assessment team, the process of conducting assessments comprises a series of steps. Although different authors use different words to describe those steps (Bailey et al., 1986; Greenspan & Meisels, 1994; Kjerland & Kovach, 1990; Simeonsson, 1986), there is little variation in what must be done to plan and implement an exemplary assessment. Conceptualizing entry into early intervention services as a flow of activities with a variety of entry points rather than a rigid system of identification referral, eligibility assessment, and so on, provides a more responsive system (Hurth et al., 1988). This promising practice enables families to be more fully involved in the assessment, to determine when they are ready to take the next steps, and to enter a more flexible service delivery system. Table 8.1 highlights the content of a five-stage, family-focused assessment process, and each stage is explained in the paragraphs that follow.

Table 8.1. Stages and Activities in the Assessment Process

Stages	Activities
Planning	Meet with family to determine their concerns, priorities, and resources.
	Clarify family's concerns, questions, priorities, and sociocultural preferences.
	Determine, with family, whether assessment is what is needed or requested.
	Review existing information with family.
	Determine roles and responsibilities of other team members including family if assessment is deemed appropriate.
	Arrange for sign or language interpreters/translators as needed.
	Develop assessment objectives with family.
	Develop assessment strategies with family.
	Obtain parental consent for assessment.
	Schedule assessment.
	Obtain assessment instruments/materials.
Conducting	Organize materials and environment.
	Meet with child and family; establish rapport; explain assessment processes and procedures.
	Observe/interview or alter plans as needed based on child's state, parental concerns and priorities, new information.
	Encourage parent/caregiver input, suggestions, questions throughout.
	Close session with debriefing of the assessment, clear specifications of next steps in the process, time lines, and contact person.
Interpreting	Review notes, protocols, videotapes, language samples, work samples collected in relation to referral questions and assessment objectives.
	If interim meetings are held to discuss the assessment, include family.
	Review anything learned not related to specific referral questions and objectives for importance and relevance to program planning.
	Incorporate all information into a jargon-free written report that can be shared in full with family.
	Review written report for clarity, accuracy, and relevance to program development.
Sharing	Provide written report to family and team members: The report should be provided before any meeting in which it is discussed and should be followed by one-to-one interpretation with family.
	Discuss findings with team members and parents/caregivers in relation to family's concerns and priorities related to child's and family's strengths and needs.
	Encourage parent/caregiver input and participation by facilitating their inclusion in the process.
	Determine appropriate services and placement in collaboration with family.
Following Up	Check on performance in setting, family satisfaction, staff perceptions/concerns.

Planning

The planning stage of the assessment process is often the most neglected; however, time spent with the family clarifying referral questions, determining assessment objectives and strategies, and reviewing existing information is time well spent. The planning stage enables the assessors, family, and child to get acquainted. Planning time can also be used to coordinate roles and responsibilities to ensure that information is gathered in multiple settings using a variety of approaches that respect the child's and family's needs and preferences.

Conducting

There are several compelling reasons to assess infants and toddlers in their own homes. Because these children often require more time than older children to adjust to unfamiliar situations and environments, home-based assessments minimize the amount of warm-up time for the child. Because preferred practice dictates that infants and toddlers be assessed with the parent(s) or primary caregiver(s) present, the home provides an ideal setting. Being in the home also enables team members to learn more about family priorities, concerns, and resources and to incorporate family members into the assessment process.

Conducting assessments of infants and toddlers often requires several sessions. According to studies by Parmelee, Werner, and Schulz (1964), children under 12 months are optimally alert for only 4 to 7 hours in a 24-hour period. Children who are at risk or who have identified disabilities may have even shorter periods of optimal alertness. Infant states, as described by Brazelton (1973), Prechtl (1974), and Simeonsson, Huntington, and Parse (1980), provide helpful information about the best times to assess infants. However, the bottom line has not changed: Never waken or assess a drowsy or sleeping baby!

Flexibility is the hallmark of an expert in assessing young children (Ulrey & Rogers, 1982). Very young children require the assessor's total involvement; she or he must be a sensitive and skilled observer of the child's cues and the parent–child interactions (Hanson & Krentz, 1986). Careful attention to the child's cues is particularly important with premature or small-for-gestational-age infants or children who usually have limited tolerance for interaction and social demands (Harrison, 1983; VandenBerg & Hanson, 1993). An infant who is stressed by the demands of the task or environment cannot perform optimally. Thus, the assessor has to be alert to changes in state, tone, and interactions. Cues as subtle as looking away or closing eyes may be the infant's signal that the demands are too great. If the subtle cues are overlooked, the infant's cues may become more dramatic and endangering to the child. Crying, fussing, projectile vomiting, and apnea are all ways that infants communicate that they have had enough. Careful observation that prevents assessors from stressing a fragile infant is critical not only to the assessment process but to the infant and family as well.

Although, as Greenspan and Meisels (1994) pointed out, "formal tests or tools should not be the cornerstone of the assessment of an infant or young child" (p. 8), sometimes a standardized test might be selected as one element of a comprehensive assessment. If a standardized test is used, the items must be administered in standardized ways. However, once the item has been presented and scored in the prescribed manner, assessors may modify the task to learn more about the conditions necessary for the child to respond. Knowing when and when not to alter items, having a repertoire of modifications available, and being able to switch order and task are all part of the flexibility necessary to assess young children with suspected or diagnosed developmental difficulties.

Assessments are always stressful to families, but assessors can use several strategies to minimize that stress. Involving the parents and/or caregivers, accepting and using their knowledge about the child, and explaining assessment items and procedures can eliminate some of the mystery. Being clear about the next steps can also reduce anxiety. Written information about who will contact the family next, when the team will discuss detailed assessment findings with them, when the program planning will take place, and whom they can call with questions provides something tangible for parents as they wait for the next step in what is often a painful process.

Interpreting

Assessment team members need time to individually and collectively review their assessment findings. The first level of review is checking the accuracy of interpretation or scoring, clarity of notes, and completeness of the information gathered. Where there are gaps, other members of the team or the families may be called upon for additional information. The next step is writing a report. Some teams elect to write a single, comprehensive report; other teams write several coordinated reports dealing with different aspects of the child's and/or family's needs. Because the purpose of the report is communication, it should be free of jargon, clear, concise, and useful to the family and others who will be planning the child's program (Rocco, 1994). Figure 8.1 provides a sample format for an integrated child and family assessment report.

Assessment reports are incorporated into records that follow the child and family for many years. Therefore, it is particularly important that interpretations of the data are based on observations and actual findings, with complete discussions of family corroboration or differing perceptions of the assessment or child's performance. Hunches about a family's functioning or the child's performance should not be written until they can be documented, and information that is not relevant to developing the IFSP should be eliminated or minimized.

Sharing

Sharing the findings of the assessment involves discussion among all of the team members including the family. Some programs have elected to have one or two team members meet with family members to discuss the information and help them develop questions prior to the IFSP meeting. Regardless of how this sharing of assessment findings is done, it is essential that families not be expected to hear the findings for the first time and then move directly into program and placement issues. Because few people can assimilate so much information at one time, particularly when it is emotion-laden, preferred practice dictates that a follow-up meeting be scheduled within a few days to respond to those concerns that have surfaced after families have had an opportunity to process assessment information.

Descriptions of assessment findings should be clear, stated in lay language, and relevant to the child's program needs. The emphasis

Family-Centered Child Assessment Report

Information for the Record

Child's Name: _____

Those Present, Relationships and Roles:

Name: _____ Relationship/Role: _____

Name: _____ Relationship/Role: _____

Name: _____ Relationship/Role: _____

Name: _____ Relationship/Role: _____

Assessment Dates: _____ Child's Birthdate: _____

Child's Age: _____ Adjusted Age: _____ (if appropriate) Gender: _____

Family Concerns, Priorities, and Resources

Include the following:

- What are the family's concerns about their child or the child in the context of their family?
- What do family members hope the assessment will answer or address?
- What are the family's highest priorities right now in relation to the child and their family?
- What are the family's strengths and resources that will assist in planning for and implementing early intervention programs and services?

Relevant Background Information

Include the following:

- Birth information that may be important in relation to the family's concerns and the child's development or health status.
- Child's current status, including health, as described by the family and/or mentioned in other assessment reports.
- Programs and services in which the child and family participate.

Assessment Objectives and Strategies

Include the following:

- Why is the assessment being conducted (initial assessment, 6-month review, addressing specific concerns raised by the family, monitoring progress, etc.)?
- What approaches and strategies were used to gather the information (family interview, play-based assessment, observation in day care setting, parent–child interaction, etc.)?
- How was each strategy employed, i.e., describe in detail how data gathering was done.

Observations and Findings

Include the following:

- Family observations and perspectives of the child's performance during the assessment process.
- Professional observations and perspectives of the child's performance during the assessment process.
- Results and/or interpretations of the findings from each of the assessment strategies used.

(continues)

Figure 8.1. Format for an integrated child and family assessment report.

Summary and Suggested Next Steps

Include the following:

- Summary of the assessment objectives, strategies, and findings, including family input.

- Suggestions for next steps in relation to the child's needs and the family's concerns, priorities, and resources. Recommendations may be included subject to review and revision at the Individualized Family Service Plan meeting.

Figure 8.1. continued

should be on the positive aspects of the child's functioning and the child–family interaction, with suggestions of ways to enhance development. Because learning that one's child is disabled or at risk for a disability is never good news, it is important that early interventionists deliver the news as honestly and sensitively as possible.

Written information about resources that may be helpful, including names and phone numbers of other parents who have children with similar problems, can also be shared at this time. Although families may not choose to use those resources immediately, they will have information about what is available when it is needed.

Following up

Assessment is the beginning, not the end, of early intervention. Although appropriate assessment should lead to appropriate programs and services, it is important to follow up to assure that the child is performing well in the setting and the family and staff members are satisfied with the program and the placement. This follow-up also provides an opportunity for family members to ask additional questions and for resources to be discussed.

Assessment Strategies and Techniques

Because no single source of information is adequate for making judgments about a child's or family's needs, assessors work with families to develop an assessment plan that incorporates a variety of strategies and techniques matched to the questions to be answered. Informal techniques may be commercially available or locally developed instruments, and they provide information about the child's performance in relation to the demands of the environment. Formal assessment instruments compare the child's performance with that of a norm group (McLoughlin & Lewis, 1994). Consequently, for diagnostic, eligibility, and some program evaluation decisions, formal instruments are included in the assessment; however, for planning day-to-day activities and determining family priorities and concerns, informal procedures are more appropriate.

All of the techniques described in this section need to be considered in the context of current thinking about the assessment of young children. Several key practices now define assessment, and these practices provide the framework for considering specific assessment strategies and techniques. The first key practice is the belief in *authentic assessment*—that is, assessment that is functional, uses tasks that are typical in the child's daily life experience, and is conducted in familiar surroundings with familiar people. Authentic assessment not only is being adopted in early childhood settings, but is part of a growing movement within the whole field of assessment (e.g., McLoughlin & Lewis, 1994) that emphasizes the social and treatment validity of what is being measured (Bagnato et al., 1993).

Arena assessment is a strategy for conducting assessments that is frequently used in early intervention programs. Foley (1990) described arena assessment as "the simultaneous assessment of the child by multiple professionals of differing disciplines" (p. 277). Because of the transdisciplinary nature of quality programs, roles are expanded and released in ways that enable professionals from a variety of disciplines to share assessment responsibilities. In this approach, one individual is selected to have primary, hands-on contact with the child during the administration of structured tasks. Other staff members observe, question, and interpret the child's responses. In some instances other assessors may move in and out of the arena and spend some time interacting directly with the child. For some infants or toddlers, the parent or primary caregiver may be the one who holds and handles the child. This approach allows the family's and professionals' perspectives to be shared, limits the stress placed on the child by reducing the number of adults who are handling him or her, and creates a dialogue during the assessment process that can produce insights into the child's behaviors and caregiver–child interactions.

As emphasized throughout this chapter, a single interaction with a child, the administration of a test, or one observation does not constitute an assessment. Assessments of young children require *multiple measures and strategies employed over time* (Meisels & Provence, 1989). A holistic view of development and the interplay of child, family, and environmental variables dictates the need for a variety of data gathering strategies and techniques.

A final key practice that is foundational to assessment of young children is assessment that is *culturally competent*. To be culturally competent, assessors and the practices that they use must understand, respect, and honor sociocultural and linguistic diversity and tailor their approaches to accommodate different life experiences, worldviews, and beliefs.

The diversity of children and families in early intervention programs continues to be far greater than the diversity represented among those who provide services, so it is incumbent upon interventionists to work individually and collectively to enhance their ability to work with families who differ from themselves in terms of culture, ethnicity, language, family structure, and economic status. For a more complete discussion of these issues, refer to Chapter 3 of this book and to Lynch and Hanson (1992). For additional references related to assessment and diversity, see Barrera (1994), Hanson, Lynch, and Wayman (1990), and Lynch and Hanson (in press).

The paragraphs that follow highlight some of the most common strategies and techniques used in the assessment of young children. No single technique should be used in isolation, and any technique should be selected for its value in addressing the concerns and priorities of families and interventionists alike. As discussed earlier, current thinking suggests that less formal measures may have greater utility than some of the traditional measures and measurement strategies that have been used in the past.

Observation

Systematic observations made by sensitive and knowledgeable observers are more powerful than any other technique in determining a child's strengths and needs; however, critical to good observation is knowing what to observe and recording the information for later reference. Usually, observations can be done unobtrusively while the child interacts with caregivers, plays, and is fed in the natural setting. Sometimes, situations may have to be contrived to provide the information about specific behaviors. Deciding what to observe determines whether the observation can be natural or contrived. Very young children are often observed to determine their level of interest in and response to the environment, their ability to solve problems and apply formerly learned solutions to new problems, communication skills, motor functioning, and social skills. Another major area of observation is in parent–child interaction; observation is the primary strategy used to examine infants' and parents' ability to communicate, cue, and interact with each other synchronously.

Several strategies are used to structure information gathered during observations. These include event recording, time sampling, checklists and rating scales, and coded observations. *Event recordings* may be continuous, narrative records of the child's behaviors and responses or a detailed recording of a single event. For example, behaviors of concern such as temper tantrums and seizures may occur infrequently, but it is important to capture the details of the antecedent conditions, the behaviors during the tantrum or seizure, and the consequent events in order to develop appropriate management and treatment plans.

Time sampling, often called interval recording, is used when behaviors occur more frequently and the observer is interested in their frequency of occurrence. For example, the interventionist may be concerned about a toddler who seldom plays with toys but seems to spend most of his time spinning objects. To develop a more complete picture of the child's behavior, the interventionist may decide to observe the child using a time sampling approach. Prior to the observation, the interventionist must develop a form for recording observations and select the times to observe. Forms are usually quite simple. They are typically divided into smaller intervals of 15 seconds to 1 minute, and behaviors may be preprinted on the form so that the observer can circle what is observed during each interval. Forms may also have blank spaces for the observer to write in the child's behavior at the end of each interval. The observation period may last from several minutes at different times throughout the day to an hour or more every day for several weeks.

Using a stopwatch or other timer, the observer records what the child is doing at the end of each interval. At the end of the observation period, the percentage of time that the child has spent in the behaviors of interest can be determined. For example, the percentage of time that the child spent whirling objects versus playing with a toy could be calculated. Time sampling can be used to determine the percentage of time that the child spends in a wide variety of behaviors, such as interacting with others, crying, or smiling at a caregiver during feeding.

Checklists and rating scales can be used to determine the presence or absence of a particular skill or behavior or to rate the quality of the behavior or setting. Checklists of developmental milestones can be used as children are observed at play to determine which skills they have mastered, which are emerging, and which remain to be learned. Rating scales can be used to evaluate the quality of the home or toddler program setting across many dimensions. Figure 8.2 provides an example of a brief rating scale that might be used to evaluate a home-based, infant day care setting.

Coded observations are often used to study multiple interactions or behaviors occurring within a specified period of time. In observations of this kind, the behaviors of interest are specified prior to the observation. The number and types of behaviors can range from very few, simple behaviors to many complex interactional patterns. For example, a mother and infant may be observed in a quiet play time. In this situation the observer may be interested in a wide range of complex interactional patterns such as face-to-face engagement between mother and child, child-initiated vocalizations and maternal response, mother-initiated vocalizations and infant response, and interactional tempo. All of these behaviors would be operationally defined, and in situations of this level of complexity, the session would typically be videotaped and coded later by individuals trained in the coding system. When fewer or less complex

Brief Rating Scale of a Home-Based, Infant Child Care Setting

Visit a home-based, infant child care setting when children are present. Observe the environment and the interactions between caregivers and children, between caregivers and parents, and between caregivers if there is more than one. After your observation, use this form to record your impressions of the setting. Circle the number that most closely corresponds to your impressions.

Factor	Strongly Disagree	Disagree	Agree	Strongly Agree
Quality of Caregiving				
1. Children are encouraged to explore and play.	1	2	3	4
2. Caregivers are actively involved with children.	1	2	3	4
3. Human comfort is provided.	1	2	3	4
4. Interactions with children are sensitive and tailored to individual.	1	2	3	4
5. Atmosphere is secure, warm, and nurturing.	1	2	3	4
Staff and Staff Interactions				
6. Staff have training or supervised experience in working with young children.	1	2	3	4
7. Staff work well together.	1	2	3	4
8. Staff respect and work well with parents.	1	2	3	4
9. Staff are bonded/licensed or hold other required credentials.	1	2	3	4
10. Staff provide information about the child's day when parents arrive for pickup.	1	2	3	4
11. Number of staff is adequate for number of children being cared for.	1	2	3	4
Safety				
12. Plugs and outlets are covered.	1	2	3	4
13. No low, pointed corners or objects.	1	2	3	4
14. No objects to be pulled down.	1	2	3	4
15. Pools and other attractive hazards are gated off.	1	2	3	4
16. Cupboard doors are childproofed.	1	2	3	4
17. Stairs are gated off.	1	2	3	4
18. Pets are friendly and under control.	1	2	3	4
Health and Sanitation				
19. Diapering area is clean and disinfected between changes.	1	2	3	4
20. Food is properly stored.	1	2	3	4
21. Children are kept clean except for normal mess of playing.	1	2	3	4
22. Equipment and toys are clean and disinfected.	1	2	3	4
23. Children who are ill are not served or are cared for in a separate area.	1	2	3	4
24. General environment is well scrubbed.	1	2	3	4
25. Caregivers observe universal health precautions.	1	2	3	4
Materials, Equipment, and Space				
26. Adequate space for naps.	1	2	3	4
27. Adequate space for indoor and outdoor play.	1	2	3	4
28. Age-appropriate toys are available.	1	2	3	4
29. Adequate number of toys for number of children.	1	2	3	4
Overall				
30. As a parent, I would feel comfortable having my child in this setting.	1	2	3	4

Figure 8.2. Sample rating scale.

interactions or behaviors are being studied, coding can be done as the behaviors occur. For example, the interactions between children who are disabled and those who are not disabled in an inclusive toddler program might be coded during a free play period.

Key to all observational techniques is a clear set of definitions of what is being observed. If fussiness is to be observed, what constitutes fussiness must be specified. What does fussiness look like? How does the observer know when it is occurring? For example, is fussiness whining, turning away, crying, hitting, throwing things, refusing attempts to comfort, or some combination of all of these? Prior to the observation these categories and their definitions must be developed, and all who use the observational instrument must be trained and skilled in its use.

Interviews

A major part of every assessment of a young child is an interview with the child's parents and/or primary caregivers. An interview of this nature can be viewed as a structured conversation in which those closest to the child have an opportunity to share information and the interviewer has a chance to benefit from the family's knowledge and experience with the child. Interviews about young children typically include questions related to pregnancy and birth, medical and health history, developmental history, current status, and the family's concerns and priorities (Fallen & Umansky, 1985; Lerner, Mardell-Czudnowski, & Goldenberg, 1987).

With the more recent emphasis on ecological assessment, interviews have begun to examine the relationship of children to their environment. Assessors may want to use ecological inventories to collect information about the infant or toddler in relation to the environment and the family's concerns and priorities.

How parents are treated in initial contacts with professionals who will be working with their child shapes their current and future attitudes and behaviors (Parker & Zuckerman, 1990). Thus, planning and conducting the interview thoughtfully and sensitively is an important investment. Interviews should allow time for rapport building or "warming-up" for both the interviewer and the interviewee (Molyneaux & Lane, 1982). The purpose of the interview should be reviewed and an overview of the kinds of questions provided. The interviewer should inform those being interviewed that notes will be taken to assist recall; this often relieves the interviewee's anxiety about what is being written down. Some interviewers suggest that notes always be kept visible to the interviewee and that they be shared at the close of the interview as a sort of summary.

Active listening is one of the keys to success in interviewing. Characteristics of active listening include being attentive to the speaker; communicating a genuine desire to understand the speaker and her or his point of view; willingness to accept all information without being judgmental; and checking understanding by repeating, rephrasing, and questioning (Molyneaux & Lane, 1982). Often the content of what is being said is less important than the feelings that are being shared. Although the early interventionist's role is not one of therapist or counselor, it is appropriate to acknowledge the feelings that are being communicated. For example, if a family member appears to be near tears, the interviewer may say, "It must be very difficult to talk about this. Do you want to go on, or shall we move to something else?" Or, if a family member is angry, the interviewer might say, "It seems there are a lot of things about that situation that still make you angry."

There are times in interviews when silence says far more than words. A person often uses silence to process the question, gather and organize thoughts, or decide whether to respond to a question in a particularly sensitive area (Molyneaux & Lane, 1982). Silence is not a void to be filled; rather, it is a space to be respected and honored.

During the body of the interview, the purpose is usually to gather and give information, and it is the interviewer's job to guide all participants through the process. When an interview seems to be drifting away from its intended purpose, the interviewer should consider three questions: Is it drifting because I am not being clear? Is it drifting because the interviewee cannot or does not want to respond to the questions? Or is it drifting from the original purpose because more important issues have arisen? If either of the first two is true, it is important to determine what the problem is and rectify that. If the third is true, that something more important has come up, then it is probably most fruitful to set aside the original objectives and pursue the issue(s) that the family has identified as more important.

Throughout the interview family members should be encouraged to talk, discuss, question, and disagree; in the closing minutes of the interview, the interviewer may want to again solicit their input. This is also the time to summarize what has been said, clarify responses, and share the next steps in the assessment process. Before the interviewer leaves, family members should have a telephone number where the interviewer can be reached and a clear understanding of what will happen next along with the time lines.

Interviewing is a skill and, like all other skills, it takes practice to become good at it. Interviews that result in more knowledge about the child and family that will help

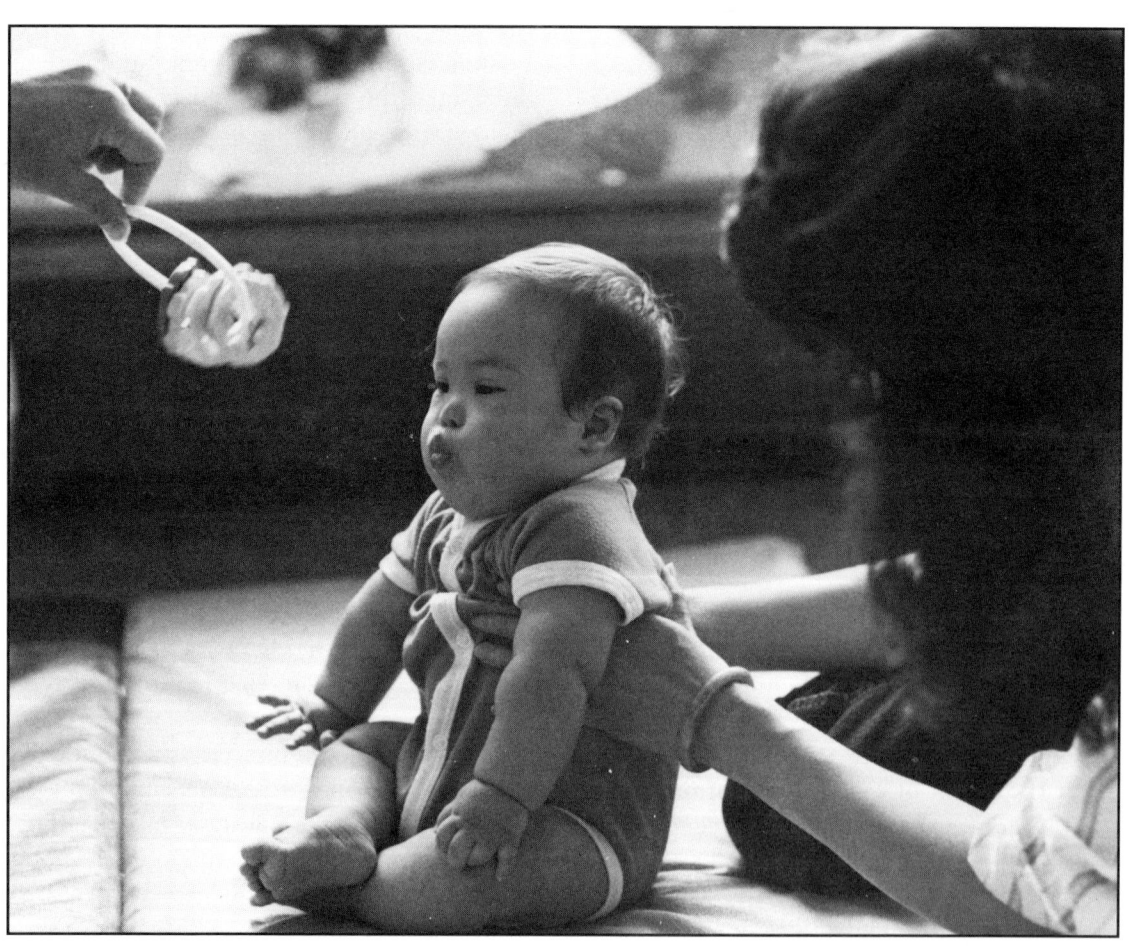

build an appropriate plan are very rewarding both for the family and the interventionist. Table 8.2 provides some practical suggestions for novice interviewers.

Tests

Four different types of tests are used most often in early intervention programs: standardized or norm referenced, criterion referenced, curriculum based, and task analyses. *Standardized* tests are typically administered as one measure of the child's eligibility for services, because they compare an individual's performance with that of a norm group. They must be administered following very specific directions presented in the test manual, and the conditions of the test should approximate the standardization conditions as closely as possible (McLoughlin & Lewis, 1994). If the conditions are changed (i.e., materials substituted, items altered, or order of presentation changed), the norms cannot be used for comparison. Those administering standardized tests should have training and supervised experience in measurement, the particular test being used, and the assessment of young children.

Table 8.2. Survival Guide for Interviewers

1. Write down the address, directions, and a phone number where you can reach or leave a message for the family that you are interviewing. It's easy to get lost when you're busy and nervous.

2. There are different cultural rules related to being in someone's home. Don't be surprised if the father or an elder does all the talking in some situations or if a male interventionist cannot visit the home unless the husband is present. In some cultures, it is important to tell the questioner what he or she wants to hear, so don't be surprised if what you see and what you hear don't match.

3. If you are conducting the interview through an interpreter, allow time to discuss the interview questions with the interpreter first. Give the family and interpreter time to get acquainted and comfortable with one another, and be sure that you address your questions and comments to the family, not the interpreter.

4. Dress professionally yet in keeping with the norms of the family and community.

5. If you are taking toys or materials into the home, take something that can remain (picture book, crayons, animal crackers, etc.), remembering that there may be several brothers and sisters who will be very interested in what you are doing and what you have brought.

6. Don't be afraid to admit it if you're nervous. Parents always recognize bluffing.

7. It's not okay to tell your own stories or say that you know just how they feel, but it is okay to laugh and cry with someone who is sharing joy or pain.

8. Don't feel that you have to have answers to all of the family's concerns or questions. For some you may be able to find answers; for others you may be able to help them find answers; and for some there never will be an answer.

9. If you do not feel safe in a neighborhood, take someone with you for the interview or arrange to conduct it outside the home.

10. Remember the Golden Rule as you embark on any interview: Interview others as you would like to be interviewed.

Criterion-referenced tests are designed around specific criteria of performance. In this type of test, the required performance is specified and the child's performance is measured against it. For example, in assessing the child's verbal imitation skills, the criterion for successful performance might be saying "ba ba ba" or "ma ma ma" in response to an adult's saying those sounds three out of four times. Many developmental tests are criterion referenced, with expected skills listed in order of difficulty. Children are observed or assessed to determine whether they have acquired those skills. Scoring systems often include ways to denote emerging skills and skills for which there has been no opportunity to practice in addition to noting passes and failures. Unlike norm-referenced tests, which compare the child's performance with that of others, criterion-referenced tests compare the child's performance with the criterion or standard.

Curriculum-based assessments are a variation on criterion-referenced tests. These assessments use the curricular objectives as the standard for performance. Because they assure that assessment and programming are linked, curriculum-based assessments are the most frequently used in early intervention programs. These instruments are tied directly to the overall skills and knowledge that constitute the curriculum, thus making assessment relevant to curriculum (Bagnato et al., 1993).

Task analysis is a procedure used in assessment and in instruction. A task analysis is a sequentially ordered list of steps required to perform a given task or skill (Hanson, 1987). Once a task has been broken into small steps, the child can be observed or assessed to determine whether he or she can perform each step. When task analysis is used for instruction, a single step is taught until the child gains mastery on it; then the next step is added, taught, and practiced. This progression, or chaining, allows the child to learn more quickly and receive reinforcement for mastery of each of the smaller steps. Table 8.3 depicts a typical task analysis for eating a cracker independently. As an assessment procedure, task analysis provides a way to target very specific behaviors that need to be taught and, by its very nature, it is intrinsically related to the curriculum.

As these descriptions indicate, testing is only one part of assessment, and there is considerable variety in types of tests. Table 8.4 provides a list of selected assessment instruments frequently used in early intervention programs. Although the list is not exhaustive, it provides a good sampling of standardized, criterion-referenced, and curriculum-based assessment instruments. For a more comprehensive review, see Cohen and Spenciner (1994).

Characteristics of good measuring instruments

Although standardized test instruments and many criterion-referenced tests should have gone through a rigorous process of development, field testing, and refinement, this is not always the case. It is up to the assessor to determine whether the test is a "good" test. The "goodness" of a test is determined by several criteria, with its *validity* and *reliability* being paramount. A test is valid only for the purpose for which it is written. A test designed to measure receptive vocabulary is not valid for determining a child's intelligence. A test designed to record interactions between an infant and a parent is not valid for assessing the child's social skills. Thus, any standardized test selected for use in an early intervention program must be used for the purpose for which it was created.

Other types of validity to consider when selecting a standardized test include content, concurrent, predictive, construct, and discriminate. *Content validity* refers to the instrument's scope, sequence, and relationship to the entire set of skills in an area. For example, a test of adaptive skills that included only dressing and toileting would not have

Table 8.3. Task Analysis

Task: Eating cracker independently from tray

1. Child visually notices cracker.
2. Child extends arm and reaches for cracker.
3. Child opens hand and positions it over cracker.
4. Child lowers fingers/hand over cracker until hand touches cracker.
5. Child uses palm or fingers to secure/grasp cracker.
6. Child maintains grasp and lifts cracker toward mouth, rotating the palm of the hand toward the mouth while lifting.
7. Child opens mouth.
8. Child puts cracker in mouth (whole or part).
9. Child closes mouth around cracker and bites or gums cracker.
10. Child lowers hand from mouth.
11. Child chews cracker.
12. Child swallows cracker.

good content validity because the area of adaptive or self-help includes many additional areas, such as bathing, eating, and oral hygiene. Likewise, a test that purports to assess cognitive skills must have a wider range of content than simply pointing to pictures.

Concurrent validity is determined by comparing one test with another that has established validity. If the two tests are highly correlated—that is, a child earns very similar scores on both tests—the test is said to have good concurrent validity. This measure of validity is used when new tests are created. New instruments are compared and correlated with older, established tests.

Predictive validity refers to the success with which the instrument predicts future performance. For example, tests that are used to determine whether a child is cognitively delayed need to be accurate predictors, because such information has a major impact on the lives of the child and family and influences others' attitudes and behaviors. Infant tests are notoriously poor predictors of later intelligence in all but the most severely impaired because of the limited range of skills that can be tested and the instability and discontinuity in development (Dunst & Rheingrover, 1981). This is particularly true of infants and toddlers who are at risk. Because little is yet known about the later performance of infants born under 1,500 grams, those who are technology dependent, and those who are born prenatally exposed to drugs, all test results should be viewed with extreme caution.

Construct validity relates to the theory or construct on which the test is based. For example, an instrument based on Piaget's theory of cognitive development would be quite different from one that views cognition as simply a compilation of skills. Early intervention programs may want to select instruments that are compatible with the model and theories upon which their program is based.

Discriminate validity is a measure of the independence of each of the subtests or subscales of an assessment instrument. In other words, is the language subscale measuring

Table 8.4. Selected Instruments for Assessing Infants and Toddlers

Instrument Name and Publisher	Author(s)	Age Range	Purpose/Skills	Examiner
Neonatal Assessments				
Assessment of Preterm Infant Behavior Plenum Press	H. Als, B. M. Lester, E. C. Tronick, & T. B. Brazelton	Preterm and high-risk newborns	Extension of *The Neonatal Behavioral Assessment Scale* to address issues related to premature and high-risk infants.	Professional trained in the instrument
The Neonatal Behavioral Assessment Scale–Second Edition J. B. Lippincott	T. B. Brazelton	Birth–1 mo.	Observational scale that assesses newborn reflexes, motor responses, and patterns of interaction.	Professional trained in instrument
Screening and Diagnostic Assessments				
Battelle Developmental Inventory Screening Test Riverside Publishing Co.	J. Newborg, J. R. Stock, L. Wnek, J. Guidubaldi, & J. Svinicki	Birth–8.5 years	Screening instrument that assesses personal-social, adaptive, motor, communication, and cognitive performance.	Professional trained in the instrument
Denver II Denver Developmental Materials	W. Frankenburg & J. Dodds	Birth–6 yrs.	Screening instrument that provides gross assessment of personal-social, fine motor, adaptive, language, and gross motor skills.	Professional or trained paraprofessional who has passed a proficiency test
Developmental Activities Screening Inventory–II PRO-ED	R. R. Fewell & M. B. Langley	1 mo.–5 yrs.	Assesses cognitive, academic, perceptual motor, and basic skills. Can be modified for children with vision or hearing impairments.	Professional
Norm-Referenced Developmental Assessments				
Battelle Developmental Inventory Riverside Publishing Co.	J. Newborg, J. Stock, L. Wnek, J. Guidubaldi, & J. Svinicki	Birth–8 yrs.	Developmental status in personal-social, motor, adaptive, communication, and cognitive domains.	Professional
Bayley Scales of Infant Development II Psychological Corp.	N. Bayley	1–42 mos.	Provides clinical picture of child's developmental status using three scales: Mental, Motor, and Behavior.	Psychologist or professional trained in instrument
Kaufman Assessment Battery for Children American Guidance Service		2.5 yrs.–12.5 yrs.	Measures achievement and intelligence.	Professional

(*continues*)

Table 8.4. *Continued*

Instrument Name and Publisher	Author(s)	Age Range	Purpose/Skills	Examiner
Stanford–Binet Intelligence Scale (4th ed.) Riverside Publishing Co.	R. L. Thorndike, E. P. Hagen, & J. M. Sattler	2 yrs.–Adult	Measure of intelligence.	Psychologist
Vineland Adaptive Behavior Scales American Guidance Service	S. S. Sparrow, D. A. Balla, & D. V. Cicchetti	Birth–18+ yrs.	Assesses adaptive behavior skills in communication, daily living, socialization, play and leisure, and coping.	Professional
Comprehensive Developmental and Skill Assessments for Program Planning				
Assessment, Evaluation, and Programming System for Infants and Children Paul H. Brookes	D. Bricker	Birth–3 yrs.	Assesses performance in fine motor, gross motor, adaptive, cognitive, social-communication, and social areas of development with strong link to programming.	Professional trained in the instrument and working directly with the child
Brigance Diagnostic Inventory of Early Development Curriculum Associates	A. H. Brigance	Birth–7 yrs.	Assesses child's development in motor, self-help, speech and language domains.	Professional
Callier-Azusa Scale: G Form Callier Center for Communication Disorders	R. Stillman (Ed.)	Items begin under 1 yr.	Assesses development in children who are deaf-blind and/or multiply handicapped.	Professional
Carolina Curriculum for Infants and Toddlers with Special Needs Paul H. Brookes	N. M. Johnson-Martin, K. G. Jens, S. M. Attermeir, & B. J. Hacker	Birth–24 mos.	Assesses cognitive, adaptive, communication, social, fine motor, and gross motor skills.	Professional trained in the instrument and familiar with the child
Developmental Programming for Infants and Young Children (Vols. 1–3) University of Michigan Press	D. S. Schaefer & M. S. Moersch (Eds.)	Birth–3 yrs.	Developmental status in cognitive, fine motor/perceptual, gross motor, self-help, cognition, language, and personal-social domains.	Professionals on an interdisciplinary team
Hawaii Early Learning Profile (HELP) VORT Corp.	S. Furuno, K. O'Reilly, C. Hosaka, T. Inatsuka, P. Allman, & B. Zeisloft	Birth–3 yrs.	Developmental status in all developmental areas.	Professionals on interdisciplinary team

(*continues*)

Table 8.4. *Continued*

Instrument Name and Publisher	Author(s)	Age Range	Purpose/Skills	Examiner
Learning Accomplishment Profile (LAP) and Infant LAP (LAP-I) Kaplan Press	A. Sanford, E. M. Glover, & A. Preminger	Birth–6 yrs.	Developmental status in six areas: fine and gross motor, social, self-help, language, and cognition.	Professional or trained paraprofessional
Single Domain Assessments				
Preschool Language Scale–3 Psychological Corp.	I. L. Zimmerman, V. G. Steiner, & R. E. Pond	Birth–6 yrs. 11 mos.	Assesses receptive and expressive language.	Professional
Receptive-Expressive Emergent Language Test–2 (REEL–2) PRO-ED	K. R. Bzoch & R. League	1 mo.–36 mos.	Assesses language development.	Professional
Uzgiris–Hunt Scales of Infant Psychological Development University of Illinois	I. Uzgiris & J. Hunt with Manual by C. Dunst	2 wks.–2 yrs.	Assesses cognitive development during sensorimotor period.	Professional

different skills than the cognitive subscale? In some areas, such as language and cognition, there is often overlap, but one would expect that each should be tapping into some different aspects of the child's functioning.

An instrument's reliability, which can be thought of as its dependability or consistency, is also important when one is selecting a test. Types of reliability include interrater, test–retest, and equivalent forms. *Interrater reliability* refers to the ability of different raters to get the same results. For example, if a child's motor skills are being assessed, the directions for assessing and the criteria for passing and failing items should be clear enough that all of the assessors get the same results for the child. In addition to being an important consideration in standardized tests, interrater reliability is equally important in locally developed instruments. Whenever a program develops or uses such an instrument, all staff members who will use it should be trained so that all are assessing the same behaviors and using the same criteria.

Test–retest reliability describes the test's stability over time. Although one would expect changes over time in developmental and achievement tests, scores should show gradual progression rather than wide variations from one assessment to the next. When results do fluctuate dramatically without apparent reason, it may be because the test is not reliably measuring what it purports to measure.

Equivalent forms reliability is relevant only when the test has more than one form. When tests are published in several forms, it is important that they yield nearly identical results. If one form is more difficult than another, changing forms would not provide comparable or reliable results.

Validity and reliability are critical concerns when selecting or developing tests. Additional issues, such as the size of the standardization sample; its characteristics in terms of age, gender, primary language, and ethnicity; and the demands of test items, should also be considered. A test that has been normed on very few children or one with a standardization sample that is not representative of the age, gender, primary language, and ethnicity of the children served by the early intervention program should be regarded with skepticism.

Test Use and Abuse

Many issues have been raised about the use of standardized tests with all children, but particular concerns have emerged about their use with very young children who are disabled or at risk for disabilities. Although tests can provide information that helps all involved understand the child more completely, they can also be used inappropriately or in ways that could be damaging to the child. Thus, in any assessment, whether it is formal or informal, standardized or criterion referenced, and locally developed or commercially available, the primary question is whether what can be learned through assessment outweighs any potential harm.

Summary

Assessments of young children are conducted to learn more about their strengths and needs. Information gathered in the assessment process should be directly related to the family's concerns and priorities and the child's intervention program. A variety of approaches can be used to collect information from commercially available, standardized instruments to locally developed rating scales or checklists. The instruments or strategies selected should be matched to the information needed, as well as to the child's age, abilities, and disabilities.

Tests are only as good as their developers and users. Instruments' validity and reliability, stated purpose, and other psychometric properties should be reviewed. Attractive packaging does not assure high quality, so assessors must carefully review test instruments and strategies that they are considering to determine their appropriateness. This is especially true when the child and family do not share the same culture and language as the assessors. Because assessors can also influence a child's performance, anyone doing assessment should be trained and experienced in working with typically and atypically developing young children as well as in the technical aspects of assessment.

Preferably assessments are conducted by inter- or transdisciplinary teams, and the team composition is determined by the child's needs and the family's concerns and priorities. Although the assessment team in any program may include many staff members, the team assigned to any child and family should be limited in number, and family members should be integral members of the team. Often two or three team members can gather the information needed for the initial assessment, and other team members can serve as consultants to them. Limiting the numbers of new people with whom the family and young child must interact initially reduces intrusiveness and stress.

The assessment process includes several steps. Choosing assessment strategies and instruments, determining which team member will collect various pieces of information, and making arrangements for the assessment are all part of the planning process. Conducting the assessment and interpreting the findings follow. After the information from each of the assessments has been summarized and synthesized, families and staff members work together to develop the IFSP. This step leads to program planning and placement. The final step is follow-up—a time to check on programming and placement decisions as well as the family's satisfaction with the program.

Assessing all children is fraught with controversy. Because young children grow and change so rapidly, many parents and professionals are concerned that early assessment could lead to misdiagnosis and labeling that would limit the child's opportunities. Yet, assessment that leads to appropriate intervention improves the child's chances to function optimally. Perhaps the best rule is to view assessment findings as guidelines for developing the next steps in working with the child instead of predictions of or answers about the child's future.

Identifying Family Concerns, Priorities, and Resources

The previous sections focused on assessing children. Until recently that was the only assessment conducted in many early intervention programs. However, with the passage of Part H, P.L. 99-457, now incorporated into IDEA, early intervention programs became responsible for assessing, with the family's concurrence, family concerns and priorities as well as the child's strengths and needs. For many professionals, assessing family concerns and priorities is a new role. Most early interventionists were originally trained to be child centered rather than family centered, and most viewed the child, rather than the family, as their client. Although university training programs throughout the country have been shifting to a family-centered approach, the numbers of people trained in this model do not approach the numbers needed for new and growing early intervention programs. Likewise, many of the existing early intervention programs are staffed by professionals who were trained in programs that were exclusively child oriented (Bailey et al., 1986). Thus, staff development and inservice education are needed for even the most experienced professionals. The final portion of this chapter presents the rationale for identifying family concerns, priorities, and resources; approaches that can be utilized; and related concerns. It provides techniques and strategies that have been used successfully.

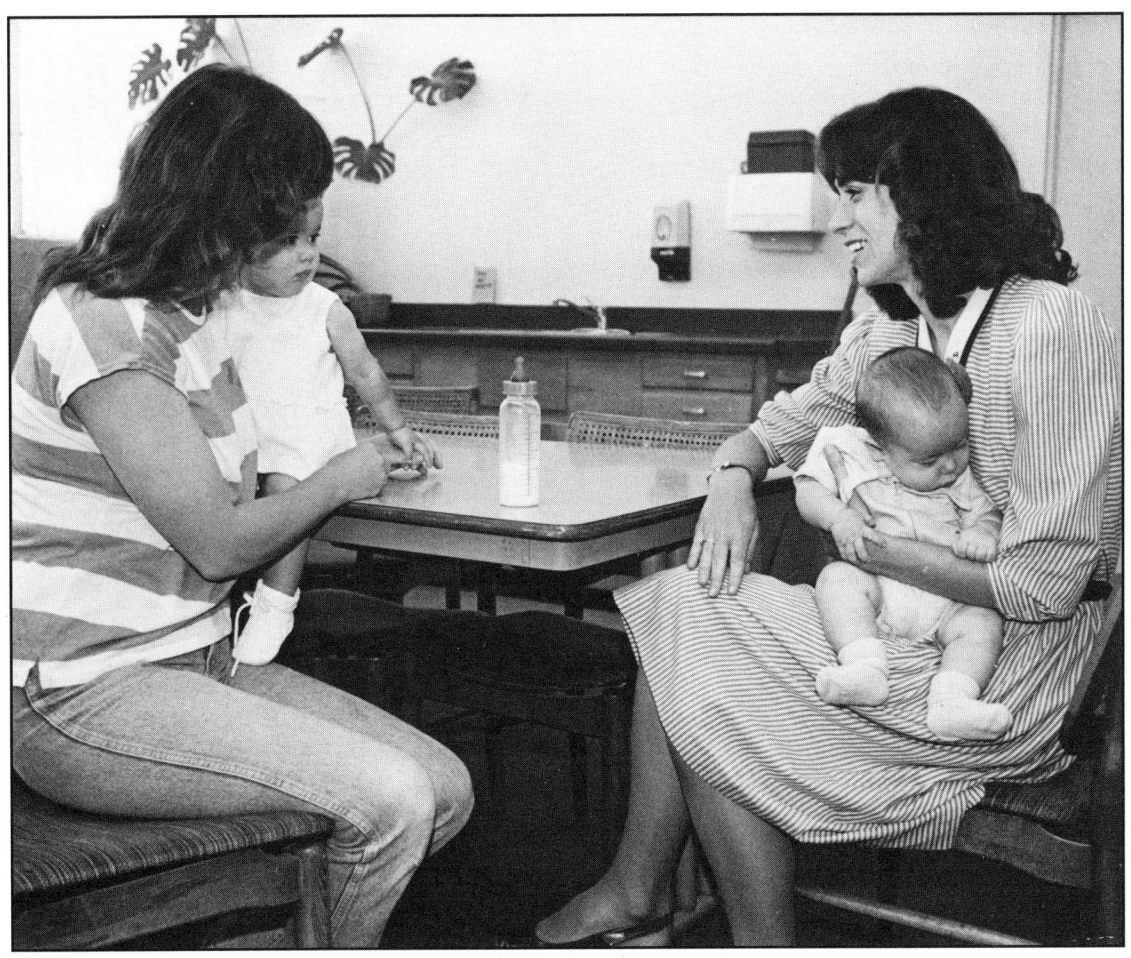

Rationale for Identifying Family Concerns, Priorities, and Resources

One of the first questions raised is why an early intervention program would be identifying the family's concerns, priorities, and resources? Early interventionists have been taught that it is the child's special needs that are of concern and that the child, not the family, is the client. In fact, some of the first model demonstration projects sponsored by the federally funded Handicapped Children's Early Education Program did focus on families (Trohanis, Cox, & Meyer, 1982). It was only during the period from 1975 to 1985 when the focus shifted away from families and into developing interdisciplinary teams, establishing curricula, creating assessment tools, and writing IEPs that the child and family came to be viewed separately (Vincent, 1988).

Part H mandates that an IFSP be developed for each infant, toddler, and his or her family (see Appendix A). This aspect of the legislation came about because family members advocated for the importance of their role in decision making about their child's life and for the concerns of the family as a whole instead of the needs of only one member. At the same time, professionals began to apply the family systems literature to early intervention. This combination of forces resulted in a mandate to develop programs that are responsive to both child needs and family concerns and priorities.

Family systems theory has grown out of the disciplines of sociology and psychology and the work of researchers, psychologists, social workers, and counselors who have worked with families and individual family members (e.g., Carter & McGoldrick, 1980; Kantor & Lehr, 1975; Lee, 1982; McCubbin et al., 1980; Minuchin, 1974; Olson et al., 1983). Key to understanding this theory is the recognition that each family is a system, and all parts of the system are interrelated. As a consequence of these interrelationships, anything that affects one family member affects all family members. Imagine dropping a stone into a small puddle of water; regardless of where the stone is dropped, it creates ripples that affect each droplet of water in the pond. The same can be said of families; anything that happens to one family member has an effect on all other family members. For example, a couple's new baby changes the way in which they live and relate. Neither partner now has the exclusive attention of the other; schedules change to accommodate the baby's routines; and financial changes may occur because of the temporary or long-term loss of one partner's income. Likewise, the illness of a grandparent has an impact on the entire family. Time taken to care for the grandparent may take time away from other family members, may reduce the time available for renewing and replenishing the caregivers' energy, and may cause serious financial adjustments. Many times the roles of family members change in response to the changing needs. Brothers and sisters may take on additional responsibilities for child care and household maintenance, and grandparents in poor health may be parented by their own child.

Having a child with a disability has an impact on every family member. The disability creates ripples that touch the entire family system and often spread beyond it to friends and the community (Turnbull et al., 1993; Turnbull & Turnbull, 1990). Because individuals with disabilities most often remain in their own homes and the family is the most involved with the child over the longest period of time, it is inherently sensible to focus interventions on the concerns and priorities of the entire family. Thus, early interventionists must find ways to assess families' concerns, priorities, and resources and determine how they want to be served.

Approaches to Identifying Family Concerns, Priorities, and Resources

Identifying the family's concerns, priorities, and resources in early intervention programs is still new. A variety of approaches are being used, but no single approach has become the standard for the field. Although professional ethics and procedures related to helping families articulate their concerns and priorities probably do need to be standardized, the techniques and strategies used need to be diverse, flexible, and individualized to fit the wide range of families served in early intervention programs.

Bailey et al. (1986) suggested specific goals related to developing, implementing, and monitoring family-focused early intervention programs. The first goal is to assist the family to cope with those needs that are directly related to parenting and caring for their child with disabilities. The second goal is to help families understand their child's development as an individual and as a member of the family. The third is to promote positive parent–child interaction, and the fourth is to maintain and strengthen the family's dignity through respect, responsiveness, and a process of mutual goal setting.

As with child assessment, the strategies and techniques selected to identify the family's concerns, priorities, and resources should be matched to the information required. Therefore, to meet the first goal outlined by Bailey et al. (1986), information about the family's skill needs as well as about the family's personal, social, and/or emotional concerns related to the child who is at risk or disabled might be collected. This particular area encompasses a wide range of possible skills, ranging from needing to know how to catheterize the child, to managing behavior, to preparing a specialized formula. The range of a family's personal, social, and emotional needs could be equally wide reaching, varying from questions about how to tell the grandparents about the child to reconciling the birth of a child with a disability with their own self- and family images.

The second goal is to help families understand the child's growth and development as an individual and as a member of the family. Gathering information in this area may focus on informational as well as personal support needs. Families may want basic information about child development, or they may want information about differences in developmental patterns in infants who are blind or deaf. All or some family members may also request support to examine the child's place within the family.

The third goal relates to promoting positive parent–child interactions. Information gathering in this area might focus on the quality and quantity of interactions between the young child and the parents and can range from parents' expressed concerns about interactions with the child to observations by professionals trained in this area.

The fourth goal describes the process that should be used rather than the information to be collected. This goal simply reinforces the need to be sensitive, responsive, and collaborative in all interactions with families. As found by Summers et al. (1990) in a study that included 102 family members, families' number one request was for professionals to "be supportive of families experiencing a wide range of emotions, to be accepting, and nonjudgmental" (p. 85).

Bailey et al. (1986) suggested that this model provides a framework that can be used to determine what kinds of information should be included as a part of the identification of family concerns. Although many areas can be assessed, Bailey et al. (1986) recommended that information be collected in three areas: (a) child variables that affect family functioning; (b) the family's needs for information, support, or specific training; and (c) parent–child interaction. The families themselves must determine whether they want to participate in this type of assessment, and families and professionals in partnership determine the content, range, and depth of the information that will be gathered.

Assessor Characteristics, Skills, and Attitudes

The approach a program selects to identify family concerns, priorities, and resources will depend to a great extent on the program's theoretical base, the training and experience of professional staff, and the characteristics of the children and families being served. Just as assessment strategies must be matched to the individual and the information needed, so too must the approach be matched to those who will be doing the assessment. At this time few early intervention programs have staff members who are clinically trained at the post-master's or doctoral level in family assessment and intervention. Consequently, certain approaches to data gathering are automatically ruled out. In-depth interviews that deal with all aspects of the family's life, instruments that require clinical interpretation, and quasi-therapeutic approaches have been designed to be used only by those who have had the prerequisite training. Even if personnel were available, clinical interviewing and in-depth analysis of family functioning do not reflect the intent of the legislation. The purpose of identifying family strengths, concerns, priorities, and resources is to empower and support families surrounding issues related to raising a child with a disability, not to treat family members as clinical entities.

Of equal importance when considering how to gather information about families' concerns, priorities, and resources is the issue of diversity. When families agree to participate in identifying their concerns and priorities, the ways in which information will be gathered must be tailored to their preferences. Given the considerable diversity of families who participate in early intervention programs, interventionists need to have a variety of methods and procedures that they can use. The family's cultural and ethnic background, educational level, socioeconomic status, familiarity with human services programs, and past experiences with professionals will all affect the strategies selected. (For a more complete discussion of issues associated with family diversity, see Chapter 3.)

What then are the skills that are needed to help families identify their concerns, priorities, and resources? Perhaps the most important skill is being a *good listener*. In books, articles, speeches, and individual contacts, parents report that they want professionals to *listen* to them. Simons (1987) reported that "not being treated like an individual—not being listened to—is parents' greatest complaint about professionals" (p. 47). The ability to listen actively is one of the critical skills that assessors need.

In addition to listening actively, assessors need to observe the *principle of neutrality* in their interactions with families (Bailey, 1988). Simply stated, this principle, which appears frequently in family therapy literature, means that the interventionist does not take sides. Aligning oneself with one family member only results in losing the others. In many early intervention programs, staff members have more contact with mothers than with fathers. To the father who cannot be part of the sessions, this imbalance in time spent can be viewed as an alliance between the staff member and his wife. Thus, it becomes increasingly important to include both parents or primary caregivers and to remain neutral in any disputes.

A third skill required in conducting family needs assessments is the ability to be *nonjudgmental*. Although the interventionist may not share the family's approach to child rearing, housekeeping, or life in general, it is not her or his role to evaluate the family's approach. Differences in culture, geographic region, socioeconomic status, religion, values, priorities, and ideology all influence family patterns and behaviors. Even though a particular pattern or behavior may not be ideal, unless it constitutes abuse or neglect, it is the family's choice. As part of the intervention program, staff members may help families develop more constructive patterns of behavior, but even this is done without judging their current behaviors.

Viewing *parents as equal partners* in early intervention programs and services is a quality that is essential. Each parent is a specialist regarding her or his own child (Beckman, 1984; Lynch, 1978; McGonigel et al., 1991; Vincent, 1984), and modeling and supporting that collaborative stance from the initial contact with families is a key ingredient to success. Equality does not mean that each member of the partnership has equal knowledge and information in all areas, but it does mean that each partner's contributions are of equal value. For example, the parents' and family's input about the child's temperament and sleep patterns would be valued as highly as the technical skills of the physical therapist related to positioning and handling.

The final assessor characteristic that leads to effective identification of family concerns, priorities, and resources is a composite of many related skills and attitudes. It includes competence, openness, and a genuine desire to help families maintain or regain control over their own lives. It is an attitude and state of being that engenders hope, self-confidence, and empowerment. Although this characteristic is perhaps less easily measured or taught than the others discussed, it too is an essential ingredient in working effectively with families.

Techniques and Strategies

Although identifying family concerns, priorities, and resources is relatively new to early intervention programs, a variety of approaches have been tried. Several of the early approaches were drawn directly from clinical practice or research and have not been demonstrated to be effective strategies in early intervention settings. Others are drawn from sound practices in information gathering that incorporate families as partners in assessment and problem solving.

Assessing family strengths and identifying concerns, priorities, and resources

One of the first strategies professionals use to solve new problems is to label the problem and impose some sort of structure upon it. In the past, that is often what professionals did to families. Many programs labeled problems they thought families had—stress, coping, multiple responsibilities, limited support networks—and attempted to find tools to measure the extent of the families' problems in these areas. Consequently, many strategies and techniques designed to be used solely as research tools or by trained clinicians were suggested for use in the family needs assessment process. For example, the *State-Trait Anxiety Scale* (Spielberger, Gorsuch, & Lushene, 1970), *F–COPES—Family Crisis Oriented Personal Scale* (McCubbin, Olson, & Larsen, 1981), *FIRM—Family Inventory of Resources for Management* (McCubbin, Comeau, & Harkins, 1981), *FACES—Family Adaptability and Cohesion Evaluation Scales* (Olson, Portner, & Bell, no date), *Questionnaire on Resources and Stress* (Holyroyd, 1974), and *Parenting Stress Index* (Abidin, 1983) were suggested as ways to gather information about the family's concerns, priorities, and resources. Our position is that many of these instruments are inappropriate, and using them is inappropriate practice. These instruments were not developed to ascertain information about particular families that can assist in early intervention programming; instead, they were designed to measure overall characteristics of individuals or family members. Consequently, using them in ways that are inconsistent with their purpose is not a valid practice. Additionally, several of the measures are quite intrusive and invade family privacy.

What then is appropriate? How can family strengths and concerns be assessed in ways that are technically sound, culturally appropriate, respectful of families, and useful for developing programs and locating resources? At this time, a focused interview with the primary caregivers (mother and father or others who take the parental role) is recommended as the best practice for early intervention programs to use in collecting information about child variables that affect the family's functioning and the family's needs for information, support, or training (Bailey & Simeonsson, 1988). Interviews have several advantages over pencil-and-paper tests. The intrusiveness of an interview can be monitored by the interviewer; the language and questions can be changed to more closely fit the family's values and culture; and family members can select what to share without making that selection process obvious. In contrast, pencil-and-paper tests are often quite intrusive, but there is no way for the assessor to monitor their effects. Some pencil-and-paper tests are inappropriate for members of certain cultures, and it is more difficult for families to screen their responses on written instruments. In addition, written tests require literacy, making it difficult, if not impossible, for some family members to respond.

Although a focused interview is structured, the interviewer has considerable flexibility to pursue areas of particular concern to families or to focus on feelings that emerge during the conversation. Prior to the interview the interviewer identifies broad topics to be covered as well as critical events that are upcoming. The interviewer may ask about the family's strengths, their concerns, the resources that they have available and use, and their perceptions of their situation and needs. As family members respond to broad questions, other areas of importance to them often emerge, enabling the interviewer to pursue the family's concerns. For some families the initial interview may be extensive; for others it may be abbreviated and elaborated over time. Bailey et al. (1986) summarized the specific skills they believe are necessary to conduct an interview of this kind:

1. responding empathetically to family concerns;
2. following feelings expressed by family members;
3. probing for details in a sensitive fashion;
4. utilizing both open-ended and closed-ended questions effectively;
5. focusing in depth on issues of particular concern;
6. utilizing strengths to reinforce family members' efforts and provide a basis for suggestions;
7. summarizing topics discussed as well as future plans; and
8. artfully blending all of these skills into a naturally flowing, comfortable interview. (p. 162)

An example of a focused interview is presented in Table 8.5.

As a part of or at the conclusion of the interview, family members are asked to articulate their goals or desired outcomes in relation to the family and the child who is at risk or has a disability. After the interview is conducted, the team generates possible resources to meet the family's concerns and priorities that build upon family strengths. In many cases the resources will not be within the program itself, but will exist within the community. For example, some families may request information about special equipment for their child. There are many ways to provide that information, and families will have varying preferences. Some may want to talk one-to-one with a physical or occupational therapist; others may want to read books; and others may prefer to talk with another parent whose child has had special equipment. Another family may want supportive counseling to help them adjust to the changes in their lives. Some families' needs will be met by a psychologist, social worker, psychotherapist, or counselor; others may prefer to work with their spiritual leader, priest, rabbi, or minister; and other families may be able to meet their counseling needs by attending a parent support group. The staff's job is to develop a menu, or list of alternatives, for the family to choose from based on the identified issues and the family's preferred methods of solving problems and getting information. It is not the program's job to provide all the services and all the answers; rather, it is the program's role to help families find the resources they need. Appendix E presents an example of an Individualized Family Service Plan that includes family outcomes.

One of the key components of family strength is the social support system that families have available to help them to meet their individual and collective needs. Social support has been found to result in more positive outcomes for both children and families, and identifying the supports that exist or the absence of supports in families who are socially isolated can help interventionists and families design more effective interventions (Dunst, Leet, & Trivette, 1988; Dunst & Trivette, 1990). Because of the strong correlation between family support and improved outcomes, assessing supports by mapping kinship, friendship, and other networks may be a strategy that interventionists and families select as part of the identification of the family's concerns, priorities, and resources.

Bailey and Simeonsson (1988) proposed Goal Attainment Scaling to measure the success of family-determined outcomes. This method, which has been used extensively in mental health, allows those who set the goal to evaluate the extent to which it has been met. After the family goals have been specified, each goal is weighted or prioritized by the family and a continuum of possible outcomes specified. The continuum of outcomes with numeri-

Table 8.5. Example of Focused Interview Format

The questions that follow elicit the kinds of information that may be helpful in identifying a family's concerns, priorities, and resources. Although the items are presented as questions, it is not intended to be a formal interview. The types of questions that are important and the way in which they are asked will be tailored to the individual family, and often the responses to many questions are embedded in the answer to another one.

1. Let's begin by talking about *name of child who is at risk or disabled*. Tell me about *him or her*.
2. Who else is in your family or an important part of your life? Tell me about them and their relationship to *name of child who is at risk or disabled*.
3. Now that I know a little bit more about *name of child who is at risk or disabled*, let's talk about a typical day with *him or her*. How does it begin? What happens next? [Continue through the day and night.]
4. What are your greatest concerns in relation to *name of child who is at risk or disabled*?
5. What do you see as the strengths of *name of child who is at risk or disabled*?
6. Families are responsible for many things, and sometimes it helps to know about resources that are available to help. Let me mention several areas, and if it is something that you would like to know more about, we can talk about it.
   - Anything related to daily care such as feeding, bathing, comforting, or using equipment?
   - Anything related to health care or medical concerns?
   - Anything related to opportunities to talk with other parents who have children who have experienced similar difficulties?
   - Anything related to financial support for health care, therapy, equipment, transportation, and so forth?
   - Anything related to your own needs for rest, relaxation, or time to be with your partner or other family members?
   - Anything related to your own personal, educational, or vocational goals?
   - Anything related to information or support for other family members such as brothers and sisters, grandparents, and so forth?
7. How do you and your family like to tackle problems or get information (e.g., books, lectures, videotapes, conversations with other people who have had the same experience)?
8. Are there questions that you have or other concerns that you would like to discuss?

---

cal weightings typically includes five levels of success ranging from the best expected outcome to an outcome that is worse than expected. The family's current level of success with the goal is assessed, intervention is provided, and the family's success in accomplishing the goal following intervention is assessed. For example, the Martin family may want to find ways to encourage Emily's involvement in family activities. To do this they have identified the goal of positioning Emily so that she can see other family members at mealtimes with the intent that it will become a habit to position Emily near the table and interact with her as the family eats together. At the end of the 6-week period, the Martins would be asked to discuss how it had worked and to rate the effectiveness of the intervention on the following 5-point scale: best expected outcome (2 points), more than expected outcome (1 point), expected outcome (0 points), less than expected outcome (–1 point), and worst expected outcome (–2 points). The results of that goal and the others the Martins had identified would then be plotted on a graph to depict their accomplishments. A system of this kind is appropriate for some families and inappropriate for others; however, it is a promising evaluation strategy for helping family and early intervention staff members measure progress.

Supporting families by assessing parent–child interaction

A growing body of research supports the belief that the nature and quality of parent–child interactions have a strong influence on the child's development (Bromwich, 1981; Zeanah, 1993). These interactions form the basis for attachment and the foundation for communication and social-emotional development. In most parent–infant dyads, mutually satisfying interactions develop naturally. The parents learn to "read" their baby's cues; the baby, in turn, responds to the attention, giving parents a sense of competence and further strengthening the relationship and the desire for continued interaction (Healy, Keesee, & Smith, 1985).

When the infant is born prematurely, at risk for developmental problems, or disabled, the nature and quality of parent–infant interactions may be jeopardized (see Hanson, 1984, for review). Goldberg (1977), describing typically developing infants, proposed that they varied in three dimensions including readability, predictability, and responsiveness. Infants who are at risk or disabled may vary even more dramatically across each of these continua. Their cues may be subtle and fleeting, and thereby more difficult to read and interpret. Because of their general lability, these children may be less predictable, and they may have fewer resources to marshal for interactions, thus making them less responsive. Consequently, parent–infant interaction may be less satisfying to both parent and child, resulting in a deterioration in both quantity and quality.

When parents come to the early intervention program with questions about parent–child interactions, the team may want to include assessments of parent–infant interactions in the family assessment. Paradigms for these assessments have been developed for research and for clinical practice. Ainsworth's Strange Situation (Ainsworth, Blehar, Waters, & Wall, 1978), Sander's (1962) model, Bromwich's (1981) *Parent Behavior Progression Scale*, Barnard and Bee's (1981) *Nursing Child Assessment Scales*, and Greenspan and Greenspan's (1985) stages are all useful ways to measure parent–infant interaction. However, each requires considerable training to conduct and interpret and should not be used unless the assessor has been appropriately trained and formally supervised in the method. (For a description of each, see Hanson & Krentz, 1986.)

One system of parent–infant interaction that has been used successfully in a community-based infant program is described by Hanson and Krentz (1986). A staff member trained in observation and interviewing works with the family to generate concerns they might have about the parent–infant relationship. Through interviews and observations, the parents and staff member together examine the infant's abilities, the parents' abilities, and the components of parent–infant interaction in the context of the developmental level, the effect on the child, the effect on the parent, and the effect on the relationship (Hanson & Krentz, 1986). Table 8.6 describes this assessment framework.

As with all assessments in early intervention, the assessment of parent–infant interaction should lead to interventions that enhance those interactions. Many of the strategies for determining parent–child interactions are clinical or experimental in nature and require the expertise of someone highly trained and experienced in their use. Although some assessments, such as the *Nursing Child Assessment Scales* (Barnard & Bee, 1981) or the *Parent Behavior Progression* (Bromwich, 1981), may be useful in certain situations or settings, direct observations of behavior and interviews with parents are typically less intrusive and more helpful. Given that a major goal of identifying family strengths and concerns is to empower parents and assist them to become more effec-

Table 8.6. Assessment Framework

Infant Abilities	Parent Abilities	Components of the Interaction
Responsiveness	Parent's awareness of the child's development	Predominant affect
Signaling	Parent's ability to function in the larger environment	Affectual changes
Communication	Level of parenting skills	Initiation of interaction
Cognitive	Meaning of the disabling condition to the parents and parents' ability to understand the condition	Continuation of interaction
Motor		Contingent responsiveness
Emotion		Pace
Social		Turn-taking
Temperament		Use of communicative modalities
Appearance		

From *Supporting Parent–Child Interactions—A Guide for Early Intervention Program Personnel* by M. J. Hanson and M. Krentz, 1986, Project ISIS, San Francisco State University. Reprinted by permission.

tive in meeting family needs, it is imperative that professional instruments and strategies do not work against that goal. Assessments that do not include the parents' own observations and participation or those that focus on their deficits may be counterproductive.

Assessing Home Environments

Some attempts have been made to assess children's home environments—for example, *Home Observation for Measurement of the Environment* (Caldwell, Bradley, & Staff, 1978). Although the importance of the home environment and the need for safe, nurturing conditions cannot be underestimated, the instruments that have been developed tend to evaluate the home from a middle class perspective, which does not allow for cultural, ethnic, or socioeconomic differences. At this time evaluation of the home should probably be done only through observation within the cultural and economic context.

Issues and Concerns

Identifying family concerns, priorities, and resources is a new role for many professionals in early intervention programs. The new role brings both opportunity and anxiety. Assessments that are well planned, incorporate family members as equal partners, are sensitively conducted, and lead to enhanced functioning for both the child and the family open new frontiers in early intervention. Those that are not can close doors. As programs develop a more family-focused approach and make these assessments a routine part of the process, the following issues may be considered:

- Who should conduct assessments that identify family concerns, priorities, and resources?
- How should this person be trained?
- What assessment methods (interview, pencil-and-paper, combination) are most appropriate for the families served?
- What method is least intrusive?
- What information should be gathered, particularly in relationship to program planning?
- How can the IFSP be written to honor families' wishes and remain fluid rather than cast in stone?
- How can strategies be tailored to address the diversity among families served?

Each of these issues has a set of related concerns that program staff with the families' help must confront. The identification of family strengths and resources as well as concerns and priorities has evolved as a way to incorporate families into early intervention, as a way to help them empower themselves, and as a way to plan programs that are sensitive to the entire family system. When assessments do those things, they are working. When they do not, they need to be reviewed and changed.

Summary

Infants and toddlers cannot be viewed separately from their families; thus, a family-focused approach to early intervention has become the model for practice. Programs that incorporate families have a greater likelihood of enhancing both the child's and family's functioning and of addressing the concerns that are of greatest importance to families. To develop family-centered interventions, programs need to learn more about families' strengths, needs, concerns, priorities, and resources. Furthermore, gathering information about families requires different skills from those that have been a traditional part of the training of early intervention professionals.

Perhaps the key ingredient in identifying family concerns, priorities, and resources is the assessor. Because she or he will be entering homes and talking with families about their strengths, needs, worries, and dreams, it is important that the assessor be well trained and comfortable in the role. Some basic char-

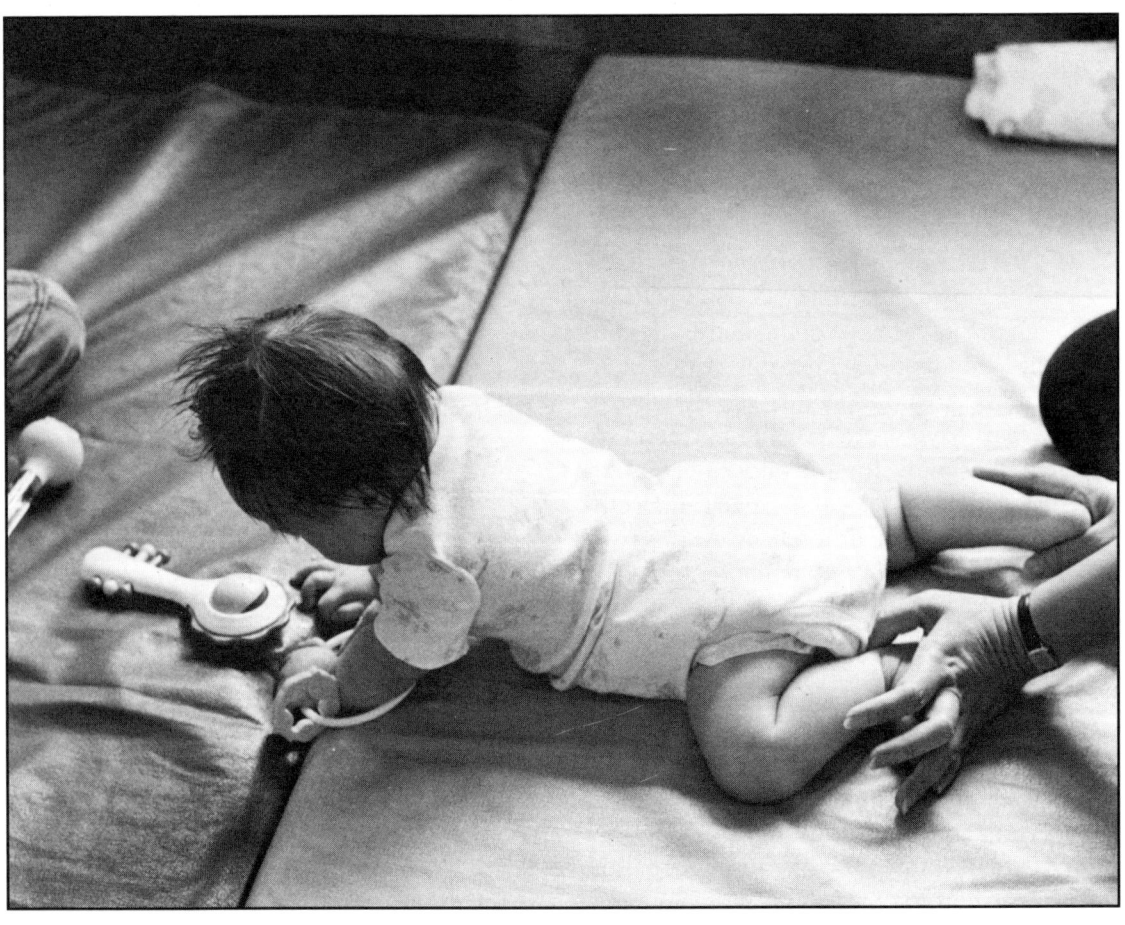

acteristics, skills, and attitudes, such as active listening, observing the principle of neutrality, remaining nonjudgmental, treating parents as equals, and demonstrating competence as well as a sincere desire to work together, can help assure that these interactions go well.

Three types of data may be gathered in the process of helping families identify their concerns, priorities, and resources: (a) information about child variables that may affect the family's functioning, (b) information about the family's strengths and needs, and (c) information about parent–child interaction. Different methods have been developed in each of these areas.

How information is collected will depend on the staff's training and experience, as well as on the families that are being served. In a few instances pencil-and-paper assessment instruments may be used, but a well-conducted, structured interview is often a less intrusive and more effective way to collect information. If pencil-and-paper instruments are selected, it is important that the results lead directly to intervention. Currently, many of those that are commercially available were designed for research or clinical practice and tend to be extremely intrusive without leading to potential interventions.

Parent–child interactions are critical elements in the child's development and later performance. Assessments of parent–child interaction are not designed to judge parents' skills but to help parents and infants find mutually satisfying ways of interacting.

The purpose of identifying families' concerns, priorities, and resources is to make programs more responsive to child and family needs. Exemplary strategies are those that are supportive, empowering, and linked to interventions.

Preferred Practices

The following questions can be used to review and evaluate procedures used to assess young children and identify family concerns, priorities, and resources.

1. Are diagnostic or eligibility assessment procedures clearly defined?
2. Are child assessment and family procedures linked to programming?
3. Are staff members conducting child assessments trained in measurement, the particular strategies being used, and assessment of infants and young children?
4. Are the assessment instruments being used valid and reliable?
5. Is the assessment being conducted by an inter- or transdisciplinary team that includes the parents or primary caregivers as equal partners on the team?
6. Is adequate time allocated for the team to jointly plan assessments with the family?
7. Are assessments conducted in a setting that is familiar to the child (preferably at home), with the parents or primary caregivers present and assisting?
8. Are assessment data collected in a variety of ways (e.g., observation, interview, play)?
9. Are assessments of the child's strengths and needs and the family's concerns, priorities, and resources culturally and linguistically appropriate?
10. Is there a standard procedure for writing reports and sharing the findings with all team members including the parents?
11. Are written and verbal reports free of judgments, stereotyping, and negative labeling?
12. Is ample time allocated for discussing and sharing findings and making programming decisions?
13. Is follow-up done soon after placement to determine the appropriateness of the program, the child's performance, and

the family's and staff's satisfaction with the program?

14. Is the identification of family concerns, priorities, and resources nonintrusive, nonjudgmental, and conducted with sensitivity?

15. Does the information collected about the family's concerns, priorities, and resources assist in finding resources or developing programs?

16. Are parent–child interaction data being collected when that is an area of concern?

17. Is the assessment process fluid and individualized for families to respect their privacy, values, and concerns?

18. Are families viewed and treated as equal partners throughout the assessment process?

References

Abidin, R. (1983). *Parenting Stress Index*. Charlottesville, VA: Pediatric Psychology Press.

Ainsworth, M. D. S., Blehar, M. C., Waters, E., & Wall, S. (1978). *Patterns of attachment*. Hillsdale, NJ: Erlbaum.

Bagnato, S. J., Neisworth, J. T., & Munson, S. M. (1993). Sensible strategies for assessment in early intervention. In D. M. Bryant & M. A. Graham (Eds.), *Implementing early intervention: From research to effective practice* (pp. 148–156). New York: Guilford Press.

Bailey, D. B. (1988, April). *Professionals working collaboratively with parents*. Presentation at the Family Service Delivery Training Institute, San Diego.

Bailey, D. B., & Simeonsson, R. J. (1988). *Family assessment in early intervention*. Columbus, OH: Merrill.

Bailey, D. B., Simeonsson, R. J., Winton, P. J., Huntington, G. S., Comfort, M., Isbell, P., O'Donnell, K. J., & Helm, J. M. (1986). Family-focused intervention: A functional model for planning, implementing, and evaluating individualized family services in early intervention. *Journal of the Division of Early Childhood, 10,* 156–171.

Barnard, K., & Bee, H. (1981). *The assessment of parent–infant interaction by observation of feeding and teaching*. Unpublished manuscript, University of Washington School of Nursing and the Child Development and Mental Retardation Center, Seattle.

Barrera, I. (1994). Thoughts on the assessment of young children whose sociocultural background is unfamiliar to the assessor. *Zero to Three, 14*(6), 9–13.

Beckman, P. (1984). Perceptions of young children with handicaps: A comparison of mothers and program staff. *Mental Retardation, 22,* 176–181.

Brazelton, T. B. (1973). *Neonatal Behavioral Assessment Scale: Clinics in Developmental Medicine*, No. 50. London: Heineman.

Bromwich, R. (1981). *Working with parents and infants*. Austin, TX: PRO-ED.

Caldwell, B., Bradley, R. H., & Staff. (1978). *Home observation for measurement of the environment*. Syracuse, NY: Syracuse University Press.

Carter, E., & McGoldrick, M. (Eds.). (1980). *The family life cycle: A framework for family therapy*. New York: Gardner.

Cohen, L. G., & Spenciner, L. J. (1994). *Assessment of young children*. New York: Longman.

DuBose, R. F. (1981). Assessment of severely impaired young children: Problems and recommendations. *Topics in Early Childhood Special Education, 1*(2), 9–21.

Dunst, C. J., Leet, H., & Trivette, C. M. (1988). Family resources, personal well-being, and early intervention. *Journal of Special Education, 22,* 108–116.

Dunst, C. J., & Rheingrover, R. M. (1981). Discontinuity and instability in early development: Implications for assessment. *Topics in Early Childhood Special Education, 1*(2), 49–60.

Dunst, C. J., & Trivette, C. M. (1990). Assessment of social support in early intervention programs. In S. J. Meisels & J. P. Shonkoff (Eds.), *Handbook of early childhood intervention* (pp. 326–349). New York: Cambridge University Press.

Dunst, C. J., Trivette, C., & Deal, A. (1988). *Enabling and empowering families: Principles and guidelines for practice*. Cambridge, MA: Brookline.

Fallen, N. H., & Umansky, W. (1985). *Young children with special needs* (2nd ed.). Columbus, OH: Merrill.

Foley, G. (1990). Portrait of the arena evaluation: Assessment in the transdisciplinary approach. In E. D. Gibbs & D. M. Teti (Eds.), *Interdisciplinary assessment of infants: A guide for early intervention professionals* (pp. 271–286). Baltimore: Brookes.

Garwood, S. G. (1982). Piaget and play. *Topics in Early Childhood Special Education, 2*(3), 1–13.

Gibbs, E. D., & Teti, D. M. (1990). *Interdisciplinary assessment of infants: A guide for early intervention professionals*. Baltimore: Brookes.

Goldberg, S. (1977). Social competence in infancy: A model of parent–infant interaction. *Merrill-Palmer Quarterly, 23,* 163–177.

Greenspan, S., & Greenspan, N. (1985). *First feelings*. New York: Viking.

Greenspan, S. I., & Meisels, S. (Eds.). (1994). Toward a new vision for the developmental assessment of infants and young children. *Zero to Three, 14*(6), 1–8.

Hanson, M. J. (1984). Parent–infant interaction. In M. J. Hanson (Ed.), *Atypical infant development* (pp. 179–206). Austin, TX: PRO-ED.

Hanson, M. J. (1987). *Teaching the infant with Down syndrome: A guide for parents and professionals* (2nd ed.). Austin, TX: PRO-ED.

Hanson, M. J., & Krentz, M. S. (1986). *Supporting parent–child interactions*. San Francisco: Project ISIS (Integrated Special Infant Services), Department of Special Education, San Francisco State University.

Hanson, M. J., Lynch, E. W., & Wayman, K. I. (1990). Honoring cultural diversity of families when gathering data. *Topics in Early Childhood Special Education, 10,* 112–131.

Harrison, H. (1983). *The premature baby book*. New York: St. Martin's Press.

Hayes, A. (1990). The context and future of judgment-based assessment. *Topics in Early Childhood Special Education, 10,* 1–12.

Healy, A., Keesee, P. D., & Smith, B. S. (1985). *Early services for children with special needs—Transactions for family support*. Iowa City, IA: Division of Developmental Disabilities, University Hospital School.

Holyroyd, J. (1974). The Questionnaire on Resources and Stress: An instrument to measure family response to a handicapped member. *Journal of Community Psychology, 2,* 92–94.

Hunt, S. (1976). Environmental risk in fetal and neonatal life and measured intelligence. In M. Lewis (Ed.), *Origins of intelligence: Infancy and early childhood* (pp. 223–258). New York: Plenum.

Hurth, J., Bailey, D., Kaufman, R., McGonigel, M., Brown, C., & Rasbold, R. A. (1988, November). *IFSPs and case management: An analysis of implementation issues, best practices and implications for state policy and procedural guidelines*. International Early Childhood Conference on Children with Special Needs, Nashville, TN.

Kantor, D., & Lehr, W. (1975). *Inside the family*. San Francisco: Jossey-Bass.

Kjerland, L., & Kovach, J. (1990). Family–staff collaboration for tailored infant assessment. In E. D. Gibbs & D. M. Teti (Eds.), *Interdisciplinary assessment of infants: A guide for early intervention professionals* (pp. 287–297). Baltimore: Brookes.

Lee, G. R. (1982). *Family structure and interaction: A comparative analysis*. Minneapolis: University of Minnesota Press.

Lerner, J., Mardell-Czudnowski, C., & Goldenberg, D. (1987). *Special education for the early childhood years* (2nd ed.). Englewood Cliffs, NJ: Prentice-Hall.

Linder, T. W. (1990). *Transdisciplinary play-based assessment: A functional approach to working with young children*. Baltimore: Brookes.

Lynch, E. W. (1978). The home–school partnership. In S. L. Brown & M. S. Moersch (Eds.), *Parents on the team* (pp. 21–24). Ann Arbor: University of Michigan Press.

Lynch, E. W., & Hanson, M. J. (1992). *Developing cross-cultural competence: A guide to working with young children and their families*. Baltimore: Brookes.

Lynch, E. W., & Hanson, M. J. (in press). Ensuring cultural competence in assessment. In M. McClean, D. B. Bailey, & M. Wolery (Eds.), *Assessing infants and toddlers with special needs* (2nd ed.). Columbus, OH: Merrill.

McCubbin, H. I., Comeau, J. K., & Harkins, J. A. (1981). *FIRM—Family Inventory of Resources for Management*. St. Paul: Family Social Science, University of Minnesota.

McCubbin, H. I., Joy, C. B., Cauble, A. E., Comeau, J. K., Patterson, J. M., & Needles, R. H. (1980). Family stress and coping: A decade review. *Journal of Marriage and the Family, 42*(4), 855–871.

McCubbin, H. I., Olson, D. H., & Larsen, A. S. (1981). *F–COPES—Family Crisis Oriented Per-*

sonal Scale. St. Paul: Family Social Science, University of Minnesota.

McGonigel, M. J., Kaufmann, R. K., & Johnson, B. H. (1991). *Guidelines and recommended practices for the individualized family service plan* (2nd ed.). Bethesda, MD: Association for the Care of Children's Health.

McLoughlin, J. A., & Lewis, R. B. (1994). *Assessing special students* (4th ed.). Columbus, OH: Merrill.

Meisels, S. J., & Provence, S. (1989). *Screening and assessment: Guidelines for identifying young disabled and developmentally vulnerable children and their families*. Arlington, VA: National Center for Clinical Infant Programs.

Minuchin, S. (1974). *Families and family therapy*. Cambridge, MA: Harvard University Press.

Molyneaux, D., & Lane, V. W. (1982). *Effective interviewing—Techniques and analysis*. Boston: Allyn & Bacon.

Neisworth, J. T., & Bagnato, S. J. (1988). Assessment in early childhood special education: A typology of dependent measures. In S. L. Odom & M. B. Karnes (Eds.), *Early intervention for infants and children with handicaps* (pp. 23–49). Baltimore: Brookes.

Olson, D. H., McCubbin, H. I., Barnes, H., Larsen, A., Muxen, M., & Wilson. M. (1983). *Families: What makes them work*. Beverly Hills, CA: Sage.

Olson, D. H., Portner, J., & Bell, R. (no date). *FACES*. St. Paul: Family Social Science, University of Minnesota.

Parker, S. J., & Zuckerman, B. S. (1990). Therapeutic aspects of the assessment process. In S. J. Meisels & J. P. Shonkoff (Eds.), *Handbook of early childhood intervention* (pp. 350–369). New York: Cambridge University Press.

Parmelee, A., Werner, W., & Schulz, H. (1964). Infant sleep patterns from birth to 16 weeks of age. *Journal of Pediatrics, 65*, 576–582.

Prechtl, H. (1974). The behavioral states of the newborn infant (a review). *Brain Research, 76*, 185–212.

Rocco, S. (1994). New visions for the developmental assessment of infants and young children: A parent's perspective. *Zero to Three, 14*(6), 13–15.

Sander, L. (1962). Issues in early mother–child interaction. *Journal of the American Academy of Child Psychiatry, 1*, 141–166.

Simeonsson, R. J. (1986). *Psychological and developmental assessment of special children*. Boston: Allyn & Bacon.

Simeonsson, J., Huntington, G., & Parse, S. (1980). Expanding the developmental assessment of young handicapped children. In J. J. Gallagher (Ed.), *New directions for exceptional children—Young exceptional children No. 3*. (pp. 51–74). San Francisco: Jossey-Bass.

Simons, R. (1987). *After the tears—Parents talk about raising a child with a disability*. San Diego: Harcourt Brace Jovanovich.

Spielberger, C. D., Gorsuch, R. L., & Lushene, R. E. (1970). *State-Trait Anxiety Inventory*. Palo Alto, CA: Consulting Psychologists Press.

StevensDominguez, M., Beam, G., & Thomas, P. (1989). *Guide for family-centered services*. Albuquerque: University of New Mexico.

Summers, J. A., Dell'Oliver, C., Turnbull, A. P., Benson, H. A., Santelli, E., Campbell, M., & Siegel-Causey, E. (1990). Examining the Individualized Family Service Plan process: What are family and practitioner preferences? *Topics in Early Childhood Special Education, 10*, 78–99.

Teti, D. M., & Gibbs, E. D. (1990). Infant assessment: Historical antecedents and contemporary issues. In E. D. Gibbs & D. M. Teti (Eds.), *Interdisciplinary assessment of infants: A guide for early intervention professionals* (pp. 3–13). Baltimore: Brookes.

Thurman, S. K., & Widerstrom, A. H. (1990). *Infants and young children with special needs: A developmental and ecological approach* (2nd ed.). Baltimore: Brookes.

Trohanis, P. L., Cox, J. O., & Meyer, R. A. (1982). A report on selected demonstration programs for infant intervention. In C. T. Ramey & P. L. Trohanis (Eds.), *Finding and educating high-risk and handicapped infants* (pp. 163–191). Austin, TX: PRO-ED.

Turnbull, A. P., Patterson, J. M., Behr, S. K., Murphy, D. L., Marquis, J. G., & Blue-Banning, M. J. (Eds.). (1993). *Cognitive coping, families, and disability*. Baltimore: Brookes.

Turnbull, A. P., & Turnbull, H. R. (1990). *Families, professionals, and exceptionality: A special partnership* (2nd ed.). Columbus, OH: Merrill.

Ulrey, G., & Rogers, S. J. (1982). *Psychological assessment of handicapped infants and young children*. New York: Thieme-Stratton.

VandenBerg, K. A., & Hanson, M. J. (1993). *Homecoming for babies after the neonatal intensive care nursery: A guide for professionals in supporting families and their infants' early development.* Austin, TX: PRO-ED.

Vincent, L. (1984, December). *Family relationships.* Paper presented at the Conference on Comprehensive Approaches to Disabled and At-Risk Infants, Toddlers and Their Families, jointly sponsored by Maternal and Child Health, Office of Special Education and Rehabilitative Services, Health and Human Services, and National Center for Clinical Infant Programs, Washington, DC.

Vincent, L. (1988, April). *Changing role of the professional in working with families.* Paper presented at the Family Service Delivery Training Institute, San Diego.

Zeanah, Jr., C. H. (Ed.). (1993). *Handbook of infant mental health.* New York: Guilford Press.

Zelazo, P. (1979). Reactivity to perceptual-cognitive events: Application for infant assessment. In R. B. Kearsley & I. Sigel (Eds.), *Infants at risk: The assessment of cognitive functioning* (pp. 49–83). Hillsdale, NJ: Erlbaum.

Selected Readings

General References on Educational Measurement

Kubiszyn, T., & Borich, G. (1987). *Educational testing and measurement* (2nd ed.). Glenview, IL: Scott, Foresman.

Walsh, W. B. (1989). *Tests and measurements* (4th ed.). Englewood Cliffs, NJ: Prentice-Hall.

Assessment of Young Children Who Are At Risk or Disabled

Cohen, L. G., & Spenciner, L. J. (1994). *Assessment of young children.* New York: Longman.

Gibbs, E. D., & Teti, D. M. (1990). *Interdisciplinary assessment of infants: A guide for early intervention professionals.* Baltimore: Brookes.

McLean, M., Bailey, D. B., & Wolery, M. (in press). *Assessing infants and toddlers with special needs* (2nd ed.). Columbus, OH: Merrill.

Meisels, S. J., & Provence, S. (1989). *Screening and assessment: Guidelines for identifying young disabled and developmentally vulnerable children and their families.* Arlington, VA: National Center for Clinical Infant Programs.

Rossetti, L. M. (1990). *Infant–toddler assessment: An interdisciplinary approach.* Austin, TX: PRO-ED.

Special Topics

Bailey, D. B., & Simeonsson, R. J. (1988). *Family assessment in early intervention.* Columbus, OH: Merrill.

Linder, T. W. (1990). *Transdisciplinary play-based assessment: A functional approach to working with young children.* Baltimore: Brookes.

Wodrich, D. L., & Kush, S. A. (1990). *Children's psychological testing: A guide for nonpsychologists* (2nd ed.). Baltimore: Brookes.

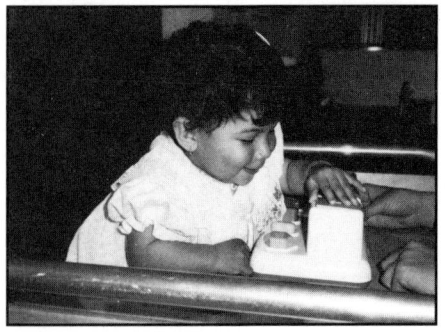

Designing the Curriculum

CHAPTER 9

It looks like a cyclone struck! Balls, tubes, and tents are covering the floor! Louis is inside one large tube trying to make echoes with his voice and banging on the sides of the tube like a drum. Jamal is on the outside of the tube laughing and banging back whenever Louis makes a sound. Beth is creeping over to enter the tube to see what the commotion is about. Miguel is busy trying to take little tennis balls out of the clothes basket as quickly as Cynthia can put them in.

Mireya, the early intervention special educator, places a roadway mat and several houses and building sets on the floor. She also brings out little plastic people and cars. Sudha toddles over and begins moving the cars around the roads, saying "vroom, vroom." This attracts Wei-min, who comes to join her in making the cars go around the roadway and into the garages. Joyce sits propped to the side and occasionally giggles when a car crashes and points as if to ask for a car too. Mireya says, "Joyce, do you want a car? Here, let's find one for you to drive!" as she places a sturdy car in front of Joyce and repositions her so that her car can also be on the roadway.

To the outside observer, these activities appear to be children merely playing together; they may even seem a bit chaotic. Someone with a trained eye, however, can see a myriad of individual teaching objectives being addressed through a carefully orchestrated and planned environment. Some children have goals for increasing the sounds they make and some for their movements. Still other objectives and goals are social and interactional. These are the plans and activities that make up a curriculum.

In this chapter and Chapter 10, the following questions will be addressed: What should the focus of early intervention be? What do young children need to learn? What strategies are appropriate for use in teaching the very young child? Who should do the "teaching"? The curricular design of a program addresses these issues and provides the framework around which all intervention activities are structured.

This chapter presents an overview of curriculum development issues and strategies for curriculum planning and implementation. After defining curriculum, the major theoretical approaches that underlie most early intervention curricula are reviewed and developmentally appropriate practice is described. Next, both the content, or an analysis of *what* should be included in the curriculum, and the method, or *how* intervention should be conducted, are discussed. Finally, an evaluation checklist is given for analyzing best practices in curricular designs, and a list of selected exemplary curricular packages is furnished.

Definition of Curriculum

Several definitions of a curriculum have been articulated (Dunst, 1981; Lillie, 1975; Mori & Neisworth, 1983). All outline the components that follow here. A curriculum is an organized set of activities and experiences designed to achieve particular developmental or learning objectives. This organizational structure dictates both the content (what should be included) and the method (how the targets are to be taught) for intervention implementation. As such, it involves a carefully planned and arranged sequence of events. This design of activities and experiences should flow from the philosophical and theoretical principles upon which the program is developed. Theoretical approaches that have primarily influenced early intervention structures are reviewed below.

Theoretical Approaches

Most early intervention programs practice a rather eclectic approach to service delivery. However, central programmatic components may be structured around a particular theoretical view. Educational models, such as those described in Chapter 4, and curricula often are derived from these theoretical perspectives.

The major theoretical constructs that underlie commonly utilized curricula are examined in terms of their influence on curricular design. Specifically, these theoretical perspectives include the following: developmental,

cognitive (also referred to as cognitive-developmental), behavioral, and functional or ecological approaches.

Developmental

The developmental approach derives from an ideological perspective that views development as genetically predetermined in a specific sequence. Theorists such as Arnold Gesell (1925; Gesell & Amatruda, 1947) are representative of this viewpoint. Curricula based on this approach typically contain an ordered listing of developmental milestones, and educational programs are aimed at providing an environment in which the child is supported to engage in self-directed play and learning activities.

With regard to curricula for infant intervention programs, the developmental influence is seen primarily in the content of the curricular package. Many curricula include a listing of milestones and advocate an additive approach to teaching—teaching one milestone after another, each building successively on the previous less complex behavior. Milestones have been gleaned to a large degree from developmental assessment tools such as the *Cattell Infant Intelligence Scale* (Cattell, 1969) and the *Bayley Scales of Infant Development, Second Edition* (Bayley, 1993). This approach also is considered a diagnostic-prescriptive approach to education, because developmental assessment tools are used to determine the skills the child possesses or lacks compared with age-related norms. From this information, age-related developmental training goals are identified.

Cognitive

The cognitive or cognitive-developmental approach is typically associated with the theory of Jean Piaget (1952, 1970; Phillips, 1975). According to this theoretical perspective, development proceeds from the child's interaction with the environment through the continual reorganization of psychological structures that result from this interaction. The child is viewed as an active and intrinsically motivated learner. This theoretical approach has had a tremendous influence on both the content and the implementation of curricula. Specifically, many cognitive curricula focus on the enhancement of sensorimotor skills through the young child's active, guided interaction with a planned, enriched environment.

Behavioral

The behavioral theory of development and its application to education are most closely associated with the work of B. F. Skinner (1972). The behavioral approach emphasizes the importance of environmental factors as determinants of child behavior. The child is seen as extrinsically motivated, and the child's active involvement with a carefully planned environment is paramount. This influence is seen in curricula aimed at direct instruction of children through a prescribed series of structured activities. Typically, target behaviors are identified and instructional strategies designed to change (i.e., accelerate, decelerate, initiate) the behaviors are implemented. This approach has most influenced the method, rather than the content, of curriculum implementation.

Functional

In recent years attention has been directed to identifying curricular goals that teach the child functional skills for daily living. These are skills that the child will need to interact in a more typical fashion with the environment and also skills that are geared more to daily living experiences than to particular academic or developmental sequences. Examples of functional skills for infants and toddlers include reaching to obtain a desired object, having a means of locomotion, and self-care skills such as toileting, to name a few. This approach is not a theoretical approach to child development in the same sense as the previous three approaches reviewed. Rather, it provides a practical perspective to guide assessment and goal selection for educational activities. For children with severe and/or multiple impairments, whose development may not proceed according to a typical developmental sequence and rate, this perspective is particularly useful.

Summary

In practice most early intervention programs combine theoretical approaches. Curricular content, for instance, is most often gleaned from the developmental, cognitive, and/or functional approaches. The behavioral approach, on the other hand, is often used in designing instructional strategies. Bricker and Bricker's (1976) work in early intervention provides a good example of combined theoretical perspectives. In their intervention approach, cognitive (Piagetian) theories of child development provided the theoretical bases for content, whereas instructional strategies were implemented utilizing a behavioral base.

Regardless of the primary theoretical rationale selected by a given intervention program, the identification of the program philosophy is an essential first step in curriculum planning, because it is from this theoretical base that decisions regarding content, child learning, child motivation, instructional techniques, and the roles of the child, parent, and staff in the learning process are derived.

Developmentally Appropriate Practice

Early childhood education programs have received great scrutiny in recent years due to political, social, economic, and demographic shifts. The National Association for the Education of Young Children (NAEYC), in response to concerns about early childhood education programs, issued a position statement and set of guidelines for reviewing developmentally appropriate practices for young children (Bredekamp, 1987). Briefly, these guidelines include the following principles with respect to curricula in early childhood education programs (rephrased from Bredekamp, 1987, pp. 3–8):

1. Curricula include all areas of development (physical, emotional, social, cognitive) in an integrated approach.//
2. Curricula are based on teacher's observations of children's interests and progress.
3. Emphasis is placed on learning as interactive, and environments are constructed to encourage active exploration and interaction with all facets of the environment.
4. Activities are concrete and relevant to children's lives.
5. Activities and programs include a wide range of interests and abilities to accommodate the needs of all children regardless of developmental level.
6. A variety of activities and materials are provided to encourage and provide challenges for child exploration and learning.
7. Opportunities are given for children to choose among a range of activities, and children are encouraged to become actively involved.
8. Materials and activities reflect multicultural and nonsexist experiences.
9. Opportunity for a balance of rest and active movement is provided.
10. Outdoor experiences are provided.

The NAEYC guidelines also discuss the role of adults in early childhood education programs as nurturing, responsive, supportive, and facilitative of children's opportunities to explore and learn through their unique styles and abilities.

Developmental and learning theories, regardless of particular theoretical perspective, all recognize that infants and toddlers learn through their active experiences. Furthermore, adult caregivers are viewed as highly influential in supporting early development and in the primary socialization of the young child. Nurturing, responsive, and supportive relationships are crucial to the optimal development of the young child.

These developmentally appropriate practice guidelines provide a foundation for all early education programs. They are as relevant for early intervention settings as for settings whose primary focus is typically developing children. Additional factors may need to be considered in the development and implementation of curricula and learning environments for young children with special needs and their families (Carta, Schwartz, Atwater, & McConnell, 1991).

Curricular Content

Curricular content refers to what is taught. Goals for children are derived from developmental theory and knowledge of child development. Attention is given to goals that are functional for the child and priorities for the family.

Developmental Principles

The developmental principles articulated by Lewis (1984) (previously reviewed in Chapter 1) provide the foundation for examining curricular content. Lewis described the infant as competent, social, and active. These concepts turn the early interventionist full circle away from a deficit-based model for looking at infant development, to a model that focuses on what infants bring to the interactions in their environment—their strengths, unique characteristics, temperament, and individual styles. Thus, curricula approaches can be developed around the notion that infants are active learners and seekers and participants in their own development. Activities and materials that are social in nature and foster active opportunities for infants to initiate and interact are seen as optimal.

Lewis (1984) also used the metaphor of a tree to describe development. Although the areas of development become increasingly differentiated with growth and change, they are nevertheless interrelated and joined like the branches of a tree are to the tree's trunk. Thus, the planning and implementation of curricular goals and strategies must link areas of development and recognize the overlapping quality.

Finally, Lewis (1984) discussed the interactional nature of development (also referred to as the transactional model, described in Chapter 1). Families and program staff members, working together as partners in designing strategies and goals for infants with special needs, can influence the child's development and support family functions and priorities. These mechanisms provide the structure for positive transactions. Babies who are more competent may have more learning opportunities. Families who are supported in their caregiving and who feel confident and competent in their roles and relationships, will have more opportunities and support for promoting the infant's development.

Goals for Infants and Toddlers

The early years represent a period of enormous growth and developmental change. The infant moves from an organism with largely uncoordinated motor movements but with the abilities to process sensory information to a highly organized processor of information able to engage in symbolic and abstract thought and problem solving. This early period of development, the sensorimotor period as defined by Piaget (1952), encompasses the first several years. Changes during this period include such behaviors as the development of visual pursuit (tracking), an awareness of object permanence (i.e., objects exist even when not visible), knowledge of means–ends or cause–effect relationships, vocal and gestural imitation, and awareness of the spatial relationships of objects (e.g., tracking sounds, grasping). At this time the infant learns to coordinate sensory and motor systems. At the end of this period, the young child solves simple problems and demonstrates some symbolic and abstract thinking. The next developmental period, referred to as the preoperational period by Piaget, is characterized by the child's ability to use mental symbols and words and by symbolic play activities.

Particularly with the very young infant, areas of development are highly integrated and interrelated. For instance, in the beginning the baby communicates through motor gestural movements and exercises control over objects by exploring them with the mouth and hands and moving them in various ways (e.g., pounding, waving, dropping, throwing). As the child grows and develops, areas of development (e.g., motor, speech and language, cognition) become increasingly differentiated. However, as Lewis (1984) explained, the structure of development can be likened to a tree. At the core or trunk level all functions of the organism—biological, social, cognitive—are interrelated and a part of one another. As the child grows and develops "branches," these functions become more differentiated and independent. Nevertheless, the underlying skills and functions remain intertwined and related.

Most early intervention programs recognize that all areas of development must be addressed and that areas of development are interrelated and interdependent. This is a particularly important point given the populations served in early intervention services. The disability or at-risk condition is likely to influence several developmental areas, not only the primary area affected by the disability. For instance, the child who is born visually impaired usually also manifests delays or differences in development in the motor and language areas, not only in the ability to orient to or process visual stimuli. Thus, early intervention services typically employ professionals from several disciplines and with expertise across developmental areas who work together to provide a coordinated program that addresses the needs of the whole child.

Generally, areas of development for curricula are grouped into the following categories: motor (gross and fine), cognitive, communication (speech and language), social-emotional, and self-help. Although curricular content may be separated by area of development for purposes of discussion and presentation, in practice goals and objectives across areas often are combined. For example, an individualized program for an infant might suggest working on speech and language skills (communication) at the same time a feeding goal (self-help/oral motor) is implemented, or practicing standing up to a furniture support (gross motor) to obtain a puzzle with which to play (cognitive and fine motor).

Appendix F provides a listing of major long-range goals in specific areas of development. This appendix provides the reader with a guide to major developmental achievements in the early years. More complete resources for information on typical developmental milestones or sequences include Cohen, Gross, and Haring (1976); Hanson and Hanline (1984); and Knobloch and Pasamanick (1974).

The behaviors outlined in Appendix F include general, long-range behavioral goals rather than specific goals and objectives. As such, the list provides a guide for examining curricula to ensure that the full range of behavioral domains is addressed. The reader also is referred to the publication, *DEC Recommended Practices: Indicators of Quality in Programs for Infants and Young Children with Special Needs and Their Families* (Division for Early Childhood, Council for Exceptional Children, 1993). This monograph provides recommended practice guidelines for programs, including curricula and intervention strategies in early intervention.

Method

In addition to identifying the content or what to teach, the curriculum also should specify the method or how to implement the intervention. Issues discussed in this section include general guidelines for implementation, curricular structure, and instructional strategies.

Guidelines for Implementation

Several general underlying principles govern the selection of curricular content and strategies. These guidelines for implementation follow.

1. *Each child has individual needs. Each child and family should have an Individualized Family Service Plan.* Although every early intervention program will have a core curriculum content based on the program's philosophy, the selection of goals and strategies will vary from child to child based on each child's individual needs. The needs of no two children served in early intervention programs are exactly alike regardless of their diagnoses. The goals for each Individualized Family Service Plan (IFSP) will be developed by the family and professionals from a transdisciplinary assessment of the child's strengths and areas of need and from family input regarding their concerns, priorities, and resources. Implementation strategies and issues, such as the rate at which the child should perform a specific behavior (e.g., how long the child should be expected to sit independently or in what time interval the child should be expected to feed), will depend upon extensive observations and input from both family and staff members.

2. *Family involvement in all aspects of curriculum planning and implementation is vital.* Early intervention services are designed both for the young child *and* the family. The needs of the young child and the environment in which the young child grows and learns cannot and should not be separated from that of the family unit. As such, intervention strategies must promote the needs and priorities expressed by families; provide an ongoing vehicle for the open expression of those goals; and take into account the culture, ethnicity, values, and language of the particular family. Although it is beyond the expectations of any intervention program to provide for the complete needs of a given family, an open system of communication and referral to other services as necessary must be established to ensure flexible and responsive service delivery. Such a system allows for various levels and types of family involvement ranging from parents who wish to learn technical teaching skills to those who are uninterested or unavailable for active participation in their child's program. Families, like children, have changing needs. An interest or need at a particular point in time may be markedly different at another point.

3. *Services should be delivered around the view of the child as a whole person.* Although a specific disability may primarily affect one portion of the body or child's development (e.g., audition, vision, movement in upper and/or lower body), other behavioral and developmental domains are likely to be affected as well. As discussed earlier, curricular content areas cannot be viewed as discrete and unrelated. Rather, areas of development are integrally related.

In practice, when parents and early intervention personnel develop strategies for teaching, several points must be taken into account. First, all areas of development must be assessed and observed and, from that assessment, goals set in all areas in which a need exists. Second, as strategies are implemented, the combination of goals is helpful to ensure a more natural and reinforcing learning setting. For example, a child with cerebral palsy may be placed in a chair with special supports. As careful positioning is being implemented, the child can be helped to reach for a toy that is operated by pushing a button (fine motor and cognitive goals) or to reach and point to a picture board to communicate requesting a desired object (communication goal). In such ways goals across areas of development can be effectively combined to enhance the teaching and learning processes. At the same time the needs of the whole child, in all developmental areas, are being considered. This approach varies from past practices in special education and health-related fields when professionals concentrated solely on the primary effects of the specific disability.

4. *Given that the development of the young child occurs largely in the social context, emphasis should be placed on teaching in a natural environment and with a focus on social-communicative goals.* The young child who is at risk or disabled must be viewed as a child first. Like all parents, the parents of these children are concerned with routine caregiving, feeding, sleeping, disciplining, and loving. Not only are these major areas of concern for families in their daily living, but they also offer ideal opportunities for interaction and "teaching." Curricular goals and activities should be integrated into these naturally occurring situations so that parents experience interactions that are as typical of early child-rearing interactions as possible. Furthermore, the young infant appears particularly attuned to social stimuli—the parent's voice, a human face, molding to a human body and touch when held. The young child spends most of the time in the home with these important human caregivers. Thus, it is this context that represents the optimal teaching and learning environment.

Also during the early years, the child acquires the abilities to communicate and to relate to others and a sense of self. For these reasons intervention goals must emphasize the development of social-communicative behavior.

5. *Goals and strategies selected for intervention must be both developmentally appropriate for the child and functionally appropriate and important for the child and family.* Because the early years are a time of rapid developmental change and because many developmental goals are achieved only after prerequisite developmental changes have occurred (e.g., the child is able to walk only if he or she has prerequisite head and trunk control and the ability to stand and bear weight and coordinate movements), early intervention regimens emphasize a developmental approach. A second factor that should be considered is how functional the goal or strategy is to the child or family. For instance, it may be developmentally appropriate given the child's age that he or she learn to crawl; however, the child may be so physically involved that teaching crawling may consume months or years of teaching and therapy time. If this is the case, the child may be blocked from having a way to locomote in the environment. A more functional goal may be for the child to learn to operate a scooter board to move forward or to move via a walker or wheelchair device. Another example comes in the use of materials. Putting pegs in a pegboard and building towers of small cubes are common curriculum items in early intervention programs. These items are selected for their developmental appropriateness because they are commonly found on infant development tests. However, their functional relevance can be debated. Certainly the abilities to attend, to grasp and release objects, and to rotate the wrist are functional skills. However, these skills may be more appropriately taught for some children with more functional materials

(e.g., feeding utensils; switches, buttons, or levers to operate toys) and in a more functional context (e.g., operating a button on a toy or wheelchair). Thus, when goals and strategies are developed, they should meet the twin tests of being both developmentally and functionally appropriate and important to the child.

6. *Early intervention activities that include a mix of structured and unstructured experiences are more likely to meet the diverse needs of young children in the program.* Different children will require differing degrees of structure to enhance their learning. Furthermore, these instructional requirements will likely change over time. Some young children are able to learn when placed in a supportive, enriched environment where they are allowed to engage in self-directed play and interactions. Other children have limited behavioral repertoires that prevent them from initiating effective interactions in their environments. For these children a more contrived and structured approach may be needed to teach skills that will allow them to actively initiate and respond to persons and events.

7. *To ensure generalization of newly learned behaviors to new situations, places, and/or people, children should be provided with many different instances, materials, and settings in which they can practice.* Too often in the past, children were taught to respond in a highly specific fashion to a highly structured instructional task. Research indicated that these practices often failed to produce generalization of the newly acquired skills to other experiences. Furthermore, especially with young children, their attention was never captured or quickly waned under such stylized conditions. Once again, if "teaching" occurs in situations that are as natural and typical as possible across variable conditions and people, the child is apt to demonstrate skills across situations while also experiencing a more normalized teaching and learning environment.

8. *Early intervention curricular strategies should emphasize the process of learning, not merely the product.* Traditionally, educational programs focused on the teaching of specific skills—typically skills in which the child was deficient. A more contemporary approach emphasizes the processes through which children learn. Assisting the young child in gaining control over the environment, learning about causal relationships, and attaining feelings of competence are important early intervention goals. Thus, devising a responsive environment that facilitates the child's active role in learning is needed. For instance, instead of teaching a child to label objects such as a comb or ball as an isolated speech activity, a parent or early interventionist may ask the child to name the object within the context of play or the object's use (e.g., combing the hair in the morning or playing ball). Then the child would be encouraged to show and/or discuss the object's use as well. In this way the activity is functional for the child and more motivating. It also emphasizes the process of learning and the child's active involvement rather than merely the product—being able to say "comb" or "ball."

9. *A team approach to the delivery of early intervention services is optimal.* Early intervention services run a wide gamut. They may include educational planning and teaching typically performed by a teacher, physical and occupational therapy, speech–language therapy, health care, and social services (e.g., counseling). To deliver services to the child across developmental areas and assist families, a coordinated team approach is necessary. Through such an approach, input from a variety of professionals is available to parents in a manner that represents a synthesis of various perspectives and viewpoints and an efficient scheme for teaching.

10. *Early intervention strategies should be implemented in coordination with other service needs of the child and family.* Particularly for the very young child with special needs, service areas encompass a range of professions and agencies. These children are likely to have considerable health care and educational needs, and perhaps the family will be served by social service agencies as well. Thus, professionals in early intervention must take the role of collaborators in the larger service delivery arena so that parents are supported and assisted in their quest to obtain and coordinate services. Too often parents report that one professional tells them one thing and another tells them something else. This advice, delivered in isolation, often puts professionals and agencies in conflict and parents in a dilemma. As with teaming within an early intervention staff, service delivery methods that reflect joint decisions and goals across professions best serve the child and family.

Early intervention involves a complex network of services for the young child. Emphasis is placed on individualizing services, providing opportunities for active family involvement and participation, and selecting goals and strategies that reflect developmental needs and the child's ability to function in the daily environment. Moreover, collaboration among professionals and a focus on the whole child to ensure a comprehensive and appropriate delivery of services are stressed.

Curricular Structure

Curricula vary greatly in terms of the degree and type of structure for implementation. Four considerations in determining program structure are discussed in the following sections: the role of the child, the role of the environment, the role of the parent, and the role of staff members. Depending upon program purpose and philosophy, the structure can vary from very open, child-directed learning to learning that is highly planned and organized by adults. The following discussion pinpoints preferred practices in early intervention in terms of child development theory and clinical experiences.

Role of the child

Contemporary research on the capabilities of infants and developmental growth in the early years highlights the importance of *viewing the infant as an active, competent learner.* Even infants with the most severe disabilities and few behaviors in their repertoires for affecting the environment must be encouraged to initiate and develop an awareness of environmental control. Through such interactions, young children develop a sense of competence and control and the motivation to continue to learn through environmental interactions. Infants who are given few or no opportunities to exhibit control over their immediate environment are in jeopardy of developing a "learned helplessness" characterized by extreme passivity and withdrawal. On the other hand, the infant who is the active learner, rather than the passive recipient of stimuli, continues to engage the environment and learn.

Role of the environment

Environments vary as to the degree of organization designed to promote specified child behaviors and also the degree to which the environment is responsive to child behavior. The amount of structure in this area will depend upon the teaching goal. For instance, if the goal is to teach children to arrange or classify items sequentially along some dimension or characteristic, environmental cues or prompts may be provided in the form of patterns or the materials themselves may be self-correcting. In the case of Montessori cylinders, for example, wooden cylinders are arranged from largest to smallest and fit only in the ordered precut holes to which they match. An example of prompts may be a puzzle board that provides an outline or silhouette of the object shape and size such that the child can match the object and outline and order objects by size. If, on the other hand, the teaching goal is for children to play near peers, talk to one another, or play cooperatively, toys may be selected that require two or more children for optimal operation (e.g., teeter-totter or see-saw; tea set for doll play) but allow a lot of leeway in terms of how, how long, and when children operate them.

No one type of structural arrangement is appropriate for all children or for all goals. Rather, environmental arrangements can be modified to suit the individual child's needs and the teaching goals. Most young children with special needs require some degree of environmental structure to "get a behavior going." Many, for example, would not initiate a cooperative play session with another child. However, if armed with the skills to do so and encouragement—words they can say, toys that enhance play, praise for their efforts—they may successfully make a new initiation.

Role of the parent

The rule of thumb is that no one role is appropriate for all parents. Some parents choose to become active teachers in their children's learning programs, and others do not wish to participate. A full range of options must be made available to accommodate various families' needs. Furthermore, these options must be flexibly exercised so that parents are free to modify the degree and terms of their involvement as family circumstances change and dictate. However, all parents should be given the opportunity to be well informed in a manner in which they can understand (i.e., in their native language) the early intervention options for their child. Moreover, a mechanism for an open and continual exchange of ideas between families and early interventionists is needed to ensure family participation as appropriate to the families' needs and wishes.

Role of staff members

The roles of early intervention staff members typically center on the degree to which they plan or organize the learning environment. Staff members may plan an environment to enhance or enrich the child's development by facilitating interactions with it, or they may plan a highly structured activity of staff-directed instruction or therapy. Again, their roles depend upon the teaching goal. However, preferred practices would dictate viewing the child as an active initiator and enhancing the involvement of family members in decision making regarding goal setting and implementation of strategies. Intervention staff members in this sense function as consultants to families.

Instructional Strategies

Some children learn optimally through incidental observations of their environment and others do not. A child may require highly prepared learning situations to establish a new behavior or increase (or decrease) an existing one in her or his repertoire. This section outlines specific teaching strategies for use when more direct instruction is needed. The supplemental reading section at the end of this chapter provides references for more detailed information on these strategies and their usage.

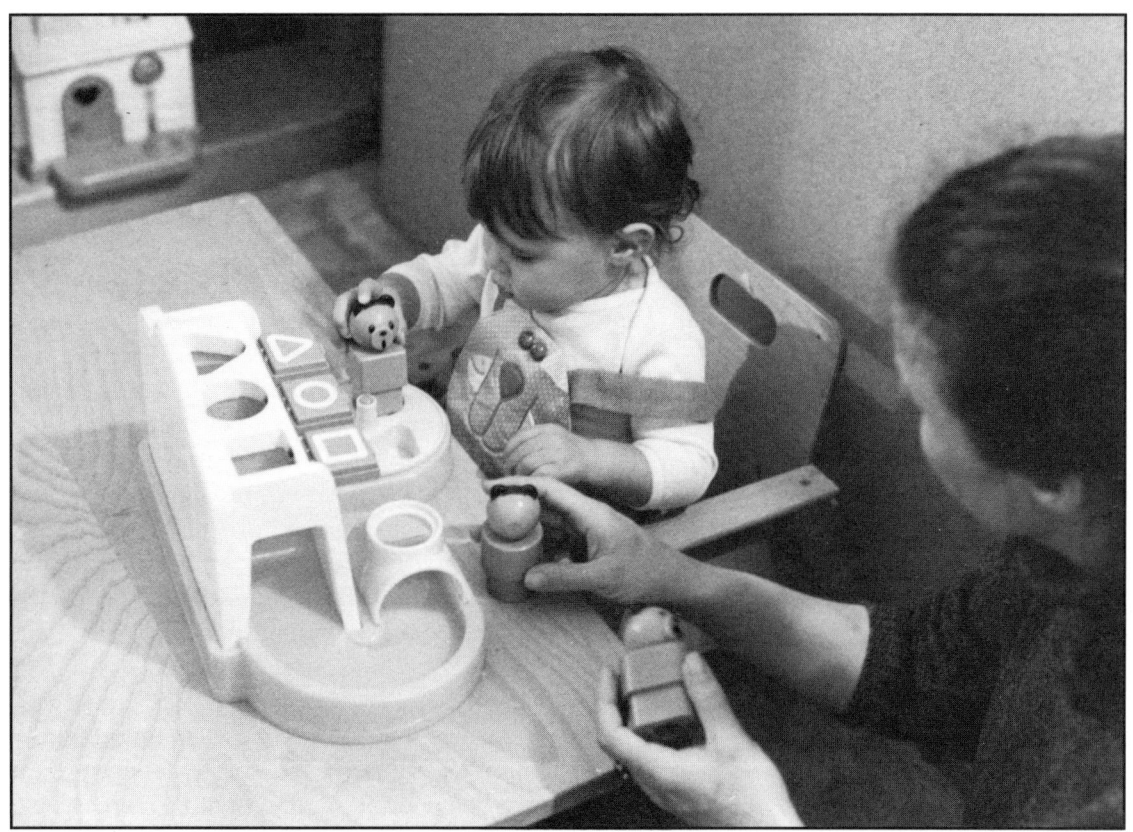

Instructional and behavioral objectives

Before beginning instruction the interventionist must have a clear plan or idea of the behavior to be taught. Objectives are derived from the assessments and observations of family members and staff members and include those goals family members select as targets. Each objective must be written in clear, concise words in such a fashion that it is apparent to everyone what is expected of the child. Furthermore, the behavior specified in the objective must be observable and measurable.

Instructional or behavioral objectives have three major component parts:

1. The *behavior* (e.g., baby will reach)
2. The *conditions* under which the behavior will occur (e.g., when placed in a supported sitting position)
3. The *standard or criterion* for evaluation (e.g., on four of five occasions when the rattle is presented for 3 consecutive days)

Each of these components is necessary for an objective to be complete.

Selection and sequencing of instructional goals

The first step in the teaching process is to establish a specific goal or objective that is appropriate to the needs of the child. Then the instructional process must be designed. This involves an ordering or sequencing of a series of teaching steps. Teaching objectives may be ordered or sequenced along several dimensions, such as by level of difficulty. One process for sequencing is called *task analysis*, which involves breaking down an instructional objective into the small steps necessary to teach it. The series of steps may be different for different children depending upon the rate at which each child learns and the degree to which the behavior must be broken into smaller steps in order to teach the behavior. This process involves four steps (Hanson, 1987):

1. Deciding what behavior to teach
2. Breaking the behavior into small steps and ordering the steps
3. Deciding how well the child must do the behavior
4. Observing what the child can do and establishing with which step the instruction must begin

An example follows:

Instructional Objective to Be Taught: When placed in front of chair with a toy on it (condition), Jillian will pull herself independently to standing to see the toy (behavior) on three of four occasions for 3 consecutive days (standard or criterion).

Task Analysis:

1. Child kneels at chair.
2. Child pulls self from kneeling to half-kneeling (one knee up).
3. Child pulls self from kneeling to half-kneeling to standing.

For the child in need of more assistance or smaller steps, several variations could be added. The child could be physically or verbally prompted or assisted to stand. For example, an additional step might be (2a) pulls from kneeling to half-kneeling when parent holds hands and tugs *or* pulls from kneeling to half-kneeling when parent supports child at the hips, taps knee and helps child lift knee to half-kneeling position. Any of a number of variations and smaller steps can be added depending upon what is needed and appropriate for a particular child. More complete discussions of this process are presented with examples in Hanson (1987) and Hanson and Harris (1986).

Teaching techniques

Teaching techniques involve the use of consequation and of various antecedent events or prompts. Although associated with a behavioral theoretical model, these techniques are so important and so widely used in educational settings for all age groups that their systematic use has become almost universal. However, the degree of program structure associated with their usage varies greatly and is reflected in differing models. These techniques are considered individually.

The type of consequation most used in teaching is reinforcement. Briefly, *reinforcement* is any consequence that immediately follows a behavior and serves to strengthen that behavior or, in other words, increase the likelihood the behavior will occur again. For example, when a child (or adult for that matter) is praised, she or he is likely to repeat the behavior. Typical reinforcers for young children include verbal praise, hugs, adult attention, food (though more natural social consequences are preferred), and producing a change or outcome in an object (e.g., watching the top spin, hearing the toy squeak).

Antecedent events also can be used for instructional purposes. These events or actions can set the occasion for a behavior to occur. These events are typically termed *prompts* or *cues*. For purposes of this discussion, these terms will be used interchangeably. These prompts or cues may be verbal or physical actions on the part of the early interventionist or the parent, or they may involve a structuring of the environment or materials in the environment. For example, providing a tug or a tap on the knee or leg to encourage the child to stand is a physical prompt or cue. Saying "stand up" is a verbal prompt or cue. Another instance is saying "bbb" to encourage the child to use the label "ball." Examples of environmental prompts or cues may include color coding a formboard so that the outside of the hole is the same color as the shape to be placed there or providing a toy that requires two children to operate the lever in order to encourage cooperative interactions. These antecedent events can be used effectively in a variety of settings to enhance the child's ability to perform a particular behavior.

The use of these antecedent events (prompts and cues) and consequation events is also effective in shaping more complex behavior. *Shaping* is a process whereby the child is reinforced for demonstrating successive approximations to the final instructional goal. For example, the final goal may be that the child says "milk" when she wants a glass of milk. The mother might provide a prompt, such as "What do you want?" or a prompt that models the response such as "Milk? Do you want milk?" At first, if the child looks to the refrigerator and signs milk or points, the mother may reinforce the child by getting the milk. Later, she might require the child to make a vocalization. Still later, the child may be required to say "mmm" to get the milk. At each step the child is reinforced for making a closer and closer approximation to the goal of clearly saying "milk."

These strategies represent major instructional techniques that are used often with young children. All offer parents and early interventionists opportunities for structuring the instructional environment (home, classroom) to facilitate certain instructional goals or behavior.

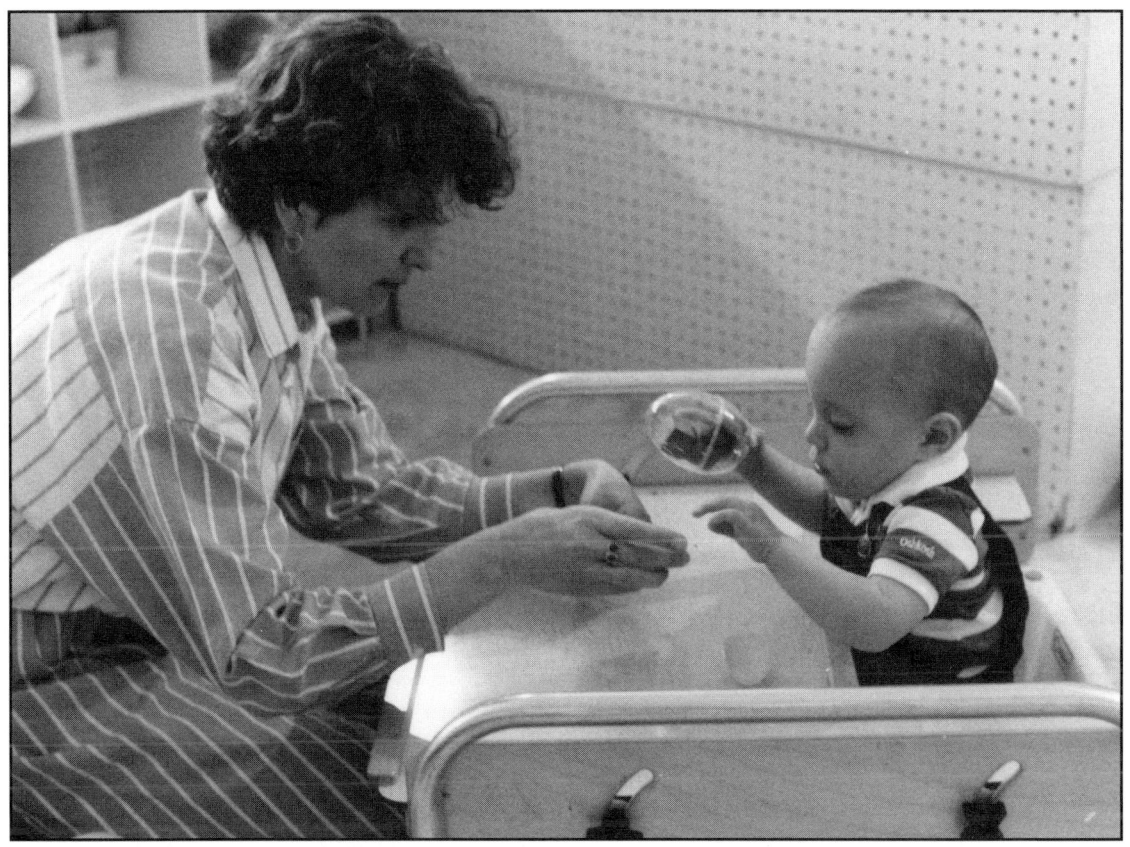

Activity-Based Intervention

Early childhood education programs have long advocated teaching through providing children with motivating activities and materials that encourage their active participation and engagement. As previously discussed in the section Developmentally Appropriate Practice, providing these types of experiences is seen as exemplary practice.

The use of everyday events and activities as opportunities for facilitating specific teaching goals also has been explored systematically through a number of research studies, particularly in the area of communication development (Snyder-McLean, Solomonson, McLean, & Sack, 1984; Warren & Rogers-Warren, 1985). Warren and Kaiser (1988) reviewed and discussed the use of natural methods in a "milieu approach" in the area of language intervention. This body of literature has helped focus attention on naturally occurring activities and events as appropriate experiences for teaching behavioral goals for children with special needs.

Bricker and Cripe (1992) articulated an approach for using natural environments and events in early intervention. The term *activity-based intervention* describes these methods. Briefly, an activity-based intervention is characterized by the following elements: (a) child-directed transactions; (b) training goals embedded in routine activities that may be planned and/or child initiated; (c) activities that incorporate naturally occurring antecedents and consequences; and (d) activities that develop functional and generative skills that will enable children to function more independently (Bricker & Cripe, 1992). The examples of activities found at the beginning of this chapter could be considered activity-based interventions.

This approach represents an appropriate blend of child development principles with strategies for facilitating the development of children with special needs. It provides a synthesis of the elements discussed in this volume and is advocated as an optimal approach to early intervention.

Putting It All Together

A curriculum is not implemented in isolation. As previously described, objectives and goals are formulated after careful observation and assessment by family members and early intervention staff members. From these observations and assessments, families select goals and objectives based on their concerns, priorities, and resources. Early interventionists provide expertise in the subject area and support for families in identifying the goals most appropriate to their child and situation. After the curriculum is implemented, the procedures are monitored and evaluated to determine if they are effective or if changes should be made. This process is linked and continuous in an exemplary early intervention approach. Such a linked system is described by Bricker (1989). This approach linking assessment, intervention, and evaluation is put into practice in the *Assessment, Evaluation, and Programming System* (Bricker, 1993; Cripe, Slentz, & Bricker, 1993), which is a good resource for early intervention programs.

Summary

All curricula should be anchored in a theoretical framework. From this framework, programmatic decisions regarding environmental design and the roles of the child, early intervention staff members, and family members in the learning process are defined. In addition to outlining these issues, this chapter has focused on the content appropriate to a curriculum for young children and on methods for implementing the curriculum. This curriculum represents the set of educational learning experiences or tasks in the early intervention program. The greater the degree to which goals and strategies are embedded in the child's and family's daily activities, the greater the likelihood these goals will be met and in a manner valued by the family.

Preferred Practices

The following list of questions provides guidance to the reader in evaluating the quality and appropriateness of curricular approaches. Although not every question is equally important or relevant to a given program or situation, early intervention program personnel can use the list as a reference when selecting curricula.

1. Is the curriculum organized around a theoretical rationale? Is this philosophical approach clearly stated?
2. Is the philosophical approach consistent with or appropriate to the early intervention program's approach and the population to be served?
3. Does the curriculum include a wide range of items (scope), such that the needs of the full range of children in the program will be met? Are items appropriate for use with children with different disabilities (if so, which ones) and ages?
4. Are the directions for curriculum use clearly and specifically stated?
5. Are the curricular items sequenced in a developmentally appropriate order?
6. Can items be further "branched" or broken down to accommodate children for whom items may be too difficult? Are instructions for this branching provided?
7. Do items meet the test of being both developmentally and functionally appropriate for young children?
8. Is family involvement encouraged and a central focus? If so, how?
9. Is the selection of curricular items integrally linked with assessments and observations of child behavior? Are the goals and objectives clearly stated so that child progress can be assessed?
10. Are the goals and activities written in a clear, jargon-free manner so that they can be easily and consistently used?
11. Is the amount of time needed to implement the curriculum appropriate to the needs of the program?
12. Are the target environments or settings in which the curriculum is to be implemented appropriate to the goals and needs of the program?
13. Are the teaching techniques and areas of expertise required to implement the curriculum consistent with those of the staff members?
14. Are special materials or equipment needed? If so, are these readily available to early intervention program staff members and/or family members?
15. Is the curricular package economically feasible for the program?
16. Are the curricular items nonracist, nonsexist, and culturally nonbiased?
17. Does the curriculum foster generalization of skills?
18. Has the curriculum been tested on the populations for which it was designed? Are these validation data presented?
19. Were different specialists and specialties involved with and reflected in the curricular content?
20. Can the curriculum be used in formative and summative evaluations of child progress? Can the effectiveness of the curricular approach be evaluated for program evaluation?

References

Bayley, N. (1993). *The Bayley Scales of Infant Development* (2nd ed.). San Antonio, TX: Psychological Corp.

Bredekamp, S. (1987). *Developmentally appropriate practice in early childhood programs serving children from birth through age 8.* Washington, DC: National Association for the Education of Young Children.

Bricker, D. (1989). *Early intervention for at-risk and handicapped infants, toddlers, and preschool children* (2nd ed.). Palo Alto, CA: VORT.

Bricker, D. (1993). *Assessment, Evaluation, and Programming System for Infants and Children, Volume 1: AEPS measurement for birth to three years.* Baltimore: Brookes.

Bricker, D., & Cripe, J. J. W. (1992). *An activity-based approach to early intervention.* Baltimore: Brookes.

Bricker, W. A., & Bricker, D. D. (1976). The infant, toddler, and preschool research and intervention project. In T. Tjossem (Ed.), *Intervention strategies for high-risk infants and young children* (pp. 545–572). Baltimore: University Park Press.

Carta, J. J., Schwartz, I. S., Atwater, J. B., & McConnell, S. R. (1991). Developmentally appropriate practice: Appraising its usefulness for young children with disabilities. *Topics in Early Childhood Special Education, 11*(1), 1–20.

Cattell, P. (1969). *Cattell Infant Intelligence Scale.* San Antonio, TX: Psychological Corp.

Cohen, M. A., Gross, P. J., & Haring, N. G. (1976). In N. G. Haring & L. J. Brown (Eds.), *Teaching the severely handicapped* (Vol. 1, pp. 35–110). New York: Grune & Stratton.

Cripe, J., Slentz, K., & Bricker, D. (1993). *Assessment, Evaluation, and Programming System for Infants and Children, Volume 2: AEPS curriculum for birth to three years.* Baltimore: Brookes.

Division for Early Childhood, Council for Exceptional Children. (1993). *DEC recommended practices: Indicators of quality in programs for infants and young children with special needs and their families.* Reston, VA: Author.

Dunst, C. J. (1981). *Infant learning: A cognitive-linguistic intervention strategy.* Hingham, MA: Teaching Resources.

Gesell, A. (1925). *The mental growth of the preschool child.* New York: Macmillan.

Gesell, A., & Amatruda, C. S. (1947). *Developmental diagnosis.* New York: Paul B. Holder.

Hanson, M. J. (1987). *Teaching the infant with Down syndrome: A guide for parents and professionals* (2nd ed.). Austin, TX: PRO-ED.

Hanson, M. J., & Hanline, M. F. (1984). Behavioral competencies and outcomes: The effects of disorders. In M. J. Hanson (Ed.), *Atypical infant development* (pp. 109–177). Austin, TX: PRO-ED.

Hanson, M. J., & Harris, S. R. (1986). *Teaching the young child with motor delays: A guide for parents and professionals.* Austin, TX: PRO-ED.

Knobloch, H., & Pasamanick, B. (Eds.). (1974). *Gesell and Amatruda's developmental diagnosis* (3rd ed.). Hagerstown, MD: Harper & Row.

Lewis, M. (1984). Developmental principles and their implications for at-risk and handicapped infants. In M. J. Hanson (Ed.), *Atypical infant development* (pp. 3–24). Austin, TX: PRO-ED.

Lillie, D. L. (1975). *Early childhood curriculum: An individual approach.* Chicago: Science Research Associates.

Mori, A. A., & Neisworth, J. T. (1983). Curricula in early childhood education: Some generic and special considerations. *Topics in Early Childhood Special Education, 2*(4), 1–8.

Piaget, J. (1952). *The origins of intelligence in children.* (M. Cook, Trans.). New York: International Universities Press. (Original work published 1936)

Piaget, J. (1970). Piaget's theory. In P. H. Mussen (Ed.), *Carmichael's manual of child psychology* (Vol. 1, 3rd ed., pp. 703–732). New York: Wiley.

Phillips, J. L. (1975). *The origins of intellect: Piaget's theory* (2nd ed.). San Francisco: W. H. Freeman.

Skinner, B. F. (1972). *Cumulative record: A selection of papers* (3rd ed.). New York: Appleton-Century-Crofts.

Snyder-McLean, L., Solomonson, B., McLean, J., & Sack, S. (1984). Structuring joint action routines. *Seminars in Speech and Language, 5*(3) 213–228.

Warren, S., & Kaiser, A. P. (1988). Research in early language intervention. In S. L. Odom & M. B. Karnes (Eds.), *Early intervention for in-*

fants and children with handicaps (pp. 89–108). Baltimore: Brookes.

Warren, S., & Rogers-Warren, A. (Eds.). (1985). *Teaching functional language*. Austin, TX: PRO-ED.

Selected Readings

Curriculum Implementation

The following texts discuss both *what* should be included in early intervention curricula and *how* such content can be implemented.

Bagnato, S. J., & Neisworth, J. T. (1981). *Linking developmental assessment and curricula*. Rockville, MD: Aspen.

Bailey, D. B., & Wolery, M. (1984). *Teaching infants and preschoolers with handicaps*. Columbus, OH: Merrill.

Bredekamp, S. (1987). *Developmentally appropriate practice in early childhood programs serving children from birth through age 8*. Washington, DC: National Association for the Education of Young Children.

Bricker, D., & Cripe, J. J. W. (1992). *An activity-based approach to early intervention*. Baltimore: Brookes.

Cook, R. E., Tessier, A., & Klein, M. D. (1992). *Adapting early childhood curricula for children with special needs* (3rd ed.). New York: Macmillan.

Cripe, J., Slentz, K., & Bricker, D. (1993). *Assessment, Evaluation, and Programming System for Infants and Children, Volume 2: AEPS curriculum for birth to three years*. Baltimore: Brookes.

Deiner, P. L. (1993). *Resources for teaching children with diverse abilities* (2nd ed.). Fort Worth, TX: Harcourt Brace College Publishers.

Division for Early Childhood, Council for Exceptional Children. (1993). *DEC recommended practices: Indicators of quality in programs for infants and young children with special needs and their families*. Reston, VA: Author.

Dunst, C. J. (1981). *Infant learning: A cognitive-linguistic intervention strategy*. Hingham, MA: Teaching Resources.

Instructional Strategies

These references provide information on *how* to teach. Detailed instruction on how to plan and implement a teaching task is given, and many cases are presented.

Bailey, D. B., & Wolery, M. (1984). *Teaching infants and preschoolers with handicaps*. Columbus, OH: Merrill. (Chapter 2, Determining Instructional Targets, and Chapter 3, Implementing Direct Instruction, are particularly helpful.)

Becker, W. C. (1971). *An empirical basis for change in education*. Chicago: Science Research Associates.

Becker, W. C., Engelmann, S., & Thomas, D. R. (1975). *Teaching 1: Classroom management*. Chicago: Science Research Associates.

Becker, W. C., Engelmann, S., & Thomas, D. R. (1975). *Teaching 2: Cognitive learning and instruction*. Chicago: Science Research Associates.

Becker, W. C., Engelmann, S., & Thomas, D. R. (1976). *Teaching 3: Evaluation of instruction*. Chicago: Science Research Associates.

Mager, R. F. (1984). *Preparing instructional objectives*. Belmont, CA: David S. Lake.

Behavior Management

These paperbacks are written for parents and professionals and provide easy-to-read descriptions of strategies for effectively teaching children and managing children's behavior.

Becker, W. C. (1971). *Parents are teachers*. Champaign, IL: Research Press.

Madsen, C. K., & Madsen, C. H. (1970). *Parents/children/discipline: A positive approach*. Boston: Allyn & Bacon.

Patterson, G. R. (1971). *Families*. Champaign, IL: Research Press.

Patterson, G. R. (1976). *Living with children*. Champaign, IL: Research Press.

These paperbacks provide a comprehensive discussion of behavior management strategies.

Deibert, A. N., & Harmon, A. J. (1973). *New tools for changing behavior.* Champaign, IL: Research Press.

Krumboltz, J. D., & Krumboltz, H. B. (1972). *Changing children's behavior.* Englewood Cliffs, NJ: Prentice-Hall.

Child Development

These resources provide general information on typical child development and child care. They are useful to both parents and professionals as reference materials.

Brazelton, T. B. (1969). *Infants and mothers.* New York: Dell.

Brazelton, T. B. (1992). *Touchpoints.* Reading, MA: Addison-Wesley.

Caplan, F. (1973). *The first twelve months of life.* New York: Grosset & Dunlap.

Caplan, F., & Caplan, T. (1977). *The second twelve months of life.* New York: Grosset & Dunlap.

Leach, P. (1977). *Your baby and child from birth to age five.* New York: Knopf.

Leach, P. (1983). *Babyhood* (2nd ed.). New York: Knopf.

McCall, R. B. (1979). *Infants.* New York: Vintage Books.

Activities for Infants

These books feature activities that parents and professionals can use when teaching and playing with infants. Several references describe easy-to-make toys.

Burtt, K. G., & Kalkstein, K. (1981). *Smart toys for babies from birth to two.* New York: Harper Colophon.

Cunningham, C., & Sloper, P. (1978). *Helping your exceptional baby.* New York: Pantheon.

Fewell, R. R., & Vadasy, P. F. (1983). *Learning through play.* Hingham, MA: Teaching Resources.

Goldberg, S. (1981). *Teaching with toys.* Ann Arbor: University of Michigan Press.

Gordon, I. J. (1970). *Baby learning through baby play: A parent's guide for the first two years.* New York: St. Martin's Press.

Gordon, I. J., Guinagh, B., & Jester, J. E. (1972). *Child learning through child play: Learning activities for two- and three-year-olds.* New York: St. Martin's Press.

MacDonald, J. D., & Gillette, Y. (1984). *Ecological Communication System.* Toledo, OH: ECO-LETTER.

McConkey, R., & Jeffree, D. (1981). *Making toys for handicapped children: A guide for parents and teachers.* Englewood Cliffs, NJ: Prentice-Hall.

Moyer, I. D. (1983). *Responding to infants.* Minneapolis, MN: T. S. Denison.

Musselwhite, C. R. (1986). *Adaptive play for special needs children.* Austin, TX: PRO-ED.

Segal, M. (1983). *Your child at play: Birth to one year.* New York: Newmarket.

Segal, M., & Adcock, D. (1985). *Your child at play: Birth to two years.* New York: Newmarket.

Curriculum, Equipment, and Supply Resources

Extensive lists of resources are provided in Appendix G and at the end of Chapter 10.

Selected Early Intervention Curricula[1]

***Assessment, Evaluation, and Programming System for Infants and Children, Volume 2:** AEPS Curriculum for Birth to Three Years* by Juliann Cripe, Kristine Slentz, and Diane Bricker (1993)

Publisher: Paul H. Brookes Publishing Co., P.O. Box 10624, Baltimore, MD 21285-0624, (800) 638-3775.

---

[1] Sandra Petersen is gratefully acknowledged for compiling a major portion of this list.

Items:

AEPS Measurement for Birth to Three Years—Volume 1 (Edited by D. Bricker, 1993)	$39.00
AEPS Curriculum for Birth to Three Years—Volume 2 (Edited by J. Cripe, K. Slentz, & D. Bricker, 1993)	$59.00
AEPS Data Recording Forms, Birth to Three Years	3/$21.00
AEPS Family Report, Birth to Three Years	3/$15.00
AEPS Family Interest Survey, Birth to Three Years	3/$10.00
AEPS Child Progress Record, Birth to Three Years	3/$16.00

Age: Birth to 36 months.

Target Population: Infants and toddlers with special needs.

Curriculum Areas: Fine motor, gross motor, adaptive, cognitive, social-communication, social.

Carolina Curriculum for Handicapped Infants and Infants at Risk

Publisher: Paul H. Brookes Publishing Co., P.O. Box 10624, Baltimore, MD 21285-0624, (800) 638-3775.

Items:

Carolina Curriculum for Handicapped Infants and Infants At Risk — $40.00
  Developmentally based (drawing on Piaget, Uzgiris, and Hunt); logical teaching sequences; adaptive skills.

Age: Birth to 24-month developmental age range.

Target Population: Children with disabilities and their families—for use in homes and centers.

Curriculum Areas: 20 sequences, including Social Skills, Tactile Integration and Manipulation, Object Permanence, Functional Use of Objects and Symbolic Play, Control over Physical Environment, Imitation, Communication, Self-Direction, Reaching and Grasping, Gross Motor.

Developmental Programming for Infants and Young Children

Publisher: University of Michigan Press, 839 Greene Street, P.O. Box 1104, Ann Arbor, MI 48109, (313) 764-4394.

Items:

Volume 1: Assessment and Application — $14.95
  Guide in moving from assessment to individualized programming; includes discussion of theoretical basis and section on specific disabilities.

Volume 2: Early Intervention Developmental Profile — $2.10
  (min order of 5)
  Covers perceptual/fine motor, cognition, language, social-emotional, self-care, gross motor. Should be administered by interdisciplinary team.

Volume 3: Stimulation Activities — $15.95
  Activities by curriculum area by age (2- to 3-month ranges)
  Complete set — $24.95

Age: Birth to 36 months.

Target Population: Children with disabilities and their families—for use in homes and centers.

Curriculum Areas: Perceptual/fine motor, cognition, language, social-emotional, self-care, gross motor.

Early Learning Accomplishment Profile

Publisher: Kaplan School Supply Corporation, P.O. Box 609, Lewisville, NC 27023-0609, (800) 334-2014.

Items:

Early Learning Accomplishment Profile (Early LAP) — $7.50
  Criterion-referenced tool that provides guidance in programming for infants, young children, and children with special needs.

Early LAP Scoring Booklet — 20/$20.50

Early LAP Developmental Kit — $275.00
  Provides basic assessment materials recommended by the Early LAP.

Early Learning Activity Cards $39.95
     Sequenced cards that provide instructional activities and direct teaching procedures.

Age: Birth to 36 months.

Target Population: Infants, toddlers, and young children with special needs.

Curriculum Areas: Motor, cognitive, language, self-help, social-emotional.

Hawaii Early Learning Profile (HELP) and Activities

Publisher: Vort Corporation, P.O. Box 60880, Palo Alto, CA 94306, (415) 322-8282.

Items:

HELP Activity Guide $22.95
     Task-analyzed curriculum guide.

HELP Charts $2.95/1–9; $2.45/10–99; $1.95/100+
     Recording/visually tracking progress; 650 skills sequenced on horizontal continuum.

HELP Checklist $2.95
     Same 650 skills; space for assessment dates and comments, especially for setting objectives.

HELP: When the Parent Is Handicapped $25.95
     Offers alternative activities and training techniques for parents who are blind, deaf, physically disabled, or mentally retarded.

HELP for Parents (of Children with Special Needs) $3.95
     Booklet with information on child health, immunization, nutrition, safety, sleep patterns, behaviors, illness. Room for parents to record milestones.

Age: Birth to 3 years; month-by-month increments.

Target Population: Children with all different disabilities.

Curriculum Areas: Cognitive, expressive language, gross motor, fine motor, social-emotional, self-help.

Parent–Infant Communication

Publisher: Infant Hearing Resource, Portland Center for Speech and Hearing, 3515 SW Veteran's Hospital Road, Portland, OR 97210, (503) 228-6479.

Items:

Parent–Infant Communication Manual $39.95
     A program of clinical and home training for parents of infants with hearing impairments.

Age: Birth to 4 years.

Target Population: Infants with hearing impairments and their parents.

Curriculum Areas: Auditory development, presymbolic communication, receptive language, expressive language.

Growing: Birth to Three Portage Project

Publisher: Portage Project, CESA 5, 626 East Slifer Street, Portage, WI 53901, phone: (608) 742-8811 ext. 264, fax: (608) 742-2384.

Items:

Piecing It All Together $5.00
     Describes the research and literature foundation, as well as provides an introduction to Growing: Birth to Three.

Ecological Planner (set of 10, with Master Forms) $44.00
     Provides guidelines for observation and communication, forms for gathering information, and formats for intervention planning.

Interactive Grow Pack $10.00
     Provides suggestions for interactions between parent or caregiver and child.

Interactions & Daily Routines Books $40.00
     Four books that provide suggestions for daily activities.

Nurturing Journals (10 sets) $13.00
     Open-ended questions and statements help parents reflect on the process of parenting. Includes information on child nutrition and immunization.

Complete Set $110.00

Age: Birth to three.

Target Population: Children with disabilities and their families—for use at home.

Curriculum Areas: Spans all developmental areas.

Small Wonder

Publisher: American Guidance Service, Publisher's Building, P.O. Box 99, Circle Pines, MN 55014-1796, (800) 328 2560.

Items:

You and Your Small Wonder

Book 1: Activities for Busy Parents and Babies $14.95
(Birth to 18 months)

Book 2: Activities for Parents and Toddlers on the Go $14.95
(18 to 36 months)

More than 150 activities in each for parents to integrate into daily routines.

Small Wonder Program $174.95 each level; $299.95 complete set

Levels 1 (birth to 18 months) and 2 (18 to 36 months)

The complete program includes a user's guide, activity cards, look book and picture cards, diary or progress charts, puppets, songs, card stories, and storage box. Activities incorporate a variety of games, exercises, songs, picture stories, and puppet plays.

Age: Birth to 36 months.

Target Population: Normal and developmentally delayed.

Curriculum Areas: Spans all developmental areas.

Teaching the Infant with Down Syndrome: A Guide for Parents and Professionals (2nd ed.) by Marci J. Hanson (1987)

Publisher: PRO-ED, 8700 Shoal Creek Boulevard, Austin, TX 78757, (512) 451-3246.

Items:

Step-by-step guide for parents to help children with Down syndrome develop as normally as possible, plus additional resource information sections. $27.00

Age: Birth to 3 years.

Target Population: Infants and toddlers with Down syndrome and their families.

Curriculum Areas: Gross motor, cognitive and fine motor, communication, social and self-help.

Teaching the Young Child with Motor Delays: A Guide for Parents and Professionals by Marci J. Hanson and Susan R. Harris (1986)

Publisher: PRO-ED, 8700 Shoal Creek Boulevard, Austin, TX 78757, (512) 451-3246.

Items:

Guide provides information to parents on how motor development influences other areas of development and provides teaching strategies and activities for use in the home.

Age: Birth through 3 years.

Target Population: Young children with motor difficulties and/or delayed motor development.

Curriculum Areas: Emphasis on gross and fine motor; activities also provided in the social, cognitive, and communication areas.

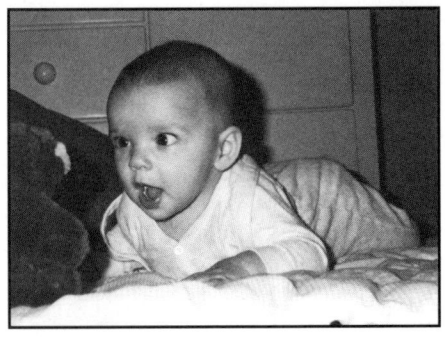

Creating Learning Environments

CHAPTER 10

Jaree is holding little Alisha on her lap. When she says, "Hello little cutie" with a smile, Alisha's face lights up and she smiles back. Soon Alisha gurgles out a coo sound. Jaree coos back for a moment as she smiles at her baby girl. Alisha coos again and kicks with excitement. On and on the exchange goes, each happy in "conversation" with the other.

The baby doll is being fed in her highchair by Jillian. Justin stands at the child-sized stove and stirs a pot while Laura puts dishes on the table. The routine continues until Anhthu decides that she wants to play with the stove. She grabs the spoon from Justin who tugs back at the spoon and screams. Maria, the early interventionist, asks Anhthu if she can ask Justin if she can play with the spoon and pan. She also points to another set of dishes with which Anhthu can play.

Each of these examples demonstrates an optimal learning environment for infants and toddlers. Both are engaging and provide opportunities for children to practice skills as well as expand their behavioral repertoires. These environments also are appropriate for the age of the children and allow them to have enjoyable social exchanges. Although they are examples of routine play activities, they have many individualized goals and objectives embedded in them for children with developmental delays.

Early intervention services do not resemble more structured services for school-aged children. They are unique. A major focus of the intervention will include the child's caregivers (typically the parents) and the home environment because the home environment is the primary environment for the infant and toddler. The purpose of this chapter is to describe major components that characterize quality learning environments for infants and toddlers, both in homes and centers, and to discuss specific techniques for designing and enhancing these environments.

Learning Through Social Interactions and Play

Learning is social in nature. Major child development theorists have highlighted the importance of play to child growth and development in that play provides a means for children to develop and expand their cognitive, problem-solving, language, and social skills (Bruner, 1972; Piaget, 1962; Vygotsky, 1967).

Much attention has been focused in recent years on the use of play activities for instruction and to enhance the development of children with disabilities. Fewell and Kaminski (1988) reviewed the research in this area and also the research conducted on the play behavior of children with disabilities. They defined play as having the following characteristics: (a) it is intrinsically motivated; (b) it is done by choice and as such is voluntary and spontaneous; (c) it involves active engagement by the child and is self-generated; and (d) it is enjoyable for the child (adapted from Fewell & Kaminski, 1988, p. 146). They further described the developmental sequence of play in the first year as progressing from visual to manual exploration by the infant in the early months, followed by manipulation of objects particularly those that are responsive. Toward the end of the first year, infants begin to act on objects according to the function of the object (e.g., stir with a spoon, push a toy car). This functional play is followed by the emergence of symbolic play whereby children imitate lifelike situations and use objects or signals in symbolic ways. An example is pretending to drink from a cuplike object or pretending to be asleep. Symbolic play becomes increasingly complex and decontextualized as the child develops.

Fewell and Kaminski (1988) discussed the use of play in the assessment of young infants and the design of interventions aimed at facilitating play in infants and toddlers with disabilities. Selected Readings of Chapter 9 in this book also presented a number of

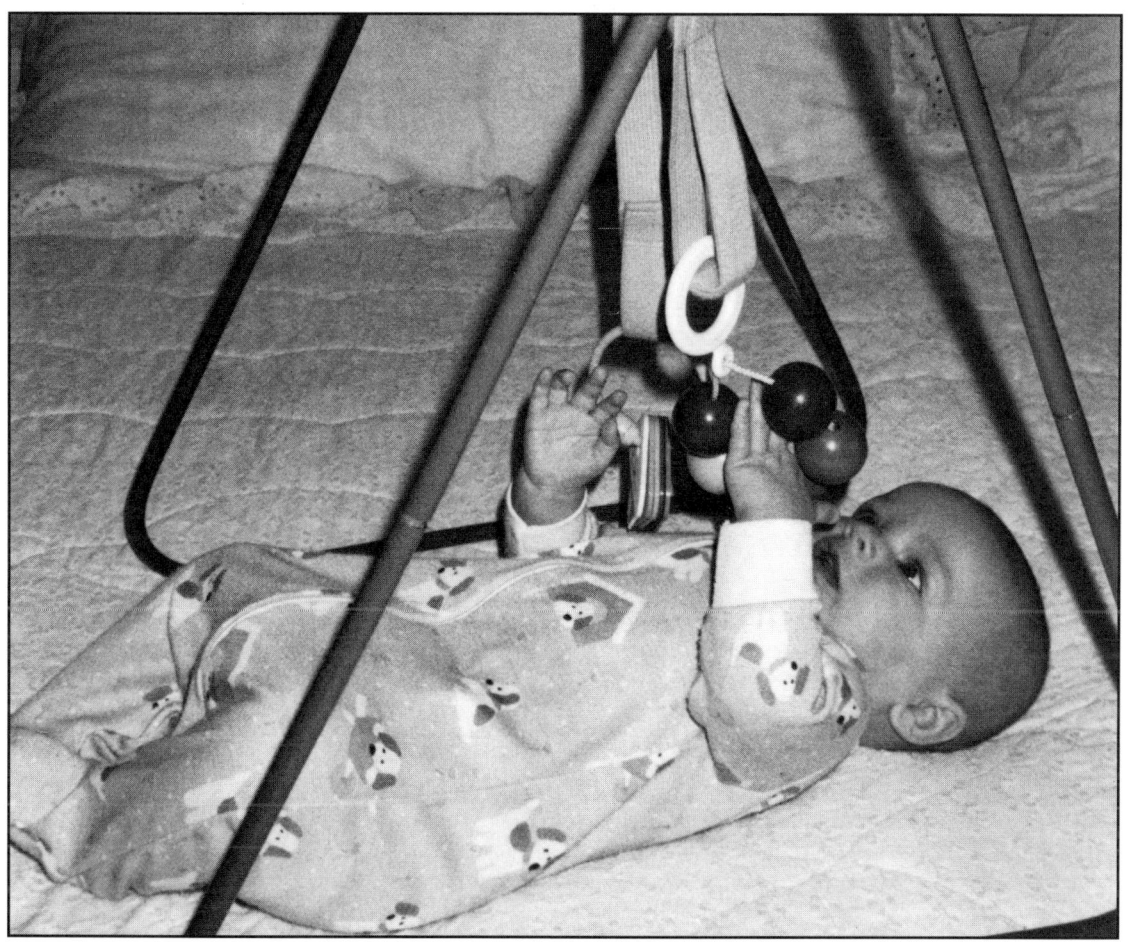

resources to guide parents and interventionists in supporting and enhancing play with young children.

Play provides a means for motivating and engaging young children with materials and people. Play routines in homes and centers can be optimal opportunities for children to practice behaviors and learn new ones.

Characteristics of Quality Learning Environments

Several important factors must be considered in selecting or designing an exemplary learning environment for infants and toddlers with special needs. These factors are applicable regardless of the environmental setting—home or center. Specifically, these factors are grouped into six areas: (a) contingency and responsiveness; (b) health, safety, and hygiene; (c) age appropriateness for infants and toddlers and their families; (d) availability of specialized equipment; (e) physical arrangement; and (f) opportunities for social inclusion for infants and toddlers and their families.

Contingent and Responsive Environments

Ample empirical evidence exists documenting the importance of responsive environments for optimal infant development. Responsive, contingent environments are those in which the infant's actions cause something predictable to happen. Correlational studies of infant development have linked mothers' contingent responding to their infants' behaviors to more advanced infant cognitive and social development (Clarke-Stewart, 1973; Lewis & Goldberg, 1969; Yarrow, Rubenstein, Pedersen, & Jankowski, 1972). Furthermore, White (1959) theorized that infants are motivated to continue interactions when they experience control over their environment (effectance motivation).

A series of landmark studies by Watson (1966, 1967, 1972) established that infants develop "contingency awareness" when they repeatedly experience an interesting spectacle as a result of their behaviors. In Watson's primary studies, young typically developing infants learned to repeat a behavior (a head movement) in order to operate a mobile that

turned, contingent upon the infants' movements. The babies also began to coo and smile at the mobile during the response-contingent action situations. The infants appeared to develop an awareness of this relationship and showed enjoyment at this feeling of competence. Watson (1972) discussed the importance of this awareness to the infant's cognitive and social development. He further theorized that people become important to the babies because they play "The Game" of contingent interactions.

Other researchers have examined the effects of the contingent learning experiences on subsequent learning. These studies provided evidence that experience with response-contingent stimulation resulted in retention and enhanced learning ability in other learning situations for young infants (Finkelstein & Ramey, 1977; Ramey & Finkelstein, 1978; Rovee & Fagan, 1976).

Research on the importance of response-contingent interactions to infant development has tremendous implications for the development of interventions during infancy. This work has created a shift from looking solely at the products of learning (i.e., the development of specific behavioral milestones or skills) to an examination of the importance of the process of learning—the infant's ability to "learn to learn." Infants who experience these response-contingent situations appear to develop a motivation to continue such interactions. Conversely, infants who receive only noncontingent stimulation or little stimulation may withdraw from interactions. This is closely akin to the phenomenon described by Seligman (1975) as "learned helplessness." Clinical evidence for this phenomenon with infants is provided in studies of institutionalized infants, such as that by Provence and Lipton (1962). In this study, home-reared and institutionalized infants were compared as to their development. The researchers found that although many of the babies in institutions developed skills (e.g., standing up) at ages similar to their home-reared peers, they showed little desire to use the skills.

Children with disabilities appear particularly at risk for developing learned helplessness. Because of limitations in their behavioral repertoire due to the disabling condition(s), they often have fewer means for interacting with and controlling their environment. Also, their initiations may be so different or so slight when compared with those of the typically developing infant (e.g., an abrupt arm lunge as opposed to a directed reach; a fleeting look as opposed to prolonged and sustained attention to a caregiver) that their behaviors fail to produce an outcome (e.g., operation of a toy, attention by an adult). If these babies fail repeatedly to effectively control their environment (both social and nonsocial), it is likely that they will withdraw and make fewer attempts. Consequently, they will receive less feedback, and a negative spiral of withdrawal will develop. Early intervention can arrest this negative spiral of fewer and fewer interactions by developing opportunities for infants—even those with severe and multiple disabilities—to experience control over their environment and receive contingent feedback for their actions.

Support for the use of response-contingent feedback for infants with disabilities also is provided by the "learning to learn" curricula developed by Brinker and Lewis (1982) and Sullivan and Lewis (1990). Infants were linked to equipment that provided them with response-contingent outcomes for targeted behavioral responses. This type of program was shown to provide motivation to infants and enhance babies' responses.

Interventions aimed at creating responsive and contingent environments can be developed around both social interactions (e.g., caregivers and infants) and nonsocial environmental interactions (e.g., infant playing with toys). Caregivers can be assisted to read babies' cues and respond immediately and consistently to those cues. For example, a young infant may make several different types of cries. In time, responsive caregivers learn to differentiate

which cries signal pain or distress and necessitate an immediate response versus those cries that indicate fussiness or tiredness that may not constitute an emergency response. For babies whose states are very labile or for babies who are almost continually fussy, this process of discriminating various cries may be more difficult. Early interventionists may help parents and other significant caregivers to understand how difficult this is and also assist them to "read" the various cries. Once the caregiver can differentiate and respond consistently to a specific cry, the communication system between the infant and caregiver is enhanced. Many babies with disabilities or those born at risk present atypical behavioral cues and/or labile and agitated states. This can cause interactional difficulties. Strategies for assisting caregivers are described more fully later in this chapter in the section on optimizing home environments.

The child's physical or nonsocial environment also can be modified to be more responsive. On a basic level, babies can be positioned so that they are more likely to use their limbs for reaching or swiping. The side-lying position, for example, often allows for more reaching opportunities, particularly at midline position, than do other positions such as back-lying. Early interventionists can provide these suggestions to the baby's caregivers. The environment of toys and materials also can be specially constructed to be more responsive. Babies should be provided with toys that provide immediate and contingent feedback. Good examples of these toys and materials include rattles, busy boxes, chime balls, mobiles that move when baby moves, and squeaker toys. The important feature is that something happens when the baby acts. Some toys, such as tops or wind-up toys, have this characteristic; however, they may be difficult to operate for very young children or for children with physical disabilities. A number of these toys can be easily modified (particularly battery-operated ones) to respond to a more subtle or different type of infant movement. Several references (e.g., Burkhart, 1980, 1982) are provided in the selected readings section of this chapter. These are excellent resources that present detailed plans for adapting toys that are commonly available so that the special needs of these children can be met.

In summary, research on the effects of contingent and noncontingent stimulation on infant learning suggests that infants need responsive, contingent environments to learn and be motivated to learn. Conversely, environments in which they receive only noncontingent stimulation (i.e., handling, auditory, and visual stimuli that are made available to the infants but are in no way linked to or contingent on the infant's actions) may produce adverse effects and cause babies to "tune out" or withdraw. The provision of a responsive, contingent environment is consistent with the view of infant development upheld in this book—the view of the infant as an *active* learner.

Health, Safety, and Hygiene

All young children are entitled to receive services in a healthful and safe environment.

However, for children who have disabilities or those born at risk, these health and safety issues may be particularly important. Some adaptations and precautions are necessary because of the disabilities; some are necessitated by the young age of the children; and others are dictated by health and safety needs inherent in group care for children.

Disability-related alterations

Specific environmental alterations may be needed for children with physical and sensory impairments. Children with visual impairments and motor delays may need environments, for example, that are predictable (i.e., equipment and furniture remain in place and are not moved often) and noncluttered. These environments should provide opportunities for play and exploration at the floor level to minimize the dangers of falling and should include padding for any sharp edges or points. Children also should be able to get feedback from the environment through several sensory channels. For example, play toys should have both auditory and visual components so that children with impairments in one modality can receive feedback through another. When necessary, special adaptive equipment, such as corner chairs, transport chairs, wedges, and bolsters, can be used to position children safely and in postures that allow them to play and/or engage in daily living tasks, such as feeding and dressing. Specialized equipment needs are discussed more fully later in this chapter.

Childproofing the environment

Due to the age of children served in early intervention programs (birth to 3 years), special safety considerations are necessary. Guidelines for parents and caregivers in childproofing an environment include the following:

1. Toys, furniture, and materials with sharp edges should be removed or modified with padding.

2. Materials with small, removable parts should be used only under careful supervision to avoid swallowing and choking incidents.

3. All paint used on toys, materials, furniture, and walls should be lead free.

4. Electrical outlets, plugs, and cords should be covered with childproof protectors or placed out of reach of children.

5. All cabinets containing medical or cleaning supplies should be locked and out of reach of children. Only needed supplies should be kept on hand.

6. Protectors should be placed over hot water faucet outlets, or children should have access only to cold water faucets under supervision.

7. Water play tables and climbing and other playground equipment should be carefully supervised at all times.

8. Activities should be designated primarily around floor play with only safe standing and climbing structures provided. Floor surfaces should be clean and carpeted or padded.

In addition to these safety issues related to creating a childproof environment, several other safety concerns are warranted. Emergency protocols and procedures should be carefully planned and reviewed with all parents and program staff members. Procedures should be outlined for possible evacuations in the case of fire, explosion, or natural disaster (e.g., earthquake, tornado) and for medical emergencies. Information on special procedures and contact persons for each child should be available in a spot that is within easy access. Staff members should be trained and prepared to administer basic first aid, cardiopulmonary resuscitation (CPR), and infant emergency care procedures in the case of choking.

Applying universal health precautions

A number of precautionary standards also are necessary to ensure a hygienic environment. Many children with disabilities or those born at risk are more prone to infections. Therefore, every effort should be made to avoid the spread of disease. It is recommended that group care centers receive consultation from a health care professional as to implementation of appropriate health care standards. Some health standards for environments in which young children are served include the following:

1. All toys and materials should be washed daily in soap and water after being handled by each child to avoid the spread of disease from child to child.

2. All dishes and feeding materials should be washed in hot water and soap at temperatures necessary to kill bacteria.

3. Eating tables, changing tables, toilets, and activity surfaces should be scrubbed after each use with appropriate cleansers and water.

4. Care providers should wash their hands with soap and water before and after each feeding or diaper changing. Disposable gloves and bags should be available in the toileting or changing areas and used by staff members. Hand-washing techniques should include the application of liquid soap and warm water and the use of circular motion and friction for 15 to 30 seconds, followed by wiping with a clean paper towel. Diapering procedures should include placing the baby on a clean surface, removal of soiled diaper and placement in appropriate receptacle (i.e., lined, closed container), removal of any soiled clothing and placement in plastic bags, cleansing of child's body with soap and water or wipes, and use of a disinfectant on the changing surface following the diapering. Any abnormal conditions, such as blood, rashes, or watery stools, should be reported to parents and the supervisor.

5. In classrooms, smocks can be used by staff members to promote cleanliness. Any staff members with cuts or weeping lesions should wear disposable plastic gloves. Because long fingernails and ornate rings provide places for bacteria to collect and grow, they should be avoided.

6. Food preparation and serving areas should be separate from diapering areas.

7. Each child's personal grooming items (e.g., toothbrush, hairbrush) should be stored separately. At centers, soiled clothing should also be stored separately in a marked bag and sent home each day for proper laundering.

These steps can help prevent the spread of infectious diseases in both home and group care settings.

These precautions are particularly important in center-based programs, given the opportunity for spread of bacterial and viral diseases (e.g., cytomegalovirus or CMV, hepatitis B infection, herpes simplex, rubella). Some young children may be placed in early intervention programs due to disabilities resulting from these infectious agents, and in some cases (e.g., CMV, rubella) children may continue to shed the virus. Proper precautions and hygiene will greatly reduce the risks of infecting others.

Other environmental adaptations include the provision of appropriate temperatures and proper clothing. Additionally, children should be observed carefully for allergic reactions to substances in the environment, and these substances should be removed or avoided when possible.

Many children served in early intervention programs have significant health risks (e.g., susceptibility to respiratory disorders). Therefore, health as well as safety factors are extremely important when providing care and early intervention services to these very young children.

Age Appropriateness for Infants and Toddlers and Their Families

Early intervention programs can be found in many different settings—public or private schools, clinics, special centers, hospitals, and homes. A number of different types of settings can be appropriately designed for serving very young children and their families. However, by necessity these environments will be quite different from traditional school environments with desks and chairs. Some considerations include the following:

1. Most activities for infants and toddlers will be best performed on the floor or at low toddler-sized tables and chairs. Floors should be comfortable, clean, and carpeted or cushioned. Mats are also useful. Tables and chairs should be lightweight but sturdy, durable, cleanable, and easily accessible to infants and toddlers. Many well-designed, well-supported chairs are available through educational supply catalogs or stores for children (see resources at the end of this chapter and in Appendix G). These chairs are often made of durable, easy-to-clean plastic and have supports around the back and sides. Furthermore, many can be adjusted or turned upside down to adjust seat height. A good example is the plastic cube chair that functions as a chair or can be turned to become a little table.

2. Infants and toddlers need access to many items that provide opportunities for manipulation (e.g., mouthing, touching, banging, throwing, waving, rolling) and sensory experiences (e.g., visual, auditory, tactile). Toys should provide movement or feedback and be colorful, easily washable, and safe. Good examples include form balls, rattles, texture toys, chime balls, blocks, puzzles, busy boxes, and activity quilts. Today, toy manufacturers are becoming increasingly well informed about the developmental and safety needs of infants and toddlers, and many quality toy materials are available. These materials are quite appropriate for use in early intervention programs, and special designs are not needed in most cases. Again, these materials can be found in local stores and through the resources listed in Appendix G.

Many toys and materials also can be constructed from items found around the household, such as measuring cups and spoons, spools, pieces of cloth, magazine pictures pasted on cardboard and covered with contact paper, plastic bowls and containers, boxes, and cardboard rolls.

3. Equipment should be available for large- and small-muscle activities. Toddlers like to climb, swing, and play actively. They also enjoy opportunities for pouring, sifting, stacking, and the like. Sand and water play areas are ideal for these activities and learning experiences.

4. Areas for reading, art, and imaginative or dramatic play activities also should be available. A quiet corner equipped with a beanbag chair, rocker, and/or pillows can be an ideal spot for looking at books and pictures. Other equipment, such as a tape recorder, recorder player, flannel boards, and puppets, are also appropriate for this age group. Dress-up areas and areas for playing house or other imaginative activities are well

suited to the learning needs of toddlers. This area may include child-size furniture such as a sink and stove, and old clothes, such as dresses, shirts, shoes, hats, sunglasses, and gloves. Finally, opportunities should be provided for art activities in areas with close access to clean-up supplies and water. Tables with materials for drawing, pasting, painting, and cutting can provide many learning options in the fine motor, cognitive, and social development areas.

5. Materials are best utilized when organized according to function and presented to children in small doses. Shelving, baskets, buckets, and boxes are useful for storing toys and materials. Children can be allowed to choose materials or be presented with specific items depending upon the goal. However, it is best to use only a few items at a time. A floor full of toys is likely to be overwhelming to the child and may result in the child "tuning out" rather than becoming engaged in play.

6. Environments that are bright and cheerful, and allow for child exploration, are most conducive to learning activities for young children. If children can safely and freely explore, they are most likely to experience new learning opportunities. These types of environments also are best for family members. They can relax in comfort without concern about their child's safety.

In summary, young children learn through play and actively engaging their environment. Many opportunities should be provided for manipulating toys and materials, experiencing feedback through all the senses, and moving around the environment. It is through this active and repetitive engagement with people and things in the environment that the young child learns about spatial relationships, cause and effect, the permanence of objects even when they are not visible, and other means for relating to people and things in the environment. Infants and toddlers who get these experiences are likely to be motivated to continue to explore their environment.

Specialized Equipment Needs

Few special adaptations in toys and equipment are needed in early intervention settings beyond those typically available for infants and toddlers. However, in some cases, special equipment and materials or simple modifications are necessary to make the environment more accessible to children with disabilities.

With regard to equipment and materials, a number of commercially available items can be purchased for use in early intervention settings particularly with children with motor impairments. The most common types of adaptive equipment that may be needed include wedges, abductor seats (seats that position the child so that the legs are separated and not crossed), and prone boards or standing tables

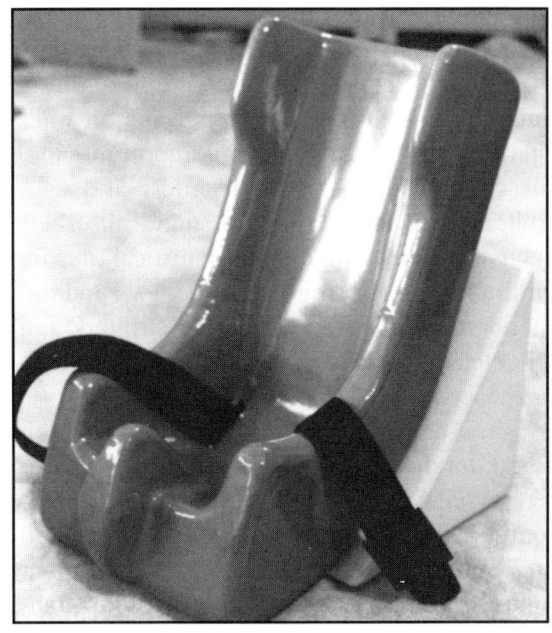

Teaching the Young Child with Motor Delays (Hanson & Harris, 1986).

Although a great many resources are available commercially, inexpensive and effective adaptations often can be made by staff members and parents. Creative occupational and physical therapists can use foam inserts or cardboard to provide appropriate chair and table supports and adaptations for some children. These temporary and "homemade" adaptations are particularly useful with this young age group, because children grow so quickly that they often outgrow their equipment. Furthermore, adaptations to baby spoons and cups (e.g., placing tape or a cork on spoon handle to make it easier to grasp, cutting out space for mouth and nose around rim of plastic cup to facilitate drinking) can be easily accomplished by trained staff members and caregivers. Additionally, materials such as dycem, foam rubber pads, suction cups, or Velcro strips can be purchased inexpensively to reduce slippage of plates and cups on eating surfaces or provide suction for toys and materials on tables. Finally, toys can be adapted in such ways as using

(boards that hold a child in standing position up to a table's surface). Special chairs for feeding and transportation also can be bought that allow for adjustments at head, shoulders, trunk, hips, and legs so that an individual child can be appropriately positioned. Self-help devices, such as special spoons, cups, and plates, can be purchased as well.

Augmentative communication devices also are made increasingly available and usable by very young children. Some involve microcomputer technology and others are simple communication boards that may be commercially produced or in some cases constructed by hand for individual children's needs. Communication boards provide opportunities for children to point to pictures or symbols to communicate their wants or needs to others. Even toddlers and preschool-aged children are beginning to use microcomputers, and some software programs are available for the early user.

Resources for commercially available adaptive equipment, electronic devices, and communication boards are provided at the end of this chapter. Positioning and handling considerations and the use and purchase of adaptive equipment are discussed in more detail in

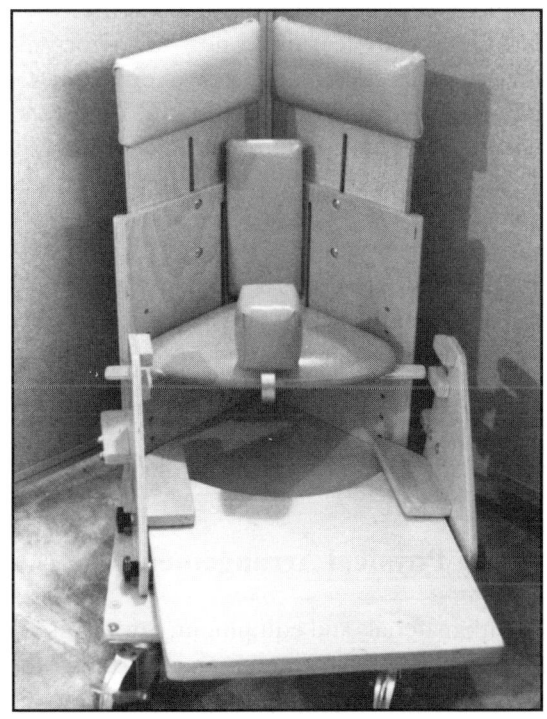

knobs on puzzles, switches (previously discussed), handles that are enlarged with tape or padding, and tabs for zippers or openers. The list of selected readings at the end of this chapter provides references on building and adapting equipment and materials.

Other special adaptations include cues or prompts built into instructional materials. As discussed in Chapter 9, modification of materials or settings often is desirable to enhance the learning process. For example, puzzles and formboards can be color coded so that the child is given a prompt as to where to place the shape. Also, distractors in the environment can be minimized to assist the children as they are learning a new behavior. All puzzle pieces except one or two, for instance, may be taped down until the child masters placing one shape, then gradually the puzzle can be made more difficult with more options.

In reality, few adaptations of equipment and materials are necessary in early intervention settings regardless of whether programs are home or center based. Nevertheless, most modifications are simple and inexpensive, and many represent common sense and creative ideas by professionals and parents.

Physical Arrangement

As with materials and equipment, few physical environmental adjustments are necessary in early intervention programs. However, several important features must be taken into consideration. These features include the availability of adequate lighting and tactile and auditory cues (e.g., railings or textured strips on walls that can be used to guide children in moving) for children with visual disorders and controlled noise levels through sound absorbers such as carpets, drapes, and acoustical tiles for children with hearing impairments. Environments should be accessible to strollers and wheelchairs and free of unnecessary obstacles or barriers.

Some babies with disabilities or those born at risk for developmental delay are very sensitive to outside stimuli. For these babies, environmental stimuli must be carefully monitored and modulated. High noise levels, bright lights, too much movement, or too much handling can cause them to become agitated or in some cases to "shut down." Given that these babies need to conserve their energy for growth and development, such disruptions should be minimized. Quiet places where infants and their parents can go to interact should be available in homes and centers. In these areas distractors and extraneous stimuli can be diminished, allowing for the babies' states to become more regulated and beneficial interactions to occur.

Homes by their very nature tend to be organized into zones for various activities—kitchens for eating, bedrooms for sleeping, family rooms for group activities and active play. The organization of center-based programs into specific areas is also useful. Young children learn that different areas signal different activities. For example, the quiet reading corner is a place to relax and play quietly; the playground is a place for rough and tumble play; and the tables and chairs are for playing with toys and materials. Organization of the home or center environment into various functional zones is useful so that young children have a place to go for various predictable types of activities that vary from highly stimulating activities, such as climbing and tumbling, to quiet, restful activities.

Opportunities for Social Inclusion for Infants and Toddlers and Their Families

Research on the effects of providing educational activities for children with and without disabilities together substantiates the importance of this integration practice. Documented benefits to children with disabilities from participating in integrated experiences with their nondisabled peers include advances in communicative behavior, attention, social behavior, and learning skills (Guralnick, 1981a, 1982; Odom & McEvoy, 1988; Strain & Odom, 1986). Furthermore, as discussed elsewhere in this book, current legal mandates call for the education of children with disabilities in the least restrictive environment. Thus, the provision of services to infants and toddlers and their families in the most typical situations possible with other children who are not disabled is considered important for an exemplary learning environment.

Given the very young age of the children in early intervention settings—birth to 3 years—inclusion opportunities are often different from those available to school-aged children. Children with disabilities may be provided opportunities for play and learning experiences together with nondisabled peers through various programmatic options. Some options include participation in Head Start programs, integration of special classes with regular classes located on the same site for a full day or a portion of the day, and reverse mainstreaming where nondisabled children are integrated into special programs. Other community options include group and family child care, baby and toddler "gym" classes, and parent–infant classes in the community. Guidelines and suggestions for enhancing these earlier inclusion opportunities are provided later in this chapter.

Home Environments

For the young child the primary environment is the home. It is in this environment that the baby or toddler spends most of the time and that the people most important to that child's nurturance and development—the parents and other family members—live. Regardless of the model of the early intervention program (home based, center based, combination), attention to the needs and situations in the home environment is paramount.

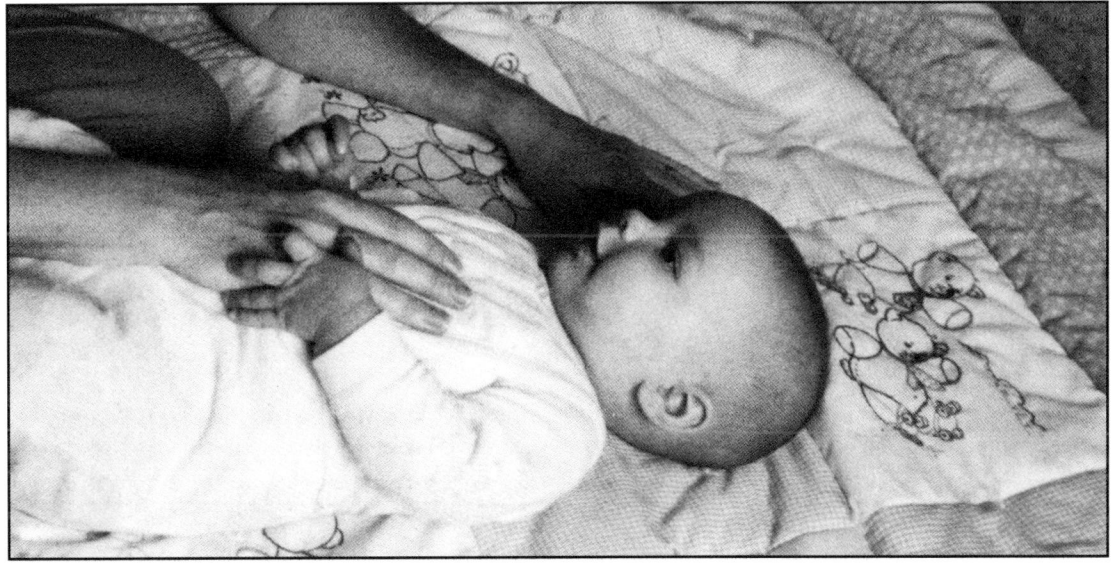

Parents are first and foremost parents. They have the primary responsibility for care of the child, and that responsibility by its very nature involves providing physical, emotional, and financial support as well as food, shelter, and basic caregiving. Parenting brings immeasurable joys, challenges, new experiences, and responsibilities. It can be exciting and tremendously enjoyable, as well as taxing and frustrating. No other responsibility than the care for the life of another human being can bring such a range of roles and responses.

Early intervention practices must be carefully and thoughtfully integrated into the lives of families so that special circumstances necessitated by the interventions do not unduly interfere with the family's functions. Thus, the creation of quality learning environments in homes will focus on two related dimensions: enhancing parent–child interactions and establishing "teachable moments" in daily living situations.

Caregiver–Child Interactions

Babies by their very nature are social creatures, and much of what they learn comes from their interactions with people. For most parents and infants, these interactions are immensely enjoyable and are characterized by playful bouts and social exchanges. For parents and their babies whose interactional skills may be limited or different from the typically developing infant due to disabilities or at-risk conditions, these interactions may be less enjoyable and fruitful. For some the typical "match" or "fit" between the two partners does not occur. Early intervention efforts are aimed at assisting the child to become more competent and develop more normally. However, developing competencies may take a long time, and for some infants typical interactional skills may never develop. Therefore, another goal of intervention is helping parents to modify their interactional patterns and read and understand their babies' cues so that more enjoyable interactions can occur.

Although relatively few empirical investigations have focused on examining critical components of parent–child interaction in the early years, some important indications are available in the existing studies. The descriptive literature on parent–child interactions in dyads where the young child is disabled suggests that, although interactions are not dramatically different from those in dyads where children are not disabled, parents of children with disabilities show some differences in teaching style, play, and/or language patterns (Buium, Rynders, & Turnure, 1974; Cunningham, Reuler, Blackwell, & Deck, 1981; Eheart, 1982; Garrard, 1989; Gutmann & Rondal, 1979; Mahoney & Robenalt, 1986; Marshall, Hegrenes, & Goldstein, 1973; McCollum, 1987; Rosenberg & Robinson, 1988). In general, these interactions are characterized as more directive than interactions with nonhandicapped children. Parents may be adapting their interactions to their child's developmental level and characteristics. The potential differences in interactions between parents and their children with disabilities and the effects of these differences on the children's development are debated (Brooks-Gunn & Lewis, 1984; Crawley & Spiker, 1983; Maurer & Sherrod, 1987). Some researchers (Mahoney, Finger, & Powell, 1985; Mahoney & Powell, 1988) have suggested that a directive or didactic style of interaction is less beneficial to the child's development than is a more child-oriented responsive style.

Researchers and clinicians have turned their attention in recent years to defining strategies for the enhancement of parent–child interaction (Bromwich, 1981; Hanson & Krentz, 1986; Mahoney & Powell, 1986, 1988; McCollum & Stayton, 1985). From this work, as well as the literature on normal child development (e.g., Brazelton, Koslowski, & Main, 1974), several themes or intervention areas emerge. These areas include reading of and responsiveness to infant's cues, turn-taking or reciprocity, pacing, and imitation or matching of interactions. Although interventions are continually aimed at helping infants to become more competent initiators and effective communicators, the major focus of intervention is on caregiver-oriented strategies. Early intervention assistance and support to caregivers who express frustrations or experience difficulties in these early interactions are the most simple and efficient means of getting caregiver–child interactions off to the right start. Interventions around specific interactional components are discussed below.

Reading and responding to infant's cues

Many infants born at risk or with disabilities behave differently from babies born without difficulties. For instance, these babies may be more irritable, labile, less easily soothed, or less responsive by virtue of the risk conditions. Furthermore, those with sensory or motor impairments are unable to effectively interact with their environment through those modalities. These differences can present interactional difficulties to caregivers. Early interventionists can work with caregivers to assist them to observe, to understand, and in some cases to redefine their babies' cues. For example, a baby with motor impairments may stiffen when picked up. The caregivers may have had experience with other babies and expect the common response of the baby molding to the body when held. The baby with motor impairments could be perceived as angry, unloving, or rejecting of the holding. Caregivers could be helped to redefine the stiffening behavior as an involuntary response that does not indicate negativism on the part of the child. They also could be assisted to look for other cues (e.g., child orienting eyes toward parent) that are indicative of the child's wanting to communicate or receive attention. Often, these babies present tremendous challenges, especially babies who are severely and multiply disabled. It is through experience that caregivers and professionals can come to understand the unique signaling systems and interpret the cues of these infants.

Turn-taking or reciprocity

Just as communication between adults involves turn-taking and reciprocal exchange, so does the communication between caregivers and children. Sometimes babies are unable to take their turn, and sometimes parents override their babies' communicative attempts and do not encourage this reciprocity. Caregivers can be assisted to more effectively communicate with their children by encouraging the baby's response through gaze, smiling, touch, or vocalizing. When baby does attempt to communicate through any modality (e.g., vocalizing, reaching, gazing), caregivers can be assisted to give the baby time to respond and also be responsive to the baby's signal by smiling, talking back, touching, and/or gazing back after the baby makes a response.

In the child development literature, these typical parent–child exchanges have been likened to a dancing couple with each partner in tune with and responsive to the moves of the other. Developing this synchrony or partnership can take time and may be difficult for some caregivers and infants because of the unresponsive nature of the child or the child's lability. Early interventionists can support caregivers through this process and help them to discover positive interactional patterns, and thus feel more competent as parents and caregivers.

Pacing

Closely akin to the notion of turn-taking or reciprocity is the issue of pacing. Some children will need a great deal of time in which to make a response, and others will shift attention and state very quickly. The same child may even show both extremes at different times and on different occasions. Again, this can be a frustrating experience for caregivers, particularly if there is a mismatch between the interactional paces of the caregiver and the infant. Caregivers can be helped to observe the infant's style and timing needs and then provide stimulation and feedback in a carefully modulated manner. For example, during feeding the caregiver may be helped to learn that if baby turns away, looks away, spits up, or fusses, the baby is trying to disengage and "take a break." When the baby's attention or equilibrium returns, the caregiver can offer another bite of food or a communicative exchange. Establishing this fine-tuned pacing or synchrony is not always easy. Staff members can assist by speaking for the baby and helping caregivers understand what the baby is trying to say (e.g., turning away because she needs a break, not because she does not like the food or the caregiver's attention). Experimentation with different methods and paces is often needed so that caregivers and professionals together can solve difficult situations. Having access to videotape recorders can be useful in this process. If caregivers are able to sit back and view the interaction in a nonthreatening environment, they often can pinpoint areas of difficulty and develop strategies for overcoming them.

Matching or imitation

Another method for enhancing caregiver–child interactions is the caregiver's matching or imitating the child's behavior. For instance, if a baby is playing with blocks, the caregiver may also build a tower with two cubes and knock it over, or if the baby says "ah, ah, ah," the caregiver may imitate these vocalizations. This process allows caregivers to become very responsive to child-oriented or child-directed behaviors. Caregivers learn to "start where the child is," thus capitalizing on the child's interest and developmental level. Children also learn that their behaviors produce attention and responses from caregivers.

In summary, these areas represent several strategies for enhancing caregiver–child interactions. Social exchanges are the most important part of a child's home environment, because it is through this experience that babies form relationships with others and learn about the world. Methods for communicating with parents and working with family members are discussed further in Chapter 5.

Teachable Moments

As we discussed earlier, the role of a parent is many-faceted. Certainly, parents have a great many things to do in addition to helping their children learn. Parents' needs and resources change, too, and they may be more able at particular times than at other times to work with their children. Having a young child with disabilities or a child born at risk may necessitate extra or different activities on the part of the parent as well. The child may need to be positioned or handled differently or fed in a special way, and the child may present interactional differences. Early interventionists can best assist parents and caregivers by helping them to discover ways to integrate therapeutic or learning activities into their typical and daily routines. Identifying these *teachable moments* will help parents and caregivers to effectively "teach" their children while not placing a burden on or modifying family functions.

Teachable moments can occur during any daily activity. Diapering, feeding, and dressing, for instance, are all prime times for interacting with children and providing learning opportunities. During any trip to the grocery store, one can witness some parents "teaching." The parent, for example, may discuss food types with the child, ask the child to identify or label fruits and vegetables, practice naming colors or classifying foods, or even provide the child with practice sitting well supported in the cart and learning to reach across midline to grab an item when it is presented.

This one activity of going to the grocery store may involve a number of designated teaching goals and objectives for the child. Many parents provide these rich experiences for their children on an ongoing basis and do so as a matter of course without receiving training. For the infant or toddler with special needs, such a rich environment may be particularly important, because these children often need more practice or opportunities to learn a new behavior than do nondisabled children.

The early interventionist can assist parents by mapping out the daily routines of the family and, together with parents, discussing ways in which goals for the child can be integrated into these routines. During diapering, for instance, a mother or father may give the baby a toy to practice reaching and then pull the baby to sitting in a therapeutic manner. Feeding time can be an excellent time to encourage speech and language as well as enhance oral-motor development. Also, playtime is great for learning to communicate, learning about objects and people, and learning to move one's body in space—all important goals for infants.

The emphasis in these teachable moments is not so much on the product of the child's learning, such as pointing to a book when asked to do so, but rather on the process. In other words, the child learns to be motivated and engaged in the environment and to seek interactions both with the social aspects of the environment—people—and with the nonsocial or physical environment of toys, materials, and household items.

Parents and caregivers who use these teachable moments can greatly benefit their children's development. However, we do not mean to imply that all parents must be superparents. All people have good days and bad days, and sometimes parents have the resources and motivation to provide these experiences and other times they do not. Parents can be assisted to capitalize on these moments while recognizing that "teaching" need not and cannot occur at all times.

Scheduling and Implementing Home Visits

Home visits by early intervention staff members may serve different functions. Typically, the staff member and family members together observe the child, and plan educational and therapeutic activities that will be implemented in the home. They may discuss particular problem areas such as feeding, sleeping, or behavior. A home visit also can be used as a time for the child to receive one-to-one instruction or therapy from the staff member if that is needed. Regardless of the major purpose for a given home session, the visit typically lasts 1 to 2 hours and is organized around the following activities:

1. *Arrival and greeting.* The home visitor is greeted by the family member(s), and they exchange information and pleasantries.

2. *Information exchange and review.* The visitor and the family members review and discuss the prior programs and activities. The parent may explain any concerns or irregularities in the program, and any notes or information that is pertinent may be presented. The visitor and parent may then observe the child performing the educational goals and review and reassess the appropriateness and success of the program.

3. *Development of new goals and strategies.* Based on the review of the prior educational goals and strategies, new strategies can be developed. This phase may include time for role modeling by the home visitor and time for extensive discussions and questions by both the visitor and the parent. The visitor should remain sensitive to the individual needs of the family and the circumstances in the home in the development of these plans. These are ideal times to plan teachable moments.

4. *Closure.* At the end of the home visit, the visitor should summarize the discussion and

allow parents to provide any additional input or questions. The plan for the next appointment or visit should be made before the home visitor's departure if possible.

The tenor of the home visit should always be friendly but professional. Visitors must judge when the situation may become too personal or inappropriate. For example, involvement in marital problems or discussions would be considered an inappropriate role of the early intervention provider. The service boundaries must be clearly identified and established with families for successful interventions to occur.

Although most home visits will have a definite beginning and end as described above, the type of greetings, style of communication and exchange, length of exchange, participants in the visit, and parent's role with respect to the early interventionist, will all change from home to home. Variables including cultural background, languages spoken, socioeconomic status, and geographic location, to name a few, will have significant influence on the way a home visit is conducted.

As home visitors move from home to home, they may even feel as if they are moving from country to country due to the diverse U.S. population. Several publications offer detailed information and suggestions for providing services in a competent manner to families of a wide range of cultures (Hanson, Lynch, & Wayman, 1990; Lynch & Hanson, 1992; Wayman, Lynch, & Hanson, 1990). These considerations also are addressed in more detail in Chapter 3 of this book.

Regardless of the family served or the service delivery model used, the following suggestions for home visitation may apply.

1. *Be flexible.* A family-centered approach involves responding to families' concerns and needs. For every family, each day is dynamic. Families are constantly undergoing change as the needs of each member are considered. For families with children with disabilities, meeting the many appointments they must keep is often a juggling act.

2. *Be respectful, sensitive, and nonjudgmental.* Visiting a family's home is a highly personal matter. The family's lifeways and lifestyles may differ radically from those of the early interventionist. Safety and health concerns aside, in most respects, there is no right or wrong way of conducting a household. Early interventionists may be exposed to sights, sounds, and smells that appear foreign. They may be asked to participate in family routines such as the taking of tea or a meal. The family may suggest interventions that may appear unusual or inappropriate. If a harmful or neglectful situation is apparent, the early interventionist must report it. In other circumstances, however, the interventionist should show respect and sensitivity to the family's wishes, concerns, and methods, and should follow household rules, such as taking off one's shoes when entering the home and avoiding smoking.

3. *Offer services to families in their primary language or language of choice and in the setting they select.* Communication is a critical issue in early intervention. Unless families feel comfortable and competent in communicating, a meaningful partnership between the family and early interventionist cannot exist. Often the interventionist will need to rely on a translator. In Chapter 3, the issue of translation is discussed more fully. Often members of the community can serve as community liaisons or community guides in helping the family and interventionist communicate and plan together.

4. *Be a good listener and encourage family members to participate if they wish to do so.* If family members wish to actively participate, they must be given the opportunity. Families need to be asked, not told, what their concerns, priorities, and resources are. Even the means whereby they are asked (e.g., through interview, questionnaire, intermediary) will depend on the family's preferences.

5. *Be prompt, consistent, and prepared.* The early interventionist is a professional and must exhibit high standards of professional conduct. Families have many roles and responsibilities;

working with the home visitor is only one of many. Therefore, the visitor should prepare materials and activities as appropriate before the meeting and follow through at the appointed time and place. Families need to know that they can count on the early interventionist.

6. *Take the time that families need to discuss their concerns and schedule additional appointments or services as needed.* Sometimes families need a great deal of time to discuss an issue; at other times only a very short visit is needed or warranted. Although early intervention services are not limitless, adjustment as much as possible to the needs of the families is important. If the scheduled visit does not allow sufficient time for the exchange or if the parent wishes to communicate with other types of staff members, additional appointments and services can be scheduled at another time.

7. *Maintain confidentiality.* When working with families in their homes, early interventionists will receive a great deal of personal information and impressions about the family. It is of the utmost importance that high standards of confidentiality be maintained.

8. *Avoid using jargon, technical terms, and postures or gestures that the family may view as inappropriate.* Effective communication must respect the great variability in linguistic abilities and literacy levels of family members. Early interventionists are cautioned to communicate in a manner that is simple, informal but professional, and valued by the family.

9. *Consider safety issues.* Not all families live in safe environments. The early interventionist should dress and act in a manner that does not draw attention to her or him in the neighborhood and should exercise the greatest care in parking the car, walking through the neighborhood, and entering and exiting buildings. The early intervention program is advised to conduct inservice training on methods for ensuring safety of staff members.

10. *Maintain a sense of humor.* Anyone who works with human beings must have a sense of humor to be effective. Things change; people make mistakes. Early interventionists may be unfamiliar with routines, practices, or priorities that a family holds dear; they may make honest mistakes or conduct themselves in a manner that feels uncomfortable. Maintaining a sense of humor and tackling an issue honestly will most likely lead to a solution to any predicament.

Summary

The natural daily living activities that occur in home environments represent the major settings for working with the young child in need of early intervention services. It is through interactions with parents and other significant caregivers that the young child learns. Relatively few environmental modifications are needed in homes to assist the young child's development. Rather, it is the mutually enjoyable and responsive interactions with others and opportunities to manipulate and get feedback from things in the environment that constitute quality learning environments for young children in home settings.

Center Environments

A number of different settings can be appropriate for early intervention programs. The organization of materials, people, and activities will determine the program's worth. In addition to the general components common across quality learning environments previously described, the following issues specific to center-based programs are discussed: selection of sites, design of program space, scheduling, and adult-to-child ratios.

Selecting a Site

Early intervention services are located in a variety of sites—schools, hospitals, clinics, homes, and child care settings, to name a few.

Regardless of the location, several factors are important in selecting a site for an early childhood center. In addition to the safety factors and the physical environmental needs previously presented, the site should have access to hot and cold running water; toileting facilities appropriate to young children; an area for diapering and cleanup; a place for simple food preparation; a large surface that can be easily partitioned or divided into various areas; an outdoor play area; areas for storage of materials and supplies, toys, equipment, and children's personal items; office space for staff members; and a small meeting space for family members and/or caregivers and staff members. Ideally, the site will be well lighted, cheerful, and easily accessible to parents and caregivers transporting child materials, strollers, and children. Insofar as possible, it is desirable that early intervention programs be located in public facilities or facilities that provide access to community-based activities, rather than in facilities that have stigmatizing labels such as programs for the "crippled," "retarded," or "handicapped." These labels can be particularly troubling to the family who has just given birth to a child with difficulties and who is struggling to find appropriate and normalizing experiences for the child. Such settings can set the tenor for the expectations for the child. Families should be supported to raise their children in their homes and provide them with typical daily living experiences, rather than segregating the children or feeling isolated from the rest of society.

Designing the Program Space

Both the division and organization of space are important to program design. Most early

education or intervention settings are divided into various zones or areas with different functions, which may include the following: greeting children and storing their materials, diapering and toileting, snacks and feeding, group activities such as circle time, large-muscle activities, learning activities, quiet activities, free play including dramatic play, and art activities. An area also should be designated for private one-to-one meetings with parents and caregivers. This area may double as an office or quiet area where parents and caregivers or staff members can bring children who need to rest or quiet down. The important issue is that discrete areas need to be identified and separated so that various functions or activities can occur in the intervention setting.

Another consideration may be access for observers. Other family members or visitors often wish to see early intervention programs. If dividers or partitions between areas are low, observers can view the program without distracting children. The benefit of low partitions needs to be weighed, however, against the needs for the reduction of noise and other distractors for children in any given room. A sample of a floor plan for a center-based early intervention program is provided in Figure 10.1.

The organization of materials, equipment, and people within the room(s) is critical as well. The organization of this physical space must be consistent with the program's goals (e.g., to provide space for meetings with family members, to provide developmental activities). Furthermore, the space should be functional for parents and caregivers, staff members, and children, and laid out so that the program can be effectively and efficiently implemented. Materials and supplies should be stored near the activities in which they will be used. Diapers, for example, should be in the diapering area; art supplies nearby that area; and pictures, toys for fine motor tasks, and other instructional items in the area for small group instruction. Time spent by staff members hunting for items or walking across the room to obtain items is time wasted. Such disruptions also may prove disturbing to child activities.

The organization of space should also be functional for children and should foster independence. Toys should be located on small, reachable shelves for easy access by children. The space should be designed to allow for locomotion, including rolling, crawling, walking, and climbing, to attain desired objects. Self-care areas for toileting and handwashing and cubbies for storage of personal items should be accessible to children to foster independent behavior and self-initiation. The safety and developmental issues previously described in the discussion of characteristics of quality learning environments should be applied in selecting and arranging toys, equipment, and materials.

Scheduling

Scheduling requires a careful balance of one-to-one opportunities and small group activities. Quiet times and active times, as well as structured and unstructured times, also need to be balanced. Finally, the need for making efficient transitions from activity to activity must be considered. These factors, coupled with the fact that the young child has a short attention span, dictate a series of 15- to 30-minute sessions. A sample schedule is presented below.

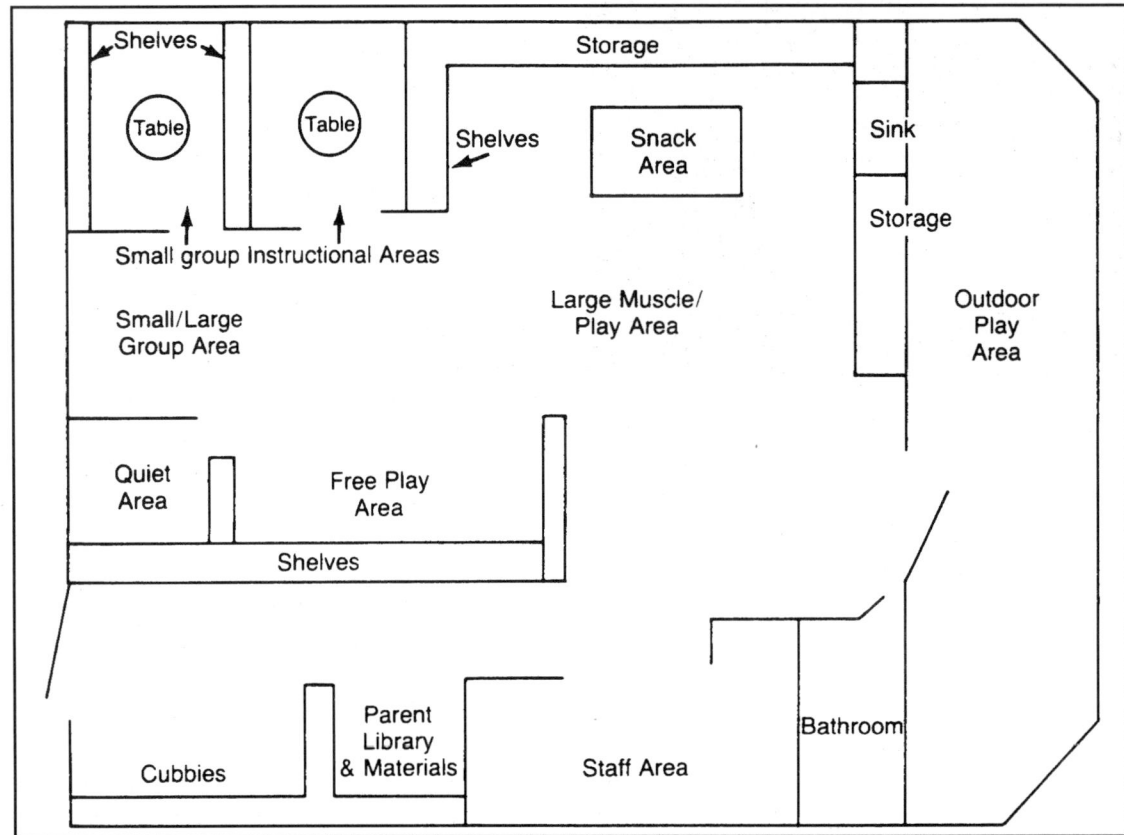

Figure 10.1. Example of a center-based program floor plan.

9:00–9:15 *Arrival and Free Play*
Families and caregivers are greeted, and children are assisted to remove coats and hang them up. Any needed diapering or toileting is done, and children are encouraged to play, with parents and caregivers observing or participating as desired.

9:15–9:30 *Circle Time*
Children and parents and caregivers participate in large group opening activities that include singing, finger plays, puppets, and signing.

9:30–9:50 *Activity-Based Instruction* (2 to 4 Areas as Needed)
Instructional activities embedded in typical child play activities with goals in cognitive, communication, motor, and social domains. One-to-one instruction can be scheduled for particular children, as well as for physical therapy, communication therapy, and cognitive tasks or for individual consultation with a parent and child.

9:50–10:10 *Activity-Based Instruction*

10:10–10:30 *Outside Play or Large Group Indoor Play Activity*
Large-muscle activities and peer interactions are encouraged.

10:30–10:45 *Toileting/Diapering*
Independent toileting is encouraged as appropriate, as are hand-washing and dressing.

10:45–11:10 *Snack and Transitions*
Children are provided snacks by staff members, but they are encouraged to communicate their needs, feed independently as appropriate (including activities such as pouring), clean up, and move to a reading, art, or free play activity.

11:10–11:30 *Activity-Based Instruction*

11:30–11:50 *Activity-Based Instruction*

11:50–12:00 *Closing Group Circle Activity*

Staff may find it useful to post a large washable bulletin board upon which the daily schedule can be written and modified. Different activities (e.g., motor = balance reactions on a large ball; cognitive = learning about common objects; communication = talking about animals and playing with a farm set; social = taking turns in game) as well as the person responsible for the activity can be designated.

This schedule is merely an example of one common to center-based early intervention programs. Variation across programs will take into account diverse philosophical approaches and models. As can be noted, early intervention programs typically are scheduled only for a partial day given the young age of the children served. Furthermore, such programs may meet daily or only several times per week depending upon the population needs and the program model.

For the young infant whose state is very labile, a more appropriate schedule is a visit to the center with the parents or caregivers for a 1- to 2-hour session either individually with staff members or in a very small group (i.e., two to three infants and parents together with staff members). Such meetings can be staggered through a morning or afternoon as scheduling permits. The focus of the center-based program for the young infant (under 1 year of age) most likely will be one-to-one sessions with the parent or caregiver and staff members, rather than small group activities, given the lack of peer interactions with this age group.

Adult-to-Child Ratios

Standards for adult-to-child ratios vary depending upon state and local regulations. Such ratios are usually based on the age of the children served, the severity of their disabilities, and the program model (home vs. center based). Generally, the adult-to-child ratio for an early intervention program is one adult to two to four children. Given the team model and the participation of parents and caregivers in the program, the ratio may even be richer at various times.

Summary

Centers for early intervention are located in a variety of settings. Important considerations for selecting and designing the space include safety, appropriateness for infants and toddlers and their families, accessibility for children and families, functionality, and efficiency. Many different settings can be adapted to meet these needs.

Working in Inclusive Settings

The value of integrated or inclusive learning opportunities has been established for preschool-aged and older children (Guralnick, 1981a, 1981b; Odom, McConnell, & McEvoy, 1992; Odom & McEvoy, 1988; Strain & Odom, 1986). Less information is available on the effects for younger children. One must keep in mind that the primary relationships for infants in the first year of life are with parents and other significant adults rather than with peers. In fact, establishing and supporting these early parent–infant relationships should be a major goal of early intervention programs. Integration and least restrictive environment in these early years focus on the family. The family must be supported in making the child an integral part of the family and also in participating in community activities of choice just as other families do. By 2 years of age, however, most children demonstrate an awareness of other children and enjoy watching and in some cases imitating certain peer actions. Cooperative play, however, does not generally begin until the late 2s and 3s. It is during this toddler period that peer–peer interactions can provide effective learning experiences. Thus, an optimal practice for early intervention programs is the provision of opportunities for children with disabilities to learn and interact with nondisabled children as part of their educational experience. Many children in need of special services may receive these services in the context of their daily child care program as well.

Families of children with disabilities should have access to the same community-based supports and programs as do families of other children. These community programs may include parenting classes, general health services, play groups, and family and group child care centers. Unfortunately, these services are often woefully lacking or limited for all families. Nevertheless, we are advocating equal access to and participation in these community-based services for families of children with disabilities who elect to participate.

The design of integration opportunities for very young children with disabilities necessitates several special considerations (Hanson &

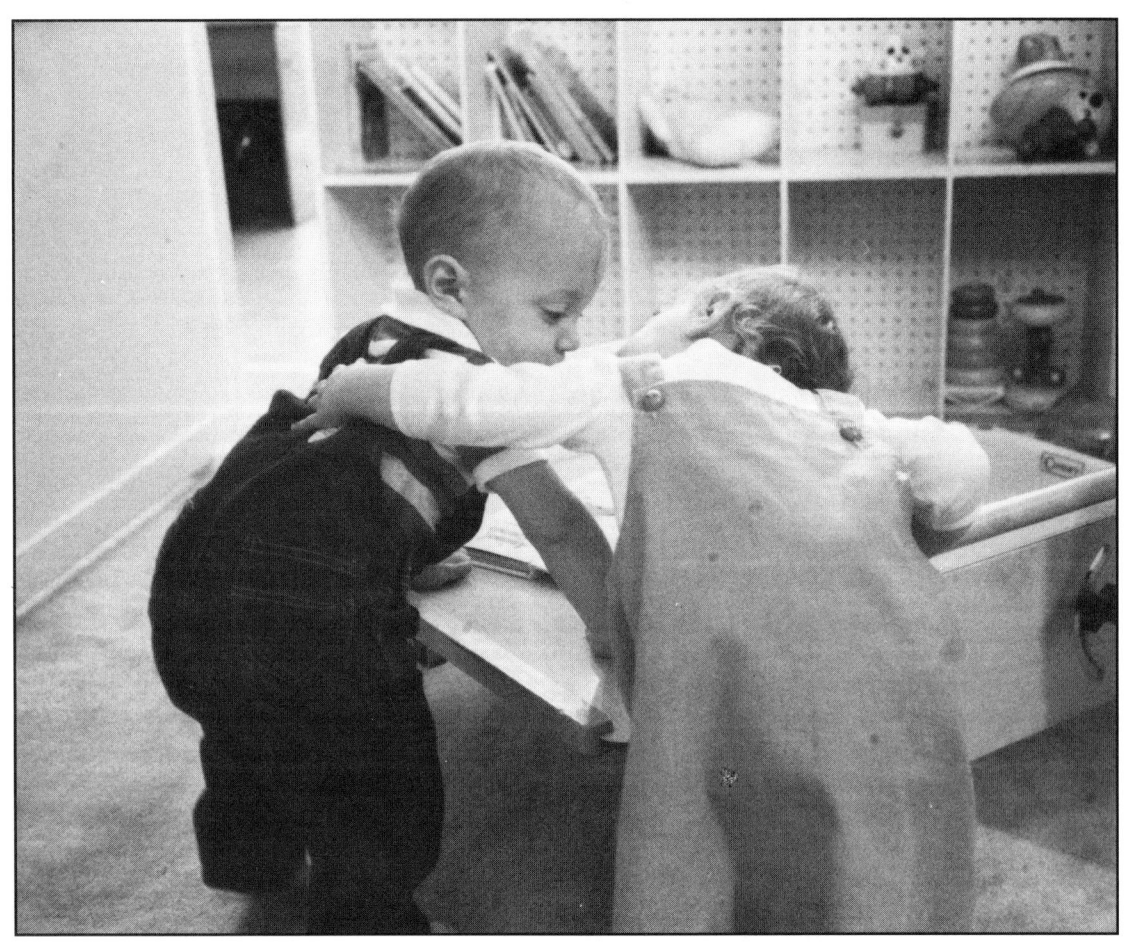

Hanline, 1989). First, intervention activities in the early years should be developed in conjunction with the child's parents. Parents should be provided with integration options, and then the decision must rest with the parents as to the type of integration and initiation of the integration activities. Parental input and decisions are as much a part of planning for integration as they are for other aspects of early intervention. Second, access to nondisabled peers for very young children is often difficult to achieve. Few nondisabled children under age 3 attend programs in school sites or other public settings. However, these children increasingly are in other types of group experience such as child care. The creative early interventionist can pursue integration and inclusion opportunities with a variety of program options that may be located in the community, such as Head Start for infants and toddlers, family child care, center-based group child care programs, and organized play groups (Bruder, 1993; Hanson & Widerstrom, 1993). A third consideration in the design of integration opportunities for this age group centers on health and safety issues. Given the age of the children and the health risks posed by some of these children, integration should be undertaken cautiously. Very young children or children who are unusually prone to contracting infections, for instance, may not be able to cope well with exposure to other young children in group care and educational experiences until their immunological systems are more stable. Finally, integration activities require carefully trained and prepared staff members. Merely placing children with disabilities in programs for nondisabled children may not accomplish helpful goals. The children with disabilities or those at risk are by definition in need of special services. Children do not necessarily interact with one another or interact positively unless planned activities and interventions to promote these interactions are implemented (Guralnick, 1981a, 1981b; Peterson, 1982; Peterson & Haralick, 1977; van den Pol, Crow, Rider, & Offner, 1985). Therefore, staff members should have a knowledge of both typical and atypical child development and training in methods of promoting social interactions among children.

Several strategies can be employed to encourage social interactions among children. Teacher attention and prompts, the selection of specific activities and materials, and patterns for grouping children can all influence the degree of interaction (Fredericks et al., 1978; Guralnick, 1982; Hanline, 1985; Strain & Odom, 1986). Teacher encouragement and prompting of social interactions, for example, can be useful when interaction opportunities between children with and without disabilities occurs, such as during play in the sandbox or the block area. Furthermore, certain activities and materials encourage interactions more than others. These include dramatic or imaginative play activities, such as playing house or dressing up, and pieces of equipment that require two or more children to operate or play, such as a see-saw or rocking boat or play with tea sets. Several research studies have documented the effectiveness of using normal peers as peer models also (Cooke, Apolloni, & Cooke, 1977; Cooke, Cooke, & Apolloni, 1977; Strain & Kerr, 1981). In these studies peer models were trained to model behaviors, encourage imitation by peers with disabilities, and tutor children on specific learning activities. Finally, the size of the group and ratio of disabled to nondisabled children may influence interactions. Additionally, small group activities appear to be more conducive to interactions than large group activities.

Very young children with disabilities and their families have the same rights to participate in community-based activities as do other children and families. Sometimes, special adaptations or organizational considerations are needed to ensure that these activities are beneficial or implemented appropriately. However, legislative mandates and research findings clearly support the need for these inclusion efforts.

Summary

The primary environment for the young child is the young child's home. It is here that relationships with parents and other family members are formed and vital early learning opportunities occur. Assisting parents to provide these learning experiences in the context of their daily routines and supporting early interactions and relationships are prime goals of early intervention. Although few special adaptations are necessary in either home or center environments for early intervention services, several important factors must be considered, such as the need to construct a responsive environment, health and safety issues, appropriateness for infants and toddlers and their families, specialized equipment needs, physical arrangements, and opportunities for social inclusion. Attention to these factors in the organization of people, materials, and space is necessary in the design of exemplary learning environments for infants and toddlers with special needs.

Preferred Practices

The following list of questions can be used to guide the reader in selecting and designing quality learning environments. These items provide a general checklist for analyzing the learning opportunities and organization of environments for early intervention services. The importance of individual items and areas of emphasis will depend on the program model and objectives.

1. Does the environment (both social and nonsocial aspects) provide contingent feedback to the child for initiating and responding?
2. Is the environment responsive to even slight or small initiations on the part of the child?
3. Is the environment safe and hygienic? Is it childproofed and sanitary? Are universal health precautions observed?
4. Are the materials, equipment, and supplies organized to promote safe, efficient use?
5. Are the materials, equipment, and supplies appropriate for infants and toddlers and their families?
6. Do infants and toddlers have ample access to the materials to learn functional responses and independence?
7. Are the specialized needs of children with various disabilities being met (e.g., adaptations for sensory impairments and motor disorders in materials, equipment, and space)?
8. Is the physical environment conducive to early intervention services (e.g., cheerful and bright, sound and lights carefully modulated)?
9. Are opportunities for inclusion of children who have disabilities with nondisabled children available and appropriately planned and implemented?
10. Are parents and caregivers being supported in their interactions with their infants and toddlers and assisted in making these interactions enjoyable and fruitful?
11. Are parents and caregivers being helped to integrate learning opportunities for their infants and toddlers into their daily routines?
12. Are center program sites located in public, nonstigmatizing settings that are appropriate for young children?
13. Are settings designed for flexibility, for efficiency, and with the program objectives in mind?
14. Is a written schedule of each day's activities, including the organization of staff, children, space, and teaching activities, available?

References

Brazelton, T. B., Koslowski, B., & Main, M. (1974). The origins of reciprocity: The early mother–infant interaction. In M. L. Lewis & L. A. Rosenblum (Eds.), *The effect of the infant on its caregiver* (pp. 49–76). New York: Wiley.

Brinker, R. P., & Lewis, M. (1982). Discovering the competent handicapped infant: A process approach to assessment and intervention. *Topics in Early Childhood Special Education, 2*(2), 1–6.

Bromwich, R. (1981). *Working with parents and infants*. Austin, TX: PRO-ED.

Brooks-Gunn, J., & Lewis, M. (1984). Maternal responsivity in interactions with handicapped infants. *Child Development, 55*, 782–793.

Bruder, M. B. (1993). The provision of early intervention and early childhood special education within the community early childhood special education programs: Characteristics of effective service delivery. *Topics in Early Childhood Special Education, 13*(1), 19–37.

Bruner, J. S. (1972). The nature and uses of immaturity. *American Psychologist, 27*, 687–708.

Buium, N., Rynders, J., & Turnure, J. (1974). Early maternal linguistic environment of normal and Down's syndrome language learning children. *American Journal of Mental Deficiency, 79*, 52–58.

Burkhart, L. J. (1980). *Homemade battery-powered toys and educational devices for severely handicapped children*. (Available from Linda Burkhart, 8503 Rhode Island Ave., College Park, MD 20740)

Burkhart, L. J. (1982). *More homemade battery devices for severely handicapped children with suggested activities*. (Available from Linda Burkhart, 8503 Rhode Island Ave., College Park, MD 20740)

Clarke-Stewart, A. K. (1973). Interactions between mothers and their young children: Characteristics and consequences. *Monographs of the Society for Research in Child Development, 38*(6–7, Serial No. 153).

Cooke, T. P., Apolloni, T., & Cooke, S. A. (1977). Normal preschool children as behavior models for retarded peers. *Exceptional Children, 43*, 531–532.

Cooke, S. A., Cooke, T. P., & Apolloni, T. (1977). Developing nonretarded toddlers as verbal models for retarded classmates. *Child Study Journal, 8*, 1–8.

Crawley, S. B., & Spiker, D. (1983). Mother–child interactions involving two year olds with Down syndrome: A look at individual differences. *Child Development, 54*, 1313–1323.

Cunningham, C. E., Reuler, E., Blackwell, J., & Deck, J. (1981). Behavioral and linguistic developments in the interactions of normal and retarded children with their mothers. *Child Development, 52*, 62–70.

Eheart, B. K. (1982). Mother–child interactions with nonretarded and mentally retarded preschoolers. *American Journal of Mental Deficiency, 87*, 20–25.

Fewell, R. R., & Kaminski, R. (1988). Play skills development and instruction for young children with handicaps. In S. L. Odom & M. B. Karnes (Eds.), *Early intervention for infants and children with handicaps* (pp. 145–158). Baltimore: Brookes.

Finkelstein, N. W., & Ramey, C. T. (1977). Learning to control the environment in infancy. *Child Development, 48*, 806–819.

Fredericks, H. D., Baldwin, V., Grove, D., Moore, W., Riggs, C., & Lyons, B. (1978). Integrating moderately and severely handicapped preschool children into a normal day care center. In M. J. Guralnick (Ed.), *Early intervention and the integration of handicapped and nonhandicapped children* (pp. 191–206). Baltimore: University Park Press.

Garrard, K. R. (1989). Mothers' verbal directives to delayed and nondelayed children. *Mental Retardation, 27*(1), 11–18.

Guralnick, M. J. (1981a). The efficacy of integrating handicapped children in early childhood settings: Research implications. *Topics in Early Childhood Special Education, 1*(1), 57–71.

Guralnick, M. J. (1981b). The social behavior of preschool children at different developmental levels: Effects of group composition. *American Journal of Child Psychology, 31*(1), 115–130.

Guralnick, M. J. (1982). Programmatic factors affecting child–child social interactions in mainstreamed preschool programs. In P. S. Strain (Ed.), *Social development of exceptional children* (pp. 71–92). Rockville, MD: Aspen.

Gutmann, A. J., & Rondal, J. A. (1979). Verbal operants in mothers' speech to nonretarded and Down's syndrome children matched for linguistic level. *American Journal of Mental Deficiency, 83*, 446–452.

Hanline, M. F. (1985). Integrating disabled children. *Young Children, 40*(2), 45–48.

Hanson, M. J., & Hanline, M. F. (1989). Integration options for the very young child. In R. Gaylord-

Ross (Ed.), *Integration strategies for persons with handicaps* (pp. 177–193). Baltimore: Brookes.

Hanson, M. J., & Harris, S. R. (1986). *Teaching the young child with motor delays*. Austin, TX: PRO-ED.

Hanson, M. J., & Krentz, M. K. (1986). *Supporting parent–child interactions: A guide for early intervention program personnel*. San Francisco: Department of Special Education, San Francisco State University.

Hanson, M. J., Lynch, E. W., & Wayman, K. I. (1990). Honoring the cultural diversity of families when gathering data. *Topics in Early Childhood Special Education, 10*(1), 112–131.

Hanson, M. J., & Widerstrom, A. H. (1993). Consultation and collaboration: Essentials of integration efforts for young children. In C. A. Peck, S. L. Odom, & D. D. Bricker, (Eds.), *Integrating young children with disabilities into community programs: Ecological perspectives on research and implementation* (pp. 149–168). Baltimore: Brookes.

Lewis, M., & Goldberg, S. (1969). Perceptual-cognitive development in infancy: A generalized expectancy model as a function of the mother–infant interaction. *Merrill-Palmer Quarterly of Behavior and Development, 15*, 81–100.

Lynch, E. W., & Hanson, M. J. (Eds.). (1992). *Developing cross-cultural competence: A guide for working with young children and their families*. Baltimore: Brookes.

Mahoney, G., Finger, I., & Powell, A. (1985). Relationship of maternal behavioral style to the development of organically impaired mentally retarded infants. *American Journal of Mental Deficiency, 90*, 296–302.

Mahoney, G., & Powell, A. (1986). *Transactional intervention program teacher's guide*. Farmington, CT: Pediatric Research and Training Center.

Mahoney, G., & Powell, A. (1988). Modifying parent–child interactions: Enhancing the development of handicapped children. *The Journal of Special Education, 22*(1), 82–96.

Mahoney, G., & Robenalt, K. (1986). A comparison of conversational patterns between mothers and their Down syndrome and normal infants. *Journal of the Division for Early Childhood, 10*, 172–180.

Marshall, N. R., Hegrenes, J. R., & Goldstein, S. (1973). Verbal interactions: Mothers and their retarded children vs. mothers and their nonretarded children. *American Journal of Mental Deficiency, 77*, 415–419.

Maurer, H., & Sherrod, K. B. (1987). Context of directives given to young children with Down syndrome and nonretarded children: Development over two years. *American Journal of Mental Deficiency, 91*, 579–590.

McCollum, J. A. (1987). Looking patterns of mentally retarded and nonretarded infants in play and instructional interactions. *American Journal of Mental Deficiency, 91*, 516–523.

McCollum, J. A., & Stayton, V. D. (1985, Spring). Infant/parent interactions: Studies and intervention guidelines based on the SIAI model. *Journal of the Division for Early Childhood*, pp. 125–135.

Odom, S. L., McConnell, S. R., & McEvoy, M. A. (1992). *Social competence of young children with disabilities: Issues and strategies for intervention*. Baltimore: Brookes.

Odom, S. L., & McEvoy, M. A. (1988). Integration of young children with handicaps and normally developing children. In S. L. Odom & M. B. Karnes (Eds.), *Early intervention for infants and children with handicaps* (pp. 241–267). Baltimore: Brookes.

Peterson, N. L. (1982). Social integration of handicapped and nonhandicapped preschoolers: A study of playmate preferences. *Topics in Early Childhood Special Education, 2*(2), 56–69.

Peterson, N. L., & Haralick, J. G. (1977). Integration of handicapped and nonhandicapped preschoolers: An analysis of play behavior and social interaction. *Education and Training of the Mentally Retarded, 12*, 235–245.

Piaget, J. (1962). *Play, dreams, and imitation in children*. New York: Norton.

Provence, S., & Lipton, R. C. (1962). *Infants in institutions*. New York: International Universities Press.

Ramey, C. T., & Finkelstein, N. W. (1978). Contingent stimulation and infant competence. *Journal of Pediatric Psychology, 3*(2), 89–96.

Rosenberg, S. A., & Robinson, C. C. (1988). Interactions of parents with their young handicapped children. In S. L. Odom & M. B. Karnes (Eds.), *Early intervention for infants and children with handicaps* (pp. 159–177). Baltimore: Brookes.

Rovee, C. K., & Fagan, J. W. (1976). Extended conditioning and 24-hour retention in infancy. *Journal of Experimental Child Psychology, 21*, 1–11.

Seligman, M. (1975). *Helplessness: On depression, development and death*. San Francisco: W. H. Freeman.

Strain, P. S., & Kerr, M. M. (1981). *Mainstreaming of children in schools: Research and programmatic issues*. New York: Academic Press.

Strain, P. S., & Odom, S. L. (1986). Peer social initiations: Effective intervention for social skills development of exceptional children. *Exceptional Children, 52*(6), 543–551.

Sullivan, M. W., & Lewis, M. (1990). Contingency intervention: A program portrait. *Journal of Early Intervention, 14*(4), 367–375.

van den Pol, R. A., Crow, R. E., Rider, D. P., & Offner, R. B. (1985). Social interaction research in integrated preschool: Implications and applications. *Topics in Early Childhood Special Education, 4*(4), 59–75.

Vygotsky, L. S. (1967). Play and its role in the mental development of the child. *Soviet Psychology, 5*(3), 6–18.

Watson, J. S. (1966). The development and generalization of contingency awareness in early infancy: Some hypotheses. *Merrill-Palmer Quarterly, 12*, 123–135.

Watson, J. S. (1967). Memory and "contingency analysis" in infant learning. *Merrill-Palmer Quarterly, 13*, 55–76.

Watson, J. S. (1972). Smiling, cooing, and "the game." *Merrill-Palmer Quarterly, 18*, 323–339.

Wayman, K. I., Lynch, E. W., & Hanson, M. J. (1991). Home-based early childhood services: Cultural sensitivity in a family systems approach. *Topics in Early Childhood Special Education, 10*(4), 56–75.

White, R. W. (1959). Motivation reconsidered: The concept of competence. *Psychological Review, 66*, 297–333.

Yarrow, L. J., Rubenstein, J. L., Pedersen, F. A., & Jankowski, J. J. (1972). Dimensions of early stimulation and their different effect on infant development. *Merrill-Palmer Quarterly, 18*, 205–218.

Selected Readings

Adaptive Equipment

The following books and manuals describe the use of adaptive equipment for young children with disabilities. Several explain how to make pieces of equipment and how to modify common household items that may be available.

Connor, F., Williamson, G., & Siepp, J. (1978). *Program guide for infants and toddlers with neuromotor and other development disabilities*. New York: Teachers College Press.

Finnie, N. (1975). *Handling the young cerebral palsied child at home*. New York: Dutton.

Fraser, B. A., Galka, G., & Hensinger, R. N. (1980). *Gross motor management of severely multiply impaired students* (Vol. 1). Austin, TX: PRO-ED.

Fraser, B. A., Hensinger, R. N., & Phelps, J. A. (1987). *A professional's guide: Physical management of multiple handicaps*. Baltimore: Brookes.

Golbin, A. (Ed.). (1977). *Cerebral palsy and communication: What parents can do*. Washington, DC: Job Development Laboratory, George Washington University.

Hanson, M. J., & Harris, S. R. (1986). *Teaching the young child with motor delays*. Austin, TX: PRO-ED.

High, E. C. (1977). *A resource guide to habilitative techniques and aids for cerebral palsied persons of all ages*. Washington, DC: Job Development Laboratory, George Washington University.

Morris, S. E. (1977). *Program guidelines for children with feeding problems*. (Available from Childcraft Education Corporation, 20 Kilmer Rd., Edison, NJ 08818)

Robinault, I. P. (1973). *Functional aids for the multiply handicapped*. New York: Harper & Row.

Williamson, G. G. (1987). *Children with spina bifida*. Baltimore: Brookes.

Home-Constructed Electronic Devices

These books and manuals outline how to build toys and electronic devices for use with young children. Most provide simple-to-use plans for construction or modification of toys and objects commonly found in households and intervention programs. These devices provide ideal playthings for young children, particularly those with severe disabilities that impair ability to play with typical toys and receive feedback from the environment.

Burkhart, L. J. (1980). *Homemade battery-powered toys and educational devices for severely handicapped children.* (Available from Linda Burkhart, 8503 Rhode Island Ave., College Park, MD 20740)

Burkhart, L. J. (1982). *More homemade battery devices for severely handicapped children with suggested activities.* (Available from Linda Burkhart, 8503 Rhode Island Ave., College Park, MD 20740)

Campbell, P. H., Bricker, W. A., Simmons, T., & Esposito, L. (1981). *Electronic aids for teaching the severely motorically impaired student.* Akron, OH: Children's Hospital Medical Center.

Shein, G. F. (1980, November). *Instructions for constructing a large area flap switch to allow disabled children to control battery-operated toys.* Toronto, Ontario, Canada: Rehabilitation Engineering Department, Ontario Crippled Children's Centre, 350 Rumsey Rd., Toronto, Ontario, Canada, M4G 1R8.

Wright, C., & Nomura, M. (1985). *From toys to computers: Access for the physically disabled child.* (Available for $17.00 from Christine Wright, P.O. Box 700242, San Jose, CA 95170)

Communication Devices

Blackstone, S. (Ed.). (1986). *Augmentative communication: An introduction.* Rockville, MD: American Speech, Hearing, and Language Association.

Brandenburg, S. A., Bengston, D. A., & Vanderheiden, G. C. (1987). *The rehab/education technology resourcebook series: Communication, control, and computer access for disabled individuals, 1986–87.* (Book 1—Communication aids; Book 2—Switches, training, and environmental control; Book 3—Software and hardware.) Madison, WI: Trace Research and Development Center on Communication, Control, and Computer Access for Handicapped Individuals, University of Wisconsin.

Burkhart, L. J. (1987). *Using computers and speech synthesis to facilitate communicative interaction with young and/or severely handicapped children.* (Available from Linda Burkhart, 8503 Rhode Island Ave., College Park, MD 20740)

Porter, P. B., Carter, S., Goolsby, E., Martin, N. J., Reed, M., Stowers, H., & Wurth, B. (1986). *Prerequisites to augmentative communication.* Chapel Hill: Division for Disorders of Development and Learning, Biological Sciences Research Center 220-H, University of North Carolina.

Vanderheiden, G. C., & Krause, L. A. (Eds.). (1983). *Non-vocal communication resource book.* Baltimore: University Park Press.

Recommended Equipment and Materials

The following list provides a guideline for the types of equipment and materials that are useful in an early intervention program.

Equipment

Mats

Bolsters

Large therapy/beach balls

Small, toddler-sized table

Chair with support (e.g., cube chairs)

Special chairs (e.g., corner chairs, chairs with adductor and abductor blocks)

Climbing equipment

Wheeled toys (e.g., wagons, trikes, push toys)

Sandbox

Water play tray/tub

Easel

Materials and Toys

Rattles

Small balls

Chime balls

Tactile quilts and balls

Blocks

Busy boxes and activity centers

Toys with cause–effect components

Books for infants and toddlers

Tapes and records for infants and toddlers

Small wheeled toys (e.g., cars, trucks)

Dolls

Stuffed animals

Cloth toys that rattle or move

Color cubes

Flannel and felt boards

Animals—farm, zoo

Knob puzzles

Noninterlocking and simple interlocking puzzles

Dressing frames

Lacing and tying frames

Nesting toys

Pictures and photographs

Puppets

Shape-sorting toys

Telephones

Sound boxes and shapes

Pop-up toys

Containers and safe small objects for sorting and retrieving

Push and pull toys

Resources for Adaptive Equipment

These companies sell adaptive equipment appropriate for young children with disabilities. Most provide catalogs at no charge.

Achievement Products for Children
P.O. Box 9033
1621 Warner Ave. SE
Canton, OH 44711

Adaptive Equipment Company
175 Parker Ct.
Chardon, OH 44204

Adaptive Therapeutic Systems
683 Boston Post Rd.
Madison, CT 06443

Crestwood Company
Communication Aids for Children and Adults
6625 N. Sidney Pl.
Milwaukee, WI 53209-3259

Equipment Shop
P.O. Box 33
Bedford, MA 01730

Everest & Jennings, Inc.
3233 E. Mission Oaks Blvd.
Camarillo, CA 93010

Fred Sammons
145 Tower Dr.
Burr Ridge, IL 60521

J. A. Preston, Inc.
P.O. Box 89
Jackson, MI 49204

Jesana Ltd.
P.O. Box 17
Irvington, NY 10533

Kay Products, Inc.
535 Dimmocks Mill Rd.
Hillsborough, NC 27278

Lakeshore Learning Materials
2695 E. Dominguez St.
P.O. Box 6261
Carson, CA 90749

Orth-Kinetics, Inc.
P.O. Box 436
W220 N507 Springdale Rd.
Waukesha, WI 53187

Rifton, Inc.
P.O. Box 901
Rifton, NY 12471-0901

Safety Travel Chairs
147 Eady Ct.
Elyria, OH 44035

Therapy Skill Builders
3830 E. Bellevue
P.O. Box 42050-P92
Tucson, AZ 85733

Toys for Special Children
385 Warburton Ave.
Hastings-on-Hudson, NY 10706

SECTION III

Administrative Issues

Managing Program Components

CHAPTER 11

Early intervention programs are characterized by diversity across program features, such as types of settings, program models, and staff composition. Comprehensive, developmentally and educationally oriented programs with multiple service delivery options and family support opportunities include a variety of services that must be managed, coordinated, supervised, and evaluated. Equally varied are the responsibilities of the manager of the early intervention program. Thus, the manager must possess a broad range of management skills. Managers need disciplinary knowledge including information about infant development, assessment, curriculum design and implementation, and evaluation.

Managers must also possess good "people skills." They must be flexible and have the ability to work and communicate effectively with various groups of people including staff members, families, and personnel from other agencies. The manager must be a creative problem solver who is able to develop and consider a wide range of options for effective use of both human and fiscal resources. The leadership skills of most individuals in this role extend beyond their own program and are manifested by a deep commitment to developing, improving, and expanding services to infants and toddlers with special needs and their families.

In addition, early intervention program managers must have excellent organizational skills. The numbers of children and families being served, the wide range of staff employed, the multiplicity of services provided, and the diversity of community constituents require that the manager be organized almost to the point of compulsivity. These organizational skills are particularly important because most programs operate with limited resources.

Finally, program managers must be advocates for *all* children and families. They must welcome diversity and invest time in ensuring that the programs and services that they are managing are responsive to the diversity of families, of staff, and of organizational cultures that are encountered in any interagency effort. Because there are still shortages of early intervention personnel from diverse cultural and language backgrounds, program managers must be committed to recruiting and retaining staff from underrepresented groups. As part of their advocacy, they must know state and federal legislation that pertains to the programs

---

The authors would like to acknowledge contributions to this chapter by Patrick J. Harrison, Department of Educational Technology, San Diego State University.

that they operate, and they must be creative developers of policies that support the intent and spirit of the law instead of dogmatic implementors of the letter of the law.

Program managers of early intervention services come from a variety of educational and professional backgrounds. Given the range of professions represented in early intervention services, the supervisor or manager may come from any of a number of disciplines (e.g., early childhood special education; physical, occupational, or speech–language therapy; psychology; social work; nursing; medicine). Managers' experience and training, however, must extend beyond that of their primary area of professional training to include leadership skills in all aspects of the program.

Managers of early intervention programs have many of the same responsibilities as supervisors in business and industry as well as managers of other human service programs. In general, these responsibilities can be grouped into four functions: planning, organizing, directing, and controlling (Frame, 1987). In the

following sections of this chapter, each of these functions is discussed in terms of early intervention program management.

Strategic Planning

Throughout this book the importance of planning has been stressed. Thus, one of the manager's critical roles is strategic planning. "Strategic planning determines where your organization should be going so that all organizational efforts can be pointed in that direction" (Below, Morrisey, & Acomb, 1987, p. 1). Strategic planning differs from operational planning in that strategic planning is visionary and focused or directional (Below et al., 1987). Such planning efforts are usually done with a team and occur periodically throughout the life of the program. All decisions that are made in a program should be consistent with the plan that has been formulated, and the program manager should take the leadership in developing strategic plans. For example, if the strategic plan calls for the program to move to a much more family-focused approach, staff development, resource allocation, assessment, and evaluation should focus on this outcome.

Operational Planning

Another type of planning focuses more on developing the day-to-day policies and procedures that enable the program to function. Operational planning defines in detail what will be accomplished and who is accountable. It is the implementation arm of strategic planning (Morrisey, Below, & Acomb, 1988).

Goals and Objectives

Developing program goals, objectives, and policies is part of operational planning. These are derived from multiple sources including the strategic and operational plans; community needs; and the various laws, rules, and regulations under which programs must operate. The goals and objectives are inextricably bound to the program's mission and philosophy as well as to the daily demands of program operation. Overall goals and objectives are set by the manager during the planning process in consultation with staff, advisory boards, supervisors, and community needs.

Policies

As the program leader, the manager is responsible for policy planning in all programmatic areas. Given the importance of close teamwork in early intervention settings, many policies are developed with extensive input from the team members and consumers of the services (i.e., the parents). A number of programs also have a formal advisory board. The board's members typically include parents of children in the program and professionals from the community. It is the responsibility of the advisory board to provide input to the manager on the various program components and to assist in program planning. Because of the interagency nature of the infant and toddler sections of the Individuals with Disabilities Education Act (IDEA), policies often have to reflect relationships with other agencies and coordinated approaches to service delivery.

Regulations

It is the manager's responsibility to ensure that the early intervention program complies with state and federal regulations as well as those of its funding agency. Part of the operational planning process is determining what these regulations are and deciding how they will be translated into policies and procedures. Such regulations typically involve establishing child eligibility criteria for participation according to agency regulations, adhering to attendance or other funding requirements, implementing services according to guidelines (staff-to-child ratios, type of services, etc.), following nonbiased assessment procedures, recording child and family participation, ensuring that staff are appropriately licensed or credentialed, and reporting appropriate budget information.

Legal Compliance

Programs funded with state and federal moneys also must be in compliance with specific state and federal laws. Again, becoming knowledgeable about these laws and developing operating policies and procedures consistent with them form part of the planning process. These laws and their regulations pertain to parental rights, eligibility for participation, due process procedures, and stipulations related to staffing, assessment procedures, and program planning and implementation.

Safety and Health

The manager also must develop and supervise the utilization of policies related to the welfare and safety of personnel and program participants. Such issues as program safety, sanitation, emergency procedures, and insurance must be addressed for the particular program setting and an administrative protocol adopted. Preplanning in each of these areas helps assure that programs will operate safely with reduced liability.

Alternatives and Choices

For every activity in a program, a series of decisions must be made. Ultimately, the program manager is responsible for making those decisions and seeing that they are carried out; however, planning about the decision-making process, such as who will give input, how the input will be structured, and who makes what sorts of decisions, provides a framework for choosing alternatives.

Task Definition and Delegation

Although the preceding paragraphs imply that the managers do everything, in reality a good manager defines tasks clearly and delegates many of them to others. One of the keys to successful delegation is the ability to chunk tasks, define clearly what needs to be done, and specify optimal performance. Even when managers are skilled in chunking, defining, and specifying performance criteria, delegation often presents management dilemmas (Mintzberg, 1980). Those who do not delegate are doomed to increasing workloads and staff dependency; those who do delegate must be willing to accept that others may perform tasks differently than they themselves might have performed them.

Task and Resource Scheduling

Forecasting what needs to be accomplished in an early intervention program and developing schedules for utilization of personnel, space, transportation, clerical support, and the myriad other details that make programs run smoothly or chaotically require advance planning. One of the first steps in scheduling is to list all of the tasks that need to be accomplished. This listing, often referred to as a work breakdown structure, starts at a global level and adds layers of details until it can serve as a checklist or blueprint for operation. Figure 11.1 provides an example of a work breakdown structure for planning a family–professional training program.

Planning staff members' schedules needs equal attention. The program manager and the staff must be creative and flexible to divide their time between home-based activities,

Planning a Family–Professional Training Program

1.0 Determine need for program
    1.1 Develop draft needs assessment questionnaire
        1.1.1 Program manager and family coordinator list questions
        1.1.2 Share questionnaire with entire staff
    1.2 Pilot needs assessment questionnaire
    1.3 Revise questionnaire
    1.4 Determine distribution and return strategies
    1.5 Duplicate questionnaires
        1.5.1 Prepare return envelopes
    1.6 Distribute questionnaires
    1.7 Prompt nonrespondents as necessary
    1.8 Analyze responses on returned questionnaires

2.0 Develop program content
    2.1 Contact professional and family member trainers who will be developing and delivering the program
    2.2 Chunk needs assessment findings into content themes
    2.3 Develop overall outline of program
    2.4 Develop each session
        2.4.1 Outline content
        2.4.2 Detail content areas as needed (in some cases detail to level of script)
        2.4.3 Develop handouts
        2.4.4 Determine equipment/materials needed
        2.4.5 Share draft with program manager and family coordinator
        2.4.6 Revise as needed
        2.4.7 Have final draft reproduced for use
    2.5 Compile final copies of each session in program file/notebook

3.0 Organize logistics
    3.1 Calendar sessions
    3.2 Secure space and equipment/materials for scheduled times
    3.3 Make plans for transportation for families
    3.4 Make plans for child care
    3.5 Develop procedures for notifying families
    3.6 Develop invitations
        3.6.1 Write invitations
        3.6.2 Send invitations
        3.6.3 Do telephone follow-ups
        3.6.4 Do telephone confirmations the day before the session
    3.7 Notify security and get keys to unlock building
    3.8 Pack materials for sessions
        3.8.1 Pack name tags and other session materials
        3.8.2 Bring coffee pot, cups/cream/sugar/lemonade, and other snacks

Figure 11.1. Work breakdown structure.

center-based activities, and consultation; equalize workloads; and develop schedules that enable families to participate in the program.

Budgets

Early intervention programs may be funded by a single agency (e.g., state-level department of education or department of health) or by multiple agencies or sources. Many programs also have affiliations with private, nonprofit agencies, such as the Easter Seal Society, Parent to Parent, or Association for Retarded Citizens. The manager is responsible for soliciting or applying for funding, coordinating with funding agencies, managing moneys, and accounting for expenditures. Typically, the manager has access to a bookkeeper or accountant with technical expertise in budgeting. However, the manager must do the planning and make the vital decisions regarding allocation of resources and coordination with fiscal agents.

Organizing

Implementing the operational plan requires systems and procedures that can be easily routinized into the day-to-day functioning of the project. The program manager is responsible for guiding the overall development of these procedures and overseeing their implementation. These procedures provide a backbone for program operation and help assure that necessary tasks are being performed without disruption or confusion.

Managing the Service Delivery System

The program manager must supervise the development and implementation of all program services—assessment, curriculum, direct services to children, and services to families. Although these services will be delivered by the entire staff, it is the manager's role to ensure that services are delivered appropriately and adequately. These components are fully discussed in Chapters 4 through 10. The following paragraphs suggest some standard operating procedures for referral, intake, and exit procedures.

First contacts

Each program should appoint a primary contact person for referral sources. This may be the program manager or a designated staff member. A *single, primary* contact is preferred so that consistent and complete information can be provided for each referral. The contact person is responsible for describing program services and procedures to referring professionals or prospective families. In some communities, the primary contact from an early intervention program or service may participate in an interagency group that receives all referrals and works with families to expedite their introduction to the early intervention system. In this case, it is typically that individual's responsibility to speak for her or his agency when explaining eligibility criteria, services that can be offered, and the way the program works.

The description of services includes an overview of the ages of children served, eligibility requirements, program philosophy, and types and range of services available. Following this brief, factual explanation, which may occur over the telephone or in an interagency meeting, interested families and/or referring persons typically are invited to arrange for a home visit or to visit the program site. Written descriptions of the program and procedures may be mailed to them as well. During subsequent visits or conversations, the program can be explained more fully.

If the services are inappropriate for a given family, the contact person should be prepared to provide information on other community services. The infant and toddler sections of IDEA require that states maintain a central directory, and it is recommended that programs keep directories of community service agencies and that contact persons remain well informed as to available service options in their locality. Such assistance to families ensures that families do not get lost in the shuffle. This assistance is particularly important for parents of infants, because the time and effort needed to learn about services and make initiations to agencies may be overwhelming or difficult at best when the child is very young.

During the period of first contacts, time should be allowed for families to become acquainted with the service system and determine what they want the next steps to be. Some families will be eager for the assessment process to begin and eager to have their child participate in early intervention programs and services. Others may feel that they would like some time together as a family before they commit to assessment and participation in early intervention. Providing families with the information that they need to make a decision, giving them time to decide, and supporting their decision are all part of family-centered early intervention. Developing and implementing policies and procedures that allow the initial contacts to proceed at the family's pace is not as easy as it sounds. Early intervention programs typically are not reimbursed for time spent with children and families who are not enrolled in their program. As a result, this critical time prior to assessment and possible enrollment is often not financially supported by funding sources. In addition, regulations specify time lines within which programs must complete assessments and develop Individualized Family Service Plans (IFSPs). Although slowdowns requested by the family are permissible, they must be carefully documented. The paperwork may tempt some intervention programs to push families into time frames that are more comfortable for the program than the family.

During this period of first contacts, or after the family has decided that they want to have their child assessed, a family service coordinator is assigned. The service coordinator may be the person with whom the family has been working or another professional whose only role is service coordination. This person works with the family to determine their concerns; arranges for the needed assessments; supports the family through the assessment process, providing them with information and opportunities to participate as fully as they choose; and ensures that the family's voice is heard in the IFSP.

Intake procedures

Once families have been referred and expressed their interest in participating in the assessment, detailed intake procedures can be implemented. These procedures involve two steps. The first step is for a program staff member or the initial family service coordinator to *completely and thoroughly explain program services and requirements*. This information should be provided both verbally and in writing for families' future reference. It should also be provided in a language that families can understand, and in ways that are suited to the family's cultural preferences.

In the second step a program staff member or the initial family service coordinator is assigned to *collect descriptive family information* including such things as family members' names and addresses; siblings' names and ages; and information on the child such as diagnosis, medical problems, and special conditions that must be noted such as seizures or allergies. This information may be obtained using a written questionnaire, an interview, or both. However, an interview in the parents' native language is recommended. This ensures that parents are given ample time to ask and answer questions, and their responses are likely to be less limited by language difficulties or reading skills. Furthermore, it serves as the beginning of a partnership relationship between the professional staff of the program and the parents.

In addition to the descriptive information, the initial family service coordinator or other staff member, with the family's permission, gathers information about the family's concerns, priorities, and resources. This information will be used to help determine the questions that should be addressed in the child's assessment. It will also be used to set priorities and to ensure that interventions build upon family strengths. This information can be obtained through several methods, such as a questionnaire or needs assessment or through a detailed interview. Again, personal contact and discussion are recommended. At this point, parents are asked to indicate their concerns about their child, their understanding of the child's diagnosis or reason for referral, their goals and hopes for their child, and their perceptions of how program services may be of use to the child and family. It is useful to procure information regarding typical child and family activities, such as persons and toys the child prefers, a description of a typical day for the child and family, activities the family enjoys, and support systems and difficulties the family encounters from others such as relatives, friends, and other service providers. Figure 11.2 is a sample interview questionnaire that may be incorporated into the intake process.

The intake process may take place across several meetings so that parents are not fatigued or overwhelmed by the process. Unless the family has another preference, at least part of the intake should take place in the child's home where the child is most comfortable and also where the parent and professional can openly discuss and/or observe difficulties and areas of concern. As mentioned, it is recommended that the intake process be conducted by a single, primary contact person or initial family service coordinator so that parents can relate on a one-to-one basis to the staff member and be made to feel comfortable. Most persons are uncomfortable if confronted with a room full of professionals asking questions or different persons at different times conducting a personal interview. The initial contact person or family service coordinator needs to remember that many parents have been interviewed and observed numerous times by various professionals from various agencies often asking the same questions. Such contact may be frustrating, emotional, or even frightening to parents. Therefore, the more that parents are given the opportunity to express their goals and concerns in a nonthreatening and comfortable environment, the more likely it is that a true partnership between the parent and the program staff will develop.

In some communities committed to an interagency approach to implementing the infant and toddler sections of IDEA, all of the agencies involved in services to children under 3 who are at risk or disabled and their families have come together to develop a multiagency intake questionnaire. This form provides the intake information needed by each of the participating agencies so that families do not have to fill out different forms asking the same questions at every agency from which they receive services. This procedure makes the intake process far more family friendly and efficient.

After or concurrent with the intake process, a *transdisciplinary team assessment* of the child's development can be conducted. Again, it is useful to designate one staff member as the primary assessor along with appropriate family members, with other staff members observing and perhaps asking questions. A coordinated team approach to assessment prevents duplication of assessment efforts and provides a more efficient and comfortable situation for families to become involved. During and after the assessment, the family service coordinator or primary assessor should discuss findings and identified areas of need with parents. Again, families are more likely to become fully involved if they are able to relate to someone

INFANT PROGRAM
INTAKE QUESTIONNAIRE

I. **GENERAL INFORMATION:** Date: _____

Child's Name: _____ Birth Date: _____
Address: _____
_____
Phone: _____
Parents/Guardian: _____
_____
Referred by: _____ From: _____
Reason for Referral: _____
Child's Physician: _____
Address: _____
_____
Phone: _____
Child's General Health: _____
Height: _____ Weight: _____
Developmental Concerns: _____
Medical Concerns: _____
_____
_____
Medication: _____
_____
Immunizations: _____
_____

Child has had or shown (check all that apply):

Allergies—food, drugs	☐	German Measles	☐
Mumps	☐	Scarlet Fever	☐
Chicken Pox	☐	Seizures or Convulsions	☐
Whooping Cough	☐	High Fever	☐
Asthma	☐	Speech Problems	☐
Headaches or Dizziness	☐	Motor Problems	☐
Skin Disease or Condition	☐	Accidents	☐
Eye or Visual Problems	☐	Operations or Hospitalization	☐
Ear or Hearing Problems	☐		

Other agencies you have contacted with regard to your child (assessment, medical, educational, etc.): _____
_____
_____
_____

(continues)

Figure 11.2. Intake questionnaire.

Are you still in contact with these agencies? If so, which ones and with whom do you work? _____

Family Information

Child's primary caregiver(s) and relationship to child: _____

Other persons who care for the child and relationship to child: _____

Mother's Name: _____ Birth Date: _____
   Address: _____

   Home Phone: _____ Work Phone: _____
   Years of Education: _____
   Occupation: _____ Income: _____
   Ethnic Identity: _____

Father's Name: _____ Birth Date: _____
   Address: _____

   Home Phone: _____ Work Phone: _____
   Years of Education: _____
   Occupation: _____ Income: _____
   Ethnic Identity: _____

Brothers' and Sisters' Names: Birth Dates:

_____   _____

_____   _____

_____   _____

_____   _____

                 (Use back of form for more space)

Other people living in home:
   Permanently: _____

   Temporarily: _____

                 (Use back of form for more space)

Language spoken in home: _____

If any of the following have occurred or are now happening, please give a brief account and date of: adoption, marital problems, divorce, long absence of an important family member or close friend, change of residence, serious physical illness, death in the family, or other important events not mentioned elsewhere.

(continues)

Figure 11.2.   continued

II. **Birth History:** When my infant was born, s/he was (check all that apply):

                                                                              Comments

- premature ☐
- overdue ☐
- breech (feet first) ☐
- an odd color ☐
- having respiratory difficulty ☐
- functioning normally ☐
- attended to by a physician ☐
- attended to by others (specify) ☐

_____ lbs.   _____ oz.   _____ inches long

III. **Neonatal Behavior:** My newborn infant
had: **Comments**
- convulsions ☐
- an absent, weak, or unusual cry ☐
- an absent, weak, or unusual suck ☐
- difficulties feeding ☐
- difficulties sleeping ☐
- to be hospitalized (prolonged) ☐
- to have special care ☐
- to have oxygen ☐

was:
- inactive ☐
- irritable ☐
- cuddly ☐
- floppy ☐

IV. **Developmental Milestones**

	Age When It Happened	**Description** (e.g., emerging skill, under what conditions)
Motor:		
lifts head when on belly		
rolls prone to back		
sits alone		
crawls, belly touches floor		
creeps, hands and knees on floor only		
pulls up to stand using furniture		
cruises (side-steps holding on)		
walks (falls a lot)		
walks (a few falls a day)		
uses riding toys		

(continues)

Figure 11.2. continued

	Age When It Happened	**Description** (e.g., emerging skill, under what conditions)
Any other things you would like your child to do?		

Interaction with Objects:
- grasps objects
- mouths objects
- swipes at objects
- reaches and grasps objects
- shakes and bangs objects
- transfers objects hand to hand
- brings hands together
- takes objects out of container
- puts objects into container
- plays with manipulative toys (e.g., knobs and buttons on busy box)

Any other things you would like your child to do?

Social Interaction:
- smiles
- smiles at me
- smiles at others
- smiles when I smile
- watches me
- watches others
- demands attention
- is shy with others
- prefers to play alone
- prefers to play with me
- prefers to play with others
- plays "baby" games peek/pat-a-cake

Any other things you would like your child to do?

Language:
- reacts to sound (listens)
- coos, laughs, yells, cries differentially
- repeats certain sounds (mama, dada)
- imitates new sounds

(*continues*)

Figure 11.2.   continued

	Age When It Happened	**Description** (e.g., emerging skill, under what conditions)
understands "no"		
uses words and gestures meaningfully to communicate needs		
follows simple directions		

Any other things you would like your child to do?

Feeding:

sucks well from breast/bottle		
weaned from breast/bottle		
eats strained foods		
holds own bottle		
eats mashed table food		
finger feeds		
puts hand on spoon to help		
holds own cup (spills)		
spoon feeds with spilling		
eats independently		

Any other things you would like your child to do?

Toileting:

cries to be changed		
indicates need for diaper change		
stays dry for 2-hour periods		
has bladder control during day		
has bowel control		
takes self to bathroom		

Any other things you would like your child to do?

Behavior (Check all that apply):

- watches own hands ☐
- rocks self ☐
- doesn't seem to focus ☐
- focuses with one eye only ☐
- is awkward ☐
- seems withdrawn ☐
- tantrums ☐
- spins ☐
- makes no noise ☐
- is extremely active ☐

(*continues*)

Figure 11.2. continued

Please describe briefly a typical day in your child's life: _____

For the time periods listed below, please indicate (1) *what* child is usually doing, (2) *when* it occurs, (3) *whom* your child is with, and (4) *how* your child does this. Describe any special problems (e.g., eating problems) that usually come up.

	What	When	With Whom	Where	How
Waking					
Morning					
Lunch					
Afternoon					
Dinner					
Evening					
Bedtime					

What types of things does your child especially like—food, toys, games, activities? _____

Are there people with whom your child especially seems to like to be? _____

What does your child do outside the home (e.g., relatives' homes, friends' homes, park, doctor's office, etc.)? _____

Has your child ever shown fear of strangers? _____
If so, when and of whom? _____

What do you like doing with your child? _____

What do you dislike doing with your child? _____

(*continues*)

Figure 11.2. continued

Does your child have any particular behaviors about which you are worried? _____
_____

Please describe your child's condition. _____
_____

Are there any other particular concerns that you have about your child for the present time or for the future?
_____

What would you like your child to learn or be able to do this year? _____
_____
_____

Figure 11.2.   continued

on a one-to-one basis. As with every other procedure discussed in this book, recommendations need to be adjusted to fit the diverse preferences of families. This process may be considered an extension of the intake process.

Transition and exit procedures

IDEA requires that a transition plan be developed prior to the child's moving from infant and toddler services to preschool services at age 3. The plan is included in the IFSP as the child approaches the third birthday. The plan provides a blueprint for the transition process so that families, the infant program staff, and receiving districts or other services will be prepared to meet the child's needs. However, in addition to the transition plan that addresses next steps for the child, it is useful to conduct an exit interview with parents or other family members whenever a child leaves the program.

An exit interview can accomplish several objectives. First, it gives the program staff members and family members a chance to discuss issues and bring closure to the relationship that they have had. The interview may take place informally or formally depending upon program procedures. At the least, information should be obtained regarding reasons why the child is leaving the program, simple descriptive information on the child's next environment, and an assessment of what the family perceives the early intervention program's major strengths and weaknesses to be. The information provided by parents can be valuable to the program in assessing how well the program is meeting the needs of families in the community.

Staff members can be valuable resources to parents as they leave the program and make the transition to other services or out of the service network. Providing specific information and referral to other services, developing transition plans, and serving as a sounding board for parental concerns are but a few of the ways in which early interventionists can assist families during this time.

Exiting from the program often is not easy for families or staff. Special relationships frequently form between families and their children's "first teachers." However, the more staff members prepare families for the new environment and support and assist them to become involved with the next program, the better able families and staff will be to make the transition.

Keeping Records

In addition to records related to budgeting, the program must maintain a variety of other records. Numerous types of records are needed in an early intervention setting. They include demographic family data, child health and medical history information, records regarding community contacts and referrals, financial and budgeting records, data on child performance and progress, and information on family usage and satisfaction with the services.

There are many reasons for maintaining records. First, specific types of records are required by administrative/regulatory and funding agencies for program continuation (e.g., income and expenditures, client attendance, hours of participation, staffing patterns). Second, certain types of information are needed for practical purposes in program operation, such as logs of community contacts and data on child progress. Finally, information obtained on the effectiveness of services offered provides valuable feedback for evaluating services both on an ongoing basis and summatively over time. The types of information that may be collected are more fully described in the sections that follow; once again, it is the program manager's responsibility to see that appropriate records are kept.

Although extensive records are vital to program operation, record keeping can be cumbersome and add a significant burden to staff members who often have precious little time. Therefore, data collection and record keeping must be efficiently designed and managed.

Several considerations must be noted in the design of record-keeping systems. The first issue is that of utility. A rule of thumb should be observed: Information that is not required or useful should not be collected. Particularly in work with children and families, it is easy to fall into the practice of taking data on all aspects of the child's history and development. If the records are not useful to intervention planning for the child, they should probably not be kept.

A second issue is efficiency. Although no "prescription" can be given for setting up a record-keeping system that is appropriate to all service settings, it is important that each program devise as streamlined a system as possible. The characteristics of an efficient system include ease of data collection and information gathering, simplicity of recording forms and procedures, integration of procedures into existing program protocol, and elimination of duplication of records (e.g., the same data gathered on two or more forms).

A third and crucial consideration in record keeping is confidentiality. Because early intervention programs are in the business of human service, records kept will pertain to specific information on children and families. Rules regarding confidentiality of information should be strictly applied, and high professional standards of record keeping should be exercised. Only necessary information should be gathered, and that information should be kept in a locked place and available only to authorized staff members. Because parents have the right to examine all records kept on the family and child, these records should be made available to them at their request.

In summary, extensive information gathering and record keeping are necessary parts of any program operation. However, the manager can enhance this process by ensuring that only pertinent records are kept and that the process of record keeping is as efficient as possible.

Given that many types of program records are necessary to program operation, each type is briefly reviewed and suggestions and examples are provided. Types of records are divided into the following categories: child and family data, community contact information, and program operation records.

Child and family data

For early interventionists to plan individualized service programs for children and their families, the professionals must obtain a detailed description of each child's current developmental level and, with family concurrence, family concerns, priorities, and resources. A specific and comprehensive account of the child's behavior is needed upon initiation of the early intervention services and during the intervention period. This is accomplished through a series of observations of the child's behavior and discussions with the family.

Extensive information on the child will be collected throughout the child's participation in the program. To facilitate usage of this information, it is recommended that a compartmentalized folder be made for each child and family and divided according to various types of information (e.g., referral, performance data). Information can be filled as it is collected and organized for easy access as it is needed. A review of the types of child and family data that are likely to be collected follows.

Intake information is the first type of information collected. When a child and family begin the early intervention program, it is necessary to obtain general family information (family members' names, addresses, telephone numbers, etc.), demographic information on the family (cultural group, occupation, language spoken at home, educational level, etc.), descriptive information on the child's developmental level and typical activities (description of a typical day, child's likes and dislikes, etc.), family concerns regarding the child's condition and development, and information on the child's health and medical history and present-day concerns. Figure 11.2 provides a sample intake interview. As suggested earlier, we recommend that the information be gathered across several sessions if necessary and through a one-on-one interview with the parent(s) or other appropriate caregivers.

Additionally, information is needed from the child's primary care physician about the child's current health status. A sample form that can be used for this purpose is provided in Figure 11.3. The physician should be asked to indicate whether any aspects of the child's medical history or current health status limit the child's participation in the program.

Many children also have been assessed or served by other service providers in the community. Staff members can benefit from an exchange of information with these programs. To receive information from other sources, written parental consent must be provided to contact the agency and procure information on a particular child. An example of a consent form for this purpose is supplied in Figure 11.4.

It is also well advised to obtain written parental permission for child participation in the program (see Figure 11.5 for a sample form). Furthermore, if the program uses photographs or videotapes of participants for instructional purposes, either within the program or outside in the community, it is necessary to obtain parents' permission for photographing and videotaping their child (see Figure 11.6 for a sample form).

The program should maintain a file that is easily accessible if an emergency occurs with a child. Emergency/health forms or cards should be available for each child, specifying parents' (or guardians') names, addresses, and telephone numbers; persons to contact in case of emergency (complete information with addresses and telephone numbers); the name and telephone number of the child's primary care physician; and any special medications to be administered or procedures to be followed in the case of any emergency.

Furthermore, it is suggested that a staff member discuss emergency procedures with families and that families be requested to provide prior written consent for these procedures (a sample form is provided in Figure 11.7). Finally, the program staff may wish to inform parents of potential health risks, such as potential exposure to tuberculosis, rubella, or cytomegalovirus, that can occur in group care settings. A sample form is furnished in Figure 11.8. If other health risks exist in a particular setting, parents should be informed both through discussion and in writing.

Child performance records in all developmental areas should be kept. Parents should be informed and included in all testing procedures,

---

Date:

RE (Child's Name):
Birth Date:

Dear Dr. _____:

The Infant Program provides services to infants and toddlers birth to 3 years of age who have identifiable disabilities or are considered "at risk" for developmental delay and includes intervention across all behavioral areas of development.

A special focus of the project is the relationship between parent and child. Parents are helped to discover and know the special unique cues of their children and to become active partners in helping their infants develop. Family involvement is further encouraged through parent training and support groups.

The parents of this child would like to participate in this project and have signed the enclosed form to allow us to contact you and request information. Before participation is finalized, we would like to obtain pertinent birth history and medical records for our confidential files in order to plan a treatment program for the child with his/her family. We also have enclosed a form requesting information to ensure there are no medical implications to contraindicate this involvement.

Please send the child's medical records and release for participation to:

Program Director
Infant Program
755 Morse Street
San Francisco, CA 94112

Information provided by you will be kept confidential. If you have any questions or wish to discuss this further, please feel free to contact us at (415) 469-0448. Thank you for your time and cooperation.

Sincerely,

Program Director

(*continues*)

Figure 11.3. Letter to physician, including health questionnaire and release form.

CURRENT HEALTH QUESTIONNAIRE

Child's name: _____
Birth date: _____ Date of last exam: _____
B.P.: _____ Wt.: _____ Ht.: _____ Head circumference: _____
General appearance and nutritional status: _____
Physical findings of significance: _____
_____
Diagnoses: _____

Significant medical problems (please note any relevant program precautions):
Seizure disorder (Type, EEG, CT, other): _____
_____
Allergies (please specify): _____
_____
Heart disease (describe): _____
_____
Sensory impairment (describe type, evaluations, treatment interventions): ____
_____
Physical disabilities (describe): _____
_____
Other (please specify): _____
_____
Medications (please include dosages): _____
_____
Hospitalizations (please list dates, hospital, diagnoses): _____
_____

Immunizations (indicate dates given):

DPT							
Polio (TOPV)							
MMR							

Other (please specify): _____
Tine/PPD date: _____ Reaction (check): Positive ☐ Negative ☐
Screening tests (please describe any abnormalities):
  Vision: Date _____ Right _____ Left _____
  Hearing: Date _____ Right _____ Left _____
  CBC/Hct.:   Date _____ Results _____
  Urinalysis: Date _____ Results _____
  Sickle cell: Date _____ Results _____
  Amino acids: Date _____ Results _____
  Others: _____

(continues)

Figure 11.3.   continued

Chromosome studies: Date _____   Results _____
Developmental/psychological assessments: _____
_____

Any unmet or anticipated medical or health care needs: _____
_____

Physician's Signature: _____
Address: _____
Date: _____ Phone: _____ FAX: _____

INFANT PROGRAM

Occupational/physical therapy services are being provided through the Infant Program. To enable these services to be provided we require your certification of the following information.

I, _____, have no medical information which would contraindicate evaluation,
        (Physician's Name)
consultation, and/or direct treatment for my patient, _____, as a participant in the
                                                              (Child's Name)
Infant Program.

Medical Diagnosis:

Medical Precautions:

Major Areas of Concern:

Medication/Side Effects:

_____
                                         (Physician's Signature)

A copy of the child's evaluation and progress notes will be sent to you on a regular basis. If you have any questions or concerns, please feel free to contact me at any time.

                    Program Director
                    Infant Program
                    755 Morse Street
                    San Francisco, CA 94112

Figure 11.3.   continued

RE (Child's Name): _____

Birth Date: _____

I hereby grant permission for

_____

_____

_____

to release my child's, _____

records to the Infant Program. I also authorize the Infant Program to exchange information with _____

_____ on an ongoing basis.

_____   _____
(Date)   (Signature)

Figure 11.4. Parent permission for release of information.

---

and their written consent for the procedures should be obtained before the procedures are implemented.

Once an IFSP is established for a child, the staff members will need to develop a system for assessing the child's progress toward the objectives on an ongoing basis. Many different types of data may be collected periodically depending upon the educational goal and the way in which the information will be used. For some educational goals, for example, the staff member may wish to collect duration data (e.g., the number of seconds the child is able to hold up her head). For other goals, a frequency count may be more appropriate (e.g., the number of times the child uses a word to get a food or drink during mealtime). Other goals will require anecdotal data or a behavioral sample, such as a listing of all the words a child says during playtime or mealtime.

Finally, for still other goals the staff member may wish to calculate the rate or percentage of correct responses achieved on an instructional task, such as the percentage of times the child matches objects that are the same or the percentage of trials in which the child sits independently without support. A useful form for collecting these data is presented in Figure 11.9. To utilize this form the staff member writes a plus sign (+) beside the number of the trial in which the child achieves a correct response and a minus sign (–) when the child fails to perform the behavior. For example, consider the following goal: "The child will sit independently without support for 20 seconds when placed on the floor."

INFANT PROGRAM
Parent Permission Form

I understand that the purpose of the Infant Program is to provide educational assistance to children from birth to 3 years with developmental delays and their families. I also understand that the program is aimed at helping families understand and facilitate their child's development. Further, this is a research, training, and observation site for professionals and graduate students in the field of early childhood special education.

I understand that my participation in the program will involve giving biographical, medical, and social information concerning my child and our family. In addition, my participation will involve bringing my child to the program for evaluation and educational activities. I also understand that staff members will be visiting my home from time to time on a prearranged basis to help facilitate my child's progress. I further understand a parent group is provided by the program for my participation.

I understand that my responses to interviews and questionnaires will be kept confidential and will be available only to authorized professional staff in the conduct of the program. Medical records will be available from my physician only upon my written authorization and will be subject to the same standards of confidentiality as other information.

I understand that, periodically, videotapes will be made for the purpose of helping me to understand my child's behavior, and for training and research purposes related to the way babies interact with caregivers. These videotapes will be kept confidential. I understand that portions of the videotape may be shown to professional audiences for training and/or research purposes. Videotapes will be kept as property of the Infant Program for the purpose of future ongoing research.

I have freely and voluntarily agreed to participate in this program. I also authorize the participation of my child,

_____. I understand that I may terminate my participation in the program at any time.

_____   _____
Child's Name   Parent's/Guardian's Signature

                                                                        _____
                                                                        Date

                                                                        _____
                                                                        Parent's/Guardian's Signature

                                                                        _____
                                                                        Date

Figure 11.5. Parent or guardian permission to participate in program.

If the child does this on two attempts and then fails on the third attempt, the staff member would place a + by the numbers 1 and 2, a / through the number 3, and so on. To calculate the percentage of correct responses, after 10 trials the staff member can simply count the number of plus signs and circle that number (e.g., 5 plus signs in Figure 11.9). In so doing the percentage of correct responses is noted and graphed. This can be done daily, and the

CONSENT TO PHOTOGRAPH AND VIDEOTAPE

The undersigned do hereby authorize the above named program and the staff members to photograph or videotape or permit other persons to photograph, audio- or videotape my child, _____, and myself while in the educational program, and agree that they may use or permit other persons to use the negatives, prints, or tapes prepared therefrom for professional purposes only.

Date: _____

_____   _____
(Signature)   (Witness)

Figure 11.6. Consent to photograph and videotape.

INFANT PROGRAM
EMERGENCY RELEASE FORM

Date: _____

In the event of an emergency, I understand that my child will be taken to General Hospital for medical treatment unless otherwise specified below:

    Name of preferred hospital: _____

    Address of hospital: _____

If in the judgment of the staff of the Infant Program, my child may be transported by private car, I hereby approve of such transport. Otherwise, I understand that an ambulance will be called, for which I will assume financial responsibility.

_____
Parent or Guardian

_____
Parent or Guardian

I give permission for staff members of the Infant Program to administer First Aid in the event of a minor injury such as a cut, bruise, insect bite, etc.

_____
Parent or Guardian

Figure 11.7. Emergency release form.

Sample Letter to Parents

Dear Parents:

Many of you participate with your child in the program and thus can be exposed to some infectious diseases that children have. I want to advise you of precautions to take, especially if you are pregnant while participating in the program.

1. *German measles* is a virus children can easily contract. It produces only a mild rash and respiratory symptoms in children; however, it can cause severe damage to an unborn child during pregnancy. As a result, we recommend that any woman of childbearing age have a blood test to determine her immunity to rubella (German measles). Women who are not already immune can then be immunized when they are not pregnant so they are protected during any future pregnancies. You can obtain a rubella blood test from your physician or from the public health department. (The rubella vaccine is routinely given to children at ages 15 months and 5 years of age in combination with measles and mumps vaccines—the MMR.)

2. *Cytomegalovirus* (CMV) is a common virus that is estimated to affect between 30% to 80% of the population. Many young children have this virus, which is transmitted by saliva or excretions. Infection with CMV has particular significance for pregnant women. There is a risk of damage to the fetus particularly when a woman is infected for the first time when pregnant. It is very important that good hygiene practices be followed in the classroom, including hand washing and toy washing. If you are considering pregnancy or are pregnant, please make an appointment with me to discuss CMV and precautions in more detail.

3. *The Hepatitis B Virus* (HBV) can be transmitted to newborns from their mother (who may not know she is carrying the virus). HBV can also be transmitted by transfusion or exposure to infected blood and/or blood products, from close contact within families of infected individuals, or from contact with open skin lesions of infected persons. The American Academy of Pediatrics and the United States Public Health Service currently recommend the immunization of all infants and children against HBV infection by the administration of the Hepatitis B vaccine.

4. *Hepatitis A Virus* can be transmitted by infected persons in their feces or body secretions. Program health procedures (careful hand washing before and after feeding, diaper changing, etc.) described in the next section are considered adequate routine precautions. If a family member of an enrolled child develops hepatitis (a.k.a. "yellow jaundice"), inform the program staff so that others in close contact with your child, such as your family members, can receive proper care from a physician.

5. *The Human Immunodeficiency Virus* (HIV) can be transmitted to newborns from their mother. The virus is transmitted to the child during pregnancy, at the time of birth, or possibly through breast milk. The virus may be present in blood or body fluids. It is important that all individuals follow strict hygiene and sanitation procedures aimed at preventing the spread of diseases. Program health procedures include those for washing toys, washing hands, and wearing disposable gloves to change a child's diaper or to provide medical treatment for an injured (bleeding) child. These procedures are outlined in detail in the Parent's Handbook. Please ask staff for specific information about hygiene practices to follow in the classroom.

It is required that all parents have a *tuberculosis screening test* and show evidence of this as part of their child's enrollment. This test is routinely given in many settings in order to avoid transmission of this disease. It is a good health practice for anyone working in close proximity to many children to have this routine test.

Although a new vaccine to prevent chicken pox (varicella) may be available within the next year or so, it is not yet available. We appreciate your cooperation in notifying the staff of any exposure of your child to chicken pox, strep

(continues)

Figure 11.8. Letter to parents regarding health risks.

infections, or other contagious diseases. This, of course, is for the protection of your child as well as for the other children and care providers in the program.

Please acknowledge the receipt of these recommendations by signing the form below, tearing it off, and returning it to me.

Sincerely,

Program Coordinator

I have been informed that San Francisco Special Infant Services has required that all parents obtain a tuberculosis screening test and recommends that all women of childbearing age obtain a rubella test. I have also been informed about the risk of cytomegalovirus, Hepatitis B, Hepatitis A, and HIV.

Parent's Name: _____

Child's Name: _____

Date: _____

Figure 11.8. continued

---

child's progress over time can be easily evaluated according to the graph. If the staff member elects to perform fewer trials, this form can be used to record, for example, 5 probe trials, and the graphs can still be used in the same fashion as for 10 trials. This form also leaves space for other notes or types of data that may be needed.

Community contact information

Extensive contact with the community is a necessary component of early intervention programs. It is often helpful to keep a record of contacts so that valuable names and information are not lost. One method is to keep a *visitor log* (see Figure 11.10 for a sample form).

A *referral log notebook* is also useful. Such a notebook includes the names, addresses, and telephone numbers of each family who is referred and who contacts the program. Also listed are any further contacts the family has with staff members and the final outcome of the referral (e.g., joins the program, elects to attend another program). In this fashion families can be followed easily until they reach a decision regarding program participation. Such data also are useful to the agency in identifying how well it is serving the community and in analyzing future program demand.

Program operation records

Each program will have a unique set of program operation record requirements depending upon the funding and regulatory sources. Records pertaining to all phases of the program's financial operations must be kept. The program also will have to keep records of child attendance and family participation as needed. In addition, such records as travel and telephone logs may be necessary. The process of establishing and maintaining

Name: _____

Area: _____

Long-Term Goal: _____

Objective: _Child will sit independently without support for 20 seconds when placed on floor_

Suggested Materials:

Date:	/	/	/	/	/	/	/
	~~10~~	10	10	10	10	10	10
	~~9~~	9	9	9	9	9	9
	+8	8	8	8	8	8	8
	+7	7	7	7	7	7	7
	~~6~~	6	6	6	6	6	6
	(5)	5	5	5	5	5	5
	+4	4	4	4	4	4	4
	~~3~~	3	3	3	3	3	3
	+2	2	2	2	2	2	2
	+1	1	1	1	1	1	1
	0	0	0	0	0	0	0

Notes:

Additional Teaching Strategies/Goals:

Figure 11.9. Data sheet.

these records will be expedited if easy-to-use forms are developed and if the number and types of forms are kept at a minimum.

In summary, extensive data collection and record keeping are necessary components of any service delivery program. The program manager can facilitate the process of information gathering by designing an efficient and practical system for keeping records. This process is enhanced when responsibilities are clearly defined and delegated to various staff members. Records kept should be those that are useful to program development and maintenance.

INFANT PROGRAM VISITOR LOG

Date	Program Person/ Phone Number	Referral Source	Request	Scheduled Visitation Date(s)	Confirmation/ Cancellations

Figure 11.10. Visitor log.

Training and Supervising Staff

The quality of early intervention services is determined largely by the skills of the staff members and their ability to work together, with families, and with other community agencies. The program manager's job is to facilitate teamwork and supervise all aspects of the staff members' performance. This includes making decisions regarding hiring, firing, and promotions; clearly communicating job responsibilities to staff members; and providing evaluations of the staff members' performance at regular intervals. Several job description samples are provided in Figure 11.11 to demonstrate an outline of job responsibilities. A sample staff evaluation form is furnished in Figure 11.12. Although priorities for staff functions and competencies will vary somewhat from program to program, this staff evaluation form serves as an example of the type of evaluation that can be performed regularly (e.g., at 6-month intervals). Such an evaluation provides a vehicle for regular discussions between manager and staff member.

Staff development is also a crucial component of early intervention programs, and it is the manager who is responsible for designing staff development plans. Staff development issues and activities are discussed fully in Chapter 6.

Beyond the typical managerial responsibilities related to staff supervision is a set of supervisory characteristics that are particularly important in early intervention settings. The manager is in charge of allocating resources, planning schedules, and problem solving. The manager must solicit input from staff members as well as families, be open to feedback, and make fair and honest decisions surrounding issues. Early intervention personnel must deal with many difficult situations, such as children who are ill, families who are at risk, and limited resources. These daily concerns make burnout common. The competent manager tries to provide resources, guidance, and understanding to staff members to build the team and ease tensions, while at the same time functioning as the primary decision maker regarding policy decisions.

Directing

The third function of a manager is directing. In this role the early intervention program director establishes the organizational climate; motivates, guides, and team builds; resolves conflicts; and develops networks and serves as head of public relations for the program. Although each of these activities is dramatically shaped by the program administrator's personal style, a general discussion of each is provided in the sections that follow.

Establishing the Organizational Culture

Although organizational climate and organizational culture are phrases that are most often associated with business and industry, every organization has its own personality and view of the world. Campbell, Dunnette, Lawler, and Weick (1970) described seven characteristics or organizational values, which have been modified by Robbins (1986). Each represents a continuum; the position of the organization on the continuum is heavily influenced by the administrator's leadership. The characteristics as outlined by Robbins (1986, p. 431) include individuals' autonomy, structure, support, identity, performance reward, conflict tolerance, and risk tolerance. Individual autonomy refers to the degree of freedom that staff members have in decision making, their level of responsibility, and their degree of independence. In most early intervention programs, as in most educational programs, there is a high degree of individual autonomy. Staff members may work with families on a one-to-one basis, make home visits far from the program's administrative offices, and conduct assessments and keep records on their own. Although this level of autonomy is appropriate for most professionals, it is not appropriate for paraprofessionals within a program. There may also be variations in staff members' comfort with autonomy. Professionals such as physical therapists have retained strong ties to the medical profession and often work only under a physician's orders; thus, the autonomy may be uncomfortable at best, and unethical or illegal at worst.

The autonomy that has characterized most early interventionists must now be reexamined

EARLY CHILDHOOD SPECIAL EDUCATOR/EARLY INTERVENTIONIST

Participate as transdisciplinary team member in early intervention program

DUTIES:

Education
- Conduct home visits.
- Plan and coordinate educational activities for each infant in partnership with family.
- Collect data on infants.
- Establish home programs for children in partnership with families.
- Coordinate weekly schedule planning.

Evaluation
- Schedule evaluations with families.
- Obtain releases from parents for medical and other records.
- Obtain medical records for each infant.
- Evaluate infant cognitive, fine motor, self-help, and feeding skills in partnership with families.
- Prepare these sections of reports.
- Schedule starting date with each family.

Referrals
- Schedule parents to visit program.
- Take intake calls.

Record Keeping
- Record school attendance.
- Prepare IFSPs as per model from school district upon entry, at review, and upon exit.
- Prepare monthly logs for school district.
- Update monthly class list.
- Assist in research activities.

Training
- Schedule visitors to the program.
- Meet with visitors and orient to program.
- Keep record of visitors attending.
- Supervise and train master's degree interns in classroom.

FAMILY SERVICE COORDINATOR

Participate as transdisciplinary team member in early intervention program

DUTIES:
- Develop and lead toddler–parent groups on twice monthly basis each.
- Develop and maintain parent educational library.
- Serve as service coordinator to selected toddler families.
- Participate in team assessments/evaluation.
- Prepare social-emotional section of reports, IFSPs, and goals.

(continues)

Figure 11.11. Sample job descriptions

- Participate as needed in scoring criterion-referenced checklist.
- Prepare introductory section of toddler reports.
- Conduct surveys of parent satisfaction.
- Consult with other staff members regarding social-emotional goals and psychological issues.
- Collect data as required.
- Assist in research activities.
- Confer or consult with other service providers as necessary.

SPEECH THERAPIST

Participate as transdisciplinary team member in early intervention program

DUTIES:
- Assess language, communicative competence, and screen hearing status of children during evaluation.
- Provide information to parents regarding communicative competence of child and plan language and communication programs in partnership with the family.
- Prepare speech and language section of reports, IFSPs, and goals. Prepare hearing section of reports.
- Evaluate feeding and plan intervention programs in conjunction with other staff and family members.
- Participate as necessary in scoring criterion-referenced checklist.
- Participate in conferences and IFSPs.
- Monitor equipment and toy needs for language development and prepare orders.
- Conduct Signing Exact English (SEE) signing classes for parents during program.
- Conduct SEE signing classes for staff members.
- Develop adaptive equipment and photo library for language development.
- Supervise and train students.
- Collect data as required.
- Assist in research activities.
- Confer and/or consult with other service providers.
- Coordinate trainings with project.
- Plan agenda for trainings.
- Serve as contact person with trainees.
- Report to project director regarding training plans.
- Participate in evaluation of master's degree interns.

Reports
- Write introductory sections of reports.
- Obtain sections of reports from other staff members.
- Integrate report into cohesive whole.
- Proofread reports.
- Mail final reports to collaterals.

Collateral Contact
- Serve as liaison to other service providers advising them of pertinent information and obtaining information from them.
- Schedule caseworker visits.

(continues)

Figure 11.11. continued

PHYSICAL THERAPIST

Participate as transdisciplinary team member in early intervention program

DUTIES:
- Assess motor needs during evaluation in partnership with families.
- Provide information to family regarding motor needs of child and provide educational/motor programs for children.
- Prepare motor section of reports, IFSPs, and goals.
- Participate as necessary in scoring criterion-referenced checklist.
- Participate in conferences and IFSPs.
- Monitor equipment and toy needs for motor development and prepare orders.
- Develop adaptive equipment library for parents.
- Supervise and train students.
- Collect data as required.
- Plan, build, and obtain adaptive equipment.
- Assist in research activities.
- Confer and/or advise other service providers as necessary.

Figure 11.11. continued

in the context of family-centered, transdisciplinary services. If both of these goals are to be realized in service delivery systems, early interventionists will have to become more effective team players as well as better collaborators with families. Teaming and collaboration require different skills and sometimes demand changes in interpersonal interactions. Program administrators now have an added responsibility of ensuring that their staff are well prepared and effective in these new roles.

Structure relates to the degree of regulation or supervision used by management to control employees. As mentioned in the previous paragraph, the amount of supervision must vary with the professionals hired, but even within these variations there is a general climate or feeling surrounding individuals' perceptions of this control.

Support from managers is another of the organizational culture continua. Some organizations spend little time supporting employees, being friendly, and facilitating individuals' development. Early intervention programs tend to be very supportive environments. The general concern for children and families is often translated into policies for employees that are nurturing and supportive. One often finds close and warm relationships between the staff members and the "boss."

Identity comes from affiliation with one's own expertise or the organization as a whole. In early intervention programs, one of the goals is to help professionals blend their disciplinary skills with those of others to form a new, transdisciplinary identity. A manager who has strong disciplinary skills yet models transdisciplinary functioning helps shape the group identity. Identity is also important as programs become more interagency in their makeup. Too strong an identity with one agency can inhibit the collaboration required for interagency coordination.

Performance reward is the degree to which the rewards or compensations provided by the organization reflect employees' performance. In other words, are rewards based on merit? Most social and educational programs

INFANT PROGRAM
STAFF PERFORMANCE EVALUATION

EMPLOYEE: _____

Rate by circling the appropriate number:
  1 = outstanding   4 = needs work
  2 = strong   5 = unsatisfactory
  3 = satisfactory   0 = not observed

General Attitude
1. Enthusiasm 1 2 3 4 5 0
2. Accepts responsibility 1 2 3 4 5 0
3. Exhibits initiative 1 2 3 4 5 0
4. Willingness to learn 1 2 3 4 5 0
5. Ability to evaluate own performance realistically and accurately 1 2 3 4 5 0
6. Reacts positively and constructively to suggestions 1 2 3 4 5 0
7. Adapts own behavior in response to suggestions 1 2 3 4 5 0

Professional Conduct
1. Behaves appropriately for professional role 1 2 3 4 5 0
2. Punctuality 1 2 3 4 5 0
3. Attendance 1 2 3 4 5 0
4. Prepares for responsibilities 1 2 3 4 5 0
5. Meets deadlines 1 2 3 4 5 0
6. Responds promptly to requests 1 2 3 4 5 0
7. Makes use of available resources 1 2 3 4 5 0
8. Asks relevant questions 1 2 3 4 5 0
9. Performance under stress or in "crisis" situations 1 2 3 4 5 0
10. Flexibility and adaptability 1 2 3 4 5 0

Interaction with Colleagues
1. General rapport with colleagues 1 2 3 4 5 0
2. Communicates effectively with colleagues 1 2 3 4 5 0
3. Addresses areas of disagreement professionally 1 2 3 4 5 0
4. Provides support for colleagues 1 2 3 4 5 0
5. Interaction with transdisciplinary team 1 2 3 4 5 0

Interaction with Parents
1. General rapport with parents and families 1 2 3 4 5 0
2. Communicates effectively with family members 1 2 3 4 5 0
3. Addresses areas of disagreement professionally 1 2 3 4 5 0
4. Respects values, culture, suggestions, and priorities of families 1 2 3 4 5 0
5. Interacts in nonjudgmental manner 1 2 3 4 5 0
6. Maintains satisfactory working relationships with parents and
   other family members 1 2 3 4 5 0
7. Encourages family–professional collaboration 1 2 3 4 5 0
8. Provides parents and other family members with useful and
   appropriate information 1 2 3 4 5 0

(continues)

Figure 11.12. Staff performance evaluation. Form adapted from the Intern Performance Evaluation Form, Early Childhood Special Education, San Francisco State University.

Interaction with Children

1. Uses varied, stimulating learning experiences. 1 2 3 4 5 0
2. Interacts positively with children 1 2 3 4 5 0
3. Uses "unplanned" activities for learning experiences 1 2 3 4 5 0
4. Responds appropriately to child's initiations and cues 1 2 3 4 5 0
5. Provides opportunities for children to learn through exploration 1 2 3 4 5 0
6. Is reinforced by children 1 2 3 4 5 0
7. Group management skills 1 2 3 4 5 0
8. Reinforcement appropriate 1 2 3 4 5 0
9. Reinforcement effective 1 2 3 4 5 0

Development of Child Intervention Programs

1. Identifies behaviors for intervention 1 2 3 4 5 0
2. Writes behavioral objectives correctly and completely. 1 2 3 4 5 0
3. Writes task analyses correctly and completely. 1 2 3 4 5 0
4. Writes activity plans correctly and completely 1 2 3 4 5 0
5. Writes activities appropriate for child and family 1 2 3 4 5 0

Implementation of Individual Intervention Programs

1. Ability to carry out established programs. 1 2 3 4 5 0
2. Effectiveness of programs 1 2 3 4 5 0
3. Efficiency of programs. 1 2 3 4 5 0
4. Data collection 1 2 3 4 5 0
5. Modification of programs based on observations of child. 1 2 3 4 5 0

Classroom Organization

1. Provides distraction-free learning environment 1 2 3 4 5 0
2. Appropriateness of instructional grouping. 1 2 3 4 5 0
3. Selection of materials. 1 2 3 4 5 0
4. Utilization of materials. 1 2 3 4 5 0
5. Efficient use of time 1 2 3 4 5 0
6. Effectively handles transition periods 1 2 3 4 5 0
7. Scheduling 1 2 3 4 5 0
8. Use of other adults in the classroom. 1 2 3 4 5 0

Professional Knowledge

1. Typical child development 1 2 3 4 5 0
2. Atypical child development. 1 2 3 4 5 0
3. Assessment 1 2 3 4 5 0
4. Program planning and implementation 1 2 3 4 5 0
5. Family involvement. 1 2 3 4 5 0

Figure 11.12. continued

are operated within frameworks that have little flexibility in their reward system. Often, salary and wage structures are preset, leaving intangible rewards as the only manipulable variables that managers have. As a consequence managers must develop reward and incentive systems for their own staff members independent of the larger system.

Organizations have varying toleration for conflict and differing rules and mores related to open, honest communication. The manager sets the tone for the style of interacting and debate. Although open, honest communications probably contribute to effective functioning, few people thrive in a constantly conflict-ridden environment.

The final characteristic of the organization is risk tolerance. To what extent are staff members encouraged to try new procedures or develop innovative practices? A balance between established procedures and more experimental approaches that may succeed or fail is probably the hallmark of exemplary programs. However, evaluation must be a part of any approach, and practices that do not achieve progress must be abandoned.

The early intervention manager has the responsibility to set the tone of the program. The manager may want to consider this challenge and responsibility and review some of the more recent works from business and industry that have addressed the issues of organizational culture. (For suggestions, see the Selected Readings section at the end of this chapter.)

Motivating, Guiding, and Team Building

One primary responsibility of the program manager is helping staff members be the best that they can be. Supporting, training, coaching, and caring are all elements of this role. The ways in which this is done depend upon the individual manager, and how it is done is far less important than that it is done consistently. All programs have their ups and downs, but a team that is motivated and supported by its administrator tends to emerge from the worst times as a stronger, more positive unit.

Resolving Conflicts

Conflicts occur in every program and organization. In fact, sometimes conflicts come from positive origins such as a strong belief in what is best practice, a commitment to families, or an individual's own ethical standards. At other times, conflicts come from different priorities, feelings of inadequacy, or interpersonal conflicts. It is the manager's job to create a climate that minimizes negative conflict and to provide leadership in resolving the conflicts that do arise. Literature on conflict provides a range of conflict-handling behaviors, which must be adapted to differing situations and different management styles (Robbins, 1986). In most instances in early intervention programs, strategies that use collaboration and compromise are the most effective, but there will be times when the manager must make a decision that is neither collaborative nor a compromise.

Networking and Public Relations

No early intervention program can stand isolated from other services. Program staff members must work closely with other agencies and professionals to gain referrals, and coordination with others is absolutely essential to ensure that families obtain the full complement of services needed. The program manager is the primary person responsible for developing ties and networks both within the parent agency (e.g., school, hospital, private organization) and with outside agencies (e.g., community and state educational, health, and social services). These activities may involve frequent meetings and presentations in the community, membership and attendance at professional gatherings within the state and local community, and outreach to other agencies and professionals. Because the program manager is likely to be the major person with whom others meet, it is crucial that the manager be comfortable and capable of making public presentations and initiating contacts with others. Such networks ensure that families in need of services will be given information about the program and a full spectrum of services, and they enhance community support for the continued operation of the program.

Controlling

The final function of a manager is controlling. This aspect of management includes anticipating and detecting problems and implementing solutions. Good managers are good listeners, good forecasters, visionaries, and pragmatists. In the controlling function managers attend to all of their constituents, recognize the politics of various situations, and avert errors whenever possible. When difficult decisions need to be made, they are willing to make them and willing to explain their thinking without wavering. As a controller, the manager may not always be popular, but popularity is not the goal in early intervention leadership.

Summary

The role of the program manager is varied and multifaceted and includes the four functions of planning, organizing, directing, and controlling. Competent performance requires great skill at working with a wide variety of individuals and the ability to coordinate and supervise different types of program operations. In many programs the managerial responsibilities will be assumed by a single individual; in other programs several persons may share administrative duties. Regardless of the administrative model, the managerial position is challenging and necessitates both technical knowledge of early intervention issues and the knowledge and skills to supervise other professionals performing a variety of program services.

Preferred Practices

The following questions may be used to examine the management of early intervention programs.

1. Has the program staff done any strategic planning (i.e., are the mission and direction clear)?
2. Were families included in the planning process?
3. Have plans been made for all aspects of the operation of the program?
4. Have systems and procedures been developed to facilitate program intake, program participation, record keeping, and program exit?
5. Are all staff members aware of the systems and procedures of record keeping?
6. Are records related to children and families secured in locked file cabinets and confidentiality procedures enforced?
7. Are health and emergency action forms maintained for each child?
8. Is ongoing staff development available, and are new employees trained in the systems and procedures used in the program?
9. Is the organizational culture one in which services are provided efficiently and humanely and staff members are enthusiastic about their jobs?

10. Does the manager spend time motivating, guiding, team building, and appreciating staff members?
11. Is a high degree of respect and caring demonstrated among program staff?
12. Are procedures for resolving conflict effective?
13. Is the manager skilled at networking and public relations?
14. Are most problems anticipated and resolved before they become serious?
15. Is there a clear and consistent respect for diversity?
16. Are the ethnic, cultural, and languages of families being served represented in the staff?
17. Are all policies, procedures, and practices family centered and family friendly?

References

Below, P. J., Morrisey, G. L., & Acomb, B. L. (1987). *The executive guide to strategic planning.* San Francisco: Jossey-Bass.
Campbell, J. P., Dunnette, M. D., Lawler III, E. E., & Weick, K. E. (1970). *Managerial behavior, performance, and effectiveness.* New York: McGraw-Hill.
Frame, J. D. (1987). *Managing projects in organizations.* San Francisco: Jossey-Bass.
Mintzberg, H. (1980). *The nature of managerial work.* Englewood Cliffs, NJ: Prentice-Hall.
Morrisey, G. L., Below, P. J., & Acomb, B. L. (1988). *The executive guide to operational planning.* San Francisco: Jossey-Bass.
Robbins, S. P. (1986). *Organizational behavior—Concepts, controversies, and applications* (3rd ed.). Englewood Cliffs, NJ: Prentice-Hall.

Selected Readings

Fisher, R., & Ury, W. (1981). *Getting to yes.* Boston: Houghton-Mifflin.
Peters, T., & Austin, N. (1985). *A passion for excellence—The leadership difference.* New York: Random House.
Senge, P. M. (1990). *The fifth discipline: The art and practice of the learning organization.* New York: Doubleday/Currency.

Developing Community Collaboration

CHAPTER 12

Infants and toddlers who are at risk or disabled and their families present a complex picture of service needs. Medical services are often the first, most intense needs in the early days, weeks, or months of life, particularly for infants who are premature, small for gestational age, or born with a life-threatening problem. As long as the infant is hospitalized, highly skilled teams of specialists work to maintain the baby's life and function, and other support staff work with the family to help them through this difficult period. As the infant's health improves, an early childhood special educator from a community early intervention program may visit the infant and family in the hospital. These visits focus on the child's needs and the family's priorities, and on making plans for the infant's return home. When the infant is determined to be stable enough to leave the hospital, she or he is discharged.

Some infants with disabilities do not have intensive medical needs. Many children with Down syndrome or other disabilities that are genetically caused may be quite healthy and not require prolonged hospitalization. Other children will appear to be developing normally for the first few months, and a diagnosis of disability will not be made until they fail to achieve the normal developmental milestones.

Whether the child's problems are diagnosed at birth or months or years later, the discharge from the hospital or the eventual diagnosis activates multiple service delivery systems. Follow-up health care, ongoing physical or occupational therapy, social support services such as respite care or counseling, financial assistance, parent-to-parent outreach, and educationally oriented early intervention programs are provided by different community agencies. As a consequence, at a time when families are typically in crisis, it is likely that one of two things will happen: (a) Families in large, urban areas may face a multitude of different service agencies with differing rules, regulations, and eligibility criteria (Coulter, Wallace, & Laude, 1993; Nordyke, 1982), or (b) families in remote or rural areas may discover that resources and services are limited, and that very little help is available as they struggle with the added demands of the child's disability. To make it easier for families in both sets of circumstances, interagency coordination and collaboration have become goals of all those who provide services to young children who are at risk or disabled and their families. One of the primary goals of Part H of P.L. 99-457 (now revised and titled the Individuals with Disabilities Education Act [IDEA]) is to develop a comprehensive, coordinated system of early intervention within each state and territory of the United States.

Why Collaborate?

In addition to IDEA, which mandates interagency collaboration in the delivery of early intervention services, there are at least four reasons for agencies to collaborate and to develop coordinated service delivery systems. This chapter discusses those reasons, outlines barriers to interagency collaboration, provides successful models of collaboration, and suggests strategies for developing effective community collaboration. The four primary reasons for working collaboratively are described in the following sections.

Improve Services to Children and Families

As mentioned in the opening paragraphs of this chapter, the needs of young children who are at risk or disabled and their families are complex; no single professional discipline or agency has the skills, resources, or staff to meet those needs (Lynch & Harrison, 1986). As a result many agencies have been created to provide services that meet needs in the areas of health, education, or social services (Flynn & Harbin, 1987). Although each of

these agencies and services is an important component in the network of service delivery,

> too often the multiple agency roles, functions, eligibility requirements, and service mandates are fragmented, overlapping, and confusing. When one considers that staff of one agency often have only a vague idea of what other agencies do because there is no time to investigate and programs, services, and personnel change quickly, it is no wonder that parents seeking services have difficulty finding the right service at the right time. The service delivery system has become a maze of seemingly independent units that do not relate, communicate, or coordinate with one another. (Lynch & Harrison, 1986, pp. 6–7)

Parents report they have learned about services in a piecemeal fashion; that eligibility criteria from one system to another differ and are unclear; and that they spend hours completing forms, having their child assessed, and participating in one intake interview after another (Lynch & Harrison, 1986). Simplifying the process and helping families get accurate information as quickly and efficiently as they want or need it is crucial. Reducing the amount of time family members spend attending to institutional bureaucracies instead of to themselves and their families is the most compelling reason for agencies to work together to develop a coordinated service delivery system.

Reduce Duplication of Services

Each agency has a set of policies and procedures that enables it to operate (McNulty, 1989). Among human service agencies that serve young children who are at risk or disabled, several procedures related to new clients are common. When new clients come to the agency, they are usually asked to complete detailed forms that request information about the prenatal, birth, and developmental history of the child; information about the parents' health, education, and employment; and information about the family's financial resources. Although not every agency collects financial information, almost all collect the other data mentioned. After the forms have been completed, an assessment of the child's and family's eligibility for service and their service needs is usually conducted by a team of professionals. Following the assessment the team typically meets with the parents or primary caregivers to discuss assessment findings, the family's eligibility for services, and the programs available.

For a more complete picture of what is meant by duplication of services, imagine that the steps outlined above take place at a regional center which helps find services for individuals with disabilities, at the public health department which provides home visits by public health nurses, at the local school district which operates the early intervention program, and at a therapy services agency which provides physical and occupational therapy to eligible clients. To develop a plan of services that meets the child's and family's needs, the family has gone through an intrusive and time-consuming process at each of four agencies, and the professional and clerical time expended has also been multiplied by four. The parents have completed four sets of similar forms; the child has been assessed four times by teams of highly trained professionals; and four different meetings have been held to discuss the assessment findings and next steps. Still, however, the child and family are not receiving any intervention services.

Until very recently this duplication was the rule rather than the exception in communities throughout the country (Rossi, Gilmartin, & Dayton, 1982). However, Part H of PL 99-457, now IDEA, was crafted to eliminate this duplication and put more resources into services than into getting into them. In the example above, so many financial resources and so much personnel time are going into intake, assessment, and staffing that the energy and dollars available for programs and services are no doubt reduced. The question and the answer are simple. Which makes more sense: four assessments over 4 weeks without a day of intervention, or one assessment followed by 3 weeks of intervention? Reducing the duplication—moving from four sets of forms, assessments, and meetings to one that would include all agencies—would be a positive outcome for families and agencies alike; this is exactly what IDEA encourages (Lynch, Jackson, Mendoza, & English, 1991).

In remote and rural areas where few services exist, collaboration can increase resources. An early childhood special educator from the nearest city who visits a home twice monthly may collaborate with the city's public health department to bring to the family information on nutrition, immunizations, and general health care. Conversely, with the family's permission, the early childhood special educator may send packets of activities and information to the family via an agricultural extension agent who makes weekly trips through the region.

Develop a More Comprehensive Service System

Systems that have duplication in services usually have the opposite problem as well—gaps in service (Audette, 1980). When services are duplicated, it reduces the amount of money available for more comprehensive services and for initiating new services as they are needed. In most communities there are fewer social service programs than there are needs for those programs. For example, the kinds of transition programs needed when an infant who is technology dependent leaves the hospital are often not available. The intensive monitoring and intervention required when infants who are prenatally exposed to drugs, infants born to parents with mental retardation, and premature infants leave the hospital are not there. Respite care for infants who are medically fragile or technology dependent, which enables families to go to the grocery, visit the dentist, or spend a few hours away from the demands of caretaking, is nonexistent in many communities. In cities where those services have been developed, the demand is often far greater than their availability.

The services mentioned above describe some of the gaps that exist in many communities today. However, these gaps are not static; they shift as medical technology and family resources change. The need for hospital-to-home transition programs for infants who are technology dependent, was not predicted 10 years ago; and only within the last 5 years have predictions been made about the extensive resources that will be required to care for infants with AIDS. These needs and those in the future will create gaps in the service delivery system that will require creative, coordinated efforts.

Reduce the Costs of Services

A final reason to develop a service delivery system that is collaborative and coordinated is fiscal (Healy, Keesee, & Smith, 1985). There are ever-increasing demands on the limited dollars available for social and educational services. Although one might argue that social programs and services are not getting an adequate piece of the national pie, the fact remains that money is a limited resource. As economic analysis and cost-effectiveness become increasingly important factors in budgetary decision making, the larger economy will be less likely to tolerate programs that are economically inefficient (Audette, 1980; Barnett & Escobar, 1988; Rossi et al., 1982).

In summary, making it easier for families to obtain service in a timely, efficient, and humane manner; reducing duplication; filling gaps; and reducing costs are all arguments for interagency collaboration. The strength of these arguments is reflected in IDEA, which mandates that services to infants and toddlers who are at risk or disabled and their families be provided through a coordinated, collaborative model.

How to Develop Community Collaboration

Whom to Involve

Every community has a slightly different array of services that might be needed by families with young children who are at risk or disabled. Even though the names of the agencies differ from one state or community to another, often similar types of services are offered. One of the first steps in developing collaborative services in a community is determining whom to involve. (See Swan & Morgan, 1993, for additional ideas.)

Magrab, Kazuk, and Greene (1981), under the sponsorship of the American Association of University Affiliated Programs, suggested a group of agencies that should be included in interagency planning efforts. They listed the following agencies as active in providing services to preschoolers with disabilities:

1. Mental Health Centers
2. University Affiliated Facilities (UAF)
3. Resource Access Projects (RAP)
4. Community medical leadership

5. Preschools and day care centers, including handicapped children's early education projects
6. Parent, foster parent, and citizen organizations
7. Other local providers and other referral sources. (p. 5)

For infants and toddlers who are at risk or disabled, the list might be expanded to include neonatal intensive care units; the public health or maternal and child health department; the social services department; alcohol and drug recovery programs for women; existing early intervention programs; parent support groups; ethnic advocacy groups such as the Urban League, National Association for the Advancement of Colored People (NAACP), Union of Pan-Asian Communities, Chicano Federation, or Tribal Council; and college and university training programs.

Bringing Groups Together

The next step in the process is to bring together a group to begin to consider a more collaborative service delivery model (Elder & Kazuk, no date). Making decisions about who should convene the first meeting, whom to invite, where it should be held, and how it should be structured presents major challenges. The final decisions will vary depending upon each community's size, existing services, history, politics, and the competing demands that each agency and agency administrator are confronting. In some situations having various state department staff convene the meeting is the most effective strategy; in others several respected individuals representing two or more agencies may be the conveners; and in still others inviting agency administrators to coffee after a ball game may be the best way to begin.

In developing community collaboration, there is no single right answer. The strategies for each community must be as individualized as the programs for children and families. However, a variety of models have been developed for getting started (e.g., Commission for Cooperative Services for Young Handicapped Children and Their Families, 1988; Georgetown University Child Development Center, 1981–1984; Swan & Morgan, 1993), and these provide suggestions that can be adapted for any community.

Although the law requires interagency coordination, it is important to make it attractive to participants. The planners of the initial meeting may want to consider some of the following issues.

1. Does the convening group have adequate power within the community to call together the people who are being invited? If not, who could be selected—a government official, a state department staff member, two or more agency administrators, a local university?

2. Is there a clear purpose for the meeting, or does it provide an incentive to attend, such as a well-known speaker, opportunities to socialize, a setting that people would like to see?

3. Who will preside at the meeting? Several people from different agencies who are widely respected in the community may choose to preside jointly.

4. Where should the meeting be held? A neutral meeting site that is not affiliated with any of the service delivery agencies reduces territoriality and the tension that accompanies it. The setting should also be pleasant and accessible for individuals with disabilities.

5. What should be included in the meeting? Both time for focusing on the meeting's purpose and time to socialize and get to know one another more informally should be part of the schedule.

6. What happens next? Next steps depend upon the people that were called together and the particular community. Often, the most important outcome of the initial meeting is sanction to proceed. Leaving the meeting with verbal support from the key decision makers in the service delivery community is a commendable accomplishment.

Determining Needs

As the collaborative efforts develop, determining community needs becomes an important task. Needs can be described in two different ways—by the numbers of children and families needing services and by the types of services needed. Both pieces of information are important in developing collaborative planning and implementation. Projections about the numbers needing service can be developed from a combination of national prevalence and incidence figures, the numbers of children and families currently being served, and census figures. In some states and communities, more sophisticated forecasting, which is already being done by groups as diverse as epidemiologists and property developers, can be used to strengthen the prediction.

In addition to knowing the approximate numbers of children and families needing service, it is important to know what services are needed. Communities may want to develop a schema for determining needs that includes a wide range of services with questions about availability, adequacy, and concerns about the service. Such a schema can be used to help communities discover duplication, identify gaps, and develop priorities for new services.

Planning a Collaborative Venture

The ultimate goal of interagency collaboration is a comprehensive, coordinated service delivery system that operates humanely and efficiently, making it easy for families to obtain services, reducing duplication and fragmentation, and operating cost effectively. This does not happen overnight; any change brings about resistance (Fessler, 1976; McNulty, 1989). The slowness of the process presents some special difficulties. Lasting progress is slow, time-consuming, and often frustrating; however, many of the people who see the need for collaborative efforts are action oriented and want to see things fixed in a short period of time. To compensate for these competing needs, many communities have found that identifying a single concern, project, goal, need, or population for the first collaborative venture is the most effective way to begin. Focusing the effort, establishing a goal, and developing an action plan provide a sense of movement without rushing the entire process (Pelosi, no date).

Some communities have selected an awareness campaign about disabilities as a way to begin; some have planned forums that included agency administrators and local and state politicians; others have developed multiagency intake forms to reduce the paperwork that families encounter. Although these efforts may not seem like major breakthroughs in collaborative efforts, they were effective in each of the communities where they were used. Working together over a period of months or years on a specific goal enabled the communities to move toward much more comprehensive collaborative planning and implementation of services for infants and toddlers who are at risk or disabled and their families.

Developing Collaborative Agreements

The initial understandings and agreements in interagency collaboration may be unwritten. Attending meetings, working on a task force, or even beginning to develop a specific collaborative grant or project may require only that one's supervisor is informed and sanctions the activity. However, as collaborative activities take more time or involve the exchange of personnel or other expensive resources, it may be necessary to develop written agreements. These agreements will vary not only in their content but also in their formality. In some instances a short letter from one agency administrator to another outlining the collaboration with a return letter of acknowledgment and support is enough. In other situations a memorandum of understanding (MOU) with somewhat more detail, signed by the authorized administrator at each of the agencies, is appropriate (see Figure 12.1 for an example MOU). In still other instances, a complete contract approved by the legal department of each agency at the local and state levels may be required. The formality and extent of legal scrutiny has increased in some states with the implementation of the infant and toddler sections of IDEA. Because responsibilities are shared and many of those responsibilities carry financial obligations, policies and agreements have had to be carefully reviewed (Lynch et al., 1991).

Regardless of the formality or informality of the agreement, it is important to have all parties "buy in" and support the effort. Even the most complicated and legalistic MOUs and contracts are real evidence of progress toward a collaborative service delivery system.

The Collaboration Cascade

No single model of interagency collaboration exists. Instead, collaborative efforts are tailored to fit the needs of the community. As a result of this individualization, a cascade of collaborative relationships exists. In some communities the linkages are loose. For example, a task force composed of early intervention staff from the local school district, nurses from the public health department, social workers from Child Protective Services, case managers from the regional center, and advocates from the Association for Retarded Citizens concerned about services for young children whose mothers are mentally retarded may meet monthly to discuss ways in which the community could respond more effectively to these families' needs. Figure 12.2 depicts a cascade of collaborative arrangements.

In other communities the collaboration may be more intensive. Gans and Horton (cited in Nordyke, 1982), in an analysis of 30 case studies of grants given to communities for service integration, found six different types of collaboration. First, some communities had developed fiscal linkages, which involved joint budgeting and funding. Funds from one agency might be used to purchase services from another.

Second, other communities had developed ways to collaborate through innovative personnel practices. In some, staff were shared and paid jointly by two or more agencies; in others, individual staff members from one agency were housed in another agency. In still other instances, satellite offices were shared by staff from two or more related agencies. Such co-location facilitates interaction, communication, and service delivery. It may also make it easier for families to access services if they can work with several different providers in the same location.

The third model involved joint planning and programming. Policies, programs, and program evaluations were developed and conducted jointly. These practices assured a greater degree of continuity in the system and often saved money by eliminating duplication.

Agencies in some communities had found ways to share central support services such as record keeping, grants management, and purchasing. This represented a fourth type of collaboration model. For example, for small to medium-size agencies, a shared accounting system and clerical staff may be feasible, or publishing a joint newsletter may save staff and clerical time.

MEMORANDUM OF UNDERSTANDING

Participating Agencies:

Peninsula Regional Center
4380 Wharf Way
Coastal, CA 92102

Surfside School District
1612 Bayview Dr.
Coastal, CA 92107

Association of Retarded Citizens
Suite 330 A
930 Bridge St.
Coastal, CA 92116

Peninsula County Department
of Public Health
876 Wave St.
Coastal, CA 92116

A recent needs assessment in Peninsula County including the city of Surfside determined that approximately 200 adults with mental retardation are parents of children under the age of 3 years. Although fewer than 5% of the children currently show any indications of developmental delay, employees and/or advocates from each of the agencies listed above have expressed concern about their continued growth and development without additional support for the parents.

As a result of these concerns, agency staff and advocates and chief administrators from each of the above-mentioned agencies have met to develop a plan to improve services to these children and their families. After negotiations, a Special Parents Team was proposed, and the following agreements have been reached.

1. Each of the above-named agencies will allocate a .25 FTE staff position to serve as its representative on the Special Parents Team. That staff member will be responsible for communicating all team activities to his or her agency, for managing and coordinating services to families as assigned by the Special Parents Team, for working with his or her home agency and the Special Parents Team to streamline documentation and reporting procedures, and for attending and participating in Special Parents Team meetings and other activities.

2. The Special Parents Team will develop streamlined methods of record keeping which are not duplicative and will assign a service coordinator to serve as home visitor to each of the identified families. With parental permission, information will be exchanged among agencies.

3. Following 18 months of planning, service, and collaboration, the Special Parents Team will provide a joint report to each of the collaborating agencies that evaluates the effectiveness of the model and provides suggestions and recommendations for continuance or discontinuance of the program.

4. The Surfside School District will provide space for staff and secretarial offices and a conference room for the duration of the program.

5. The Peninsula Regional Center and the Peninsula Department of Public Health will each provide .50 FTE in salary dollars for secretarial support.

6. The Association for Retarded Citizens (ARC) will contribute furniture and equipment (desks, chairs, conference table, FAX, computer and printer, file cabinets) to the program. These items will remain with the program for its lifetime. If the program is discontinued, these items will be returned to the ARC or redistributed as ARC management specifies.

7. Mileage for home visits will be reimbursed by the staff member's home agency.

Based on the understandings outlined above, we the undersigned, as the authorized administrative representative of our agency, agree to participate in the Special Parents Team program.

Hannah Melville, M.D., M.B.A.
Director, Peninsula Regional Center

Jonah Johnson, Ph.D.
Director of Special Education, Surfside School District

Jaime Martinez, Ph.D.
Executive Director, Association for Retarded Citizens

Isa Rakajoni, M.D., M.P.H.
Chief, Peninsula County Department of Public Health

Figure 12.1. Memorandum of understanding.

Informal groups of individuals from different agencies who meet to discuss issues and concerns; often groups are organized by professional discipline.

More formalized groups representing different agencies meet to work on a specific issue or task. These task forces or work groups may work together to bring attention and a solution to a particular community need, such as respite services for families of infants who are technology-dependent, an improved system of information and referral, or a program for teen parents with infants who are at risk.

Co-location of staff members from different agencies at a single site or housing a staff member at another agency. By being physically located within another agency or sharing facilities, staff members can learn more about each other and about each agency. This may also simplify communication and improve access for families.

Sharing staff members with agencies, sharing salary and other costs associated with the position. Shared staff members can provide formal and informal linkages between the agencies and work to reduce barriers on a daily basis.

Eliminating duplication via joint intake, assessment planning, assessment, conferencing, implementation, and follow-up on all children and families to whom they provide services. In this instance, with parental permission, all information is shared. Team members represent their own agency as well as the collaborative team.

Figure 12.2. Collaboration cascade.

A fifth model was a truly integrated delivery system in which staff members from each agency participated in the intake, assessment, and follow-up related to the child's and family's program. Although more difficult to achieve, this model has the most promise for effective service delivery.

The final model Gans and Horton (cited in Nordyke, 1982) identified was based on linkages in service coordination. This model included cross-agency conferencing, service coordination, and teaming. This level of inter-agency collaboration is the one supported by IDEA. To develop the comprehensive, coordinated system of early intervention that meets the needs of children and families, agency and bureaucratic walls will have to give way to open, flexible ways of doing business that are responsive to family and community needs.

The model or models that any community selects are not important in and of themselves. It is the effectiveness of the model within that community that is critical. Any model may need to be adapted, and many will be revised and improved over time. Loose linkages may develop into more integrated collaborative efforts, and some of the more formal structures may become less formal as people and the agencies they represent begin to understand and trust one another. Models and the people who develop them need to be willing to create new visions as the needs of the community change.

Barriers and Facilitating Factors in Interagency Collaboration

A great deal has been written about the barriers to interagency collaboration (e.g., Healy et al., 1985; Linder, 1983; McLaughlin & Covert, 1984; Wehman, Kregel, & Barcus, 1985). According to Pollard, Hall, and Keeran (1979), the following problems are cited most frequently: competitiveness, narrow or self-serving interests, lack of incentive or compelling mutual interest, lack of training and skill in coordinating efforts, difficulty in communicating across disciplines, preoccupation with the administrative structure rather than the function of the agency, concerns about client confidentiality, general resistance to change, inadequate knowledge, attitudes that are not conducive to cooperation, lack of political awareness, demands from external sources, lack of accountability, and lack of review and evaluation of policies and procedures that may facilitate or hinder collaborative efforts.

At first glance the barriers just mentioned may create their own barrier; if it is so difficult to collaborate, where do we begin? In a 3-year study of critical incidents in the collaborative process in a large, urban community, five strategies for increasing the likelihood of successful collaboration were found (Harrison, Lynch, Rosander, & Borton, 1990; Lynch & Harrison, 1986). Each of these strategies is mentioned below with several suggestions about how to apply the strategy.

The first strategy was to develop new ways to meet community needs. Many programs and agencies are trapped in their own bureaucracies. So many demands are placed upon the agency that little time is available for brainstorming new approaches to problems and needs within the community. Conducting a community needs assessment to determine how the community has changed, helping agencies or groups write small grants to fund new projects, and using faculty and students at nearby colleges and universities can help programs approach and solve problems in new and creative ways (Harrison et al., 1990; Lynch & Harrison, 1986).

Networking and increasing awareness about community issues and needs related to young children who are at risk or disabled is a second strategy that seems to enhance collaboration. Many agency and school district personnel feel bogged down by paperwork and daily demands. Many also report a sense of isolation from their professional counterparts in other agencies. Some communities have found that starting a group to read and share articles about current practices, holding forums to discuss issues, or just getting together for lunch renews energy and increases collaboration. Sometimes, simply deciding to be a catalyst in the community and helping others get together facilitates collaboration (Harrison et al., 1990; Lynch & Harrison, 1986).

Being responsive to people and agencies throughout the change process is a third strategy for increasing collaborative efforts. Many of the behaviors that people view as responsive are simply good manners. A professional can increase the likelihood that collaboration will take place by acknowledging people's accomplishments with written or telephoned congratulations, sending thank-you notes when people do something helpful for the professional or one of the families, and following through in a timely manner on any commitment that has been made (Harrison et al., 1990; Lynch & Harrison, 1986).

Acknowledging and respecting turf and territorial issues while working to decrease them is another strategy to increase collaboration. In every community there are spoken and unspoken issues of turf. Some of the issues are rooted in reality, some in perception, and some in memory. Regardless of the origins or the accuracy of the perceptions, territorial issues can interfere with the present and the future. Being sure to include all key players in activities, being sensitive to power and control needs, and being tolerant and flexible can help people develop renewed trust (Harrison et al., 1990; Lynch & Harrison, 1986).

Finally, maintaining frequent, open communications is an important strategy for increasing collaboration. Interagency efforts take time, and there are often moments of frustration. However, keeping the lines of communication open, using outside facilitators to help groups come together, and allowing time for the process to evolve all help ensure the success of collaborative efforts.

The strategies that have been suggested focus on the importance of collaboration between and among professionals and agencies, but it is important to note that family members have a role in all collaborative efforts. Their presence, wisdom, and experience are critical to creating systems that work. Whenever training, policymaking, and other collaborative ventures are being planned or conducted, family members should be at the table.

Although these suggestions have been used successfully in many communities, they represent only a beginning. Brainstorming ways that the community can operationalize each of these strategies can become one of the initial steps in developing collaboration.

Summary

Interagency collaboration is one of the hallmarks of exemplary programs for young children who are at risk or disabled and their families. It helps ensure that the service system is coordinated and easily accessible to families; reduces duplication, fragmentation, and gaps in service; and eliminates fiscal inefficiency. In addition to representing effective practice, interagency collaboration is now mandated by IDEA in programs and services for children under the age of 3 who are at risk and/or disabled and their families. Although many barriers to collaboration have been cited in the literature, many communities have found successful strategies for overcoming barriers and working collaboratively.

Preferred Practices

The following questions can be used to help programs review the collaborative efforts that are taking place within their programs and community.

1. Which agencies in the community provide services to the same families? Do collaborative relationships exist among those agencies?

2. Is there a forum where each of these agencies and family members meet to share information about their services?

3. Who is advocating for young children with special needs and their families in this community? What is the position of local governmental officials on issues related to young children who are at risk or disabled and their families? Do advocates have adequate information on child, family, and program needs and successes?

4. Is there anything that the program or community could do more effectively if agencies worked together more collaboratively?

5. What services for infants and toddlers who are at risk or disabled and their families are duplicated in the community?

6. What services for this same group do not exist but are needed?
7. Who in the community is respected, yet neutral, who could help spearhead a collaborative effort?
8. What is the best way to convince people in the community that collaboration is needed? In other words, what is in it for them?
9. Which parents in the community would be interested in working toward a more coordinated service delivery system?
10. What can be done within the next 3 months to move toward a more collaborative approach?

References

Audette, H. (1980). Interagency collaboration: The bottom line. In J. O. Elder & P. R. Magrab (Eds.), *Coordinating services to handicapped children* (pp. 25–44). Baltimore: Brookes.

Barnett, W. S., & Escobar, C. M. (1988). The economics of early intervention for handicapped children: What do we really know? *Journal of the Division for Early Childhood, 12,* 169–181.

Commission for Cooperative Services for Young Handicapped Children and Their Families. (1988). *Getting started: A guidebook for interagency collaboration.* (Available from Infant/Toddler Interagency Collaboration Project, 9245 Sky Park Court, Suite 130, San Diego, CA 92123)

Coulter, M. L., Wallace, T., & Laude, M. (1993). Early intervention services in selected Florida counties: The provider perspective. *Children's Health Care, 22,* 125–141.

Elder, J. O., & Kazuk, E. (no date). Getting started. In P. Magrab, J. Elder, E. Kazuk, J. Pelosi, & R. Wiegerink (Eds.), *Developing a community team* (pp. 1–10). (Available from Georgetown University Child Development Center, 3800 Reservoir Rd. NW, Washington, DC 20007)

Fessler, D. R. (1976). *Facilitating community change: A basic guide.* San Diego: University Associates.

Flynn, C. C., & Harbin, G. L. (1987). Evaluating interagency coordination efforts using a multi-dimensional, interactional, developmental paradigm. *Remedial and Special Education, 8*(3), 35–44.

Georgetown University Child Development Center. (1981–1984). *The workbook series for providing services to children with handicaps and their families.* (Available from Georgetown University Child Development Center, 3800 Reservoir Rd. NW, Washington, DC 20007)

Harrison, P. J., Lynch, E. W., Rosander, K., & Borton, W. (1990). Determining success in interagency collaboration: An evaluation of processes and behaviors. *Infants and Young Children, 3*(1), 69–78.

Healy, A., Keesee, P. D., & Smith, B. S. (1985). *Early services for children with special needs—Transactions for family support.* Iowa City, IA: Division of Developmental Disabilities, University Hospital School.

Linder, T. W. (1983). *Early childhood special education—Program development and administration.* Baltimore: Brookes.

Lynch, E. W., & Harrison, P. J. (1986). *Interagency collaboration: Making magic happen.* San Diego: San Diego State University.

Lynch, E. W., Jackson, J. A., Mendoza, J., & English, K. (1991). The merging of best practices and state policy in the IFSP process in California. *Topics in Early Childhood Special Education, 11,* 32–53.

Magrab, P., Kazuk, E., & Greene, L. (1981). *Community workbook for collaborative services to preschool handicapped children.* (Available from Georgetown University Child Development Center, 3800 Reservoir Rd. NW, Washington, DC 20007)

McLaughlin, J. A., & Covert, R. C. (1984). *Evaluating interagency collaboration.* (Available from Technical Assistance Development System, 500 NCNB Plaza, Chapel Hill, NC 27514)

McNulty, B. (1989). Leadership and policy strategies for interagency planning: Meeting the early childhood mandate. In J. J. Gallagher, P. L. Trohanis, & R. M. Clifford (Eds.), *Policy implementation and PL 99-457: Planning for young children with special needs* (pp. 147–167). Baltimore: Brookes.

Nordyke, N. S. (1982). Improving services for young, handicapped children through local, interagency collaboration. *Topics in Early Childhood Special Education, 2,* 63–72.

Pelosi, J. (no date). Planning for action. In P. Magrab, J. Elder, E. Kazuk, J. Pelosi, & R. Wiegerink (Eds.), *Developing a community team* (pp. 15–24). (Available from Georgetown University Child Development Center, 3800 Reservoir Rd. NW, Washington, DC 20007)

Pollard, A., Hall, H., & Keeran, C. (1979). Community service planning. In P. R. Magrab & J. O. Elder (Eds.), *Planning for services to handicapped persons: Community, education, health* (pp. 18–37). Baltimore: Brookes.

Rossi, R. J., Gilmartin, K. J., & Dayton, C. W. (1982). *Agencies working together—A guide to coordinating and planning.* Beverly Hills, CA: Sage.

Swan, W. W., & Morgan, J. L. (1993). *Collaborating for comprehensive services for young children and their families: The local interagency coordinating council.* Baltimore: Brookes.

Wehman, P., Kregel, J., & Barcus, J. M. (1985). From school to work: A vocational transition model for handicapped students. *Exceptional Children, 52,* 25–37.

Selected Readings

Elder, J., & Magrab, P. (Eds.). (1980). *Coordinating services to handicapped children: A handbook for interagency collaboration.* Baltimore: Brookes.

Georgetown University Child Development Center. (1981–1984). *The workbook series for providing services to children with handicaps and their families.* (Available from Georgetown University Child Development Center, 3800 Reservoir Rd. NW, Washington, DC 20007)

Hazel, R., Barber, P., Roberts, S., Behr, S. K., Helmstetter, E., & Guess, D. (1988). *A community approach to an integrated service system for children with special needs.* Baltimore: Brookes.

Swan, W. W., & Morgan, J. L. (1993). *Collaborating for comprehensive services for young children and their families: The local interagency coordinating council.* Baltimore: Brookes.

Evaluating Programs*

CHAPTER 13

Exemplary early intervention programs allocate time and resources to evaluation. Although evaluation may seem far removed from the day-to-day responsibilities of program management, it is an integral part of intervention. Bricker and Littman (1982) suggested that evaluation serves at least three distinct but related purposes in early intervention programs:

1. It guides development of individual programming.
2. It provides feedback about success of individual programming.
3. It provides a system for determining the value of an intervention system designed to benefit groups of children. (p. 23)

Three additional purposes may be added to their list. Program evaluations provide information that can be used to develop social policy (Takanishi & Feshbach, 1982; Johnson, 1988). Data on the efficacy of early childhood education for children who are disadvantaged and for those with disabilities provided a major impetus for expansion of early intervention programs. Thus, evaluation data have been used to influence policymakers at the highest levels of government. With the passage and implementation of Part H of P.L. 99-457 (now the Individuals with Disabilities Education Act [IDEA]), and the infusion of resources into programs for infants and toddlers who are at risk and their families, legislators and policymakers have new questions about the impact and efficacy of early intervention.

Program evaluation is also used to demonstrate program accountability and effectiveness. In times of fiscal restraint and budget reductions, social and educational programs that are outside of the mainstream of traditional services are often targeted for closure (Linder, 1983). Programs that have systematically documented their results are much more likely to be viewed favorably and funded during difficult times than those that have no data to support their claims. Program evaluation also provides an opportunity to examine all components of a program and provides a framework for pulling these components together into a meaningful whole.

Finally, evaluation is a key management tool. Program administrators must make a wide range of decisions about program operation and allocation of resources. The ability to make data-based decisions leads to wiser

---

*Contributed by Patrick J. Harrison, Department of Educational Technology, San Diego State University.

uses of resources and helps ensure that clients are well served.

Whether the evaluation is being conducted to improve the delivery of services, to monitor the progress of children in local programs, to increase understanding of the effects of various types of intervention, or to provide information to legislators about the long-term effects of early intervention, evaluation is a sound investment.

Nearly every decision that is made in programs is based on some sort of appraisal or evaluation of the situation. From the minute-to-minute decisions within a program, such as whether Melissa should be repositioned to make it easier for her to reach the rabbit or whether it is time to take Bruce to the potty, to the larger programmatic decisions about how to present the budget to the board or when to develop a new brochure, some evaluation is conducted. However, in these examples the evaluation is often internal to the person making the decision, based on professional judgment or previous experience. This chapter focuses on more formal and explicit evaluations and provides information on how to design and conduct them.

Throughout this chapter, the word *evaluator* is used to signify the person conducting the evaluation. For most programs the evaluator will be the program manager or another staff member who is given the responsibility of evaluating the program. It is this person's role to gather ongoing information about program

operation, compare outcomes with expectations, and determine whether the program is "on track." This sort of evaluation is often referred to as formative, because the information obtained helps form or shape the program. Periodically it is helpful to have an external evaluator conduct a targeted or comprehensive evaluation of program practices and outcomes. This sort of evaluation is often referred to as summative because the various aspects of the program are being compared with known standards or benchmarks. Information gathered in this type of evaluation can be used to identify areas of strength, areas that need improvement, and data on the overall performance of the program.

Determining the Kinds of Questions To Be Answered

Program evaluations can be designed to answer a broad range of questions (Brinkerhoff, Brethower, Hluchyj, & Nowakowski, 1983; Sheehan & Gallagher, 1983). Reviewing the kinds of questions that evaluations can answer is one way to begin the evaluation process.

Implementation Questions

All programs begin with an implicit or explicit set of goals, objectives, and management plans. Although the level of specificity varies widely from program to program, staff members and administrators of each have some vision of what they think will happen and how they think it will occur. Evaluations can be used to determine whether what was planned for and intended to happen is happening. Evaluations that focus on this kind of question are referred to as implementation evaluations. For example, in the conceptualization of an early intervention program, it was assumed that after the first 6 months the program would be serving 60 infants and toddlers using a home- and center-based model, that home visits would be weekly, and that each staff member would be the primary service provider for 10 families. An implementation evaluation examines whether those things are happening, and if not, why not.

Assume in this example that 60 children and families are being served but that home visits are not occurring weekly; the center-based component is almost nonexistent; and several team members are serving a disproportionate number of families. After a series of interviews with staff and parents, the evaluator learns that of the 60 children, 20 are too medically fragile to come to the center-based program, and 25 families do not have dependable transportation. The evaluator also learns that weekly home visits have become twice-monthly visits, because so many new children are being referred that staff members are spending their time on assessment rather than on intervention. Finally, the disproportionate caseload among the staff members has been brought about because many of the families are non–English speaking, and only two staff members are bilingual. As a result, they are serving all of the non–English speaking families.

On the surface it would appear that the program is not meeting its objectives; however, a more in-depth implementation evaluation can reveal why the initial objectives are not being accomplished (Johnson, 1988). With the information provided by the evaluation, program staff and administrators can rethink the service delivery system and make necessary changes.

Resource Questions

For an early intervention program to function effectively, it must have resources. The resources include space, equipment, materials, personnel, transportation, and so forth. However, in areas where population growth is high, distances great, or staff are difficult to hire, the available resources may not be adequate. The overall question is, does the program have what is necessary to make the program work? If there are questions about this, the program administrator may choose to conduct a resource evaluation.

For example, a special education director in a remote, rural part of New Mexico has been given the responsibility of developing an early intervention program for the infants and toddlers who are at risk and disabled and their families in his consortium's catchment area. The area covers several counties with isolated ranches, rugged mountains, deserts, and three designated tribal areas with small communities dotted throughout the reservations. Geographically, some 3,000 square miles are included. Although the precise number of children and families who may be eligible is unknown, it is estimated that approximately 30 children qualify for services. The school board has allocated one full-time early childhood special educator to the program and up to $25 per month in mileage reimbursement. At this point, the special education director may want to conduct a resource evaluation to determine what can be done with what has been allocated and what is needed to offer an early intervention program.

Outcome Questions

"Is what we are doing producing the desired results or outcome?" is surely one of the most frequently asked questions in early intervention. Referred to in the literature as efficacy studies, evaluations of early intervention outcomes have been conducted for over 50 years (e.g., Garber, 1988; Karnes, 1981; Lazar, Darlington, Murray, Royce, & Snipper, 1982; Skeels, 1966; Skeels & Dye, 1939). Although few programs have the resources to impose the rigorous methodology required to demonstrate effectiveness free of all confounding variables, every program should be examining its effectiveness in terms of child, family, and community outcomes. The primary question in this sort of evaluation is whether the things the program is doing are having the desired results.

Although some equate outcome evaluation with educational research because its goal is to demonstrate that the intervention "is the most likely explanation for the child or family outcomes" (Johnson, 1988, p. 200), outcome evaluation seldom takes this form in early intervention programs. Conducting research of this nature is extremely challenging because of the conflict between daily program implementation that is responsive to children and families and the demands of research. Therefore, in the discussion that follows, outcome evaluation is not equated with traditional research paradigms. (For a review that links outcome evaluation to research, see Johnson, 1988.)

Consider the Lollipop Program in a medium-size Midwestern university community. Many of the young children being served have intensive medical needs, and they are frequently hospitalized. One of the goals of the program is to help parents become empowered, to be more involved in decision making about their child, and ultimately to serve as the child's primary resource coordinator. One of the program's practices has been to visit the children during their hospitalizations and to accompany the parents when they take their children to the physician for follow-up visits or reevaluations. At a staff meeting several staff members expressed concern about some of the families' growing dependence on them. One mentioned that whenever a toddler had the sniffles, one of the parents called to ask if they should go to the doctor. As the staff discussed their concerns, they began to ask why this was happening and to consider how they might be contributing to the problem.

Although the answer to the Lollipop Program's problem seems fairly simple, there are many times when professionals are not sure what the effects of their interventions are. Is the child making progress? Is the family achieving the outcomes they have set for themselves, or is the child making progress at great psychic and physical costs to the rest of the family? It is these issues—from how many and how quickly the Individualized Family Service Plan (IFSP) outcomes are being met to what the effects of the program are on the family system—that need to be subjected to outcome evaluations.

Educational Focus, Validity, and Philosophical Questions

Preferred practice in all fields shifts as the knowledge base grows and as outcome evaluations validate some practices and invalidate others. However, in programs that must be responsive to the day-to-day responsibilities and demands of working with children and families, there is seldom time to reflect on practice—to reexamine what is being done, how it is being done, and why. The question associated with this kind of evaluation is whether the interventions being used are the ones that should be used. Even if the other forms of evaluation show that a program is doing a good job, there is still the question of whether the program is doing a good job at the right thing. Even though a program may be operating smoothly, children and families may be making gains on mutually agreed-upon objectives, and everyone may be satisfied, the intervention may not be appropriate philosophically in terms of its educational validity or in relation to its functionality for the child and family in the future.

A potent example of this concern over the validity of the intervention comes from programs for older students with moderate to severe mental retardation. For many years those programs used a developmental approach in teaching students. Teachers used developmental assessment instruments to determine the student's mental age, then developed programming matched to that developmental level. It was typical to see a group of adolescents coloring, playing with preschool toys, or being treated and behaving in ways far below their chronological age level. Although this practice continued for several decades, in the late 1970s a number of leaders in the field began reflecting on and questioning this practice (e.g., Brown et al., 1979; Holvoet, Guess, Mulligan, & Brown, 1980; Wehman, Schleinen, & Kiernan, 1980). The developmental approach for these students was not educationally valid nor did it match the emerging philosophy of age-appropriate, community-based instruction, which focuses on functional skills that students need in present and future environments. As a result of this reflection, practice began to change.

Similar questions are being asked in early intervention programs. Can a child-focused approach be considered valid when one examines the literature on family systems? Can highly directed approaches be appropriate when one considers the literature on the importance of play and early choice making? Do full-day, center-based programs for children from 18 months to 3 years of age make sense in terms of what is known about all young children? These and many other questions about early intervention practice are being evaluated, and programs are being redesigned in terms of the findings.

Satisfaction Questions

One of the goals of most administrators is that, in addition to having a program that is effective and highly regarded, it also should be one that everyone feels good about. However unrealistic such a goal may be, it would be nice to know that consumers are satisfied with service, that staff members enjoy their jobs, and that others in the community feel the program is doing a good job. Evaluations that focus on satisfaction are frequently used in early intervention programs. The overall question is how satisfied the various constituents are with the program.

Imagine you are directing an early intervention program that serves children under the age of 3 who are at risk and disabled. In addition to the services to children, there is a comprehensive array of services for families, a large collaborative component that includes four other agencies, and a training component that works with staff at child care centers and preschools. At the last meeting with your board, there were rumblings that more money needed to be spent on awareness campaigns with the possible result that fewer dollars would be available for your services. As you consider how to counter the proposal, it occurs to you that you hear success stories on a daily basis, but that they are not recorded anywhere. Many children are now in inclusive toddler programs because of your staff's work with teachers at the preschool. Four of your families who had been referred to Child Protective Services 2 years ago are now coaching other parents on how to be better parents. The collaborative component of the program has been the impetus for the development of a community-wide tracking system for high-risk infants, and one of the interagency task forces has completed an agreement that will enable families to apply for a number of different services on the same, simple form. Systematically collecting data related to constituents' satisfaction with the program can provide an excellent buffer against cutbacks. Conversely, if there are problems in any area, such satisfaction measures can find them so that they can be corrected.

Finally, periodic and systematic collection of evaluation data can help build team spirit and ensure that the occasional negative incident does not have undue effect. For example, family satisfaction data and success stories can bolster the early intervention staff's morale. In an area in which progress is often slow, positive feedback is particularly welcome. Systematic data collection can help all staff members put isolated, negative comments into perspective. The "they" who are dissatisfied with programs often turn out to be two or three disgruntled individuals. Although it may be important to continue to improve services and respond to the complaints, knowing that only two people are dissatisfied provides an important perspective.

Cost Questions

The costs of programs and services are an important issue to program administrators, legislators, and the general public. As resources become more limited, questions of resources loom larger, and early intervention programs have not escaped scrutiny. Although there are many ways to figure costs, three methods are typically used to examine programs for young children: cost analysis, cost effectiveness, and cost benefit.

Cost analysis is the method that is probably most appropriate for the majority of programs. In this method the costs of all of the human and other resources used by the program are simply tallied. The costs of salaries and benefits for staff, transportation, material and supplies, space, equipment, and so forth are added and divided by the number of children or families served. This kind of analysis provides information about the per capita costs of services. For example, programs may want to compare the costs of a home-based program with the costs of an inclusive center-based program. Other community agencies may want to determine the cost differences of keeping a child who is technology dependent at home instead of in a skilled nursing facility. The cost analysis method provides a detailed measure of the actual costs of a program or service.

Cost effectiveness is a measure of how much it costs to get a set amount of gain or change (Levin, 1983). For example, how many dollars in human and other resources does it take for a child who is at risk or disabled to make 6 months progress in language, or how much does it cost to prepare a 3-year-old who is at risk to enter a regular preschool rather than a special education program? In other words, cost-effectiveness evaluations examine alternatives in terms of costs and effects.

The most involved and sophisticated cost measures are referred to as *cost-benefit analyses*. In this method the cost of the inputs and the value of the outputs are calculated and compared. The most significant cost benefit of an early intervention program has been a longitudinal study of the Perry Preschool graduates and their control group developed by David Weikart and his colleagues (Schweinhart & Weikart, 1981, 1993). The costs of the intervention have been calculated, and the experimental and control group subjects have been studied for over 24 years to determine the benefits of the intervention. Using sophisticated accounting procedures and teams of evaluators including economists, the effects have been studied across a wide range of variables such as school achievement, parental reinforcement, school conduct, and delinquent behavior. In this example, the costs of the early intervention program were compared with the real benefits to society in terms of reduced public assistance, reduced incarcerations, fewer unwanted pregnancies, vocational aspiration and achievement, and so forth. Although most programs do not have the resources to conduct evaluations of this magnitude, the data from the Perry Preschool provide strong support for the long-term cost effectiveness of preschool programs for children who have or are at risk for developmental delays.

Program Description Questions

A final question that a program administrator may want to ask—what is happening as a result of the program?—is less precise than those previously discussed. This type of evaluation is more descriptive, and the answers provide information about unplanned outcomes. In such an evaluation prejudgments are avoided, and the evaluator simply looks at the program as it is.

Imagine that a family-focused program has been developed in conjunction with a neonatal intensive care unit in the community. The early childhood educators, therapists, nurses, and physicians work side-by-side on the unit with the infants and families. The program was initiated on a shoestring as a way to improve communication among health providers, education providers, and families. No one was really sure about what to expect, but now that the program has been operating fairly smoothly for a year the staff are beginning to sense positive changes for everyone involved. At this point they may want to evaluate what is happening in the program—how it is affecting the participants, whether there have been unplanned benefits, and how the components could be described to others.

In summary, the general evaluation questions that need to be answered are critical in the selection of an evaluation approach, model, and even the evaluator. Determining the global questions is a beginning step in planning and conducting an evaluation.

Approaches to Evaluation

Two approaches to evaluation are often described in the literature: formative and summative (Fitz-Gibbon & Morris, 1987). *Formative evaluation* is used to provide information about the program's progress, and the information is used to make midcourse corrections or adjustments as needed. For example, as programs refine their approach to developing IFSPs, they may pilot test several ways to gather information and write the plan. To determine whether the process and the outcome are working, the program administrator, designated staff member, or outside evaluator may interview families and staff members who participated to determine their satisfaction with the process, procedures, and outcome. Such a formative evaluation enables program staff to determine what is working and what is not and adjust the process and procedures to improve the program.

Summative evaluation examines the final results of a program or project. Summative evaluation data are often presented in a final report or as a summation of outcomes. For example, a report to the program's agency board might include summative evaluation data. Board members typically would want to know how many children and families were served and some of the demographic information about them, such as children's ages, diagnoses, geographic areas represented, and ethnicity. They would also want to know how much progress children had made and how satisfied families were with the program. Information that describes a program and its effectiveness is summative in nature. Its primary purpose is to describe what has been accomplished rather than suggest strategies for change.

Although a distinction is usually made between the two, the strategies used to collect the data are often the same. The difference is in how the results or findings are used and sometimes in who collects the information. A formative evaluation could be summative if the program ended at that time, and summative data could be used formatively to guide the development of another cycle of the program. Typically, members of the program staff collect formative evaluation making the process more internal, whereas external evaluators are more likely to be recruited to collect summative data.

Evaluation Models

Many different models of evaluation have been used, and as Wolery (1994) pointed out, the field of early intervention is dealing with complex research and evaluation questions with new and diverse measurement methods. Because it would not be possible, or sensible, to try to remember each model, many leaders in the field have proposed schema for categorizing the various models. The schema on which this section of the chapter is structured was developed by Popham (1988), who proposed five classes of educational evaluation models:

1. Goal-Attainment Models
2. Judgmental Models Emphasizing Inputs
3. Judgmental Models Emphasizing Outputs
4. Decision-Facilitation Models
5. Naturalistic Models. (p. 24)

Each of these models is described briefly. For a more thorough treatment, see Popham (1988).

Goal-attainment models focus on the extent to which a program's goals are being accomplished, and they rely on clearly specified behavioral objectives against which the program's progress is measured. For example, in an early intervention program, goals and objectives may be related to child progress, family attainment of the outcomes they have specified, numbers of children being served, staff development, and interagency collaboration. If a goal-attainment model of evaluation were used, the evaluator would measure the program's effectiveness based on the extent to which the prespecified goals and objectives were achieved.

Judgmental models that emphasize inputs rely heavily on professional judgments of what is required to operate an adequate to exemplary program. For example, a state-level interagency task force may develop a list of input criteria that an early intervention program must meet to receive state funds. Input criteria generally refer to things that a program must have. In this instance, the state may include the following criteria: a 1-to-3 adult-to-child ratio, a specified number of square feet per child for all center-based programs, a professional staff that includes members of at least three professional disciplines who hold the appropriate certification or licensure for practice in their field, and so forth. To determine whether a program qualifies for funding, an evaluator reviews the program based on whether it meets those criteria or possesses these internal characteristics.

Judgmental models emphasizing outputs assess not only the attainment of goals but the goals themselves. According to proponents of these models, the worthiness of the goals themselves is an important part of the evaluation. More boldly put, if the goals are inappropriate, how well they are achieved does not really matter. These models are often used to compare different program models. For example, the evaluator might (a) examine child progress in home-based versus center-based programs or (b) compare child change in a mainstreamed, play-oriented program versus a segregated, data-based classroom.

In *decision-facilitation models* the evaluator's primary job is to provide information to decision makers without including personal judgments. In this model the evaluator is a data gatherer who supplies information to managers. Two of the best known decision-facilitation models are the Context, Input, Process, Product Model, referred to as CIPP (Stufflebeam & Guba, 1970), and the Discrepancy Evaluation Model (Provus, 1971). Because both of these models are rather rigidly formulated and do not include external standards of best practice, they are probably less useful to administrators of early intervention programs.

Naturalistic or qualitative evaluation models focus on why and how data are collected. Naturalistic models developed by Lincoln and Guba (1985) and Eisner (cited in Popham, 1988), as well as numerous ethnographic approaches, use strategies borrowed from areas as diverse as anthropology and art criticism. Case studies, participant-observational strategies, surveys, and interviewing are all techniques that are used.

These methods can be applied as a way to evaluate the context of early intervention programs (Odom & Shuster, 1986). For example, in a mainstreamed toddler program, evaluators may elect to become participant observers. In this role they would spend time in the setting participating in the day-to-day activities of the program in an attempt to get an understanding of the interactions and environment. Like anthropologists, they would record their observations as field notes and continue to refine and add to the description. The case study methodology can also be profitably applied in early intervention programs to examine the impact of interventions on children and families.

Focus groups represent one qualitative evaluation strategy that has gained popularity in early intervention settings. Focus groups emerged from marketing, but the methodology is being adapted to fit many other settings. A focus group is a way to solicit opinions about a service or product from a group of people in an informal setting through a semi-structured interview. Because the interview is conducted with a group and group interaction is encouraged, often more can be learned and greater insights gained than through a series of individual interviews (Krueger, 1994). Summers and colleagues (1990) used the method to gather information from families and practitioners about their preferences regarding the IFSP, and Brotherson (1994) provided an excellent description of the method in its application to early intervention. Like many evaluation techniques, focus group interviewing sounds simple; however, many aspects of the procedures and analysis require training and sophistication in the method. Focus groups are not merely group conversations that anyone can conduct.

Each type of evaluation model has its strengths and weaknesses, and each is more appropriate for some evaluation questions than for others. Although some information can be gathered by staff members without training in evaluation, any comprehensive evaluation should be developed jointly by the program staff and a professional in evaluation.

Planning and Conducting an Evaluation

The paragraphs that follow outline a step-by-step procedure for planning and conducting evaluations and using the results. Although the time spent on each step will vary depending on the questions that are to be answered and the resources available, each step is critical in assuring that the evaluation provides the needed information.

Planning Evaluations

Determining what to evaluate

The first step in any evaluation is to determine what needs to be evaluated. Most programs have multiple components such as services to children, services to families, transitions to preschool, or collaborative activities. Starting the evaluation process by depicting the program components graphically often helps focus the relative importance of each of the potential areas of evaluation. Using the Discrepancy Evaluation Model, Yavorsky (1984) suggested depicting the various program components as networks. Although the Discrepancy Evaluation Model is not ideal for evaluating early intervention programs, a visual display of program components is often helpful. Figure 13.1 is based on the multiple components of Project IINTACT (Infant Interagency Network Through Accessing Computer Technology), an early intervention program funded by the Handicapped Children's Early Education Program of the Department of Education. Each large box represents a major program component, and the subcomponents or tasks related to each are identified in smaller boxes. This view of the project assists program administrators and evaluators to determine evaluation needs and priorities.

Determining the target audience and how the information will be used

The next step in planning is deciding who will use the evaluation findings and how they will be used. Will findings be used internally to guide decisions and make any needed modifications in the program (formative uses), or will they be used to present to outside decision makers (summative uses)? In some instances the information will be shared only with the program administrator and staff and used to review and improve the existing program. In other instances it will be used as an accountability measure and shared with parent groups, boards, or agency administrators. In some instances the evaluation findings will be shared with legislators or funders and used to make decisions about program continuance or discontinuance. In each instance the accuracy and integrity of the information is equally important, but the specific questions would change.

For example, if the program is going to evaluate its program for children for its own internal use to assure that the program is working effectively, the questions might include the following: Are children accomplishing outcomes written in the IFSP? Are families satisfied with the program for their children? If, however, programs were evaluating the child intervention program in order to present information to funders, the following questions might be included: What percentage of IFSP child outcomes are being attained? What is the rate of attainment of these IFSP objectives? What are the per capita costs of the program (cost analysis)? What does it cost to get 6 months' growth developmentally (cost effectiveness)? What percentage of children enter a regular rather than a special education preschool program at age 3? As this example suggests, the people with whom the results are to be shared, and the decisions that will be made based on the results of the evaluation, shape the questions that will be asked.

Developing evaluation questions

The next step is to determine what questions need to be answered by the evaluation. Does the program need information about child progress, cost, family satisfaction, the image of the program in the community, or the staff's feelings of competence? Each of these

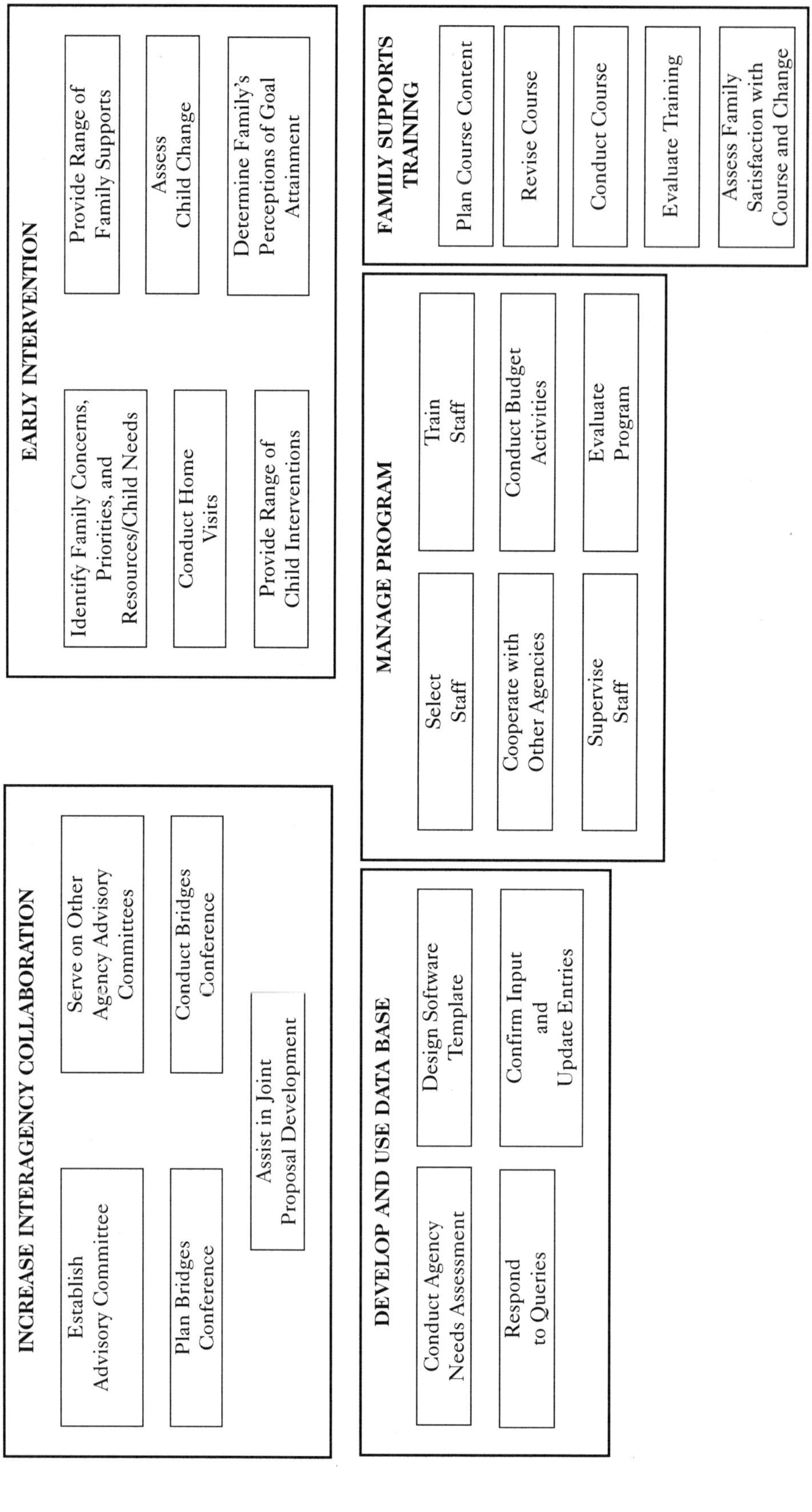

INCREASE INTERAGENCY COLLABORATION

- Establish Advisory Committee
- Serve on Other Agency Advisory Committees
- Plan Bridges Conference
- Conduct Bridges Conference
- Assist in Joint Proposal Development

EARLY INTERVENTION

- Identify Family Concerns, Priorities, and Resources/Child Needs
- Provide Range of Family Supports
- Conduct Home Visits
- Assess Child Change
- Provide Range of Child Interventions
- Determine Family's Perceptions of Goal Attainment

FAMILY SUPPORTS TRAINING

- Plan Course Content
- Revise Course
- Conduct Course
- Evaluate Training
- Assess Family Satisfaction with Course and Change

DEVELOP AND USE DATA BASE

- Conduct Agency Needs Assessment
- Design Software Template
- Respond to Queries
- Confirm Input and Update Entries

MANAGE PROGRAM

- Select Staff
- Train Staff
- Conduct Budget Activities
- Cooperate with Other Agencies
- Supervise Staff
- Evaluate Program

Figure 13.1. Evaluation schema.

questions may demand a different evaluation model and different methods of data collection.

Sample questions based on Project IINTACT are listed in the first column of Table 13.1. In this evaluation it was determined that four of the five project components needed evaluation, so evaluation questions related to the intervention with children, family supports training, the development of the data base, and interagency collaboration were developed. Because the findings were going to be used by several target audiences—by the program administrator and staff to improve the program and services, by funders, and by a more general audience looking for models to adopt—the questions vary in their nature and sophistication.

Developing an evaluation design

Designing an evaluation requires much of the same rigor and attention to detail that is required in conducting research. In fact, exemplary evaluations often employ experimental or quasi-experimental designs. (For a detailed treatment of the types of designs and their uses, see Campbell & Stanley, 1963.) Experimental designs are highly controlled using randomization and control of as many variables as possible in an attempt to focus on the causes of change. Quasi-experimental designs are used when the experimenter or evaluator cannot randomly assign individuals to various groups or exercise a high degree of control over the variables. Most evaluations of early intervention programs fall into the latter category.

One of the most helpful ways to approach evaluation design is to focus on what questions need to be answered. The design will change depending on whether the program administrator wants to answer questions related to description, differences, or relationships (Charles, 1988). Questions of description are the most frequently asked. They deal with program and client profiles and trends. Questions of description are reported using means, standard deviations, ranges, medians, modes, percentages, and frequencies. The following are typical questions of description:

What was the average gain in motor performance of children participating in the program each month for the first 6 months of their participation?

What was the average length of time it took families to go through the program's intake process?

How many reports of stress (e.g., child abuse, abandonment, parent flight) were there after implementation of the parent respite program was introduced?

Questions of differences examine pre- and posttest scores or scores from two or more different groups using statistical techniques such as the chi square, t-test, or analysis of variance (ANOVA). Typical questions of difference are:

Do more children whose families participate in the Family Partnerships Program achieve 85% or more of their IFSP goals than children whose parents do not participate?

Is there a difference in the coping strategies used by parents who participate in a family support group compared with parents who do not participate?

Do staff members who receive individual consultation from the manager differ in their willingness to participate in the community involvement program from those who receive group training?

When children are given the opportunity to immediately perform the social skills tasks taught in the program, will their performance be significantly improved?

Questions of relationship are concerned with the association among child, family

Table 13.1. Evaluation Plan

Evaluation Questions	Instrument
Early Intervention Data	
1. What progress has the child made?	1a. Early Intervention Developmental Profile 1b. Home visit log 1c. Check on family–child objectives and outcomes
2. How many children and families have been served?	2a. Numer of intake forms 2b. Number of exit interviews
3. What types of services are being provided?	3a. Number and type of home visits Number of phone consultations Number of resources mobilized
Family Support Training	
4. Are family members learning skills useful in caring for their children?	4a. Observation 4b. Family members' self-assessment of skills
5. Are family members experiencing competence and positive feelings about parenting?	5a. Family members' self-assessment and discussion with staff members
Data Base	
6. Does the directory represent the range of services and agencies in San Diego County?	6a. Community needs assessment data 6b. Annual confirmation check with agencies
7. Are agencies and family members accessing the directory?	7a. Inquiry log
8. Is the directory providing useful information?	8a. Feedback form mailed; printout of search request data
Interagency Collaboration	
9. Is Project IINTACT having a positive effect on interagency collaboration?	9a. Key events questionnaire 9b. Critical incident interviews and reports
10. Is the Project IINTACT advisory board having a positive effect on collaboration?	10a. Questionnaire on advisory committee members' perceptions and attitudes
11. What are the strategies, events, and activities that have had a positive or negative impact on interagency collaboration?	11a. Critical incident interviews and reports
12. Was BRIDGES conference well received and perceived to have a positive effect on interagency collaboration?	12a. Conference evaluation forms 12b. Log of presenters and attendance demographics

member, or early interventionist characteristics, program practices, and performance variables. Statistical tests such as the Spearman *r*, the Pearson *r*, or the biserial *r* are used to analyze the data. Typical questions of relationship include:

Is the child's performance related to the number of home visits made by an early intervention team member?

Is there a relationship between the amount of time that children spend in the program (full day vs. half day) and their performance on a measure of prelinguistic and language behavior?

Is there a relationship between the number of children in the family and parental satisfaction with the program?

Is there a relationship between the type of disability and the level of satisfaction with the program that family members report?

The design of the evaluation must fit the questions and the resources and provide data that are valid for use within the program or outside of it. Because of the complexities of these decisions, professional evaluators should be consulted when comprehensive evaluations are being conducted.

Selecting or developing instruments

The methods used to collect the information depend upon the design that has been selected. Norm- or criterion-referenced measures may be used to collect information on child change. Interview instruments, paper-and-pencil inventories, logs of referrals to agencies such as Child Protective Services, or parent reports may be used to evaluate the effectiveness of family support services. Survey questionnaires may be used to evaluate satisfaction, perception, knowledge, or information about the program. Several examples are included in Figures 13.2, 13.3, 13.4, and 13.5. The examples may not fit the needs of every program, but they may provide ideas for those writing evaluation instruments. Although survey questionnaires sound simple to write, good ones are extremely difficult to develop. Because they must take into account the reading level, language, and general comprehension of respondents, as well as how to ask questions that are clear, their presumed simplicity is deceptive. (For a fuller treatment of questionnaire writing, see Sudman & Bradburn, 1982.)

Often instruments that can serve as the basis for data collection are already used in the program. For example, assessment instruments used to determine eligibility or to plan the child's program may be used as measures of child change. Forms that are used to identify family concerns, priorities, and resources may be compared at specified intervals to examine families' success accomplishing the outcomes that they have set for themselves, and logs of services provided can be used to estimate program costs. Perhaps the three most important rules in instrument selection are to (a) be sure that it is a reliable and valid measurement of what one wants to know; (b) keep it simple; and (c) use as much of what is already used in the program as possible. Because many evaluation headaches would be prevented by preplanning, attention to evaluation at the earliest stages of the program can help to assure that instruments used in the program can also serve an evaluation function. If instruments do have to be developed, they should be piloted and their reliability and validity examined to ensure that they will provide information that is sound enough for decision making. The second column of Table 13.1 lists the instruments used in the evaluation of Project IINTACT.

Developing the data collection plan

Developing a plan for managing the data collection in any evaluation is part of the planning process. Determining who will gather data, where it will be kept, what the collection

Family Survey

The Infant Development Program at the Sacramento County Office of Education has made some changes in the past several years. These changes were made to improve our programs and services for the children and families that we serve. As someone who participates in our program, we'd like your help in our continuing efforts to improve our services. Please help us determine what we are doing well and what we can do to improve.

Please tell us exactly what you think. What you say will never be identified with you or your child. The information that you provide will only be used to help us do a better job. When you have completed the survey, return it to the evaluators in the enclosed envelope by June 7th.

Thank you for your time and your help. We look forward to receiving your response.

This form is divided into several parts. Each one asks about different parts of the Infant Development Program or about how you and your child have participated in it. Please circle the answer that is closest to your opinion. If there is something that you want to write in, please write it in or put it on the back of a page.

✎ GETTING STARTED IN THE PROGRAM

The very first meeting between your family and the staff of the infant program can be very important. Please think back to the first contacts and meetings you had with the Infant Development Program and give us your impressions.

Circle the number that is closest to your thoughts or feelings.

1. The staff member(s) listened to us.
4	3	2	1	0
Strongly Agree	Agree	Disagree	Strongly Disagree	Not Sure, or Don't Remember

2. After the meeting I understood what the Infant Program had to offer.
4	3	2	1	0
Strongly Agree	Agree	Disagree	Strongly Disagree	Not Sure, or Don't Remember

3. We were given too much information during the first meeting.
4	3	2	1	0
Strongly Agree	Agree	Disagree	Strongly Disagree	Not Sure, or Don't Remember

4. The first meeting was a confusing experience.
4	3	2	1	0
Strongly Agree	Agree	Disagree	Strongly Disagree	Not Sure, or Don't Remember

5. I felt better after the first meeting.
4	3	2	1	0
Strongly Agree	Agree	Disagree	Strongly Disagree	Not Sure, or Don't Remember

6. What do you remember most about your first contacts with Infant Program staff?
   _____
   _____

(continues)

Figure 13.2. Family survey. Copyright Patrick Harrison & Eleanor Lynch. Developed with input from Gary Johnson, administrator, and staff of the Sacramento County Office of Education Infant Development Program.

ASSESSMENTS & UPDATES

The assessment or update process is supposed to help both you and the Infant Program Team members learn more about your child and your family's concerns and priorities.

Think about the last time that your child and family participated in an assessment or update in the Infant Program and answer the questions based on that experience.

Planning for Your Child's Assessment/Update

7. I was encouraged to actively participate in the assessment/update process.
4	3	2	1	0
Strongly Agree	Agree	Disagree	Strongly Disagree	Not Sure, or Don't Remember

8. The staff expected me to participate more in the planning process than I really wanted to.
4	3	2	1	0
Strongly Agree	Agree	Disagree	Strongly Disagree	Not Sure, or Don't Remember

9. The staff did not pay any attention to what I had to say.
4	3	2	1	0
Strongly Agree	Agree	Disagree	Strongly Disagree	Not Sure, or Don't Remember

10. I felt left out of the assessment/update planning process.
4	3	2	1	0
Strongly Agree	Agree	Disagree	Strongly Disagree	Not Sure, or Don't Remember

11. I feel that I understood what was happening during the assessment/update planning process.
4	3	2	1	0
Strongly Agree	Agree	Disagree	Strongly Disagree	Not Sure, or Don't Remember

12. What do you remember most about planning the assessment/update?
    _____
    _____

Your Child's Assessment or Update

13. During the assessment/update the staff seemed to really care about my child.
4	3	2	1	0
Strongly Agree	Agree	Disagree	Strongly Disagree	Not Sure, or Don't Remember

14. The whole assessment/update was a confusing experience.
4	3	2	1	0
Strongly Agree	Agree	Disagree	Strongly Disagree	Not Sure, or Don't Remember

15. I think that the assessment/update that was done on my child was accurate.
4	3	2	1	0
Strongly Agree	Agree	Disagree	Strongly Disagree	Not Sure, or Don't Remember

16. I felt that the information that I shared about my child was an important part of the assessment/update.
4	3	2	1	0
Strongly Agree	Agree	Disagree	Strongly Disagree	Not Sure, or Don't Remember

17. I was involved in the assessment/update.
4	3	2	1	0
Strongly Agree	Agree	Disagree	Strongly Disagree	Not Sure, or Don't Remember

18. My feelings were important to the assessment/update team.
4	3	2	1	0
Strongly Agree	Agree	Disagree	Strongly Disagree	Not Sure, or Don't Remember

(*continues*)

Figure 13.2. continued

19. I learned a lot about my child from the assessment/update

4	3	2	1	0
Strongly Agree	Agree	Disagree	Strongly Disagree	Not Sure, or Don't Remember

20. The staff members explained what they were doing.

4	3	2	1	0
Strongly Agree	Agree	Disagree	Strongly Disagree	Not Sure, or Don't Remember

21. My child's assessment/update was fair.

4	3	2	1	0
Strongly Agree	Agree	Disagree	Strongly Disagree	Not Sure, or Don't Remember

22. What do you remember most about your child's last assessment/update?

    _____

    _____

Sharing Your Family's Concerns and Priorities

23. The staff cared about our whole family.

4	3	2	1	0
Strongly Agree	Agree	Disagree	Strongly Disagree	Not Sure, or Don't Remember

24. The staff tried to help me find the services I requested.

4	3	2	1	0
Strongly Agree	Agree	Disagree	Strongly Disagree	Not Sure, or Don't Remember

25. The staff made suggestions that helped our family.

4	3	2	1	0
Strongly Agree	Agree	Disagree	Strongly Disagree	Not Sure, or Don't Remember

26. The staff listened to me and my family and made suggestions based on what we said.

4	3	2	1	0
Strongly Agree	Agree	Disagree	Strongly Disagree	Not Sure, or Don't Remember

27. The staff asked questions about things that were none of their business.

4	3	2	1	0
Strongly Agree	Agree	Disagree	Strongly Disagree	Not Sure, or Don't Remember

28. The staff's concern for our whole family made me feel good.

4	3	2	1	0
Strongly Agree	Agree	Disagree	Strongly Disagree	Not Sure, or Don't Remember

29. What do you remember most about sharing your family's concerns and priorities with Infant Program staff?

    _____

    _____

✎ DEVELOPING THE INDIVIDUALIZED FAMILY SERVICE PLAN

After the assessment or update, you and some of the Infant Program staff members met to write a plan called an Individualized Family Service Plan or IFSP. The plan describes your child's strengths and needs, your concerns and priorities, and the services that will be provided. Think about the last IFSP meeting that you attended and answer the questions based on your experience.

30. Staff members encouraged me to participate in the IFSP meeting.

4	3	2	1	0
Strongly Agree	Agree	Disagree	Strongly Disagree	Not Sure, or Don't Remember

(continues)

31. I was confused by the technical terms that staff members used.
   | 4 | 3 | 2 | 1 | 0 |
   | Strongly Agree | Agree | Disagree | Strongly Disagree | Not Sure, or Don't Remember |

32. Staff members respected our family's concerns and priorities.
   | 4 | 3 | 2 | 1 | 0 |
   | Strongly Agree | Agree | Disagree | Strongly Disagree | Not Sure, or Don't Remember |

33. I felt left out when the plan was being written.
   | 4 | 3 | 2 | 1 | 0 |
   | Strongly Agree | Agree | Disagree | Strongly Disagree | Not Sure, or Don't Remember |

34. The IFSP is helpful to the staff, but it isn't important to me.
   | 4 | 3 | 2 | 1 | 0 |
   | Strongly Agree | Agree | Disagree | Strongly Disagree | Not Sure, or Don't Remember |

35. Developing the IFSP was a positive process.
   | 4 | 3 | 2 | 1 | 0 |
   | Strongly Agree | Agree | Disagree | Strongly Disagree | Not Sure, or Don't Remember |

36. The IFSP includes the things that I think are most important for my child's development.
   | 4 | 3 | 2 | 1 | 0 |
   | Strongly Agree | Agree | Disagree | Strongly Disagree | Not Sure, or Don't Remember |

37. The IFSP includes things that are important to our whole family.
   | 4 | 3 | 2 | 1 | 0 |
   | Strongly Agree | Agree | Disagree | Strongly Disagree | Not Sure, or Don't Remember |

38. What can you tell us about your experience writing the IFSP that would help us improve our service?

_____
_____

HOME PROGRAM

In a home program, a home visitor from the Infant Program comes to your house regularly to talk with you and work with you and your baby on the things that are included in the IFSP. Think about your experience with a home program and answer the questions based on that experience.

39. I like that I don't have to take my child somewhere else.
   | 4 | 3 | 2 | 1 | 0 |
   | Strongly Agree | Agree | Disagree | Strongly Disagree | Not Sure, or Don't Remember |

40. Home visits give me the opportunity to talk with someone about my child.
   | 4 | 3 | 2 | 1 | 0 |
   | Strongly Agree | Agree | Disagree | Strongly Disagree | Not Sure, or Don't Remember |

41. During home visits we talk about our whole family.
   | 4 | 3 | 2 | 1 | 0 |
   | Strongly Agree | Agree | Disagree | Strongly Disagree | Not Sure, or Don't Remember |

42. During home visits we should talk about my child and not the whole family.
   | 4 | 3 | 2 | 1 | 0 |
   | Strongly Agree | Agree | Disagree | Strongly Disagree | Not Sure, or Don't Remember |

43. The home visitor makes good suggestions.
   | 4 | 3 | 2 | 1 | 0 |
   | Strongly Agree | Agree | Disagree | Strongly Disagree | Not Sure, or Don't Remember |

44. The home visitor understands my child.
   | 4 | 3 | 2 | 1 | 0 |
   | Strongly Agree | Agree | Disagree | Strongly Disagree | Not Sure, or Don't Remember |

(*continues*)

Figure 13.2.   continued

45. The home visitor understands our family.
   | 4 | 3 | 2 | 1 | 0 |
   | Strongly Agree | Agree | Disagree | Strongly Disagree | Not Sure, or Don't Remember |

46. The home visitor comes as often as I would like.
   | 4 | 3 | 2 | 1 | 0 |
   | Strongly Agree | Agree | Disagree | Strongly Disagree | Not Sure, or Don't Remember |

47. The home visitor stays too long.
   | 4 | 3 | 2 | 1 | 0 |
   | Strongly Agree | Agree | Disagree | Strongly Disagree | Not Sure, or Don't Remember |

48. The home visits fit my schedule.
   | 4 | 3 | 2 | 1 | 0 |
   | Strongly Agree | Agree | Disagree | Strongly Disagree | Not Sure, or Don't Remember |

49. I like the privacy of home visits.
   | 4 | 3 | 2 | 1 | 0 |
   | Strongly Agree | Agree | Disagree | Strongly Disagree | Not Sure, or Don't Remember |

50. The home visitor misses too many appointments.
   | 4 | 3 | 2 | 1 | 0 |
   | Strongly Agree | Agree | Disagree | Strongly Disagree | Not Sure, or Don't Remember |

51. The home visitor expects too much of me.
   | 4 | 3 | 2 | 1 | 0 |
   | Strongly Agree | Agree | Disagree | Strongly Disagree | Not Sure, or Don't Remember |

52. I'd like more than my home visitor's opinion on things.
   | 4 | 3 | 2 | 1 | 0 |
   | Strongly Agree | Agree | Disagree | Strongly Disagree | Not Sure, or Don't Remember |

53. I'd rather meet other parents and professionals at a center than have home visits.
   | 4 | 3 | 2 | 1 | 0 |
   | Strongly Agree | Agree | Disagree | Strongly Disagree | Not Sure, or Don't Remember |

54. What advice do you have for us about the Home Program?
   _____
   _____

✏️ PLAY GROUPS

Some children attend group programs with other toddlers. If your child is attending a Play Group or has attended a Play Group that is part of the Sacramento County Infant Program, answer the questions based on your experience.

55. I like having my child with other children.
   | 4 | 3 | 2 | 1 | 0 |
   | Strongly Agree | Agree | Disagree | Strongly Disagree | Not Sure, or Don't Remember |

56. My child likes the Play Group.
   | 4 | 3 | 2 | 1 | 0 |
   | Strongly Agree | Agree | Disagree | Strongly Disagree | Not Sure, or Don't Remember |

57. My child's social skills (playing, getting along with others, sharing) have improved as a result of the Play Group.
   | 4 | 3 | 2 | 1 | 0 |
   | Strongly Agree | Agree | Disagree | Strongly Disagree | Not Sure, or Don't Remember |

58. The length of each Play Group session is about right.
   | 4 | 3 | 2 | 1 | 0 |
   | Strongly Agree | Agree | Disagree | Strongly Disagree | Not Sure, or Don't Remember |

(*continues*)

Figure 13.2. continued

59. Having children the same age without special needs in the Play Group is great.
    | 4 | 3 | 2 | 1 | 0 |
    | Strongly Agree | Agree | Disagree | Strongly Disagree | Not Sure, or Don't Remember |

60. I feel that the other children in the Play Group have more problems than my child.
    | 4 | 3 | 2 | 1 | 0 |
    | Strongly Agree | Agree | Disagree | Strongly Disagree | Not Sure, or Don't Remember |

61. My child's teacher does a good job of communicating with me.
    | 4 | 3 | 2 | 1 | 0 |
    | Strongly Agree | Agree | Disagree | Strongly Disagree | Not Sure, or Don't Remember |

62. The bus that takes my child to and from the Play Group is on time.
    | 4 | 3 | 2 | 1 | 0 |
    | Strongly Agree | Agree | Disagree | Strongly Disagree | Not Sure, or Don't Remember |

63. I am satisifed with the location of the Play Group.
    | 4 | 3 | 2 | 1 | 0 |
    | Strongly Agree | Agree | Disagree | Strongly Disagree | Not Sure, or Don't Remember |

64. If you could tell us one thing that would help us improve the Play Groups, what would it be?
    _____
    _____
    _____
    _____

✎ TRANSITIONS

Programs and services for infants and toddlers sometimes involve lots of changes. Infants often leave the hospital and begin home programs. Toddlers often go to group programs, and at age 3 children begin preschool. Think about the last transition that occurred for you and your child, and answer the questions that follow.

65. What was the last transition? _____

66. Infant Program staff members did a good job of helping us prepare for the transition.
    | 4 | 3 | 2 | 1 | 0 |
    | Strongly Agree | Agree | Disagree | Strongly Disagree | Not Sure, or Don't Remember |

67. I felt well-prepared for the change in my child's program.
    | 4 | 3 | 2 | 1 | 0 |
    | Strongly Agree | Agree | Disagree | Strongly Disagree | Not Sure, or Don't Remember |

68. Staff listened to my concerns during the transition.
    | 4 | 3 | 2 | 1 | 0 |
    | Strongly Agree | Agree | Disagree | Strongly Disagree | Not Sure, or Don't Remember |

69. Staff members followed up to make sure that the new program or service was working for my child and our family.
    | 4 | 3 | 2 | 1 | 0 |
    | Strongly Agree | Agree | Disagree | Strongly Disagree | Not Sure, or Don't Remember |

70. What advice can you give us to help improve the transition process?
    _____
    _____
    _____

(continues)

Figure 13.2. continued

FAMILY/PROFESSIONAL COLLABORATION

One of the goals of the Infant Program is to work with families in a positive, cooperative partnership. Think about all of your experiences with the Infant Program and its staff and answer the questions based on your experiences.

71. Staff members are easy to talk to.
    - 4 Strongly Agree
    - 3 Agree
    - 2 Disagree
    - 1 Strongly Disagree
    - 0 Not Sure, or Don't Remember

72. The policies and procedures seem to be family friendly.
    - 4 Strongly Agree
    - 3 Agree
    - 2 Disagree
    - 1 Strongly Disagree
    - 0 Not Sure, or Don't Remember

73. Whenever there is a problem, I feel that the staff member will work with me to solve it.
    - 4 Strongly Agree
    - 3 Agree
    - 2 Disagree
    - 1 Strongly Disagree
    - 0 Not Sure, or Don't Remember

74. Staff members are advocates for my child and me.
    - 4 Strongly Agree
    - 3 Agree
    - 2 Disagree
    - 1 Strongly Disagree
    - 0 Not Sure, or Don't Remember

75. There are opportunities for me to meet and talk with other parents.
    - 4 Strongly Agree
    - 3 Agree
    - 2 Disagree
    - 1 Strongly Disagree
    - 0 Not Sure, or Don't Remember

76. Staff members sometimes "talk down" to me.
    - 4 Strongly Agree
    - 3 Agree
    - 2 Disagree
    - 1 Strongly Disagree
    - 0 Not Sure, or Don't Remember

77. Sometimes I feel that staff members don't realize that my entire life can't revolve around my child with special needs.
    - 4 Strongly Agree
    - 3 Agree
    - 2 Disagree
    - 1 Strongly Disagree
    - 0 Not Sure, or Don't Remember

78. Staff members support me and the decisions that I make.
    - 4 Strongly Agree
    - 3 Agree
    - 2 Disagree
    - 1 Strongly Disagree
    - 0 Not Sure, or Don't Remember

79. The Infant Program has helped me feel more confident about my own opinions.
    - 4 Strongly Agree
    - 3 Agree
    - 2 Disagree
    - 1 Strongly Disagree
    - 0 Not Sure, or Don't Remember

80. The Infant Program has helped me become a better advocate for my child.
    - 4 Strongly Agree
    - 3 Agree
    - 2 Disagree
    - 1 Strongly Disagree
    - 0 Not Sure, or Don't Remember

81. If another parent asked you about the Sacramento County Infant Program, what would you tell them?
    _____
    _____

SOME INFORMATION ABOUT YOU & YOUR CHILD

Check the response that applies for each question.

82. What is your relationship to the child in the Infant Program?
    - ____ Mother
    - ____ Father
    - ____ Foster Mother
    - ____ Foster Father
    - ____ Grandmother
    - ____ Grandfather
    - ____ Aunt
    - ____ Uncle
    - ____ Other: Relationship? _____

(continues)

Figure 13.2. continued

83. What is your age?

　　___ Under 18　　　___ 35–39　　　___ 55–59
　　___ 19–24　　　　___ 40–44　　　___ 60–64
　　___ 25–29　　　　___ 45–49　　　___ 65 and above
　　___ 30–34　　　　___ 50–54

84. How old is your child?

　　___ Under 6 mos.　　　　___ 19–24 mos.
　　___ 7–12 mos.　　　　　 ___ 25–30 mos.
　　___ 13–18 mos.　　　　　___ 31–36 mos.

85. Do you consider your child's special needs to be:

　　___ Minimal　　　___ Moderate　　　___ Significant

86. Please check the diagnoses that have been used to describe your child's special needs.

　　___ Developmental delay　　　　　___ Cerebral palsy
　　___ Down syndrome　　　　　　　 ___ Medically fragile
　　___ Blind or visually impaired　　 ___ Deaf or hard of hearing
　　___ Other: What? _____

87. How long has your child been in the Infant Program?

　　___ Less than 1 yr.　　___ 1 to 2 yrs.　　___ 2 to 3 yrs.

88. What language do you speak most often at home?

　　___ English　　___ Spanish　　___ Vietnamese　　___ Other: _____

89. How would you describe your race or ethnicity?

　　___ African American　　　　　　　　___ Hispanic, Of any Race
　　___ American Indian, Eskimo, Aleut　 ___ White, Non-Hispanic
　　___ Asian　　　　　　　　　　　　　___ Other: _____

90. Which Infant Program staff member have you worked with the most? _____

Thank you for your time and your thoughts. We will use this information to review our program and improve our programs and services.

Figure 13.2. continued

schedules should be, who will enter or collate data for analysis, and so forth requires that the program administrator and the internal or external evaluator work together to develop a plan. Preplanning these details ensures the best data collection procedures while minimizing disruption of the program. Table 13.2 presents a sample form that might be used to help organize the data collection.

Reviewing the evaluation plan

Plan review may be done at several levels. Program administrators who have not had staff involvement in the development of the evaluation may want to review the whole plan with staff members. Sharing this information can result in greater cooperation and will certainly reduce anxiety about what information is being collected and how it will

PARENT QUESTIONNAIRE

Assessment Process

1. Did your child receive a complete assessment?
   ☐ yes   ☐ no

2. Please rate the usefulness of the following aspects of the evaluation:

	very useful	somewhat useful	not useful
a. Bayley Scales of Infant Development	☐	☐	☐
b. Evaluations by staff members	☐	☐	☐

3. Was there any other aspect or tool of the assessment that was useful to you? If so, please explain.
   _____
   _____

4. Was there any other aspect or tool of the assessment that was not useful to you? If so, please explain.
   _____
   _____

5. Were the results of the assessment discussed with you?
   ☐ yes   ☐ no

6. If so, did the discussion include goals for the specific areas of concern you were interested in?
   ☐ yes   ☐ no

7. After the discussion, how would you rate your understanding of your child's level of functioning (in terms of strengths and weaknesses)?
   ☐ a. much better informed   ☐ c. no change
   ☐ b. better informed   ☐ d. more confused

8. Please rate the quality of assessment in each of the following areas:

	excellent	good	fair	poor
a. cognition	☐	☐	☐	☐
b. gross motor	☐	☐	☐	☐
c. fine motor	☐	☐	☐	☐
d. speech and language	☐	☐	☐	☐
e. feeding	☐	☐	☐	☐
f. social/emotional	☐	☐	☐	☐

Intervention

1. What for you have been the most important aspects of the ISIS program? _____
   _____

2. What have been the least meaningful aspects of the program? _____
   _____

(continues)

Figure 13.3. Parent questionnaire. Developed by Patrick Harrison and the staff of Integrated Infant Services (ISIS).

3. Have you encountered any problems while participating in the ISIS program? _____

4. If so, please list them: _____

5. How did ISIS staff respond to these problems?
   a. Was staff available?   ☐ yes   ☐ no
   b. Did staff listen?   ☐ yes   ☐ no
   c. Did you feel staff understood?   ☐ yes   ☐ no
   d. Did staff help to devise a solution?   ☐ yes   ☐ no
   e. Other—please explain: _____

6. As your child's needs changed, did the ISIS program change accordingly? ☐ yes   ☐ no

7. If yes, how? Please check below any that apply.
   ☐ increase or decrease in home visits
   ☐ staff visited child and parent when hospitalized
   ☐ staff was available by phone when needed
   ☐ intervention changed with my child's development
   ☐ other—please explain: _____

The ISIS program includes both classroom work and home visits. In order that we might evaluate the effectiveness of each, please answer the following questions.

8. Are there aspects of the home visit program that you find especially useful to you? If so, please explain: _____

9. Are there aspects of the home visit program that are not useful to you? If so, please explain: _____

10. Are there aspects of the classroom program that are especially useful to you? If so, please explain: _____

11. Are there aspects of the classroom program that are not useful to you? If so, please explain: _____

12. Were there any particular times one aspect was more helpful than the other? ☐ yes   ☐ no
    If yes, please explain: _____

(continues)

Figure 13.3. continued

13. Please rate the overall degree of helpfulness of each aspect of the program.

	very helpful	somewhat helpful	not helpful
a. home visit	☐	☐	☐
b. classroom	☐	☐	☐

14. Are there any changes that you would like to see in either aspect of the program? ☐ yes ☐ no

    If yes, what would they be? _____
    _____
    _____

    How would these changes be helpful to you? _____
    _____
    _____

Work with Health Care Providers and Outside Agencies

1. Please rate the level of communication and collaboration between ISIS staff and outside agencies and practitioners:

   ☐ excellent   ☐ good   ☐ fair   ☐ poor   ☐ nonexistent

2. Please rate how well ISIS staff have used information from outside agencies and practitioners in the program they devised for you and your child.

   ☐ very well   ☐ somewhat well
   ☐ not very well   ☐ not at all well

3. Please check any of the statements below that are true. Check below any that apply.

   ☐ My doctors are aware I'm attending the ISIS program.
   ☐ ISIS staff calls doctor(s) and agencies.
   ☐ ISIS staff accompanies me on appointments.
   ☐ ISIS staff sends reports to my doctors and agencies.
   ☐ Other people I'm involved with have visited the program.
   ☐ Other—please explain: _____
   _____
   _____

4. Has ISIS staff referred you to any outside agencies or medical practitioners? ☐ yes ☐ no

   If yes, did you use the referral? ☐ yes ☐ no

   What was your overall impression of the resource?
   ☐ very pleased   ☐ somewhat pleased   ☐ neutral
   ☐ somewhat disappointed   ☐ very disappointed

   If no, would you like for the staff to refer you to an outside agency or medical practitioner? ☐ yes ☐ no

   If yes, what would be your area of concern? _____
   _____

Figure 13.3. continued

Community Survey Form

1. Have you heard of Project ISIS (Integrated Special Infant Services)? ☐ yes ☐ no
   If no, please skip to quesiton #9.

2. Please check those services you believe Project ISIS provides:
   a. Services to children in the first few months of life? ☐
   b. Services to children "at risk" for developmental problems? ☐
   c. Services to children who are disabled? ☐
   d. Services to enhance the parent–child relationship? ☐

3. Where did you first learn of Project ISIS? _____

4. How have you been involved with Project ISIS (check any that apply)?
   made a referral ☐
   visited the project ☐
   share a client or patient ☐
   other, please specify ☐ _____

5. What is your overall impression of Project ISIS?
   very positive ☐   positive ☐   neutral ☐
   negative ☐   very negative ☐

6. Please name any specific strengths or weaknesses of the project:
   _____
   _____
   _____
   _____

7. Project ISIS has included services to "high-risk" children. Please let us know the three highest areas of need you see for this population.
   1 _____
   2 _____
   3 _____

8. Based on your experience with Project ISIS, please check the quality of services in each area.

	1 High	2 Average	3 Poor
a. Child assessment	☐	☐	☐
b. Intervention with child	☐	☐	☐
c. Addressing needs of both parents and child	☐	☐	☐
d. Involving parents in the child's program	☐	☐	☐
e. Coordinating services with other professionals	☐	☐	☐

9. Would you like to receive a brochure describing the services available through Project ISIS? ☐ yes ☐ no

10. Please help us by indicating the following:
    Type or name of agency responding _____

    Discipline of person responding _____

Figure 13.4. Community survey form. Developed by Patrick Harrison and the staff of Integrated Special Infant Services (ISIS).

District and Agency Survey

The Infant Development Program at the Sacramento County Office of Education is continuing to work toward improving its programs and services for infants, toddlers, and their families. As a part of this, many components of the program are currently being evaluated. This evaluation is designed to examine the relationships that the Infant Program has with school districts and agencies with whom they work. As someone who works with the Infant Program, your feedback is extremely important. Please be candid. Your responses will never be identified with you, and only aggregated data will be presented to Infant Program staff and administration. When you have completed the survey, return it to the evaluators in the enclosed envelope by June 17th.

Thank you for your time and your help. We look forward to receiving your response.

==

This form is divided into several parts. Each one asks about different aspects of the relationship that you have with the Infant Development Program related to transitions or in day-to-day coordination and collaboration around the children and families that you serve. Please circle the answer that is closest to your opinion. If there is something that you want to add, please write it in or put it on the back of a page.

COORDINATION ACTIVITIES

Circle the number that is closest to your thoughts or feelings.

1. There is good communication between me and the Infant Program staff.
4	3	2	1	0
Strongly Agree	Agree	Disagree	Strongly Disagree	Not Sure, or Don't Remember

2. There is good communication between my district/agency and the Infant Program.
4	3	2	1	0
Strongly Agree	Agree	Disagree	Strongly Disagree	Not Sure, or Don't Remember

3. Most of the time Infant Program staff and staff from my district/agency seem to be working collaboratively.
4	3	2	1	0
Strongly Agree	Agree	Disagree	Strongly Disagree	Not Sure, or Don't Remember

4. When activities need to be coordinated between my district/agency and the Infant Program such as in the transition process, there are clear procedures that we follow.
4	3	2	1	0
Strongly Agree	Agree	Disagree	Strongly Disagree	Not Sure, or Don't Remember

5. Territorial issues sometimes interfere with coordination.
4	3	2	1	0
Strongly Agree	Agree	Disagree	Strongly Disagree	Not Sure, or Don't Remember

6. Families would probably say that the Infant Program and our district or agency are doing a good job of working together.
4	3	2	1	0
Strongly Agree	Agree	Disagree	Strongly Disagree	Not Sure, or Don't Remember

7. What advice would you like to give to the Infant Program to improve coordination activities with you or your district/agency?

   _____
   _____

(continues)

Figure 13.5. District and agency survey form. Copyright Patrick Harrison & Eleanor Lynch. Developed with input from Gary Johnson, administrator, and staff of the Sacramento County Office of Education Infant Development Program.

✎ COLLABORATION ACTIVITIES

8. The Infant Program seems to work collaboratively with families.
   | 4 | 3 | 2 | 1 | 0 |
   | Strongly Agree | Agree | Disagree | Strongly Disagree | Not Sure, or Don't Remember |

9. When my district/agency and the Infant Program are both working with families and their children, we are typically working on mutual goals.
   | 4 | 3 | 2 | 1 | 0 |
   | Strongly Agree | Agree | Disagree | Strongly Disagree | Not Sure, or Don't Remember |

10. I don't feel that I have time to collaborate.
    | 4 | 3 | 2 | 1 | 0 |
    | Strongly Agree | Agree | Disagree | Strongly Disagree | Not Sure, or Don't Remember |

11. My district's/agency's rules and regulations make it difficult to collaborate.
    | 4 | 3 | 2 | 1 | 0 |
    | Strongly Agree | Agree | Disagree | Strongly Disagree | Not Sure, or Don't Remember |

12. Collaboration with the Infant Program is increasing.
    | 4 | 3 | 2 | 1 | 0 |
    | Strongly Agree | Agree | Disagree | Strongly Disagree | Not Sure, or Don't Remember |

13. Name one thing that the Infant Program staff or administration could do to improve collaboration with you and/or your district/agency.

    _____
    _____
    _____

✎ FOLLOW-THROUGH

14. The Infant Program staff follow through on their commitments to families.
    | 4 | 3 | 2 | 1 | 0 |
    | Strongly Agree | Agree | Disagree | Strongly Disagree | Not Sure, or Don't Remember |

15. The Infant Program staff follow through on their commitments to my district/agency.
    | 4 | 3 | 2 | 1 | 0 |
    | Strongly Agree | Agree | Disagree | Strongly Disagree | Not Sure, or Don't Remember |

16. My district/agency follows through when working with families.
    | 4 | 3 | 2 | 1 | 0 |
    | Strongly Agree | Agree | Disagree | Strongly Disagree | Not Sure, or Don't Remember |

17. My district/agency follows through when working with staff at the Infant Program.
    | 4 | 3 | 2 | 1 | 0 |
    | Strongly Agree | Agree | Disagree | Strongly Disagree | Not Sure, or Don't Remember |

18. What would you suggest to improve the follow-through between the Infant Program and your district/agency?

    _____
    _____
    _____
    _____

(continues)

Figure 13.5. continued

✎ TRANSITION ISSUES

19. Infant Program staff members work with family members to help them plan for their child's transition.
4	3	2	1	0
Strongly Agree	Agree	Disagree	Strongly Disagree	Not Sure, or Don't Remember

20. Infant Program staff members typically work with me or other members of my district's/agency's staff to ensure a smooth transition.
4	3	2	1	0
Strongly Agree	Agree	Disagree	Strongly Disagree	Not Sure, or Don't Remember

21. My district/agency encourages me to participate with Infant Program staff to plan for transitions.
4	3	2	1	0
Strongly Agree	Agree	Disagree	Strongly Disagree	Not Sure, or Don't Remember

22. Transition planning between the Infant Program and my district/agency is usually done in a timely manner.
4	3	2	1	0
Strongly Agree	Agree	Disagree	Strongly Disagree	Not Sure, or Don't Remember

23. Transition planning between the Infant Program and my district/agency is usually done efficiently.
4	3	2	1	0
Strongly Agree	Agree	Disagree	Strongly Disagree	Not Sure, or Don't Remember

24. My district/agency works effectively with Infant Program staff and families to develop a transition plan.
4	3	2	1	0
Strongly Agree	Agree	Disagree	Strongly Disagree	Not Sure, or Don't Remember

25. Families would probably say that the transition between the Infant Program and my district's/agency's program is smooth and comfortable for them.
4	3	2	1	0
Strongly Agree	Agree	Disagree	Strongly Disagree	Not Sure, or Don't Remember

26. If you could change one thing in the transition process that you think would make it more effective, what would it be?

    _____

    _____

✎ GENERAL ISSUES

27. The philosophies of the Infant Program and my district/agency are very similar.
4	3	2	1	0
Strongly Agree	Agree	Disagree	Strongly Disagree	Not Sure, or Don't Remember

28. Infant Program staff have trouble letting go of the children and families that they serve.
4	3	2	1	0
Strongly Agree	Agree	Disagree	Strongly Disagree	Not Sure, or Don't Remember

29. My district/agency has a lot more rules and regulations about services than the Infant Program has.
4	3	2	1	0
Strongly Agree	Agree	Disagree	Strongly Disagree	Not Sure, or Don't Remember

30. My district/agency recognizes that collaboration takes time and provides time for that in my schedule.
4	3	2	1	0
Strongly Agree	Agree	Disagree	Strongly Disagree	Not Sure, or Don't Remember

(continues)

Figure 13.5.   continued

31. The Infant Program expects us to provide things for children and families that we can't provide.
        4   3   2   1   0
    Strongly Agree   Agree   Disagree   Strongly Disagree   Not Sure, or Don't Remember

32. There are specific staff in the Infant Program that I know and rely on.
        4   3   2   1   0
    Strongly Agree   Agree   Disagree   Strongly Disagree   Not Sure, or Don't Remember

✎ DEMOGRAPHIC INFORMATION

Check the response that applies.

33. What is your role?
    ____ Teacher   ____ Principal   ____ Social Worker
    ____ Nurse   ____ Psychologist   ____ Speech and Language Therapist
    ____ Other: What? _____

34. In what setting do you work?
    ____ School   ____ Regional Center   ____ Health Center
    ____ Other: What? _____

35. How much contact have you had with the Infant Program?
    ____ Very little   ____ Some   ____ A great deal

36. Which individual in the Infant Program have you worked with the most?
    _____

Thank you for your time and your thoughts. The information will be used to improve relationships between the Infant Program and the districts and agencies with whom they work.

Please return your completed survey in the enclosed, self-addressed, stamped envelope.

Figure 13.5. *continued*

---

be used. Program administrators may also elect to share evaluation plans with their boards or supervisors, whose input could be used to improve the plans and to get their "buy in" and cooperation.

Conducting Evaluations

Data gathering and examination consist of two steps: (a) data collection and (b) data analysis. Each of these is discussed briefly in the paragraphs that follow.

Data collection

The best evaluation plan can be jeopardized by carelessness in the data collection procedures (Law & Fowle, 1979). In addition to the plan outlined in the previous section and depicted in Table 13.2, attention must be given to several other aspects of the process. Data collectors should be trained in the use of the instruments. If the instruments that assess child and family progress are used routinely in the program, it is assumed that those using them are well trained. However, if the instruments are new to the program or if staff

Table 13.2. Sample Evaluation Plan Organizer

Instrument(s)	Date of Collection	Person(s) Responsible	Deadline Date	Percent Returned
Battelle Developmental Inventory (Newborg et al., 1984)	January	Child's primary interventionist	1/30	
Battelle Developmental Inventory	June	Child's primary interventionist	6/30	
Checklist of Family Concerns and Priorities	January	Family coordinator	1/30	
Checklist of Family Concerns and Priorities	June	Family coordinator	6/30	
Family Satisfaction Survey	November	Program administrator	11/30	
Agency Satisfaction Interviews	November	External evaluator	11/30	
Per capita cost analysis for fiscal year	September	Agency accounts officer	9/30	NA

members unfamiliar with the instruments or general measurement and evaluation procedures are helping with data collection, personnel must be trained. Training should include ample supervised practice to ensure that participants are using the instruments correctly.

If any of the data collection procedures require cooperation and coordination from others, these individuals should be informed in advance and all of the arrangements confirmed in writing. It is especially important when contacting other agencies and families that their time be respected and efficiently used. If permissions from families or clearances from human subjects committees are required, they too should be obtained well ahead of the actual data collection.

All data returned for analysis should be checked for completeness and accuracy. For example, any calculations of scores should be double-checked to avoid errors, and omitted items should be noted. If computer analysis is to be used, preparing clear and clean copies of the data to be entered helps prevent entry errors.

Because of the diversity of families served in early intervention, programs have found that face-to-face data collection strategies must be used. Structured interviews or written questionnaires that are presented orally in the family's primary language reduce difficulties for families whose primary language is not English as well as those families who have limited literacy. However, programs must consider who will conduct these interviews, because using a staff member immediately biases the response.

Finally, the entire data collection process needs to be monitored by the evaluator and/or program administrator. Checking on progress prior to deadlines, determining whether additional resources are needed, and demonstrating the importance of the evaluation through concern also contribute to an exemplary evaluation.

Data analysis

The method of data analysis selected depends upon the kinds of data that are collected and on how the information is to be used. In the earlier section on Developing an Evaluation Design, the major statistical treatments were mentioned. The analysis is another area in which a professional trained in evaluation can provide useful suggestions to program administrators.

Within the past several years a number of excellent statistical packages have been developed for microcomputers. The programs—for example, StatView (Haycock, Roth, Gagnon, Finzer, & Soper, 1992) and StatWorks (Rafferty, Norling, Tamaru, McMath, & Morganstein, 1985)—are relatively low in cost, are user friendly, and provide excellent analysis capabilities.

The analysis of qualitative data such as focus groups, ethnographies, or eco-mapping requires different procedures than empirical data. If qualitative measures are used, it is important to work with someone who is trained and experienced in the analysis. As mentioned previously, what appears to be an easy procedure actually involves many steps and considerable rigor.

Using Evaluation Data

Reporting evaluation findings and using evaluation results constitute the final phases of evaluation. The responsibility for each often resides with a different person, but each is an important aspect of the process.

Reporting findings

The evaluator is typically charged with the task of presenting evaluation findings in a way that is easy for readers to understand and use. In Popham's (1988) words, "the job of preparing evaluation reports should not be approached offhandedly" (p. 249). Because a major goal of the report is to provide findings in a manner that will facilitate decision making, clarity is of utmost importance. Report readers tend to be busy people who are often unacquainted with some of the technical jargon of evaluation; a clear, succinct report formatted so that the most important findings and recommendations are highlighted is more likely to be used than a long, academic tome.

It is also the evaluator's responsibility to interpret the findings. Particularly if statistical tests are used, it is important to explain what they mean. Providing a reader with reams of data that are not chunked into logical segments and interpreted in relation to the evaluation questions is an unacceptable practice.

It is the evaluator's job to make data-based recommendations for action. These recommendations should follow logically from the findings and should be presented in non-judgmental terms. Often the major findings and recommendations are summarized in one or two pages called an executive summary and appended to the front of the full report. This technique is an excellent strategy for calling attention to the most important findings. It also provides the program administrator with a short document that can more easily be disseminated to staff, families, supervisors, and others.

Implicit in this discussion is the understanding that evaluation reports are the property of the client who is having the evaluation conducted. The same rules of confidentiality apply as apply to other records. In other words, the program administrator can expect that her or his relationship with an external evaluator is privileged and that the evaluator will not share information with others. In some instances the evaluator may be interested in presenting evaluation findings at professional meetings or preparing them for publication in professional journals. Such requests are appropriate, and dissemination of exemplary evaluations should be encouraged; however, it is the client's right to ask that nothing about the evaluation be made public.

Applying evaluation findings

The most significant evaluation findings are meaningless unless they are used to improve programs and practices. Just as it is the evaluator's job to plan and conduct an exemplary evaluation and present the findings in a usable format, it is the decision maker's responsibility to see that findings are disseminated and used to reinforce effective practices and upgrade or change those that are ineffective.

Summary

Evaluation provides information that enables staff, families, program administrators, legislators, and the public to make informed decisions about program effectiveness. The findings of well-planned and well-conceptualized evaluations are critical to developing exemplary programs. Evaluations can be designed to answer a broad range of questions including those about implementation; resources; outcomes; validity, educational focus, and philosophy; satisfaction; cost; and what is actually occurring as a result of the program.

Approaches to evaluation are sometimes described as formative or summative. Formative evaluations tend to be more internal to the organization, and their findings are more often used to make midcourse corrections and shape the program as it goes. Summative evaluations present the overall results at the end of a program or project. However, these distinctions are not as clear-cut as they may sound. Summative evaluations are often used to guide the development of new cycles of a program.

Many evaluation models have been designed for various purposes. Those discussed in this chapter include goal-attainment models, judgmental models emphasizing inputs, judgmental models emphasizing outputs, decision-facilitation models, and naturalistic models. The model that is selected depends in large measure on the questions being asked.

To ensure that an evaluation is well conceived and conducted, a number of steps should be followed. These steps are generally organized around the three major phases of the evaluation: planning, conducting, and using evaluation findings. The planning phase includes determining what should be evaluated, determining the target audience and how the information will be used, developing evaluation questions, developing an evaluation design, selecting or developing instruments, developing the data collection plan, and reviewing that plan. Conducting the evaluation generally consists of two steps: collecting and analyzing the data. The final phase, using evaluation findings, includes reporting and utilizing the evaluation results. In each of these phases there is an important role for families.

Evaluation provides a means to examine program effectiveness and improve practice and is an important aspect of all exemplary early intervention programs.

Preferred Practices

The following questions can be used to review evaluation plans for an early intervention program.

1. What components of the program should be evaluated?

2. Can the program contract with an external evaluator to conduct or provide assistance with the evaluation?

3. What should the evaluation focus on (e.g., questions of resources, philosophy, implementation, etc.)?

4. Is the information to be used formatively or summatively?

5. What model of evaluation is most appropriate for the kinds of questions being asked?

6. Has a comprehensive evaluation plan been written?
7. Are the individuals who will be collecting the data adequately trained?
8. Have procedures for data collection, storage, and management been made?
9. Has the type of report required been specified?
10. Have previous evaluation findings been used to improve the program's effectiveness?
11. Who will use the findings of the evaluation and how will they be used?
12. Are family members included in the development, implementation, and use of the evaluation?

References

Bricker, D., & Littman, D. (1982). Intervention and education: The inseparable mix. *Topics in Early Childhood Special Education, 1,* 23–33.

Brinkerhoff, R. O., Brethower, D. M., Hluchyj, T., & Nowakowski, J. R. (1983). *Program evaluation—A practitioner's guide for trainers and educators.* Boston: Kluwer-Nijhoff.

Brotherson, M. J. (1994). Interactive focus group interviewing: A qualitative research method in early intervention. *Topics in Early Childhood Special Education, 14,* 101–118.

Brown, L., Branston-McLean, M. B., Baumgart, D., Vincent, L., Falvey, M., & Schroeder, J. (1979). Using the characteristics of current and subsequent least restrictive environments in the development of curricular content for severely handicapped students. *AAESPH Review, 4,* 407–424.

Campbell, D. T., & Stanley, J. C. (1963). *Experimental and quasi-experimental designs for research.* Chicago: Rand McNally.

Charles, C. M. (1988). *Introduction to educational research.* New York: Longman.

Fitz-Gibbon, C. T., & Morris, L. L. (1987). *How to design a program evaluation.* Beverly Hills, CA: Sage.

Garber, H. L. (1988). *The Milwaukee Project—Preventing mental retardation in children at risk.* Washington, DC: American Association on Mental Retardation.

Haycock, K. A., Roth, J., Gagnon, J., Finzer, W. F., & Soper, C. (1992). *Abacus Concepts, StatView* [Computer program]. Berkeley, CA: Abacus Concepts.

Holvoet, J., Guess, D., Mulligan, M., & Brown, F. (1980). The Individualized Curriculum Sequencing Model (II): A teaching strategy for severely handicapped students. *Journal of the Association for the Severely Handicapped, 5,* 337–351.

Johnson, L. J. (1988). Program evaluation: The key to quality programming. In J. B. Jordan, J. J. Gallagher, P. L. Hutinger, & M. B. Karnes (Eds.), *Early childhood special education: Birth to three.* Reston, VA: Council for Exceptional Children.

Karnes, M. B. (Ed.). (1981). Efficacy studies in early childhood special education [Special issue]. *Journal of the Division of Early Childhood, 4.*

Krueger, R. A. (1994). *Focus groups: A practical guide for applied research.* Thousand Oaks, CA: Sage.

Law, A. I., & Fowle, C. M. (1979). *Program evaluator's guide—The evaluation improvement program.* Princeton, NJ: Educational Testing Service.

Lazar, I., Darlington, R., Murray, H., Royce, J., & Snipper, A. (1982). Lasting effects of early education: A report from the consortium for longitudinal studies. *Monographs of the Society for Research in Child Development, 47*(2–3, Serial No. 195).

Levin, H. M. (1983). *Cost-effectiveness—A primer.* Beverly Hills, CA: Sage.

Lincoln, Y. S., & Guba, E. G. (1985). *Naturalistic inquiry.* Beverly Hills, CA: Sage.

Linder, T. W. (1983). *Early childhood special education: Program development and administration.* Baltimore: Brookes.

Newborg, J., Stock, J., Wnek, L., Guidubaldi, J., & Svinicki, J. (1984). *Battelle Development Inventory.* Chicago: Riverside.

Odom, S. L., & Shuster, S. K. (1986). Naturalistic inquiry and the assessment of young handicapped children and their families. *Topics in Early Childhood Special Education, 6*(2), 68–82.

Popham, W. J. (1988). *Educational evaluation* (2nd ed.). Englewood Cliffs, NJ: Prentice-Hall.

Provus, M. (1971). *Discrepancy evaluation for educational program improvement and assessment.* Berkeley, CA: McCutchan.

Rafferty, J., Norling, R., Tamaru, R., McMath, C., & Morganstein, D. (1985). *StatWorks* [Computer program manual]. Philadelphia: Cricket Software. (Available from 3508 Market St., Suite 206, Philadelphia, PA 19104)

Schweinhart, L. J., & Weikart, D. P. (1981). Effects of the Perry Preschool Program on youths through age 15. *Journal of the Division for Early Childhood, 4*, 29–39.

Schweinhart, L. J., & Weikart, D. P. (1993). Success by empowerment: The high/scope Perry preschool study through age 27. *Young Children, 49*(1), 54–58.

Sheehan, R., & Gallagher, R. J. (1983). Conducting evaluations of early intervention programs. In S. G. Garwood & R. R. Fewell (Eds.), *Educating handicapped infants* (pp. 495–524). Rockville, MD: Aspen.

Skeels, H. M. (1966). Adult status of children with contrasting early life experiences. *Monographs of the Society for Research in Child Development, 31*(3, Serial No. 105).

Skeels, H. M., & Dye, H. B. (1939). A study of the effects of differential stimulation on mentally retarded children. *Proceedings of the American Association on Mental Deficiency, 44*, 114–136.

Stufflebeam, D. L., & Guba, E. (1970). *Strategies for the institutionalization of the CIPP evaluation model.* Paper presented at the 11th Annual Phi Delta Kappa Symposium on Education Research, Columbus, OH.

Sudman, S., & Bradburn, N. M. (1982). *Asking questions.* San Francisco: Jossey-Bass.

Summers, J. A., Dell'Oliver, C., Turnbull, A. P., Benson, H. A., Santelli, E., Campbell, M., & Siegel-Causey, E. (1990). Examining the Individualized Family Service Plan process: What are family and practitioner preferences? *Topics in Early Childhood Special Education, 10*, 78–99.

Takanishi, R., & Feshbach, N. D. (1982). Early childhood special education programs, evaluation, and social policies. *Topics in Early Childhood Special Education, 1*, 1–9.

Wehman, P., Schleinen, S., & Kiernan, J. (1980). Age appropriate recreation programs for severely handicapped youth and adults. *Journal of the Association for the Severely Handicapped, 5*, 395–407.

Wolery, M. (Ed.). (1994). Methodological issues and advances [Special issue]. *Topics in Early Childhood Special Education, 14.*

Yavorsky, D. K. (1984). *Discrepancy evaluation: A practitioner's guide.* Charlottesville: Evaluation Research Center, School of Education, University of Virginia.

Selected Readings

Campbell, D. T., & Stanley, J. C. (1963). *Experimental and quasi-experimental designs for research.* Rand McNally.

Converse, J. M. (1986). *Survey questions—Handcrafting the standardized questionnaire.* Beverly Hills, CA: Sage.

Fitz-Gibbon, C. T., & Morris, L. L. (1987). *How to design a program evaluation.* Beverly Hills, CA: Sage.

Henerson, M. E. (1987). *How to measure attitudes.* Beverly Hills, CA: Sage.

King, J. A., Morris, L. L., & Fitz-Gibbon, C. T. (1987). *How to assess program implementation.* Beverly Hills, CA: Sage.

Krueger, R. A. (1994). *Focus groups: A practical guide for applied research.* Thousand Oaks, CA: Sage.

Levin, H. M. (1983). *Cost-effectiveness—A primer.* Beverly Hills, CA: Sage.

McWilliam, P., & Winton, P. (1991). *Brass tacks: A self-rating of family-centered practices in early intervention.* Chapel Hill: Frank Porter Graham Child Development Center, University of North Carolina at Chapel Hill.

Morris, L. L., Fitz-Gibbon, C. T., & Freeman, M. E. (1987). *How to communicate evaluation findings.* Beverly Hills, CA: Sage.

Patton, M. Q. (1990). *Qualitative evaluation and research methods* (2nd ed.). Newbury Park, CA: Sage.

Stecher, B. M., & Davis, W. A. (1987). *How to focus an evaluation.* Beverly Hills, CA: Sage.

Epilogue: Looking Back on Early Intervention from the Family's Perspective

I realize now that I would not change my challenges for anyone else's. As I look back now, I do not know whether I would have chosen this path, but it has certainly caused a lot of growth in our relationships and our family. I had to become more aggressive and determined, and that has really helped with the other kids. We have also crossed paths with many people we would never have had the privilege of knowing. And our other children are much more sensitive to everyone, not just kids with special needs, than most of their peers are.

We do not know what is down the road, so we take one step at a time. I could stew and fret continually, but then I would not have enough energy to do what needs to be done....

No one knows the child as well as the parents, and they must stand up for the child, because no one else is going to. They must get involved and make changes and make it better for their child. We have truly learned the meaning of "Life (happiness) is a journey, not a destination."

(NayDean Daily, parent,
in Hanson, 1987, p. 2)

We knew that it would be hard work. But we knew that Mellissa needed us. More than her brothers who would learn to walk and talk even without us. We began giving her mental and physical stimulation when she was 10 days old. And what a wonderful, loving child she's turning into.

(*This Baby Needs You Even More*, pamphlet,
National Down Syndrome Society)

The best thing we did for both Robbie and ourselves was to get him into an infant development program. It's so easy to sit home and tell yourself that he is just a baby and there is plenty of time for school. There isn't. We were taught ways of playing with Robbie so as not to increase the stiffness in his limbs along with a physical therapy program of exercises. We learned how to assess his present developmental skills, how to set goals for future tasks . . . , and how to encourage achievement of these milestones. Most important, we got to know our son and assumed some control of his development and future.

I'm not going to say that we're not still frustrated at times and that doing his "homework" is all fun and games; it isn't. In fact, it's a lot of work. We are always conscious of what Robbie is doing and how he is doing it. We don't like the fact that our child has problems—no one does—but working with Robbie and teaching him new things has helped relieve our feelings of inadequacy. And sharing our frustrations by talking with other parents in the program lets us know we are not alone....

We realize that the education of parents in teaching and working for their child is that child's only hope. We see Robbie smile while playing with his trucks, and we want to share the joy.

(Laura Repke, parent, in
Hanson & Harris, 1986, p. 5)

We also have a deep sense of contentment with our early intervention program, a feeling of trust and joy of working with Mark as he goes from goal to goal, climbing higher and higher on the musical scale of his little life. The program has helped us to look at not only Mark's life but our own lives. We have been trained to take life in smaller chords, day-by-day "notes," if you will. . . . The program focuses us on what Mark is right now, doing something a step at a time, not Mark's entire life. Life will be a series of these growing steps, little bits that we look at all day. Each step that we are concentrating on will lead to the final goal, certainly, but projecting too far into the future only overwhelms us. Our trust is to each small individualized program goal, which will eventually lead to an independent Mark Sullivan.

(Timothy & Marilyn Sullivan, parents, in Hanson & Harris, 1986, p. 8)

These parents' statements underscore several crucial functions of early intervention services. First, and perhaps most important, these services provide support and assistance to families *early on*. This support helps families to move beyond shattered hopes and dreams for their children to providing direct assistance to the babies. Parents who participate in early intervention services often report how much they valued someone giving them hope for their children as well as specific help. The opportunity to meet with and gain information from other parents and professionals specially trained in work with young children is frequently cited as critical to the abilities of the family members to move forward in getting to know and care for their new babies.

Second, the quotes from parents demonstrate the importance of carefully planned early assessment, goal setting, and teaching for young infants with developmental difficulties. It is through individually designed programs that the needs of each child and family can be addressed. The importance of close partnerships with families is paramount so that early intervention activities can be responsive to family values and integrated into family routines.

Third, these parent quotations allude to early uncertainty and the need for easy access to services within the community. Early intervention services must be community based and part of an interagency network so that families who need these services are identified and referred for appropriate services at their earliest point of need and contact. Particularly for family members with a newborn child with special needs, it is difficult and challenging to seek out and identify potential sources of support and assistance.

Finally, early intervention is not a single protocol or procedure for all families. Rather, the term should assume a continuum of services within the community that are provided by a range of professionals. It is this continuum and breadth of service that is demanded to fully meet the multiple and varied needs of young children who are disabled or at risk for developing disabilities and their families.

For a number of years early intervention services have been offered in various parts of the country. With federal legislation (Public Law 99-457, Amendments to the Education of the Handicapped Act, revised as the Individuals with Disabilities Education Act) and states' overwhelming response to this national program, early intervention services are expanding to provide assistance to more children. This commitment stems largely from the needs expressed by families and from evidence that children who are given early support and assistance need less intensive and expensive services in later years and go on to lead lives characterized by higher quality.

Many questions remain regarding the identification of children who will benefit from services, the design of early services, and the timing and duration of these services. However, early support and assistance in the form of family-centered early intervention programs are recognized as worthy and necessary in society.

Like the children served in early intervention programs, the field is in its infancy. It is a time for learning, growing, and developing the

skills, competencies, and attitudes that will shape the future. It is a time of excitement and enthusiasm as well as a time for nurturing. We hope that this book will assist early interventionists to develop exemplary programs for young children who are at risk or disabled and their families.

References

Hanson, M. J. (1987). *Teaching the infant with Down syndrome: A guide for parents and professionals* (2nd ed.). Austin, TX: PRO-ED.

Hanson, M. J., & Harris, S. R. (1986). *Teaching the young child with motor delays.* Austin, TX: PRO-ED.

APPENDIX A

Public Law 99-457 (Title 1, Part H)

This appendix presents the amendments to the Education of the Handicapped Act (EHA) which authorized an early intervention program for infants and toddlers with disabilities and their families. Since its passage in 1986, P.L. 99-457 has been amended. The most recent amendments are found in Public Law 102-119 (October 7, 1991). The EHA also has been retitled *Individuals with Disabilities Education Act*.

Among the amendments (now found in P.L. 102-119) the following additions and changes in terminology were made:

(a) "handicapped infants and toddlers" was changed to "infants and toddlers with disabilities";

(b) "case management services" are now referred to as "service coordination services";

(c) "language and speech" is replaced by "communication";

(d) "psychosocial" is replaced by "social or emotional";

(e) "self-help skills" is replaced by "adaptive development";

(f) the following early intervention services are added: social work services, vision services, assistive technology devices and assistive technology services, transportation and related costs that are necessary to enable an infant or toddler and the infant's or toddler's family to receive early intervention services;

(g) the following personnel are added as providing early intervention services: family therapists, orientation and mobility specialists, and pediatricians and other physicians;

(h) a statement describing early intervention services is added: "to the maximum extent appropriate, are provided in natural environments, including the home, and community settings in which children without disabilities participate."

Other amendments found in P.L. 102-119 pertain to the Individualized Family Service Plan, state application and assurances, use of funds, procedural safeguards, state interagency coordinating council, allocation of funds, authorization of appropriations, and the federal interagency coordinating council.

Public Law 99-457
99th Congress

An Act

To amend the Education of the Handicapped Act to reauthorize the discretionary programs under that Act, to authorize an early intervention program under that Act for handicapped infants and toddlers and their families, and for other purposes.

Oct. 8, 1986

[S. 2294]

Be it enacted by the Senate and House of Representatives of the United States of America in Congress assembled,

Education of the Handicapped Act Amendments of 1986. Contracts. Grants. 20 USC 1400 note. 20 USC 1400.

SECTION 1. SHORT TITLE: REFERENCE.

(a) SHORT TITLE.—This Act may be cited as the "Education of the Handicapped Act Amendments of 1986".

(b) REFERENCE.—References in this Act to "the Act" are references to the Education of the Handicapped Act.

TITLE I—HANDICAPPED INFANTS AND TODDLERS

SEC. 101. ADDITION OF A NEW PART RELATING TO HANDICAPPED INFANTS AND TODDLERS.

(a) AMENDMENT.—The Act is amended by inserting after the part added by section 316 the following new part:

"PART H—HANDICAPPED INFANTS AND TODDLERS

"FINDINGS AND POLICY

"SEC. 671. (a) FINDINGS.—The Congress finds that there is an urgent and substantial need—

20 USC 1471.

"(1) to enhance the development of handicapped infants and toddlers and to minimize their potential for developmental delay,

"(2) to reduce the educational costs to our society, including our Nation's schools, by minimizing the need for special education and related services after handicapped infants and toddlers reach school age,

"(3) to minimize the likelihood of institutionalization of handicapped individuals and maximize the potential for their independent living in society, and

"(4) to enhance the capacity of families to meet the special needs of their infants and toddlers with handicaps.

"(b) POLICY.—It is therefore the policy of the United States to provide financial assistance to States—

State and local governments.

"(1) to develop and implement a statewide, comprehensive, coordinated, multidisciplinary, interagency program of early intervention services for handicapped infants and toddlers and their families,

"(2) to facilitate the coordination of payment for early intervention services from Federal, State, local, and private sources (including public and private insurance coverage), and

"(3) to enhance its capacity to provide quality early intervention services and expand and improve existing early intervention services being provided to handicapped infants, toddlers, and their families.

"DEFINITIONS

"SEC. 672. As used in this part—

"(1) The term 'handicapped infants and toddlers' means individuals from birth to age 2, inclusive, who need early intervention services because they—

"(A) are experiencing developmental delays, as measured by appropriate diagnostic instruments and procedures in one or more of the following areas: Cognitive development, physical development, language and speech development, psychosocial development, or self-help skills, or

"(B) have a diagnosed physical or mental condition which has a high probability of resulting in developmental delay.

Such term may also include, at a State's discretion, individuals from birth to age 2, inclusive, who are at risk of having substantial developmental delays if early intervention services are not provided.

"(2) 'Early intervention services' are developmental services which—

"(A) are provided under public supervision,

"(B) are provided at no cost except where Federal or State law provides for a system of payments by families, including a schedule of sliding fees,

"(C) are designed to meet a handicapped infant's or toddler's developmental needs in any one or more of the following areas:

"(i) physical development,
"(ii) cognitive development,
"(iii) language and speech development,
"(iv) psycho-social development, or
"(v) self-help skills,

"(D) meet the standards of the State, including the requirements of this part,

"(E) include—

"(i) family training, counseling, and home visits,
"(ii) special instruction,
"(iii) speech pathology and audiology,
"(iv) occupational therapy,
"(v) physical therapy,
"(vi) psychological services,
"(vii) case management services,
"(viii) medical services only for diagnostic or evaluation purposes,
"(ix) early identification, screening, and assessment services, and
"(x) health services necessary to enable the infant or toddler to benefit from the other early intervention services,

"(F) are provided by qualified personnel, including—

"(i) special educators,
"(ii) speech and language pathologists and audiologists,
"(iii) occupational therapists,
"(iv) physical therapists,
"(v) psychologists,

"(vi) social workers,
"(vii) nurses, and
"(viii) nutritionists, and
"(G) are provided in conformity with an individualized family service plan adopted in accordance with section 677.

"(3) The term 'developmental delay' has the meaning given such term by a State under section 676(b)(1).

"(4) The term 'Council' means the State Interagency Coordinating Council established under section 682.

"GENERAL AUTHORITY

"SEC. 673. The Secretary shall, in accordance with this part, make grants to States (from their allocations under section 684) to assist each State to develop a statewide, comprehensive, coordinated, multidisciplinary, interagency system to provide early intervention services for handicapped infants and toddlers and their families.

State and local governments. Grants. 20 USC 1473.

"GENERAL ELIGIBILITY

"SEC. 674. In order to be eligible for a grant under section 673 for any fiscal year, a State shall demonstrate to the Secretary (in its application under section 678) that the State has established a State Interagency Coordinating Council which meets the requirements of section 682.

State and local governments. Grants. 20 USC 1474.

"CONTINUING ELIGIBILITY

"SEC. 675. (a) FIRST TWO YEARS.—In order to be eligible for a grant under section 673 for the first or second year of a State's participation under this part, a State shall include in its application under section 678 for that year assurances that funds received under section 673 shall be used to assist the State to plan, develop, and implement the statewide system required by section 676.

State and local governments. Grants. 20 USC 1475.

"(b) THIRD AND FOURTH YEAR.—(1) In order to be eligible for a grant under section 673 for the third or fourth year of a State's participation under this part, a State shall include in its application under section 678 for that year information and assurances demonstrating to the satisfaction of the Secretary that—

"(A) the State has adopted a policy which incorporates all of the components of a statewide system in accordance with section 676 or obtained a waiver from the Secretary under paragraph (2),

"(B) funds shall be used to plan, develop, and implement the statewide system required by section 676, and

"(C) such statewide system will be in effect no later than the beginning of the fourth year of the State's participation under section 673, except that with respect to section 676(b)(4), a State need only conduct multidisciplinary assessments, develop individualized family service plans, and make available case management services.

"(2) Notwithstanding paragraph (1), the Secretary may permit a State to continue to receive assistance under section 673 during such third year even if the State has not adopted the policy required by paragraph (1)(A) before receiving assistance if the State demonstrates in its application—

"(A) that the State has made a good faith effort to adopt such a policy,

"(B) the reasons why it was unable to meet the timeline and the steps remaining before such a policy will be adopted, and

"(C) an assurance that the policy will be adopted and go into effect before the fourth year of such assistance.

"(c) FIFTH AND SUCCEEDING YEARS.—In order to be eligible for a grant under section 673 for a fifth and any succeeding year of a State's participation under this part, a State shall include in its application under section 678 for that year information and assurances demonstrating to the satisfaction of the Secretary that the State has in effect the statewide system required by section 676 and a description of services to be provided under section 676(b)(2).

"(d) EXCEPTION.—Notwithstanding subsections (a) and (b), a State which has in effect a State law, enacted before September 1, 1986, that requires the provision of free appropriate public education to handicapped children from birth through age 2, inclusive, shall be eligible for a grant under section 673 for the first through fourth years of a State's participation under this part.

"REQUIREMENTS FOR STATEWIDE SYSTEM

20 USC 1476.

"SEC. 676. (a) IN GENERAL.—A statewide system of coordinated, comprehensive, multidisciplinary, interagency programs providing appropriate early intervention services to all handicapped infants and toddlers and their families shall include the minimum components under subsection (b).

"(b) MINIMUM COMPONENTS.—The statewide system required by subsection (a) shall include, at a minimum—

"(1) a definition of the term 'developmentally delayed' that will be used by the State in carrying out programs under this part,

"(2) timetables for ensuring that appropriate early intervention services will be available to all handicapped infants and toddlers in the State before the beginning of the fifth year of a State's participation under this part,

"(3) a timely, comprehensive, multidisciplinary evaluation of the functioning of each handicapped infant and toddler in the State and the needs of the families to appropriately assist in the development of the handicapped infant or toddler,

"(4) for each handicapped infant and toddler in the State, an individualized family service plan in accordance with section 677, including case management services in accordance with such service plan,

"(5) a comprehensive child find system, consistent with part B, including a system for making referrals to service providers that includes timelines and provides for the participation by primary referral sources,

Public information.

"(6) a public awareness program focusing on early identification of handicapped infants and toddlers,

"(7) a central directory which includes early intervention services, resources, and experts available in the State and research and demonstration projects being conducted in the State,

"(8) a comprehensive system of personnel development,

"(9) a single line of responsibility in a lead agency designated or established by the Governor for carrying out—

"(A) the general administration, supervision, and monitoring of programs and activities receiving assistance under section 673 to ensure compliance with this part,

"(B) the identification and coordination of all available resources within the State from Federal, State, local and private sources,

"(C) the assignment of financial responsibility to the appropriate agency,

"(D) the development of procedures to ensure that services are provided to handicapped infants and toddlers and their families in a timely manner pending the resolution of any disputes among public agencies or service providers,

"(E) the resolution of intra- and interagency disputes, and

"(F) the entry into formal interagency agreements that define the financial responsibility of each agency for paying for early intervention services (consistent with State law) and procedures for resolving disputes and that include all additional components necessary to ensure meaningful cooperation and coordination,

"(10) a policy pertaining to the contracting or making of other arrangements with service providers to provide early intervention services in the State, consistent with the provisions of this part, including the contents of the application used and the conditions of the contract or other arrangements,

"(11) a procedure for securing timely reimbursement of funds used under this part in accordance with section 681(a),

"(12) procedural safeguards with respect to programs under this part as required by section 680, and

"(13) policies and procedures relating to the establishment and maintenance of standards to ensure that personnel necessary to carry out this part are appropriately and adequately prepared and trained, including—

"(A) the establishment and maintenance of standards which are consistent with any State approved or recognized certification, licensing, registration, or other comparable requirements which apply to the area in which such personnel are providing early intervention services, and

"(B) to the extent such standards are not based on the highest requirements in the State applicable to a specific profession or discipline, the steps the State is taking to require the retraining or hiring of personnel that meet appropriate professional requirements in the State, and

"(14) a system for compiling data on the numbers of handicapped infants and toddlers and their families in the State in need of appropriate early intervention services (which may be based on a sampling of data), the numbers of such infants and toddlers and their families served, the types of services provided (which may be based on a sampling of data), and other information required by the Secretary.

"INDIVIDUALIZED FAMILY SERVICE PLAN

"SEC. 677. (a) ASSESSMENT AND PROGRAM DEVELOPMENT.—Each handicapped infant or toddler and the infant or toddler's family shall receive—

20 USC 1477.

"(1) a multidisciplinary assessment of unique needs and the identification of services appropriate to meet such needs, and

"(2) a written individualized family service plan developed by a multidisciplinary team, including the parent or guardian, as required by subsection (d).

"(b) PERIODIC REVIEW.—The individualized family service plan shall be evaluated once a year and the family shall be provided a review of the plan at 6 month-intervals (or more often where appropriate based on infant and toddler and family needs).

"(c) PROMPTNESS AFTER ASSESSMENT.—The individualized family service plan shall be developed within a reasonable time after the assessment required by subsection (a)(1) is completed. With the parent's consent, early intervention services may commence prior to the completion of such assessment.

"(d) CONTENT OF PLAN.—The individualized family service plan shall be in writing and contain—

"(1) a statement of the infant's or toddler's present levels of physical development, cognitive development, language and speech development, psycho-social development, and self-help skills, based on acceptable objective criteria,

"(2) a statement of the family's strengths and needs relating to enhancing the development of the family's handicapped infant or toddler,

"(3) a statement of the major outcomes expected to be achieved for the infant and toddler and the family, and the criteria, procedures, and timelines used to determine the degree to which progress toward achieving the outcomes are being made and whether modifications or revisions of the outcomes or services are necessary,

"(4) a statement of specific early intervention services necessary to meet the unique needs of the infant or toddler and the family, including the frequency, intensity, and the method of delivering services,

"(5) the projected dates for initiation of services and the anticipated duration of such services,

"(6) the name of the case manager from the profession most immediately relevant to the infant's and toddler's or family's needs who will be responsible for the implementation of the plan and coordination with other agencies and persons, and

"(7) the steps to be taken supporting the transition of the handicapped toddler to services provided under part B to the extent such services are considered appropriate.

"STATE APPLICATION AND ASSURANCES

"SEC. 678. (a) APPLICATION.—Any State desiring to receive a grant under section 673 for any year shall submit an application to the Secretary at such time and in such manner as the Secretary may reasonably require by regulation. Such an application shall contain—

"(1) a designation of the lead agency in the State that will be responsible for the administration of funds provided under section 673,

"(2) information demonstrating eligibility of the State under section 674,

"(3) the information or assurances required to demonstrate eligibility of the State for the particular year of participation under section 675, and

"(4)(A) information demonstrating that the State has provided (i) public hearings, (ii) adequate notice of such hearings, and (iii) an opportunity for comment to the general public before the submission of such application and before the adoption by the

State of the policies described in such application, and (B) a summary of the public comments and the State's responses,

"(5) a description of the uses for which funds will be expended in accordance with this part and for the fifth and succeeding fiscal years a description of the services to be provided,

"(6) a description of the procedure used to ensure an equitable distribution of resources made available under this part among all geographic areas within the State, and

"(7) such other information and assurances as the Secretary may reasonably require by regulation.

"(b) STATEMENT OF ASSURANCES.—Any State desiring to receive a grant under section 673 shall file with the Secretary a statement at such time and in such manner as the Secretary may reasonably require by regulation. Such statement shall— [Regulations.]

"(1) assure that funds paid to the State under section 673 will be expended in accordance with this part,

"(2) contain assurances that the State will comply with the requirements of section 681,

"(3) provide satisfactory assurance that the control of funds provided under section 673, and title to property derived therefrom, shall be in a public agency for the uses and purposes provided in this part and that a public agency will administer such funds and property,

"(4) provide for (A) making such reports in such form and containing such information as the Secretary may require to carry out the Secretary's functions under this part, and (B) keeping such records and affording such access thereto as the Secretary may find necessary to assure the correctness and verification of such reports and proper disbursement of Federal funds under this part,

"(5) provide satisfactory assurance that Federal funds made available under section 673 (A) will not be commingled with State funds, and (B) will be so used as to supplement and increase the level of State and local funds expended for handicapped infants and toddlers and their families and in no case to supplant such State and local funds,

"(6) provide satisfactory assurance that such fiscal control and fund accounting procedures will be adopted as may be necessary to assure proper disbursement of, and accounting for, Federal funds paid under section 673 to the State, and

"(7) such other information and assurances as the Secretary may reasonably require by regulation.

"(c) APPROVAL OF APPLICATION AND ASSURANCES REQUIRED.—No State may receive a grant under section 673 unless the Secretary has approved the application and statement of assurances of that State. The Secretary shall not disapprove such an application or statement of assurances unless the Secretary determines, after notice and opportunity for a hearing, that the application or statement of assurances fails to comply with the requirements of this section.

"USES OF FUNDS

"SEC. 679. In addition to using funds provided under section 673 to plan, develop, and implement the statewide system required by section 676, a State may use such funds— [State and local governments. 20 USC 1479.]

"(1) for direct services for handicapped infants and toddlers that are not otherwise provided from other public or private sources, and

"(2) to expand and improve on services for handicapped infants and toddlers that are otherwise available.

"PROCEDURAL SAFEGUARDS

State and local governments.
20 USC 1480.

"SEC. 680. The procedural safeguards required to be included in a statewide system under section 676(b)(12) shall provide, at a minimum, the following:

"(1) The timely administrative resolution of complaints by parents. Any party aggrieved by the findings and decision regarding an administrative complaint shall have the right to bring a civil action with respect to the complaint, which action may be brought in any State court of competent jurisdiction or in a district court of the United States without regard to the amount in controversy. In any action brought under this paragraph, the court shall receive the records of the administrative proceedings, shall hear additional evidence at the request of a party, and, basing its decision on the preponderance of the evidence, shall grant such relief as the court determines is appropriate.

Confidentiality.

"(2) The right to confidentiality of personally identifiable information.

"(3) The opportunity for parents and a guardian to examine records relating to assessment, screening, eligibility determinations, and the development and implementation of the individualized family service plan.

"(4) Procedures to protect the rights of the handicapped infant and toddlers whenever the parents or guardian of the child are not known or unavailable or the child is a ward of the State, including the assignment of an individual (who shall not be an employee of the State agency providing services) to act as a surrogate for the parents or guardian.

"(5) Written prior notice to the parents or guardian of the handicapped infant or toddler whenever the State agency or service provider proposes to initiate or change or refuses to initiate or change the identification, evaluation, placement, or the provision of appropriate early intervention services to the handicapped infant or toddler.

"(6) Procedures designed to assure that the notice required by paragraph (5) fully informs the parents or guardian, in the parents' or guardian's native language, unless it clearly is not feasible to do so, of all procedures available pursuant to this section.

"(7) During the pendency of any proceeding or action involving a complaint, unless the State agency and the parents or guardian otherwise agree, the child shall continue to receive the appropriate early intervention services currently being provided or if applying for initial services shall receive the services not in dispute.

"PAYOR OF LAST RESORT

20 USC 1481.

"SEC. 681. (a) NONSUBSTITUTION.—Funds provided under section 673 may not be used to satisfy a financial commitment for services which would have been paid for from another public or private source but for the enactment of this part, except that whenever considered necessary to prevent the delay in the receipt of appropriate early intervention services by the infant or toddler or family in a timely fashion, funds provided under section 673 may be used to pay the provider of services pending reimbursement from the agency which has ultimate responsibility for the payment.

"(b) REDUCTION OF OTHER BENEFITS.—Nothing in this part shall be construed to permit the State to reduce medical or other assistance available or to alter eligibility under title V of the Social Security Act (relating to maternal and child health) or title XIX of the Social Security Act (relating to medicaid for handicapped infants and toddlers) within the State.

42 USC 701.
42 USC 1396.

"STATE INTERAGENCY COORDINATING COUNCIL

"SEC. 682. (a) ESTABLISHMENT.—(1) Any State which desires to receive financial assistance under section 673 shall establish a State Interagency Coordinating Council composed of 15 members.

20 USC 1482.

"(2) The Council and the chairperson of the Council shall be appointed by the Governor. In making appointments to the Council, the Governor shall ensure that the membership of the Council reasonably represents the population of the State.

"(b) COMPOSITION.—The Council shall be composed of—
    "(1) at least 3 parents of handicapped infants or toddlers or handicapped children aged 3 through 6, inclusive,
    "(2) at least 3 public or private providers of early intervention services,
    "(3) at least one representative from the State legislature,
    "(4) at least one person involved in personnel preparation, and
    "(5) other members representing each of the appropriate agencies involved in the provision of or payment for early intervention services to handicapped infants and toddlers and their families and others selected by the Governor.

"(c) MEETINGS.—The Council shall meet at least quarterly and in such places as it deems necessary. The meetings shall be publicly announced, and, to the extent appropriate, open and accessible to the general public.

"(d) MANAGEMENT AUTHORITY.—Subject to the approval of the Governor, the Council may prepare and approve a budget using funds under this part to hire staff, and obtain the services of such professional, technical, and clerical personnel as may be necessary to carry out its functions under this part.

"(e) FUNCTIONS OF COUNCIL.—The Council shall—
    "(1) advise and assist the lead agency designated or established under section 676(b)(9) in the performance of the responsibilities set out in such section, particularly the identification of the sources of fiscal and other support for services for early intervention programs, assignment of financial responsibility to the appropriate agency, and the promotion of the interagency agreements,
    "(2) advise and assist the lead agency in the preparation of applications and amendments thereto, and
    "(3) prepare and submit an annual report to the Governor and to the Secretary on the status of early intervention programs for handicapped infants and toddlers and their families operated within the State.

Report.

"(f) CONFLICT OF INTEREST.—No member of the Council shall cast a vote on any matter which would provide direct financial benefit to that member or otherwise give the appearance of a conflict of interest under State law.

"(g) USE OF EXISTING COUNCILS.—To the extent that a State has established a Council before September 1, 1986, that is comparable to the Council described in this section, such Council shall be considered to be in compliance with this section. Within 4 years after the date the State accepts funds under section 673, such State shall establish a council that complies in full with this section.

"FEDERAL ADMINISTRATION

"SEC. 683. Sections 616, 617, and 620 shall, to the extent not inconsistent with this part, apply to the program authorized by this part, except that—

"(1) any reference to a State educational agency shall be deemed to be a reference to the State agency established or designated under section 676(b)(9),

"(2) any reference to the education of handicapped children and the education of all handicapped children and the provision of free public education to all handicapped children shall be deemed to be a reference to the provision of services to handicapped infants and toddlers in accordance with this part, and

"(3) any reference to local educational agencies and intermediate educational agencies shall be deemed to be a reference to local service providers under this part.

"ALLOCATION OF FUNDS

"SEC. 684. (a) From the sums appropriated to carry out this part for any fiscal year, the Secretary may reserve 1 percent for payments to Guam, American Samoa, the Virgin Islands, the Republic of the Marshall Islands, the Federated States of Micronesia, the Republic of Palau, and the Commonwealth of the Northern Mariana Islands in accordance with their respective needs.

"(b)(1) The Secretary shall make payments to the Secretary of the Interior according to the need for such assistance for the provision of early intervention services to handicapped infants and toddlers and their families on reservations serviced by the elementary and secondary schools operated for Indians by the Department of the Interior. The amount of such payment for any fiscal year shall be 1.25 percent of the aggregate of the amount available to all States under this part for that fiscal year.

"(2) The Secretary of the Interior may receive an allotment under paragraph (1) only after submitting to the Secretary an application which meets the requirements of section 678 and which is approved by the Secretary. Section 616 shall apply to any such application.

"(c)(1) For each of the fiscal years 1987 through 1991 from the funds remaining after the reservation and payments under subsections (a) and (b), the Secretary shall allot to each State an amount which bears the same ratio to the amount of such remainder as the number of infants and toddlers in the State bears to the number of infants and toddlers in all States, except that no State shall receive less than 0.5 percent of such remainder.

"(2) For the purpose of paragraph (1)—

"(A) the terms 'infants' and 'toddlers' mean children from birth to age 2, inclusive, and

"(B) the term 'State' does not include the jurisdictions described in subsection (a).

"(d) If any State elects not to receive its allotment under subsection (c)(1), the Secretary shall reallot, among the remaining States, amounts from such State in accordance with such subsection.

"AUTHORIZATION OF APPROPRIATIONS

"SEC. 685. There are authorized to be appropriated to carry out this part $50,000,000 for fiscal year 1987, $75,000,000 for fiscal year 1988, and such sums as may be necessary for each of the 3 succeeding fiscal years.". 20 USC 1485.

(b) STUDY OF SERVICES; COORDINATION OF ACTIONS.—(1) The Secretary of Education and the Secretary of Health and Human Services shall conduct a joint study of Federal funding sources and services for early intervention programs currently available and shall jointly act to facilitate interagency coordination of Federal resources for such programs and to ensure that funding available to handicapped infants, toddlers, children, and youth from Federal programs, other than programs under the Education of the Handicapped Act, is not being withdrawn or reduced. 20 USC 1485 note.

(2) Not later than 18 months after the date of the enactment of this Act, the Secretary of Education and the Secretary of Health and Human Services shall submit a joint report to the Congress describing the findings of the study conducted under paragraph (1) and describing the joint action taken under that paragraph. 20 USC 1400. Report.

APPENDIX B

Professional and Parent Organizations and Information Resources

Alexander Graham Bell Association for
the Deaf
(includes International Parent Organization)
3417 Volta Pl. NW
Washington, DC 20007

American Academy of Pediatrics
P. O. Box 927
Oak Grove Village, IL 60009

American Association of University
Affiliated Programs
8630 Fenton St., Suite 410
Silver Spring, MD 20910

American Foundation for the Blind
15 W. 16th St.
New York, NY 10011

American Medical Association
515 N. State St.
Chicago, IL 60610

American Occupational Therapy Association
1383 Piccard Dr./P.O. Box 1725
Rockville, MD 20849-1725

American Physical Therapy Association
1111 N. Fairfax St.
Alexandria, VA 22314

American Psychiatric Association
1400 K St. NW
Washington, DC 20005

American Psychological Association
750 1st St. NE
Washington, DC 20002-4242

American Speech-Language-Hearing
Association
10801 Rockville Pike
Rockville, MD 20852

Association for the Care of Children's Health
7910 Woodmont Ave., Suite 300
Bethesda, MD 20814

Association for the Education and Rehabilitation of the Blind and Visually Impaired
206 N. Washington St., Suite 320
Alexandria, VA 22314

Association for Persons with Severe
Disabilities
11201 Greenwood Ave. North
Seattle, WA 98133

Association for Retarded Citizens National
Headquarters
500 E. Border St., Suite 300
Arlington, TX 76010

Autism Society of America
8601 Georgia Ave., Suite 503
Silver Spring, MD 20910

Children's Defense Fund
25 E St. NW
Washington, DC 20001

Council for Exceptional Children
1920 Association Dr.
Reston, VA 22091

Epilepsy Foundation of America
4351 Garden City Dr., Suite 406
Landover, MD 20785

ERIC Clearinghouse on Handicapped and
Gifted Children
Council for Exceptional Children
1920 Association Dr.
Reston, VA 22091

Federation of the Blind
1800 Johnson St.
Baltimore, MD 21230

Library of Congress
Division for the Blind and Physically
Handicapped
Washington, DC 20542

March of Dimes Birth Defects Foundation
1275 Mamaroneck Ave.
White Plains, NY 10605

Muscular Dystrophy Association
3300 E. Sunrise Dr.
Tucson, AZ 85718

National Association for the Deaf
814 Thayer Ave.
Silver Spring, MD 20910

National Association for the Education of Young Children
1834 Connecticut Ave. NW
Washington, DC 20009

National Association for Parents of the Visually Impaired
2180 Linway
Beloit, WI 53511

National Association of Parents of the Deaf
814 Thayer Ave.
Silver Spring, MD 20910

National Association of the Physically Handicapped
Bethesda Scarlet Oaks/No. 6A4
440 Lafayette Ave.
Cincinnati, OH 45220-1000

National Center for Clinical Infant Programs
2000 14th St. North
Arlington, VA 22201-2500

National Down Syndrome Congress
1800 Dempster St.
Park Ridge, IL 60068-1146

National Down Syndrome Society
666 Broadway
New York, NY 10012

National Easter Seal Society, Inc.
230 W. Monroe
Chicago, IL 60606

National Information Center for Handicapped Children and Youth
P.O. Box 1492
Washington, DC 20013-1492

National Institute of Child Health and Human Development
National Institutes of Health
Public Health Service
U.S. Department of Health and Human Services
Bethesda, MD 20014

National Rehabilitation Information Center
8455 Colesville Rd., Suite 935
Silver Spring, MD 20910-3319

Office of Human Development Services
U.S. Department of Health and Human Services
309F Hubert H. Humphrey Bldg.
200 Independence Ave., SW
Washington, DC 20201

Office of Special Education and Rehabilitative Services
U.S. Department of Education
Donohue Bldg.
400 Maryland Ave., SW
Washington, DC 20202

Parent Care
9041 Colgate St.
Indianapolis, IN 46268-1210

Spina Bifida Association of America
4590 MacArthur Blvd., NW
Washington, DC 20007-4226

United Cerebral Palsy Association
1522 K St. NW, Suite 1112
Washington, DC 20005

APPENDIX C

Council for Exceptional Children (CEC) Code of Ethics and Standards for Educators

CEC Code of Ethics

We declare the following principles to be the Code of Ethics for educators of exceptional persons. Members of the special education profession are responsible for upholding and advancing these principles. Members of The Council for Exceptional Children agree to judge by them in accordance with the spirit and provisions of this Code.

   I. Special education professionals are committed to developing the highest educational and quality of life potential of exceptional individuals.
   II. Special education professionals promote and maintain a high level of competence and integrity in practicing their profession.
   III. Special education professionals engage in professional activities which benefit exceptional individuals, their families, other colleagues, students, or research subjects.
   IV. Special education professionals exercise objective professional judgment in the practice of their profession.
   V. Special education professionals strive to advance their knowledge and skills regarding the education of exceptional individuals.
   VI. Special education professionals work within the standards and policies of their profession.
   VII. Special education professionals seek to uphold and improve where necessary the laws, regulations, and policies governing the delivery of special education and related services and the practice of their profession.
   VIII. Special education professionals do not condone or participate in unethical or illegal acts, nor violate professional standards adopted by the Delegate Assembly of CEC.

CEC Standards for Professional Practice

1. Professionals in Relation to Exceptional Persons and Their Families

1.1 Instructional Responsibilities

1.1.1 Special education personnel are committed to the application of professional expertise to ensure the provision of quality education for all exceptional individuals. Professionals strive to:

1.1.1.1 Identify and use instructional methods and curricula that are appropriate to their area of professional practice and effective in meeting the needs of exceptional persons.

1.1.1.2 Participate in the selection and use of appropriate instructional materials, equipment, supplies, and other resources needed in the effective practice of their profession.

1.1.1.3 Create safe and effective learning environments which contribute to fulfillment of needs, stimulation of learning and of self-concept.

1.1.1.4 Maintain class size and caseloads which are conducive to meeting the individual instructional needs of exceptional persons.

1.1.1.5 Use assessment instruments and procedures that do not discriminate against exceptional persons on the basis of race, color, creed, sex, national origin, age, political practices, family or social background, sexual orientation, or exceptionality.

1.1.1.6 Base grading, promotion, graduation, and/or movement out of the program on the individual goals and objectives for the exceptional individual.

1.1.1.7 Provide accurate program data to administrators, colleagues, and parents, based on efficient and objective record keeping practices, for the purpose of decision making.

1.1.1.8 Maintain confidentiality of information except where information is released under specific conditions of written consent and statutory confidentiality requirements.

1.2 Management of Behavior

1.2.1 Special education professionals participate with other professionals and with parents in an interdisciplinary effort in the management of behavior. Professionals:

1.2.1.1 Apply only those disciplinary methods and behavioral procedures which they have been instructed to use and which do not undermine the dignity of the individual or the basic human rights of exceptional persons (such as corporal punishment).

1.2.1.2 Clearly specify the goals and objectives for behavior management practices in the exceptional person's Individualized Education Program.

1.2.1.3 Conform to policies, statutes, and rules established by state/provincial and local agencies relating to judicious application of disciplinary methods and behavioral procedures.

1.2.1.4 Take adequate measures to discourage, prevent, and intervene when a colleague's behavior is perceived as being detrimental to exceptional persons.

1.2.1.5 Refrain from aversive techniques unless repeated trials of other methods have failed and then only after consultation with parents and appropriate agency officials.

1.3 Support Procedures

1.3.1 Adequate instruction and supervision shall be provided to professionals before they are required to perform support services for which they have not been previously prepared.

1.3.2 Professionals may administer medication, where state/provincial policies do not preclude such action, if qualified to do so or if written instructions are on file which state the purpose of the medication, the conditions under which it may be administered, possible side effects, the physician's name and phone number, and the professional liability if a mistake is made. The professional will not be required to administer medication.

1.3.3 Professionals note and report to those concerned whenever changes in behavior occur in conjunction with the administration of medication or at any other time.

1.4 Parent Relationships

1.4.1 Professionals seek to develop relationships with parents based on mutual respect for their roles in achieving benefits for the exceptional person. Special education professionals:

1.4.1.1 Develop effective communication with parents, avoiding technical terminology, using the primary language of the home, and other modes of communication when appropriate.

1.4.1.2 Seek and use parents' knowledge and expertise in planning, conducting, and evaluating special education and related services for exceptional persons.

1.4.1.3 Maintain communications between parents and professionals with appropriate respect for privacy and confidentiality.

1.4.1.4 Extend opportunities for parent education, utilizing accurate information and professional methods.

1.4.1.5 Inform parents of the educational rights of their children and of any proposed or actual practices which violate those rights.

1.4.1.6 Recognize and respect cultural diversities which exist in some families with exceptional persons.

1.4.1.7 Recognize that the relationship of home and community environmental conditions affects the behavior and outlook of the exceptional person.

1.5. Advocacy

1.5.1 Special education professionals serve as advocates for exceptional persons by speaking, writing, and acting in a variety of situations on their behalf. Professionals:

1.5.1.1 Continually seek to improve government provisions for the education of exceptional persons while ensuring that public statements by professionals as individuals are not construed to represent official policy statements of the agency by which they are employed.

1.5.1.2 Work cooperatively with and encourage other professionals to improve the provision of special education and related services to exceptional persons.

1.5.1.3 Document and objectively report to their supervisors or administrators inadequacies in resources and promote appropriate corrective action.

1.5.1.4 Monitor for inappropriate placements in special education and intervene at the appropriate level to correct the condition when such inappropriate placements exist.

1.5.1.5 Follow local, state/provincial, and federal laws and regulations which mandate a free appropriate public education to exceptional students and the protection of the rights of exceptional persons to equal opportunities in our society.

2. Professional Employment

2.1 Certification and Qualification

2.1.1 Professionals ensure that only persons deemed qualified by having met state/provincial minimal standards are employed as teachers, administrators, and related-service providers for persons with exceptionalities.

2.2. Employment

2.2.1 Professionals do not discriminate in hiring on the basis of race, color, creed, sex, national origin, age, political practices, family or social background, sexual orientation, or exceptionality.

2.2.2 Professionals represent themselves in an ethical and legal manner in regard to their training and experience when seeking new employment.

2.2.3 Professionals give notice consistent with local education agency policies when intending to leave employment.

APPENDIX D

Early Childhood Special Education Journals

Many journals that focus on general or categorical areas of special education also publish articles about infants and preschoolers, but the following are directed specifically toward young children.

Child Development
Society for Research in Child Development
University of Chicago Press—Journals Division
P.O. Box 37005
Chicago, IL 60637

Child Development Abstracts and Bibliography
Society for Research in Child Development
University of Chicago Press—Journals Division
P.O. Box 37005
Chicago, IL 60637

Children's Health Care
Association for the Care of Children's Health
7910 Woodmont Ave., Suite 300
Bethesda, MD 20814

Infant Behavior and Development
Ablex Publishing Corporation
355 Chestnut St.
Norwood, NJ 07648

Infants and Young Children
Aspen Publishers, Inc.
7201 McKinney Circle
Frederick, MD 21701

Journal of Developmental and Behavioral Pediatrics
Society for Behavioral Pediatrics
c/o Noreen M. Spota
241 E. Gravers Ln.
Philadelphia, PA 19118

Journal of the Division for Early Childhood
Division for Early Childhood—Council for Exceptional Children
2500 Baldwick Rd., Suite 15
Pittsburgh, PA 15205

Monographs of the Society for Research in Child Development
Society for Research in Child Development
University of Chicago Press—Journals Division
P.O. Box 37005
Chicago, IL 60637

Topics in Early Childhood Special Education
PRO-ED, Inc.
8700 Shoal Creek Blvd.
Austin, TX 78757-6897

Young Children
National Association for the Education of Young Children
1834 Connecticut Ave., NW
Washington, DC 20009

Zero to Three
National Center for Clinical Infant Programs
2000 14th St. North
Arlington, VA 22201-2500

APPENDIX E

Individualized Family Service Plan

The Individualized Family Service Plan

for

Kamala Jackson

and His or Her Family

May 1, 1995
Date

Developed by a Family–Professional Team That Included

Team Member	Relationship/Agency
Leona Jackson	Mother
Marshall Jackson	Father
Gloria Thomas	Grandmother
Rhonda Martin	Infant Tchr.-Bay Schools
Connie Lopez	SLP-Bay Schools

Team Member	Relationship/Agency
Doug Parker	PT-Regional Center
Maurine Boxer	Nurse-Public Health
Jane Harrison	Admin.-Bay Schools
Jenny Flynn	Service Coordinator-Community
	Interagency Team

Information About Kamala
Child's Name

Date of Birth: Mar. 2, 1994   Age Today: 1 yr. 2 mos.   Boy or (Girl)

Language(s) Spoken at Home: English _____ (Circle the primary language)

Address: 6025 Skyline Dr. _____ Apt. # _____ Linda Vista _____ 92141
        Street   City   Zip Code

Telephone # at Home: (619) 876-1234

Directions to House:

Information About Kamala   Family
Child's Name

Parent/Guardian: Leona Jackson, Mother

Address: 6025 Skyline Dr. _____ Apt. # _____ Linda Vista _____ 92141
        Street   City   Zip Code

Telephone # at Home: (619) 876-1234   Telephone # at Work: (619) 473-1604

Preferred Language: English

Parent/Guardian: Marshall Jackson

Address: same as above _____ Apt. # _____ City _____ Zip Code
        Street

Telephone # at Home: (619) 876-1234   Telephone # at Work: (619) 584-1945

Preferred Language: English

Information About _Kamala_   Service Coordinator at This Meeting

Child's Name

Name: _Jenny Flynn_   Agency: _Community Interagency Team_   Telephone: _(619) 473-1819_

Address: _4032 West Bay Dr._   _100_   _Linda Vista_   _92121_
         Street   Office #   City   Zip Code

Date Appointed: __/__/__

As _Kamala's_ Parents or Family Members, We Are Concerned About
Child's Name

- learning to talk
- learning to walk
- gaining weight—she needs to weigh more before heart surgery can be done
- heart surgery within the next year
- paying medical bills

As _Kamala's_ Parents or Family Members, Our Priorities Are
Child's Name

- gaining weight so she can have surgery
- sitting up by herself
- crawling (on her hands and knees)
- saying "mama" and "papa"
- getting help to pay medical bills

As a Family, Our Strengths and Resources Include

- Leona's mother, Gloria, takes care of Kamala while Leona and Marshall are at work
- Leona works for an insurance company—she knows about billing for Kamala's medical needs
- Kamala likes to play with her cousins, and she gets to see them a lot
- Close family and faith that things will work out

What We Know About ____Kamala's____ Early Life and Current Abilities
Child's Name

- Kamala has Down syndrome
- She gets sick easily and has been sick a lot since she was born
- Kamala's muscles seem weak, and she gets tired easily
- She needs to gain more weight before she can have heart surgery
- She says "aah" and "ooh" and makes sounds when her mother, father, or her grandmother talks to her
- Kamala has ways of telling you what she wants

Things about Pregnancy, Delivery, and Early Life That Are Important for the Team to Consider:

- Kamala was born prematurely (at 30 weeks) and stayed in the hospital for 2 months after birth
- She has a heart defect and will have surgery within the next year
- Kamala's pediatrician has recommended a special formula to increase her intake of calories

Current Abilities

Learning, and solving problems (Cognitive):

- Takes turns making sounds with a familiar person
- Claps her hands when her grandmother sings and claps

Moving around and interacting with toys and objects (Gross Motor and Fine Motor):

- Sits by herself after an adult helps her sit up
- Rolls to get a toy
- Holds, shakes, and mouths toys

Communicating, letting us know what is needed, or understanding what is being said (Receptive and Expressive Language):

- Says "ooh" and "aah"
- Listens when you talk to her

Taking care of own needs (Self-Help):

- Accepts food from a spoon
- Holds her bottle

Getting along with self and others (Social-Emotional):

- Smiles at others
- Likes to be near a familiar person

Health Issues that the Team Should Consider

- Kamala's heart defect is being monitored by a cardiologist. The cardiologist has placed no limitations on her activities. However, whenever Kamala shows any sign of fatigue, she should be allowed to rest.
- Since Kamala gets sick easily, the family prefers to re-schedule appointments if any staff members have symptoms of illness

Any Other Issues that the Team Wants to Record or Consider

- Kamala's weight gain and motor development are concerns of the team. Her parents wonder if she will use up too many calories by being more physically active. Team members feel they need input from Kamala's physicians about these issues.
- Kamala has not yet received a hearing evaluation or an assessment of her vision. However, her parents have no concerns about hearing or vision at this time.

As Service Providers on the Team, We Are Concerned About

- Ensuring that health concerns are addressed as strategies and activities are planned
- Providing information and support to Kamala's family
- Monitoring hearing and vision status
- Helping Kamala learn the skills that come before talking and walking

What Outcomes Would the Family–Professional Team Like to Accomplish in the Next 6 Months?

1. Obtain more information about Kamala's heart condition, weight gain, and implications for intervention

2. Help Kamala learn to sit by herself

3. Help Kamala learn to crawl (on her hands and knees)

4. Help Kamala learn to say "mama" and "papa"

5. Explore and confirm various options for payment of medical bills

How We Plan to Accomplish the Outcomes

Outcome 1 Obtain more information about Kamala's heart condition, weight gain, and implications for intervention

Strategies/Activities To Be Used	Specific Service & Agency/Person Responsible	Evaluation Criteria & Target Date (How We'll Know If We Met the Goal & When We'll Formally Check Progress)	
• Talk with physicians about the issues	Leona & Marshall Jackson, Doug Parker, Maurine Boxer	Conversations held and reported	6/1/95
• Obtain recent medical reports and disseminate	Maurine Boxer, Leona & Marshall Jackson	Reports obtained and disseminated	6/1/95

Outcome 2 Help Kamala learn to sit up by herself

Strategies/Activities To Be Used	Specific Service & Agency/Person Responsible	Evaluation Criteria & Target Date (How We'll Know If We Met the Goal & When We'll Formally Check Progress)
Provide physical assistance as Kamala moves into and out of sitting	Family and infant program staff with consultation from Doug Parker	Able to transition into and out of sitting independently 11/1/95

Outcome 3 Help Kamala learn to crawl (on her hands and knees)

Strategies/Activities To Be Used	Specific Service & Agency/Person Responsible	Evaluation Criteria & Target Date (How We'll Know If We Met the Goal & When We'll Formally Check Progress)
Position Kamala on her stomach for play Then, encourage her to reach and grasp a toy (using one hand)	Family and infant program staff with consultation from Doug Parker	Able to creep 11/1/95

Outcome 4 Help Kamala learn to say "mama" and "papa"

Strategies/Activities To Be Used	Specific Service & Agency/Person Responsible	Evaluation Criteria & Target Date (How We'll Know If We Met the Goal & When We'll Formally Check Progress)	
• Model saying "mama" and "papa" as you look for and find them	Family and infant program staff with consultation from Connie Lopez	Recognition of family members when they are named	11/1/95
• Play peek-a-boo and re-appear each time Kamala makes a sound	(same as above)	Use of voice to call for her mother or father	11/1/95

Outcome 5 Explore and confirm various options for payment of medical bills

Strategies/Activities To Be Used	Specific Service & Agency/Person Responsible	Evaluation Criteria & Target Date (How We'll Know If We Met the Goal & When We'll Formally Check Progress)	
• Provide the parents with the name and number of the SSI coordinator.	Jenny Flynn, Leona and Marshall Jackson	Information provided	5/8/95
• Assist the parents in completing the SSI application packet (or other packets) if desired.		Assistance provided	6/1/95
• Explore other options for assistance.		Options confirmed and parents linked to appropriate agencies	6/1/95

In Developing this Plan, the Family–Professional Team

- Considered and agreed upon eligibility under P.L. 99-457   (Yes)   No   NA
- Made arrangements for translators or interpreters as needed   Yes   No   (NA)

- Used settings that are integrated and age appropriate — (Yes) / No / NA
- Based programs and services on family priorities, concerns, and resources — (Yes) / No / NA
- Included representatives from other agencies providing services — (Yes) / No / NA
- Developed and included or attached a transition plan — Yes / No / (NA)

Service Coordinator Responsible for Assisting in Implementing This Plan

Name: _Jenny Flynn_ Agency: _Community Interagency Team_ Telephone: _(619) 473-1819_

Address: _4032 West Bay Dr._ _____ _100_ _Linda Vista_ _92121_
           Street   Office #   City   Zip Code

Date Appointed: _5 / 1 / 95_

As _Kamala's_ **Authorized Family Members,**
    Child's Name

We (I) feel that we (I) have had an opportunity to cooperatively develop this plan and that the outcomes reflect our (my) concerns and priorities. We (I) understand that this plan can be amended at any time at our (my) request and that it will be formally reviewed by _Nov. 1, 1995_. Based on these understandings, we (I) give permission for the plan to be implemented.

✓ Yes   ___ No

Leona Jackson   _5/1/95_   _Marshall Jackson_   _5/1/95_
Signature   Date   Signature   Date

NOTE: Thanks are extended to Maria Morgan for her input on the IFSP.

APPENDIX F

Typical Developmental Milestones

Motor Development

Motor development proceeds in a cephalocaudal and proximal to distal direction. In other words, voluntary control develops from head to foot and from body midline to limbs. Finally, large-muscle control precedes control of small muscles.

Gross Motor

Gross motor development typically proceeds in the following sequences: head righting and control from prone (stomach), supine (back), and upright (sitting) positions; trunk control and joint stability, trunk, hips, arms, and legs; rotation lying down (rolling), sitting, standing; locomotion (movement) on stomach with arms and legs, on hands and knees, to sitting, to standing, walking, jumping, and throwing and catching objects.

Head Control

Moves head side to side

Lifts head up when lying on stomach

Sitting

Sits fully supported

Holds head steady in sitting position

Sits without support

Raises self to sitting from back and stomach lying positions

Climbs into and out of child-sized chair

Locomotion from Stomach and Back Lying (Rolling, Crawling)

Turns from side to side and back to side

Rolls from stomach to back

Rolls from back to stomach

Crawls forward (stomach down)

Creeps forward (up on "all fours")

Creeps up and down stairs

Climbs

Standing and Walking

Bears own weight

Stands at furniture supports

Pulls self to standing

Stands without support

Stoops and recovers

Cruises (walks alongside furniture supports)

Walks with support (e.g., hands held)

Walks without support

Walks sideways

Walks up and down stairs

Coordinated Movements from Standing

Runs

Kicks

Jumps

Throws and catches objects (e.g., ball) with two hands

Fine Motor

Developmental progressions in fine motor skills include reaching, grasping, releasing, coordinating the use of two hands at once, differential object use, and refined thumb-finger opposition for drawing and writing.

Reaching, Grasping, Releasing

Reaches (including across midline)

Grasps using full hand

Brings objects in hand together at midline

Transfers objects from hand to hand

Grasps with thumb and finger (including pincer grasp with forefinger)

Takes objects in and out of containers

Stacks (places and releases) one object on top of another

Manipulating Objects in Functional Ways

Explores objects with hands and mouth

Moves objects by pushing, pulling, dangling, banging, etc.

Pushes buttons or levers to activate switches or toys

Puts parts/pieces of toys together (e.g., lids on containers, puzzles)

Turns pages and looks at books and pictures

Scribbles

Cognitive and Preacademic

Developmental progressions in the cognitive and preacademic areas include orienting to and following stimuli (tactile, visual, auditory), object permanence, causality, means–ends, relations of objects in space, imitation, classification of objects by characteristics, one-to-one correspondence, and symbolic play.

Sensory Exploration

Orients to and follows visual stimuli

Orients to auditory stimuli

Responds to touch

Object Permanence

Looks at a person or object as it's disappearing

Finds an object partially hidden

Finds an object that child sees being hidden

Finds an object that child sees being hidden in one place and then is moved

Causality and Means–Ends

Repeats an action to produce an interesting outcome

Moves to retrieve or get an object

Manipulates or moves a simple object or toy to produce an obvious outcome (e.g., shakes rattle, bangs, pushes)

Manipulates a mechanical object or toy (e.g., pushes button, turns switch) to produce an outcome that is not obvious (e.g., toy bear plays drum, music plays on cassette recorder)

Uses an object to obtain another (e.g., a string to pull a toy, a stick to reach a toy)

Relations of Objects in Space

Places objects in and out of containers

Builds vertical and horizontal structures

Moves around barriers

Imitation

Imitates motor movements (i.e., gestures)

    Imitates actions both in repertoire and new actions

    Imitates actions that are both visible and invisible to child

Imitates vocalizations

    Imitates familiar sounds and sounds in repertoire

    Imitates new sounds

    Imitates words

Preacademic Skills

Sorts objects and puts objects that are the same together

    Classifies by shape, color, function, size

Matches an object to one that is the same when given a sample

Shows beginning one-to-one correspondence

Selects a specified object from a group

Groups objects according to simple categories or classes (e.g., things to eat)

Orders objects (e.g., big to little)

Symbolic

Engages in pretend play

Uses imaginary objects

Communication

Communication includes both language and speech development and includes the developmental progression of orienting and responding to persons speaking, comprehending sound and word usage, and producing single words then multiple word combinations and complex word productions.

Social Interactions

Looks at a person speaking

Maintains reciprocal gaze with a person

Engages in reciprocal vocalization exchanges

Uses a gestural or vocal signal to gain attention of someone or get something

Receptive Language

Identifies self and family members through pointing

Finds/identifies common pictures, persons, objects, or events by pointing

Follows simple (one- and two-step directions) (e.g., come here, pick up the toys and put them in the box)

Points to body parts—both visible and invisible to infant

Expressive Language

Makes sounds or gestures

Uses words or gestures

Names objects, persons, events—vocally or through gesture

Combines words/gestures into two- or three-word phrases

Uses combinations that include agent-action (e.g., Doggie runs), action-object (e.g., push car), agent-object (e.g., Kate food)

Social-Emotional

Developmental progression in the social-emotional area includes recognition of familiar adults, making signaling behaviors and differential responses to people, differentiation of self, expanding independence from familiar adults, independent play, parallel play alongside peers, and cooperative play and peer interactions.

Interactions with Adults

Recognizes familiar adults

Engages in reciprocal interactions with familiar adults

Shows affection with familiar adults

Initiates interactions and communications with familiar adults

Establishes some independence from familiar adults (moves away while still in proximity)

Interactions with Peers

Plays beside peers (no or little interaction)

Initiates interactions with peers

Initiates communications with peers

Plays cooperatively with peers

Self-Help

Feeding proceeds from coordinated sucking and swallowing to independent management of feeding utensils (e.g., spoon and cup). Other self-help subdomains include hygiene or personal care and dressing.

Feeding

Drinks from bottle/breast using coordinated tongue and lip movements

Takes food in and swallows using coordinated tongue and lip movements

Munches (chews up and down)

Feeds self with fingers

Drinks from a cup being held

Drinks from a cup independently

Feeds self with spoon

Chews crunchy or chewy foods using rotary motions of jaw

Hygiene

Toilets

Cooperates in toothbrushing

Washes and dries hand and face

Dressing

Cooperates in dressing and undressing

Removes simple garments

Zips and unzips

Pulls on simple garments

Fastens and unfastens garments

APPENDIX G

Resources for Equipment and Education Materials

The following companies supply books, assessment measures, learning materials, equipment, and toys that are appropriate for use with young children with disabilities. Catalogs are available from all for price and ordering information.

Achievement Products, Inc.
1621 Warner Ave., SE
Box 9033
Canton, OH 44707

American Guidance Service
4201 Woodland Rd.
Box 99
Circle Pines, MN 55014-1796

Childcraft Education Corp.
10 Kilmer Rd./P.O. Box 3081
Edison, NJ 08818-3081

Communication Skill Builders
3830 E. Bellevue
P.O. Box 42050-CS4
Tucson, AZ 85733

Constructive Playthings
1227 East 119th St.
Grandview, MO 64030-1117

Council for Exceptional Children
Publication Sales
1920 Association Dr.
Reston, VA 22091-1589

Curriculum Associates, Inc.
5 Esquire Rd.
North Billerica, MA 01862-2589

DLM Teaching Resources
One DLM Park
Allen, TX 75002

Edmark
P.O. Box 3218
Redmond, WA 98073-3218

Educational Productions, Inc.
7412 SW Beaverton Hillsdale Hwy., Suite 210
Portland, OR 97225

Flaghorse, Inc.
150 N. Mac Question Pkwy.
Mt. Vernon, NY 10550

Fred Sammons, Inc.
145 Tower Drive
Burr Ridge, IL 60521

Harcourt Brace Jovanovich
301 Commerce St., Suite 3700
Ft. Worth, TX 76105

Houghton Mifflin Co.
Wayside Rd.
Burlington, MA 01803

J. B. Lippincott Co.
P.O. Box 1530
Hagerstown, MD 21740

Kaplan School Supply Corp./East Coast Division
P.O. Box 609
Lewisville, NC 27023-0609

Kaplan School Supply Corp./West Coast Division
5360 Eastgate Mall, Suite E
San Diego, CA 92121

Lakeshore Learning Materials Co.
2695 E. Dominguez St.
P.O. Box 6261
Carson, CA 90749

Macmillan Publishing Group
Front and Brown Sts.
Riverside, NJ 08075

McGraw-Hill Inc.
Princeton Rd.
Hightstown, NY 08520

National Lekotek Center
2100 Ridge Ave.
Evanston, IL 60204

Paul H. Brookes Publishing Co.
P.O. Box 10624
Baltimore, MD 21285-0624

Play Fair
P.O. Box 1821D
Boulder, CO 80308

Portage Project Materials
CESA 5-626 E. Slifer St.
Portage, WI 53901

Prentice-Hall School Division
6900 E. 30th St.
Indianapolis, IN 46219

PRO-ED, Inc.
8700 Shoal Creek Blvd.
Austin, TX 78757-6897

Psychological Corporation
555 Academic Ct.
San Antonio, TX 78204-2498

Research Press
P.O. Box 9177, Dept. N
Champaign, IL 61826

Rifton, Inc.
P.O. Box 901
Rifton, NY 12471-0901

Science Research Associates
P.O. Box 5380
Chicago, IL 60680

Sensational Beginnings
P.O. Box 2009
300 Detroit, Suite 6
Monroe, MI 48161

Simon & Schuster
1230 Avenue of the Americas
New York, NY 10020

St. Martin's Press
175 5th Ave.
New York, NY 10010

Toys for Special Children
385 Werburton Ave.
Hastings-on-Hudson, NY 10706

Toys to Grow On
P.O. Box 17
Long Beach, CA 90801

Vort Corp.
P.O. Box 60880
Palo Alto, CA 94306

Western Psychological Corp.
12031 Wilshire Blvd.
Los Angeles, CA 90025

Author Index

Abidin, R., 173
Abroms, K. I., 82
Accardo, P. J., 42
Ackerman, P. R., Jr., 72
Acomb, B. L., 240
Adcock, D., 202
Adelson, E., 12
Ainsworth, M. D. S., 92, 93, 176
Alberto, P. A., 72
Alford, C. A., 29
Algozzine, B., 54
Allen, K. E., 118
Allen, L. M., 12
Allman, P., 165
Als, H., 34, 164
Amatruda, C. S., 186
Anastasiow, N. J., 62, 72, 138
Anderson, P. P., 48, 52, 53
Anderson, R., 12
Apolloni, T., 229
Aronson, M., 12
Attermeir, S. M., 165
Atwater, J. B., 72, 188
Audette, H., 277
Austin, N., 273

Bagnato, S. J., 78, 148, 149, 155, 162, 201
Bailey, D. B., 72, 73, 78, 110, 114, 121, 123, 135, 150, 168, 170, 171, 172, 173, 174, 183, 201
Bailey, E. J., 11
Bakeman, R., 94
Baker, B., 13
Bakley, S., 60, 61
Baldwin, V., 12
Balla, D. A., 165
Balzer-Martin, L., 84
Bane, M. J., 46
Banet, B., 73
Barber, P., 287
Barcus, J. M., 284
Barnard, K., 142, 176
Barnes, H. V., 9, 11
Barnett, W. S., 9, 277
Barocas, R., 140
Barrera, I., 54, 156
Baskiewicz, A., 95
Batshaw, M. L., 22, 24, 25, 28, 30, 31, 42, 81
Bayley, N., 164, 186
Beam, G., 149
Becker, W. C., 201
Beckman, A. A., 24
Beckman, P., 78, 84, 95, 172

Beckman-Bell, P. J., 84
Bee, H., 176
Behr, S., 115, 287
Bell, R., 92, 93, 173
Beller, E. K., 11
Belous, R. S., 46
Below, P. J., 240
Bengston, D. A., 234
Bennett, T., 78
Bernier, J. C., 116
Berrueta-Clement, J. R., 9
Bidder, R. T., 12, 13
Blacher, J., 84
Blackman, J. A., 21, 24, 26, 27, 32, 33, 42
Blackstone, S., 234
Blackwell, J., 218
Blehar, M. C., 176
Bloch, M., 63
Blue-Banning, M. J., 115
Boese, R. J., 115
Borich, G., 183
Borton, W., 284
Bowlby, F., 92
Bradburn, N. M., 301
Bradley, R. H., 177
Brandenburg, S. A., 234
Brandt, P. A., 123
Branston, M. B., 74
Branston-McLean, M., 74
Brazelton, T. B., 152, 164, 202, 218
Bredekamp, S., 72, 187, 201
Brekken, L., 121, 124, 126
Brent, R. L., 24
Brenton, D. P., 24
Brethower, D. M., 290
Bricker, 288
Bricker, D. D., 10, 11, 12, 73, 74, 121, 123, 165, 187, 198, 201, 202–203
Bricker, W. A., 73, 187, 234
Bridges, F. A., 94
Brigance, A. H., 165
Briggs, T., 72
Brinker, R. P., 110, 209
Brinkerhoff, R. O., 290
Bristol, M. M., 78, 107
Bromwich, R., 84, 108, 176, 218
Bronfenbrenner, U., 11, 96
Brooks-Gunn, J., 62, 138, 218
Brotherson, M. J., 97, 110, 296
Brown, E. R., 63
Brown, F., 74, 292
Brown, J. V., 94

Brown, L., 74, 292
Bruder, M., 123, 229
Bruner, J. S., 206
Bryant, G., 12, 13
Buium, N., 94, 218
Burgess, D. M., 63
Burke, J., 135
Burkhart, L. J., 210, 234
Burns, K. A., 36
Burns, W. J., 36
Burrell, B., 95
Burtt, K. G., 202
Butcher, S. D., 34, 35, 43
Buyse, M. L., 24
Bzoch, K. R., 166

Cabello, B., 72
Cahill, M., 135
Caldwell, B., 177
Caldwell, M. B., 28
Calvelli, T. A., 28
Campbell, D. T., 299, 322
Campbell, F. A., 11
Campbell, J. P., 265
Campbell, P., 73
Campbell, P. H., 118, 234
Caplan, F., 202
Caplan, T., 202
Capute, A. J., 42
Carbin, C. F., 115
Carithers, T., 123
Carson, A. T., 64
Carta, J. J., 37, 72, 188
Carter, E., 170
Carter, S., 234
Casto, G., 11, 12
Catardi, C., 82
Cattell, P., 186
Cavallaro, C. C., 72
Centers for Disease Control, 29
Chan, S., 57, 67
Chandler, M. J., xii, 6, 8, 38
Charles, C. M., 299
Charney, E. B., 26
Chasnoff, I. J., 36
Chatlin-McNichols, J. P., 73
Chauvel, P., 26
Child Welfare League of America, 38
Children's Defense Fund, 33, 38, 45, 46, 62, 63–64
Chu, 28
Cicchetti, D., 72, 79, 94, 165
Clarke, A. D. B., 7
Clarke, A. M., 7
Clarke, J. T., 24
Clarke-Stewart, K. A., 92, 208

Clarren, S. K., 36
Cleveland, J. O., 53, 58
Cloud, H. H., 123
Clunies-Ross, G. G., 12
Cohen, L. G., 150, 162, 183
Cohen, M. A., 189
Comeau, J. K., 173
Commission for Cooperative Services for Young Handicapped Children and Their Families, 143, 279
Committee for Economic Development, 45
Committee on Genetics, 26
Conlon, C. J., 28
Connolly, B., 12
Connor, F., 233
Converse, J. M., 322
Cook, R. E., 201
Cooke, S. A., 229
Cooke, T. P., 229
Cooper, D. H., 12
Coulter, M. L., 274
Council for Exceptional Children (CEC), 190, 201, 345–348
Covert, R. C., 284
Covitz, F. E., 92
Cox, J. O., 120, 169
Coye, R. W., 135
Crain, L. S., 22
Crais, E. R., 123, 135
Crawley, S., 94, 218
Cripe, J., 74, 198, 201, 202–203
Crow, R. E., 229
Cummins, J., 54
Cunningham, C., 202
Cunningham, C. C., 101
Cunningham, C. E., 218
Cunningham, D., 115
Czeizel, A. E., 26

Darling, R. B., 115
Darlington, R., 11, 13, 82, 291
Davis, W. A., 322
Dawson, D. A., 46
Day, N. L., 36
Dayton, C. W., 83, 276
Deal, A., 149
Deal, A. G., 78, 103
Deck, J., 218
Deibert, A. N., 202
Deiner, P. L., 201
Deitz, J., 123
Demmitt, A., 110
Demmler, G. J., 27, 29, 30
Denhoff, E., 14
Dewey, J., 4, 73, 74

Division for Early Childhood, Council for Exceptional Children, 190, 201
DiVitto, B., 43, 94
Dmitriev, V., 12
Dodds, J., 164
Donahue-Kilburg, G., 135
Dopyera, J. E., 81
Dow, M. G., 12
Drotar, D., 95, 123
Du Verglas, G., 121
DuBose, R. F., 150
Dubowitz, L. M. S., 32
Dudas, I., 26
Duesberg, P., 28
Dumars, K. W., 137, 138
Dunn, W., 123
Dunnette, M. D., 265
Dunst, C. J., 12, 78, 103, 110, 148, 149, 163, 166, 174, 185, 201
Duran-Flores, D., 137
Dye, H. B., 7, 291

Edelman, L., 135
Eggbeer, L., 123, 135
Eheart, B. K., 218
Eisner, 296
Elder, J., 83, 279, 287
Elsayed, S. S., 135
Emde, R. N., 94
Engelmann, S., 201
English, K., 52, 79, 143, 277
Epstein, A. S., 9
Erba, G., 116
Erikson, E., 73
Escalona, S. K., 54
Escobar, C. M., 277
Espe-Sherwindt, M., 60, 61
Esposito, L., 234
Evans, I. M., 74

Fagan, J. W., 209
Fallen, N. H., 159
Fallstrom, K., 12
Fanaroff, A. A., 71
Fandal, A. W., 138
Farel, A., 121, 123
Featherstone, H., 115
Fenichel, E. S., 48, 52, 53, 79, 123, 130, 135
Feshbach, N. D., 288
Fessler, D. R., 280
Fewell, R. R., 79, 81, 82, 84, 114, 121, 164, 202, 207
Field, T., 13, 94
Figueroa, R. A., 54
Filler, J. W., 83
Finger, I., 94, 218

Finkelstein, N. W., 209
Finnie, N., 115, 233
Finzer, W. F., 319
Fisher, R., 273
Fitz-Gibbon, C. T., 294, 322
Flushman, B., 42–43
Flynn, C. C., 275
Foley, G., 156
Foster, C., 137
Foster, P. W., 9
Fowle, C. M., 317
Fraiberg, S., 12, 94
Frame, J. D., 239
Frankenburg, W., 138, 164
Fraser, B. A., 30, 233
Fraser, B. S., 115
Fredericks, B., 12
Fredericks, H. D., 229
Freeman, M., 322
Freeman, R. D., 115, 116
Freud, A., 73
Freund, L., 23
Froebel, 4
Furono, S., 165
Furstenberg, F. F., 62

Gabarino, J., 140
Gagnon, J., 319
Gale, G., 42
Galka, G., 233
Gallagher, J. J., 20, 114, 145
Gallagher, R. J., 290
Gallo, F., 46
Gans, 281, 283
Garber, H. L., 291
Gargiulo, R. M., 115
Garland, C., 9
Garrard, K. R., 94, 218
Garwood, S. G., 82, 150
Georgetown University Child Development Center, 287
Gesell, A., 186
Gfroerer, J., 35
Gibbs, E. D., 148, 183
Gillette, Y., 202
Gilmartin, K. J., 83, 276
Glover, E. M., 166
Golbin, A., 115, 233
Goldberg, S., 43, 94, 105, 176, 202, 208
Goldenberg, D., 73, 159
Goldman, R., 118
Goldstein, D., 72
Goldstein, S., 94, 218
Gonsalves, S. V., 62
Goolsby, E., 234

Gordon, I. J., 202
Gordon, N., 13
Gorski, P. A., 12, 13, 33
Gorsuch, R. L., 173
Gray, O. P., 12, 13
Green, J. W., 52
Greenberg, M. T., 94
Greenberg, R., 13
Greene, L., 278
Greenland, B., 135
Greenspan, N., 176
Greenspan, S. I., 63, 79, 140, 149, 150, 153, 176
Gross, P. J., 189
Guba, E., 296
Guess, D., 287, 292
Guidubaldi, J., 164
Guinagh, B., 202
Guralnick, M. J., 217, 227, 229
Guthrie, R., 24
Gutmann, A. J., 94, 218

Hacker, B. J., 165
Hagen, E. P., 165
Hall, B., 95
Hall, H., 284
Haney, M., 72
Hanft, B. E., 123, 135
Hanley, W. B., 24
Hanline, M. F., 95, 120, 189, 229
Hann, D. M., 62
Hanson, M. J., 2, 12, 13, 34, 35, 37, 42, 44, 45, 46, 47, 48, 49, 50, 51, 53, 54, 56, 57, 58, 59, 68, 77, 79, 84, 90, 94, 95, 101, 108, 114, 116, 120, 121, 123, 124, 126, 152, 156, 162, 176, 177, 189, 196, 205, 215, 218, 222, 228, 233, 323–324
Haralick, J. G., 229
Harbin, G. L., 20, 145, 229, 275
Haring, N. G., 189
Harkins, J. A., 173
Harmon, A. J., 202
Harris, J., 79
Harris, S. R., 2, 79, 90, 116, 196, 205, 215, 233, 323–324
Harrison, H., 43, 116, 122, 152
Harrison, P. J., 57, 83, 129, 275, 276, 284, 285
Harry, B., 57, 67–68
Haseler, M., 24
Hauser-Cram, P., 12, 13, 120
Haycock, K. A., 319
Hayden, A. H., 12
Hayes, A., 149
Hazel, R., 287
Healy, A., 79, 84, 176, 277, 284
Hegrenes, J. R., 94, 218
Heifetz, L., 13

Heinrich, J., 84
Helmstetter, E., 287
Hemmeter, M. L., 110
Henerson, M. E., 322
Hensinger, R. N., 30, 115, 233
Heyne, E., 33
Hickey, C., 123
High, E. C., 233
Hilliard, A. G., III, 54
Hine, R. J., 123
Hinton, A. W., 123
Hluchyj, T., 290
Hobbs, N., 54
Hohman, M., 73
Hole, W. T., 33
Holloway, E., 32
Holm, V. A., 118
Holvoet, J., 292
Holyroyd, J., 173
Horrobin, J. M., 12
Horton, 281, 283
Horton, K., 12
Hosaka, C., 165
Humphry, R., 123, 135
Hunt, J., 7, 166
Hunt, S., 148
Huntington, G., 123, 152
Hurth, J., 52, 151
Hussey, B., 34, 35, 43

Inatsuka, T., 165
Infant Health and Development Program, 12
Irvin, L. K., 115
Irvin, N., 95
Isaacs, S., 73

Jackson, J. A., 52, 79, 143, 277
Jan, J. E., 116
Jankowski, J. J., 92, 208
Jeffree, D., 202
Jens, K. G., 165
Jester, J. E., 202
Joanning, H., 110
Johnson, 288, 290, 291
Johnson, B. H., 143, 149
Johnson, B. J., 78
Johnson, C. B., 28, 63
Johnson-Martin, N. M., 165
Joint Center for Urban Studies, 46
Jones, M. H., 123
Jones, O. H. M., 94
Jones, R. L., 54

Kaiser, A. P., 110, 198
Kaiser, C., 123

Kalkstein, K., 202
Kaltenbach, K., 79
Kaminski, R., 207
Kantor, D., 170
Karnes, M. B., 291
Katz, E. L., 94
Kaufman, A. S., 164
Kaufman, M., 123
Kaufman, N. L., 164
Kaufmann, R. K., 52, 78, 143, 149
Kazuk, E., 278, 279
Keeran, C., 284
Keesee, P. D., 79, 176, 277
Kelly, J. F., 83
Kelly, M., 90
Kennell, J. H., 84, 95
Kerlin, S. L., 60
Kerr, M. M., 229
Khalsa, J. H., 35
Kiernan, J., 292
King, J. A., 322
Kjerland, L., 150–151
Klaus, M. H., 71, 84, 95
Klein, M. D., 31, 201
Klein, N., 73
Klerman, L. V., 38
Knobloch, H., 189
Kogan, K., 13
Kornblatt, E. S., 84
Kositsky, A., 122
Koslowski, B., 218
Kovach, J., 150–151
Krause, L. A., 234
Krauss, M., 12
Kregel, J., 284
Krener, P., 28
Krentz, M., 108, 152, 176, 177, 218
Kroth, R. L., 115
Krueger, R. A., 296, 322
Krumboltz, H. B., 202
Krumboltz, J. D., 202
Krywawych, S., 24
Kubiszyn, T., 183
Kurtz, L. A., 30
Kush, S. A., 183

Lackey, S., 42
Lane, V. W., 159
Langley, M. B., 164
Larsen, A. S., 173
Laude, M., 274
Law, A. I., 317
Lawler, E. E., III, 265
Lay-Dopyera, M., 81
Layton, C., 46

Lazar, I., 11, 13, 82, 291
Leach, P., 202
League, R., 166
Lee, G. R., 170
Leet, H., 174
Lehr, W., 170
Leonard, C. H., 33
Leonard, C. R., 123
Lerner, J., 73, 159
Lesar, S., 29, 63
Lester, B. M., 164
Levin, H. M., 322
Levitan, S. A., 46
Lewis, H. C., 127
Lewis, M., 6, 138, 188, 189, 208, 209, 218
Lewis, R. B., 82, 120, 147, 155, 161
Lidz, C. S., 54
Lillie, D. L., 138, 185
Lincoln, Y. S., 296
Linder, T. W., 71, 73, 101, 120, 121, 123, 150, 183, 284, 288
Lingerfelt, B. V., 78
Lipton, H. L., 101
Lipton, R. C., 209
Littman, 288
Liu, J., 46
Long, J. G., 33
Lorenz, K. Z., 7
Lovett, D., 121
Lubs, H. A., 23
Lucas, B. L., 123
Lucey, J. F., 33
Ludlow, J. R., 12
Lushene, R. E., 173
Lynch, E. W., 44, 45, 46, 49, 50, 51, 52, 53, 54, 56, 57, 58, 59, 60, 68, 79, 82, 83, 114, 120, 122, 123, 129, 143, 156, 172, 222, 275, 276, 277, 281, 284, 285
Lyon, G., 118
Lyon, S., 118

MacDonald, J. D., 202
MacMillan sisters, 4
MacPhee, D., 13
Madsen, C. H., 201
Madsen, C. K., 201
Mager, R. F., 201
Magrab, P., 83, 278, 287
Magyary, D. L., 123, 142
Mahoney, G., 94, 218
Main, M., 218
Maldonado, Y. A., 29, 63
Mardell-Czudnowski, C., 73, 159
Marquis, J. G., 115
Marshall, N. R., 94, 218
Martin, N. J., 234

Martin, S. L., 11
Marvin, R. S., 94
Masi, W., 13
Masnick, G., 46
Mastropieri, M. A., 12
Maurer, H., 94, 218
Maza, R., 84
Mazzocco, M. M., 23
McBride, S. L., 110
McCall, R. B., 202
McCartan, K., 123
McCollum, J., 94, 123, 218
McConkey, R., 115, 202
McConnell, S. R., 72, 188, 227
McCormick, L., 118
McCubbin, H. I., 170, 173
McEvoy, M. A., 217, 227
McGoldrick, M., 170
McGonigel, M. J., 52, 78, 135, 143, 149, 172
McKinney, L. E., 37
McLaughlin, J. A., 284
McLean, J., 198
McLean, M., 123, 183
McLean, M. E., 72
McLoughlin, J. A., 147, 155, 161
McMath, C., 319
McNulty, B., 276, 280
McWilliam, P., 322
McWilliam, P. J., 114
Meadow, K. P., 94
Meisels, S. J., 145, 149, 150, 153, 156, 183
Mendoza, J., 52, 79, 143, 277
Mercer, C. D., 54
Merkel-Holguin, L. A., 38
Meyer, D. J., 84
Meyer, R. A., 120, 169
Milburn, D., 32
Miller, C., 121
Miller, F. B., 28
Mills, B. L., 135
Mintzberg, H., 241
Minuchin, S., 97, 170
Moersch, M. S., 123, 165
Molyneaux, D., 159
Montessori, M., 4, 72
Moore, M. G., 72
Moore, W., 12
Morgan, J. L., 278, 279, 287
Morganstein, D., 319
Mori, A. A., 82, 115, 185
Morris, L. L., 294, 322
Morris, S. E., 233
Morrisey, G. L., 240
Morton, K., 92
Moyer, I. D., 202

Mullick, J. A., 115
Mulligan, M., 292
Munson, S. M., 148
Murphy, D., 13
Murphy, D. L., 115
Murphy, L. B., 7
Murray, H., 291
Musselwhite, C. R., 202
Myers, B. J., 79
Myers, J. J., 29

National Association for the Education of Young Children, 72, 187
National Center for Children in Poverty, 38
National Center for Health Statistics, 33
National Down Syndrome Society, 323
National Health Interview Survey, 46
Neisworth, J. T., 4, 78, 81, 82, 148, 149, 185, 201
Nelson, D. E., 78
Newborg, J., 164
Nomura, M., 234
Nordyke, N. S., 274, 281, 283
Norling, R., 319
Nover, A. R., 123
Nowakowski, J. R., 290

O'Connor, R., 23
Odom, S. L., 72, 217, 227, 229, 296
O'Donnell, K., 121
Offner, R. B., 229
Ogle, P. A., 115
Olson, D. H., 170, 173
Olson, H. C., 63, 79
O'Reilly, K., 165
Osofsky, J. D., 62, 63, 79
Owen, V., 74

Palsha, S. A., 123
Parker, M., 38
Parker, S. J., 159
Parmelee, A., 152
Parse, S., 152
Parsons, E., 90
Pasamanick, B., 189
Pass, R. F., 29
Patterson, G. R., 201
Patterson, J. M., 115
Patton, M. Q., 322
Paul, J. L., 115
Pedersen, F. A., 92, 208
Peebles, C., 62
Pelosi, J., 280
Perret, Y. M., 22, 23, 24, 25, 28, 30, 42, 81
Peters, D. L., 4
Peters, T., 273

Petersen, S., 120
Peterson, N. L., 4, 145, 229
Phelps, J. A., 233
Phi Delta Kappa, 135
Philip, A. G., 33
Phillips, J. L., 8, 186
Piaget, J., 8, 73, 74, 186, 189, 206
Piersel, W., 36
Pokorni, J., 84
Pollard, A., 284
Pond, R. E., 166
Popham, W. J., 295, 296, 319
Porter, P. B., 234
Portner, J., 173
Poulsen, M. K., 37, 141
Powell, A., 94, 218
Powell, T. H., 115
Powers, L. E., 79, 115
Prechtl, H., 152
Preminger, A., 166
Provence, S., 149, 156, 183, 209
Provus, M., 296
Public Health Service, 24
Pueschel, S. M., 115, 116

Rafferty, J., 319
Ramey, C. T., 11, 12, 13, 209
Ramey, S. L., 11, 13
Raver, S. A., 75
Reed, M., 234
Reis, K., 127
Reiss, A. L., 23
Research and Policy Committee of the Committee for Economic Development, 45
Reuler, E., 218
Rheingrover, R. M., 12, 148, 163
Richardson, G. A., 36
Rider, D. P., 229
Robbins, S. P., 265, 271
Robenalt, K., 218
Roberts, H., 95
Roberts, S., 287
Robinault, I. P., 233
Robinson, C. C., 94, 218
Rocco, S., 153
Rogers, M. F., 28
Rogers, S. J., 127, 152
Rogers-Warren, A., 72, 198
Rondal, J. A., 94, 218
Rosa, F. W., 25
Rosander, K., 284
Rosenbaum, S., 46
Rosenberg, S. A., 94, 218
Rossetti, L. M., 183
Rossi, R. J., 83, 276, 277

Roth, J., 319
Rothbart, M. K., 94
Rouse, L., 78
Rovee, C. K., 209
Royce, J., 291
Rubenstein, A., 28
Rubenstein, J. L., 92, 208
Russell, F., 12
Rynders, J., 12, 94, 218

Sack, S., 198
Salisbury, C., 84
Sameroff, A. J., xii, 6, 8, 38, 140
Sandall, S. R., 79
Sander, L., 93, 176
Sanford, A., 166
Sattler, J. M., 165
Schacht, R., 52
Schaefer, D. S., 165
Scheiner, A. P., 12
Schiefelbusch, R. L., 118
Schleichkorn, J., 116
Schleinen, S., 292
Schlesinger, H. S., 94
Schnoll, S. H., 36
Schoonheyt, W., 24
Schopler, E., 107
Schroeder, S., 95
Schulz, H., 152
Schulz, J. B., 115
Schwartz, I. S., 72, 188
Schwarz, R. H., 12, 13
Schweinhart, L. J., 9, 11, 294
Scott, E. P., 116
Scott, K., 13
Scull, S., 123
Segal, M., 202
Seifer, R., 140
Seligman, M., 115, 209
Semmler, C. J., 34, 35, 43
Senge, P. M., 273
Sexton, D., 95
Sharpton, W. R., 95
Sheehan, R., 290
Shein, G. F., 234
Sherrod, K. B., 94, 218
Shonkoff, J., 12, 13, 120
Showstack, J., 95
Shriver, M. D., 36
Shuster, S. K., 296
Siepp, J., 233
Simeonsson, R., 12, 121, 148, 149, 151, 152, 173, 174, 183
Simmons, T., 234
Simons, R., 115, 122, 172

Simpson, C., 122
Simpson, R. L., 115
Singer, G. H. S., 79, 115
Skeels, H. M., 7, 291
Skinner, B. F., 186
Slavik, B., 32
Slentz, K., 123, 198, 201, 202–203
Sloper, P., 202
Sloper, T., 101
Smith, B., 12
Smith, B. S., 79, 176, 277
Smith, H. T., 7
Snell, M. E., 73
Snipper, A., 291
Snyder, S. W., 12
Snyder-McLean, L., 198
Sobel, A. J., 38
Solnit, A., 95
Solomonson, B., 198
Sontag, J. C., 52
Soper, C., 319
Sparling, J. J., 13
Sparrow, S. S., 165
Spencer, P. E., 135
Spenciner, L. J., 150, 162, 183
Spielberger, C. D., 173
Spiker, D., 94, 218
Sroufe, A., 72
Sroufe, L. A., 94
Stagno, A., 29
Stanley, J. C., 299, 322
Stark, M., 95
Stecher, B. M., 322
Steiner, V. G., 166
StevensDominguez, M., 149
Stewart, J. C., 115
Stillman, R., 165
Stills, S., 137
Stock, J. R., 164
Stoller, S., 13
Stone, J. L., 7
Stone, N. W., 9
Stoneman, Z., 122
Stowers, H., 234
Strain, P., 12, 72, 217, 227, 229
Stray-Gundersen, K., 116
Strayton, V. D., 218
Streissguth, A. P., 36, 63
Stufflebeam, D. L., 296
Sturm, L., 123
Sudman, S., 301
Sullivan, M. W., 209
Summers, J. A., 97, 171, 296
Susi, A., 24
Svarstad, B., 101

Svinicki, J., 164
Swan, W. W., 278, 279, 287
Swanson, J., 9
Sweet, N., 42
Swenson-Miller, K., 135

Takanishi, R., 288
Tamaru, R., 319
Taylor, P., 95
Templeman, T., 12
Terry, D. V., 20, 145
Tessier, A., 201
Teti, D. M., 148, 183
Thom, V. A., 32, 35
Thomas, D. R., 201
Thomas, P., 149
Thompson, B., 95
Thorndike, R. L., 165
Thorp, E. K., 123
Thorpe, J. K., 94
Thurman, S. K., 62, 138, 150
Timberlake, E. M., 123
Tjossem, T. D., xi, 11, 20, 138
Toth, S. L., 79
Trifiletti, J. J., 54
Trivette, C. M., 78, 103, 149, 174
Trohanis, P. L., 120, 169
Tronick, E. C., 164
Tulkin, S. R., 92
Turnbull, A. P., 78, 79, 97, 98, 107, 115, 170
Turnbull, H. R., 98, 115, 170
Turnure, J., 94, 218
Tyler, N., 13

Ulrey, G., 152
Umansky, W., 159
U.S. Department of Commerce, 44
U.S. Department of Health and Human Services, 24, 33, 38
U.S. General Accounting Office, 63
Upshur, C., 12
Ury, W., 273
Uzgiris, I., 166

Vadasy, P. F., 84, 114, 202
Van den Pol, R. A., 229
VandenBerg, K. A., 34, 35, 42–43, 152
Vanderheiden, G. C., 234
Verkerk, A. J. M., 23
Vietze, P. M., 114
Vincent, L., 169, 172
Vygotsky, L. S., 74, 206

Walker, D. K., 81
Wall, S., 176

Wallace, T., 274
Walsh, W. B., 183
Warren, S., 198
Warren, S. F., 72
Wasik, B., 13, 145
Waters, E., 176
Watson, J. S., 208–209
Wayman, K. I., 45, 56, 156, 222
Weber, C. U., 9
Weed, K. A., 74
Wehman, P., 284, 292
Weick, K. E., 265
Weidenman, L. E., 116
Weikart, D. P., 9, 11, 73, 82, 292
Werner, E. E., 140, 141
Werner, W., 152
Whiddon, D., 110
White, K., 11, 12
White, R. W., 208
Widerstrom, A. H., 138, 150, 229
Widmayer, S., 13
Williamson, G., 233
Williamson, G. G., 233
Williamson, W. D., 27, 29, 30
Willis, W., 53
Wilson, 27
Wimpelberg, R. K., 82
Windhover, R., 121

Winton, P., 107, 322
Winton, P. J., 78
Wnek, L., 164
Wodrich, D. L., 183
Wolery, M., 59, 72, 73, 183, 201, 295
Woodruff, G., 9
Wright, C., 234
Wurth, B., 234

Yando, R., 84
Yarrow, L. J., 92, 208
Yavorsky, D. K., 297
Yawkey, T. D., 4
Yeates, K., 13
Yonemitsu, D. M., 53, 58

Zax, M., 140
Zeanah, C. H., Jr., 176
Zeisloft, B., 165
Zeitlin, S., 121, 124
Zelazo, P., 148
Ziegler, R. G., 116
Zigler, E., 84
Zimmerman, I. L., 166
Zirpoli, T. J., 73
Ziskin, L., 91
Zuckerman, B., 63, 159

Subject Index

Abecedarian Project, 11, 13
Accutane, 25
Achievement Products for Children, 235
Acquired immune deficiency syndrome (AIDS), 28–29, 63, 131
Active listening, 159, 172
Activity-based intervention, 198
Activity-Based Model, 73–74
Adaptive Equipment Company, 235
Adaptive Therapeutic Systems, 235
Administration and management. *See also* Staffing
  alternatives and choices, 241
  budgets, 243
  conflict resolution, 271
  controlling function, 272
  directing function, 265, 268, 271–272
  educational and professional backgrounds of managers, 239
  evaluation function, 288–290
  goals and objectives, 240
  legal compliance, 241
  motivating, guiding, and team building function, 271
  networking, 271–272
  operational planning, 240–243
  optimal model for, 81–82, 86
  organizational culture, 265, 268, 271
  organizing function, 243–265
  policies, 240
  preferred practices for, 272–273
  public relations, 271–272
  record keeping, 253–264
  regulations, 240–241
  responsibilities of managers, 239–240
  safety and health, 241
  of service delivery system, 243–253
  skills necessary for managers, 238–239
  staff training and supervision, 264–265
  strategic planning, 240
  task and resource scheduling, 241–243
  task definition and delegation, 241
AFP levels, 26
African American children, 33, 44–45
Age of childbearing, 45–46
Agreements for collaboration, 280–281, 282
AIDS, 28–29, 63, 131
Alcohol exposure, prenatal, 35, 36, 63
Alerting, in intervention process, 109
Alexander Graham Bell Association for the Deaf, 342
Alpha-fetoprotein (AFP) levels, 26
American Academy of Pediatrics, 342
American Association of University Affiliated Programs, 342
American Foundation for the Blind, 342
American Indian families, 53
American Medical Association, 342
American Occupational Therapy Association, 342
American Physical Therapy Association, 342
American Psychiatric Association, 342
American Psychological Association, 342
American Speech-Language-Hearing Association, 342
Amniocentesis, 26
Anticonvulsant medications, 25
Applied Behavioral Analysis Model, 73
Arena assessment, 156
Asian families, 53
Assessment. *See also* Identification; Screening
  arena assessment, 156
  authentic assessment, 155
  behavioral approach to, 148
  and characteristics, skills, and attitudes of assessors, 171–172, 178–179
  child assessment, 54, 57, 146, 147–168
  conducting stage of, 151, 152–153
  cross-cultural competence and, 54, 57–58, 156
  curriculum-based assessment, 78, 148
  curriculum-based assessments, 162
  diagnostic assessments, 142, 148, 164
  ecological assessments, 149–150
  eligibility assessments, 78, 142, 144, 148
  of family concerns, priorities, and resources, 57–58, 78, 101, 146–147, 168–179
  family-focused, child assessment process, 150–155
  follow-up stage of, 151, 155
  of home environments, 177
  interactive, family-focused approaches to, 148–150
  interpreting stage of, 151, 153
  in intervention process, 110
  interviews, 159–161, 171–176
  list of assessment instruments, 164–166
  methodological difficulties in, 10
  observation, 156–159
  optimal model of, 77–78
  of parent–child interaction, 176–177
  planning stage of, 151, 152
  play-based assessment, 150
  preferred practices in, 179–180
  psychometric approach to, 148
  purposes of, 147–148
  qualitative-developmental approach to, 149
  reports of, 153, 154–155
  sharing stage of, 151, 153, 155
  for staff development, 125, 127, 128
  stages and activities in, 151–155, 168
  strategies and techniques for, 155–167, 172–177

383

team for, 150, 168, 245, 252
tests, 161–167
Assessment, Evaluation, and Programming System for Infants and Children, 165, 198, 202–203
Assessment of Preterm Infant Behavior, 164
Assessment reports, 153, 154–155
Assessment teams, 150, 168, 245, 252
Association for Persons with Severe Disabilities, 342
Association for Retarded Citizens, 342
Association for the Care of Children's Health, 342
Association for the Education and Rehabilitation of the Blind and Visually Impaired, 342
Associations, 341–343
At Risk Does Not Mean Doomed, 11
Attachment, 92–93
Attention system, of premature or low birth weight infants, 34
Augmentative communication devices, 215, 234
Authentic assessment, 155
Autism Society of America, 342

Basic Competencies for Personnel in Early Intervention (Zeitlin), 123–124
Battelle Developmental Inventory, 164
Bayley Scales of Infant Development II, 164, 186
Behavioral approach
  to assessment, 148
  to curriculum design, 186
Behavioral objectives, 195
Biological risk, xi, 12–13, 20, 32–37, 140
Brigance Diagnostic Inventory of Early Development, 165
Budgets, 243
Burnout, 130

California Early Intervention Personnel Study Project, 124
Callier-Azusa Scale, 165
Caregivers. *See* Parents
Carolina Curriculum for Infants and Toddlers with Special Needs, 165, 203
Cattell Infant Intelligence Scale, 186
CEC (Council for Exceptional Children), 342, 345–348
CEC Code of Ethics, 346
CEC Standards for Professional Practice, 346–348
Center environments
  adult-to-child ratios in, 227
  design of program space, 224–225
  floor plan for, 226
  scheduling in, 225–227
  site selection for, 223–224
Center-based services, 83
Cerebral palsy (CP), 30–31
Checklists, 157
Chicano Federation, 279

Child abuse, 63
Child care movement, 4
Child Development, 350
Child Development Abstracts and Bibliography, 350
Child Development Model, 72
Child-find systems, 77, 138. *See also* Identification; Screening
Child rearing, 47, 55
Childbearing, age of, 45–46
Childproofing, 211
Children. *See* Infants and toddlers
Children's Defense Fund, 342
Children's Health Care, 350
Chromosomal disorders, 22–24
CIPP (Context, Input, Process, Product Model), 296
CMV infection, 27, 29–30, 131, 212
Cocaine exposure, prenatal, 36, 63
Code of Ethics (CEC), 346
Coded observations, 157, 159
Cognitive and preacademic milestones, 365–366
Cognitive approach to curriculum design, 186
Cognitive Model, 73
Collaboration
  agencies to be involved in, 278–279
  agreements for, 280–281, 282
  barriers to, 284
  cascade of, 281, 283–284
  for comprehensive service system, 277
  development of community collaboration, 278–281
  facilitating factors in, 284–285
  family–professional collaboration, 79, 85, 107–110
  group meetings for, 279–280
  for improving services to children and families, 275–276
  models of, 281, 283–284
  needs assessment and, 280
  planning for, 280
  as preferred practice, xii, 15, 83–84
  preferred practices in, 285–286
  rationale for community collaboration, 274–278
  for reducing costs of services, 277–278
  for reducing duplication of services, 276–277
  referrals and, 143
  in staff development, 127, 129
Collaboration cascade, 281, 283–284
Collaborative agreements, 280–281, 282
Commenting, in intervention process, 109
Communication
  augmentative communication devices, 215, 234
  collaboration and, 285
  and cross-cultural competence, 50, 52, 53
  cultural differences in, 48, 53, 56
  developmental milestones in, 371
  home visitors and, 56, 221–223
  interpreters and, 57, 58

pacing, in parent–child interaction, 219–220
parent–child communication, 94, 105
parent–professional communication, 79, 85, 107–110
reading and responding to infant's cues, 35, 219
turn-taking and reciprocity in parent–child interaction, 219
Community collaboration. *See* Collaboration
Community contact information, 262, 264
Community resources, xii, 105–106, 244
Community Survey Form, 313
Compensatory education movement, 5
Concurrent validity, 163
Conducting stage of assessment, 151, 152–153
Confidentiality, 223, 253
Conflict resolution, 271
Congenital infections, 27–31
Congenital malformations, 24–25
Construct validity, 163
Content validity, 162–163
Context, Input, Process, Product Model (CIPP), 296
Contingency awareness, 208–209
Contracts, as collaborative agreements, 281
Cost analysis, 293
Cost effectiveness, 293
Cost questions, 293–294
Cost-benefit analyses, 293–294
Costs, of early intervention, 9–10, 293–294
Council for Exceptional Children (CEC), 342, 345–348
CP (cerebral palsy), 30–31
Credentialing and licensure, 129–130
Crestwood Company, 235
Criterion-referenced tests, 162
Critical periods of human development, 7
Cross-cultural competence
   and application of new cultural knowledge, 50
   assessment and, 54, 57–58, 156, 171–172
   attributes of, 50, 52
   "Cultural Journey," 51
   development of, 49–52
   first contacts and, 52–54
   of home visitors, 55–56
   and the Individualized Family Service Plan (IFSP), 52–60
   information about specific cultures, 50
   principles of, applied to early intervention, 52–60
   program planning and, 59
   values clarification and, 49–50, 51
Cues
   in instruction, 196–197
   reading and responding to infant's cues, 35, 219
Cultural diversity, 44–45
"Cultural Journey," 51
Culture. *See also* Cross-cultural competence
   application of new cultural knowledge, 50
   applications to early intervention practices, 52–60
   attributes of cross-cultural competence, 50, 52
   child rearing and, 47, 55
   cross-cultural competence, 49–52
   "Cultural Journey," 51
   definition of, 48
   and definition of family and family roles, 48, 55
   development of cross-cultural competence, 49–52
   help-seeking and intervention and, 47–48, 56
   importance of cultural competence, 46–52
   information about specific cultures, 50
   and language and communication styles, 48–49, 56
   meaning and influence of, 48–49
   meaning of disability and, 47, 56
   medicine and healing and, 48, 56
   values clarification and, 49–50, 51
Curriculum, definitions of, 185
Curriculum-based assessments, 78, 148, 162
Curriculum design. *See also* Learning environments
   activity-based intervention, 198
   behavioral approach to, 186
   child's role and, 193
   cognitive approach to, 186
   content, 188–190
   definition of curriculum, 185
   developmental approach to, 15, 186, 187–188, 191–192
   environment's role and, 193–194
   functional approach to, 15, 186–187
   goals for infants and toddlers, 188–190
   implementation guidelines, 190–193
   instructional and behavioral objectives, 195
   instructional strategies, 194–197
   list of early intervention curricula, 202–205
   optimal model of, 78–79, 85
   parent's role and, 194
   preferred practices in, 199
   selection and sequencing of instructional goals, 195–196
   staff members' role and, 194
   structure of curriculum, 193–194
   teaching techniques, 196–197
   theoretical approaches to, 185–187
Cystic fibrosis, 30
Cytomegalovirus (CMV) infection, 27, 29–30, 131, 212

Data analysis, 319
Data collection, 301, 309, 317–319
Data sheet on child performance, 258–259, 262, 263
DEC Recommended Practices, 190
Decision-facilitation evaluation models, 296
Denver II, 164
Developmental Activities Screening Inventory–II, 164
Developmental milestones, 363–367

Developmental principles
  Child Development Model, 72
  Cognitive Developmental Model, 73
  critical periods of human development, 7
  curriculum design and, 15, 186, 188–189, 191–192
  for early intervention, 6–7
  importance of early year to later development, 7–8
  milestones of development, 363–367
  in parent–infant relationship, 93
  transactional model of development, xi–xii, 6–7, 8
Developmental Programming for Infants and Young Children, 165, 203
Diagnosis, definition of, 148. *See also* Assessment
Diagnostic assessment, 142, 148, 164
Disabilities and disorders. *See also* Risk conditions; and specific disabilities
  cerebral palsy, 30–31
  chromosomal disorders, 22–24
  congenital infections, 27–31
  congenital malformations, 24–25
  cytomegalovirus (CMV) infection, 27, 29–30
  definition of disability, 141
  Down syndrome, 12, 20–21, 22–23, 94
  Fragile X syndrome, 23
  meaning of disability to families, 47, 56
  neural tube defects, 26–27
  phenylketonuria (PKU), 23–24
  rubella, 27, 29
  secondary disabilities, 8–9
  toxoplasmosis, 27
Discrepancy Evaluation Model, 297
Discriminate validity, 163, 167
Distance education, 129
District and Agency Survey, 314–317
Diversity. *See also* Cross-cultural competence
  applications to early intervention practices, 52–60
  assessment and, 54, 57–58, 156, 171–172
  and attributes of cross-cultural competence, 50, 52
  and changing demographics, 44–46
  in child rearing practices, 47, 55
  and cross-cultural competence, 49–52
  in definition of family and family roles, 48, 55
  families with multiple risks, 63–64
  in family characteristics, 45–46, 106–107
  first contacts and, 52–54
  guidelines for home visitor, 55–56
  help-seeking and intervention and, 47–48, 56
  in language and communication styles, 48–49, 56
  and meaning and influence of culture, 48–49
  in meaning of disability, 47, 56
  medicine and healing and, 48, 56
  and parents with mental retardation, 60–62
  population statistics on, 44–45
  preferred practices regarding, 65
  program planning and, 59
  respect for, 46–52
  teen parents, 62–63
  and values clarification, 49–50, 51
Down syndrome, 12, 20–21, 22–23, 94, 205
Drug exposure, prenatal, 35–37, 63

Early Childhood Research Institute of Substance Abuse, 37
Early childhood special educator job description, 266–267
Early intervention. *See also* Administration and management; Assessment; Collaboration; Curriculum design; Family-centered approach; Learning environments; Program evaluation; Screening; Staffing
  Activity-Based Model of, 73–74
  Applied Behavioral Analysis Model of, 73
  and benefits to children, 10–13
  and benefits to families, 13–14
  and benefits to society, 9–10
  Child Development Model of, 72
  Cognitive Model of, 73
  components of optimal model for, 70–82, 84–86
  costs of, 9–10
  current perspectives on, 3–4
  definition of, xi
  developmental principles in, 6–7
  Ecological Model of, 74
  effectiveness of, 10–14
  and family concerns and priorities, 9
  family-professional collaboration in, 79
  first contacts in, 52–54
  health and safety and, 81
  historical roots of, 4–6
  implementation and monitoring in, 59
  importance of, 3–10, 323–324
  and importance of early years to later development, 7–8
  and inclusion with nondisabled peers, 79–80, 85
  interface between referral source and, 142–143
  legislation on, 3–6
  Medical Model of, 71–72
  methodological difficulties in assessment of, 10
  Montessori Model of, 72–73
  parents' comments on, 323–324
  preferred practices in, xi–xiii, 14–15, 65, 86, 111–112, 132–133, 144–145, 179–180, 199, 230, 272–273, 285–286, 320–321
  and prevention of secondary disabilities or effects, 8–9
  principles of, xi–xiii
  program philosophy for, 70–75
  program planning in, 59
  rationale for, 7–10
  service delivery systems for, 82–84

synthesized, dynamic approach to, 84
Early Intervention Research Institute, 12
Early interventionist job description, 266–267
Early LAP, 203–204
Early Learning Accomplishment Profile (Early LAP), 203–204
Eating utensils, 215–216
Ecological assessments, 149–150
Ecological Model, 74
Economic Opportunity Amendments (P.L. 92-424), 5
Education for All Handicapped Children Act (P.L. 94-142), 5, 79, 99, 138
Education for parents, 103–105
Education of the Handicapped Act (EHA) Amendments (P.L. 99-457), 3, 77, 78, 80–81, 83, 99, 138, 168, 169, 274, 276, 327–339
Educational focus questions, 292
Educational materials suppliers, 369–371
EHA Amendments. *See* Education of the Handicapped Act (EHA) Amendments (P.L. 99-457)
Eligibility assessment, 78, 142, 144, 148
Emergency release form, 254, 260
Environmental risk, xi, 11, 20, 38–39, 139–140
Epilepsy Foundation of America, 342
Equipment, for learning environments, 214–216, 233–236, 369–371
Equipment Shop, 235
Equivalent forms reliability, 167
ERIC Clearinghouse on Handicapped and Gifted Children, 342
Established risk, xi, 11–12, 20, 21–31, 139
Ethics, code of (CEC), 346
Ethnicity, 44–45. *See also* African American children; American Indian families; Asian families; Diversity; Hispanic children
Evaluation. *See* Assessment; Program evaluation; Staff performance evaluation form
Event recordings, 157
Everest & Jennings, Inc., 235
Exit procedures, 252–253
Exosystem, 96
Experimenting, in intervention process, 109

F-COPES (*Family Crisis Oriented Personal Scale*), 173
FACES (*Family Adaptability and Cohesion Evaluation Scales*), 173
FAE (fetal alcohol effects), 36
Families. *See also* Parents
 adjustments of, 90–96
 and age of childbearing, 45–46
 assessment of concerns, priorities, and resources of, 57–58, 78, 101, 146–147, 168–179
 and changing demographics, 44–46, 79
 characteristics of, 45–46, 55

child rearing practices in, 47, 55
collaboration with professionals, 79, 85, 107–110
cultural differences in definition of, and family roles in, 48, 55
disclosure level of, 58
early attachment in, 92–93
functions of, 98
and inclusion, 80
interactional processes in, 93–95, 98, 105, 176–177, 218–220
life cycle of, 98
and meaning of disability, 47
needs of, 84
parents with mental retardation, 60–62
principles in working with, 106–108
records of data on, 254–263
resources of, 98
roles in, 48, 55
size of, 46
staff's tendency to become overprotective of or overresponsible for, 131–132
strategies for working with, 106–110
stress in, 95–96
structure of, 46, 55
subsystems in, 97–98
systems theory of, 96–99, 107, 169–170
as team members, 123
teen parents, 13, 46, 62–63
and views on change and intervention, 47–48
Family Adaptability and Cohesion Evaluation Scales (FACES), 173
Family-centered approach
 in assessment, 150–155, 168–179
 benefits to families, 13–14
 curriculum design and, 190
 and diversity among families, 44–65
 and family concerns and priorities, 9
 and family–professional collaboration, 79, 85, 107–110
 goals of, 170–171
 and inclusion issues, 80
 optimal model of, 79, 85, 110–111
 preferred practices on, xii, 14–15, 110–112
 principles of, 106–108
 rationale for, 99–100
 strategies for working with families, 106–110
Family Crisis Oriented Personal Scale (F-COPES), 173
Family Inventory of Resources for Management (FIRM), 173
Family services. *See also* Service delivery systems
 community resources, 105–106
 education and training, 103–105
 general information, 52–53, 101–102
 parent–child interaction, 105
 support, 102–103
 types of, 100–106

FAS (fetal alcohol syndrome), 36
Fathers. *See* Family-centered approach; Parents
Fatigue, cues for, in infants, 35
Federation of the Blind, 342
Fetal alcohol effects (FAE), 36
Fetal alcohol syndrome (FAS), 36
FIRM (*Family Inventory of Resources for Management*), 173
First Chance Programs, 5
First contacts, 52–54, 243–244
Focalization, 93
Focus groups, 296
Focused interviews, 173–176
Follow-Through, 5
Follow-up stage of assessment, 151, 155
Formative evaluation, 290, 294, 295, 320
Fragile X syndrome, 23
Functional approach to curriculum design, 186–187
Functional Model, 74

Goal-attainment evaluation models, 295
Goal Attainment Scaling, 174–176
Goals
   in approach to early intervention, xii–xiii
   home visits and, 221
   in instruction, 195–196
   in operational planning, 240
Grandparents, 84
Growing: Birth to Three Portage Project, 204
Guiding, in intervention process, 109

Handicapped Children's Early Education Assistance Act (HCEEAA) (P.L. 90-538), 5
Handicapped Children's Early Education Program (HCEEP) Model Demonstration Programs, 5, 297
Handicaps. *See* Disabilities and disorders
Hawaii Early Learning Profile (HELP), 165, 204
HCEEAA. *See* Handicapped Children's Early Education Assistance Act (HCEEAA) (P.L. 90-538)
HCEEP Model Demonstration Programs, 5, 297
Head Start, 5–6
Healing, cultural differences in views on, 48, 56
Health issues
   for children, 81, 85–86
   learning environments and, 210–213, 229
   letter to parents on, 255, 261–262
   management concerns about, 241
   for staff, 131, 212–213
Health Questionnaire, 256–257
Hearing impairments, 12, 94
HELP (*Hawaii Early Learning Profile*), 165, 204
Hepatitis B infection, 212
Heroin exposure, prenatal, 36, 63

Herpes, 27, 131, 212
High/Scope Perry Preschool Project, 11
Highlighting, in intervention process, 109–110
Hispanic children, 44–45
HIV, 28–29, 63, 131
Home-based services, 82–83
Home environments
   assessment of, 177
   caregiver–child interactions in, 218–220
   as learning environments, 217–223
   matching or imitation in, 220
   pacing in, 219–220
   reading and responding to infant's cues in, 219
   scheduling and implementing home visits, 221–223
   teachable moments in, 220–221
   turn-taking or reciprocity in, 219
Home Observation for Measurement of the Environment, 177
Home visitors
   first contacts by, 52–54
   guidelines for, 55–56
   scheduling and implementing of home visits, 221–223
Homelessness, 38, 63
Human immunodeficiency virus (HIV), 28–29, 63, 131
Humor, 223
Hygiene, and learning environments, 210–213

IDEA. *See* Individuals with Disabilities Education Act (IDEA) (P.L. 102-119)
Identification. *See also* Assessment; Screening
   as legal requirement, 136
   optimal model of, 77, 85
   preferred practices for, 144–145
   and referral for further assessment and diagnosis, 141–142
IFSP. *See* Individualized Family Service Plan (IFSP)
IINTACT (Infant Interagency Network Through Accessing Computer Technology), 297, 298, 299, 300
Illness at birth, 33–35
Imitation, in parent–child interaction, 220
Implementation questions, 290
Inclusion, 79–80, 85, 217, 227–229
Individualized Family Service Plan (IFSP)
   and assessment, 142, 258
   and cross-cultural competence, 52–60
   curriculum design and, 190
   family concerns and goals included in, 78, 101
   forms for, 351–361
   as legal requirement, 4, 96, 99
   and parents with mental retardation, 61–62
   steps in, 52–60
   and transition services, 81

Individuals with Disabilities Education Act (IDEA) (P.L. 102-119), 3–4, 77, 83–84, 96, 136, 138, 142–144, 146, 168, 169, 244, 274–277
Infant Behavior and Development, 350
Infant Interagency Network Through Accessing Computer Technology (IINTACT), 297, 298, 299, 300
Infant LAP (LAP-I), 166
Infant Studies Project (UCLA), 108
Infants and toddlers. *See also* Assessment; Early intervention; Learning environments; Families; Family-centered approach
  adjustment of environment for early development of, 35
  attachment with parents, 92–93
  attention system of premature or low birth weight infants, 34
  and biological risk, xi, 12–13, 20, 32–37, 140
  cues for stress or fatigue, 35
  cues indicating stability and readiness, 35
  and environmental risk, xi, 11, 20, 38–39, 139–140
  and established risk, xi, 11–12, 20, 21–31, 139
  and illness at birth, 33–35
  low birth weight infants, 12–13, 33–35
  motor system of, 34
  parents' interactions with, 93–95, 105, 176–177, 218–220
  physiological signs of premature or low birth weight infants, 34
  predictability of, 105
  premature infants, 12–13, 32–35, 94
  and prenatal drug exposure, 35–37
  readability of, 105
  reading cues of, 35
  records of data on, 254–263
  responsiveness of, 105
  self-regulatory system of premature or low birth weight infants, 34–35
  very low birth weight of, 13, 33
Infants and Young Children, 350
Infections, congenital, 27–31, 131, 212, 255, 261–262
Information services, 52–53, 101–102
Informing, 109
Initial regulation, 93
Initiative, 93
Instructional goals, 195–196
Instructional objectives, 195
Instructional strategies, 194–197. *See also* Learning environments
Intake procedures, 244–252, 254–262
Intake Questionnaire, 246–252
Integration, 80, 227–229
Intelligence and Experience (Hunt), 7
INTER-ACT, 123
Interagency collaboration. *See* Collaboration

Interdisciplinary teams, xii, 75, 119
Interpreters, 57, 58
Interpreting stage of assessment, 151, 153
Interrater reliability, 167
Intervention process, steps in, 108–109. *See also* Early intervention
Interviews
  in assessment, 159–161, 171–176
  focus groups for, 296
Isotretinoin, 25

J. A. Preston, Inc., 235
Jesana Ltd., 235
Job descriptions, 265, 266–268
Journal of Developmental and Behavioral Pediatrics, 350
Journal of the Division for Early Childhood, 350
Journals, 349–350
Judgmental evaluation models, 295–296

Kaufman Assessment Battery for Children, 164
Kay Products, Inc., 235
Kindergarten programs, 4

Lakeshore Learning Materials, 235
Language
  diversity in, 44–45, 48, 56
  guidelines on, for home visitors, 52–53, 56, 222, 223
  of information sources, 52–53
  interpreters and, 57, 58
LAP (*Learning Accomplishment Profile*), 166
LAP-I (*Infant LAP*), 166
Laws. *See* Legislation; and specific laws
Learned helplessness, 209
Learning Accomplishment Profile (LAP), 166
Learning environments. *See also* Instructional strategies
  age appropriateness of, 213–214
  center environments, 223–227
  characteristics of, 208–217
  childproofing of, 211
  contingency and responsiveness of, 208–210
  disability-related alterations in, 211
  equipment needs for, 214–216, 233–236
  health, safety, and hygiene of, 210–213
  home environments as, 217–223
  inclusion and, 217
  inclusive settings, 227–229
  and learning through social interactions and play, 206–208
  list of resources for, 233–236
  matching or imitation in parent–child interaction, 220
  pacing in parent–child interaction, 219–220
  physical arrangement of, 216
  preferred practice in, 230

reading and responding to infant's cues, 219
teachable moments in, 220–221
turn-taking and reciprocity in parent–child interaction, 219
Least restrictive environment (LRE), 79–80
Legal compliance, 241
Legislation, 3–6, 77, 99, 138. *See also* specific laws
Letters
    to parents, 255, 261–262
    to physician, 254, 255
Library of Congress, 342
Library services, 101
Licensure, 129–130
Listening
    in home visits, 222
    in interviewing, 159, 172
Low birth weight infants, 12–13, 33–35
LRE (Least restrictive environment), 79–80

Macrosystem, 96
Mainstreaming, 80
Malformations, congenital, 24–25
Management. *See* Administration and management
March of Dimes Birth Defects Foundation, 343
Marijuana exposure, prenatal, 36
Matching, in parent–child interaction, 220
Medicaid, 138
Medical Model, 71–72
Medical Questionnaire, 256–257
Medicine, cultural differences in views on, 48, 56
Memorandum of understanding (MOU), 281, 282
Mental health centers, 278
Mental retardation, parents with, 60–62
Mentoring, 130
Mesosystem, 96
Methamphetamine exposure, prenatal, 63
Microsystem, 96
Minorities. *See* African American children; American Indian families; Asian families; Diversity; Hispanic children
Modeling, 109
Monographs of the Society for Research in Child Development, 350
Montessori Model, 72–73
Mothers. *See* Family-centered approach; Parents
Motor development milestones, 364–365
Motor system, of premature or low birth weight infants, 34
MOU (Memorandum of understanding), 281, 282
Multidisciplinary teams, 75, 118–119
Multiple disabilities, 12
Multiple drug use exposure, prenatal, 36–37
Muscular dystrophy, 30
Muscular Dystrophy Association, 343
Myelomeningocele, 26

NAACP, 279
NAEYC. *See* National Association for the Education of Young Children (NAEYC)
National Association for the Advancement of Colored People (NAACP), 279
National Association for the Deaf, 343
National Association for the Education of Young Children (NAEYC), 72, 187–188, 343
National Association of Parents of Deaf, 343
National Association of the Physically Handicapped, 343
National Down Syndrome Congress, 343
National Down Syndrome Society, 343
National Easter Seal Society, Inc., 343
National Information Center for Handicapped Children and Youth, 343
National Institute of Child Health and Human Development, 343
National Rehabilitation Information Center, 343
Naturalistic evaluation models, 296
Neonatal Behavioral Assessment Scale—Second Edition, 164
Neonatal intensive care units (NICUs), 33–34
Networking
    collaboration and, 284
    manager's responsibility for, 271–272
    parent-to-parent networks, 102
    support networks, 102–103
Neural tube defects, 26–27
Neutrality, in family assessment, 172
Nicotine exposure, prenatal, 35, 63
NICUs (neonatal intensive care units), 33–34
Nonjudgmental attitude, 172–173, 222
Nursery school movement, 4
Nursing Child Assessment Scales, 176

Objectives
    in instruction, 195
    in operational planning, 240
Observation, for assessment, 156–159
Office of Human Development Services, 343
Office of Special Education and Rehabilitative Services, 343
Organizational culture, 265, 268, 271
Organizations, 341–343
Orth-Kinetics, Inc., 235
Outcome questions, 291–292

Pacing, in parent–child interaction, 219–220
Paraprofessionals, 76, 122–123
Parent Behavior Progression Scale, 176
Parent Care, 343
Parent consent to photograph or videotape, 254, 260
Parent education and training, 103–105
Parent groups, 101

Parent–Infant Communication, 204
Parent permission for release of information, 254, 258
Parent permission to participate in program, 254, 259
Parent Questionnaire, 310–312
Parent-to-parent networks, 102
Parenting Stress Index, 173
Parents. *See also* Families; Family-centered approach
   age of childbearing, 45–46
   and benefits of early intervention, 13–14
   and child rearing practices, 47
   communication with professionals, 79, 85, 107–110
   curriculum design and, 194
   education and training for, 103–105
   and home environments as learning environments, 217–223
   importance of, in early intervention, 99–100
   infants' attachment with, 92–93
   information for, 52–53, 101–102
   interaction with children, 93–95, 105, 176–177, 218–220
   interviewing of, 159–161
   letter to, regarding health risks, 255, 261–262
   maternal drug use during pregnancy, 35–37, 63
   maternal stress, 13–14
   with mental retardation, 60–62
   needs of, 84
   organizations for, 341–343
   principles in working with, 106–108
   questionnaire for, 310–312
   reading and responding to infant's cues, 35, 219
   services for, 100–106
   stress of, 95–96
   support for, 102–103
   as team members, 123
   teen parents, 13, 46, 62–63
   training of, 13
Pennsylvania Association for Retarded Children (PARC) v. Commonwealth of Pennsylvania, 5
Perry Preschool, 9, 11
Personnel. *See* Staffing
Phenylketonuria (PKU), 23–24
Philosophical questions, 292
Philosophy, of early intervention program, 70–75
Photographing, parent consent for, 254, 260
Physical therapist job description, 268
Physicians
   health questionnaire to, 256–257
   letter to, 254, 255
Physiological signs, of premature or low birth weight infants, 34
PKU (phenylketonuria), 23–24
Planning
   of assessment, 151, 152
   of collaborative venture, 280
   diversity and, 59
   operational planning, 240–243
   of program evaluation, 297–318
   strategic planning, 240
Play, 206–208, 226, 229
Play-based assessment, 150
Policies, 240
Polydrug use exposure, prenatal, 36–37
Poverty, 38–39, 63
Practicing, in intervention process, 110
Predictability, of infants, 105
Predictive validity, 163
Premature infants, 12–13, 32–35, 94
Prenatal drug exposure, 35–37, 63
Preschool Language Scale–3, 166
Preschool programs, 80–81, 279
Professional organizations, 341–343
Professionals. *See* Staffing
Program administration and management. *See* Administration and management
Program description questions, 294
Program evaluation
   applying evaluation findings, 320
   Community Survey Form, 313
   conducting phase of, 317–319
   cost analysis, 293
   cost effectiveness, 293
   cost questions for, 293–294
   cost-benefit analyses, 293–294
   data analysis in, 319
   data collection for, 301, 309, 317–319
   decision-facilitation models of, 296
   design of, 299, 301
   determining what to evaluate, 297
   District and Agency Survey, 314–317
   educational focus questions for, 292
   Family Survey Form, 302–309
   formative evaluation, 290, 294, 295, 320
   goal-attainment models of, 295
   implementation questions for, 290
   instrument selection or development, 301, 302–317
   judgmental models of, emphasizing inputs, 295
   judgmental models of, emphasizing outputs, 295–296
   as management tool, 288–290
   models of, 295–296
   naturalistic evaluation models of, 296
   optimal model for, 82, 86
   outcome questions for, 291–292
   Parent Questionnaire, 310–312
   philosophical questions for, 292
   planning phase of, 297–318
   preferred practices for, 320–321
   program description questions for, 294
   purposes of, 288–289
   qualitative evaluation models of, 296

questions for, 297, 299, 300
questions to be answered by, 290–294
reports of, 319–320
resource questions for, 290–291
sample instruments, 302–317
satisfaction questions for, 292–293
summative evaluation, 290, 294–295, 320
target audience for, and how information will be used, 297
using evaluation data phase of, 319–320
validity questions for, 292
Program operation records, 262–263
Program philosophy, 70–75
Program planning. *See* Planning
Project CARE, 11
Prompts, 196
Psychometric approach to assessment, 148
Public Law 90-538 (Handicapped Children's Early Education Assistance Act), 5
Public Law 92-424 (Economic Opportunity Amendments), 5
Public Law 94-142 (Education for all Handicapped Children Act), 5, 79, 99, 138
Public Law 99-457 (Education of the Handicapped Act Amendments), 3, 77, 78, 80–81, 83, 99, 138, 146, 168, 274, 276, 327–339
Public Law 102-119 (Individuals with Disabilities Education Act), 3–4, 77, 83–84, 96, 136, 138, 142–144, 146, 168, 169, 244, 274–277
Public relations, 271–272

Qualitative-developmental approach to assessment, 149
Qualitative evaluation models, 296
Questionnaire on Resources and Stress, 173

Radiation, 25
RAP (Resource access projects), 278
Rating scales, 157, 158
Readability, of infants, 105
Receptive-Expressive Emergent Language Test–2 (REEL–2), 166
Reciprocal exchange, 93
Reciprocity, in parent–child interaction, 219
Record keeping
  of child and family data, 254–263
  child performance records, 255, 258–259, 262, 263
  community contact information, 262, 264
  confidentiality and, 253
  data sheet on child performance, 258–259, 262, 263
  design of systems for, 253
  emergency release form, 254, 260
  health questionnaire, 256–257
  intake information, 254–266
  intake questionnaire, 246–252

letter to parents on health risks, 255, 261–262
letter to physician, 254, 255
parent consent to photograph or videotape, 254, 260
parent permission for release of information, 254, 258
parent permission to participate in program, 254, 259
program operation records, 262–263
referral log notebook, 262
types of records, 253
visitor log, 262, 264
REEL–2 (*Receptive-Expressive Emergent Language Test–2*), 166
Referral log notebook, 262
Referrals, 141–143
Reframing a behavior, 109
Regulations, 240–241
Reinforcement, 196
Release of information, parent permission for, 254, 258
Reliability of tests, 167
Reports
  of assessment, 153, 154–155
  of program evaluation data, 319–320
Resource access projects (RAP), 278
Resource questions, 290–291
Responsiveness in learning environments, 209–210
Responsiveness, of infants, 105
Rifton, Inc., 236
Risk conditions
  biological risk, xi, 12–13, 20, 32–37, 140
  definitions of, 138–141
  environmental risk, xi, 11, 20, 38–39, 139–140
  established risk, xi, 11–12, 20, 21–31, 139
  list of, 140
Rubella, 27, 29, 131, 212

Safety issues
  for children, 81, 85–86
  learning environments and, 210–213, 229
  management concerns about, 241
  for staff, 131
Safety Travel Chairs, 236
Sammons, Fred, 235
Satisfaction questions, 292–293
Scheduling
  in center environments, 225–227
  task and resource scheduling, 241–243
Screening. *See also* Assessment; Identification
  criteria for exemplary programs, 138, 139
  definition of, 137–138
  and definitions of disability, 141
  and definitions of risk, 138–141
  and identification and referral for further assessment and diagnosis, 141–142

legal requirements for, 138, 143–144
preferred practices for, 144–145
tests for, 164
Secondary disabilities, 8–9
Self-assertion, 93
Self-help milestones, 367
Self-regulatory system, of premature or low birth weight infants, 34–35
Sensory Cognitive Model, 72–73
Service delivery systems
    collaboration and, 276–278
    comprehensiveness of, 277
    cost of, 277–278
    family services, 52–53, 100–106
    first contacts, 52–54, 243–244
    improvement of, through collaboration, 275–276
    intake procedures, 244–252, 254–266
    management of, 243–253
    reduction of duplication of, 276–277
    transition and exit procedures, 252–253
    types of, 82–84
Severe disabilities, 12
Shaping, 197
Sharing stage of assessment, 151, 153, 155
Siblings, 84
Small Wonder, 205
Social ecology model of families, 96–97
Socio-emotional milestones, 366–367
Special education movement, 5
Speech therapist job description, 267
Spina Bifida Association of America, 343
Spina bifida with myelomeningocele, 26
Staff development
    collaborative options in, 127, 129
    manager's responsibilities for, 265
    needs assessment for, 125, 127, 128
    optimal model for, 76–77
    required activities in, 127
    as team-building activity, 127
Staff performance evaluation form, 265, 269–270
Staffing. *See also* Cross-cultural competence
    attributes of cross-cultural competence, 50, 52
    burnout, 130
    competencies of staff, 123–126
    credentialing and licensure, 129–130
    curriculum design and, 194
    guidelines for home visitors, 52–54
    health and safety precautions, 131, 212–213
    home visitors, 52–56, 221–223
    interdisciplinary teams in, 75, 119
    job descriptions, 265, 266–268
    mentoring and support, 130
    multidisciplinary teams in, 75, 118–119
    optimal model for, 75–77, 85, 120
    paraprofessionals, 76, 122–123
    parent–professional collaboration, 79, 85, 107–110
    performance evaluation form, 265, 269–270
    and personal needs of staff, 131–132
    personnel issues, 129–132
    personnel standards, 123–124
    preferred practices regarding, 132–133
    professional skills and disciplines, 120–122
    supervision of staff, 264–265
    team approach to, 75–76, 118–123
    and tendency to become overprotective or overresponsible, 131–132
    transdisciplinary teams in, 15, 75, 119–120
    turnover and continuity, 130–131
    and working with interpreters, 57, 58
Standardized tests, 151
Standards for Professional Practice (CEC), 346–348
Stanford-Binet Intelligence Scale, 165
State-Trait Anxiety Scale, 173
StatView, 319
StatWorks, 319
STORCH infections, 27–31
Strategic planning, 240
Stress
    cues for, in infants, 35
    in families, 95–96
Substance abuse. *See* Prenatal drug exposure
Summative evaluation, 290, 294–295, 320
Support networks, 102–103
Syphilis, 27
Systems approach to families, 96–99, 107, 169–170

Task analysis, 162, 163, 195–196
Teachable moments, 220–221
Teaching techniques, 196–197
Teaching the Infant with Down Syndrome, 205
Teaching the Young Child with Motor Delays, 205
Team building, 271
Teams
    assessment team, 150, 168, 245, 252
    curriculum design and, 193
    development of, 271
    interdisciplinary teams, 75, 119
    multidisciplinary teams, 75, 118–119
    optimal model for use of, in staffing, 75–76
    paraprofessionals on, 76, 122–123
    parents and families on, 123
    professional skills and disciplines on, 120–122
    staff development as team-building activity, 127
    transdisciplinary teams, 75, 119–120, 245, 252
Teen parents, 13, 46, 62–63
Teratogens, 24–25
Test–retest reliability, 167
Tests. *See also* Assessment
    characteristics of good measuring instruments, 162–163, 167

criterion-referenced tests, 162
curriculum-based assessments, 162
list of assessment instruments, 164–166
reliability of, 167
standardized tests, 151
task analysis, 162, 163
use and abuse of, 167
validity of, 162–163, 167
Tetracycline, 25
Thalidomide, 25
Therapy Skill Builders, 236
Time sampling, 157
Tobacco exposure, prenatal, 35, 63
Toddlers. *See* Early intervention; Infants and toddlers
Topics in Early Childhood Special Education, 37, 350
TORCH-S infections, 27–31
Toxoplasmosis, 27
Toys, 210, 213, 225, 234–235
Toys for Special Children, 236
Training for parents, 103–105
Training of staff. *See* Staff development
Transactional model of development, xi–xii, 6–7, 8
Transdisciplinary teams, 15, 75, 119–120, 245, 252
Transition services, 59–60, 80–81, 85, 252
Translators, 57, 58
Tribal Council, 279
Turnover in staff, 130–131
Turn-taking, in parent–child interaction, 219

UAF (University affiliated facilities), 278
UCLA (University of California, Los Angeles), 108

Ultrasonography, 25, 26
Union of Pan-Asian Communities, 279
United Cerebral Palsy Association, 343
U.S. Department of Education, 297, 343
U.S. Department of Health and Human Services, 343
University affiliated facilities (UAF), 278
University of California, Los Angeles (UCLA), 108
University of Kansas, 37
University of Minnesota, 37
University of South Dakota, 37
Urban League, 279
Utah State University, 12
Uzgiris-Hunt Scales of Infant Psychological Development, 166

Validity of tests, 162–163, 167
Validity questions, 292
Values clarification, 49–50, 51
Very low birth weight, 13, 33
Videotaping, parent consent for, 254, 260
Vineland Adaptive Behavior Scales, 165
Violence, 38, 63–64
Visitor log, 262, 264
Visual impairments, 12, 94

Young Children, 350
Ypsilanti Perry Preschool Project, 9

Zero to Three, 350